TRAJAN
Optimus Princeps

TRAJAN
OPTIMUS PRINCEPS
A Life and Times

Julian Bennett

ROUTLEDGE

London and New York

First published 1997
by Routledge
11 New Fetter Lane, London EC4P 4EE

Designed and typeset by David Seabourne

Printed and bound in Great Britain by
Butler & Tanner, Frome, Somerset

British Library Cataloguing in Publication Data
A catalogue record for this book is available from the British Library

Library of Congress Cataloguing in Publication Data
Bennett, Julian.
    Trajan, optimus princeps: a life and times/Julian Bennett.
        p.   cm.
    Includes bibliographical references and index.
    1. Trajan, Emperor of Rome, 53–117. 2. Rome—History—98–117.
    3. Roman emperors—Biography.   I. Title.
    DG294.B46 1997
    937'.07'092—dc20

                            96-31094

ISBN 0-415-165245

CONTENTS

FIGURES AND MAPS
(BY MARGARET FINCH)

PLATES

(BETWEEN PAGES 142 AND 143)

OUTLINE
OF SIGNIFICANT
EVENTS

Conjectured dates of attested events are indicated by *italics*.

c. 50		Marriage of Marcus Ulpius Traianus *pater* and 'Marcia', ?daughter of Barea Soranus
		Birth of Ulpia Marciana (?Traiana)
54	13 October	Death of Claudius, accession of Nero
56	18 September	Birth of Marcus Ulpius Traianus *filius* (hereafter Trajan)
c. 60		Marcus Ulpius Traianus *pater* appointed *proconsul* of Baetica
c. 67		Marcus Ulpius Traianus *pater* appointed *legatus legionis X Fretensis*, in Syria. Placed under Vespasian's command for the Judaean War
68	9 June	Nero commits suicide
69		The 'Year of the Four Emperors'
	Beginning of July	The eastern armies declare for Vespasian
70	June	Vespasian enters Rome
	September/October	Marcus Ulpius Traianus *pater* takes office as suffect consul
	Autumn	Marcus Ulpius Traianus *pater* appointed *legatus Augusti* of Cappadocia
c. 73		Marcus Ulpius Traianus *pater* adlected to the patriciate, and appointed *quindecemvir sacris faciundis*
	Autumn	Marcus Ulpius Traianus *pater* appointed *legatus Augusti* of Syria
c. 74		Trajan enters vigintivirate as ?*triumvir monetalis*
c. 75		Trajan assigned to a legion in Syria with the rank of *tribunus laticlavius*
c. 76		Marcus Ulpius Traianus *pater* wins triumphal *ornamenta* in an unspecified military action in the east which involves Trajan as *tribunus laticlavius*
c. 77		Trajan transferred as *tribunus laticlavius* to a legion in Germany

c. 78		Marriage of Trajan and Pompeia Plotina
79	24 June	Death of Vespasian, accession of Titus. Shortly after, Marcus Ulpius Traianus *pater* appointed *sodalis Flavialis*
	24 August	Eruption of Mount Vesuvius, destroying Pompeii, Herculaneum and many other settlements
81	January	Trajan in office as *quaestor* (?as *imperatoris*)
	13 September	Death of Titus, accession of Domitian
86	January	Trajan in office as praetor
c. 87		Trajan appointed *legatus legionis VII Geminae*
89	January	Trajan takes the *VII Gemina* to Moguntiacum in response to the revolt of Saturninus
		?Trajan takes part in punitive campaign against the Chatti
91	January	Trajan opens year as ordinary consul with Acilius Glabrio
92/93		?Trajan appointed *legatus Augusti* of either Germania Inferior or Superior
95/96		?Trajan appointed *legatus Augusti* of Pannonia
96	18 September	Death of Domitian, accession of Nerva
97	*September*	?Trajan victorious in campaign against the Suebi. On hearing the news, Nerva adopts Trajan *in absentia* with the names Nerva Caesar
	25 October	Nerva formally adopts Trajan, and confers on him *proconsulare imperium maius* and the tribunician power. ?Trajan shortly after departs for Germany with the purpose of restoring the frontier
98	1 January	Trajan opens year as ordinary consul (*iterum*) with Nerva
	28 January	Death of Nerva
	February	Hadrian brings news of Nerva's death to Trajan, then at Colonia Agrippina, Germania Inferior
	Spring	Trajan commences a tour of inspection of the Danube frontier
99	*September/ October*	Trajan enters Rome as *princeps* Distribution of the first *congiarium*
	Autumn	?Trajan implements change to the renewal date of his tribunician power. Opens calendar year as *Trib. Pot. II*, moves up to *III* in October, then to *IIII* on 10 December ?
100	1 January	Trajan takes his third consulship with Julius Frontinus
	September	Pliny delivers the *gratiarum actio*, which later becomes the *Panegyricus*

101	1 January	Trajan takes his fourth consulship with Articuleius Paetus
	25 March	Trajan departs for the First Dacian War
	September	Battle of Tapae and second imperatorial salutation
102		Third and fourth imperatorial salutations
	10/31 December	Trajan returns to Rome, and is voted the title *Dacicus*
	10/28 December	Trajan celebrates Dacian triumph
103	1 January	Trajan takes his fifth consulship with Laberius Maximus. During this term as consul, Trajan initiates the Concordat with the senate, resulting in his coinage bearing the rubric *SPQR OPTIMO PRINC(ipi)*
		The second *congiarium* is distributed
105	4 June	Trajan departs for the Second Dacian War
106	*March*	Trajan's fifth imperatorial salutation
	Early July	Reduction of Sarmizegethusa Regia and Trajan's sixth imperatorial salutation
	September/October	Death of Decebalus
107	January	Hadrian appointed praetor and organizes the first games in celebration of the Dacian victory
	Mid-June	Trajan returns to Rome
	26 June	Third *congiarium* and beginning of the second Dacian games
109	22 June	Thermae Traiani dedicated
	24 June	Aqua Traiana dedicated
	11 November	Trajan's *naumachia* inaugurated
112	1 January	Trajan takes his sixth consulship with Sextius Africanus and dedicates the Forum and Basilica Traiani
113	12 May	Trajan's Column dedicated and the Temple of Venus reopened
	29 August	Death of Marciana
	September/October	Trajan departs for Parthia
114	*7 January*	Trajan enters Antioch
	Spring	Trajan departs for Satala
		Reduction of Arsamosata
	May	Trajan arrives at Satala
	Summer	Trajan arrives at Elegeia. Shortly after he publicly humiliates and deposes Parthamasiris, for which he takes his seventh imperatorial salutation
		The senate again votes Trajan the title *Optimus* and he now formally incorporates it into his titulature

115		Trajan on campaign in Mesopotamia
		Eighth, ninth, tenth and eleventh (and twelfth?) imperatorial salutations
	13 December	Trajan is almost killed in the Antioch earthquake
116	21 February	Trajan voted *Parthicus* and a triumph by the senate
	Summer	Trajan enters Ctesiphon, and receives his thirteenth imperatorial salutation
	Autumn	Parthian revanche, and abandonment of territories beyond the Euphrates and much of Armenia, which are now given client status
117	*Spring*	Trajan falls ill and suffers a stroke
	July	Trajan sets sail for Rome
	9/11 August	Death of Trajan at Selinus
	12 August	Hadrian receives news of Trajan's death and declares himself emperor
	Mid-August	Trajan cremated at Seleucia in Pieria, and his ashes returned to Rome for the postponed Parthian triumph. They are then placed in the chamber at the base of the eponymous Column

PREFACE
AND
ACKNOWLEDGEMENTS

Many will agree that the historian's duty, of establishing cause and effect, is best done through the investigation of the characters of those individuals who specifically influenced their contemporary circumstances. This is especially true of the imperial Roman period, a time when autocrats ruled the known world. By reconstructing the characters of individual emperors, and understanding their own particular environment, it becomes possible to establish the reasoning behind the policies they adopted to direct the greatest and most successful empire the western world has ever seen. The emperor Trajan is a notable case in point. In his own lifetime he was termed *Optimus Princeps*, 'greatest of princes', and as the second of Edward Gibbon's 'Five Good Emperors', he initiated an epoch described by that celebrated historian as 'the period in history during which the human race was most happy and prosperous'. Small surprise, then, that subsequent emperors often endeavoured to glorify their own reign by association with Trajan: Septimius Severus, for example, thought it necessary to include in his official titulature the phrase *divi Traiani Parth(ici) abnepoti* – 'great-great-grandson of the deified Trajan, conqueror of Parthia'. To appropriate Ariosto, 'Natura Traiano fece, e poi ruppe la stampa.'[1]

As it is, there is nothing harder for a historian than to recapture his subject's personality and ideology. Thus, while we can meditate endlessly about Trajan's motives and policies while *princeps*, the 'first citizen' of Rome, only those who actually experienced his physical and mental presence would have known the ambition and persuasiveness which prompted them. Then it needs remembering that the literary sources for Trajan's principate are singularly deficient, even by the general standards applying to the Roman empire. As the late Sir Ronald Syme wrote, 'It is the historian deprived of their help who is least contemptuous of the name of Suetonius and the *Historia Augusta*, as he bitterly recalls the famous lament of Gibbon (who himself did not attempt the task), that he must "collect the actions of Trajan from the glimmerings of an abridgement or the doubtful light of a panegyric".'[2]

Indeed, the principal contemporary literary account of Trajan's reign is Pliny the Younger's *Panegyricus*, a work which uncritically expands upon the virtues of our subject; and his tenth volume of *Letters*, devoted to his personal and official correspondence with the emperor. Otherwise all that can be gleaned concerning Trajan's political virtues comes from the four orations on rulership delivered to Trajan by Dio Chrysostom.[3] Then there is Book 68 of Cassius Dio's *Roman History*, written a century after Trajan's demise, using the contemporary senatorial and imperial archives. But Dio rarely indicates the nature of his sources, nor does he always distinguish between fact and hearsay. More seriously, Book 68 survives only as a series of abridgements collated for the emperor Constantine

VII Porphyrogenitus (912–59), and as an 'epitome', a discontinuous and selective narrative prepared by John Xiphilinus for the emperor Michael VII Parapinaces (1071–8). It is generally accepted, however, that these synopses generally embody faithful verbatim quotations, and their value is thus not necessarily totally compromised.[4]

Other than these, the literary sources for Trajan's reign are almost non-existent. From the imperial period they are effectively restricted to three mid-third-century epitomes: Eutropius' *Breviarium ad urbe condita*, dedicated to the emperor Valens in 369; Aurelius Victor's *Liber de Caesaribus*, dated from internal references to between February and 9 September 360; and the anonymous *Epitome de Caesaribus*, which ends with the burial of Theodosius, 8 November 395. The first two apparently derive their information at first hand from an inferred earlier work, known to classical scholars as the 'kaisergeschichte'; the anonymous, in turn, based his work on Victor's compilation, but may well have also used the 'kaisergeschichte' or another similar work, for he provides ancillary information that neither Victor nor Eutropius seems to have considered worth while reporting. Of the three, Eutropius is generally credited with having produced the more accurate résumé, but all are plagued with errors.[5]

Finally there are the assorted excerpts and details found in certain Byzantine annals, such as the *History of the World* prepared *c*. 1118 by Zonaras for Alexis I Commenus, or the earlier *Chronicon Paschale*. Some of these contain passages that appear to be verbatim quotations from the original text of Cassius Dio; others are evidently copied or derived from Xiphilinus' own abstract; a few are annalistic compilations using a variety of sources. Insofar as it can be established, these excerptors did not invent or embellish their sources, although they did frequently miscopy them, in which case the basic information they provide might well be correct, and they should not be neglected.

The fragmentary and eclectic nature of the literary sources helps to explain the almost complete absence of any modern biography of Trajan, a void which this book can only partly attempt to fill. None the less, no matter how poor the sources, the historian's duty is clear. Consequently, while we lack a Suetonius or even a *Historia Augusta* to assemble an uncritical compendium, that 'doubtful light of panegyric', supplemented by assorted anecdotal commentaries, must remain the basic source material from which to recreate the dynamics of Trajan's reign. And without the breadth of literary detail needed to assess Trajan's personality and the personal ambition which motivated him, conjecture, albeit augmented by the results of epigraphical prospection and archaeological excavation, becomes the primary tool in assessing the character and policies of this most perfect of *principes*. For this reason, it is inevitable that any investigation must perforce be built upon a huge foundation supplied by other people's knowledge: not only is it impossible for one person to be an expert in everything pertaining to the period, but it is doubtful that he or she could ever attain the objectivity demanded by the contrariness of the available material. A corollary is that the author might perchance have inadvertently subsumed and regurgitated to some degree the labours of these others who have expressed the matter in question much better than he could – *pereant qui ante nos nostra dixerunt*! Due pardon is therefore sought in the case of any such unintentional infringements, and may it be noted in passing that, as Oscar Wilde observed, 'Imitation is the sincerest form of flattery.'

As it is, then, the few facts available for Trajan's life do not allow for a purely annalistic explanation, and might even allow for many interpretations. Even so, a conscious effort has been made to maintain the general spirit of the series to which this book belongs. While aimed at the general reader with an interest in Roman history, and Trajan in particular, it is also intended to promote wider discussion among specialists concerning the more obscure aspects of Trajan's reign. But, to stay within the necessary format, it was necessary to make a choice as to what should be included and discussed in detail, while not entirely neglecting the other aspects of Trajan's reign. Not all will agree with the choice of emphasis, or the depth of coverage, but without passing over in relative silence some highly complex and fundamental issues, no overall assessment of Trajan's reign would ever be possible. Likewise, it is imperative to include some material which specialists would consider superfluous to their own needs: only by doing so can a wider readership be reached and informed about what is too often presented in the most recondite fashion. On the other hand, a conscious effort has been made to avoid the jargon of modern sociology and semiotics, in which fashionable keywords and dialectical excesses are frequently substituted for information and fact. This author does not completely agree with the prevailing tendency of adapting the invocations of French philosophers to explain social processes which are often already well documented in the historical and archaeological record. That is not to imply that an uncritical 'literalist' approach has been embraced: merely that in the absence of any proof to the contrary, it is far better to accept at face value the statements of contemporary observers, even if we are sometimes at a loss to explain certain well-documented affairs and incidents.

With all this in mind, it is recognized that the analysis presented here will not satisfy everyone, not least because the format of this series quite rightly precludes erudite discussion of arcane matters to explain each and every view presented. But it is necessary to take a stand on ambiguous issues, even if, as John Locke divined, 'New opinions are always suspected, and usually opposed, without any other reason but because they are not already common.'[6] Thus, while it is hoped that the ideas set forth here will be found reasonable and acceptable by most, notwithstanding the reliance upon speculation and conjecture necessary to interpret some aspects of Trajan's reign, it is freely acknowledged that many will find cause for disputation over certain of the explanations offered.

The suggestion that I write this book came from Peter Kemmis Betty, and I appreciate his proposition that I attempt what has proved a most recalcitrant yet invigorating subject, as well as his continued encouragement and understanding at the delays in its completion. The research was done using the materials held in the following institutions: the New York Public Library; the Avery and Butler Libraries at Columbia University, New York; the Library of Congress, Washington, DC; the Haverfield Library at the Ashmolean Museum, Oxford; the Joint Library of the Hellenic and Roman Societies, London; the University Library, Leeds; the University Library, Sheffield; and the J. D. Cowen Library at the Department of Archaeology, the University of Newcastle upon Tyne. I am most grateful to the staffs of these foundations for their courtesy and assistance at all stages in my research.

For their help during the vital early stages of preparation and writing this book, I was fortunate to be able to call upon the wide experience and knowledge of my friends at Newcastle University's Department of Archaeology, especially Charles Daniels, Jim Crow and Pat Southern. Mr Daniels, along with Richard Barcham, Valerie Harte and Marilyn

Stokstad, also made many useful, perceptive and improving comments and suggestions concerning the text, for which I am most grateful. Joe Schork, of the University of Massachusetts, clarified certain obscurities in Latin and Greek, and my colleague Jean Özturk has improved my Latin. Mark and Deborah Beale generously loaned me their house in Florida, which allowed me three months of sustained and uninterrupted writing at a crucial period, while Richard, Karen, Basil and Nigel Barcham, of Dallas, Texas; Peter and Barbara Bennett, of Wakefield; Charles and Miriam Daniels, of Newcastle upon Tyne; and David and Vicky Dawson and family, of Taunton, have all made me equally at home and provided working space at various times during the period the book was written. My former employers, Raymond and Whitcomb of New York, encouraged my academic pursuits, in particular in assisting with the necessary travel involved, and it is a pleasure to acknowledge the special help I have received from William Watson, Emilia Laboda and Edguardo Sensi. I also gladly acknowledge the assistance I have received from Ahmet Yilmaz Firtina, of Diana Travel, Kuşadası, Turkey, who paved the way for me to visit certain pertinent sites in Asia Minor; Paula Kraft, of Meta Felix, Naples, Italy, who assisted my excursions in Campania; and especially to Captain Giuseppe Casini-Lemmi, and his officers and crew aboard the *M/V Regina Renaissance*, who have wholeheartedly shared in satisfying my esoteric demands in the process of writing this book. I also wish to thank various anonymous readers, who so diligently and promptly read through the final draft, submitted in 1995, and corrected several howlers. The line illustrations were prepared by Margaret Finch, and certain slides were provided by Charles Daniels and Jon Coulston: their help in this way is profoundly appreciated.

Throughout the years I have studied the fascinating events of the late first–early second century, and especially during the preparation of this book, I have been able to draw upon the valued companionship, encouragement, support and knowledge of many friends, both directly and indirectly. Thus, despite the risk of producing what might seem akin to a Homeric catalogue of ships and doughty warriors, I thank in particular Lindsay Allason-Jones, Margaret Bertin, Lene Blegen, Christina Cerna, Laura Gillespie, Louise Graff, Cheryl Haldane, Nancy Levinson, Susana Mendes de Matos, Diana Moore, Julie O'Sullivan, Theresa Thompson, Gill Walker, Paul Bidwell, Mike Bishop, Jon Coulston, Nick Hodgson, Andre Lessard, Ian Paterson, Ralf Tranninger and Derek Welsby. If I have failed to live up to their unfailing hospitality, wisdom, wit and advice, the fault is mine, not theirs. And they will understand why I dedicate the book to my daughter, who probably suffered the most during its gestation.

Julian Bennett,
Bilkent University, Ankara,
Dies imperii Traiani 1996

PROLEGOMENON

The emperor Trajan was indubitably well liked in his own lifetime, when he was termed *Optimus Princeps*, the 'perfect prince'. After his death it was said that no other emperor had excelled or even equalled him in popularity with the people, and his memory remained green for centuries. In the mid-fourth century, it was said that he displayed the utmost integrity and virtue in affairs of state, and total fortitude in matters of arms, while the Roman senate is said to have greeted the accession of each new emperor with the wish that he surpass the felicity of Augustus and the excellence of Trajan. Trajan's constructions impressed those who came long after his time: the emperor Constantius II, when visiting Trajan's Forum at Rome, remarked it was 'the most exquisite structure under the canopy of heaven, admired even by the gods themselves', while Cassiodorus wrote, 'The Forum of Trajan, no matter how often we see it, is always wonderful.' [7]

Medieval legend enshrined Trajan's memory with even greater affection. A twelfth-century chronicler talks of how the emperor was venerated in times of yore on account of the many buildings he contributed for the benefit of mankind. And just as among the Muslims it remains a mark of sanctity to provide charitable structures, such as fountains, wells, khans and roads, he goes on to provide an account of how St Gregory was impelled to pray for Trajan's salvation because of the belief that he had built so many of the bridges at Rome. That anecdote, in fact, is a variant of a more common legend, one of the favourite tales of the Middle Ages, concerning the quality of Trajan's justice. The story, as related to Pope Gregory, when visiting Trajan's Forum, is that Trajan was about to ride from Rome with his army to defend the empire when a poor and elderly widow, full of tears, clutched his horse's bridle, and begged him for justice against the murderers of her son. Trajan answered that justice would be done on his return, but she would not loosen her grip, saying 'And if you do not return?' 'Then whosoever wears my crown will right the wrong', he replied, to which she responded, 'And can the good deed another does grace and profit him who shuns his own responsibility to do good?' At that, the emperor paused, dismounted, and announced, 'Rest assured. It is clear to me that this duty is to be done before I leave. Justice calls me, pity binds me here.' Gregory was so moved by the tale, we are told, that he promptly prayed for intercession on Trajan's behalf – a rarity indeed for a theologian who had insisted that prayers for the damned were futile: 'Forgive, O dear and almighty God, the errors of Trajan, because he always maintained right and justice.' His prayers were immediately answered: the clouds parted, and God, in his infinite Mystery and Wisdom, proclaimed, 'I hear your petition and pardon Trajan' – but divinely warned Gregory never to intercede again for those who died in paganism.[8]

Thus did Gregory triumph over Hell, and in so doing create a major theological problem: how could anyone, even a saint, release by prayer a long-dead and damned pagan? To admit of such a miracle was to place Gregory on a par with the Saviour himself, when he released thousands of lost souls during the Harrowing of Hell, since which time all who lived had had the option of being Christian, unlike those who predeceased the event. The account was viewed with suspicion – some even thought the story an invention of the English Church, for Gregory had been responsible for the conversion of the southern English, and he was highly venerated there. The Church deliberated. Finally, it was decided to circumvent the theological problems by agreeing that Gregory had only wept for Trajan's soul, not prayed for divine intervention, and it was allowed that Trajan might indeed have been released from Hell for his past good deeds – but only to reach Purgatory, where he was to wait until the Last Judgement. Yet as Dante realized, since God had granted the pardon, the event must have been predestined. Trajan, therefore, was never truly damned, for no prayer can help the damned, and only those pagans present when Christ harrowed Hell could ever be released from there to Heaven. Consequently, he must have been restored to solid flesh long enough to be converted to Christ before making his way to Heaven, where the poet accordingly placed the emperor among the Just and Temperate Rulers in the sixth sphere.[9]

The publication of the *Divine Comedy* gave greater currency to the legend, and the 'Resurrection and Conversion of Trajan' quickly became a favourite subject among moralists and artists of the Middle Ages. It is referred to in Langland's *Piers Plowman*, for example, and Wycliff used the theme in certain of his sermons.[10] It quickly appeared in religious art. An altar piece of *c.* 1365 by Jacopo Avanzi, for one, now in the Pinacoteca di Bologna, shows Gregory and four supplicants kneeling in prayer beside a tomb clearly marked *Sepulcrum Traiani Imperatoris*, and the Hand of God is shown responding to their petition. Another instance is a triptych of the Fathers of the Church by Michael Pacher (*c.* 1435–89), now hanging in the Alte Pinakothek in Munich: a seated St Gregory is shown in the centre, while Trajan, depicted as a bearded and crowned figure, surrounded by flames and naked save for a loincloth, emerges from Hell in response to Gregory's prayers. Indeed, it proved a popular subject in other media: Trajan's dispensation of justice, for example, forming the main subject of a mid-fifteenth-century Flanders tapestry diptych now in the Bern Historical Museum.[11]

The greenness of Trajan's memory continued even, indeed, into the Age of Enlightenment and the modern period. Gibbon was to describe how Trajan's principate inaugurated the Golden Age of the Roman empire, and Niccolini and Prunetti were inspired to compose an opera, *Trajano in Dacia*, in celebration of his achievements. And when Italian marble-workers sought suitable subjects for a bas-relief in the Supreme Court in Washington, DC in the 1930s, who better to exemplify the spirit of equal Justice before all in the Roman period than Trajan? That the story recounted to Gregory about Trajan actually originates in a mid-third-century account relating to his successor, Hadrian, perhaps inspired by an overly fanciful interpretation of scenes represented on Trajan's many monuments – the reliefs in the Forum, the Arch at Beneventum – is neither here nor there. What counts is the spirit and admiration in which Trajan's memory was held, and it is to investigating the substance of his glorious reputation that this book is devoted.[12]

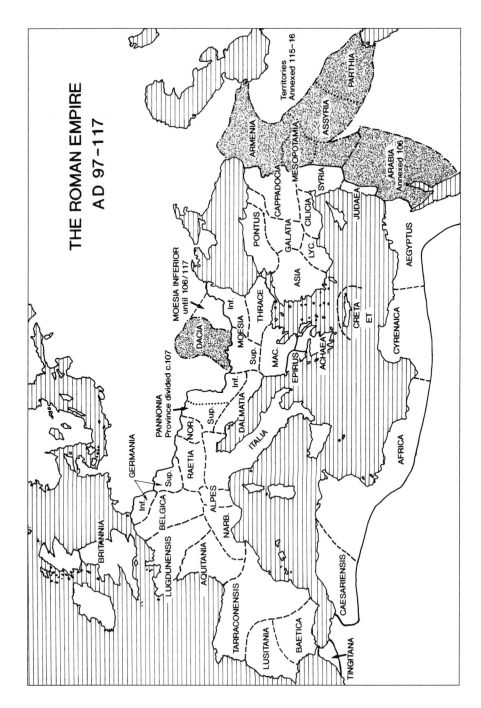

Fig. 1 The Roman empire under Trajan

I
THE
MAKING OF A NEW
ARISTOCRACY

The third-century historian Cassius Dio, himself of provincial origin, had little respect for the phylogeny of the emperor Trajan, observing with barely disguised contempt that he was 'an Iberian, and neither an Italian nor even an Italiot'. In fact one ancient account derives Trajan's paternal family, the *gens Ulpia*, from Tuder (modern Todi), on the northern border of ancient Umbria, an area where the clan is independently recorded.[1] Moreover, his own formal nomenclature, Marcus Ulpius Traianus, can be adduced in support of the asseveration: while the *praenomen*, or personal name, of Marcus was common enough throughout the Roman world, his other names seem specific to the same region. The *gentilicium* Ulpius, for example, is cognate with the Latin *lupus* (wolf) and probably derives from the Osco-Umbrian group of Italic languages. Likewise his personal name, or *cognomen*, Traianus, used to differentiate him from any kin who might share the same *praenomen* and *nomen*.

It belongs to a group in which the suffix *-anus* denotes derivation from a *gentilicium*, in this case Traius, and it can be conjectured it was introduced into the family when Trajan's grandfather married a member of that *gens*. Yet, like Ulpius, while not especially common, it occurs with some frequency in northern Italy, notably at Tuder, and at the nearby municipality of Ameria, the probable *origo* of Trajan's mother, strengthening the possibility of close family ties with the region.[2] Even so, while an Italian pedigree for the *gens Ulpia* seems certain, the family was not especially illustrious or distinguished in the affairs of Rome. His homonymous father (referred to here throughout as Traianus) was apparently the first of the blood-line to achieve consular rank, and at that through imperial patronage rather than by free vote of the senate.[3]

Whatever their ultimate origins, at the time of Trajan's birth his family had settled at Italica (Santiponce) in southern Spain, a few miles east of modern Seville. The town, located on the right bank of the River Baetis, adjacent to an existing Turdetanian emporium, had been founded in 206 BC by P. Cornelius Scipio after he defeated the Carthaginians at the battle of Ilipa (Alcalá del Rio). It was only natural that the first colonists, a mixture of wounded and sick Roman citizen soldiers and their Italian allies, should name it after their common homeland. Likewise, it was a foregone conclusion that the settlement would prosper. At the time, Rome's armies were made up of men who were first and foremost farmers, and Italica, on the same latitude as Sicily, occupied a prominent spur at the very heart of the fertile flood-plain of the Baetis. The location guaranteed cool breezes throughout the summer in an otherwise sun-baked landscape; the river allowed easy access to the Bay of Cadiz and the Atlantic, some sixty miles downstream, whence travel and trade were possible south into the

Mediterranean and north to Gaul. But it should not be thought that Scipio's motives in founding Italica were entirely altruistic. The area was still potentially hostile, and the veterans formed a reservoir of trained men, should the need ever arise. More importantly, the urban complex provided a focus for the religious, social, political and commercial development of the region as the first step in exploiting its reserves to the benefit of the Roman economy. By the first century AD, Baetica was famed for its agricultural and metallurgical wealth, and Iberia was recognized as Rome's richest and most important overseas territory.[4]

Systematic exploitation of the peninsula's agricultural resources began *c.* 175 BC, with the introduction of regular taxation into Hispania Ulterior, and greatly increased after the territorial reforms of 16/13 BC, when the area centred on the Baetis become the province of Baetica. Cereals were the dominant crop in the region, but the torrid plains around Italica were especially suited to the olive tree, and the production of olive oil probably started within decades of the Roman conquest. It was of a high quality, both Strabo and the elder Pliny holding it to be the finest outside of Italy, and within a short time Baetican olive oil was being traded throughout the Roman world, much of it going to Rome.[5] It was transported in distinctive locally made bulbous amphorae, often stamped with the maker's mark, and after delivery to the Emporium at Rome, once the contents had been transferred to a larger storage jar, these were usually discarded behind the imperial store-houses. With time, they formed a 115ft (35m) high hill, Monte Testaccio, estimated to contain the sherds (*testae*) of 40 million amphorae. Study of its make-up suggests that the Baetican oil trade with Rome reached its apogee in the final decades of the second century AD, by when perhaps as many as 130,000 Baetican amphorae were being dumped at the site every year.[6] Given that each held some 15.5 gallons (70 litres) of oil, they represent the import of not less than 2 million gallons (9,000 hectolitres) of Baetican olive oil per annum. The prosperity the trade brought to Baetica is amply demonstrated by increased expenditure on municipal and private building projects throughout the region. It is especially tangible at Italica, where the final decades of the first century AD saw the construction of what was effectively a new town to the north of the existing settlement, which eventually became the fourth largest community in the peninsula. Hardly surprising, then, that the *Italicenses* sought, and gained, colonial status from Hadrian shortly after he became emperor.[7]

Given the military origin of Italica, it is a reasonable conjecture that the first Ulpius settled there after service with Scipio's army. Later immigration cannot be excluded, for the complete conquest of Iberia was not achieved for another century after Ilipa. The absence of a consistent policy for settling retired veterans during that time meant that many naturally made their way to thriving towns with an existing complement of Italian immigrants. It is equally possible that the first Ulpius arrived at Italica as a civilian: several of the Spanish foundations, especially those created after the Civil Wars of the late first century BC, attracted their own quota of camp-followers, traders, speculators and entrepreneurs, although few of these latecomers seem to have been attracted to the older communities, such as Italica.[8] But no matter how he first arrived, there is a chance that the descendants of the first Ulpius might well have lost their citizenship by the early first century BC. Until the reign of Caracalla, only the children of two citizen parents, or of a citizen and non-citizen with *connubium*, the legal right of marriage, could claim the status of a

Roman or Latin citizen by inheritance. It might seem demographically improbable that sufficient enfranchised families existed in Italica in its early days to provide the number of eligible brides required for the number of retired soldiers now settling there. Miscegenation is to be expected, the *hybridae* having no rights whatsoever to their parents' civil status. If this indeed happened to the *Ulpia*, it is unlikely that they regained Latin citizenship until the mid-first century BC, when Italica was elevated to municipal rank with Latin rights.[9] Under the *ius Latii*, all free-born inhabitants received the Latin franchise, and the decurions or magistrates became eligible for Roman citizenship *per honorem*, allowing them or their sons to enter the equestrian order, the first step towards senatorial status.

According to Eutropius, Trajan's father was not the first member of the family to belong to the senatorial order. True or not, Traianus himself must have been a wealthy man to have achieved that status: the necessary property qualification was one million *sesterces* (*HS*) – ten times that needed to be a decurion, at a time when a workman's average daily pay was between *HS* 2–3 and a legionary's about the same before deductions.[10] Traianus or his parents, therefore, must have accumulated considerable wealth as well as social status, for a surplus over and above the required minimum was necessary to maintain a reasonable standard of living.[11] The likely source for the family fortune was the olive oil industry, perhaps augmented through judicious matrimonial alliances. As we have already seen, it was probably a marriage with a member of the *gens Traia* which introduced the *cognomen* Traianus into the family: in which case, it should be noted that a certain Traius is attested elsewhere in Baetica as the proprietor of an amphora manufactory.[12] Whatever, it can be reasonably assumed that the end of the first century BC saw the *Ulpia* prominent amongst the local nobility and the colonial élite. Their advancement from Italica to Rome, however, was due entirely to the reforms of one man: the first emperor, Augustus.

The Imperial System of Government

To understand how this was so, it is necessary to survey the origins and function of the imperial system of government.[13] As with any explanation of bureaucratic procedure, the task is inevitably irksome – but germane to all that follows. Its origin can be traced to the end of the Triumviral War in 31 BC, when victory for Octavian saw him in control of a Rome that longed for security and stability. Shamelessly manipulating these desires, he retained the powers voted him at the outset of the crisis and shrewdly appropriated the title *imperator* into his own name, and emphasized his somewhat tenuous filial relationship to the popular dictator Julius Caesar, assassinated and now *divus* – deified. In January 27 BC, when his supremacy was universally acknowledged, Octavian formally 'restored' the government of Rome to the senate and the people. In return, he was acclaimed *Augustus*, or worshipful, adding this title to his existing nomenclature to become known henceforth as 'Imperator Caesar divi filius Augustus'.[14] But, if the truth be known, he had only nominally relinquished power. Outside of Italy, he continued to command by proxy those territories where the bulk of the legions were stationed, the so-called 'imperial' provinces, while at Rome itself his power was overtly expressed through repeated annual election as one of the two consuls, the senior magisterial posts in the Roman world.[15] Four years later, when he renounced the continuous consulate after a near-fatal illness, the senate augmented his supremacy by voting him the supreme honour of the tribunician power in perpetuity, giving Augustus absolute authority in most spheres of public life.

It was no dictatorship, however. From the beginning, in spite of his very real powers, Augustus accepted that he could not maintain his position as *primus inter pares* – first among equals – without appeasing the senate, or survive long without the support of the *Curia*. Not only was the senate (at least in theory) the sovereign constitutional authority in Rome,[16] but its ranks supplied his most important subordinates, the men who saw to the military and civil administration of the assimilated territories. Consequently, it was essential for his continued power that the senate produce a flow of acceptable candidates to administer the provinces on his behalf. Using his wealth and prestige, but mindful throughout to maintain the semblance of the senate's overall authority, he accordingly began to reform the system and secure his position as first citizen – *princeps*. Many members welcomed the changes for the sake of equilibrium, and their own subsequent advancement. Others, especially the nobility, were not fooled by Augustus' constitutional measures, and resented his monarchical and dynastic aspirations. None the less, through adroit diplomacy, political acumen and natural duplicity, he achieved his aims without losing primacy.

Augustus' method was simplicity itself. First, he reduced the size of the senate, ostensibly to create a smaller and more manageable body, but in the process dismissing many whom he considered to be enemies or so impoverished as to reflect adversely on the dignity of the *Curia*. Then, he regulated and refined the system of appointments and length of tenure of the traditional magistracies, the quaestors, praetors and consuls. Finally, by 5 BC he had organized the suffect, or substitute, consulship so that it became a regular institution of the senatorial *cursus*. Now one or both of the eponymous ordinary consuls regularly resigned after six months, allowing the election of a replacement who served the remainder of the year, enabling a greater number of men to achieve their ambition of the senior magistracy, even if only as one of the *consules suffecti*.[17]

The measures were welcomed by the more ambitious senators, but Augustus made them conditional on the senate's support for another reform, one designed to admit a greater number of his partisans to the *Curia*. Hitherto, entry had been primarily by inheritance, despite a tradition, rarely exercised, of welcoming and advancing men of valour and substance.[18] Caesar, however, had made full use of the principle. By these means, he enlarged the senate with his supporters, mainly men of high standing in the *municipia* outside Italy, in Gaul and Hispania, some of them only recently elevated to Latin and then Roman status. What Augustus now proposed was to regulate the existing *ad hoc* methods of entry so that suitable candidates could be advanced according to a consistent system – provided they satisfied certain criteria. These included a record of public service and the property qualification of *HS* 1,000,000, but the significant factor in securing election was partisanship: Augustus' main aim, after all, was to ensure support in the *Curia* for his long-term policies as well as to provide competent and loyal officials for the increasing number of imperial administrative offices. Notwithstanding that, the reforms fundamentally influenced the subsequent development of the empire in ensuring the future dominance of the *novi homines*, 'the new men', those senators who either lacked consular ancestors or who first entered the *Curia* during Augustus' principate.

The Equestrian Order

Yet while it was now theoretically within the grasp of any plebeian male citizen to aspire to the *latus clavus*, the broad purple stripe which denoted senatorial rank, the actual procedure required both considerable wealth and influential advocacy. To begin with, it was necessary to accumulate property to the value of *HS* 100,000, one of the requirements for election as a *duovir*, or local magistrate.[19] Then, having secured entry into the decurionate, the local gentry, a man had to procure the support and further wealth essential for entering the equestrian order, the urban aristocracy of Italy and the Romanized provinces, for which there was a property census of *HS* 400,000.

Originating in the cavalry arm of the Republican army, the equestrian order now provided the majority of the civil jurors, most of the junior military officers and all the lower grades of administrative officials in the expanding empire. At first it was a rather loosely defined body, less homogeneous than the senate, but both Caesar and Augustus had taken measures to create a regulated system of promotion to satisfy the political ambitions of their equestrian supporters. By the middle of the first century AD, it had developed a full and complex career structure, which began with the *tres militiae*, a graded series of military posts each of which was generally held for between two and four years.[20] The first was that of prefect, the commander of a *cohors quingenaria*, one of the one hundred and fifty or so auxiliary infantry and part-mounted units, each five hundred men strong, constituted from among Rome's non-citizen allies.[21] Afterwards, those who wished to proceed any further in the equestrian hierarchy would transfer into a legion as a *tribunus angusticlavius*, the epithet alluding to the narrow stripe, the *angustus clavus*, that knights wore on the toga to distinguish them from members of the senatorial class. There were five angusticlave tribunes in each of the thirty or so legions, but perhaps not more than twenty vacancies every year. Alternatively, from the reign of Vespasian on, a youth might be appointed as an auxiliary tribune, in command of one of the thirty *cohortes milliariae*, those regiments with a nominal strength of a thousand men. Then followed the 'third' and final *militia*, the prefecture of an *ala*, one of seventy or so cavalry regiments, each of five hundred men, although for exceptional men there was a fourth promotion, as prefect of a milliary *ala*, of a thousand men, of which there were fewer than ten in the entire empire.

After completing the *tres militiae*, by which time most equestrians were in their mid-thirties at the very least, the majority chose to return to their home town and seek further distinction in the social, administrative and business affairs of their communities. The ambitious, however, sought a career in the imperial secretariat, holding one of several administrative posts which eventually became exclusive to suitably qualified equestrians. To judge from epigraphic evidence, fewer than twenty-five of these élite positions existed in the early empire. But by the third quarter of the first century AD, the growing demands of administering an increasingly complex polity resulted in their number rising to about sixty, and then to over a hundred.[22] They were classed in one of three ascending grades, each identified according to the commensurate salary. Those in the lowest grade, the *sexagenarii*, were paid a salary of *HS* 60,000; the *centenarii* received *HS* 100,000; the *ducenarii*, HS 200,000. Within the three grades there was evidently a pecking order of sorts, for some men held as many as three posts in each before progressing to the next.

On the other hand, the lack of a definable sequence in the offices held at any one grade suggests that there was no official ranking, even if the duties sometimes widely differed. For example, it was theoretically possible for a man to begin his career at the sexagenarian grade with the administration of Corsica, before going on to command the Alexandrian Fleet. Promotion to the centenarian grade could start with the administration of Achaea, followed by the charge of the Chersonesus region, and finish with the jurisdiction of Judaea. On progressing to the ducenarian scale, charge of the imperial library might be followed by the prefecture of the Ravenna Fleet, and end with the administration of Mauretania Caesariensis.

Not many procurators, if any, followed such a path: the majority held just one post in no more than two grades. Nor does it seem that the individual appointments were held for any substantive length of time, at least not those at the lower end of the scale. At the end of the first century AD, for example, there were fewer than twenty sexagenarian posts, somewhat more centenarian and over thirty at the ducenarian grade, a top-heavy distribution which strongly suggests that the junior posts were rarely held for more than twelve months. The senior posts, on the other hand, could be held for a considerably longer period, and there are instances of ducenarian procurators holding their office for as much as eleven years.[23] The length of tenure was evidently at the behest of the emperor. Likewise the eventual promotion for really exceptional men to one or more of the three senior equestrian offices: as prefect of the *vigiles* of Rome (strictly speaking, the imperial fire brigade, but in practice a para-military force); then prefect of Egypt; finally as one of the two commanders of the Praetorian Guard (the élite and only regular army unit stationed within Rome).[24] Only skilled and favoured candidates might expect these appointments, and their term of office evidently varied according to the particular demands of the emperor they served.

The Senate

It was during his tenure of one of the procuratorial posts that an *eques* might seek entry into the senate, either for himself or for one or more of his sons. True, the senate had gradually lost many of its legislative powers, but it still provided the basis for the mechanism of government and constituted the élite from whom the *princeps* chose his senior administrators. At this time it was made up of about 600 members, and it was usual to maintain the strength with replacements from the equestrian order as and when the body politic became depleted through natural and other causes. An *eques* might achieve entry by one of two means, adlection or direct election. Adlection was the process whereby individuals were nominated to the senate as a reward for some special service or other – provided they could satisfy the necessary property census. Caesar regenerated the procedure to reward his provincial allies, as did Augustus, Tiberius and Gaius, while Claudius made the process an institution. Many of the *novi homines* who characterized the early imperial senate entered by this procedure, and were usually adlected into the rank of quaestor, although older and more experienced men often entered as praetor.[25]

The more usual method of entry for an equestrian, however, was by election at the age of eighteen or above to the vigintivirate, the twenty junior magistrates who were in charge of the four law courts at Rome. Unless adlected, a year's service as one of the *vigintiviri* (literally, 'the twenty men') was compulsory for all those who wished to enter the senate. Consequently any aspiring equestrian candidates were in direct and presumably fierce competition with the sons of existing senators, who might expect their election to be a mere formality. As it was, the *princeps* would naturally ensure his own preferences were noted and advanced any whom he chose, regardless of origin, even to the extent of deciding which of the four judicial benches the *vigintivir* was elected to: *tresviri monetales*, the three men charged with overseeing the mint; *quattuorviri viarum curandarum*, the board of four responsible for the streets of Rome; *decemviri stlitibus iudicandis*, the ten attached to the Centumviral Court; or *tresviri capitales*, the three men responsible for capital cases. Moreover, while it seems probable that the particular board a candidate entered was to some extent determined by his social status, it certainly had an important effect on his subsequent career. It can hardly be coincidence, for example, that the *triumviri monetales* were almost exclusively of patrician origin – and thus usually went on to the ordinary consulship close to the minimum age, following this with higher command as the governor of one or more of the imperial consular provinces. Similarly, it would seem that whereas several of the *decemviri* came from the upper echelons of society, they were more often than not from a plebeian background, and recurrently pursued a judicial career rather than seeking the consulship and military office; unless marked out for advancement as *candidati imperatoris*, which guaranteed their eventual election to higher office. By way of contrast, the two remaining colleges were almost entirely drawn from the ranks of plebeian candidates, and while some of the *quattuorviri* eventually attained a consular command, few of the *triumviri capitales* were appointed to offices of high distinction, and those only through abnormal circumstances. More importantly, whatever board the young man belonged to, it allowed him access to the regular meetings of the *Curia*, where he could acquire new patrons and augment his relationship with existing ones, thus easing his passage when elections were held for entry into the senate proper.[26]

There was a compulsory five-year interval between the vigintivirate and the quaestorship, the next stage in the senatorial *cursus*, although as Roman law allowed that 'a year once begun counts as a year completed', this could be effectively shortened to three full years.[27] Some prospective senators utilized this interval to further their legal career, but most would enter the army, as *tribunus laticlavius* in one of the legions. Wearing the broad stripe of senatorial rank, the laticlave tribune was theoretically second in command of his legion, for only the *legatus legionis*, always an ex-praetor, was his social superior. None the less, like his angusticlave colleagues, he was more likely to be involved with mundane but necessary administrative details rather than active military service, particularly as he might be commissioned for as little as six months, although between two and three years seems more usual. On the other hand, the commission was often in a legion or province commanded by a relative, which would ensure some advancement, while a select number served in two or even more legions, presumably to gain wider experience.[28]

The compulsory quinquennium after the vigintivirate meant that a candidate was in his twenty-fourth year, which started on his twenty-third birthday, before he was eligible for election as quaestor. As there were only twenty annual quaestorships available, not all candidates were guaranteed entry at the first attempt, especially not the *novi homines*, who were once again in direct competition with the sons of existing senators, both those of their own peer group and those who had failed to be elected in earlier years. Much depended on patronage, the emperor and consuls having a significant say in who was elected: a well-placed *novus homo* might well be chosen in preference to an obscure member of the nobility.[29] They also determined which of the twenty quaestorial offices the successful candidate was awarded. He might be commissioned as one of the ten allowed to the proconsular governors, giving him practical training in provincial administration, or he would serve his term of office at Rome, in duties that ranged from service with one of the financial offices to reading aloud the emperor's public speeches.

For those who wished to pursue a political career, a second statutory quinquennium intervened between the quaestorship and the next magisterial appointment, as praetor. During this period, a man could choose to stand for an intermediate office at Rome, as aedile or tribune of the plebs, once again after an obligatory interim had elapsed, in this case a biennium. There were sixteen such posts, the six aediles being concerned with municipal administration and the ten tribunes assuming nominal responsibility for protecting the common people against abuses of power by the senate. Men of patrician birth, however, the scions of particularly ancient and distinguished families, were not allowed to hold either office – but neither were they excused the statutory pause in the senatorial *cursus*. Some seem to have been employed in an *ad hoc* capacity by the emperor, for example, as custodian of the proceedings of the senate, but the majority would have no formal employment.

Thus it was at the age of twenty-eight or above that a man could expect to be elected as one of the eighteen annual praetors, the senior jurisdictional office in ancient Rome. The praetors were the mainstay of the imperial system, for it was from amongst their ranks, after their term of office ended, that the emperor chose his second tier of provincial commanders and the senate designated its senior administrative functionaries. Those appointments within the purview of the senate – mainly annual – included six or so posts in Rome with the rank of prefect, as many as nine connected with overseeing the roads of Italy, and up to twenty-two assigned to the senatorial provinces, as *legati pro praetore* and *proconsules*. More important positions were in the gift of the emperor. He employed between twenty-five and thirty ex-praetors as *legati legionis* in command of his legions, and between seven and fifteen as *legati Augusti pro praetore*, to administer certain of the imperial provinces: whichever was taken, the command lasted from one to three years (or even more).

Generally speaking, whether an imperial or senatorial appointee, a propraetor would immediately commence his new duties unless it was one of those involving provincial command, which required a quinquennium between the two successive offices. That said, by this stage any married candidate could remit part of this term, or any of the others, through use of the *ius trium liberorum*, the legal statute whereby each legitimate child cancelled a year in the mandatory intervals between certain posts. While it is not certain how many men might have used this device, it is perhaps significant that several praetors held more than one praetorian office, for example following a term as legionary legate with service as proconsul of a senatorial province, which suggests it was rarely employed.[30]

A third and final compulsory interval elapsed before a senator became eligible for the consulship, the pre-eminent political office. The interlude varied according to social rank, as the prescribed minimum age was set at thirty-one for a patrician and forty-two for those who did not belong to the nobility, although once again use of the *ius trium liberorum* made entry at an earlier age possible.[31] Most patrician candidates could expect to become one of the two *consules ordinarii*, the eponymous consuls who gave their name to the legal year, while the others generally had to be satisfied with the substitute consulship, as *consul suffectus*. In the early empire, competition for these posts was especially fierce, as Augustus had originally allowed for only two suffect consuls in any one year. The number gradually increased in subsequent reigns, so that by the Flavian period there were as many as seven or eight – and even more in times of imperial crisis or dynastic change.

After the consulship, some senators would look forward to one of the five or six senior administrative posts available in the capital. Others might be appointed to posts generally held by a propraetor, or to some special *ex officio* position. The majority, however, particularly those desirous of further advancement, would seek selection for a three-year term as a *legatus Augusti pro praetore*, in charge of one of the ten or so larger imperial provinces. There was a ranking hierarchy of sorts, the provinces of Britannia, Syria and Hispania Citerior, for example, usually being held after one of the other propraetorian administrations. Only then might a particularly competent man attain the summit of the consular career, the senatorial proconsulship of either Asia or Africa. Both were held for a single year only, and in the normal course of events would not become available until ten or even more years after being consul.[32]

As we have already noted, as early as the mid-first century BC, Caesar had diluted the purely Roman nature of the senate through the addition of provincials, many of them wealthy and politically astute *novi homines* only recently elevated to the citizenship. The process, now regulated by Augustus, continued under his successors, and those senators whose immediate origins lay outside the Italian peninsula and among the provincial élite soon formed a significant proportion of the *Curia*. Several cases might be cited to show the possibilities and the potential for rapid advancement. One pertinent to our study is the family Annaeus from Corduba. The patriarch, the equestrian L. Annaeus Seneca, better known as Seneca the Elder, secured eminence as an orator under Tiberius, but seems never to have aspired to the senate. Nor did his youngest son, Mela, father of the poet Lucan, who was content to remain an equestrian, believing – probably with some justice – that he could accumulate more money by pursuing a procuratorial career rather than political office. His two remaining sons, on the other hand, both embraced the senatorial *cursus*. The older, Lucius Annaeus Novatus (who later took the name Gallio after adoption by the eponymous orator), became proconsul of Achaea *c.* 52, in which office he was responsible for the trial of St Paul. The homonymous second son, Seneca the Younger, besides being the leading literary figure of his generation, and renowned as a Stoic philosopher, was appointed as tutor to the future emperor Nero in 49, becoming his confidant and adviser after he took the purple.[33]

Significantly more *novi homines* owed their elevation to Gaius, who, faced with a reduction in the numbers of those eligible for equestrian and senatorial rank, sought and promoted numerous recruits from outside Italy.[34] Claudius continued the pattern, but it was the reign of Nero which saw non-Romans elevated to the more important offices of state in increasing numbers. Not least because the political importance of the republican nobility seems to have diminished considerably during the early principate, some of Rome's greatest families having apparently become extinct before Nero's accession.

A possible reason for this demographic change might have been fundamental economics. As the Romans did not recognize the principle of primogeniture, it was natural, on the one hand, for older and wealthier families to limit the number of their heirs to maintain the property intact, which in turn, in a period when early death was frequent, and when summary executions and exiles during dynastic intrigues were common, increased the risk of leaving no heir whatsoever. Then, on the other hand, if more than one male heir survived their parents, it could well be that the distribution of property between them meant that none could satisfy the necessary census to secure election to the senate.

The new provincial aristocracy filled the void, partly through natural evolution, as the sons of existing provincial senators reached maturity, but also through the efforts of influential patrons. One of these was the younger Seneca, who, together with Agrippina, Nero's mother, and Sex. Afranius Burrus, the Praetorian Prefect, had a firm grasp on imperial appointments by the time Nero became emperor in 54. It might reasonably be suspected that at the very least he was hospitable and kind to those hopefuls from his homeland who sought his advocacy, and it is not unlikely that he actively helped their careers wherever possible. It certainly seems possible that only his retirement, *c.* 62, prevented the consulship from being entirely dominated by descendants of Rome's erstwhile allies.[35]

How and when the *Ulpia* first attained more than local prominence is hidden from view. They might have already secured sufficient dignity and wealth to enter the equestrian order by the beginning of the first century BC, a time when the first Spanish knights are recorded. It could have been later, in the middle years of the century, when this group is more frequently mentioned in the epigraphic and literary record.[36] There is simply no evidence. Either way, if the family were astute enough in acquiring the necessary patronage and fortune for advancement, entry into the senate might well have followed within a generation, after which they or their descendants could advance comparatively swiftly, if politically and socially adroit. The case of one Publius Vitellius, equestrian procurator under Augustus, is instructive: his four sons all became senators, two achieving consular status (one on three occasions), while his grandson became emperor. As for the *Ulpia*, all that one can be certain about is that they owed their rise in some part to an influential benefactor, and it would be natural to look for one amongst powerful senators from their own homeland. Certain clues are available: if a man held a specific rank in a given year, then his *minimum* age at the time can be deduced, and thus the approximate date when he began the senatorial *cursus*. With that knowledge, an attempt can be made to identify those members of the nobility influential enough to promote his advancement. It therefore becomes necessary to examine the career of Trajan's father in order to establish when and what patronage he might have benefited from, hazardous though it is to guess at a man's friends from the date and sequence of his *cursus honorum* alone.

II

THE RISE
OF THE ULPII

Patronage and ability were the ways by which *novi homines* gained access to high society, obtaining prominence and securing the advancement of their family. Consequently the career of Trajan's father is germane to our understanding of how his son eventually reached his own eminence. In fact, few tangible facts survive for Traianus' *cursus honorum*, but Roman society being fairly stratified at this time, it can none the less be reconstructed reasonably accurately from the scant literary and epigraphic sources available.[1] To begin with, in the year 70 (probably), he was elected consul. As a non-patrician, he must then have been not less than forty-two years old, although, as we will see, he had already fathered at least two children by that time, in which case the *ius trium liberorum* reduced the qualifying age to forty. Simple calculation, therefore, assuming the rigid application of the *leges annales*, reveals he was born *c*. 30 at the very latest, although an earlier date is quite probable, as few senators could expect to reach the consulship at the minimum age.[2] For our purposes, we need no fine-tuned precision, and it will be assumed for convenience that Traianus was born *c*. 25.

Passing through the vigintivirate,[3] and then the military tribunate, Traianus became quaestor at the age of twenty-five or so in about the year 50. It can be deduced that his first child was born about the same year, which suggests that he married between the tribunate and the quaestorship. That was normal, for most prospective senators took a wife at this point in their career, when their political and financial future was reasonably well secured and self-evident, as the earlier the marriage the better the chance of rapid advancement through the privileges afforded by the *ius trium liberorum*.[4] But, while it can be conjectured that the lady is likely to have been ten or more years younger than Traianus, almost nothing can be said about her, as she is nowhere named by any of the ancient historians.[5] From their daughters' nomenclature, Ulpia Marciana, it is deduced she was a member of the *gens Marcia*, and it might be assumed she was of Iberian stock: local influence and regional predominance were normally advanced through matrimonial links between neighbouring families of wealth and standing. There again, when Trajan was emperor, he owned an estate known as the *figlinae Marcianae* ('the potters' fields of the Marcian family') in the vicinity of Ameria, 15 miles from Tuder, the ancestral home of the Ulpii. It most probably came to him through matrilinear inheritance as part of his mother's dowry, and as other estates in the same area were owned by a prominent local land-owning family of the first century AD, the *Marcii Bareae*, it might be stretching coincidence to presume that there were two unrelated families of the same *gens* in such a limited area. The possibility exists, therefore, that Trajan's mother was to some degree intimately connected to the then patriarch of the *Marcii Bareae*, the younger Q. Marcius Barea Soranus.[6]

If this could be demonstrated, it was a most propitious union for Traianus, and would confirm that he had by then achieved a modicum of social and financial status. The *Marcii Bareae* were no minor provincial clan, but were of consular rank: the elder Barea Soranus was suffect consul in 34 and proconsul of Africa in 42–3, and his son was destined to be consul in 52, before advancing to the Asian proconsulship. As it is, the limited evidence available can certainly be marshalled to support the premise. To begin with, prosopographical prospection reveals that Soranus sired at least two daughters, Marcia Servilia and Marcia Furnilla. Of the two, we know that Servilia was in her nineteenth year in 65/66, that is, she was born *c.* 46. And it can be deduced that Furnilla was probably the younger sister. Immediately before 66 she had been both married (for the first time) and quickly divorced by the younger Flavius Titus, elder son and successor of the future emperor Vespasian, having produced a daughter Julia in the meantime, all of which suggests she was probably no more than sixteen by then, and thus born *c.* 50.[7] Traianus' Marcia, on the other hand, must have been born at least twelve years before Servilia and perhaps fifteen before Furnilla, for we will see that she entered matrimony and delivered her eldest child *c.* 50. Given the contemporary dangers of late childbirth, it is unlikely that she, Servilia and Furnilla all shared the same mother,[8] but analysis reveals that Barea Soranus was somewhat older than his two known daughters. His consulship in 52 indicates he was born before the year 10, and thus was at least 36 years old when Servilia was conceived.[9] This raises the possibility that she and Furnilla were born of a second marriage, unremarkable in a time when re-marriages occasioned by death or divorce were a common occurrence. Thus it is not stretching credulity to identify Traianus' Marcia as the child of an earlier alliance of Soranus', and therefore the elder half-sister of Servilia and Furnilla. Verification is unlikely to be forthcoming, but the supposition is certainly strengthened by the circumstances surrounding Traianus' later career: a matrimonial link through Marcia to her half-sister Furnilla would help explain the evident rapport between Traianus and Vespasian at the time of the Jewish War in 66, and his well-rewarded adherence to the Flavian cause in subsequent years.

Whatever her origins, Marcia had at least two children before the decade was out. The eldest was evidently the aforementioned daughter, Ulpia Marciana. She married a Matidius, perhaps C. Salonius Matidius Patruinus, *magister* of the Arval Brethren on his death in 78, and they had one daughter, Matidia, who was married at least twice: first to a Mindius, by whom she had a daughter also named Matidia; then to L. Vibius Sabinus, consul in 97(?), by whom she had a second daughter, Vibia Sabina, born 85/87, who went on to marry the future emperor Publius Aelius Hadrianus (her second cousin) in 100, presumably – as then customary – when in her early teens. Already having had issue from her first marriage, therefore, Matidia was probably eighteen or so when Sabina was born, and so her own birth was presumably *c.* 67. Assuming Ulpia Marciana was sixteen at the very least when she gave birth to Matidia, her own nativity can therefore be assigned to *c.* 50.

A broader chronology is available for the year of Trajan's birth, even if the *Fasti Philocali* secures his *dies natalis* as the fourteenth day before the Kalends of October, 18 September by modern reckoning.[10] The difficulty arises chiefly from the contradictory accounts concerning his age at death. John Malalas, for example, a sixth-century historian from Antioch (Antakya), states that Trajan was sixty-six years old when he died, signalling 50 for his birth, but the *Chronicon Paschale* of *c.* 630 notes he was sixty-five, which would make the year 51. Later dates are implied by two mid-fourth-century writers: the anonymous *Epitome de Caesaribus* states that Trajan died in his sixty-fourth year, which allows either 52 or 53 to be entertained, but Eutropius, who used the same source(s), says he was sixty-three, fixing the year at 53. Against these records should be set the categoric statement of the historian Cassius Dio, as abbreviated by Xiphilinus: Trajan was in his forty-second year when he succeeded Nerva in January 98, and as Dio (or his epitomator) was generally fastidious in the use of ordinal and cardinal enumeration, this would fix his birth in the year 56.[11]

Which (if any) of these authorities should be believed? The post-Roman chroniclers can probably be disregarded: they are frequently erroneous and confused, and prone to the copyist's errors that bedevil compilations of that period and of that type. It might well be the same with Dio's account, for the relevant section survives only in the form of eleventh-century and later abstracts, known to contain several inaccuracies, even if their original source was usually meticulous on matters demanding mathematical precision. The fourth-century historians, on the other hand, apparently derived their information from the same original(s), even if Eutropius' work is generally regarded as the more responsible rendition.[12] Understandably, therefore, most modern historians have settled on the year 53 for Trajan's birth.

Validation of one or the other might seem confounded. Yet to anticipate Trajan's progress through the senatorial *cursus*, clues are available which point to a later date for his birth as being the more probable. For example, Pliny informs us that Trajan served his military tribunate while Traianus was governor of Syria, that is, Trajan was eighteen sometime between 73–6/77. He went on to become praetor in 86/87, by when the family had been advanced to the patriciate, which suggests that he was then at or near the statutory minimum of the twenty-eighth year, the usual age for a member of the nobility to take the post. Finally, he became *consul ordinarius* in 91; again, as a patrician, it is likely that he was elected close to the applicable minimum age, in this case the thirty-second year. Now, it can be rightly objected that not every candidate for senatorial office inevitably took the relevant post at or even close to the minimum legal age. But Trajan was a special case. When he embarked on the senatorial *cursus*, he was both a patrician and the son of a consul, and the members of such families were generally assured an accelerated career. Moreover, as will be shown, Trajan's father had proved instrumental in elevating the Flavian dynasty to the principate; as the son sought magisterial office under that dynasty, it would have been unusual at the very least if he were he not favoured for rapid promotion, at least in the early stages. The claim of Dio, that Trajan was forty-one when he became emperor, therefore becomes decisive, and verifies 56 as the probable year of Trajan's birth.

Meanwhile, assuming regular progression, Traianus probably entered the praetorship in *c*. 59/60, which made him eligible for a propraetorian command. The first secured date in his career, however, is in the spring of 67, when he was made commander of the *legio X Fretensis*, apparently his only senior military commission. He was then not less than thirty-seven, if not older, a somewhat advanced age for the post if he had progressed through the normal sequence of senatorial appointments, and it can reasonably be conjectured that he held a propraetorian office in the civil administration before his legionary command. As we have already seen, there was an obligatory quinquennium between the praetorship (at thirty or thereabouts) and any other magisterial duty, during which time Traianus might well have been aedile or plebeian tribune.[13] But this statutory pause in his career expired in 65 at the latest, allowing for another propraetorian office before he was appointed to the *X Fretensis*, probably as proconsul of Baetica, a one-year senatorial office, attested on a fragmentary inscription from Miletus (Turkey).[14]

The appointment was doubly significant. Traianus was quite probably the first citizen born outside Italy to hold the position and also one of the very few senators who were ever entrusted with administering their place of birth. Moreover, there were only eight such appointments available. That he was chosen in direct competition with more noble candidates testifies to his skills and patronage, especially as it seems that the Baetican office was reserved for men of promise, destined for the consulship.[15] A suspicious mind would expect the advocacy of some influential person to have played a part here, given that the patron–client system was fundamental to Roman society and to the achievements of *novi homines*. While the influence and identity of any inferred benefactors need to be kept in perspective, one can perhaps detect the manipulations of an influential compatriot – Seneca himself? – determined to reward a compatriot with a senior and presageful appointment in their common *patria*.

But, if Seneca was involved in Traianus' extraordinary promotion to the Baetican proconsulship, then it must have been before 65, the year Seneca was implicated in the Pisonian conspiracy, denounced and forced to commit suicide along with many other prominent men. Moreover, Traianus himself, if we have correctly identified his wife's family, would have been touched by the unravelling of the plot, for by the end of the same year, Marcia Servilia's husband, Annius Pollio, and his brother, Annius Vinicianus, had been respectively exiled and executed for their complicity.[16] Then, the following year Barea Soranus too was tried for sedition and, found guilty, was executed forthwith. It was an uncertain period for anyone linked however tenuously to those connected to the intrigue: an intimate relationship might suggest participation in treasonable acts – indeed, it may be that Titus only divorced Marcia Furnilla at this juncture to preserve the integrity and position of the Flavii.[17] Both the Ulpii and the Flavii, however, evidently escaped implication, for 67 saw Traianus and Titus in charge of legions in Judaea under the overall leadership of Vespasian himself. And whatever advocacy and skill made Traianus proconsul of Baetica, it was his role in the Jewish and Civil Wars, and the subsequent rise of the Flavian dynasty, with Vespasian as their first emperor, which marked the turning point in his family's fortunes.

Revolt broke out in Judaea in 66 for a number of reasons, not least hatred of Roman domination and internecine strife.[18] Initial attempts at suppression by Cestius Gallus, governor of Syria, proved unsuccessful, and in February 67 the emperor Nero replaced him with Vespasian, then one of Rome's most celebrated living marshals.[19] Vespasian chose three legions for the task. Command of one, the *XV Apollinaris*, was given to his eldest son, Titus, then twenty-seven, while the other two, the *V Macedonica* and the *X Fretensis*, were placed under Sex. Vettulenus Civica Cerialis and M. Ulpius Traianus respectively. It is natural to assume these two also owed their commands to Vespasian, given the probable Sabine origins of the first and the deduced matrimonial connection of the second, but the seriousness of the situation makes it unlikely. Titus was relatively inexperienced, and Vespasian needed tried and proven commanders for the remainder of his army; in which case, it might be that both Cerialis and Traianus had already proved their own military abilities and skill and were already in place as commanders of their respective legions.[20]

From Josephus we learn that Vespasian marshalled his army at Ptolemais (Akko), and then secured Galilee by capturing Jotapata, the centre of the northern resistance. While he was thus engaged, certain neighbouring towns, emboldened by Vespasian's decision to concentrate his forces on Jotapata, also rebelled. Traianus was sent against Japha, the nearest and largest of these, which he took on 25 June 67, after shrewdly requesting and receiving the support of the tyro Titus. With Japha in Roman hands, operations intensified, and other strongholds were stormed before the winter intervened, Titus again ostensibly playing a major part in many of the actions. The end of the year saw much of Judaea occupied and the legions in semi-permanent bases, Traianus, with the *X Fretensis* at Scythopolis (Beat Shean), positioned to control the main western route into Peraea, the others at Caesarea Maritima. The following year, Vespasian marched west with Traianus to subdue Peraea, a feat accomplished when the capital, Gadara (Um Qeis), was taken on 4 March. Leaving Traianus to continue south to prosecute the reduction of Jericho, Vespasian returned to Caesarea in the middle of March to plan his further strategy, arriving there in time to receive the news of a revolt in Gaul against the emperor Nero. It was the beginning of a sequence of events which were to change drastically the destiny of the Flavii and the Ulpii.

Opposition to Nero can be traced back to an early stage in his reign. His accession in 54, after the alleged poisoning of his stepfather Claudius, was at first welcomed by the people of Rome, and his principate was initially noted for its benevolence. Unprepared for rule, however, the child-prince was prone to extreme acts when thwarted in his personal aims. Tyranny ensued as he ruthlessly hounded those who opposed him, some into exile, others to death. Among the latter was his own mother, Agrippina, one of the first victims of his vengeful nature, but he was careful throughout to cultivate the common people assiduously, and retained their support through frequent largesse until the great fire at Rome in 64. The common belief was that Nero had deliberately started it in order to build anew a grandiose capital for the empire, and his popularity deteriorated dramatically, not least because of his decision to reserve some 250 acres (100ha) of central Rome for a palace, the Domus Aurea. The fortuitous discovery the following year of the Pisonian conspiracy gave him the opportunity to place the blame for the fire elsewhere, and simultaneously remove all those remaining who sought to restrict his whims: but the disgust, horror and fear engendered by his fierce persecution of those allegedly connected with the intrigue rebounded. Instead of securing his position it prompted greater dissent throughout the empire.

Even so, none seemed prepared to act until Julius Vindex, governor of Gallia Lugdunensis, proclaimed rebellion.[21] Having no regular army himself, Vindex canvassed support from the commanders of the larger 'imperial' provinces. Vespasian was probably among them, but whatever his personal thoughts on the matter, he was then fully occupied in Judaea. Most of the other governors chose to bide their time to see which way the wind would blow, and only Sulpicius Galba, governor of Hispania Tarraconensis, and Salvius Otho, administrator of Lusitania, were prepared to declare for Vindex. Galba, on account of his dignity (he was the descendant of an ancient republican family), was chosen as emperor-elect, but that April, before the conspirators could combine their forces, Vindex's native levies were defeated near Vesontio by the Upper German legions. They, in their turn, proclaimed their commander, Verginius Rufus, as emperor, but he refused the nomination, and returned with his army to Germany, leaving Galba in position in Spain. Nero panicked at the growing evidence of his declining authority. Losing the confidence of the Praetorian Guard and faced with the hostility of the senate, he despaired and on 9 June 68, with the help of his secretary Epaphroditus, took his own life, thus ending the Julio-Claudian dynasty.

Galba, who had himself contemplated suicide after Vindex's defeat, was now declared emperor by the senate, and after a slow and acrimonious march to Rome, entered the capital that October. The resulting parsimonious administration, although honest, did little to enhance his now bloody reputation or fulfil people's expectations. Some felt overlooked by the new emperor in his distribution of honours, and the military were embittered by his refusal to pay the customary accession donative.[22] The Upper German legions especially were indignant at their lack of profit for having eased Galba's eventual victory, an attitude not enhanced by the summary dismissal of Verginius Rufus, replaced in office by Hordeonis Flaccus. Dissent in the other provinces grew with the delay in confirming many of the existing commanders in their posts, Vespasian amongst them. It was further exacerbated by the execution of the Lower German incumbent, Fonteius Capito, and his replacement with one of the new emperor's own friends, a man of no real military experience, Aulus Vitellius. At the beginning of 69, the German legions gave voice and substance to the growing dissatisfaction, and mutinied. Somewhat surprisingly, given their resentment over the dispatch of Capito, they nominated Vitellius as emperor, and he immediately commenced a march on Rome.

Seeking to avert his own overthrow, Galba thought to disarm his opponents by adopting Piso Licinianus, a scion of ancient republican nobility, as his partner and heir, but the act only served to worsen the political crisis. Otho, for one, felt especially slighted, and successfully sought the support of the Guard. Galba was murdered at his behest on 15 January 69, and two months later, Otho, now emperor in Rome, marched forth with what troops he could raise to meet Vitellius, emperor of the German legions. Neither Otho nor his army proved a match for the hard-trained legionaries from the Rhine, and the bloody battle of Bedriacum (Cremona), on 14 April, ended in defeat, Otho taking his own life two days later. The way to Rome was now open to Vitellius, who foolishly entered the capital more as a conqueror than a saviour. It was a portent, for his bloody reign was distinguished from the start by its extravagances of debauchery and incompetence, even when set against the examples of Gaius and Nero.

The events of 68/69 revealed to all the well-hidden secret of the principate: an emperor could be chosen from outside Rome.[23] Whereas Galba owed his eventual acclamation to his long pedigree, his military experience and his high social and personal standing with all the rulers since Augustus, neither Otho nor Vitellius could boast of such prominence. Municipal in origin, they derived their earlier prestige solely from patronage, and before Nero's death neither had commanded an army. They acquired the principate only through the support of the armies they won over to their cause. Since the imperial throne was open to all and any prepared to fight for it, it is hardly surprising that those provincial governors with their own armies felt they too had the right to the purple. One was Vespasian, who had immediately postponed active operations in Judaea on the news of Nero's suicide. Another was his reputed rival, Licinius Mucianus, then governor of Syria. But the potential horrors of continued civil war and anarchy were enough to make many erstwhile foes become allies and support a single candidate who could restore the equilibrium, and the eastern commanders agreed between them to support Vespasian in a bid for the principate. In the first two weeks of July 69, the Egyptian, Judaean and Syrian legions declared in his favour, the Danubian army following suit shortly after. Titus was now sent to Egypt to control the vital grain shipments which Rome depended on, while Traianus was entrusted with supervising operations in Judaea in Vespasian's place.

Meanwhile, the Danubian legions under Antonius Primus, being the closest to Rome, marched west to confront Vitellius. Thereafter, events moved quickly. On 24 October, Vitellius was defeated at the second battle of Bedriacum, and by December, Primus was in Rome, where Vitellius committed suicide on the twenty-second of that month. Licinius Mucianus then took the capital on Vespasian's behalf and established the provisional administration that inaugurated the Flavian dynasty. Receiving the news of his proclamation, the new emperor assigned control of the Judaean conflict to Titus, and began his return to Rome, simultaneously replacing Traianus with A. Larcius Lepidus Sulpicianus, thus allowing the Baetican to join his entourage with the rank of *comes*.[24]

Vespasian arrived at Rome in June 70, and his powers were quickly confirmed and defined by the *senatus consultum* known today as the *lex de imperio Vespasiani*.[25] He then set about securing his position by appointing placemen in strategic positions, and in particular in the more important consular provinces. Thus, 'speedy consulates now came to the sound men among the legionary legates of the Danubian and eastern armies'.[26] Among them was Traianus, elected *consul suffectus* for September–October 70, in reward for the unstinting support he had given Vespasian in the previous years. He was further distinguished by advancement to the *quindecimviri sacris faciundis*. It was a priestly institution of great antiquity, ranking third among the senior religious colleges in Rome, and connected with the worship of Apollo and the curatorship of the books containing the Sibylline Oracles, and the supervision of all foreign religious cults.[27]

Traianus was now eligible for a consular jurisdiction. His next attested office, however, was not until three years later, when he was given the administration of Syria, as *legatus Augusti pro praetore*. An intermediate post seems probable, and may have been the governorship of Cappadocia, apparently made a consular province shortly after the autumn of 70. A gap in the provincial *fasti* allows the possibility, and the circumstances seem appropriate. The change in status meant a competent man was needed who could integrate the existing civil structure with the incoming military forces and attend to the re-ordering of the eastern frontier, particularly along the border with Armenia. Traianus' previous duties in Baetica and Judaea had given him sound experience in both fields, making it quite likely that he did indeed hold the position.[28]

The successful administration of Cappadocia would have been instrumental in the accrual of another honour for Traianus, namely adlection into the patriciate. The precise date of the award has not been secured, but was probably 73/74, the period when Vespasian and Titus held office as censors. One of their incumbent duties was the reorganization of the senatorial and equestrian orders, a reform long overdue, and occasioned by the weakening of both owing to 'frequent murders and continuous neglect' during the previous regimes. Hence, many of Vespasian's equestrian supporters were now honoured by adlection into the senate either *inter tribunicios* or *inter praetorios*, while a select few among the *ordo senatorius*, especially those who had helped Vespasian in the Jewish and/or Civil War, were adlected *inter patricios*.[29]

The award therefore probably coincided with a further signal honour for Traianus when he was made governor of Syria. It was among Rome's most prestigious appointments, as the administrator was charged with defending the province against Rome's traditional eastern enemy, the Parthians. Traianus is recorded in the post in late 73/74, perhaps replacing a predecessor who died in harness, and remained there until *c*. 76/77. Little can be said about his tour of duty, however, except that he received triumphal honours, a rare distinction at this period. By their very nature, *ornamenta triumphalia* were normally only awarded at the conclusion of a particularly significant campaign, although other circumstances are attested, yet it is difficult to identify the particular occurrence which might have given rise to Traianus' distinction. Apart from veiled allusions to the Parthians being somewhat troublesome at this time (*plus ça change, plus c'est la même chose*), the ancient historians are silent about any warfare on the eastern frontier now, even though Traianus' triumphal laurels are specifically associated with a military campaign in Parthia. They may have been awarded in connection with an invasion of Parthian territory by the Alani in *c*. 75. The event occasioned the dispatch of Roman troops to refortify towns in the adjacent client-kingdom of Iberia, and possibly the secondment of troops to the kingdom of Albania, on the lower Cyrus river and western coast of the Caspian Sea, where a Flavian inscription records the presence of legionaries from the *legio XII Fulminata*. On the other hand, Vespasian had refused to involve himself directly in affairs beyond Rome's borders, and had rejected a request for help from the Parthians. Perhaps the effective encirclement of northern Armenia, a tributary state of Parthia, which was brought about by these movements – Roman and Alan – gave rise to further apprehension amongst the Parthians themselves, leading to threatening military movements on their own part along the upper Euphrates. As Syme divined, in such circumstances, triumphal honours would be in order as much for a combination of skilful diplomacy and limited military action as for full-scale warfare.[30]

Whatever the event that occasioned the award, Traianus' tenure of Syria was considered both masterful and successful. He was promoted to the proconsulship of Asia, one of the twin pinnacles of the senatorial provincial career, succeeding to the office in 79, a bare eight years from the consulship. Most proconsuls waited ten if not fifteen years or more for the honour – further proof, if needed, of the esteem in which he was held by Vespasian. From inscriptions we learn that Marcia accompanied her husband to the province, and there are many records of his administration, including the construction of a stadium at Laodicea, the Nymphaeum at Miletus and an aqueduct at Nicaea, as well as the rebuilding of the Imperial Temple enclosure wall at Ephesus.[31]

The proconsulship could well have been Traianus' final senatorial duty. After Vespasian's death on 24 June 79, his successor, Titus, surrounded himself with his own placemen, and Traianus did not receive the second consulship he might have expected. He was, however, made a *sodalis Flavialis*, one of the fifteen priests attached to the cult of the deified Vespasian established by Titus in his father's memory, and perhaps remained in Rome for his retirement, as his priestly duties required his presence on occasion.[32]

He could well have died there, even if the year of his death defies precision. Coins issued between 112 and 114 give Traianus the epithet *divus*, or deified, although an inscription of the same general period mentions him without that appellation. Thus, it might be thought that he died some time between 112 and 114 – but if so, then certainly in the early months of 112: his daughter Marciana died on 29 August of that year, and the record of her death and apotheosis (on the same day) provided by the *Fasti Ostienses* contain no reference to her father.[33] In fact, the absence of any record of Traianus' death whatsoever from the admittedly incomplete *Fasti* or other annals is presumptive proof of his death before his son received imperial honours, that is, before 98. There is some evidence to support the contention. A passage in Pliny's *Panegyricus*, delivered on 1 September 100, evokes a picture of Nerva with Traianus in the starry firmament, from where both could look down on their mutual heir.[34] On balance, therefore, it seems that the coins of 112–14 record Traianus' delayed apotheosis – and it will be argued later that it was done purely for political reasons.

Trajan's Career to 89

Just as Traianus' career has to be restored from the few salient details available, so too must we reconstruct the early life of his son. We are singularly ill-informed about Trajan's activities prior to 89, when he first enters history, in connection with the German mutiny of that year. Much can be deduced from the few anecdotes that survive, when set against contemporary practices. His education, for example, was likely to have been along traditional lines, even if by his time few *patres familiae* followed that paragon Cato in personally instructing their sons in all branches of the curriculum. Instead, the nobility now generally used their own specially trained slaves. Lesser families either hired teachers for home tuition or sent their children out to the *ludus*, those at Rome often in a rented shop or portico, and some even co-educational, although usually only the male offspring was given any detailed education.[35]

The educational procedure was both privileged and specific. Until the first century AD, most teachers followed the precepts espoused by Livius Andronicus, that a solid grounding in the Greek and Latin classics was essential to produce a civilized person. As Roman society became more political in its orientation, however, so the teaching system expanded to accommodate the demand for greater instruction in the arts of public speaking. When Trajan received his education, the different schools of pedagogy had developed their own increasingly formal curriculum. The principal exponent of the new methods was one M. Fabius Quintilianus (Quintilian), who much later distilled his thoughts on the matter in his *Institutiones Oratoriones* – 'The Education of an Orator'.[36] Born *c.* 35 in Calagurris (Calahorra), Hispania Tarraconensis, Quintilian had quickly achieved prominence at Rome on account of his rhetorical skills, and in 72, Vespasian made him one of the first State Professors of Rhetoric, with a salary of *HS* 100,000.[37] It was in this capacity that he taught the younger Pliny, among others who probably included Juvenal, Tacitus and Suetonius, and it was his experience in teaching which prompted him to devote his retirement to writing 'great works for the young', presumably the *Institutiones*.

According to the *Institutiones*, the first stage in the child's formal education should begin when he was seven or thereabouts, when he was placed under the guidance of a *paedagogus,* often a man of Greek origin, responsible for teaching the elements of reading and writing.[38] Both Greek and Latin were taught as a matter of course, as every well-bred Roman was expected to be bilingual, but the greater emphasis was on Greek, as the child could be expected to pick up Latin at home.[39] Between the tenth and twelfth year, he would begin further instruction under a *grammaticus,* who provided a thorough grounding in literature, with particular stress on appreciation, paraphrase and critical analysis, although the value of athletics, music and geometry to ensure a well-rounded education was also recognized.[40] Only when an acceptable degree of progress had been made under the *grammaticus* did the boy graduate to his last formal teacher, the *rhetor,* from whom he learnt the art of declamation:[41] oratorical skill was the *sine qua non* for a public career, and it was Vespasian's recognition of the fact that prompted him to appoint public teachers of rhetoric. This stage was usually completed by the youth's fifteenth year, when he assumed the plain white *toga virilis* that denoted manhood, by tradition at a public ceremony in the Roman Forum on the Festival of the Liberalia (17 March). He was now ready to enter public service, although most young men would first enrol in the *collegium iuvenum,* a youth organization founded by Augustus to teach the concepts of *Romanitas* and basic military skills.[42]

From anecdotal evidence, it can be inferred that Trajan was no more than an adequate pupil, even if he used Greek familiarly – at least when making legal pronouncements.[43] Indeed, there are grounds for suspecting that his education might not have progressed beyond more than cursory tuition from a *rhetor.* Cassius Dio, for example, claims that '[Trajan's] education did not extend to the level of oratorical discourse, but he understood and applied its basic principles.' Later sources concur: 'His intelligence was more intuitive than learned [yet] while sparing in his knowledge, he was an eloquent and adequate speaker on many matters', and when emperor, he routinely employed others to research and write his speeches. Another anecdote has him amiably remarking to the philosopher Dio Chrysostom that he could not understand a word of his rhetoric – but none the less held him in the highest regard.[44] To be set against these somewhat negative citations, however, is the unvarnished yet lucid style of the fifty-plus letters sent by Trajan, when emperor, to the younger Pliny, when governor of Bithynia. They are generally believed to have been composed and dictated by Trajan himself, not least because their familiarity reveals a personal touch rather than an anonymous chancery hand.[45] If indeed so, they not only reflect skilful tuition from the *grammaticus,* but also provide a clue as to the literary works used in Trajan's education: their terse prose directly recalls that of Caesar, whose masterpieces survive to this day as models of concise and perfect Latin composition. But whether or not Trajan consciously modelled his everyday prose on that of Caesar, the influence of the great dictator's 'Commentaries' is certainly reflected in the title he chose for his published account of the Dacian Wars, the *Dacica,* and in the single peremptory sentence that survives from it: 'inde Berzobim deinde Aizi processimus': 'From there we proceeded to Berzobis and thence to Aizi.'[46]

In September 73, when Trajan was seventeen, he automatically became eligible for the *latus clavus* and election to the vigintivirate. There is no direct evidence as to which of the four boards he was assigned to, and R. Paribeni, among others, has wisely decided not to speculate on this.[47] Even so, some prospection is possible. To begin with, it was probably about now that the family was elevated to the patriciate, in which case it might be expected that Trajan was made *triumvir monetalis*, the usual bench for members of that social class. Election to the decemvirate, however, cannot be excluded, as Trajan is reported to have been a diligent jurist, and many of his later judicial reforms proved to be of great importance:[48] on the other hand, there is no indication that Trajan ever practised law or intended to pursue a legal career, and as so few *decemviri* attained high military rank, this college might seem unlikely. Similarly with the other two boards, for almost none of the *tresviri* or the *quattuorviri* ever took a senior command. Thus, in view of Traianus' social status, and the subsequent course of Trajan's own career, it can reasonably be conjectured that the son secured election as *triumvir monetalis*.

Usually, most *vigintiviri* went almost directly into military service as a *tribunus laticlavius* in one of the thirty or so legions.[49] The commission was technically the gift of the emperor, but personal patronage played its part, some tribunes evidently being designated by the various provincial governors and other influential persons, while many served in legions and provinces commanded by a close relative or family friend.[50] Despite the circumstances of his appointment and age – anywhere between nineteen and twenty-three – the laticlave tribune was the nominal second-in-command of his unit. True, the importance of the legionary tribunate as a military office had dramatically declined from the days of the republic: then, only citizens already skilled in warfare were appointed; now it was held as a matter of course in both the equestrian and senatorial *cursus*. Further, whereas the angusticlavian tribunes came to a legion after some military service with an auxiliary regiment, and usually received their legionary commission as a preliminary to another military command in the *tres militiae*, the laticlave tribune took his senior position purely on account of his social class, and there was no professional military career as such for him to pursue afterwards. What, then, was the purpose of the laticlave tribunate? Some would hold that it was intended to give a youth serious military training, and therefore it was usually held for between two and three years. If so, the value of such instruction doubtless depended on when and where the commission was held, for not every legion was involved in active military campaigning. Others have suggested that the rank was retained merely to provide a young man with a taste of army life as a useful step on the road to future honours, and could be held for as little as one year or even less. This would certainly agree with Tacitus' allegation that many tribunes used their period of office as an excuse for debauchery.[51] The truth should – as usual – lie somewhere between the two extremes; after all, the office not only involved formal military procedures, but also entailed certain administrative duties. For example, Pliny the Younger, when tribune with the *legio III Gallica*, audited the accounts of the auxiliary regiments stationed in Syria, while those laticlave tribunes in single-legion provinces might well have served as the governor's deputy in his absence.[52]

Whatever the purpose of the post, a short tribunate would hardly have contributed to the military efficiency of either the tribune or the legion involved. Indeed, two reliable sources suggest the normal period was not less than eighteen months, even if a man might only hold the commission for half the usual time.[53] Pliny the Younger, for example, while implying that his own laticlave commission lasted for a single year, must have served somewhat longer to allow for the time he spent studying with two Greek philosophers as well as to complete the audit already referred to.[54] Eighteen months might seem appropriate, and seems to be confirmed by the three successive tribunates held by the future emperor Hadrian. He began service with the *legio II Adiutrix* in 95, perhaps that spring, and then transferred to the *legio V Macedonica* in Moesia Inferior, where he remained from before September 96 to October 97, after which he was retrospectively seconded to the *legio XII Primigenia* until sometime in 98/99.[55] He therefore probably served not less than forty-six months in all, and perhaps between thirteen and eighteen months with each unit. Hadrian is hardly a typical case, however, whatever the reasons behind his successive transfers, as few tribunes served in more than one legion. Thus, the varied tenure of each of his assignments is not necessarily to be taken as an accurate guide to whatever term existed. In short, much probably depended on the particular ambition and aptitude of the individuals involved, but a minimum term of eighteen months might be accepted as the usual term of service.[56]

With regard to Trajan's own military tribunate, our sole information comes from the younger Pliny's *Panegyricus*. The relevant passages consequently require careful dissection to establish where and for how long Trajan served his commission. To begin with, Pliny claims that:

> you were scarcely out of your swaddling bands when you augmented the glory which won your father his laurels, when you already deserved the name Germanicus, when the sound of your approach struck terror into the supercilious hearts of the savage Parthians, and when the Rhine and Euphrates united in their admiration of you.[57]

Then:

> Indeed, as a tribune when still at a tender age, you served and proved your manhood at the far-flung boundaries of the empire, for fortune set you to study closely, without haste, the lessons which later you would have to teach. It was not enough for you to take a distant look at a camp, a stroll through a short period of duty: while a tribune you desired the qualifications for command, so that nothing was left to learn when the moment came for passing on your knowledge to others. Through ten years' service you learnt the customs of peoples, the localities of countries, the opportunities of topography, and you accustomed yourself to cross every kind of river and endure all kinds of weather as if these were the springs and climate of your native land. So many times you changed your steed, so many times your weapons, worn out in service![58]

Pliny's laudation cannot be simply dismissed as hyperbole. The *Panegyricus*, in its original and published form, was addressed to an audience which contained men who had a long and deep personal knowledge of Trajan. Some exaggeration was allowable, but falsification was not, and as in all political oratory there would have to be a kernel of truth for the speaker to maintain intellectual credibility with his audience. As it is, hidden within the panegyrist's luxuriant extolment are three claims which can be disengaged as pertinent to this stage of Trajan's career.

For one, Pliny specifically refers to Trajan's youth at the time he commenced his tribunate, and notes that he was involved in the campaign which won Traianus *ornamenta triumphalia*. From this we deduce that Trajan was in his late teens when he took his commission, and that he was appointed to a Syrian legion during his father's administration of the province.[59] This indicates the period between 73 and 76, when he was aged 17–20, even if we cannot determine which of the four legions he served with – the *III Gallica*, *IV Scythica*, *VI Ferrata* or *XVI Flavia*. But, whereas most tribunes might not expect to see much more than routine frontier work – the supervision of patrols and standing garrisons, the occasional skirmish – Pliny's remark, that Trajan's approach 'struck terror into the supercilious hearts of the savage Parthians', need not be pure rhetoric. As already noted, the award of triumphal insignia to Traianus should be seen in the context of some military action, even if exactly when and where is unclear.

Pliny then tells us that Trajan followed his service in Syria by transferring to a legion stationed on the Rhine frontier. For a tribune to serve in two legions is not unknown, albeit unusual: at least thirty cases are recorded of young men who took this particular path, among them Hadrian, who served in three, a distinction shared with only one other, the younger Minicius Natalis.[60] There were three occasions which might give rise to such a sequence of posts at this stage in a man's career: firstly, in following his legionary commander or provincial governor on his mentor's promotion to another command;[61] secondly, through displacement when his commander was replaced by another, bringing his own protégé as *tribunus laticlavius*; thirdly, by transfer as part of a body of reinforcements to an active or intended battle front.[62] Of the three, the first option can be immediately discounted, for Traianus never held a western command, while whosoever was Trajan's *legatus legionis* in Syria could not have been promoted from that post direct to one of the German administrations without first serving as consul. There is little to choose between the remaining two possibilities, but if Trajan was appointed in the final biennium of his father's Syrian administration, then Traianus' replacement as governor *c.* 77 could well have signalled Trajan's transfer to a Rhine province. It just so happens that about this time the legions of Germania Superior were involved in various unspecified campaigns in the Black Forest area, while those in Germania Inferior were fighting the Bructeri.[63] Either theatre would have been appropriate for Trajan, by now a skilled junior officer with active combat duty to his credit, but of the two, the last seems more apposite. The governor of Germania Inferior was Rutilius Gallicus, an exact contemporary of Traianus, and it is to be expected that patronage would play its part in Trajan's second commission.

Such speculation aside, Trajan's probable transfer from one legion to another would at least help explain the third and most puzzling of Pliny's claims about his tribunate, namely his 'stipendia decem', or ten years' sustained military service. Superficially, this is as baffling as it is without parallel: after the reign of Tiberius, not even senior generals held their command that long, except in rare cases of national emergency. Even if some laticlave tribunes served in more than one legion, there was no such thing as a regular senatorial military career, and consequently nothing to be gained from serving a lengthier commission than normal. Pliny's 'stipendia decem', therefore, seems to be nothing more than the rhetorical exploitation of an ancient principle, that ten years should elapse between an individual assuming the *toga virilis*, in his fifteenth year, and entering the senate with the office of quaestor, at twenty-five.[64] On the other hand, it does not exclude the possibility that Trajan did serve as *tribunus laticlavius* for a longer period than was usual, especially as the panegyrist stresses how Trajan was dissatisfied with the usual 'short term of service', however long that was. On the contrary, if Trajan did indeed serve in more than one legion, then his tour of duty is likely to have lasted longer than was customary, providing Pliny with an opportunity to exploit the anachronism of the ten years' service which traditionally prepared a man for mature command.

It will be assumed, therefore, that Trajan completed his formal military career *c.* 78, when in his twenty-second year. This was also the usual age for male members of the senatorial class to marry, and there is no reason to doubt that Trajan conformed to accepted custom. He took to wife one Pompeia Plotina, but beyond the fact that her father was one L. Pompeius, her origins are obscure. Nomenclature suggests that she came from the province of Gallia Narbonensis, and perhaps Nemausus (Nîmes), where her protégé Hadrian built a basilica in her honour after her death in 123.[65] The connections between the Ulpii and the Pompeii which brought about the marriage are unknown, although there is a possibility that the two families might already have been related: an Ulpia Plotina, possibly an aunt of Trajan's, is attested at Herculaneum in the years immediately before the eruption of Mount Vesuvius in 79.[66]

In September 79, Trajan entered his twenty-fourth year and became eligible for election to the annual quaestorship. The twenty quaestors performed a range of bureaucratic functions, twelve as financial officers in the senatorial provinces, two as *quaestores urbani*, with administrative duties at the *Curia*, four as assistants to the consuls, and two as members of the imperial secretariat. Election to the quaestorship probably took place sometime after 12 January, the office being held for a twelve-month term from the following December.[67] Trajan apparently entered the quaestorship at the first available opportunity, in January 81, for there was a compulsory five-year interval between this stage of the senatorial *cursus* and the praetorship, and it can be demonstrated that he was most probably praetor in the year 86. In view of his patrician status and his family's long-standing links with the Flavian dynasty, he may even have been nominated as one of the *candidati Caesaris*, one of those men assured election by the emperor's personal recommendation.[68] Likewise, it is possible that he served as one of the two imperial quaestors, as these men, the *quaestores Caesaris* or *Augusti*, were normally drawn from the patriciate. It was not an excessively demanding duty, for it involved little more than the reading of imperial speeches in the senate. None the less, although technically of low status in the senatorial hierarchy, it was an influential post, as the holders frequently acted as the emperor's personal agent in a variety of other capacities.

Trajan's quaestorship ended in January 82, after which he needed to endure a further compulsory quinquennium before the praetorship. As a patrician, he was denied a civil office; his plebeian colleagues, on the other hand, could occupy part of this period with service as an aedile or plebeian tribune. How Trajan and others of like status might have used this enforced retirement from public life is unclear. His later predisposition to the military life allows the speculation that he may have been involved in Domitian's wars against the Chatti and the Dacians. If so, it would have been in some supernumerary capacity, for there was no formal military position available for a man at this stage of his career.

In 85, Trajan became eligible for election as praetor, and there is every reason to believe that he was immediately elected to the duty. This can be deduced from the *Vita Hadriani* in the *Historia Augusta*, which tells us that Hadrian was left fatherless when in his tenth year, and was placed in the guardianship of P. Acilius Attianus and Trajan, his first cousin once removed, and by then of praetorian rank. Now Hadrian was born on 24 January 76; his tenth year, therefore, might be either that commencing 24 January 85 or the following year, depending on whether the reckoning is cardinal or ordinal. It is usually the latter in the *Historia Augusta*, but as the praetorship was held from the month of January the exact year, 85 or 86, might yet defy precision – were it not for Dio's statement that Trajan was forty-one in January 98, in which case the year January 86–January 87 saw Trajan as praetor.[69]

The praetorship required Trajan to reside at Rome for at least the bulk of the year. The praetors had retained much of their original significance after the Augustan reforms and continued to preside over the permanent courts, the *quaestiones*. They also sponsored the six principal 'games' that took place every year, each lasting between six and sixteen days, and consisting of a mixture of gladiatorial shows, chariot-racing and fun-fair.[70] Their quality evidently varied: some were lavish, others not. Most praetors probably aimed simply to please. Wherefore, we read of Agricola's term as praetor that

> In sponsoring the games, he steered mid-way between cold reason and opulence; on the one side he was far from extravagant, but at the same time he was sensitive to public opinion.[71]

A middle course is to be expected. While some state aid was available towards the cost of certain games, up to *HS* 600,000 in the case of the longest, the *ludi Romani* or *Magni*, the praetors between them had to find the remainder, even if absent from Rome.[72] It could be a substantial sum, for a typical contribution seems to have been in the order of *HS* 100,000 per show, although one praetor managed to spend three times this amount on a single occasion; hardly surprising, therefore, that we learn of praetors who depended on their relatives and friends to help out with the costs involved.[73] Yet despite the financial burden involved, the office was eagerly sought: only ex-praetors could hold the senior imperial duties and proceed to the consulship, the highest magistracy.

In so far as it can be reconstructed, therefore, Trajan's career up to the praetorship was probably fairly unexceptional, apart for a lengthy period as *tribunus laticlavius* in two (if not more) legions. His subsequent employment, however, was anything but regular. In the normal course of events, patricians could expect the ordinary consulship shortly after the praetorship, and consequently only a small number took any intervening post.[74] Trajan belonged to that select minority, for between 86 and 89, he was commissioned as commander of the *legio VII Gemina*, the only patrician, in fact, to be so signalled by Domitian, who generally seems to have pursued a policy of promoting *novi homines* at the expense of the nobility.[75] Why Trajan sought the appointment is not at all clear. True, throughout his life he showed a preference for the campaign mess, and was to spend almost half his reign absent from Rome on one campaign or another, but this alone cannot explain it. Moreover, the particular post was hardly a promising one if Trajan was deliberately seeking to enhance his position through military duty. For one thing, the legion's record was not especially auspicious.[76] Recruited as the *legio VII Galbiana* in Spain on 10 June 68, it was decimated at the second battle of Cremona, and re-formed with a stiffening of loyal elements from another legion (if the title *Gemina* really means that it was made up from elements of two existing legions, instead of distinguishing it as the 'twin' by enumeration with the *VII Claudia*). For another, it was by now based at

Legio (Léon), in Hispania Tarraconensis, far removed from any potential or active front where a man might win fame.

The real explanation for Trajan's appointment to a legionary command, therefore, should lie elsewhere, and might be sought in connection with the then critical situation on the Danube. The resolution of the crisis required the presence of Domitian's best generals, and doubtless involved several transfers amongst men of senior rank, the experienced *legati* from the frontier provinces, to provide governors for the lower Danube territories of Moesia and Pannonia, and the divisional commanders for his armies. Transfers of this type inevitably advanced the careers of lower-ranking men, now promoted to fill the ensuing vacancies. The command of the *VII Gemina* could well have been one of these – and one especially suited for an aspiring tyro such as Trajan. In short, Trajan's extraordinary appointment probably occurred as much by default as through any overt military ambition. Even so, if we are to credit the panegyrist, it was later to prove crucial for Domitian: Pliny claims that Trajan was the emperor's surest aid when Saturninus threatened civil war on the Rhine.[77] Moreover, it was but the first step in a series of appointments that ultimately ended with Trajan's unchallenged nomination as heir to the *imperium* eight years later. Hence, it becomes necessary to review the events of the intervening years, and especially the circumstances leading up to Saturninus' revolt and the aftermath. Not only does this allow us to understand the stages whereby Trajan ultimately acquired the supreme power but, as K. H. Waters has shown, 'It is quite impossible to estimate correctly the reign of Trajan without first establishing the true nature of the reign of Domitian.'[78]

III
IMPERIAL EXPANSION
AND CRISIS

The emperor Titus had unexpectedly died on 13 September 81 while Trajan was quaestor, and was succeeded with indecent haste by his brother Domitian. Domitian himself was a most complex person, who combined militant intolerance with puritanical fanaticism, a blend which resulted in the last years of his reign declining into bloody persecution. He was abhorred by many in his lifetime; the episodic commentaries and undisguised bias of the principal literary testators for the period – Tacitus, Pliny the Younger and Suetonius – hinder an objective assessment of his policies or even the establishment of an accurate chronicle for his fifteen-year reign.[1] Even so, just as the accession of Vespasian was germane to the advancement of Traianus, so that of Domitian heralded a period which saw Trajan steadily augment the distinction of the Ulpii, confirming their status as loyal adherents to the Flavian dynasty as he too was gradually elevated to the highest offices of the state.

Now it cannot be disputed that the sour and cynical Domitian promoted a social and political ideology less transparent and more absolute than that of his predecessors. In the manner of Louis XIV, he identified the state with himself, and deemed that autocratic rule through his own functionaries, rather than by the senate, was the means whereby Rome's prestige and greatness could be best increased. It was this interpretation of the ruler's *auctoritas* which gave substance to later claims of an unmitigatedly despotic and imperious reign, as freedmen and equestrians began to assume greater responsibility for the developing bureaucracy within and outside the imperial household. Then, Domitian's reputation was hardly helped by his increasing tendency to appoint provincial *novi homines* to praetorian and consular rank, for it further diminished the power of the established Italian aristocracy. Even so, while both trends might well have been influenced by a desire for revenge – for the senate had treated Domitian with undisguised contempt while his father and brother were alive – his administrators, whether freedmen, equestrian or senatorial, generally proved themselves to be exceedingly competent. So much so that many were retained in office by his immediate successors. None the less, neither development endeared Domitian to a fundamentally reactionary *Curia*, and if we are to credit Dio and Eusebius, discontent with the emperor's autocracy quickly surfaced – and was dealt with summarily: Flavius Sabinus, his first cousin once removed, being among those soon executed for the crime of *maiestas,* or *lèse-majesté*.[2]

Yet even Domitian's greatest detractor admits that the beginning of his reign was marked with a display of *clementia* and *abstinentia*, indulgence and restraint, an acknowledgement perhaps intended to disguise the erstwhile complaisance of those senators whose own careers were significantly advanced in the reign.[3] Indeed, if the polemical diatribes are put to one side, there stands revealed an emperor responsible for far-reaching changes in domestic administration and foreign policy, most of which were happily adopted by his successors. Typical was the decision to cancel outstanding debts to the imperial treasury, the annulment of particularly harsh judgements, and the scrupulous opposition to public bribery and corruption.[4] Concomitantly, Domitian reaffirmed social distinctions and public decorum, and actively campaigned for a restoration of public morality: one equestrian was expelled from the order for taking back his wife after openly accusing her of adultery, while a senator was removed from the curial roll on account of his passion for dancing and pantomime.[5]

More noteworthy were Domitian's attempts to restore the dignity of Rome by resuming military operations in north-western Europe. Since the Varan disaster, when Augustus lost his confidence in the eventual occupation of Germany west of the Elbe, the legions had effectively remained stalled on the left bank of the Rhine. A tradition of reciprocity had developed between Rome and the tribes of Free Germany, the two sides happily co-existing so long as neither showed naked hostility or territorial ambition affecting the other's interest – a Roman Monroe Doctrine, as it were. While Vespasian had moved troops across the Rhine to annex the territory known as the Agri Decumantes, it was Domitian who made the decisive break with that legacy, deciding upon a military campaign against the Chatti.[6] His justification is hidden by the contempt of Tacitus and others, but the claim that the operation lacked a strategic objective and was undertaken purely for Domitian's own military prestige seems unconvincing: the Chatti were considered the most formidable of the western German tribes.[7] Moreover, they occupied the eastern Hercynian massif (Hesse), a wooded and mountainous region, riven by steep-sided water courses, and ideal terrain for the guerrilla warfare which had previously proved so deleterious to the tactics used by the Roman army. On the other hand, the reduction of the Chatti was an essential preliminary to any strategy that visualized the future occupation of the North German Plain, and the territory west of the Elbe.

Domitian began his Chattan War in 83 with a surprise attack across the Rhine. By September 84, he was able to celebrate a triumph, taking the title *Germanicus* and renaming the month after the victory. He may well have intended to advance further east the following year. Instead he was forced to a rapid accommodation with the Chatti, as a raid by the Dacians into Moesia, and the loss of an army, along with the governor, C. Oppius Sabinus, diverted his attention to the Danube. The Danubian counter-offensive began in mid-85, and was initially successful, Domitian taking the field and assuming his tenth and eleventh imperial salutations before the end of 85, and a twelfth between March and May 86. Diurpaneaus, the Dacian king, subsequently abdicated in favour of a certain Decebalus, who twice proposed a negotiated peace to the emperor. Both offers were peremptorily dismissed by Domitian, who now left the region for Rome, on account of increasing dissatisfaction with his administration, leaving his Praetorian Prefect, Cornelius Fuscus, with instructions to press home the advantage.[8]

Discontent at Rome was probably aroused by the seemingly endless pillaging of state revenues to subsidize Domitian's military endeavours. It was not alleviated by his attempts to restore confidence in the exchequer: first, by devaluating the bullion coinage a mere three years after its revaluation; then by increasing direct taxation and resorting to naked extortion of the nobility; finally by raising the provincial tribute, which in Numidia at least resulted in rebellion.[9] If Domitian had won tangible success against the Chatti and the Dacians, then the rumblings could have been countered, using that wave of popular support which commonly results from the successful military enterprises of rulers, even among the most politically isolated. Instead, the armchair strategists were glibly able to belittle and negate the limited territorial gains of the Chattan War, and the ignoble accommodation made with them in 85, when it seemed to all that conclusive victory was imminent. Their greatest grievance, however, was with the emperor's rejection of the peace terms offered by Decebalus. An already disenchanted aristocracy now feared a waste of the state's energy and resources, which threatened all the gains of past decades for one man's vainglorious pursuit of personal military fame.[10]

As it was, any disquiet at Rome quickly paled into insignificance compared with events in the east. Fuscus had crossed the Danube by pontoon bridge to launch an attack on the Dacians from their rear, but no field commander, he lost his life and much of his army in the subsequent battle.[11] The *princeps* was forced to return in person to retrieve the situation, winning his thirteenth and fourteenth salutations before the year was out. Nothing less than a conclusive victory over the Dacians would repair the harm, and so Domitian devoted 87 to preparations for a full-scale campaign against Decebalus. Moesia was now partitioned to form two new provinces, and up to six legions converged on the Lower Danube ready for the invasion in 88. Assembling this force could only be achieved by reducing the garrisons in other operational theatres, among them Britannia, which now lost the *legio II Adiutrix*, bringing about the abandonment of the island north of the Tyne–Solway line: as Tacitus gloomily assessed the consequence, 'perdomita Britannia et statim omissa' – 'All Britain had been subdued, but was then abandoned.'[12]

Domitian, however, was once more cheated of personal victory. Rumours of a conspiracy at Rome compelled his return, and he returned to the capital, leaving L. Tettius Julianus, a general of proven ability, in charge of the campaign. While history remains silent on the identities and aims of the conspirators at home, there can be little doubt concerning the substance of the plot suppressed that September. Shortly after, news reached Rome of Julianus' victory over the Dacians at Tapae, only the lateness of the season preventing him from pressing home the advantage. Domitian took his fifteenth and sixteenth imperial salutations at the end of the year, and with the gateway to the Dacian *Basileion* stormed, could reasonably look forward that winter to outright victory in the coming season – only to be distracted from achieving his aims once again, this time by an insurrection fomented by L. Antoninus Saturninus, army commander of Moguntiacum (Mainz) and Upper Germany. [13]

The meagre episodic fragments that survive tell us very little about Saturninus' revolt. It was activated at the very beginning of January 89, when he seized the combined funds of his two legions – the *XIV Gemina Martia Victrix* and the *XXI Rapax* – and declared against the emperor, but his motives are nowhere reported. If we are to accept our sources uncritically, his personal circumstances render him an unlikely candidate of a wider plot to replace the emperor. Equestrian by origin, elevated to the senate by Vespasian, and made suffect consul by Domitian in 82, he was allegedly a disgusting and scandalous fellow, not to be trusted with state funds, and had been publicly condemned on account of his homosexuality. Whatever prompted his move now (an attempt to forestall further prosecution by an increasingly moralistic *princeps*?), Saturninus singularly failed to secure the allegiance of the other Upper German legions, the *VIII Augusta* at Argentorate (Strasbourg), and the *XI Claudia* at Vindonissa (Windisch). Nor could he elicit the support of any other army commanders, which forced him to recruit the Chatti to his side.[14]

Domitian was at Rome when he received the news of the uprising. By 12 January 89, he had left for Moguntiacum, having ordered Trajan, at this time commander of the *legio VII Gemina* in Hispania Tarraconensis, to organize a counter-attack from the south.[15] In the event, the presence of neither Domitian nor Trajan was needed. Before 29 January 89, Saturninus was outflanked and defeated by his northern colleague, Aulus Bucius Lappius Maximus, a sudden thaw of the Rhine preventing the Chatti from crossing to the rebels' aid.[16] Domitian none the less continued on his journey, as did Trajan, and the surviving literary sources suggest some limited follow-up action against the Chatti. They also reveal the emperor's revenge on the principal surviving conspirators at Moguntiacum – some being tortured with hot iron rods inserted in their private parts.[17]

Domitian allegedly used the pretext of the revolt to remove many of those at Rome who were opposed to him, claiming it was the manifestation of a wider senatorial conspiracy. True, Lappius is said to have burnt many incriminating documents when he took Moguntiacum: but the charge seems unfounded, for he held Domitian's trust and was rewarded for his prompt action with the administration of Syria, receiving a second consulship in 95.[18] Similarly, Domitian evidently retained confidence in, and the support of, his other senior commanders, and it has proved impossible to identify any senators who suffered for their putative connivance, which suggests that any alleged conspiracy was a fabrication.[19] On the other hand, it could well be significant that Domitian chose Marcus Cocceius Nerva as his fellow consul in 90. All the Flavians seem to have been loath to share the consulship with those not of their *gens*, yet Nerva, while of an ancient lineage, was certainly no relative, which makes his election superficially somewhat startling. The reason probably lay with his nature and reputation: he was a consummate diplomat and distinguished consul of Vespasian's, and a man of proven expertise in smoothing over discord between *princeps* and *Curia*.

The revolt suppressed, Domitian was again able to devote his attention to the Danube, where he faced a steadily worsening situation. The Suebic Marcomanni and Quadi had refused to honour their treaty obligations during his earlier campaign against Decebalus, and were now proving directly hostile. Both tribes revised their attitude when Domitian arrived in Pannonia, but their peace emissaries were put to death.[20] An advance north against the Marcomanni began the same year, only to be reversed, perhaps because Domitian committed insufficient forces, the bulk of his army remaining in Moesia to forestall any action on the part of the Dacians. To recover the situation, he hastily concluded a peace treaty with Decebalus and the tribes beyond the Marcomanni, allowing him to move reinforcements to the Upper Danube.[21] Sabinus and Fuscus might lie unavenged, but with the threat of war on two fronts removed, the emperor's representatives could devote their attention to the Marcomanni while Domitian himself returned to the capital.

Little is known about the subsequent conduct of the Marcomannic War, except that it did not go as expected. In May 92, the 'Suebi', by whom the Quadi are presumably meant, allied themselves with the Sarmatian Iazyges and prepared to cross the Ister, the name given to the Lower Danube, and attack Pannonia and/or Moesia Superior.[22] A legion and its commander were lost in action in 'Sarmatia' about this time, probably the *legio XXI Rapax*, recently transferred east in disgrace from Moguntiacum and henceforth absent from all records; the 'Sarmatians' in question, however, might well have been the Roxolani rather than the Iazyges.[23] Domitian once more made his way to the Danube, remaining there for eight months to co-ordinate the response. Nine legions, plus detachments from the Rhine army, were now assembled to counter the Sarmatian threat, one force moving through part of Dacia, apparently with the agreement of Decebalus, to attack the Quadi and their Iazygian allies from the east. In the face of such odds, they elected for peace: Domitian took an *ovatio* on his return to Rome in December 92/January 93, instead of a triumph, denoting that his business with them was not yet complete.[24]

Despite the derision of contemporary observers, all writing after the fact, it is clear that Domitian's Suebic–Sarmatic wars were the necessary preliminaries to an intended military settlement of the Dacian problem. And such a settlement was required, to avenge the defeats of Sabinus and Fuscus and to escape the crippling subsidies agreed with Decebalus for his neutrality after the débâcle of 89, which included large sums of money 'as well as artisans of every trade pertaining to both peace and war'.[25] In the event, Domitian never resumed hostilities against the Dacians, perhaps because intermittent warfare with the Suebi continued to occupy his armies. That, at least, can be inferred from the lack of even an *ovatio* over the Suebi, and an active state of war against them seems to have continued for another five years.[26] It might have been that the Roman forces were overextended. More likely, the numerous financial burdens and obligations involved in the Danubian campaigns had exhausted the state treasuries, precluding the possibility of sustaining decisive momentum on a continuous front which stretched from Noricum to the Danube Delta.

Domitian's return to Rome in the winter of 92/93 coincided with open displays of discontent with his regime. The so-called tyranny of his reign is generally held to have commenced now with the punishment of the more vocal malcontents, some of whom were detected by *agents provocateurs*.[27] Now, while we cannot be precisely certain of the circumstances that occasioned Domitian's violent reaction, inevitable inferences can be drawn from the identity of the principals who suffered persecution, the self-professed Stoics Helvidius Priscus, Junius Arulenus Rusticus and Herennius Senecio. Whatever any latent paranoia Domitian suffered from, he had good reason to fear the wider publication of these men's Stoical beliefs. Stoicism was distinctly anti-imperialist, its adherents rejecting both monarchical rule and the hereditary system.[28] It was not the first time such doctrines had been found potentially treasonous: Vespasian had also had problems with Stoics who criticized his reign, one being the homonymous father of the self-same Helvidius Priscus, and had eventually sentenced a number of them to exile or execution for publishing beliefs 'inappropriate to the times, and ... subtly corrupting'.[29] Domitian, in his turn, had found cause to expel certain philosophers as early as 83, and thus it should not occasion surprise that he might now be mistrustful and suspicious over the activities of these three men. They were summarily tried and executed for *maiestas*, and their friends, relatives and other suspicious individuals subsequently persecuted, many being exiled.[30]

The breakdown in relations between *princeps* and senate continued into 94/95, when a number of other distinguished people were persecuted by Domitian for their suspected disloyalty.[31] It may have been that a general unhappiness with the military situation, despite the victory of Julianus, was exacerbated by the shock caused by the death of Fuscus – a popular member of the 'in-crowd' at Rome – and the loss of his army. Even at this early date, an acute shortage of manpower threatened the supply of replacements.[32] It was doubtless magnified by the withdrawal of garrisons from the uttermost parts of Britain, for no matter how severe the situation on the Danube, Domitian's actions were considered by many to be a calculated betrayal of all that Vespasian and Titus' generals had achieved in that island province. Finally, any residual equanimity was probably completely obliterated by first the banishment of the imperial secretary, Epaphroditus, on suspicion of *maiestatis*, then his forced suicide, *pour encourager les autres*.[33] To this proof of the growing mental instability on the part of the emperor, Dio adds the tradition that henceforth, he let it be known that he kept a list under his pillow of those whom he most feared, intending to have them killed whenever the opportunity arose.[34]

According to our sources, in 95 Domitian's already execrable relationship with certain sections of the aristocracy was irrevocably damaged by his persecution of several senators for their 'atheism'.[35] Impiety was something he could not personally disregard, not only because it could be construed as an active denial of his absolutism, by which he was both *Dominus* and *Deus*, 'Lord' and 'God', but also because he had consistently proclaimed religious archaism.[36] In 83, for example, he had three Vestal Virgins executed for unchastity; eight years later, the adulterous Chief Virgin, Cornelia, was buried alive, her principal accomplice being beaten to death with rods while others were exiled for their complicity.[37]

The most prominent victims of the current religious trials were no less distinguished. One was M'. Acilius Glabrio, consul with Trajan in 91. Evidently an accomplished hunter, who had trained as a gladiator with wild beasts, he was first exiled and then executed, according to Dio on trumped up charges because of Domitian's jealousy over these skills.[38] A second victim was of even greater dignity. T. Flavius Clemens was the emperor's own cousin, and had only recently shared the ordinary consulship with Domitian, while his wife, Domitilla, was the emperor's niece, and their two sons had been designated by Domitian as his heirs. According to Dio, Clemens and his family were specifically charged with having 'drifted into Jewish ways', and Glabrio and the others condemned with him had, by implication, similarly converted.[39] Whether Judaism or Christianity is meant is not certain, although the last seems more likely as a later tradition records that Domitilla suffered 'for the espousal of her Christian beliefs'.[40] Whichever, both were monotheistic faiths which disavowed the current orthodoxy – the Christians being especially notorious for their apostasy and rejection of traditional Roman religion – and adherence to either doctrine was considered potentially treasonous at best. Thus, quickly found guilty of impiety, Clemens was executed the same year: his sons, only recently renamed Vespasian and Domitian at the emperor's insistence, are heard of no more, which suggests execution or forced suicide, and Domitilla was banished to Pandateria.[41]

While Domitian's detractors would have us believe these events caused fear amongst the senate as a whole, there is no evidence that the persecution of either the Stoics or the 'impious' resulted in wholesale trials for *maiestas* amongst the *Curia*. In fact, with one possible exception, none of Domitian's military commanders or his leading administrators seems to have been implicated in what some modern commentators have seen as widespread political intrigue, and many of these men continued to support the emperor quite openly. The single exception might be the Praetorian Prefect Casperius Aelianus, who was apparently prematurely retired and replaced by one Petronius Secundus.[42] There again, the undeserved punishment meted out to Epaphroditus and the rapid downfall of two ex-consuls – one, Clemens, a man of the most contemptible sloth, with no obvious political aims – no matter how justified the charge against them, might well have given cause for alarm amongst the emperor's closest collaborators and confidants: the impetuous behaviour of Nero's last years was still fresh in many minds.[43]

Little surprise, then, that those who eventually ended Domitian's reign all belonged to his immediate entourage. According to Suetonius and Dio, the chief conspirators were Parthenius and Saturninus Saturius, both imperial chamberlains, abetted by Stephanus, a freedman of the exiled Domitilla. What prompted their action was the discovery by Domitia, the emperor's wife, of his pillow-book, and the revelation that all were included on his list of potential conspirators, and thus destined for execution.[44] To what further extent Domitia may have been involved in events cannot be gauged. She evidently treasured Domitian's memory after his death and prominently displayed her status as his widow on bricks issued from properties she owned in her own right. On the other hand, she had not played a conspicuous part in his reign after being named Augusta, and is alleged to have been adulterous and promiscuous.[45] Whatever her involvement, Dio adds that the plot was known to the two Praetorian Prefects, Norbanus and Petronius Secundus. That is to be expected. It would have been necessary for the conspirators to elicit their acquiescence at the very least, if not their active support. They commanded the only significant military forces stationed in the capital, and their agreement was necessary in any transition of power, as had been demonstrated by the elevations of Claudius, of Galba and of Domitian himself. A later tradition confirms: Petronius was to pay with his life for his complicity in the plot.[46]

Our sources are suspiciously silent about any participants of senatorial dignity. The silence betokens only that in the aftermath of the assassination it was considered essential to preserve an acquiescent senate, best done by not naming names. Time would show that no matter what opprobrium was heaped on Domitian during later reigns, his successors retained the services of several of his administrators and commanders. Neither Tacitus, Pliny nor Suetonius were so politically naïve as to extol the treasonous acts of men now serving another master. Only Dio, writing twelve decades later, hints at any collusion. He reports that M. Cocceius Nerva, Domitian's eventual successor and one of the few senators belonging to what survived of the republican nobility, was cognisant of the plot, and was offered the purple before Domitian was killed – but only after unnamed others, fearing the actions of *agents provocateurs*, had refused to take any part in the proceedings.[47] That members of the *Curia* were somehow involved seems a foregone conclusion, as only by assuming such co-operation can the subsequent unopposed transfer of power be explained; whether it resulted from extensive lobbying, or the rapidity with which the senate was presented with a strongly backed successor, however, must remain uncertain. Likewise the lack of any overt military opposition to Nerva's accession in the provinces is putative evidence for connivance between those responsible for the emperor's demise and Domitian's senior commanders and provincial governors. Their studied inactivity, when contrasted with the machinations and alliances connected with the bloody wars of 68/69, leaves little doubt that the plot was long in the making, and that an agreed successor had been selected before any action was taken. It also confirms that the conspiracy which ended Domitian's life was not simply a palace plot as is generally assumed.[48]

Whosoever was involved, the assassins struck on the afternoon of 18 September 96, coincidentally Trajan's fortieth birthday. Parthenius having beforehand removed the blade of the sword which Domitian habitually kept under his pillow, the emperor was attacked by Stephanus as he retired for his customary siesta.[49] As the emperor fell prostrate, the others came to Stephanus' aid: their victim was stabbed seven times before he expired, Stephanus also losing his life in the unseemly mêlée that developed when servants ignorant of the plot sought to save their potentate. Thus the Flavian dynasty ended, and there began the historical period which Edward Gibbon considered the 'most happy and prosperous' for the condition of the human race.

The Principate of Nerva

And yet there was by no means universal joy in the capital at the news of Domitian's death. The plebeians, for one, seemed indifferent. The Praetorian Guard, on the other hand, sought his deification and the punishment of the conspirators; only the involvement of their own commanders forestalled immediate action, and a year was to elapse before they were able to exact revenge.[50] As for the assembled senators in Rome, they could hardly disguise their euphoria. Forgetting their dignity amidst a wave of recklessness, they voted that every one of Domitian's statues and images be smashed, his memory damned, his name erased from all inscriptions, and all records of his reign revoked. That same evening they approved the choice of Marcus Cocceius Nerva as *princeps*. Having been reassured by Parthenius that Domitian was indeed dead, the new ruler made his way to the senate to be congratulated on his accession.[51] Only his contemporary and close friend, Arrius Antoninus, grandfather of the future emperor Antoninus, sounded a note of caution. After commending the senate and the provinces on the choice, he questioned why one who had escaped the designs of a tyrant should now submit himself to the inconvenience and danger of the position and the judgement of friends and enemies: not least because his friends would believe they deserved his favour, and not receiving it from so judicious a ruler, would become worse than his actual enemies.[52]

Such were the events surrounding Nerva's accession, according to the literary tradition, which was predominantly the work of existing senators. But the selection of Nerva was not the work of the senate alone, functioning as a unified body. Our sources cannot disguise the reality. Their choice was limited to a single candidate put forward by the principal conspirators, both named and nameless, and the smoothness of the operation affirms the involvement of senior senators in what was ostensibly a palace plot. Even so, given the general obfuscation of the contemporary accounts, it would be rash to claim precisely why Nerva was chosen. He could, however, attest to a most dignified lineage.[53] He was born at Narnia on 8 November 35; his homonymous great-grandfather was *consul ordinarius* in 36 BC and proconsul of Asia, and his great-great-uncle, L. Cocceius Nerva, mediated between Octavian and Antony at Brundisium (Brindisi). His immediate paternal ancestry was no less exalted. His grandfather, a close friend of Tiberius, was consul and *curator aquarum*, and both he and Nerva's father were among the leading jurists of their day. On his mother's side, he was descended from the consul Octavius Laenas, also *curator aquarum*, and his mother's brother was husband to Julia, daughter of Drusus and Livilla and granddaughter of Tiberius, thereby relating the family to Nero.

With such celebrated relations, it is understandable that Nerva was a partisan of the Julio-Claudian family in his youth and was signalled by them with rapid and prestigious advancement through the senatorial *cursus*. He became one of the twenty-four members of the ancient priestly college of the *Salii*; was made city prefect for the Latin festival and *sevir turmae equitum Romanorum* (honorary commander of one of the six squadrons of Roman knights); and was elected *quaestor urbanus*. Later, when praetor designate, he played a senior but unspecified part in the suppression of the Pisonian conspiracy, receiving triumphal honours comparable to those of the man responsible for crushing the plot, the Praetorian Prefect, Ofonius Tigellinus.[54] Yet despite this notable service, he saw neither provincial nor military command, nor does he seem to have followed the usual and most obvious alternative, a legal career. Instead, he chose the quiet life of a minor courtier, one who enjoyed his wining and dining, while practising his skills in lyricism – Martial named him the Tibullus of the age, although he was modest of his own ability.[55]

But the studied indifference of the lyrical courtier hid an astute political mind, and Nerva matured into a shrewd diplomat, capable of balancing his own position between diametrically opposed parties. He was careful not to be openly allied with any faction during the Civil Wars of 68/9, and emerged unscathed to become a favourite of the Flavian dynasty, despite his own dynastic connection and record of service to Nero and a probable marital relationship to Otho.[56] Indeed, such was his discretion that he became the only *privatus* to share the *fasces* with Vespasian – and at that in 71, the very beginning of Vespasian's rule, helping inaugurate the years of peace. It may well have been that some personal connection already existed between Nerva and the Flavii: a later anecdote claims that he had debauched Domitian, perhaps a scurrilous interpretation of a regular social institution among contemporary Hellenists, that of the *erastes* and *eromenos*.[57] Whatever the case, Nerva's principal asset to the new regime was his avowed neutrality and his marital connections to the Julio-Claudians, which on the one hand mollified and reassured those who retained a fondness for the principate's premier dynasty, and on the other alleviated the fear of their political opponents, those who had openly supported the other contenders for the *imperium*. His status as a senior member of the nobility was doubtless equally decisive: the recent advancement of the Flavii into Rome's élite from extremely humble stock was known to all, and his election satisfied the *amour propre* of the old republican nobility who saw one of their own in place as senior magistrate.

Nerva's services to the Flavian dynasty were rewarded by his election as *augur* and as *sodalis Augustalis*, one of the priests who conducted the cult of the deified Caesar and Augustus.[58] Later on, in the troubled year of 90, when Domitian saw conspiracy at every hand, his neutrality and amiability again became decisive, for he was elected to an iterated ordinary consulship with Domitian, becoming one of the few non-Flavians to be so. He was evidently a safe and quiet man; it consequently seems inherently unlikely that he was later banished to Tarentum for conspiracy, as Philostratus alleges, even if other sources also claim he was exiled during the 'tyranny'.[59] Likewise little credence should be placed in the tradition recounted by Dio, that Domitian had once placed him in peril of his life. The alleged circumstances were these. The emperor, having looked at Nerva's horoscope along with those of other leading men, established that he would become ruler and decided to have him slain along with others condemned for this same reason; except that an astrologer friendly to Nerva persuaded Domitian that he was destined to die within a few days anyway, whereupon Domitian, 'not wishing to be guilty of yet another murder, since Nerva was so soon to die regardless', allowed him to live.[60] Both of these stories, that he was exiled or placed in terror of his life, belong to a recognized genre invented to justify the principicide and yet continue the imperial system. The majority of the individual senators had actually done quite well out of Domitian's reign. They now found it necessary to exculpate themselves by denigrating their benefactor as an inherently evil person, insinuating that all who achieved prominence did so by their own means, and in spite of his hatred. If, however, Nerva had indeed aroused Domitian's displeasure by some obscure act, it could not have been very serious and any consequent 'exile' must have been little more than a period of self-imposed banishment, for otherwise he would never have won the allegiance – however reluctantly – of the pro-Domitianic faction at Rome, the Praetorian Guard and Domitian's own *consilium*. With such considerations in mind the silence of contemporary commentators on the matter is decisive and instructive.[61]

In Nerva, therefore, the conspirators ascertained the ideal candidate who satisfied all aspects of the political spectrum. He had social distinction, as a descendant of republican nobility, as a relative of the Julio-Claudian house and as a trusted confidant of the Flavian dynasty. Then, he was a man for all seasons, and consummate master in balancing the differing demands of whichever regime prevailed. He was renowned for his practised discretion; his cautious progress through the senatorial career – after the episode of the Pisonian conspiracy – ensured he had no declared enemies who might provoke civil war, nor was he identifiable with any one political faction.[62] Finally, his general affability and kindly disposition promised there would be no mass persecutions of even the closest of Domitian's advisers – especially as he was acquainted with many prominent members of the dead emperor's *consilium*, and could even be classed among his supporters.[63]

There was one further and significant advantage beside these political considerations. Nerva was by now well advanced in years, approaching the great climacteric of the sixty-third year, and already suffering the ails and illnesses associated with old age. Yet he had no immediate male or female heir, nor was he related to any of the consular legates.[64] Few among the senate could have been ignorant of the elder Pliny's comments concerning the system of government in Ceylon, where, it was alleged, a truly effective system of rule was ensured by selecting the ruler from among those advanced in years, who were childless and who displayed clemency, which prevented the establishment of a dictatorial hereditary monarchy.[65] Nerva fulfilled these requirements, and his selection perhaps allowed the conspirators, and thus the assembled senators, to delude themselves into believing they had effected a restoration of dyarchal rule.[66] Confirming in office one of their own, they had every reason to believe in a heady new dawn where they would be able to control the choice of succession.

The reality was more sobering. Nerva was openly identified as a compromise candidate: there was substance to the rumour which avowed he was not the conspirators' first choice.[67] The suspicion of temporizing is heightened by Nerva's declaration that he had done nothing to prevent him from resigning power and returning to private life, coincidentally confirming the record of his career to date as that of a person who had not sought political prerogative.[68] In which case, it can be deduced that he allowed himself to be elected only through a sense of altruism, as a transitional candidate acceptable to several contending factions, none of whom commanded overall acceptance amongst those with knowledge of the plot. While he owed his candidature to the machinations of the imperial household in consort with elements of the military command, and his social dignity and childless marriage commended him to the senate as Domitian's heir, it was his acceptability to the military above all which secured his position, as potential successors began to juggle for wider support and a more advantageous position.

The shortness of Nerva's reign precludes the identification of a defined change in imperial policy except in a few limited areas. Study of his coinage, for example, suggests that his immediate concern on accession was to reassure the general populace that all was well. Some types and legends reappeared for the first time since the Civil War of AD 69/70, and seem designed to fulfil the same purpose: to emphasize the dawn of a new age in which the peace-loving citizen could be at ease again after a period marked by absolute monarchical rule and personal and political intrigue. Others are reminiscent of early Augustan issues, suggesting a desire to associate the new regime with Augustan ideals, especially the politics of equilibrium and moral justice. It was probably no accident that these often bore a likeness of Nerva on the obverse markedly similar to that of the first *princeps*, as if to imply a personal relationship and thus confirm the legitimacy of his accession. An equal number of types were direct copies of those originally introduced by Galba, evidently intended to stress the similarities between the two men – their frugality and discreet personal reputation – and to promote a spirit of reconciliation. Above all, as incidental literary references confirm, Nerva effected a harmonization of the previously incompatible virtues of *libertas* and *principatus* – liberty within an autocracy.[69]

Nerva's inaugural political acts affirm the themes announced on his coinage.[70] Propitiation of the army by a donative is suggested by issues proclaiming *CONCORDIA EXERCITUUM*, 'The Harmony of the Armies', the first time the legend had appeared since the 68/69 Civil War, corroborating the allegiance of the army to the new government after a somewhat uncertain period.[71] The Praetorians took a large share of the largesse and were further appeased by the restoration of Casperius Aelianus as prefect in place of Norbanus and Petronius Secundus, removed from office as a nominal gesture for their complicity in Domitian's death.[72] The army commanders, meanwhile, were quickly confirmed in post, thus avoiding the uncertainty that had led to Galba's downfall in 68. Their allegiance was secured by the continuance of Domitian's military policies, at least along the Danube. This is indicated by the appearance of coins with the legend *ADLOCUTIO AUGUSTA*, 'An address to the armies by the emperor', the normal sign for the opening of a military campaign – in this case, a promised fresh season in the continuation of the Bello Suebicorum begun by Domitian.[73]

The complicity of the plebs was ensured by the customary accession gift, the *congiarium*, perhaps as much as 75 *denarii* per male citizen listed on the appropriate census, and commemorated with coins proclaiming *CONGIARIUM POPULI ROMANI*.[74] Their support was secured by the institution of a number of wide-ranging reforms aimed at diminishing the financial burden of the Italian people. Overall taxation was reduced; the abuses connected with the Jewish tax were ended and the tax only collected from those who admitted openly to the faith; the public were exempted from the expenses incurred for the *cursus publicus*; and it was decreed that the nominally neutral praetors, and not the imperial procurators, should settle disputes between individuals and the *fiscus*.[75] As part of a programme to promote the wealth and health of Rome and Italy, and to relieve the pressure of over-population at the capital, the colony at Scolacium, amongst others, was refounded; an alimentary system may have been instituted; a *lex agraria* was passed, which allowed for the allotment of land worth *HS* 60,000,000 to poor citizens under the direction of a senatorial commission in charge of purchase and distribution; the capital's water supply was reorganised; and the grain supply restructured, new granaries being built to facilitate the reform.[76]

Nor was Nerva solely concerned with the physical well-being of the urban plebs. Laws were passed allowing cities to receive legacies, forbidding castration, and restoring the pantomimes banned by Domitian. Among other measures, he turned over Domitian's house on the Palatine for public accommodation, renaming it the 'House of the People'. The grandiose Forum Transitorium, begun by Domitian, was completed; the Circus Maximus extended and improved, and new games established; and steps were taken to repair damage caused by a flood of the Tiber. In the provinces the tribute money payable on his accession was reduced, financial assistance was offered to many cities, and new citizens were excluded from the 5 per cent inheritance tax, whereby they were taxed on any monies they left to their non-citizen relatives.[77]

To implement these measures meant increasing the imperial budget. Although Nerva probably found the treasury just sufficiently wealthy to pay for his own programme and complete the expensive building projects started by Domitian, he none the less inaugurated a programme of financial austerity on the part of the imperial household. Beginning with a sale of his private and imperial property, he added the bullion content of Domitian's gold and silver statues to the *fiscus*, and set up a five-man commission, the *minuendis publicis sumptibus*, to find ways of reducing public expenditure.[78] It is doubtful that any of these specific acts had a serious effect on the treasury. More likely the policy was not so much dictated by the necessity to restore the parlous state of an ailing treasury as by Nerva's own frugal habits, as a means to restore personal confidence in the nature of the regime itself.

In his relations with the senate, Nerva continued to extol the pragmatism that had made him so valuable to Vespasian and Domitian in times of emergency. Even though a new wave of terror had begun, in which certain senators sought to resolve personal vendettas by associating their personal enemies with the name of Domitian, he refused to interfere with matters, and held back while many of Domitian's minor officials perished in the first few heady days.[79] The *Curia* was riven with accusation and counter-accusation. Typical was the attempt by Pliny the Younger to prosecute Publicius Certus for bringing the capital charge against Helvidius Priscus on Domitian's behalf:

> Once Domitian was killed, I decided on reflection that this was a truly splendid opportunity for attacking the guilty, avenging the injured, and making oneself known. And while many crimes had been committed by numerous persons, nothing seemed more shocking than the violent attack in the senate made by one senator on another, by a praetorian [*sc.*, Certus] acting as judge on a consular [*sc.*, Priscus] who had been brought to trial. [. . .] I entered the senate, requested permission to speak, and for some time won warm approval for what I was saying – until I mentioned the charge and indicated who was to be accused, when there was

a general outcry against me. 'Who is the object of your attack?', 'Who is being charged without formal notice?', 'Let the survivors [of the tyranny] live!' and so on. [. . .] All defended Certus as if I had named him, though I had not yet done so, and began refuting a charge as yet unspecified. [. . .] Then my turn came. I rose to my feet [. . .] and replied to them one by one. [. . .] I came to an end, and Veiento began to reply. No one would allow it [he had already spoken in his proper turn], and the interruption and uproar increased so much that he pleaded, 'I beg you, *patres conscripti*, not to compel me to ask for the protection of the tribunes.' At once the tribune Murena retorted, 'The honourable gentleman has my permission to continue.' Again there was an outcry, and the consul called out the names, took the division, and dismissed the *Curia*, leaving Veiento still standing and trying to speak.[80]

The thirst for revenge increasingly threatened those who had been Domitian's intimates, even the more important, who had previously saved themselves through wealth and influence. *Ad hoc* attacks of the type staged by Pliny the Younger became so prevalent that the consul Ti. Catius Fronto, a noted jurist, openly complained that the current anarchy in the *Curia* was worse than the previous tyranny. On hearing this, Nerva ordered that the prevailing state of affairs should cease forthwith. Henceforth, no formal prosecution was allowed of men summarily accused of collaboration without clear evidence of their possible involvement; furthermore, the charge of *maiestas* was suppressed, and an undertaking given that no senator would be put to death without due process.[81] It was a shrewd move on his part. The edicts had the doubtless intentional effect that any subsequent trials for complicity with the previous regime would have to be initiated by the *Curia* itself, which, like any administration, remained a body notoriously loath to condemn its own. Open dissent ceased.

Other measures quickly followed to restore the dignity of the senate. Certain of Domitian's more repressive acts were repealed, and many – but not all – of those imprisoned or exiled for impiety or other reasons were released and their property restored.[82] Even so, there was a general feeling among the public that the senate had pardoned its own while being severe to other groups, as so many of Domitian's informers, alleged and real, survived the transition. A sardonic anecdote gives substance:

> ... [At the magisterial court] that staunch champion of honesty, Junius Mauricus, declared [...] that he wished the games could be abolished at Rome. This showed great courage and resolution on his part, you will say, but that is nothing new for him. He displayed the same courage in the hearing of the emperor Nerva. Nerva was dining with a small party where Veiento [an alleged informer of Domitian's] was at his side at the table, even familiarly leaning on his shoulder: I need say no more than naming the creature. The conversation turned to the blind Catullus Messalinus [another informer] whose loss of sight had increased his already cruel disposition so much that he had neither fear, shame nor pity, and consequently had been used by Domitian to attack honest men like a weapon that flies blindly and unthinkingly to its mark. Everyone at the table was discussing his villainy and murderous decisions when the emperor Nerva said, 'I wonder what would have happened were he alive today' – 'Dining with us', replied Mauricus.[83]

Pliny's cynicism to some extent was based on fact. Nerva consolidated his tenuous hold on the imperial power and appeased any rival factions by confirming existing office-holders in their posts. But he awarded any vacant senior jurisdictions to members of his own peer group, the men associated with the reigns of Vespasian and Titus rather than Domitian. It was another shrewd move, worthy of this consummate politician, for his own candidates were not allied to any of the contending parties within the *Curia*, and could be projected as objective and neutral in all matters of government. The most illustrious among them was the foremost surviving marshal of Vespasian's reign, Julius Frontinus: now in his sixties, he was made *curator aquarum*,[84] before advancing to an iterated consulship. No less notable was Nerva's first choice to share the *fasces*, Verginius Rufus, commander of the Lower German army in 68, who took his third consulate as Nerva's colleague in 97, when aged 82/3. Arrius Antoninus, former proconsul of Asia, was also elected consul in 97 (his second term), and Vestricius Spurinna and Cn. Domitius Tullus were similarly advanced to the iterated consulship in 98.[85] Yet it was no gerontocracy: younger men were forthcoming – and were appointed. But the five named had not been conspicuously advanced by Domitian, and their advancement and rehabilitation now served the purpose of divorcing the new regime from the old while Nerva's position was secured.

Despite his attempts at appeasement, the connivance of the senior military commanders in the matter of Nerva's accession barely disguised the beginnings of a struggle for the succession. With an agreed compromise candidate in place, one whose position was inherently weakened by his advanced age, ill-health and the lack of an obvious successor, conspiracies abounded. The first signs of political weakness surfaced in 97, after Pliny's aforementioned attack on Certus. An unidentified consular took the orator aside and quietly warned him not to be so provocative: Certus had powerful friends, any one of whom might one day be emperor. A more explicit warning came to Pliny from another consular, again unidentified, who observed that the current governor of Syria, about whom rumours were already circulating concerning a plot for the *imperium*, was also one of Certus' intimates.[86] Substance for the latter putative conspiracy at least is provided by inscriptions showing that a consular governor of Syria – probably M. Cornelius Nigrinus – was replaced *c.* 97 by one A. Larcius Priscus, at the time *legatus legionis IV Scythicae*. Already having been exceptionally awarded the legionary command while quaestor in Asia, and while not yet a consular, Priscus was granted the appropriate powers as *pro legato consulare provinciae Syriae* – 'in place of the consular legate of Syria' – which indicates the need for a rapid replacement at a time of crisis.[87]

Yet another cabal involving elements of the military was led by Calpurnius Crassus. Consul in 87, he was a descendant of the famous dictator and perhaps a nephew of the Piso Licinianus belatedly adopted by Galba in 69. Apprised of the plot, Nerva caused Crassus and its leading members to sit beside him at the Circus and gave them swords to inspect, to show them he did not care what they intended. Thus exposed, they confessed their guilt and Crassus and his wife were exiled to Tarentum (Taranto), although many senators criticized Nerva for his leniency.[88]

A more serious threat materialized in the summer of 97, one that shook the very authority of the emperor: a breakdown in the discipline of the Praetorian Guard. Misled by Nerva's amiability and his continued friendship with many of those prominent under

Domitian, the Guard now sought revenge on Domitian's assassins. With Casperius Aelianus at their head, they besieged Nerva in his palace before arresting him, and demanded that the murderers be handed over. Nerva bared his throat and offered his own life in their place, saying that he would rather die than diminish his authority by surrendering them, but Casperius brushed the offer aside and Nerva was forced to accede to their demands. Those prominent in the intrigue against Domitian were immediately done to death, Petronius with a single blow, but Parthenius with extreme cruelty: first he was castrated, then his testes were stuffed into his mouth before he was slowly strangled by a guardsman. Insult followed injury: Nerva was forced to render solemn and public thanks to Casperius and the Guard for the execution of 'these most wicked and sinful men'.[89] The Praetorians seemed once again the undisputed masters of Rome.

The indiscipline of the Guard revealed the inability of Nerva to command general support for his position, for not even the senate had come to his assistance. Circumstances did not bode well for the survival of the regime or the political system it represented. None the less, after consultation with his *consilium*, Nerva eschewed abdication and, to avert a return to the unhappy years of 68/69, decided upon a successor who could command the loyalty of the legions, overawe the Praetorians, and restore authority to the principate. In the autumn of 97, he found a suitable opportunity to announce the fact when he received a laurelled-wreath signifying a victory in Pannonia, apparently the end of the '*bellum Suebicum*'.[90] He made his way to the Capitol, and there publicly proclaimed in a loud voice:

> May good success always attend the Roman Senate and People and myself. I hereby adopt Marcus Ulpius Nerva Trajan.[91]

IV
DOMITIAN'S GENERAL,
NERVA'S HEIR

The credulous were assured that the choice of Trajan was foretold by omens. According to Dio, certain (unspecified) portents had appeared when Trajan assumed the consulship in 91 which predicted his assumption of the imperial office and the death of his colleague Glabrio at the hands of Domitian. Another prognostication took the form of a dream, in which Trajan

> thought that an old man in a purple-bordered toga and vestments, and with a fillet on his head, as the senate is usually symbolically represented, took a finger-ring and impressed a seal on his neck, first on the left side, then on the right.

Pliny too knew of a prophetic indication:

> At the very moment of setting out to join your army [Trajan's first consular command] [...] the citizens gathered for other reasons hailed you with a shout as if you were already emperor, for when the doors [of the Capitoline Temple] opened for your entry, the entire crowd assembled at the threshold cried *Imperator*! At the time it was thought they were addressing [the statue of] Jupiter [...][1]

Such *dei ex machina* in the literary account seem hardly necessary, for the choice of Trajan as Nerva's heir was evidently a foregone conclusion. Pliny announces the fact – 'Your merits did indeed call for your adoption as successor long before the event.' Likewise Trajan clearly commanded respect among the *Curia* and loyalty from the military, as there was not even a whisper of opposition from either body. On the contrary: on the news of Trajan's elevation, 'every disturbance died away at once', and Nerva had his imperial authority restored on the strength of Trajan's own personality and standing.[2] Now, while Trajan might well have seemed the obvious choice to his contemporaries, the reasons for his selection are not immediately clear to the modern commentator. This is because the sources for his career between January 89 and September/October 97 are obscure and incomplete, most of what is known deriving from the *Panegyricus*, the encomium delivered by the younger Pliny in September 100. This was subsequently revised for publication; Pliny's few comments on Trajan's career as *privatus* are often proleptic, frequently contradictory and generally ambiguous. But despite these inadequacies, the *Panegyricus* and the few other available sources, when interpreted in the light of qualified conjecture and the known events of Domitian's reign, can be reconciled to demonstrate Trajan's steady progress from legionary legate to Nerva's undisputed heir.

As we have already seen, the first independently dated episode in Trajan's life is the attempted *coup d'état* against Domitian in January 89. According to Pliny, Trajan, then legate of the *VII Gemina* at Legio in Hispania Tarraconensis, was ordered by the emperor to lead a counter-attack from the south, as he was considered to be the emperor's 'surest aid' in resolving the crisis. The quick and decisive response of Lappius Maximus reveals Pliny to be somewhat economical with the *actualité*: but that our source should even admit to the emperor's reliance on Trajan at such an uncertain time none the less argues for a high degree of familiarity and trust between emperor and subject. Certainly, on this occasion Trajan made no secret of his loyalty to the Flavian dynasty. He at once marched to Domitian's aid:

> Germany was divided [from Spain] by the barrier of countless peoples and an almost infinite distance of intervening country, to say nothing of the Pyrenees and the Alps, or other mountains which, while little compared to these, were yet enormous. Throughout the entire journey you [*sc.*, Trajan] led your legions in haste – even hurried them along – and never thought of using horse or carriage.[3]

In the event neither Trajan nor his army were needed: by 29 January Saturninus had been routed and the mutiny suppressed. Trajan continued to Moguntiacum regardless, probably arriving there towards the end of February.[4] His speedy response to the crisis, in spite of the geographical odds, evidently increased his standing with Domitian as a trusty and efficient commander, and Pliny tells us he was immediately entrusted with an *expeditio*, a military campaign.[5] Unfortunately, as might be anticipated, the panegyrist provides no further details. The obfuscation may have been deliberate. Perhaps Trajan was entrusted with seeking out the remaining dissidents at Moguntiacum and restoring discipline to the disgraced rebels. A more direct reference to an endeavour of this type could have reflected badly on the spirit of liberty that characterized Trajan's regime. There again, Pliny could have been referring to an enterprise too well known to have needed more direct comment, and a more substantial and honourable field for Trajan's operations might be found in the shape of a punitive action against the Chatti. Not only had they supported Saturninus – indeed, his revolt only failed because they could not come to his aid at the crucial time – but they had recently forced Chariomerus, king of the Cherusci, to abdicate because of his pro-Roman stance. They may have been guilty of more serious matters: many of the Taunus frontier works only recently initiated by Domitian display signs of burning which are traditionally ascribed to this period.[6] Reason enough, then, for a sharp reminder of Rome's power, an action in which Trajan might have played a senior part. An offensive now would help explain why the Chatti submitted to a revised treaty about this time, giving Domitian grounds for celebrating a triumph over them later the same year. But if so, Pliny has surely exaggerated Trajan's role in the campaign, for it was his military superior, Lappius Maximus, who was honoured as *confectoris bellum Germanici*, 'the instigator of the German victory'.[7]

Pliny is mute concerning the subsequent stages of Trajan's career up to the time of his adoption by Nerva. In the normal scheme of things, a *legatus legionis* would expect to move on to the administration of an imperial praetorian province. But Trajan was a second-generation patrician, and could rightly have expected the ordinary consulship at this stage, even though Domitian, like his father, was sparing in according the honour to men outside the Flavian family. Whatever the level of any friendship between the two, however, Trajan's response to the crisis of 89, and his service in subsequent events, had left him high both in prestige and in the gratitude of the emperor and the state. It was the only reward suitable for a man who, like his father, had proved such an uncompromising supporter of the dynasty. Accordingly, although Pliny nowhere records the fact, Trajan was elected ordinary consul for 91, sharing the *fasces* with Acilius Glabrio, the two becoming only the second pair of non-'imperial' *consules ordinarii* to be elected in Domitian's reign.

After the consulship, a skilled and ambitious man, as Trajan seems to have been, could expect an appointment to one of the imperial proconsular provinces. There were eleven in all at this time, although junior consulars were generally limited to office in one of the two Germanies; the two Moesias; Cappadocia-Galatia; or Syria-Palaestina.[8] While each post was doubtless subject to availability, only in a very few cases did an ex-consul not make his way to one of these assignments relatively quickly. Yet Pliny does not record a single senatorial duty for Trajan before Nerva plucked him from apparent obscurity in 97 to be his heir. In the nature of things, it is inherently unlikely that Domitian failed to appoint Trajan to a consular command in the six intervening years. In fact it would have been a slight of great magnitude, and if Trajan had indeed been passed over or forced to withdraw from public life by that 'most treacherous of emperors', we might reasonably have expected Pliny, for one, not to have overlooked the chance of adding to the catalogue of Trajan's virtues and Domitian's vices.[9] Moreover, unless Trajan had some prior – and substantive – reputation as a *vir militaris* to his credit, it is exceedingly difficult to account for the ease with which his later adoption by Nerva was accepted by the military.

Thus Pliny's reticence on Trajan's activities between 89 and 96 might seem doubly suspect.[10] Perhaps he was being tactful in not drawing attention to an official position which Trajan would have had to actively seek from the 'tyrant'. After all, while his response to the German mutiny on Domitian's behalf could be used as an example of unswerving loyalty to duty, any reminder of how he subsequently sought consular command might reflect adversely on his personal judgement. It was better to play down his part in events at this time, hence the panegyrist's insinuation that Trajan was in Rome during the so-called 'reign of terror' from 93 to 96: 'You shared our life, our perils, our fears', a variant of the standard excuse offered to explain why so many not only survived the tyranny, but even prospered under Domitian.[11] That indeed seems to be confirmed by Pliny's anecdote that Domitian held Trajan in great admiration for his deeds, but also lived in fear of his competence, feeling the same mixed emotions towards him that Hercules inspired in Eurystheus.[12] Surely this is a veiled allusion to Trajan's administrative labours on Domitian's behalf, for Eurystheus set Hercules his several tasks to remove a popular and morally irreproachable subject from his kingdom. Some support for the belief is provided by a fourth-century tale, which reports Trajan saying that Domitian had good *amici* even if he was a bad emperor.[13] Now the emperor's *amici* were those confidants who made up his *consilium*, the informal political council by which he administered his sovereignty, and the remark, if true, would firmly place Trajan among this trusted inner circle. When all is said and done, the fact remains that no matter who was in charge at Rome, the continued administration and defence of the empire required a steady supply of competent senators, not least because the only way these men could make any progress in their career was in the service of the state. Pliny's failure to mention a junior consular command for Trajan –

or even his consulship for that matter – can therefore be explained by his perceived need to sever by deliberate omission any connection between the most liberal of emperors and the most tyrannical.

Consequently, it is conjectured that Trajan was advanced to some consular duties in the period 92–6, although what these may have been might seem to deny speculation. Yet numerous clues do exist, allowing some tentative reconstruction of his career in those years, even if the individual stages cannot be proven. For example, as we have already stressed, Trajan was evidently an acknowledged *vir militaris* when adopted by Nerva in the autumn of 97, which implies that he held some active service command in the 'missing' years. In view of the military situation on the Danube, it is natural to look for a placement on that particular front, and Trajan could well have gone there straight from his consulship, joining Domitian as one of the *comites Augusti*. On the other hand, it was not a regular rank, for the term *comes* is used to describe those senior officers who held an informal position as one of the emperor's companions on an imperial expedition.[14] Hence, such a position would hardly substitute for a consular command, and so a formal consular duty should be sought in one of the available imperial provinces. It just so happens that there is a gap at the appropriate time in the *fasti* for both Germania Superior and Inferior, two of the provinces generally reserved for a junior consul, and it may be speculated that Trajan held one or other office for the usual three-year term between 92/3 and 95/7.

Such, indeed, is the generally accepted view, and two items of 'evidence' are usually adduced to show that Trajan was probably governor of Upper Germany at the time of his adoption. The first depends on the precise interpretation of a somewhat ambiguous passage in the *Panegyricus*, which seems to state that Trajan was first acclaimed *Imperator* while in command in Germany, although in fact Pliny's account is not quite that specific.[15] The second is provided by the *Historia Augusta*, which relates how Hadrian, then a tribune with the *legio V Macedonica* on the Danube, was dispatched to Trajan with the formal congratulations of the Danubian armies after the adoption was announced, and followed this duty with secondment to the *legio XII Primigenia Pia Fidelis*, then stationed at Moguntiacum. Assuming that this place was Hadrian's final destination when he left on his mission, it is further deduced that Trajan was at Moguntiacum at the time of his adoption and was therefore in post as provincial commander of Germania Superior, notwithstanding the point that Hadrian's transfer to the *XII Primigenia* need have no actual bearing on Trajan's then whereabouts.[16]

On the other hand, the Rhine frontier was comparatively quiet at this period, and a tour of duty in the relatively junior command of Upper Germany would hardly – on its own – earn Trajan the military regard he evidently compelled from his peers at the time of his accession. Consequently, it seems more likely to us that while Trajan could well have held a consular command in one of the Germanies early in the relevant period, he held a second and senior consular post on a more active frontier. Indeed, such a duty is required to give substance to Pliny's comparison of Trajan with Gaius Fabricius, hero of the war against Pyrrhus; and the Scipios, who expelled the Carthaginians from Spain; and M. Furius Camillus, who saved Rome after the Gallic invasion of 387 BC. Otherwise, the rhetorical parallel could never have been seriously entertained by his contemporaries, never mind the emperor, in whose presence the encomium was delivered: after all, inappropriate adulation could easily be misconstrued as malicious parody, with consequent serious results. Now, it just so happens that at the precise period of Trajan's adoption, Rome was actively engaged in conflict with the Germanic Suebi, and hence a post for Trajan in Pannonia or Moesia might be essayed. Moreover, there is also a convenient *lacuna* in the Pannonian *fasti* for the period between 93/94 and February 98, and even some evidence, albeit circumstantial, to support the supposition that Trajan may have held the duty in that period. In the first place, it is known from the *Panegyricus* that Trajan's adoption coincided with the arrival of *litterae laureatae* announcing the news of a victory in Pannonia, and both Pliny and Xiphilinus' epitome of Dio's *Roman History* reveal that Trajan was absent from Rome at the time, seemingly on campaign.[17] Then, certain Byzantine compilations, in describing the events surrounding Trajan's adoption, provide the important detail that the laurels were sent by Trajan himself from 'Paeonia' (*sc.*, ?Pannonia), thus endorsing an oblique passage in the *Panegyricus* which seems to associate them with Trajan.[18] Admittedly, it is dangerous to place too much reliance on the evidence of otherwise unsupported epitomes, yet the principle of *difficilior lectio potius* might be applied. After all, not only is there little to show that the Byzantine chroniclers were prone to inventing such specific details, but these industrious scribes and scholars usually derived their information from sound historical sources, most notably in this period, Dio's *Roman History*. Furthermore, these scattered accounts of Trajan's adoption, though nowhere exactly identical, in general reproduce – if in abbreviated form – the similar wording, suggesting they may have in general faithfully reproduced an original or verbatim copy of Dio's original account. Therefore, as it stands, the likelihood of Trajan having commanded Pannonia as his second consular duty remains an attractive one, and for our purposes will be accepted as probable, if not proven.[19]

The adoption of Trajan, triggered as it was by the Praetorians' unseemly behaviour in the autumn of 97, was itself a two-stage process. It began with Nerva's receipt of the aforementioned 'laurelled letter', which he dedicated at the Capitol, laying it in Jupiter's lap and offering incense. He then made his way to the Forum Romanum, where he mounted the Rostra traditionally used for public proclamations, and before the assembled senate and plebs announced the adoption of Trajan as his son and heir by naming him (Caesar) Marcus Ulpius Nerva Traianus. 'At that one moment', Pliny tells us, '[Trajan] became son and Caesar.' We are assured by our sources that the choice was Nerva's alone, after careful consideration, inspired by divine intervention. But, there remains a suspicion that the decision to adopt an heir was not entirely his. It is most clearly expressed in a later anecdote which claims that Trajan was urged by L. Licinius Sura, probably *consul suffectus* at the time, to seize – indeed, usurp – the imperial power in order to avert a crisis. Then there is the notice of Pliny's that Trajan 'had not stirred up some activity' to become emperor, as if he were cognisant that such may indeed have been believed to be the case. Yet for comparison, there is also his observation that Trajan was initially averse to accepting the honour, and only did so to prevent the imperial system collapsing amidst widespread rioting and mutiny.[20]

These last details at least allow the inference that Nerva only reluctantly decided upon adopting a successor, and was probably forced to it, just as Galba had been forced to adopt Piso in 68.[21] If so, those behind the decision must have been the members of his imperial *consilium*, and while no record survives to indicate whose arguments might have prevailed, other than Sura's, there were many senior men available to lobby actively in Trajan's favour by virtue of kinship and shared origin. Aside from Sura, for example, Trajan could probably count on the support of at least five among the seven or so *consules suffecti* for 97, the year in question: Arrius Antoninus, a former colleague of his father and ex-proconsul of Asia; L. Vibius Sabinus, husband of his niece Matidia; M. Annius Verus, a native of Baetica, whose family was adlected into the patriciate along with Traianus; L. Neratius Priscus, a known friend of Trajan's; and Q. Glitius Atilius Agricola, *juridicus Hispaniae Tarraconensis* at the time Trajan had commanded the legion there. To these men can probably be added the name of L. Julius Ursus Servianus (*cos. suff.* 90), husband of Trajan's kinswoman Domitia (Aelia) Paulina, for the involvement of Julius Frontinus and L. Julius Ursus seems confirmed by their iterated consulships in 98, which they followed with the *summa fastigium* of a third in 100.[22]

With the adoption decided upon, Nerva sent Trajan a diamond ring as a token of the act, a ring later passed to Hadrian and used by him in turn as proof of legitimacy in the succession. It was perhaps sent with a personal letter naming Trajan as his heir in which Nerva expressed the hope 'May the Danaans, by thy shafts, requite my tears.' The allusion is to an episode recounted in Homer's *Iliad*. Chryses, the priest of Apollo, has been rebuffed in his quest for the return of his daughter from Agamemnon; he prays to Apollo and begs the archer-god to make the Greeks pay dearly for the insult: 'Your weapons, O Apollo, will pay them back for my tears.'[23] In other words, Nerva looked to Trajan to avenge the insults he had received at the hands of Aelianus and the Praetorians.

In themselves, however, neither ring nor letter, nor Nerva's public declaration, gave Trajan any right to the imperial succession. By adopting Trajan into his family, Nerva merely made him heir to his own personal property and estate, not to his position as *princeps*. This arose because there was no formal constitutional mechanism by which the *princeps* could delegate the supreme jurisdiction vested in his person. The hereditary principle being firmly opposed, as it smacked of monarchy, only the senate could bestow the twin privileges of *tribunicia potestas*, the power to initiate legislation and to exercise the veto over the senate, and *imperium maius*, which recognized an individual's authority within the city of Rome and over all the provinces, whether imperial or senatorial. It was the possession of both which gave the holder unparalleled *auctoritas*, the means whereby he could get things done without legal authorization, and exalted him with *sacrosanctitas*, supreme awe and reverence for his person and decisions. These were the attributes, spiritual and temporal, which made a man *princeps*, and it was only through their skilful exploitation that the succession had effectively been kept in one or other blood-line since the time of Augustus.

Augustus, for example, had used the imperial prerogative to grant Tiberius a limited term of *tribunicia potestas* and proconsular *imperium maius* as a means of associating him with the ruler's *auctoritas*; first in 6 BC, then in AD 4 and finally in 13. Consequently, when Augustus died, on 19 August 14, Tiberius was already in place as his successor, having virtually all the imperial powers as '*collega imperii, consors tribuniciae potestatis*' – 'imperial colleague, sharer of the tribunician power' – and was thus immediately able to handle all matters of state.[24] Tiberius in his turn granted *tribunicia potestatis* to his ill-fated son Drusus. Later on, Nero's elevation by the Guard was formally sealed when the senate voted him tribunician power and proconsular *imperium maius*. Conversely, the much later usurpers Pescennius Niger and Clodius Albinus never assumed *tribunicia potestatis* as the senate never recognized their claim to the principate.

None the less, it was the senate who enacted the *actus* by which the imperial powers were conferred on the man chosen as *princeps*. The only surviving evidence for the legal procedure is the so-called *lex de Imperio Vespasiani*, the constitutional act which enabled Vespasian to become emperor in 69/70.[25] A first step was evidently to assert the legitimacy of the accession by adopting the *nomen* Caesar. Augustus gained it by testamentary adoption, and Claudius, the first ruler not in the direct line from Augustus, assumed the filiation to justify and strengthen his otherwise weak claim to the principate. In due course 'Caesar' became a regular title signifying the junior colleague of the ruling emperor, but in Vespasian's case, it was usurped simply to signify his claim as lawful successor. Once legally installed, Vespasian had then exploited his *auctoritas* to revive the Augustan system of succession and establish his own Flavian dynasty. Titus received the tribunician power and proconsular *imperium maius* within three years of his father's accession, marking him as the heir apparent for all to see.

Nerva followed the same *modus operandi*. Trajan was first given the name of Caesar as a clear signal that he was Nerva's chosen heir to the principate, a status emphasized when both took the title *Germanicus* for the victory over the Suebi and Trajan was acclaimed *Imperator*, a title now restricted to the *princeps* and his successor.[26] Some time later, after the public statement of the adoption, Nerva convened the senate, and Trajan was

> summoned [to Rome], just as throughout the past [other] great leaders used to be recalled from foreign wars to come to the aid of the Fatherland. Thus, son and father, at one and the same time you two offered each other the greatest of gifts: he gave you the *imperium*, you restored its authority to him. [...] [S]oon you [...] shared in the tribunician power, and [were] given every authority, equally and at once, which recently a blood-father [*sc.*, Vespasian] had bestowed on the other of his two sons [*sc.*, Titus].[27]

By this process, Nerva cleverly presented the senate with a *fait accompli*, as befits a shrewd politician who throughout had shown an ability to balance his own position with the prevailing political reality. In directly associating Trajan with the role of the *princeps*, and conferring upon him a share in all the supreme powers, except that of *pontifex maximus*, which could not be delegated, Nerva had duplicated the strategy of Augustus and Vespasian. Nerva and Trajan held the principate as colleagues. There was a senior partner, Nerva, who was the civil ruler at Rome, and as junior colleague, Trajan, a military leader accustomed to active service, capable of defending the frontiers of the empire and dealing with any potential civil strife at home. In effect, Trajan now had exactly the same status as Nerva in the eyes of the law, only Nerva's position as *pontifex maximus*, chief priest, giving him the greater *sancrosanctitas*, and thus supremacy.[28]

Whatever reservations the *Curia* may have had about the way the succession was forced upon them (none is recorded), the senators could at least congratulate themselves on allowing one of their own to share the imperial power. Trajan had dignity: he was the son of a much-respected consular senator, awarded triumphal honours and adlected *inter patricios*, and had finished his public career at the very pinnacle, as proconsul of Asia. At the same time, Trajan represented a clear break with the past: like most senators at that period he came from the ranks of the *novi homines* – and from the Spanish colonial élite to boot, a group by now well represented in the *Curia*. The alternative was to accept a candidate favoured by the Praetorian Guard, one who would almost certainly be too closely identified with Domitian. In the circumstances, the assembled senate could happily and quickly accede to Nerva's wishes. Trajan was confirmed as Nerva's testamentary and imperial heir, and his distinction further enhanced by designation as Nerva's consular colleague for the coming year.

The absence of any public opposition reveals that the choice of Trajan was a popular one. It was certainly welcomed by the Moesian legions, who dispatched Trajan's kinsman Hadrian, then a tribune with the *legio V Macedonica*, to convey their acclamation. The Praetorian Guard, who indirectly controlled the situation, also found the choice acceptable. Hardly surprising if, as we surmise, Trajan was indeed governor of Pannonia at the time, with the largest single provincial army in Europe – four legions – at his call if needed to coerce any recalcitrants and crush any opposition. With a firm and unchallenged successor in place, the widespread violence and terror that had followed the action of Aelianus now ceased, and stability was restored to the principate.[29]

Consequent upon the formal ceremony of adoption before the assembled senate, it seems that Trajan was appointed to the overall command of the German provinces with full proconsular *imperium*.[30] The appointment finds several parallels. Tiberius, for example, was granted proconsular authority by Augustus over the eastern provinces in 6 BC, and he in his turn gave his adopted son Germanicus supreme authority in the same region in AD 17. In both cases, the assignment was to enable the holders to carry out missions which demanded military expertise and diplomatic tact. The reason why Trajan was now appointed to Germany, however, is obscure. Perhaps the Transrhenish Chatti were again proving troublesome, taking advantage of the Roman military commitment on the central European frontier. Or perhaps there was some anxiety about the intent of the unnamed tribes who had recently decimated the Bructeri and occupied their territory.[31] More probably Trajan was charged with formalizing the frontier system which Domitian initiated in Germany as a consequence of his reducing the German armies to garrison the Danube, for later sources credit Trajan with maintaining forces and rebuilding fortifications on the right bank of the Rhine – perhaps initiating the so-called Odenwald *limes*, linking the Main and the Neckar.[32] Only the discovery of an inscription with the necessary details will resolve the matter.

Either way, Trajan elected to spend the winter of 97/98 at Colonia Claudia Agrippina (Cologne), capital of Germania Inferior. That January, probably during the night of 27/28, Nerva died at his villa in the Horti Sallustiani, on the southern slopes of Mons Pincius. Aroused to anger by a certain Regulus, the emperor was overcome by sweating before becoming cold, his repeated and excessive shivering bringing on a fever which precipitated his death. Nerva was reportedly feeble in health, and used to vomit up his food; also he was inclined to be a heavy drinker of wine; given his lifestyle and attested infirmities, the cause might well have been aspiration of his own vomit.[33] The information came to Trajan in a rather strange fashion. The news having reached Moguntiacum, the capital of Germania Superior, his kinsman and ward Hadrian, then serving as *tribunus laticlavius* with the *legio XII Primigenia Pia Fidelis*, resolved to announce it to Trajan in person. He may have been prompted to do so in an attempt to restore his position with his guardian, for some estrangement between the two had followed reports by Hadrian's commander, L. Julianus Ursus Servianus, a noted martinet, concerning the young man's 'extravagance and indebtedness'. Servianus, however, directed that Trajan should be informed by an official messenger, and set about delaying Hadrian's departure, even going so far – it is alleged – as to sabotage his carriage to prevent him from accomplishing the mission. Servianus' actions came to naught. Hadrian continued on foot and, anticipating the official emissary, was duly rewarded. With the help of Sura and of a certain Gallus (possibly the later consul Ap. Annius Trebonius Gallus), he was restored to Trajan's favour, despite having many enemies at the imperial court. Whether or not the alleged homosexual relationship between Trajan and Hadrian was of any relevance cannot be determined, and must merely be noted.[34]

On receiving the sad tidings, Trajan at once sent a letter of goodwill to the senate, making the now customary oath to abstain from tyranny, reaffirming Nerva's principle that no senators would be put to death without due process.[35] He also requested that Nerva be granted the same funeral rites accorded to Augustus; and apotheosis, ordering that a cult be established in Nerva's honour, with altars, couches and priests, and temples erected to his memory.[36] Acceding to his instructions, members of the senate carried Nerva's body in procession after the customary five-day public wake, and then it was burnt at the imperial crematory, the *ustrinium domus Augustae*. Then, if Augustan precedent was strictly followed, the remains of the pyre were guarded for a further six days, before Nerva's ashes were gathered up by the leaders of the Equestrian Order, bare of feet and with unfastened tunics, and placed in the sole remaining niche within the Mausoleum of Augustus.

The ceremony surrounding the apotheosis presumably took place about the same time, and it can be assumed that it followed the ritual as described by Herodian.[37] According to this a wax image of the dead emperor was fashioned and left lying in state at the entrance to the palace on an ivory catafalque, covered with gold-embroidered cloth. For seven days it was guarded during the daylight hours by representatives of the senate, all wearing black, standing to the left, while their wives, in plain white cloth, and with no jewellery, stood to the right. Throughout this period, physicians 'tended' to the 'patient', and gave daily bulletins, each more serious than the last, until finally 'he' was pronounced 'dead'. Then, the noblest of the equestrians and the younger senators carried the catafalque along the via Sacra to the Forum, where choirs of noble and patrician children sang on one side of the *rostrum* in counterpoint to matrons of high repute on the other. It was then taken to the Campus Martius, where a funeral pyre of five storeyed chambers, each adorned with cloth of gold, had been erected. The catafalque was placed in the second, with spices and incense, fruit and herbs, and sweet fruit juices, and the entire Equestrian Order proceeded to parade around it, on horse or in chariots, wearing purple-bordered togas and masks representing famous generals of the past. At a given signal, the pyre was lit, and an eagle released from the topmost chamber, to take the soul of the departed to heaven.

After the official period of mourning was over, the senate met to confirm Trajan as Nerva's successor, electing him *pontifex maximus* and *Pater Patriae*, 'Father of the Fatherland'. Coins were quickly issued with a somewhat idealized bust of the new emperor (Pl. 1A) – which owe more to the portraits of Nerva (and Augustus) rather than being accurate representations – and the name Augusta was voted for both Plotina and

Marciana.[38] On hearing of all this, Trajan immediately rejected the honours, except that of *pontifex maximus*, which gave him the authority to rule in his own name.[39] His reluctance to accept the title of *Pater Patriae* was probably occasioned by a studied Augustan reverence for the ultimate accolade the senate could bestow on a citizen, one awarded in the past for especially distinguished acts. Cicero, the first recipient, for example, received it for the suppression of the Catiline conspiracy. Caesar had been similarly honoured for his services to the republic in 45 BC. When conferred upon Augustus in 2 BC, it still commanded dignity, but it had since gradually become a regular part of the imperial titulature, as successive rulers sought the prestige increasingly quickly after their accession, Nerva in fact on the very same day he was confirmed in the other imperial powers. Repeatedly pressed to accept the honour notwithstanding, Trajan eventually conceded, and before the end of 98 it was formally incorporated into his nomenclature, although he did not allow Plotina and Marciana to be granted the dignity of Augusta until a later date.[40]

In full confidence of his unchallenged authority, Trajan chose to continue with his reorganization of the Rhine frontier rather than accede to the popular demands that he make haste and return to the capital.[41] None the less, so that there should be no doubt of his *auctoritas*, he ordered the turbulent Casperius Aelianus and his accomplices to attend him in Germany. Aelianus evidently felt he had nothing to fear, perhaps because, according to Philostratus, he had served with Vespasian in Judaea and Egypt, and was thus probably known to Traianus and his son. That may have been so, but it stood him in no stead now, for Trajan had him and the ringleaders executed for the diminution of Nerva's prestige. In Aelianus' place, Trajan appointed Attius Suburanus, presenting him with a sword as symbol of the office with the highly theatrical – if sincere – command; 'Take this, so that if I rule well, you may use it for me, but if badly, against me.'[42]

Before the end of the year 98, having refused a third consulship for 99, on the grounds that he would be absent from the capital, Trajan, together with his *consilium*, had embarked on a review of the Danube frontier.[43] His ostensible purpose, if we are to believe Pliny, was twofold: firstly to 'restore the discipline' of the legions, lapsed through indifference, insolence and contempt, and secondly to acquaint himself with the legates and the prevailing situation in the other northern provinces.[44] The first reason cannot simply be dismissed as a *topos*. Morale among the Danubian army was doubtless quite low, despite the victory over the Suebi, given the loss of two legions and units of Praetorians during Domitian's reign. Indeed, a fear of mutiny had probably occasioned Nerva's *CONCORDIA EXERCITUUM* coinage. In such circumstances it was usual to rebuke the troops concerned, deal with the ring-leaders, and then lead the remainder into battle against a convenient enemy to redeem their honour and confirm the restoration of military discipline.[45] Certainly, if we are to believe the philosopher Dio Chrysostom, returning from exile in Dacia about now, the Danubian army was ready for battle. He describes the situation at a Moesian legionary base – possibly Viminacium (Kostolac) – where

> one could see swords everywhere, and cuirasses, and spears, and there were so many horses, so many weapons, so many armed men [...] all about to contend for power against opponents who fought for freedom and their native land.[46]

But it was, above all, with frontier security that Trajan probably concerned himself during his stay on the Danube, and the reason why he lingered in the northern provinces when he must have been impatiently awaited at Rome. The intermittent warfare between Rome and Dacia during Domitian's reign had shown that neighbour to be disconcertingly well-organized and militarily successful. The peace between Decebalus and Domitian had allowed the Dacian king to increase his military strength, using the technicians and the subsidy sent by Rome, and foment unrest among allied tribes. The situation was evidently somewhat tense, and an anecdote has Trajan parading an army on one bank of the frozen river to display the full power and might of Rome to a hostile tribe massed on the opposite side; suitably impressed, they refused battle, and even sent hostages to ensure peace.[47] Thus, whether or not Trajan was already contemplating a future attack on Dacia to restore Roman authority, he felt it imperative that the frontier here be secured. It was probably now that he gave orders for the reconstruction of the Djerdap tow-path on the right bank of the Danube, and for the digging of a canal to by-pass the notorious cataracts at the Iron Gates.[48] Both measures were necessary not simply to allow water transport of the supplies needed by the garrisons stationed along the river banks, but also because the job of patrolling the frontier devolved principally on the commander of the Moesian fleet. But the implementation of the new political reality could not be successfully accomplished away from the capital. Towards the end of 99, therefore, Trajan gave in to the various entreaties from Rome, laid his love of the military life to one side, and resolved to return to the capital.[49]

V

THE NEW RULER

The journey back to Rome from the Danubian provinces was quiet and unhurried, as befitted one returning in an atmosphere of secure peace, and was made famous for its modesty and dignity. Domitian had passed the same way in 92, and his progress had been likened to the plundering foray of a conquering horde, with houses forcibly emptied to provide lodgings for him and his army. Now, the commonality witnessed the ruler of the known world journeying as if a general on his way to his army, negotiating fairly for accommodation and transport and carefully recording the expenses involved to demonstrate his public accountability.[1]

Trajan's entry into the capital in the latter part of 99 was equally modest. Eschewing the palanquin or chariot favoured by his predecessors, he arrived on foot to symbolize his personal status as a citizen first and foremost, even if possessed of powers which made him *primus inter pares*.[2] He was in his prime, tall of stature, with a thick powerful neck above an athletic body, his straight hair, cut in a severe military fashion, combed forwards over his brow to conceal frontal balding (Pls 2A and 2B). He was dark of complexion, and dignified with a stern and bluff countenance; his deep-set and penetrating eyes crowned high cheekbones which emphasized the sharp planes of his forehead, despite a somewhat bulbous nose and firm mouth, with slightly fleshy folds on either side.[3]

By virtue of his status as *imperator*, Trajan was preceded by twelve lictors carrying *fasces* wreathed with laurels as he entered the city at the Porta Flamina.[4] He was greeted on arrival by an ecstatic multitude. Pliny, a witness, vividly captures the scene:

> [N]either age, nor health, nor sex held back those who wished to feast their eyes on the unexpected sight. Small children learnt who you were, young people gazed rapturously, the aged marvelled, and the bedridden, scorning their doctor's orders, left their sick-beds as if a glimpse of you could restore health. Among the crowds there were some who said that their life was fulfilled now they had caught sight of you, while others claimed that you gave them reason for living longer. Women rejoiced in their voluptuous fecundity as never before in the knowledge that now they brought forth citizens for a *princeps* to rule and soldiers for an *imperator* to command. Roofs sagged with the crowds they bore, and not a vacant inch of ground was visible except where a foot was poised to step, as the streets were reduced to a narrow passage by the excited crowds on each side, all rejoicing and cheering. All felt the same joy at your arrival, joy which increased with each step you took, your splendid physique seemingly growing with each stride.[5]

The emperor was officially welcomed by the assembled senate, the leading equestrians, and his *clientela*, those young knights and sons of senators who swelled his private household in search of future political advancement. There was unashamed delight when Trajan first embraced the senators and then greeted the knights, needing no intermediary to effect the introductions, and again when he moved forward to anticipate the welcoming congratulations of his protégés. The lictors and the escort of Praetorian Guardsmen, in civilian clothes to conceal the weapons they carried, quietly cleared a passage through the crowds for Trajan to walk to the Capitol and the Temple of Jupiter. There, a sacrifice was offered, as at the many other altars erected in Rome for the purpose, celebrating his accession and safe return. Only then did the *princeps* leave for the Imperial Palace, the Domus Tiberiana, which he entered without pomp, just as if he were a private citizen returning home, and where he immediately established a manner of life that was at once modest and popular.[6]

The Domus Tiberiana covered the north-west slope of the Germalus, the northerly of two hillocks that together constituted the Palatium, a prominent 130ft (40m) high elevation south of the Forum. It occupied an area of not less than 161,500 square ft (15,000 square m), and had been inaugurated by Tiberius as a replacement for Augustus' conspicuously simple private residence on the southern summit, the Palatine proper, which the first *princeps* had used in the manner of a republican magistrate for conducting all his official duties.[7] This building, the Domus Augustiana, had eventually developed into the centre for the imperial administration, and the name *Palatium* had gradually been transferred to the house itself, taking on the connotation of 'palace' in the sense of being the ruler's residence as well as the place where his functionaries carried out their myriad duties.[8] But the growing imperial bureaucracy had rapidly outstripped the accommodation available, causing Tiberius to replace what had become an agglomeration of rooms of all periods, scattered over a wide area, with a single and massive complex. Damaged in the fire of 80, it was reconstructed in part by Domitian, who added a reception hall at the front and connecting passages to Nero's cryptoporticus and his own Domus to the south-east, the latter being the imperial residence which Nerva gave over to public use on his own accession.[9]

Trajan and his wife Plotina shared the imperial residence with the emperor's sister, Marciana, and her immediate family, a daughter and two granddaughters.[10] While Trajan was absent in Germany, Plotina herself had probably remained in Rome, presumably at the Domus Traiana on the Aventine: it was generally frowned upon for a woman to accompany her husband to a provincial appointment, even though Traianus had taken his Marcia along with him to Asia.[11] Naturally modest, when Plotina entered the palace for the first time she at once remarked that she hoped to leave it at any time with her own personality unchanged. Pliny, apparently a personal friend, found much to praise in her. She was an 'exemplary model of the ancient wifely virtues', obedient to her husband in a spirit of reciprocal understanding and consistently faithful to the habits he inculcated in her. Demure and unassuming in her attire and entourage, she even accompanied Trajan on foot, whenever custom allowed, revealing an unswerving devotion to him and not his position.[12]

Plotina's devotion was only equalled by that of the emperor's sister Marciana, likewise a paragon of moral excellence, but in this case, we are informed, on account of her ancestry rather than the training of a husband. Now in middle life, and a widow since the death of her husband, C. Salonius Matidius Patruinus in 78, she was noted for her sincerity and candour, traits she shared with her brother. Pliny lauded the ease with which the two women shared the Palace, amicably and without envy or jealousy. Many in the same situation and proximity, he noted, would have easily succumbed to rivalry and open hatred because of the similarity yet disparity in their relevant status; but Plotina and Marciana were united in daily life and affection, content and serene as wife and sister, and mutually attentive and considerate for each other.[13]

Marciana came under Trajan's responsibility by virtue of his position as *paterfamilias* of the Ulpii. And so did her immediate family, her daughter, the twice-widowed Salonia Matidia, and her two granddaughters, (Mindia) Matidia and Vibia Sabina: the duties of the *paterfamilias* involved the care of all members of his extended family, especially the females, whether widowed or not. Salonia was by now about 32 years old, and prosopographical research has identified three husbands of hers. The first may have been a Mindius, but the fact that nothing is known of this man might suggest that he died shortly after the marriage, although he probably fathered a daughter, Matidia, *c.* 82.[14] At any rate the union was evidently short-lived, for *c.* 84 Salonia married L. Vibius Sabinus and quickly conceived and bore her second child, Vibia Sabina.[15] This man was probably related to that great survivor, L. Junius Q. Vibius Crispus, thrice suffect consul (under Nero, Vespasian and Domitian), proconsul of Africa and propraetorian legate of Hispania Citerior, who may also have been a relative of Q. Vibius Secundus, suffect consul in 86 and eventually proconsul of Asia (*c.* 113). Vibius Sabinus himself was another man of great promise, for he was honoured with a suffect consulship in the uncertain year of 97, but he seems to have died shortly after the marriage, for there seems to have been a third husband, that disputed figure Libo Rupilius Frugi. Yet Trajan was Sabina's guardian when she married her cousin Hadrian in 100, which indicates that there was no head of the family then, and Hadrian was to refer to Salonia's long widowhood when delivering the funeral eulogy in 122.[16]

Trajan's *clientela* formed a significant part of the imperial household, even if few were probably actually housed by him.[17] The client–patron system was a particular feature of the republic, when it began as a mechanism whereby aspiring politicians acquired followings of committed voters in order to enhance their career in public life. The clients were obliged to augment their patron's support among the voting tribes, walking with him to the Forum to evince his importance and prestige, and providing physical protection should the need arise. In return, the patron dispensed food and money, and sometimes employment; he also promised the advancement of his *clientela* to any minor offices of state he controlled – and beyond, when feasible. Tradition and convenience ensured the continuance of the *clientela* system into the early principate, despite the way the political franchise had been effectively reduced to the senate alone. This was partly because by now the clients were generally obligated in some way to their patron – whether as distant municipal relatives, former soldiers, tenant farmers, or even as his own freedmen or their descendants. Thus they continued to retain their importance as a sign of their patron's status and wealth, attending the morning *salutatio*, from which they might be dismissed with a hand-out (*sportula*) of food or money, if not needed to attend their patron on his daily visit to the Forum.[18]

The other members of Trajan's household, apart from the imperial slaves inherited from Domitian and Nerva, were those who constituted the palace and imperial bureaucracy.[19] Broadly speaking, the *Palatini*, or palace staff, nearly all freedmen at this period, were responsible for the management of the imperial residence, and included such functionaries as *ostiarii*, the gatekeepers; *atrienses*, who cleaned the public and private rooms; the *praegustator*, or Palace taster; and the *trichlinarcus*, the imperial maitre d'hôtel. These and others all came beneath the *a cubiculo*, or chamberlain, who controlled all access to the *princeps*, and his colleague the *procurator castrensis*, who was in charge of the household's financial matters. The imperial administration, on the other hand, formed from both freedmen and equestrians, attended to those everyday administrative tasks subsumed by the ruler's *imperium maius*. Some of these duties were limited to the Palace and its immediate environs, but others were more widespread. For example, the *procurator a muneribus* and the *procurator aquarum* were respectively managers of the imperial games and of the water-supply to Rome, while the *a rationibus* took charge of all the imperial finances. The *ab epistulis Latinis* and his colleague the *ab epistulis Graecis* likewise had particularly important positions, being responsible respectively for Latin and Greek correspondence, as did the *a libellis*, in charge of petitions, whereas the *praepositus vestis albae triumphalis* had little more to do than to take charge of the white robe worn by the *imperator* on triumphal occasions.

Trajan is known to have retained at least one household official first appointed by Domitian: this was Gn. Octavius Titinus Capito, an equestrian procurator in charge of Domitian's correspondence and the imperial patrimony, who then became *ab epistulis* to Nerva, keeping that position for a while under Trajan, before being made *Praefectus Vigilum*.[20] Another was inherited from Nerva: Ti. Claudius Classicus (Pl. 3) was a freedman of Nero's, and was successively *a cubiculo* and *procurator castrensis* to Titus (and perhaps Domitian); then *procurator voluptatibus*, the master of court ceremonies, to Nerva and then Trajan, before being promoted *procurator ludi Matutini*, in charge of the morning gladiatorial training-school, devoted to instructing *tyro bestiarii*; finally he was made procurator of Alexandria.[21] In fact, it is safe to assume that Trajan confirmed all the current members of the imperial household in their posts, not least because it was rare for an incoming *princeps* to dismiss his predecessor's *domestici* without good cause. Others, however, were now promoted by Trajan, and were subsequently given their freedom by him, adding the prefix M. Ulpius Augustus libertus ('freedman of the Augustus') to their name. Among these men we can identify a certain Aeglus, in charge of the Mausoleum of Augustus and formerly in charge of Trajan's Corinthian images while he was yet Caesar (i.e. the period between his adoption and his accession); Eutychius, a revenue clerk for the via Appia; Hermius, procurator in charge of the gold room and the reliquaries; Thaumastus, records clerk in the public works office and the office of the patrimony; and Vernius, who worked in the Latin section of the imperial secretariat.[22]

From the outset, every detail of Trajan's reign was a studied and calculated rejection of those features which had characterized Domitian's. Identifying with the example set by Augustus, of the *princeps* as the custodian of power rather than the instrument, moderation, not superiority, was his maxim. His public life was marked by a lack of pretension, as was quickly evidenced by his refusal to allow the erection of any statues to him in any metal other than bronze.[23] And while Domitian had secluded himself from the public,

Trajan championed accessibility, especially at the Palace. Long a centre of social life and recognized meeting place of politicians and philosophers, it was often thronged from sunrise for the first two hours, the period usually given over to the *salutatio*, with suppliants and the frankly curious.[24] But Trajan made no attempt to disperse them. On the contrary. The rigid protocol of Domitian's rule was dispensed with; the formalities and functionaries that previously interposed between *princeps* and *privatus* were removed for Trajan to receive 'the flower of the senatorial and equestrian order' in person, greeting them with a kiss rather than an imperious hand. An audience with the sovereign became a welcome affair, without the need for fear or obeisance, and if by chance a citizen requested that the audition be postponed, that wish was accommodated without the prejudice it had once entailed.[25]

For any senator, the third hour saw the beginning of the official working day as he made his way into the city to attend meetings of the *Curia*. Trajan seems to have continued this practice, when other matters permitted. Wearing the *toga praetexta*, the purple-bordered tunic of a consular, he made his urban peregrinations on foot, allowing all who wished to approach and talk with him freely.[26] Likewise, whether in the Forum or the Palace, he affirmed his status as a citizen in the service of the state by dealing with state affairs in full view of the citizenry. Similarly, at the sixth hour, the usual time for the midday meal, he continued the pattern of behaviour expected from a man who was first and foremost a civic magistrate. Possessed of impeccable manners, Trajan ate communally, allowing all present to share at his table. Meals were never rushed, and the soothsayers and impudent buffoons encouraged by Domitian were replaced with hospitality, culture and civilized wit for all to savour. And even if the food was served on gold and silver plate, by dint of his position, it was distinguished for its frugality in an age of ostentation. Nor was there ever any suspicion that Trajan's public moderation hid private luxury, that he might in fact have already eaten – or be about to depart for secret gluttony, as was believed of Domitian.[27] Then, with the midday meal finished, Trajan followed the example of his peers, and retired from public as, ordinarily, no business was transacted in the afternoon. Instead, it was given over to a siesta, longer in the protracted summer days and short nights, followed by other relaxing activities, such as bathing. Then the day would leisurely come to an end with a simple dinner at around the tenth hour, although formal dinner parties might begin somewhat earlier to allow the guests time to be entertained and to walk home safely through the darkening streets. And so to bed as night fell.

Yet the austere dignity projected to his subjects and so faithfully communicated by Pliny was balanced by what others might see as culpable moral laxity: Trajan's predisposition for strong wine and his predilection for young boys.[28] Trajan's capacity for potent alcohol, a characteristic he shared with Nerva, was well regarded and of long standing, and was doubtless responsible for a claret-veined protuberant nose and increasingly fleshy jowls, as well as a mid-girth which became more pronounced as the years progressed.[29] His drinking habits may well have been cultivated in the camp. Even when on active service, there were a great variety of wines available to the army, from the simple Spanish wines that dominated the market to fine vintages such as Falernian.[30] They were usually drunk with water, but those who preferred their liquor stronger imbibed undiluted wine, a particular trait of the military; the Greeks had a phrase for it, 'Drinking the Scythian way', a euphemism for getting blind drunk, after the eponymous barbarians of the Crimea whose habit of consuming their wine neat so horrified their Hellenistic peers.[31] Even so, Trajan showed an awareness of the pernicious influence of alcohol, for he avoided extreme crapulence by instructing the Palace household to cease serving him once he became intoxicated.[32]

Trajan's sexual preferences were equally well known, if also overlooked in Pliny's extolment: even Julian, the last pagan emperor of Rome, not noted for his commendation of those who indulged in 'pleasure of the vilest and most infamous sort', suggested that Zeus should be careful of the coquettish Ganymede while Trajan was in the vicinity.[33] Among his identified catamites we can certainly include Hadrian and the pageboys of the imperial household, and he was shortly to effect a liaison with an actor, Pylades, and a dancer by the name of Apolaustus. If we can trust anecdotal evidence, Nerva and Licinius Sura had already shared his bed.[34]

But whether or not Trajan was actively predisposed towards homosexuality is impossible to establish. Bisexuality, involving anal, oral or intracrural sexual congress, seems an inherent condition among Latin males, especially among those of the leisured classes. It was openly joked about in antiquity, not least by those who advanced their careers through sodomy,[35] and the practice was common enough for the Icenian Queen Boudicca, Dio tells us, to lambast the Romans as men who slept on soft couches with boys as bedfellows.[36] The Roman convention of pederasty ultimately derived from the cultural standards of ancient Greece, where women were in general considered simply as vehicles for procreation and physical lust, and where an emotional void often existed between parents and children.[37] As a direct consequence, pederasty became a vital social institution in Greek society. In the first place, it filled a natural stage in the development of the young male, whereby an older man, the *erastes*, would take for a companion an unrelated youth, or *eromenos*, and by acting as a surrogate father, nurture and guide his moral, physical and mental development, preparing him for his civil responsibilities. Then, the Greeks seeing spiritual love and sexual expression as mutually unifying forces, the *eromenos* was expected to repay his patron's care and interest through devotion and gratification of his sexual desires.

In the Roman world, however, the family was a much more cohesive force, both parents playing a prominent role in the early upbringing of their sons and tutors and patrons guiding them through the intricacies of education and civil obligations. Thus, the culture of pederasty in the Greek mode had no obvious place in Roman society. Even so, there are recorded instances of patrons forming a sexual attachment with their clients, and a simulated Greek style of patronage with pederastic overtones did develop within the upper classes. Indeed, many of Rome's rulers before and after Trajan were patently bisexual; or, at least, were popularly believed to have bisexual inclinations, which amounts to the same thing. Such rakishness was generally considered an attribute of social class, an aspect of dissoluteness rather than a singular predisposition to same-sex activities. Yet homosexuality as such was certainly not approved of: effeminacy, defined as being the willing passive partner in a homosexual relationship between two adult males, was considered deviant and a moral vice. *Machismo* was what counted. As in many an English public school, the Mediterranean and Latin America, to be the active and dominant partner was considered proof of virility and masculinity whatever the sex or age of the passive partner, rather than representative of a particular sexual orientation. Consequently, Trajan – who might well have been homosexually initiated during his military service, where sexual relationships between willing partners were not considered exceptional[38] – attracted no reproof for his sexuality from contemporary observers. His homosexual activities could be interpreted as nothing more than a functional aspect of his class.

The first political act of the emperor, once established in the Imperial Palace, was to distribute the cash bounties that traditionally marked the accession of a new *princeps*. There were two, the military *donativium* and the civil *congiarium*. Both originated in the bequests of Augustus and had been retained by his successors as an inaugural grant to confirm the status of each *princeps* as *imperator proconsulare* and *cura Urbis*, patron of both the military abroad and the citizenry in the capital. The *donativium* had effectively become a prerequisite at the beginning of every reign since the uncertain accession of Claudius in 41, when he distributed as much as *HS*747,000,000 in all, perhaps equivalent to 90 per cent of the annual imperial revenue.[39] However, the peaceful and unchallenged circumstances of Trajan's succession to the imperial power, together with the short interval that had elapsed since Nerva's own distribution, meant that, while he could not gainsay the bounty – *avaritia*, avarice, was considered the most grievous failing in a *princeps*[40] – he could at least argue that it should be somewhat less than that given by his predecessor, perhaps half the expected sum.[41]

The *congiarium*, on the other hand, had developed from the allotments of oil – *congius* – distributed to the plebs by republican *triumphatores*.[42] Since Augustus had usurped the custom, to reinforce the special patron–client relationship between the *princeps* and urban plebs, it had become usual to issue *congiaria* from the private imperial purse on any important state occasion as well as an accession. Claudius, for example, gave out a *congiarium* of *HS* 300 in 44 to commemorate the conquest of Britain, and the same amount in 51 to mark Nero's coming of age. These sums, equivalent to 75 *denarii* or 3 *aurei*, presumably reflected the expected norm. It was not an inconsiderable amount: it represented slightly less than the pay earned by a Praetorian Guardsman in a month, exactly the same as a legionary in three.[43] It certainly allowed for life on a modest level for several days, covering the cost of 600 one-pound (0.45kg) loaves of bread, or 70 bushels (560 litres) of corn – or about 4 *amphorae* (62 imperial gallons = 235 litres) of ordinary wine!

Trajan's accession *congiarium* was announced by edict and effected under his supervision towards the end of 99, perhaps on the anniversary of his adoption. It would have been a shrewd political move on his part to combine the two, as it was also the anniversary of his assumption of the tribunician power, an office charged with intercession on behalf of the plebs.[44] Pliny especially lauds Trajan's humanity and generosity in granting it so soon after that distributed by Nerva, when it could have been so easily denied.[45] The ceremony was commemorated by the striking of base metal specie which show Trajan, accompanied by an official (perhaps the *praefectus annonae*, responsible for the corn dole), presiding from a tribunal as a citizen approaches, holding out a fold in his cloak to receive the largesse. The spirit of imperial liberality watches benignly over the scene, and the legend reads *CONG(iarium) P(opulo) R(omano)*, 'A *Congiarium* for the People of Rome', none too subtly reinforcing the political significance of the grant, that the majority of the plebs had no *patronus* other than the *Pater Patriae* himself.[46] It was for the self-same reason that Trajan took pains to make sure that all who qualified shared in the bounty. Pliny records how it was granted to those unable to attend the disbursement in person through illness or business or owing to absence from Rome, and how the allotment was even extended to those whose names had been added to the qualifying register after the edict had been promulgated.[47]

The individual amount distributed at Trajan's first *congiarium* is not recorded, but it is generally agreed that the customary *HS* 300 was handed out to each recipient.[48] Nor is it known exactly who shared in the largesse – either on this or on previous occasions. Pliny talks only of the *congiarium populo*, and it has been maintained that by this he means the entire free population of Rome.[49] On the other hand, he is quite explicit that all those who received the benefit were in some way 'listed', terminology appropriate for a closely defined group, rather than deriving from any census of the population as a whole. Fronto goes further, in distinguishing the *plebs frumentaria*, who received the *congiarium*, from the populace at large.[50] By this, he seems to mean that it was restricted to the recipients of the corn dole, a registered group of 150,000 deserving people among a total citizen population of about 1,250,000. Not even the imperial treasuries, perhaps, could have borne the costs involved if the entire free population benefited from what was supposedly a gift from the personal funds of the *princeps*. Even so, 150,000 recipients still meant an outlay of *HS* 45,000,000, the equivalent of 11,250,000 *denarii* or 450,000 *aurei*, roughly the annual cost of five legions.

Fundamental economics apart, there are, in fact, historical reasons for suggesting the *plebs frumentaria* were the political constituency most likely to receive the ruler's munificence. Grain, chiefly wheat and millet, was the principal source of nutrition in ancient Rome, and the poorer citizens had always been most at risk from periodic shortages. Gaius Gracchus attempted to resolve the matter through instituting a system which guaranteed a fixed quantity always available at a set price for each and every citizen to purchase. After his lynching, the measures were amended, as they seemed to promote the dangerous ideology that all citizens were entitled to an equal share in the bounty of the expanding empire. Following a series of *ad hoc* solutions Publius Clodius Pulcher enacted a law whereby a fixed volume of free grain was distributed every month to each citizen in Rome.[51] In 46 BC, Caesar pruned it for financial reasons, and established an upper limit of 150,000 impoverished recipients, each to receive about 5 bushels (40 litres) of grain per month. Then Augustus took the system over by virtue of his *imperium maius*, and doubled the amount when he thought necessary.[52] Thus, what had begun as a state institution to provide a guaranteed minimum subsistence to the citizenry as a whole was subtly changed from the antithesis of euergetism to its embodiment, and became exclusively identified with the office of the *princeps*. By simply limiting the *congiarium*, his private munificence, to these public beneficiaries alone, the *princeps* blurred even further the line between his personal acts and those constitutionally required by his office. Since it was a good method of increasing the perceived extent of his authority without directly affecting his legal status, there can be little wonder that Trajan chose to implement what was expected of him, or that he personally oversaw the distribution of the *congiarium* to the *plebs frumentaria* and made certain that all who qualified benefited.

As sole *patronus* of the *plebs urbana*, the *princeps* was also responsible for the provision of *spectacula*. These, the imperial spectacles, are to be carefully distinguished from the *ludi*, those shows regularly given by the magistrates which had originated in religious festivals, even if an exhibition of gladiators (*ludi honorarii*) was usually added to the programme. Now, Trajan's own tastes coincided in a significant way with those of the plebs: he was exceedingly fond of gladiatorial displays.[53] They derived from the funeral celebrations associated with the deaths of prominent Etruscans, which had always involved a staged combat to the death between two adversaries, a form of displacement behaviour whereby the death of one duellist was considered to reflect the power of overcoming death – whether as victor, by dint of surviving, or as vanquished, through accepting the death blow without demur. It had become customary in the late republic for victorious generals to put on similar gladiatorial displays – *munera gladiatoria* – for the benefit of the people in the city, primarily to promote *virtus* among the onlookers, a sense of toughness and admiration for the way that the gladiators faced the perils of their craft.[54] The magistrates had gradually pre-empted the privilege as a means of gaining electoral support, and to restrict any future challenge to his own position, Augustus had appropriated the convention, as a means of demonstrating his *munificentia*, his generosity. As time went by, while the junior magistrates in Rome retained the privilege of providing gladiatorial displays as a supplement to the regular *ludi*, only the *princeps* could give the extraordinary and irregular *spectacula* that lasted one or more days: already under Claudius there was an official, the *procurator a muneribus* or *munerum*, who was responsible for staging the events. Trajan was well aware of his duty to display generosity in this field and scarcely any emperor ever excelled him in practising the art of satisfying the plebs. It was even alleged that he knew his power was based more on such futilities as providing entertainment than the attention he devoted to the serious matters of state – from neglect of the latter, only catastrophe resulted, but by ignoring the former, he risked *invidia*, unpopularity.[55]

Thus Trajan's *donativium* and *congiarium* were quickly followed with a *munus* in the great Flavian amphitheatre which we know as the Colosseum.[56] The usual sequence was for the gladiators – mostly convicted criminals or slaves – to parade through the arena, on at least one occasion, under Claudius, wearing purple cloaks embroidered with gold, and saluting the emperor with the words 'Ave imperator, morituri te salutant.' There generally followed a warm-up phase, involving mock combats (*lusarii*) with wooden weapons, before the pairs were chosen by lot, and the duel began, the contestants forced forward with whips or hot irons if they showed any reluctance. When one man was down, the sponsor of the show would indicate whether or not he was to live, although in every case he would take note of what the crowd required. At midday, condemned men were often executed – by crucifixion, or *ad bestias* (torn apart by wild beats) or *ad cremationem* (tied to a stake, coated with tar, and then burnt) – after which followed the *venationes*, the exhibition of savage beasts, some brought forth to hunt each other or to be hunted by armed men, others to show how well they had been tamed.[57]

Yet it would be wrong to conclude from either Trajan's or the people's enjoyment of the shows that the *munera* or *venationes* symbolized an inherent love of the sadistic in the populace at large or the emperor in particular. Divorced as we are from the event by nearly two millennia, we need perspective, not least because it is well recorded that watching suffering for its own sake was criticized in the Roman world.[58] Which is why Pliny was careful to observe that Trajan's inaugural *munus* was not arranged purely to satisfy his own personal inclinations or those of the audience. On the contrary, as the great Cicero had noted, the spectacles were a necessary part of masculine education, by which the 'beautiful wounds' borne by the gladiators, and the way they scorned death in fighting for glory and victory, served as a moral inspiration to those who witnessed the display.[59]

Trajan's inaugural *spectaculum* concluded with a display of some of the riches secreted by Domitian, now destined for the public purse. Then, instead of the expected public execution of condemned felons, Trajan paraded all the informers and the corrupt lawyers and treasury officials who had plagued the populace at large during Domitian's principate. Many present in the crowd that day had suffered at their hands: wills had been altered, property seized and positions lost, as the suspicions and fears of Domitian encouraged these men to benefit personally from the uncertainty of the times. Now,

> What a splendid spectacle you gave us, Caesar [...] [as] the informers marched in, like a band of robbers or brigands – only their haunts had not been the roadside of the deserted places, but the treasury and the forum.[60]

The crowd applauded as the guilty, their heads forced back to meet their accusers, trod in the blood of the criminals who had died valiantly in gladiatorial combat. Yet this experience, grim as it was, was only a prelude to their real punishment. It being considered they were too despicable to warrant the chance of redeeming themselves with a dignified death in combat, or even by execution, they were taken down to the Tiber, forced on to ships, and towed out to sea, where, sails set, they were abandoned to the mercy of the elements. The sight was unforgettable and the crowd rejoiced. Pliny, who evidently shared their sentiments, had no ethical difficulties about the punishment:

> [I]f the stormy sea casts anyone alive onto the rocks, let him eke out a wretched existence on the bare crags of a hostile shore, and suffer in the knowledge that by his departure all humanity is relieved of its cares.[61]

The *princeps*, meanwhile, having entrusted vengeance to the gods, could bask in the reflected glory of his act, free of any allegations of injustice. The demands of the people were appeased: Trajan's *providentia*, severe as it could be, was unequivocally demonstrated and *lex* was shown supreme. With his personal popularity assured, he could turn to more formal matters of government.

VI

A PUBLIC IDEOLOGY

Some have disputed that any of the early Roman emperors can be credited with initiating a personal ideology. That dictum most certainly does not apply to Trajan, who, more than any of his predecessors, *can* be credited with a personal ideology directed towards the administration of the empire. Fully comprehending the consequences of his actions, he adopted a forward-looking manifesto that was not content with simply rectifying the abuses and mistakes of previous regimes. Instead, each and every one of his many reforms was generated by a visionary speculation that conceived of a unified political, economic and military system for the Roman empire at large.

The virtues of Trajan and the ideology of a perfect ruler and his regime are set forth in the *Panegyricus* of Pliny the Younger, and complemented by the four orations on ruler-ship by Dio of Prusa. Objective judgement is needed in the analysis of these texts, which originate in the wholly laudatory excesses consequent upon the vilification of Domitian. They are propagandist in intent, for while defining the programmed agenda of the good *princeps*, both took pains to traduce the capricious Domitian, a sign that the enormity of the principicide and the legitimacy of the new reign were still matters of public concern. Then, in Pliny's case, he also needed to compensate for his own material and social advancement during the '*dominatio*', particularly as the accession of Nerva saw the return of many political exiles with whom he had once been closely allied yet failed to support publicly. Dio of Prusa, on the other hand, had been effectively exiled by Domitian for his Stoic tendencies, considered to be treasonous by the tyrant. He owed his return to Nerva and his re-establishment to Trajan, and doubtless by way of gratitude felt it incumbent upon him to justify – no matter how obliquely – the system of government through directly and firmly associating Trajan with the attributes of a divinely recognized and benevolent autocracy. Yet both orators are in striking accord concerning the ideals of the new reign, and their abstract and abstruse sentiments are supported by evidence of a con-crete nature, numismatic and epigraphic. Hence, while their oratorical utterances have often been dismissed as vaporous claptrap, little more than exercises in anaphoric encomi-ums, as manifestos of Trajan's ideology their respective treatises are indispensable for determining the broad themes of Trajan's principate.[1]

Pliny's *Panegyricus*, to begin with, does not strictly belong to that class of adulatory peroration which characterized the late Roman world, but instead originated in the *actio gratiarum* delivered when he assumed the suffect consulship on 1 September 100.[2] Born in 61/62, Gaius Plinius Caecilius Secundus was then in his thirty-eighth year, and the consulship capped a series of distinguished offices.[3] One of Domitian's imperial quaestors, and then plebeian tribune, he had been *praefectus aerarii militaris* in 94, and was promoted to the post of *praefectus aerarii Saturni* in late 97/98 at the direct and joint instigation of Nerva and Trajan.[4] His administrative skills clearly impressed Nerva, who intimated a suffect consulship as a due reward, although the change in regime meant that it was not forthcoming until 100, when he shared the honour with his erstwhile treasury colleague, the Pergian C. Julius Cornutus Tertullus.[5] But the delay added greater distinction, for Trajan himself was one of the eponymous consuls for the year, the first time since becoming emperor, thereby adding greater lustre to the suffect consulships of his successors.

For an orator of Pliny's standing, the required public speech of thanks for his own instalment provided a splendid opportunity. Taking as his model Cicero's *Pro Marcello*, he delivered an *actio gratiarum* before the emperor and assembled *Curia* that fully expounded upon the virtues of the new ruler and the ideals of his government, tactfully reminded the emperor of his constitutional position, and compared him most favourably with the notorious and autocratic Domitian. Subsequently, Pliny decided to revise, enlarge and publish the comparatively short official eulogy in the extended 95-chapter form which posterity knows as the *Panegyricus*. Numerous internal references demonstrate that this version was originally prepared in 101/102, although there are clear indications of revision in 103/4.[6] Pliny leaves no doubt that his treatise was politically motivated – 'good rulers should recognize their own deeds and bad ones should recognize what theirs should be' – explicitly stating that it was published

> to encourage our emperor in his virtues by a sincere tribute, and to show his successors what path to follow to win the same renown, not by offering instruction, but by setting his example before them.[7]

Despite the suspected anachronisms in the *Panegyricus*, it can be adduced as a faithful mirror of the state of affairs in Rome in the years 98–100. At the very least, we can be assured that Pliny, despite his superficial and simulated boldness, would not have commended actions and policies that were at odds with the new regime, and that he therefore articulated a reality which was readily apparent to his contemporaries. Otherwise, the *Panegyricus* would never have survived public ridicule. Even so, it was necessary to stress the part that divine intervention played in the advent of the perfect ruler. Pliny repeatedly associates Trajan with Jupiter, the supreme Roman deity, and his son, Hercules, and notes how the Capitol, the principal shrine of Jupiter, served as the location for an omen foretelling Trajan's adoption and Nerva's announcement of the same.[8] In saluting the emperor, it was only right to praise the gods for choosing one whose 'purity and virtue makes him their own equal', affirming that Trajan was 'divinely chosen (by Jupiter) for his task'. Yet credulity could only be stretched so far, and it was necessary to deny the force of destiny alone in favour of the workings of a divine providence which had guided Nerva in his choice.[9] None the less, the eulogist confesses himself frankly amazed at the result. He had frequently cerebrated on the qualities necessary for a ruler worthy of power that equalled that of the gods,

> yet I never envisioned the like of him whom we see before us today. Others may have shone in war, but were useless in peace, or distinguished themselves in civic duty, yet not in arms; some won respect through fear, others lost it through

seeking popularity; sometimes the honour won at home has been lost in public, other times a public reputation has been lost in private life: there has been none before in whom the virtues have not been cancelled by some villainy. Yet compare our *princeps*, in whose person all the admirable merits are found in happy concord![10]

Whereas 'we had prayed only for [a ruler] who would prove better than the worse', Trajan, Pliny now asserted, had proved greater than any could have wished for.[11] So much so, indeed, that it was only right and proper that he should be called *Pater Patriae*, 'Father of the Country', a title allied to one of the chief attributes of Jupiter, as Father of the Cosmos, and which conveyed *sancrosanctitas*, an exceptional dignity and awe.[12] It was well-deserved and confirmed by Trajan's own physical and mental qualities. He had kept up the military exercises of his youth, vying continually with his soldiers in skill and endurance.[13] Hunting and vigorous exploration were his principal recreations, and he enjoyed the effort of the chase as much as the result, unlike Domitian, who lacked the skill or the ability, and who pursued previously tamed animals in a unmitigated mockery of hunting.[14] Likewise, Trajan exulted in uninhibited ecstasy at both yachting and rowing, again so different from Domitian, who was so terrified by the sound of the water that his barge was always towed on state occasions with another at the helm, as if he were a prisoner on his own ship.[15] Then, Trajan was frugal in his meals and ostensibly free from vice, his morals, military physique and majestic comportment conforming to the plebeian concept of integrity, prejudiced as it was in favour of those who recalled ancient ideals of rustic simplicity and valour.[16] For example, there was Vespasian, commander and disciplinarian, and the first *novus homo* to become *princeps*, all the more admired for his rough exterior and frugal habits, disguising as it did a devouring ambition and a subtle, devious and tenacious personality. But it was not enough for Trajan to appear a blunt, uncompromising soldier: strength of body in itself was of little account unless that body was ruled by a mind more powerful than itself. And, just as Trajan was like Hercules in his athletic pursuits and skills, so he equalled him in wisdom.[17] Indeed, Domitian had recognized and feared these very qualities in Trajan, especially when he returned unwearied and undaunted from the assignments he had been given, feeling the simultaneous admiration and fear that Hercules had inspired in his king Eurystheus.[18]

Pliny had welcomed the dawn of a new era, a *saeculum*, at the time of Trajan's accession.[19] Previous rulers had exploited or annexed the concept of a *saeculum* commencing with the beginning of their rule, but in Trajan, Pliny found every reason to believe that the inertia and despotism of the past had been banished. At the inception of his reign, Trajan, a man of provincial origins whom strange alchemy had endowed with a specific talent and special destiny, had inaugurated a *saeculum* *'felicitas temporum'*, one in which the senate was exhorted to take up its responsibilities in sharing the governance of the empire and the establishment of *libertas*.[20] Under Domitian, the fear of retribution had substantially diminished the individual and collective authority of the senate, and a reluctance to speak out or take action on behalf of the commonality had resulted. This now changed, Pliny, reminded his peers, for Trajan 'bid us to be free, and we shall be free'.[21] The new freedom was used to the full, within its limitations, and already by 99 the senate had been able to elect its own nominees as *consules ordinarii* without fear or favour: no wonder they acclaimed the ruler *tanto maior, tanto augustior* – 'most noble, most revered'.[22]

There was also the fact that the empire was free from the insubordination of the army that had shaken Nerva's brief reign, and the military losses which had darkened Domitian's. Trajan was a *vir militaris* of the type who characterized the emergent republic, and could stand comparison with the great generals of yore – Fabricius, both of the Scipios, and Camillus.[23] His kinship with the army was personal and paternal, as commander and comrade, for he knew his soldiers by name and by their exploits.[24] His accession as commander-in-chief came none too soon. Military discipline needed to be restored. Indifference, insolence and disobedience had become all too common as successive marshals, fearful of how Domitian might interpret their deeds, had relaxed the rigorous training required to keep the army an effective fighting machine. Trajan, on the other hand, mindful of the need to be continually prepared for war, actively encouraged his legates in their restoration of discipline, sowing consternation amidst those enemies of old who had actively resisted Rome.[25] Freed from anxiety, his subordinates asserted the authority vested in them, and personally initiated manoeuvres, defence construction, recruitment and the supply of new weapons with no fear that their actions might be misconstrued by a paranoid ruler.[26]

But Pliny was able to reassure the senate that Trajan's attention to martial themes was not a device to restore tyranny. Though nurtured in the army, he was a lover of peace, and although imposed on the empire through necessity, he remained *civilis*, neither tyrant nor master, but citizen and parent, comporting himself 'as one of us': while a ruler of men, he never forgot that he was a citizen himself.[27] Furthermore, he carefully chose his personal friends from the best of his subjects, many of whom had suffered under the previous tyranny, and he was diligent in the choice of his *consilium*, taking care to encompass all shades of opinion amongst its membership.[28] But the *principatus* of Trajan being diametrically opposed to the *dominatio* of Domitian, none were compelled to serve the emperor, as had been the case in the previous regime.[29] Indeed, Pliny records with astonishment the unheard-of situation when Trajan was asked by his chosen candidate to be excused from the post of Praetorian Prefect; not only did the emperor accede to the request, albeit reluctantly, but he even went so far as to bid the man emotionally god-speed as a ship carried him into retirement.[30]

As conclusive proof of the new age, Pliny extolled the freedom granted to speak publicly and freely on all matters – even if it were to criticize the *princeps*![31] The teachers of rhetoric and the professors of philosophy were once more honoured and the liberal arts restored and embraced by the *princeps* himself.[32] Thus it was that the philosopher Claudius(?) Dio Cocceianus, posthumously surnamed Chrysostom – 'golden-mouthed' – for his eloquence, was able to deliver a series of equally laudatory sermons to the ruler in person. Born in Prusa (Bursa), Bithynia, *c.* 40, and perhaps a distant relative of the later historian Cassius Dio, he began his career as a lawyer in his hometown.[33] Making his way to Rome during the reign of Vespasian, apparently in the company of his fellow-citizen and philosopher, Archippus, he became a determined sophist whose early discourses fully supported Vespasian's expulsion of the Stoics and other philosophers.[34] Later converting to Stoicism, Chrysostom claims to have invoked Domitian's displeasure on account of his criticism of the emperor and his friendship with a member of the aristocracy executed at Domitian's behest: exile beyond the Danube resulted.[35] When he heard of Domitian's death, however, he decided to return to Rome from the northern Pontus, where he then was, to personally congratulate Nerva – a friend of long standing – on his accession.[36]

Dio's journey was evidently leisurely, for he was still outside the empire at the time of Nerva's demise.[37] He then directed himself towards Trajan, whom he met in one of the Danubian provinces in late 98. The meeting proved auspicious, for he was charged with carrying an imperial rescript to Prusa, a mission which was probably accomplished in the spring of 99. Soon afterwards, in all likelihood late summer that same year, Chrysostom returned to Rome again, now as the head of an embassy charged with obtaining from the *princeps* certain municipal favours for his home town. Apparently successful in his task, he remained in the capital until 101, when he left with Trajan for the Danube at the beginning of the First Dacian War, perhaps as an adviser on their customs, and from where he returned to Prusa. He is last heard of in 111/112, when he appeared before Pliny in a lawsuit concerning his efforts to embellish his native city at his own expense.[38]

Seventy-seven discourses credited to Dio Chrysostom have survived. Four of these, the *Peri Basileias* – 'On Sovereignty' – are concerned with the nature of autocracy, and were placed at the head of his collected works, which implies that they were considered his finest pieces.[39] That they were addressed to Trajan seems certain, even though their character as philosophical discourses precluded mention of the sovereign by name. Despite differences in style, all four seem to have been delivered to the emperor in person, a man who

> is disposed, methinks, to be not only a brave ruler but also a law-abiding one, who needs not only high courage but also a high sense of right.[40]

All four draw heavily from the works of Plato and Homer in particular and the doctrines of the Cynics and Stoics in general, and take as their subject the qualities of the ideal ruler in his many guises. The *First Discourse* takes the form of a direct address, and speaks of the divine qualities of the good ruler, a man who fears the gods and watches over his subjects even as Zeus watches over mankind, contrasted with the baseness of the tyrant. The *Second Discourse* recounts an imaginary dialogue, and in expressing the Stoic ideal, develops the theme of the *First* by showing how the true ruler should act in the practical aspects of daily life, its strongly martial tone suiting the ruler to whom it was addressed. The *Third Discourse*, also an address, then considers the nature of the true ruler, who toils for his people, contrasting him with those such as the ancient kings of Persia, who were content to enjoy pleasure and who ruled through fear. Finally, in the *Fourth Discourse*, Chrysostom evokes the Cynic doctrine through another imaginary dialogue, where it is shown that the true king, as the son of Zeus, is evidenced more by his qualities of mind and character than by his military dominance and the extent of his power.

There is no consensus that the order of the four discourses which has survived into modern times was that in which the sermons were originally delivered. Internal evidence, however, suggests the *First* at least was delivered in 98/99; the tenor of the *Second* and *Third* best fits the period before the First Dacian War; while the sentiments of the *Fourth* might suggest 104–5: all, however – and particularly the *Third* and *Fourth* – may well have been subsequently adapted to include topical allusions in later public orations, which would explain certain inconsistencies and contradictions in the texts as they now stand.[41]

Nor is there agreement on their purpose, whether they are simply adaptations of traditional Greek philosophy intended for ceremonial use, or recitations intended to guide the developing ideology of Trajan, although it can be agreed that they reflect the existing circumstances and tenets of the new ruler. Consequently, the *First*, *Second* and *Third Discourses* at least can be adduced alongside the *Panegyricus* to elucidate the ideology propounded in Rome at the beginning of Trajan's rule: they self-evidently commend a programme favoured by the ruler, if not already published.

At the same time, however, Chrysostom had his own propaganda to disseminate, as one who owed his return and re-establishment to Nerva and Trajan respectively. Hence the principal sentiments already seen in the *Panegyricus*, the splendid qualities associated with the new emperor, are constants we find repeated in all of the first four *Discourses*. Then, they reflect a prevailing – and many would say justified – tradition among the Greek-speaking east which distrusted a studied proficiency in politics. Ambition was feared, for it was a truism that those who most wanted power were least equipped for it, while those who did not seek it, as with Trajan, who considered it their duty rather than vocation, were best prepared for the responsibilities. Even so, like Pliny, Chrysostom is at pains to stress that his orations are delivered without recourse to flattery. While falsehood was necessary when declaiming in the past, now it was possible to speak the truth, and to discourse openly on the happy and god-given polity that prevailed.[42]

Predictably, therefore, the divine aspects of the perfect ruler and the relationship of such a mortal to the supreme deity and his son loom large in all four orations, although Chrysostom, reciting for a Greek audience, refers to Jupiter and Hercules by their Greek names, as Zeus and Heracles.[43] For example, in quoting Homer on the characteristics of the perfect ruler, one

> to whom the son
> Of Saturn gives the sceptre, making him
> The lawgiver, that he may rule the rest,

the rhetor implies that a good ruler could only derive his office and dignity from Zeus, with the express purpose of planning and studying for the welfare of his subjects.[44] He was nurtured by Zeus and was consequently Zeus-like in counsel. Correspondingly, all good rulers were disciples and emulators of the deity in their practice of autocracy, for Zeus alone of the gods has the deserved epithets of 'Father' and 'King', 'Protector of Cities and of Suppliants', 'God of Refuge and of Hospitality', 'Guardian of the Race' and 'Lord of Friends and Comrades'.[45] As King of Kings, therefore, Zeus personally protected the good ruler, ensuring that he would live into old age, and vouchsafed his reputation for immortality, were he somehow to be snatched away before the fullness of time.[46]

As proof of divine intervention in Trajan's advancement to the principate, Dio Chrysostom told of a myth related to him while wandering the western Peloponnesus during his exile.[47] Between the cities of Heraea and Pisa he chanced upon a country shrine to Heracles. A woman nearby, advanced in years, had the gift of divination, and prophesied that not only would his wanderings soon be ended, but so also would the tribulations of mankind, an allusion to the imminent death of Domitian. She then assured him how he would 'meet a mighty man, the ruler of very many lands and peoples', to whom he should relate the story of how Heracles was given the choice of Autocracy or Tyranny as a means of rule, and chose the first, for Tyranny was utterly odious and abominable, and should be ended. Commending his choice, Zeus gave Heracles sovereignty over all mankind, and as Deliverer of the human race and of the earth, he henceforth set out to destroy tyranny and savage and wicked men wherever he found them. Where he found just rulers, however, he protected them and their territory, and, Chrysostom concluded,

> even to this day Heracles continues this work, and in him you [*sc.*, Trajan] have a helper and protector of your government as long as it is vouchsafed you to rule.[48]

But divine choice and favour apart, what constituted a just ruler? Much depended on the form his administration took, whether 'Government', 'Monarchy' or 'Tyranny'. The first involved the equitable ordering of men in accordance with the law, while the others depended on the whims of personal will or arbitrary and lawless exploitation.[49] 'Government', therefore, being based on law and justice, was to be preferred, and enjoyed the favour of heaven and fortune. Yet much also depended on which of the three styles of government was adopted. The preferred form was that whereby

> we have a city, or a number of peoples, or the whole world, well ordered by one good man's judgement and virtue.[50]

'Aristocracy', on the other hand, the second form of government, was neither viable nor expedient, based as it was on too much diversity, with one man in charge of war, another in charge of peace, and so forth. But the least practicable had to be the third form, 'Democracy', 'a specious and inoffensive name', expecting as it did that the self-control and virtue of the common people might one day find an equitable constitution based on law.[51] In Chrysostom's mind, therefore, 'Autocracy' (although he nowhere names it as such), by which the strong were expected to govern and care for the weak, was far and above the ideal.[52] The just ruler, or *autokrator*, he concluded, was one who looked after the welfare of his subjects, had due regard for his fellow-men, and honoured the good: only by so doing could he exult in the title of 'Father' of his people.[53] It consequently behoved him to take on his subjects' cares and anxieties, as guide and shepherd, remaining ever vigilant and never idle: he was, after all, autocrat not for his own sake but for that of all men.[54] None the less, that toil and the discomfort it entailed was not to be avoided for the benefit it brought to his subjects and himself, as their ruler.[55]

Chrysostom was careful to observe that he who would rule needed to be skilful and wise, and possessed of courage and an innate sense of right to be exercised for the betterment of his subjects.[56] Sincerity and truthfulness were the qualities that most benefited the prudent and just ruler, but among the many other characteristics required of him, it was particularly necessary that he be solicitous and gentle, a guardian of the law, a promoter of friendship and peace, and a provider of wealth and substance.[57] At the same time, he was required to show due respect and reverence to the gods and hold the divine in honour.[58] It followed from this that he also needed to be above moral reproach, neither licentious nor profligate, insolent or lawless, nor disturbed by anger, pain or fear, or pleasures and lust of any kind: no wicked, dissolute or avaricious person could ever be master of himself, let alone of anyone else.[59] Hence, it was axiomatic that the autocrat, embracing virtue and rejecting vice, should not tolerate any semblance of wantonness or voluptuousness, obscene language or blasphemy, and should do away with

> indecent dancing and the lascivious posturing of women in lewd dances as well
> as the shrill and riotous measures played on the flute, syncopated music full of
> discordant turns, and the motley combination of noisy clanging instruments.[60]

Since the good ruler was chosen by providence for high office, and thus unambiguously beholden to a life of toil and service for the welfare of his subjects, citizens and soldiers, his labours and virtues brought their own rewards. Equitable and just, he was safe because he lacked enemies, and happy because he was never at fault and was beloved and adored by his fellow-men, his aura of well-being such that all wished to linger in his presence.[61] More importantly, his labours brought him perhaps the most sacred possession of all, that friendship which maintained his happy state of mind. While his wife was his helpmate in counsel and action as well as his partner in bed and his affections, and while he could select those suitably qualified from amongst his kin, his virtues meant he was able to choose his friends, representatives and administrators from amongst the multitude of men, and thus able to select none but the best.[62] If he failed to honour his obligations in this way, however, he was no better than a traitor to himself and his polity, not the least because his friends were there to help share his burden.[63] Indeed, an autocrat was dependent on them, for they alone were the ones to whom he could delegate the responsibilities of power. While a private individual could look to the law to protect him from being wronged or ill-served, the ruler must depend on the loyalty of his administrators.[64] Rich in true friends, who kept him informed, protected him, and provided companionship in times of sickness and misfortune as well as in times of pleasure, the good autocrat was further able to achieve a multiplicity of tasks at one and the same time, so that nothing was bereft of his attention.[65]

It stood to reason that one of the most important aspects of a good ruler was that he was warlike when necessary while desirous of peace: only those best prepared for war and with perfect trust in their army had the best chance of living in harmony.[66] Consequently, it was necessary that the good ruler shared the onerous duty and assignments of his soldiers, even if he was distinguished from them by his dress and armour, and that he knew those who faced peril and hardship on his behalf: only by sharing their toil, whether in military reviews or in subduing a province, could he rightly call them 'comrades'.[67] It was equally important that the good ruler saw that his army was well-trained and disciplined, for the ruler who neglected his responsibilities and pampered his soldiers was no better than a shepherd who imperils the flock by not taking care of his own guard-dogs. Possessed of a trained army, however, the good ruler was feared by his enemies, and none was prepared to acknowledge him their foe.[68] Hence, developing the theme of *mens sana in corpore sano*, Dio suggests that military training would be helped by replacing that lax and lascivious dancing and syncopated discordant music the soldiers favoured with ancient 'virile and sober' dances such as the *enoplic*, performed in full armour, or the *kouretian*, which perfected light and quick movements, all accompanied by songs of war and triumph and exhortations to battle.[69] Possessed of a trained and skilled army, and having dutifully offered warlike prayers to Zeus for the destruction of his enemy, the good ruler could then march forth in confidence, and accumulate the spoils and armour with which to adorn his palaces and temples, and thus propitiate the gods.[70]

The several coincidences in the themes explored by Dio Chrysostom and Pliny the Younger suggest that they were aware of a well-publicized manifesto already in place. True, both were influenced to some extent by their common friendship with the *princeps*, but there is nothing to indicate collaboration in the production of their disparate works. Moreover, whether their sentiments were apposite or not, there is a modicum of evidence to support the thesis that they independently report a prevailing ideology. That is the import of the reverse-types that appeared on Trajan's earliest coinage, for in the ancient world coins were often used as a convenient means of recording major events and advertising and circulating the current doctrine. Especially so amongst the military, the largest single 'consumer' of coinage, by virtue of the requirement they be paid regular sums at regular intervals. Even if they received much of their pay in ready-circulating coin, each successive *princeps* needed to propagandize his patronage to them.[71] Proof of the axiom is readily supplied and demonstrated by the relative plethora of new coin-types issued at the beginning of each successive regime, the majority of which not only record individual imperial events, but manifest and emphasize particular imperial policies, often abandoned for new models that correspond with changes in the political reality of the time. Through the medium of his coinage, therefore, the emperor could inspire, direct and censor political messages to agree with his personal programme – indeed, the types chosen might even be interpreted as short and carefully chosen abstracts of the *acta diurna*, the official proceedings of the *Curia*.[72] *Ergo*, it can be assumed that Trajan's official moneyers, under the general guidance of the emperor himself, made certain that the public at large was provided with a continuous supply of images which disseminated the events and policies he wished propagated. Hence, after some early confusion caused by his initial rejection of the title *Pater Patriae*, Trajan's coinage regularly lists the accolade among his titulature. In this way, just as Pliny and Dio Chrysostom repeatedly refer to the influence of Jupiter/Zeus, the father of the world, in Trajan's selection and accession, it confirmed that he was their proxy as ruler and protector of his people.[73]

As it was, Trajan's first specie, those coins issued between 98 and 100 inclusive, significantly developed the prevailing custom of using personifications of imperial and traditional virtues on the reverse to propagate and disseminate a personal manifesto. Indeed, his coinage is so distinct from that of Nerva's in this way that one might assume the changeover came about as a *coup d'état* rather than a peaceful transfer of power.[74] Unfortunately, the personifications which Trajan favoured are frequently of a rather general character, and rarely specifically identified, creating diverse difficulties in interpretation. Those that are descriptive certainly echo the message conveyed by the *Panegyricus* and the *Peri Basileias*, substantive proof that both perorations were in accord with the official ideals of the new regime.[75] For example, there are the coins which bear the legend *PROVID(entia)* depicting two figures, one handing the other a globe, symbolic of world government.[76] The one figure is wearing a toga and holds a scroll – the chief attribute of the *princeps* – in his free hand, and is therefore the deified Nerva; the other, receiving the globe, is in military garb, and is Trajan. Concord and the peaceful transference of power is intimated by the way the globe is passed from one to the other, and the invocation of Providence conveys Nerva's sanctified prescience; the whole, then, asserts the divine intervention that prompted Nerva to adopt Trajan as his co-ruler and heir. On the other hand, the providence implicit in a somewhat similar type, with the legend *PROVIDENTIA SENATUS*, refers to the sharing of power between senate and ruler rather than transference, as is emphasized by the way the togaed figure, lacking the scroll, and thus representing the *Curia*, has both hands on the globe.[77] None the less, it was recognized that Trajan's adoption and subsequent accession had brought peace and security to the empire at an uncertain time, hence the issue of a type showing the civic crown of oak leaves, and the legend *S(enatus) P(opulus) Q(ue) R(omanus) OB CIV(es) SERV(atos)*. A direct allusion to the similar specie of Augustus, which refers to the honour voted him for saving the state from the ravages of civil war, and meant to convey the same message,[78] it stressed the uncompromising loyalty of the army to Trajan. This loyalty was further confirmed in an issue carrying a type – borrowed from Domitian's coinage – showing the emperor receiving the oath of allegiance (*Sacramentum*) from a group of soldiers, representing the army at large, with the legend *FIDES EXERCIT(uum)* in the exurge.[79]

With those issues lacking a specific identifying legend, there are some understandable difficulties in identification and explanation, but in general they too seem to reflect the themes expressed by Pliny and Dio Chrysostom. One of the more common types depicts a woman holding the sceptre of justice and seated on a chair which has *cornucopiae* in place of arms. This innovative image does not appear again until the reign of Antoninus Pius, and the combination of horns of plenty and the sceptre suggests that she can be identified as *Iustitia-Astraea*, the spirit of a new age.[80] The appearance of *Concordia*, *Fortuna*, *Securitas* and *Felicitas* confirms the continuity of the accord between senate, army and *princeps*, and serves to reassure the population at large that their interests are not forgotten in an age that promised increased prosperity. Allied to them are coins issued in 100 at both Rome and the eastern provinces which carry a representation of a cult-statue of Hercules on the reverse, associating the emperor with the great servant of the human race, who won immortality through his labours.[81] Moreover, when Trajan raised two new legions in 102/104, one of them, the *legio II Traiana*, was given an emblem of Hercules as its regimental standard. But there is even more, for the Hercules known to Rome had come to Italy while driving the oxen of Geryon from Gades (Cadiz) in Baetica, and this cult-statue is probably that of *Hercules Gaditanus* himself. The message seems straightforward: the Baetican Trajan is a second Hercules, divinely chosen to come to Italy, where he was to labour for the benefit of the world.[82]

In addition to these less specific types, a distinct group of issues concern Trajan's image and reputation as a *vir militaris*. Mars, as *Mars Ultor*, the god of divine retribution, is perhaps a direct tribute to the martial qualities of the new emperor, while *Roma Victrix*, *Germania* and *Pax Augusti* all refer to the peace brought about by Trajan's successes on the Rhine and Danube.[83] Of the four, the *Germania* issue is especially interesting as the first ever provincial representation of its type on Roman coinage. Identified by her long braided hair and characteristic native shields, she carries a branch to signify she is *Germania Pacata et Pacifera*, that is, pacified and brought into stable and peaceful relations with the empire. Similarly, an allusion to Trajan's earlier Pannonian victories, which brought about the adoption, might be seen in the issues showing *Victrix* with a wreath and palm, while the loyalty of the army is doubtless further confirmed by issues illustrating an *Adlocutio*, the address to the army on his accession, and a *Decursio*, a military review, perhaps that undertaken along the Danube in 97/98.[84]

Trajan's coinage, therefore, might seem to confirm the broad details of his personal ideology as presented by Pliny and Dio Chrysostom. Their rhetoric, consequently, might represent a faithful reflection of Trajan's ideology up to the time of the First Dacian War, and their paeans of praise cannot be dismissed as simplistic laudations, even if they were consciously or not disseminating semi-official propaganda. The reign was divinely inspired; it marked a return to just and lawful government, with the emperor as a benevolent autocrat rather than an oppressive tyrant; it confirmed the support of the army and the emperor's care to ensure the protection of the polity. Of Holmesian interest, however, is that neither the coinage nor the eulogies stress the *libertas* so prominently emphasized in Nerva's reign. Perhaps the episode of the Praetorians had shown that too much liberty was not necessarily a desirable feature for a successful administration and the concept was quietly dropped, not least because it could be taken for granted under the benevolent rule of an autocrat whom the gods favoured.

Thus for Trajan's manifesto. It remains now to establish whether or not the independently documented inaugural measures of Trajan's reign correspond with the idea of a true and just ruler that Pliny and Dio Chrysostom described, and Trajan's coinage advertised. Or whether these laudations are little more than the corollary to the vilification of Domitian, and all that he stood for, by the Roman equivalent of the chattering classes.

VII
THE INAUGURATION
OF A NEW ERA

A distinguishing feature of the principate was the periodic usurpation by the ruler of the eponymous consulship. In theory, the consuls remained the paramount magistrates of Rome. In practice the *princeps*, through his proconsular *imperium maius* and especially by dint of his *auctoritas*, had unsurpassed ascendancy, usually reinforced by repeated possession of the eponymate to at least an equivalent number of times as any of his coevals.[1] Consequently, many rulers had openly coveted the curule chair and some even seized it on their accession. Yet, most *principes* realized that it would not do to monopolize the position. With the notable exceptions of Vespasian and Domitian, who made the ordinary consulship the virtual preserve of the Flavian family, all Augustus' successors were generally sparing in their appropriation of the distinction.

Trajan came to power during his second consulship, unusually held *in absentia* while on active service in Germany. He refused a third offered for 99 ostensibly because of his continued absence from Rome, even though there was a senator then alive who had achieved the *summum fastigium*.[2] That man was probably A. Didius Gallus Fabricius Veiento, *consul suffectus* in 72, 80 and (?)83, and Trajan may have considered that his own two terms as eponymate *ordinarius* gave him greater *auctoritas* than another's three as *suffectus*.[3] Even so, many thought it was only right that the *princeps* should be honoured at least as often as one of his ostensible peers, and after he returned to the capital Trajan was prevailed upon to take a third consulship. This time, Pliny tells us, there were no grounds for refusing the office: indeed, Trajan threatened to demean the distinction by not taking his place in the curule chair on the consul's tribunal.[4] Thus, late in 99, he duly accepted nomination.

Trajan studiously used the opportunity of his third consulship to reinforce his public image as the first servant of the state. Unlike his predecessors, who habitually disdained the traditional procedures surrounding the election, he not only attended in person, but then, at the *renuntiatio* before the assembled *comitia centuriata*, dumbfounded all – 'for he was already *princeps*' – by going up to the presiding consul and swearing the customary oath, something, Pliny claimed, no other *princeps* had done before.[5] The orator was duly eulogistic:

> Great is your glory now and forever, Caesar, whether other *principes* follow your example or not, for is it not beyond all praise that a man now thrice consul should act as if it were his first election, that a *princeps* showed himself to be no different from a *privatus*, an *imperator* no different from those in his *imperium*?[6]

74

But even more was to come, for on his first day in office, Trajan capped the *votorum non-cupatio* at the Capitol by publicly affirming the supremacy of the laws at the Rostra in the Forum, professing that even though *princeps*, he remained subject to and not above them.[7] In truth, for all Trajan's apparent unwillingness, we can be certain that he intended from the first to hold the eponymous consulship in 100: Pliny's circumlocutions fail to disguise a carefully orchestrated plan whereby Trajan's absolute sovereignty was dissembled by a legal function. As the chief officials for administering the law, the ordinary consuls were essential for forming the correct character of the regime. The additional *auctoritas* imparted to Trajan as *consul ordinarius* for the third time effectively guaranteed that any reforms he personally desired and introduced were unquestionably adopted as the deliberated measures of the first servant of the state and its most senior statesman.[8]

Yet despite his *auctoritas*, it was important that Trajan maintained a *modus vivendi* with the senate. Any potential opposition could only come from dissatisfied provincial commanders, all senators and former magistrates of one grade or another. On a practical level, the simplest method of achieving continued good relations was by reward. Consequently, Trajan used his *auctoritas* to influence the promotion of qualified individuals to appropriate positions of power which conveyed suitable prestige and distinction. An examination of the public appointments initiated by Trajan demonstrates the method, and confirms his retention of the policy established by Nerva, advancing equally those *novi homines* and *nobiles* to whom he owed favours and those who were potential rivals. The ordinary consuls for 99, for example, the Italian A. Cornelius Palma Frontonianus and the (?)Cilician Q. Sosius Senecio, not heard of before this time, went on to distinguished military and public commands, which suggests that they were the emperor's contemporaries and friends. However, of the four suffect consuls in that year – again all previously unknown – only one, A. Caecilius Faustinus, subsequently achieved high military command. As for the others, while Sulpicius Lucretius Barba and the Spaniard Senecio Mammius Afer continued their consular careers in the civil administration, the last, Q. Fabius Barbarus Valerius Magnus Julianus (also from Spain?), in Numidia at the time of Trajan's accession, does not seem to have been appointed to any subsequent consular office, which might just indicate that he was viewed as a possible rival.

A similar approach is seen in the consuls appointed for 100. The year began with Trajan and Sex. Julius Frontinus sharing the *fasces*, L. Julius Ursus Servianus replacing Frontinus a short time later as *consul suffectus*. Both men were contemporaries of Traianus, and had served iterated consulships and been otherwise exalted in the reigns of Domitian and Nerva. Frontinus, 'one of [Rome's] greatest citizens',[9] is the better known, partly on account of his two published works, *Strategemata* and *De aquae ductu urbis Romae*. A Narbonensian adlected into the senate by Galba, he was *praetor urbanus* in 69, and in 70 played a notable part in crushing the revolt of Civilis, taking the surrender of 70,000 Lingones, for which deed Vespasian elevated him into the patriciate.[10] His first consulship followed immediately, after which he was entrusted with the administration of Britain in 73/74–78/79, and then served with Domitian during the *bellum Germanicum* of 82–4, either as a member of his *consilium* or as governor of Germania Inferior.[11] After a short period of retirement, Nerva appointed him *praefectus publicis sumptibus minuendis*, one of the commissioners elected to reduce state expenditure; then *curator aquarum*, in charge of the capital's aqueducts; finally a second suffect consulship in 98.[12]

L. Julius Ursus Servianus, while not so well known, could claim a similar record of distinguished service.[13] Like Frontinus, he was an equestrian from Narbonensis, and after service under Vespasian as *praefectus annonae* and *praefectus Aegypti*, he became Praetorian Prefect, probably under Titus.[14] He was adlected into the senate by Domitian to allow his replacement by the ill-fated Cornelius Fuscus, and was appointed *consul suffectus* in 84, despite having occasioned Domitian's disfavour for his defence of the emperor's wife when she was accused of an affair with an actor. His second (suffect) consulship followed in 98, when he replaced Frontinus.[15]

In part, both Frontinus and Servianus were now honoured as a reward for their service on Trajan's behalf during the struggle for the accession.[16] However, his real purpose in preferring them was to dignify his own policies by association with those of his predecessor, for despite their provincial – and equestrian – origin, they were among the most eminent in the *Curia*, and closely identified with the return of liberality under Nerva. As such, they proved a perfect contrast to the relatively unprepossessing six men he advanced to the suffect consulship that year. Of these, only two, L. Herennius Saturninus and T. Pomponius Mamilianus, subsequently rose to a high military command, although all the others, with one exception, attained high office in the civil administration. In appointing such comparative nonentities, it seems that Trajan carefully calculated on appeasing senatorial complacency by mixing the established gerontocracy with a leavening of *arrivisti*, implying that all would stand a fair chance of the consulship in the new regime.

A somewhat different process is seen in Trajan's approach to staffing the upper echelons of provincial administration. It was essential that these were men he could trust implicitly. Thus Trajan's only serious rival, M. Cornelius Nigrinus Curiatius Maternus, governor of Syria, was replaced after his adoption.[17] Another potential adversary, Q. Fabius Barbarus Valerius Magnus Julianus, was sidelined through elevation to the consulship, after which he received no further employment. Yet almost all the other provincial commanders, many originally appointed by Domitian, remained in post until their regular term of office expired, an indication of both their loyalty and competence.[18] T. Pomponius Bassus (*cos. suff.* 94), for example, had been in charge of Cappadocia/Galatia from 94/95, and went on to become one of Trajan's first *curatores rei alimentariae*; Cn. Pinarius Aemilius Cicatricula Pompeius Longinus (*cos. suff.* 90) held Pannonia from 96/97 after administering Judaea (85–88) and Moesia Superior (93/94–96/97); P. Metilius (Sabinus) Nepos (*cos. suff.* 91), in Britain since 95/96, stayed to complete his triennium; L(?). Julius Mar(inus?) (*cos. suff.* ?93), in Pontus/Bithynia *c.* 89, likewise completed his term in Moesia Inferior (95/96–97/98), although nothing more is heard of him thereafter; C. Pompeius Planta retained his office as Prefect of Egypt, to which he had been advanced shortly before Domitian's demise.

Even though the retention of such men proved the relative soundness of the selection process adopted by Domitian, Trajan was none the less faced with serious matters of misgovernment in some spheres of provincial administration. The indulgent policy sanctioned by Nerva allowed the appointment of certain weak and rapacious men who took every opportunity to benefit from his lenient attitude.[19] The case of Marius Priscus, consular governor of Africa, is the better known. Indicted in late 98, he was accused of taking at least two bribes that amounted to *HS* 1,000,000 for procuring the punishment and death of certain equestrians for unspecified crimes.[20] Convicted on the lesser charge of extortion in 99, he was tried on the capital offences in January 100, with Trajan presiding in person. Adjudged guilty, he was exiled from Italy and fined *HS* 700,000, the sum involved in one of the bribes, a punishment many considered extremely light.[21] Less is known of the proceedings against Caecilius Classicus, Priscus' contemporary as consular governor of Baetica, as he died in suspicious circumstances before litigation was completed.[22] None the less, it was established to the court's satisfaction that he had taken bribes worth more than *HS* 4,000,000 in cases which involved rapacity and callous brutality. It was consequently decreed that his estate should forfeit all those possessions acquired after he assumed his provincial command.

Having demonstrated a concern with the integrity of the state and its officers, Trajan naturally looked to other areas where injustice offended the spirit of his *saeculum*, the 'new age'. A priority, in which he was encouraged by Plotina, was to simplify the procedure for resolving disputes between the treasuries and the public at large. Domitian had espoused a rigorous approach to the interpretation of laws concerning taxation solely to benefit the imperial treasuries, resulting in a series of protracted lawsuits against the imperial procurators who collected the taxes.[23] To expedite due process, Nerva had already instituted the office of *praetor fiscalis* to mediate in such cases.[24] Now, in order to remove any suspicion of bias, Trajan enacted a lottery to assign the magistrate responsible, allowing him to be challenged on various grounds, which included his age and his independence from the *princeps*. More significantly, Trajan initiated the replacement of existing corrupt procurators with exemplary men whose probity was beyond question.[25] The consequence was, says Pliny, that the fiscal courts now served both the principate and liberty equally. Indeed, there was now the distinct likelihood of private citizens emerging victorious from their lawsuits with the treasuries, bringing further honour to the regime.[26]

One of the taxes which had given frequent occasion for dispute was the *vicesima hereditatum*, the 5 per cent inheritance tax. Introduced by Augustus in AD 6 to replenish the recently inaugurated *aerarium militare*, the military treasury, it met opposition from the beginning as it revived memories of republican taxes that many had thought gone for ever. In response, Augustus quickly declared exemptions for direct heirs and those who inherited insubstantial estates.[27] But, as Pliny observed,

> This concession only benefited citizens of long standing. Recent ones, whether they had been granted citizenship after holding Latin rights or *per honorem* from the *princeps* himself, unless they won at the same time the right of kinship (*cognationis*) for their family, were legally alienated from those with whom they had the greatest ties. What should have been a considerable benefit became a grave injustice, as Roman citizenship came to stand for hatred, dissension and deprivation, as it parted relatives once dear to each other.[28]

This came about because of the agnatic principle of the Roman family. Every legitimate member came under the *potestas* or authority of the *paterfamilias*, the senior male ascendant, with the sole exception of his own wife and the women married to his sons, who remained under the power of their own *paterfamilias*. Hence, a man's sons owned no property in their own right, and thus could not make a will as they had no legal assets. In practice, they were often emancipated, either by virtue of *peculium*, whereby they could live away from home and were given a personal fund, although this reverted to the family at large on the death of the *paterfamilias*, or through military service, whereby they had authority over their own personal possessions. Now, a Roman citizen could only name another citizen as his lawful heir or legatee, and only those of his immediate kin who were also *sui iuris*, that is, in his *potestas* and who became legally independent on his death, were exempt from paying the inheritance tax. In the case of those citizen families of long-standing, all the immediate kin would by now have kinship rights, and therefore the heirs were usually exempt. A recently enfranchised peregrine, or non-citizen, however, who had won the right of citizenship *per beneficium*, did not always obtain it for his kin at the same time (although it was usual when receiving citizenship after holding Latin rights), and he remained liable to pay the tax on any inheritances he received from non-citizen members of his family. Furthermore, he lost the right to leave such relatives any portion of his estate, while even if he had won for them kindred rights (*ius cognationis*), it did not automatically give him *potestas* over them (although again it was usual where citizenship was awarded as part of a general grant to a Latin community), in which case any bequest between family members became liable for the tax as if they were legally strangers.[29] The inevitable consequence was, as Pliny noted, that instead of seeking it as an honour, many upstanding peregrines refused municipal office and the citizenship it conveyed as it caused families and estates to break up through the vicissitudes brought about by the tax.[30]

Recognizing the hardships that resulted from a strict interpretation of the law, Nerva had extended the degrees of exemption. Bequests between a mother and her free-born children where no kindred rights existed were now excused, so long as both were citizens, and legacies from a citizen father to his free-born sons were made exempt, even if they were not under his parental authority (*patria potestas*).[31] Trajan now expanded the immunity to a non-citizen father with respect to inheriting a citizen son's property by removing the clause requiring *in patria potestate*, on the grounds that natural law compelled children to be obedient to their fathers.[32] Then, after the principle was established with regard to the first degree of kinship, it was advanced to the second degree and immunity granted to brothers and sisters and grandparents and grandchildren in respect of each other's property. It was further amplified so that all immediate kin won *cognationis* as of right, instead of each member having to petition individually for the grant.[33] Finally, the threshold for the tax was raised and restricted to capital, and all the new provisions made retrospective, hence absolving many from accumulated debt, the books which recorded the amounts owed being ceremoniously burnt in the Forum (Pl. 4). The immediate effect was, according to Pliny, that many now eagerly sought office and citizenship, as there was no loss of family or wealth to set against the increase in status.[34]

Trajan's continued pursuit of a more liberal financial policy to set against the absolutism of Domitian might well have alarmed a former treasury official such as Pliny.[35] Yet, aside from enhancing the ruler's prestige and winning the gratitude of the people as a whole, by reducing the overall level of taxation and dismissing existing debts, Trajan calculated on overcoming the general reluctance to pay anything at all, a strategy which apparently proved successful in this case.[36] He further supplemented the treasuries by emulating Gaius and Nerva in selling state property to the public, and by deeding properties from the *patrimonium* to the state for public lease, thus ensuring that vacant estates were used again as well as securing the revenue for the state.[37]

Pliny saw this last measure solely as a means of improving the public purse. But it may well have been intended to bring back into use land long redundant and alleviate a supposed crisis in Italian agriculture whereby small peasant proprietors were losing their land to larger estate-owners. The evidence is at best circumstantial. The interpretation assumes that the expansion of the empire and the consequent introduction of provincial taxation in kind had vastly increased the supply of cheaper foodstuffs from overseas at the expense of domestic production, causing the collapse of those small- to medium-sized estates where the bulk of the cereal-growing and olive oil production traditionally took place.[38] These were then absorbed into *latifundia*, large agglomerations owned by a few wealthy men, who either turned them over to viticulture, which gave dividends of up to 10 per cent compared with the 2–3 per cent of grain; or leased them out to tenant farmers and lived off the returns of regular rents rather than directly exploiting them. Archaeological verification of the thesis is difficult – if not impossible – to come by, although the excavations at Settefinestre, among other sites, seems to bear it out.[39] The primary evidence instead comes from certain literary texts, especially the so-called 'vine-edict' of Domitian and Pliny's frequent complaints concerning his land-holdings.

Domitian's 'vine edict', to begin with, was allegedly brought about by a grain famine at the capital which coincided with a glut of wine.[40] It prohibited the extension of the existing Italian vineyards, greatly expanded since the eruption of Vesuvius had obliterated those extending from its foot, and ordered the destruction of half the vineyards in the provinces. It seems to have been quickly repealed, however, which has given currency to the claims of Statius and Philostratus that the measure was primarily intended as a moral one, to inculcate a degree of sobriety among the plebs.[41] Alternatively, it has been suggested, the measure was intended solely to compensate for a crisis in over-production.[42] Yet, on the one hand, it might reasonably be doubted that any Roman emperor would seek to reduce wine production purely on account of drunkenness: the Roman empire was not some primitive forerunner of the Nordic welfare state in which health considerations outweighed any possible gains in taxes to the *fiscus*, never mind the profits made by the emperor's land-owning peers. Then, on the other hand, it seems improbable that any emperor ever formulated an all-embracing interventionist economic policy purely to counter a surplus of one particular commodity, for Rome easily absorbed the increasing quantity available.[43] Unless, of course, as Suetonius implies, intervention was necessary because an emphasis on viticulture was interfering with the supply of grain, the chief staple of the plebs. Thus, the fact that the 'vine edict' was apparently soon repealed has little bearing on the overall thesis, for it merely signals the end of that particular agrarian crisis. Indeed, it is perhaps relevant here that Nerva revived the principle of land allotments from the *ager publicus* for the benefit of the plebs. In what was basically an agrarian society, an increase in land-ownership of this type and on this scale (land worth HS 60,000,000 was distributed) is usually indicative of a need to increase food production, at the very least as a subsistence measure for the new owners.[44] Nerva's action, therefore, supports the premise that there was a continued concern that the agrarian crisis might repeat itself.

As it is, much of Pliny's correspondence is taken up with his serious concern about the harvests in this general period. Like most senators, he relied upon his country estates as his principal source of wealth. His principal holdings, which came to him through his natural parents, were in the extremely fertile Cisalpine region of his home town, Comum (Como); his other main property, inherited from his uncle and adoptive father, Pliny the Elder, lay near Tifernum Tiberinum, in Umbria. The last earned him *HS* 400,000 in a year, and the two together have been valued at about *HS* 17,000,000.[45] Where crops are specified, viticulture is emphasized, yet the Transpadanian estates were in an area not especially noted for wine-growing, while that in Umbria was peripheral to the main centres of wine production which lay further east and south. From which we can conclude that other crops (cereals, legumes and olives) were of some importance in both properties. Pliny's letters provide a long catalogue of adverse reports concerning the liabilities of a medium-sized estate owner:

> Being dependent on the way my property is farmed, my income is small or precarious, and I make up for its deficiencies by simple living.[46]

> My mother's property is treating me badly; still I love it for being my mother's and besides, suffering has toughened me.[47]

> I hear that hail has done much damage to my Tuscan holdings [*sc.*, Tifernum], while of those in Transpadana [*sc.*, Comum], I hear that the crops are good, but the prices correspondingly low.[48]

> The necessity of letting my farms is becoming very urgent and giving me much trouble for suitable tenants can rarely be found.[49]

> Other people visit their estates to come away richer than before, but I only go to return the poorer. I had sold my grape harvest to the dealers who were eager to buy when the price quoted at the time was tempting and prospects seemed good. Their hopes were frustrated [. . .] Accordingly I returned to everyone an eighth of the sum he had spent [. . .] Then I made a special provision for those who had invested very large sums in their purchase.[50]

> I have neither time nor inclination for hunting: no time because I am busy with the grape harvest; no inclination because it is so poor.[51]

> As for me, at this very moment I am gathering in the grape harvest, which is poor.[52]

> You also say you have had a poor grape harvest, and I can join you in the complaint, even though we live so far from each other.[53]

> During the past five years, despite the large reductions I made in the rents, the arrears have increased, and as a result most of my tenants have lost interest in reducing the debt because they have no hope of ever being able to pay off the whole; they even seize and consume the entire produce of the land in the belief they will gain nothing themselves by conserving it.[54]

> I cannot postpone letting [the farms I own], especially as the new tenants should be there to see to the pruning of the vines, and this must be done soon. Moreover the series of bad harvests we have had are forcing me to reduce rents.[55]

Whichever way they are looked at, these comments provide irreducible proof for a sequence of poor harvests in Italy during the period they were written, the years *c.* 97–107. They follow on from Dio's comment that already under Claudius virtually all the grain used in Italy was imported, and the elder Pliny's assessment that the increase in *latifundia* had brought about the ruination of Italy, a reference to smaller land-holders such as himself.[56] It would be unwise to dismiss Pliny's lamentations simply as the 'complaints of a landowner [...] which might belong to any age', especially as they reveal that Pliny, for one, favoured renting his properties for a cash income, rather than developing them through a bailiff. At the very least, therefore, the circumstances which brought about the 'vine edict' of Domitian, the land allotments of Nerva and the grievances of Pliny point to the turn of the first century being a period of stagnation and poor returns from the harvests of Italy. While not proving that there was a major agricultural crisis at the time, they do at least support the conjecture that there was a need for increased productivity and capital investment. And it is in this context that Trajan's revision of the alimentary system, the major social innovation of his reign, has to be interpreted.

The concept of the *alimenta*, a scheme whereby private individuals and public corporations could assist poor families in bringing up their children, was of some antiquity.[57] It is possible that Nerva had established an imperial version still in place when Trajan became *princeps*, although the details are lost to us.[58] It may have been similar to the private arrangement made by Pliny, as *patronus* of Comum. Under this, Pliny promised a capital sum of *HS* 500,000 for the maintenance of free-born boys and girls in the city, but instead of disbursing a lump sum, he transferred property valued greatly in excess of the amount needed to the public land-agent and had it conveyed back to him at a rent of *HS* 30,000 per annum, thus securing both the principal and the interest for the town.[59]

The arrangements of Trajan's public alimentary system, already in operation by 101, are considerably better documented, thanks to the discovery of two remarkable bronze plaques which give full details of the scheme as it operated at one small town in north Italy, and an equivalent community in the south.[60] The first step at each place was evidently to set a target figure for the number of beneficiaries in each qualifying district, and then invite subscribers until the quota was reached. Both boys and girls were eligible to benefit under the scheme, although the amount of dole paid varied according to sex and legal status, *HS* 16 or 12 each month for males, and *HS* 12 or 10 for females, depending on whether legitimate or not. As is to be expected, as they brought in the greater sum, the number of legitimate males registered for the benefit vastly exceeds the other three groups.[61]

Once the quota had been filled, a sum equivalent to twenty times the amount of the benefit needed was given by the treasury to the community, and parcelled out among local landowners by the local *quaestores alimentorum*, supervised by regional senatorial *curatores rei alimentariae*.[62] It appears that the loans were initially targeted at the largest individual landowners within the specific districts and that their properties were used to secure sums equal to about 8 per cent of their value at the favourable fixed rate of 5 per cent interest per annum, compared to the more usual 6–12 per cent.[63] For example, in 101, some sixty-six mortgages were made against the fund by named landowners amongst the *Ligures Baebiani* near Macchia, Campania, to finance an overall sum of

HS 401,800 to be distributed between 110 and 120 children.[64] A typical entry is that recording the participation of one Neratius Corellius in the scheme:

> Mortgaged by Neratius Corellius: the Paccian Farm and Aurelianus's cottage, next to [the property of] Julius Saturninus. Valued at HS 22,000, [mortgaged] for HS 2,000, [the loan] administered by [his kinsman] Neratius Marcellus at HS 50 [semi-annual interest].

The interest in this case was equivalent to 5 per cent of the loan negotiated by Corellius, although at 9.09 per cent of the valuation it was somewhat higher than the average of 7.46 per cent for the table as a whole.[65] Otherwise, the mortgage corresponds in its principal details to those recorded on the *Tabula Veleia* of 103–12, which registers the scheme in the town of that name in Apulia.[66] Here, the value of the properties mortgaged against the *alimenta* was HS 1,044,000, and the interest of HS 52,000 was distributed among 300 children, 263 legitimate boys, 35 legitimate girls, 1 illegitimate boy, and 1 illegitimate girl. For example, Gaius Volumnius Memor and Volumnia Alce mortgaged

> through the agency of their freedman, Volumnius Diadumenos, their Quintiacus-Aurelianus Farm and the Hill of Muletas with its forest, in the territory of Veleia in the Ambittrebian district, bounded by [the properties of] Marcus Mommeius Persicus and Satrius Severus, and by the public [road]. [Valued at] HS 108,000: they are to receive HS 8,692 with the above-named farm as security.

The loan to the Volumenii, therefore, was 8.05 per cent of the valuation, only slightly more than the average of 8 per cent for the forty-six properties listed on the tablet.[67]

It is generally assumed that in every case the loan was perpetual, although there is no positive evidence. It seems unlikely. The effect of such a permanent charge on a unit of land was to reduce its market value considerably, both for purposes of resale and for taxation, and more probably the imperial *alimenta* incorporated some form of time-limit.[68] The interest, meanwhile, was collected by the local authority on behalf of the *princeps*, and allocated to the maintenance of those registered indigent children within the district. It seems to have been payable to the boys until they reached the age of sixteen, and to the girls until they were fourteen.[69] Then, as Pliny makes abundantly clear, in a passage sometimes dismissed as plain rhetoric, the boys were expected to enrol for military service when old enough, while the girls were expected to marry and procreate.[70]

The reformed alimentary system was welcomed as an expression of Trajan's *liberalitas* and his *indulgentia*, terms which superficially define his generosity, but which also convey distinctly paternal, religious and quasi-political overtones.[71] Unfortunately, the exact purpose of the scheme is nowhere specified in contemporary literature, and has naturally given cause for much discussion. Pliny reports that Trajan's revision was prompted by the number of begging families lining the route as he went to dispense his first *congiarium*, and is quite clear in his own mind as to what Trajan intended: inspired by the vision of the rising generation, Trajan wished it to grow at his (that is, the state's) expense to preserve the well-being of Rome and the future of the *imperium*.[72] True, according to Pliny, the security and freedom from fear already assured by his accession in themselves made it a pleasure to bear children in the new regime. But more was needed, for

> Huge rewards and greater penalties are raised to encourage the rich to procreate, but the poor are only led to this pass by the inducements and security occasioned by a good *princeps*. Yet, unless he cherishes and provides for those children that the confidence in his reign inspires, he accelerates the downfall of the *imperium* and of the *res publica*. His security is in vain if he neglects the plebs, for like a head isolated from the nourishment of the body, the system becomes unstable, and doomed to fall.[73]

To Pliny, therefore, the *alimenta* was an act of social policy, designed to provide economic security for those already born and to encourage a higher birth-rate, which in turn would secure the eternity of the *imperium*.[74] In this way, by alleviating the financial penalties of parenthood, the *alimenta* ranked alongside the *congiarium* as a means of distributing largesse for the overall benefit of the Roman people, which explains why Pliny duly associates the two schemes.[75] Even so, his seemingly rational explanation for the *alimenta*, as a measure intended fundamentally to promote a higher birth-rate, seems overly simplistic. That limited aim could have been achieved by the easier and much cheaper expedient of instituting a welfare office which granted allowances to needy families, instead of tying a large capital sum immutably to the mortgaging of agricultural land throughout the Italian peninsula. After all, even if the total required for the *alimenta* was only equivalent to, say, *HS* 311,000,000 – a sum arrived at by averaging out the costs of the *Ligures Baebiani* and Veleia schemes, multiplied by 430, the accepted figure for the maximum number of towns in Italy at the time – it was still a substantial amount, sufficient to pay for several major building schemes, or cover three-quarters of the total cost of the military for a single year – and perhaps nearly half of Rome's income from the provinces.[76]

Moreover, despite Pliny's claim, the measure *per se* did not promote an increased birth-rate; rather, it provided for the maintenance of those already born, with the possibility of grants to future children. Now, ancient demography is a minefield. We do not know for certain the population trend for either Rome or Italy at the time, and thus cannot establish if there was a real, as opposed to a perceived, need to replace a declining population. Nor do we know the rate of live births or the age range involved. But if it is assumed, just for the sake of argument, that Rome had a free population of about 1 million, and that Pliny's 5,000 beneficiaries of the *alimenta* were equally distributed across the entire juvenile age range of 0–16, then only 312 or so new additions could be made to the lists each year in a city whose free-born juveniles numbered perhaps not less than 640,000.[77] For comparison, at Veleia, while the maximum number of families who benefited was 300, a significant proportion of what must have been a population of at least 2,000, enrolment nevertheless remained a kind of lottery, even if at greatly reduced odds.[78] It would require a leap of faith of unimaginable proportions to believe the measure encouraged each and every poor family in Rome certainly, and Veleia possibly, to decide upon another child on the slight chance that the family might benefit from the lottery that was the *alimenta*. Thus, despite Pliny's contention and the views of modern scholars, the charitable intent of the *alimenta* does not seem to have been primarily 'natalist', but rather maintenance.[79]

In fact, the chief beneficiaries of the *alimenta* would appear to have been the landowners rather than indigent parents. Even if there were no way to disengage from the agreement, which seems highly unlikely, the interest liable was perhaps less than half that of a regular loan and provided a lump sum at no risk. Was, then, the *alimenta* conceived with some agrarian policy in mind? Pliny's letters certainly suggest that it may have been necessary to finance less wealthy landowners throughout the peninsula, but a simpler method could have been found – a landbank, perhaps, with a limited capital administered by the state and the interest returned to the treasury. Further, while the cash might have been intended to promote the development of the mortgagee's estate or alleviate any hardship caused by poor harvests, there are no known restrictions on how it was to be used, whether for the benefit of the property or for the benefit of the mortgagee: the concept of the selective credit advance against one's property does not seem to have been known in the ancient world. Yet it is unlikely that Trajan or his advisers intended the supply of funds to be little more than a method of financing the whims of extravagant landowners, to purchase a new chariot, say. While the *alimenta* was evidently directed at the wealthiest men in each district, none of the mortgagees held estates comparable to those of the upper classes: the largest estate recorded at Veleia, for example, at *HS* 1,600,000, equivalent to a tenth of Pliny's holdings. Consequently, while perhaps not aimed specifically at smallholders, the *alimenta* certainly benefited the owners of the smaller estates at a time when there was apparently a need for additional finance to compensate for a series of poor harvests and a shortage of suitable tenant labour. On balance, therefore, the refinancing aspect of the alimentary system can be interpreted as an avowed political policy, to promote agrarian reforms to the class of farmer who needed financing most. It may have been a crude solution to a complex problem, but what better way of furthering crop cultivation and animal husbandry, as well as promoting the welfare of the rising generation?[80]

From the outset, therefore, it seems that Trajan had a defined political and social manifesto for his regime. And in January 101, once the manifesto was firmly in place, the *princeps* took the fourth consulship so ardently requested by Pliny in his *actio gratiarum* the previous year. While little is known of his eponymous colleague, the Italian Q. Articuleius Paetus, *cos. suff.* 78 and then (?)*adiutor curatoris aquarum* 83–96, the individual who followed Trajan, as suffect consul, was quite extraordinary.[81] He was Sex. Attius Suburanus Aemilianus, an equestrian by origin, who had replaced Aelianus as Praetorian Prefect in the course of 98, but was then quickly adlected into the senate (presumably *inter praetorios*) before 100.[82] His rapid advancement reveals the trust which Trajan had in the man, not least because that March, the emperor left Rome to prosecute a military campaign in Dacia.

VIII

DACICUS[1]

The Dacians were a Thraco-Phrygian race, who originated in north-west Asia Minor.[2] They possessed a strong sense of national identity, strengthened by their location in the Transylvanian Basin, a fertile area enclosed by the Carpathians, a mountain chain ranging from 4,520 to 8,200ft (1,378–2,500m) high, with few natural access routes to the interior.[3] Trade with the Hellenistic world, based upon Dacia's considerable mineral reserves, especially of gold and silver, exposed them to more advanced technological and cultural strategies than their Celtic and German neighbours. In particular, the ashlar walls and projecting rectangular towers surrounding the Greek colonies of the Black Sea littoral influenced their own development of the unique *murus Dacicus*. Quite unlike the earthworks or palisades that fortified most towns in barbarian Europe, these drystone revetments retained a timber-reinforced rubble core, for resilience against battering-rams, and incorporated towers modelled after their Greek prototypes, for providing flanking fire for archers and missile-throwing engines. Earlier Dacian strongholds already made skilful use of natural defences, hilltops or promontories surrounded by precipitous slopes, dominating the chasm-like routes into their heartland: the addition of advanced defensive systems now made them an almost insuperable obstacle to any invader, each necessitating reduction before further passage through the extremely difficult terrain.

The introduction of the *murus Dacicus* coincided with the reign of King Burebista. He ruled from the *basileon* or royal centre of Sarmizegethusa Regia (Dealul Gradistei), a fortified complex set at 3,930ft (1,200m) in the southern Carpathians. Covering an area of 22 acres (9ha), centred on an *acropolis* of 7.5 acres (3ha), it was the largest industrial, political and religious centre of prehistoric Europe, and it was from here that Burebista unified the disparate Dacian septs and organized federations with the less-developed tribes on his frontiers, making his kingdom the nucleus of the only viable barbarian empire in Europe, and the only one powerful enough – militarily and economically – potentially to rival Rome itself.[4]

The Dacian army could never equal that of Rome in open combat, however. Dacia, like other barbarian kingdoms in Europe, never fielded a standing army, even though there was a warrior-class of sorts, the *comati*, the 'long-haired ones' (Pl. 10B). Instead, local chieftains, the *pileati* – so called because of the conical felt cap that denoted their rank (Pl. 10A) – raised a levy when required, a force only available after the harvesting season ended. The men themselves fought in everyday clothing defended merely by an oval shield, for body armour and helmets were only worn by the nobility. Even so, led into battle to the sound of the boar-headed *carnyx* war-trumpet, following the *draco*, an open-jawed zoomorphic standard streaming a wind-sock of striped and coloured cloth, the Dacian levy was renowned for its ferocity, and dreaded because of its principal weapon, the terrifying *falx*: shaped like a bill-hook (Pl. 8B), it was used in a slashing action with devastating effect against unprotected limbs.[5]

Rome had good reason to view with some disquiet the expansion of Burebista's incipient empire. They had attacked Olbia, a Greek enclave in the Crimea, and an attack on Macedonia was considered a possibility. Caesar himself made preparations for war against the king, although in the event, both men died within the same year, removing the crisis. Lacking strong leadership, the Dacian kingdom gradually splintered among warring factions and eventually collapsed. Their territory south of the Danube was taken by M. Licinius Crassus in 27 BC, the Hungarian Plain was lost to the indigenous Celtic tribes, and the Banat to the Iazyges, nomadic Sarmatians who occupied the area after 7 BC with Roman support.[6]

By 7 BC, Burebista's empire was so reduced that instead of the 200,000 warriors he fielded, only 40,000 could now be called to arms.[7] None the less, Dacia remained a formidable foe: in the winter of 10 BC, for example, a raid across the frozen Danube was barely repulsed by M. Vinicius. As a direct consequence, Lentulus established *praesidia*, permanent forts, north of the river in the area of the Iron Gates Gorge, securing a *cordon sanitaire* where no native settlements were allowed.[8] But despite the creation of one of the earliest preclusive Roman frontiers, attacks across the river continued, and the influence of Dacia again expanded, into Slovakia, Moldavia and the Wallachian Plain. Dacian aggression became more direct: a raid into Moesia in 69 was just checked by Licinius Mucianus, fortuitously passing through the province on his way to Rome to battle Vitellius at Bedriacum. Another attack in 85/86 ended with the death of the Moesian governor, Oppius Sabinus, and only the rapid response of Domitian saved the province. Then, the following year, under their new king, Decebalus, a Dacian force annihilated the Praetorian Prefect Fuscus and his army, precipitating a crisis not resolved until 88, when Tettius Julianus achieved the desperately needed victory at Tapae. But even then military superiority could not be imposed on the Dacians, because at the crucial moment, Domitian was instead diverted to engage the troublesome Suebi and the Iazyges on his left flank. They had failed to support the emperor against Decebalus, and to punish them a campaign was launched into their territories. Ironically, to ensure its success a treaty was agreed with Dacia, and a client relationship established. Decebalus sent a proxy, Diegis, to receive from Domitian the sovereignty over Dacia, 'large sums of money' were paid over with more promised in the future, and 'artisans of every trade pertaining to both peace and war' were seconded to Sarmizegethusa.[9]

This arrangement did not bring glory to Rome, nor did the subvention enhance Roman prestige. On the contrary, it confirmed the prominent and menacing position of the Dacian kingdom and Decebalus' status as Burebista's heir, for – even if the realm was nominally reduced to a client state – Dacia rapidly became the nucleus for anti-Roman sentiment, welcoming deserters and malcontents from areas already absorbed within the empire. Assured, it seemed, of Rome's unwillingness to pursue him into the tangled terrain of the Carpathians, Decebalus set about eliminating internal dissension and fortifying his kingdom, using the engineers supplied by Domitian to build up a formidable assortment of torsion weapons to add to those captured from Fuscus. The strategy of

Burebista was repeated and foreign alliances were formed, notably with the Getic Bastarnae and the Sarmatian Roxolani, although Decebalus failed to secure the support of the Quadi, Marcomanni and Iazyges. Their acquiescence was ensured, however, through treaties with the tribes to their north, trapping them between their traditional German enemies on the one side, Rome on another, and Dacia on the third.

Even before he became emperor, Trajan had recognized the special problem that Decebalus – through his personality, character and actions – constituted for the safety of the northern provinces, establishing on its borders an autocratic regime which posed a tangible threat to Roman authority in the region. This accounts for his decision, after learning of Nerva's death and his own accession, to return to Rome via the Danube provinces in order to examine and secure the situation at first hand. It was probably now that he organized the founding of *praesidia* on the left bank of the Danube across from northern Pannonia, and ordered the reconstruction of the Djerdap tow-path, the rebuilding of auxiliary forts in stone, and the cutting of the Karatash–Gradac canal to eliminate the dangers posed to river transport by the rapids of the Ister. None of these construction works in itself, however, necessarily meant that Trajan had already decided to invade Dacia: Decebalus seems to have remained content with the existing arrangements and offered no open aggression. Rather, it suggests a degree of caution on Trajan's part, the introduction of a policy to guarantee defensive and logistical support should the need arise, even if defensive measures often formed the framework – if not disguise – for an offensive strategy.

As we have seen, the need for offensive action was realized before March 101, when Trajan relinquished his ordinary consulship to launch open warfare against Dacia. Lacking a clear contemporary explanation, his aims and purpose can only be assessed pragmatically from the results he achieved: speculation on possible motives is notoriously open-ended.[10] It seems certain, however, that he deprecated conquest for its own sake and all it involved – a vast tract of land to be held for generations by many soldiers – as it had long been clear that the frontier provinces rarely returned sufficient income to pay for their standing garrisons.[11] Instead, he seems to have chosen a strategy of limited means for a specific goal, namely to bring Decebalus to terms with minimal bloodshed. As the epitome of Dio has it,

> he had taken stock of [the Dacians'] previous record, resented the annual sums of money they were getting, and saw that their powers and their pride were on the increase.[12]

These sentiments are indicative of a punitive war rather than one of conquest. A punitive campaign is likewise indicated by coin issues of 101 which bear the image of *Mars Ultor* – Mars the Avenger – referring to the need to restore Roman prestige over a people who in the past fifteen years had killed two Roman generals and countless men. It is confirmed by Trajan's failure to raise the additional legions or auxiliary troops necessary to provide a permanent garrison if conquest were indeed planned. None the less, the attack did not result from a sudden decision: logistical preparations must have begun the previous year at the latest. Concomitantly, Trajan had appointed experienced generals to the provinces directly affected, C. Cilnius Proculus to Moesia Superior, M'. Laberius Maximus to Moesia Inferior and L. Julius Ursus Servianus to Pannonia, although the last was eventually seconded to Trajan's own staff, and replaced by Q. Glitius Atilius Agricola when hostilities commenced.[13]

Trajan left Rome for Dacia on 25 March, after the Arval Brethren offered appropriate prayers for his safe journey and return:

> O Jupiter, Greatest and Best, we publicly beseech and entreat thee to cause in prosperity and felicity the safety, return and victory of the emperor, Caesar, son of the deified Nerva, Nerva Trajan Augustus Germanicus, our prince and parent, chief priest with tribunician power, Father of the Fatherland, he who speaks to us from these places and provinces to which he will go by land and sea; and to give him a goodly outcome of all those matters which now he is executing or is about to execute; and to preserve him in that condition in which he now is, or in one better than that; and to bring him back and restore him in safety to the city of Rome at the earliest possible time. And if you so do this, we vow in the name of the College of the Arval Brethren that you shall have a gilded ox.[14]

The emperor was accompanied by the Praetorian Guard, one of the Praetorian Prefects, Ti. Claudius Livianus, and his friend and confidant L. Licinius Sura, recently returned from the administration of Germania Inferior.[15] Among his entourage were a number of the most skilled generals in the empire, of whom the most notable was Q. Sosius Senecio, son-in-law of the great strategist Frontinus: now given the honorific rank of *legatus pro praetore*,[16] he had commanded the *legio I Minervia* in 97/98, and received the ordinary consulship in 99 as reward for his part in Trajan's operations across the Rhine. Another elevated to the same rank was C. Julius Quadratus Bassus, tribune in the *XIII Gemina* during Domitian's Dacian campaigns, and most recently legate of the *XI Claudia*, based at Vindonissa (Windisch). Somewhat more advanced in years – he was now in his fifties – was Cn.Pinarius Pompeius Longinus, *cos. suff.* in 90, governor of Moesia Superior between 93 and 96, and Trajan's successor in Pannonia. Of a like age was L. Julius Ursus Servianus, also *cos. suff.* in 90, promoted to Germania Superior in 96–98, then made *Comes* during Trajan's Danubian *excursus* in 98/99 and governor of Pannonia in 99/100. Completing the core of the imperial *consilium* were Lusius Quietus, commander of the irregular Moorish cavalry; the equestrian C. Manlius Felix, quartermaster for the campaign; and Trajan's cousin and the husband of his great-niece, the 25-year-old P. Aelius Hadrianus, at the time imperial quaestor after military service which had included tribunates with the *II Adiutrix* in Pannonia and the *V Macedonica* in Moesia Inferior, and now concurrently made *Comes expeditionis Dacicae*.

The imperial entourage probably travelled overland along the via Flaminia by way of Ariminum (Rimini) to Viminiacium (Kostolac), the traditional base for campaigns beyond the Ister, arriving there perhaps in late April. A considerable force was available for the campaign, with nine of the thirty legions already stationed along the front,[17] together with several auxiliary *alae* and *cohortes*. The legions were the principal fighting force of the Roman army, each comprising no fewer than 5,500 Roman citizens wearing close-fitting iron helmets and *lorica segmentata*, a cuirass of overlapping iron hoops (Pl. 6A), although some still wore the earlier *lorica hamata* or *squamata*, interlinked mail or scale armour, and a few had vambraces, to protect their arms against the Dacian *falx*.[18] Each legionary carried a rectangular *scutum*, a short stabbing *gladius* and a 6-foot-long weighted *pilum*.

A complement of artillery – arrow- and stone-throwing torsion machines, one per century – was assigned to each legion and, together with a contingent of foot archers, provided close support in open battle and harassing fire during a siege.[19]

While the legions formed the centrepiece of any set action, the initial skirmishing and combat and the responsibility for the flanks devolved upon the auxiliaries, infantry and cavalry units of non-citizens. Their infantry were accoutred with iron mail, an oval shield, and close-fitting iron or bronze helmets: they used the long *spatha* and spear (Pl. 8A), although certain specialized units retained their traditional weapons, for example the reflex bows of the Asiatic archers.[20] The cavalry, carrying a hexagonal or oval shield, and clad in a cuirass of either iron mail or bronze scales, were similarly helmeted and armed, although there were also some part-mounted regiments of archers. Riding unshod mounts similar to the present-day Icelandic pony, medium-sized beasts with short legs and stocky bodies, they did not use stirrups, retaining their position by means of a saddle with a high back and substantial projecting wings at the front.[21] In all, there were some 90 auxiliary regiments along the Ister at this date, 21 *alae*, or heavy cavalry, 5 of which were double strength; 33 *cohortes equitatae*, the mixed units of light cavalry and infantry, 9 of double strength; 25 infantry *cohortes peditatae*, 6 double strength; and 10 regiments of archers, the *cohortes sagittariae*, 3 of which were part-mounted, 1 of double strength; together, they perhaps numbered in all no fewer than 55,000 men.[22]

Finally, Trajan could call upon an unspecified number of *nationes* and *symmachiarii*, ethnic levies fighting for Rome as a result of treaty obligations by the client-kingdoms on the periphery of the empire. One literary source, *De metatione castrorum*, which apparently describes the methods used for encampment by an army group in the First Dacian War, indicates the involvement of 500 Palmyrenes, 900 Getae, 700 Daci, 500 Britons and 700 Cantabri. In addition to these, Dio attests to the involvement of the '*Mauron symmachias*', the Moorish cavalry led by Lusius Quietus, and there is figural evidence for the presence of Balearic slingmen. These national units fought in national dress, wielding their own ethnic weapons, and like the auxiliaries were used for reconnaissance and skirmishing.[23] All in all, then, the army assembled by Trajan was easily the largest ever gathered by Rome: even if half remained behind to secure the defence of the Danubian provinces, 50,000 men were available for combat.

Warfare in ancient Europe followed a certain immutable cycle, the ground rules dictated by the season's prevailing weather, which determined the state of the ground where armies manoeuvred and foraged for food. Thus May was the usual month for advance, as the first green shoots became available as fodder for the pack animals and cavalry mounts and the ground was firm and dry enough for passage of man and beast, with the bulk of the fighting commencing in June or July after harvest-time. Consequently, it can be assumed that Trajan embarked on campaign almost immediately after his arrival at Viminiacium.

Only fragmentary details survive of the war that followed: a single sentence of Trajan's own *Dacica*; little more of the *Getica* written by his doctor, T. Statilius Crito; nothing whatsoever of the poem proposed by Caninius Rufus (if it was ever written), Dio Chrysostom's *Getica* or Appian's *Dacica*. None the less, a reasonable account can be pieced together. The important if confused fragments of Dio's *Roman History*, for example, can be re-assembled to provide a basic chronological framework.[24] And then there is the

100ft Column at Rome, dedicated in Trajan's honour on 12 May 113 (Pl. 5). Incised with a 710ft-long helical bas-relief, which spirals 24 times around the shaft, more than 2,500 figures are dispersed among 155 recognized scenes, conceivably illustrating specific incidents recorded in the *Dacica*, a winged Victory at the mid-way point providing the division between the story of the two wars.[25] But such a chronicle must necessarily remain largely hypothetical. Convergences between Dio's account and the Column's scenes are few, and many of the latter are *topoi*, stock pieces, formally organized illustrations of the Roman army's superiority over the barbarians and the excellence of Trajan's leadership, rather than a historically accurate commentary. It would be erroneous to consider these scenes as historical facts: rather they represent a summary of the events that took place.

Trajan's first task was to cross the Danube, and the Column shows a benign Danuvius, the personification of the Danube, watching over the Roman army as it crosses by twin pontoon bridges, the emperor at its head.[26] The location is probably Lederata (Palanka), the confluence of the Danube and the Csernovec. This is the southern end of the easiest route to the Iron Gates Pass, and links Berzobis (Berzovia) and Aizi (Friliug) in the Banat (Fig. 2), the two way-points mentioned in the one surviving sentence of Trajan's *Dacica*.[27] Once across, the army was purified by a *suovetaurilia*, the ritual sacrifice of a boar, a ram and a bull to the god Mars, and the Column shows the emperor, wearing the veil of the *pontifex maximus*, presiding over the ceremonies with *patera* in his outstretched hand over the flaming *focus* of the altar.[28] Then, the army began its march north along the valley of the Csernovec, river valleys being the usual avenues of advance, affording fertile grazing and frequently permitting the transport of some supplies in barges. Most of the required equipment and food, however, came by mule and ass, with oxen the normal means of traction for baggage carts and wheeled torsion engines.[29]

The marching day usually began in the pre-dawn light, when tents were struck and the scouts and vanguard sent on their way to establish a camp for the evening.[30] Then the main body formed up, the rear units – the previous day's van – assembling as much as six hours after the march began. Twenty Roman miles (18.5 miles = 29.5km), with men marching six abreast, was the accepted optimum for a day's advance.[31] Between ten and twelve miles was probably more usual in the absence of paved roads, the actual distance being determined by the terrain, the availability of daylight, and the speed of the principal pack-animals, mules and oxen, only capable of about two miles per hour (3.2kph). Thus, after some six hours marching, when the rear of the column was forming up, the head had probably arrived at the location chosen for that night's encampment.[32] This had already been surveyed and apportioned by the vanguard for the several units involved, even down to the individual tent-emplacements for the eight-man *contubernium* in each unit, the smallest tactical group in the Roman army.[33] Building the defences involved almost as much effort and time as was expended on the march itself, after which baggage was unloaded and unpacked, tents erected, fires lit and the cavalry horses and baggage animals set to grazing. Only then were rations allocated and prepared by the individual *contubernia* before the army retired for the night at dusk.

All these activities are shown in great detail on the Column, the lines advancing through hilly countryside, pioneers clearing woodland and making roads and bridges, and the vanguard foraging and building fortifications as the cavalry scouts bring in prisoners

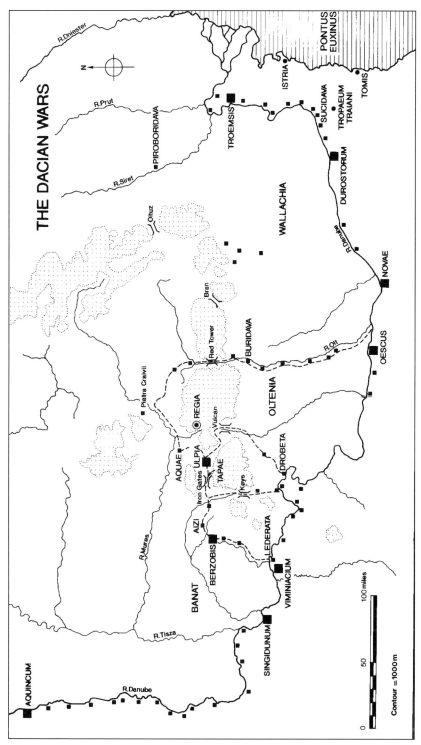

Fig. 2 The Dacian Wars

for questioning. A slow and methodical advance, consolidating as they went, was a characteristic of the Roman army; and with the memory of Fuscus' defeat still fresh in their minds, Trajan and his generals were doubly wary of being caught unprepared. Hence, Trajan's balance of grand strategy and tactical purpose, a more effective method than the rapid movement and shock tactics used by the impetuous Domitian and his generals, is emphasized on the Column. Admittedly, impetuosity and eagerness in warfare sometimes produced rapid results – but equally often ended in ignominious failure and defeat. With training, discipline and firm leadership, victory could be achieved with fewer casualties. Consequently, Trajan appears over and over again on the Column as a true *vir militaris* – marching with his troops, holding councils of war with his staff, supervising the locations of camps and bridges, receiving embassies and interrogating prisoners and spies.

According to our sources, documentary and sculptural, the Dacians offered little serious resistance during this preliminary stage of the campaign. Such a leisurely sequence of events was another characteristic of ancient warfare, when battle was only joined if both sides agreed on time and place: siege warfare was preferred, the systematic reduction of strongholds through numerical superiority in a set-piece situation, rather than the risks of open-field battle. As it was, fixed combat was easily avoided: one side could remain in rough mountainous terrain or simply march away from the field chosen by their opponents. Hence, when battle was joined, it was often as a last resort, the locale being usually dictated by the overriding constraints of communications, the approaches to mountain passes or fords, for example. None the less, battle scenes are the most common features of the Column's account of the First War, and it might be that each refers to a specific engagement. If so, the inclusion of a charming vignette of Jupiter Tonans, the Thunderer, throwing a thunderbolt, suggests the first took place in a thunderstorm.[34] But the Column's sculptors do not overlook the brutality and reality of warfare, even if the constraints of depicting the action on a cylindrical shaft meant compressing time and space. We see the Roman army emerging from a wood, pioneers clearing the ground ready for combat. The guard and the legions are held in reserve as Trajan signals the auxiliaries to advance, the standard practice since at least the time of Agricola, to minimize the loss of citizen blood.[35] The auxiliary cavalry rout the flanks of the Dacian army, while the auxiliary infantry, after a barrage of spears and arrows, use their slashing swords to drive a wedge into the Dacian centre, a band of club-wielding half-naked national troops forming the spearhead. Head trophies are taken by the auxiliaries, two of whom return to offer them to Trajan, while a third, grasping his trophy by its hair between his teeth, fights on.[36] Dacian dead bestrew the ground as their wounded are carried off to the shelter of a wood, where Decebalus himself keeps watch over the battle's progress. It ends with his defeat and retreat. A nearby Dacian fortress is then fired as the occupants flee, another river forded, and another encampment begun, where the emperor addresses his victorious troops. Then, an embassy of Dacian *comati* is received and rejected by Trajan.[37] Operations continue, cavalry laying the countryside to waste while infantry pursue the fleeing Dacians, granting no quarter to them as they try to escape across a major river, some being swept away by the flood.[38] On the other hand, the *clementia* of the emperor, when it comes to non-combatants, is stressed in a metope showing him organizing the transportation of Dacian noblewomen and their children outside the combat zone.

The fighting was not always in Rome's favour: the Column illustrates Roman auxiliaries attacked in their own forts. It also depicts Trajan's response, leading Praetorians, legionaries and auxiliaries downstream to open a counter-attack against the Iron Gates Pass from another direction, perhaps from Dierna (Orsova) via the Keys Pass, the absence of an intervening *suovetaurilia* scene demonstrating we are still in the first season's campaign.[39] Speed was evidently of the essence, signifying that the year was coming to an end: Roman troops advance at the double, the emperor on horseback. A squadron of Roxolanic cavalry are vanquished as national troops and auxiliaries make a night attack on their encampment.[40] Again the emperor displays *clementia*, allowing the non-combatants – elderly men, women and children – to leave unharmed. He also receives another embassy from Decebalus, this time of *pileati*. They are shown pleading before the emperor and his *consilium*, and Dio describes how they

> threw down their arms and cast themselves upon the ground and besought Trajan, if possible, to let Decebalus come into his presence and to speak with him in person, undertaking he would do everything that he was ordered to do; otherwise, to send someone to arrange terms of peace with him. [...] (Licinius) Sura and Claudius Livianus, the Prefect, were duly sent: but nothing came of this, for Decebalus did not venture to meet them either, but again sent intermediaries.[41]

The stage was now set for the Column's third battle, a major set-piece engagement involving legionaries and auxiliaries in which the Romans used *carroballistae*, mule-drawn missile-throwing engines.[42] Again, the sculptor depicts representative scenes of every stage of the battle, including the bringing in of prisoners for questioning and a detailed view of a Roman military field station. The inclusion of the last is particularly important in any interpretation of the Column – if it is indeed based on specific episodes retailed in Trajan's own account, the *Dacica* – for so much attention is paid to the event that it might well refer to the second battle of Tapae, where the fighting was so furious that Trajan sacrificed his own clothing for bandages (Pl. 6A).[43] After the victory Trajan addresses the assembled troops, who parade with their standards, suggesting that this is the occasion of his second imperial acclamation.[44] To complement this scene and one showing the incarceration of Dacian notables, a glimpse is afforded of the fate that awaited Roman troops who were taken prisoner: they are mercilessly tortured with clubs and pointed stakes by Dacian women.

The Column's narrative suggests that while the second battle of Tapae was a major defeat for Decebalus, the losses sustained by Trajan meant that – like Tettius Julianus before – he was unable to press home the advantage with the troops to hand. Further, it was probably late in the year, when inclement weather drove the armies into winter quarters until fodder was once more available and muddy tracks dried out again the following spring.[45] None the less, a significant victory had been won, and L. Julius Ursus Servianus and L. Licinius Sura returned to Rome, where their role in the first season was rewarded by the ordinary consulship for 102. Along with them travelled Hadrian, awarded decorations for the part he had played in the emperor's *consilium*, and now charged, as imperial quaestor, with giving the senate Trajan's own detailed account of the first season's campaign.[46]

Trajan himself remained on the Danube awaiting the arrival of reinforcements for the second season's campaign. They included the *legio I Flavia Minervia pia fidelis*, whose ram *signa* is clearly detailed on the Column; the *XI Claudia pia fidelis*, now transferred from Vindonissa; and eastern vexillations equivalent to at least one legion drawn from the *legiones IV Scythica, XII Fulminata* and one other whose name is lost.[47] The auxiliary army was likewise supplemented, the dispatch of a detachment of *pedites singulares Britanniciani*, the personal guard of the British governor, among others, proving that troops were being brought from wherever they could be spared, and also indicating that a crucial phase in the war was being forced upon the emperor either through shoddy planning, or a more determined resistance than previously bargained for.

The Column shows the new army group crossing the pontoon bridges at Lederata under the emperor's supervision, and moving forward in three divisions, the central one apparently between a rampart and a palisade.[48] After the usual formal *suovetaurilia*, the 102 campaign began, and the confused reports of Dio and the scenes represented on the Column indicate that it was much harder than the first. For example, Trajan

> stormed some mountain strongholds [where he] found the captured arms and
> engines and the standard that had been lost in the time of Fuscus. Then he set
> about scaling the very peaks of the mountains, capturing, not without danger,
> crest after crest, and drew near the Royal City of the Dacians.[49]

Even so, only a single major field engagement is shown on the Column for this phase of the war. The legionaries, for once, are in the van, and supported by *ballistae*, Palmyrene archers and Balearic slingmen. After driving a wedge through the enemy ranks, they then go on to storm a nearby stronghold, using the *testudo*, with shields locked over their heads in their assault.[50]

Meanwhile, as the emperor prosecuted the frontal attack from the Iron Gates Pass in person, pincer attacks began from other directions. Lusius Quietus and his lightly armed Moorish cavalry attacked Decebalus from the rear, perhaps via the Vulcan Pass in the eastern Carpathians, killing many Dacians and taking still more prisoners. A second attack, probably along the Olt valley and led by Laberius Maximus, took the Red Tower Pass, and succeeded in capturing Decebalus' sister and an important stronghold – but not, it would seem, without loss to Roman forces. It was presumably now, if we are to credit the story, that a surprise attack on Maximus' army resulted in the capture of Callidromus, one of his household slaves, subsequently presented by Decebalus to the Parthian king Pacorus II.[51] Eventually, however, Trajan, Quietus and Maximus joined forces at the hot springs of Aquae (Calan), a mere 20 miles from the Dacian capital.

> For these reasons [...] Decebalus sent another embassy of the top-class *pileati*
> and through them appealed to the emperor, and was ready to accept any terms
> imposed on him without exception.[52]

Dio claims that Decebalus only sought peace as a respite from his reverses. Whether that is true or not, the terms exacted were suitably punitive. He was ordered

> to surrender the arms and the engines and the engineers, to return the deserters,
> to dismantle the forts, to relinquish the [Dacian] territory already captured
> [by Rome], and for the future to have the same friends and foes as the Romans,
> and neither give refuge to any deserter nor enlist any soldier from the Romans'

dominions […] And he came into Trajan's presence and prostrated himself and did obeisance to him and cast aside his arms.[53]

The First Dacian War had succeeded in its specific aim, then, of securing a new treaty and confining the Dacians within the mountain fastness. There was no need for total conquest, as is confirmed by coins issued at the end of the war, variously depicting Victory, crowning the emperor with the victor's laurel wreath, or with one foot on a Dacian helmet, and a dejected personification of Dacia, wearing the peaked cap and long trousers of her race, sitting beneath a Roman trophy: the message is *Dacia Victa*, not *capta*, *pacata* or *adquista*, a victory over Dacia, not conquest, pacification or acquisition.[54] Even so, Trajan appreciated that any resurgent threat was best combated by a diminution of Decebalus' suzerainty, and to this end, large tracts of territory north of the Danube were now annexed. In the west, the Banat was incorporated into Moesia Superior: the area was small, and could be pacified with relatively few garrisons connected by an intensive system of communications which, it was reasoned, would deter Decebalus from attacking at will along the traditional routes into Moesia Superior and southern Pannonia. The key to the defensive strategy was the network of auxiliary forts built throughout the territory, centred on the legionary fortresses at Sarmizegethusa Ulpia and Berzobis, garrisoned by the *IIII Flavia Firma* and *XIII Gemina* respectively.[55] The system was buttressed through the construction of a permanent bridge over the Danube at Drobeta (Turnu-Severin), so that, whatever the season, reinforcements could easily be conveyed across to the further bank. It was designed and built by the Greek Apollodorus of Damascus, and consisted of a timber roadway supported by twenty ashlar piers. The construction was no easy task, for the bridge was built at a point where there were

> turbulent waters and a muddy bottom [as] the river is contracted [. . .] in its downward course from a great flood of water into a narrow gorge, to expand further downstream into a greater flood again [with] no possibility there of diverting the stream into another channel. [Yet it was] the narrowest and best adapted [point] to be bridged in the whole of that region.[56]

More substantial tracts were consolidated downstream of Oescus. To begin with, the decision was made to extend the system of forts along the Lower Danube, an area where Rome had often been forced to intervene in the past, owing to the dangers caused by folk migrations and nomadic movements.[57] Until this time, no forts existed along the right bank beyond the naval base at Sexaginta Prisca (Ruse): between here and the main port at Noviodunum (Issacea), at the apex of the Danube delta, responsibility for both banks of the river had devolved upon the *praefectus classis Flavia Moesicae et ripae Danuvii*.[58] Under Trajan, forts were now built at Carsium (Hirsova) and Sucidava (Celei), among other locations, and legionary fortresses probably now established at Durostorum (Silistra) and Troesmis (Iglita), garrisoned respectively by the *XI Claudia* and *V Macedonica*. At the same time it was realized that the river alone could not serve as a totally effective frontier. It could be easily crossed at a number of places in the summer when low, or in the winter when frozen. Instead, it was necessary to create a forward system of forts in the area, a *cordon sanitaire* in Oltenia and Wallachia, to provide advance warning of any threatening movements, and a papyrus of 105 indicates that forts were now built at

Buridava (Ocnele Mari) in Wallachia and Piroboridava (Poiana) in Moldavia, and the area considered *intra provinciam Moesiae Inferioris.*[59] They were evidently intended to cover the lines of attack from Dacia along the Olt and Siret respectively, but could not have existed in isolation, and it may be assumed that strings of others originally connected them to the main frontier line along the Lower Danube.

The emperor returned to Italy towards the very end of 102, an absence of about twenty-one months. In true republican tradition, the envoys from Decebalus were brought before the senate to ratify the peace, and

> laying down their arms they placed their hands together like manacled prisoners and uttered words of supplication; and thus they concluded the treaty and received back their arms.[60]

Between 10 and 31 December 102, Trajan was voted the title *Dacicus* and a triumph and games were held in his honour. Confirmation, if needed, that his victory was considered complete: all too often Domitian had held false triumphs; now there was cause for a genuine one, which Trajan took before the end of 102, possibly on 28 December, celebrating it with the issue of a commemorative coin depicting the *quadriga*, the triumphal chariot.[61] The right to march through Rome as a *triumphator* was the highest honour the state could bestow, even if it had long been the prerogative of the emperor alone. Events began at the Campus Martius, where the *triumphator* made speeches and awarded decorations, as trumpets sounded and white oxen were sacrificed. He then mounted a gilded *quadriga*, with his face smeared with the red paint used for the statue of the Capitoline Jupiter, allowing him to assume the attributes of the supreme deity, and wearing a purple toga over a white tunic on which were embroidered palm leaves, symbols of his victory. Consuls, magistrates and senators headed the procession, which included captured spoils, chained prisoners of war and pictures and tableaux illustrating episodes of the campaign, as they passed by the Circus Flaminius, the Porta Triumphalis, the Circus Maximus and the Palatine to the via Sacra and the Forum Romanum. The *triumphator* carried a sceptre throughout, while a slave held a golden crown over his head, whispering constantly the litany 'Remember thou art but mortal', and he was followed by marching representatives of the army, who, if tradition was followed, acclaimed their general while at the same time singing songs that ridiculed him (Pl. 14B). The whole procession, at once solemn and gaudy, climaxed at the Capitoline, where further sacrifices were made to Jupiter and a banquet was held in the temple.

Trajan was now pressed to take his fifth consulship, opening the year 103 with Laberius Maximus as his colleague and nominating Glitius Agricola as his substitute, ample reward to both men for their service in the war. He followed this with a second *congiarium*, perhaps the usual *HS* 300, and further entertainment was provided in the shape of theatrical displays.[62] Indeed, having originally banned the performance of *pantomimi* on his accession, Trajan now wholeheartedly reintroduced them, a volte-face doubtless publicly justified by precedent: his real reason may have been infatuation, for he had reputedly become enamoured with a certain Pylades, 'one of their number'. More lavish and traditional festivities, however, were provided by the inauguration of ceremonial games at the Circus Maximus, previously enlarged for the purpose.[63] Admission, as usual, was free, symbolizing the emperor's personal largesse, even if seating was strictly by rank:

senators and foreign dignitaries in the front row, equestrians in the next, and the plebs in the remaining tiers except for the very top rows, which were reserved for women. Following the *venationes* and the noon-time public executions were the gladiatorial contests. The supply of combatants may have seemed endless: while many were professional gladiators, others were probably prisoners from the Dacian campaign. The plebs exulted in the shows. That their celebration might be premature was hardly considered, although not more than two years elapsed before the situation on the Danube reached a crisis point again.

The Second Dacian War

While Trajan and Rome were celebrating the victory over Decebalus, the Dacians were already beginning to exact vengeance on those who supported the treaty of 103, following this by annexing Iazygian territory in the Hungarian Plain in revenge for their support of Rome during the First Dacian War. Further, in open breach of the treaty, Decebalus began to procure arms once more, received deserters, refortified his kingdom, and dispatched embassies to neighbouring tribes hostile to Rome – perhaps including Rome's oldest enemy, Parthia.[64] To cap it all, the following year, 105, he authorized a direct attack on Roman forces, presumably those stationed in the Banat.

This at least can be deduced from the reaction at Rome, where in the course of 105, Decebalus was duly declared an enemy by the senate. It would appear that the renewed bellicosity on the part of the Dacian king had come as a surprise, for Trajan did not leave Rome until the first week of June 105, probably on the fourth, three months into the campaigning season, and far too late to do anything more that year than consolidate existing positions.[65] The few remarks of Cassius Dio and the scenes on the Column are again the principal evidence for the ensuing events. The Column commences its account of the Second War by showing the emperor making a sea crossing at night, presumably between Brundisium (Brindisi), the southern terminus of the via Appia, and Dyrrachium (Durres), the western end of the via Egnatia, the quickest and most convenient route between mainland Italy and the Balkan peninsula. After depicting the sacrifice offered by the local citizens to celebrate his arrival, the Column shows the emperor marching with reinforcements towards the Danube and his arrival at Drobeta, probably in the autumn of 105/6. With him were his senior marshals, Licinius Sura, Claudius Livianus and Sosius Senecio: already in place were skilled consulars – L. Fabius Justus in Moesia Inferior; L. Herennius Saturninus in Moesia Superior; P. Metilus Nepos in Pannonia; and Cn. Pompeius Longinus in the Banat. The Column shows that a sacrifice was performed to celebrate his arrival in the shadow of Apollodorus' bridge, itself depicted in stylized representation in the background, the elaborate nature of the superstructure necessitated by the wide spacing of the piers being clearly illustrated.[66]

During Trajan's progress, Decebalus had continued to exert pressure through guerrilla attacks on the Roman forces stationed across the Danube. The strength report of 105 for the *cohors I Hispanorum veterana equitata*, then headquartered at Stobi in Macedonia, provides a stark bureaucratic record of events. Parts of the regiment were on detached duty within Oltenia, transdanubian Moesia Inferior, and in uncompromising language the document records how a number of men had been killed in action or wounded during the course of the year, some while on patrol or on an expedition, others while protecting crop-fields.[67] The Column amplifies the story for the Banat, transdanubian Moesia Superior. It shows Roman pioneers building forts and roads to consolidate the region, and also the construction of a series of *clausurae*, transverse ramparts laid across valleys to impede and control the movement of nomads and enemies along the natural communication routes in this mountainous terrain.[68] The Dacian response is not neglected in the illustrated record: surprise attacks are made on isolated auxiliary forts and on patrol and forage parties, while those building the *clausurae* are driven to use entrenching tools in addition to their regular weapons to repel an assault. Only the timely arrival of reinforcements under the command of a high-ranking officer prevents them from being overwhelmed.[69]

No attempt is made on the Column, however, to illustrate two events described by Dio which belong to this period: Decebalus' plan to have Trajan assassinated, and his seizure of a senior Roman commander. Dio says comparatively little about the first. Certain auxiliaries who had deserted to the Dacians were instructed to take advantage of the emperor's accessibility at the imperial headquarters and there to do him to death: the plot was disclosed when one conspirator was arrested on suspicion and under torture revealed all.[70] Dio is more forthcoming about the second incident, which is also referred to by the later orator Fronto. Through guile and treachery, Decebalus managed to capture

> a certain Longinus, the commander of the Roman force, and an officer who had served with particular distinction in the wars against him.[71]

This man can be identified as the ex-consul Cn. Pompeius Longinus, *cos. suff.* in 90, governor of Moesia Superior between 93 and 96/97, and then Pannonia until 98, and most recently probably in charge of the Banat. He had been lured into Decebalus' camp by promises of peace negotiations, but was placed under open arrest and then unsuccessfully interrogated about Trajan's strategy. Decebalus offered to repatriate Longinus and those captured with him in exchange for Trajan's withdrawal from 'the territory as far as the Danube [the Banat] and the expenses so far incurred by [Decebalus] on the war'. Trajan, for his part,

> gave him an ambiguous answer, from which Decebalus could not infer either that Longinus was of great or of little importance to him, so that he would neither be put to death nor have to be ransomed at a high price.

Sensing the impasse his unenviable position occasioned, Longinus determined to resolve the situation. Obtaining poison from one of Decebalus' own freedmen, he persuaded the king to dispatch the same man to Trajan with a letter proposing terms; after the envoy had departed, Longinus drank the poison and died. His principal hostage and major bargaining counter lost, an enraged Decebalus now sent to Trajan one of the men taken with Longinus, a centurion, demanding back the freedman in exchange for the body of Longinus and the ten remaining prisoners of war. Trajan, for his part, demurred, holding that the saving of the freedman's life was more important for the good name of the empire than the burial of Longinus' corpse, a demonstration of magnanimity designed to win over any waverers among the Dacian host.[72]

Meanwhile, the disparate components of the invasion army were making their way to Drobeta, where the emperor was assembling a force large enough to settle the Dacian problem once and for all. At about the same time, realizing that Dacia could only be held with a substantial increase in the standing forces, he ordered the creation of two new legions, the *II Traiana fortis* and *XXX Ulpia victrix*.[73] They were formed around nuclei of experienced men transferred from existing legions, probably with a forced levy from Spain, the first at some unknown location in Moesia, the second in Brigetio, and which could well have sent vexillations for the Second Dacian War.[74] Then, Trajan set about formalizing the *nationes* and *symmachiarii* as permanent units of the Roman army, the *numeri*.[75] In its abstract sense, the title *numerus* was already used to denote a number of soldiers assembled from other regular units for some specific purpose. The national *numeri*, on the other hand, were discrete military entities, distinguished by the use of an ethnic name, usually in the form of the genitive plural, and commanded by a legionary centurion given the title of *praepositus*. It is not known if there were both mounted and infantry *numeri*, although part-mounted units seem probable. Nor does it seem that each *numerus* had the same complement: analysis suggests they may have ranged from as few as 130 to perhaps as many as 1,000 men. Indeed, as P. Southern has observed, the term *numerus* may well have been used for them precisely because there was no standardization in their size, the individual units being 'tailor-made' to suit prevailing circumstances.[76]

The assembly of an even larger force than had been involved in the First War prompted increased diplomatic activity. Dio informs us that many Dacians deserted Decebalus at this time, defections which – according to Dio – induced him to sue for peace. Trajan agreed, provided that Decebalus surrendered himself and the recently acquired weapons, terms which the Dacian king found unacceptable. Instead he increased his attempts at forging military alliances with his neighbours, observing that

> if they left him in the lurch now, they would soon be imperilled, [but] by joining forces with him, while his own kingdom was intact, they would preserve their own freedom more surely and easily than by looking on idly while the Dacians were eliminated, to be subjugated later in their turn without any allies left to help them.[77]

He evidently failed. The Column shows Trajan negotiating with eleven envoys from at least six carefully characterized ethnic groups. Two are half-naked with hair-knots, a feature regarded by the Romans as distinctively Suebic, and perhaps meant to represent the Suebic Quadi. Next to them stands a Dacian *pileatus*, recognizable by his Phrygian cap and long baggy trousers, shown as a representative of those Dacians who had come over to Trajan's side. To his right is another half-naked man, perhaps Marcomannic, and behind all four stand two bearded men wearing hair-bands, evidently Greeks from the colonies along the Black Sea, the probable source of Decebalus' armoury. Three men wearing long robes and jerkins, Bastarnae or Bessarabians, or even Pontic Scythians, stand next to them, and finally two Sarmatian Iazyges are shown, fully armed and wearing conical helmets and long mail coats over baggy trousers.[78]

Diplomacy concluded, the reduction of Dacia began in the spring of 106. Dio reports even less about the Second Dacian War than he does about the First, and the Column is the basis for the reconstruction of events. It shows Trajan crossing the Danube via the Drobeta bridge, a fact confirmed by Dio, after which the army assembled on the left bank, where the usual *suovetaurilia* officially opened the campaign, perhaps the occasion for

Trajan's fifth imperial salutation (Pl. 6B).[79] The offensive was aimed directly at Sarmizegethusa Regia by way of the more direct 5,320ft (1621m) high Vulcan Pass route, rather than by way of Berzobis and the Iron Gates Pass. While guarded by the formidable fortifications of Bumbesti, the Vulcan Pass, once breached, gave easy access to the Petroseni Basin, from where a series of small valleys allowed various lines of approach to the Dacian capital.

The Column provides no hint of any resistance during the advance. Instead, it records the routine required for the systematic subjugation of hostile territory, formally organized scenes showing the Roman army involved in fieldcraft and engineering rather than battle; the protection of the flanks and supply-lines were, after all, paramount to the success of any campaign. One scene in particular hints at a particularly slow advance through Dacia, as it shows legionaries using hand scythes to cut cereal crops, not normally expected to ripen thereabouts until June or July at the earliest.[80] Like the First War, therefore, the Second was an almost leisurely, albeit guarded, progress, the now heavily outnumbered Dacians even more reluctant to field any forces against Trajan. Instead, Decebalus opted for a war of attrition, trading space for time, avoiding full-scale battle, retreating in the face of superior forces, and counter-attacking isolated outposts or small detachments: the terrain was, after all, eminently suited for small-scale guerrilla warfare of this kind. When forced to, his men sought refuge inside their strongholds, and the reduction of one stronghold after another, by siege and direct assault, seems to have taken up most of 106. Anyone who has seen the precipitous approaches to these can only admire the tenacity with which Trajan's army pursued his overall strategy. Sallies were made by the besieged communities but were repulsed, and the defence walls and towers were eventually forced by legionaries, Balearic slingmen and eastern archers providing supporting fire, fascines being manufactured to cross the ditches. The emperor throughout is never far away from the main action. He consults with his *consilium*, addresses his troops, surveys the enemy defences, and receives a kneeling *pileatus*, offering the surrender of his clan.

Finally, Trajan arrived at Sarmizegethusa Regia, the Dacian capital. Protected by deep glens on either side and a narrow steep slope leading to a single well-fortified gateway, it might have seemed impregnable, and yet the Column suggests it was given up without a fight. Perhaps the determination with which Trajan prosecuted his campaign of vengeance against the miscreant Decebalus, and the inevitability of defeat, now made itself felt. Many of Decebalus' courtiers are shown on the Column pleading with the king to come to terms with Trajan, but to no avail.[81] Instead, he fled into the mountains with his family and his personal guard, while Sarmizegethusa Regia was surrendered, looted and fired. Trajan ordered the erection of a Roman fortress over the remains and took his sixth imperial salutation, most probably in mid-July 106.[82]

Even with Sarmizegethusa Regia reduced, Decebalus continued a war of resistance. Dio speaks of a hard struggle, and the Column shows Roman forts being attacked by Decebalus and his supporters in the aftermath of Sarmizegethusa Regia. Other nobles, however, were captured or decided to surrender. They included one Biklis, who revealed the whereabouts of the Dacian royal treasury, hidden using Roman captives as labour. First, they had diverted the course of the nearby river Sargetias, and buried as 'much silver and gold and other most precious valuables such as could survive wetting' in the river bed, before bringing the Sargetias back into its old channel. The royal vestments and those items that could not survive damp were then concealed in caves adjacent to the fortress, before the men were slain to prevent them from divulging the whereabouts of the treasures. Trajan ordered the recovery of the items, which proved to be of stupendous value. According to a Byzantine epitomator, using the now lost *Getica* of Trajan's physician, T. Statilius Crito, it comprised not less than 5,000,000lb of gold and 10,000,000 of silver, as well as countless goblets and other objects impossible to value. And even if it is now accepted that these figures have been inflated tenfold through an error in transcription, the true sum being 500,000lb (226,800kg) of gold and 1,000,000 (453,600kg) of silver, it remains an extraordinary amount.[83] In weight alone the gold was equivalent to 31.5 million Trajanic *aurei*, and the silver 160 million *denarii*.

In the meantime, Decebalus withdrew into the more remote parts of the Carpathians. He was eventually tracked down sometime after 2 September 106 by a band of auxiliary cavalrymen, forestalling the ignominy of capture by cutting his throat with a *falx* just as their commander was about to seize him.[84] By a remarkable chance that man's tombstone, illustrating his version of the circumstances surrounding Decebalus' 'capture', has been found.[85] He was one Ti. Claudius Maximus, who began his military career as a cavalryman in the *legio VII Claudia*, where he attained the rank of *vexillarius* and was decorated for bravery during Domitian's Dacian campaigns. Unusually for a Roman citizen, he then transferred to the auxiliary, taking the rank of *duplicarius*, and fought in both of Trajan's Dacian Wars with the *ala II Pannoniorum*, eventually becoming an *explorator* in the same unit. Assuming he joined the auxiliary after a regular term of service in the legion, he must have been not much less than forty-five years of age at the time he caught up with Decebalus. The remnants of Decebalus' band, including his two children, were quickly rounded up, and the king's head detached from its body and taken to Trajan, who by now was at 'Ranisstorium', an otherwise unidentified Dacian settlement, perhaps Piatri Craivii. Here, Maximus received his second set of military decorations, while the grisly trophy was sent ahead to Rome, where that autumn it was hurled down the Scalae Gemoniae, the place where the bodies of Rome's defeated enemies had been regularly displayed.[86]

Dacia and Decebalus were broken and vanquished at last. Crito reported that some 500,000 Dacians were taken prisoner,[87] many to be sent to Rome to figure in the gladiatorial exhibitions (*lusiones*) that would form part of Trajan's triumph, while the systematic 'ethnic cleansing' of the conquered territory began. The manhood of Dacia exhausted, the surviving population was expelled from the core territory and the land given over to colonists invited in from nearby provinces.[88] Hadrian was again sent ahead to Rome with the news, and entering the office of praetor the following January organized the first *lusiones* to celebrate the event.[89] There remained only the mopping-up of Decebalus' northern Sarmatian allies, shown on the Column with *falces* and conical helmets (perhaps meant to represent the Agathyrsii), a series of operations which continued until at least 107, when Hadrian, now returned to the Danube as praetorian legate of Pannonia Inferior, was involved in unspecified military actions against 'Sarmatians'.[90]

Meanwhile, as a warning to the tribes of Wallachia and beyond, a masonry trophy was erected just south of the Danube in Moesia Inferior, by one of the main trade routes between *barbaricum* and *imperium*.[91] It was built on the site of an earlier battle, perhaps that of 90/91, when an army of Domitian's, probably the *XXI Rapax*, was cut down in combat against the 'Sarmatians', a defeat already solemnized on a stone altar which lists the names of over 3,000 slaughtered legionaries and auxiliaries, who died 'with great fortitude, fighting for the republic'.[92] Now, Trajan ordered a second cenotaph built, the Tropaeum Traiani – 'Trajan's Trophy' (Pls 7, 8A, 8B). A drum-shaped monument, 100ft (30m) in diameter, broadly imitating Augustus' mausoleum at Rome, it was consecrated to *Mars Ultor*, 'Mars the Avenger', in the year 107/108. With a conical top surmounted by a representation of bound captives at the foot of a military trophy, garlanded with a cuirass and helmet, it carried a frieze of fifty-four metopes. The series perhaps originally formed a continuous motif depicting the Roman army marching forth in search of vengeance against an enemy. The graphic scenes of battle, crudely carved in provincial military style, did not spare the observer the horrors of war or the inescapable wrath of a vengeful Rome. They conclude with a triumph at which the emperor watches the bound and chained captives marched by in procession. Those colonists passing by the monument to the new town which Trajan ordered founded nearby, and which took its name, Municipium Tropaeum Traiani (Adamklissi, Romania), from the trophy, could not help but be reassured of the security brought to the imperium by the emperor's military achievements.

At Rome, in the meantime, coins were quickly issued to celebrate the end of the war. They depict a seated and dejected Dacia, identified by her peaked cap and long trousers, surrounded by fallen weapons, including the *falx*: as the legend proclaims, she is no longer *Dacia Victa*, but *DAC(ia) CAP(ta)*.[93] Other issues continue the theme of victory over a long recalcitrant opponent, showing trophies and legionary eagles, assorted weapons used in the battles, the spirit of Rome as an Amazon, *Pax* (peace: Pl. 1B), Mars as Victor as well as the Avenger, and Victory, with her foot on a discarded helmet, using a palm branch to inscribe a sacred shield with the motto *DAC(ica)*, the very motif that separates the account of the two wars illustrated on Trajan's Column.[94] The propagation of the victory through the coinage infected the entire empire, and within a short time Campanian bronzesmiths were producing relief-decorated vases celebrating the event, and as were Gaulish potters working in the *terra sigillata* industry in La Graufesenque.[95]

Trajan's return to Rome was eagerly anticipated, but he did not leave the Balkans until the end of May or the beginning of June 107, arriving at the capital for a triumphal entry into the Circus Maximus in mid-June.[96] He was greeted by numerous embassies from tribes beyond the bounds of empire, including India, all seeking reassurance that they would not suffer the fate of Dacia, and he was voted his second triumph, a festival even more lavish than the first.[97] The preliminary celebrations of the second *lusiones* began on either 25 May or 26 June 107, when the emperor distributed his third and last *congiarium*, perhaps as much as 500 *denarii* per person, and exhibited at least 332.5 gladiatorial pairs in 2 *munera*, the second of 12 days.[98] A third *munus*, with 340 pairs and lasting 13 days, was completed before 30 March 108, and between 4 June the same year and 1 November 109, not less than 117 days were devoted to the main series of displays, involving 4,941.5 gladiatorial pairs and 11,000 animals – wild and tame – which were displayed and killed.[99] Finally, on 11 November 109, Trajan inaugurated a *naumachia*, a structure devoted to mock-sea battles, and exhibited a further 127.5 pairs over a period of 6 days, completing the celebrations for the conquest of Dacia on 24 November 109.[100]

The Dacian Games were an extravaganza the like of which Rome had not seen before, unashamedly designed to win the affection of the population. As Fronto later remarked, Trajan, more than any of the emperors, recognized the expectations of the common people of Rome. He knew that his unchallenged authority was effectively based on two things above all, the *annona et spectacula*, the corn supply and shows – and more especially the 'amusements' – rather than the more serious matters of state. While procrastination over the last might entail the greatest loss for the nation, and delinquency over the food largesse cause discontent among that limited number registered in the *congiarium frumentarium*, the shows satisfied all, and their neglect resulted in the greatest discontent.[101] More importantly, with peaceful frontiers and a satisfied populace in the capital, the *princeps* could now consider afresh his own contribution to the enhancement of Rome's greater glory.

IX

OPTIMUS PRINCEPS

The early Roman empire was a constitutional anomaly. For centuries Rome had been a typical Mediterranean city-state, in which elected magistrates answering to a political assembly oversaw all civic, political and military matters. Even its almost accidental acquisition of a vast hegemony – eventually covering some 1,900,000 square miles (4,920,000 square km) – did little to change matters. The *urbs* naïvely retained the pragmatic approach of a city-state, governed by a political academy and self-perpetuating assembly. The responsibility was partly Octavian's. His reforms of 27 BC shamelessly manipulated the existing political structure to ensure that the *princeps*, while legally neither magistrate nor *privatus*, commanded authority over the governing body of the city and its empire. He directly influenced and intervened in the election of candidates for the higher magisterial offices, and his *edicta* had the same power as those *consulta* passed by the senate – which in themselves were in any case little more than codified expressions of imperial prerogative, and only enforceable because the *princeps* upheld them. By the reign of Tiberius, the senate had already become little more than an honorific body, similar to the pre-1989 Supreme Soviet, possessing the trappings and potential actuality of power, but never independently exercising its authority. Thus by Trajan's time political debate had virtually ceased, and the practice of asking supplementary questions outside of the *relatio*, the proposal currently before the *Curia*, had largely been abandoned. For most senators service within the *Curia* had become little more than a prerequisite to holding one of the jurisdictions granted by the *princeps*.[1]

The senate's acquiescence was the foundation of imperial authority as formally defined in successive *leges imperii*. It was confirmed by the grant and annual renewal for each *princeps* of those offices which gave him *auctoritas* and extraordinary *sancrosanctitas*, namely the tribunician power, the proconsular *imperium maius*, and the position of *pontifex maximus*. Some idea of the extent of the imperial prerogative can be gleaned from the surviving part of the so-called *lex de imperio Vespasiani*, the eight surviving clauses of which confirm that similar powers had been extended to one or all of the previous 'good' emperors – Augustus, Tiberius and Claudius.[2] The first two gave the *princeps* full authority to make treaties, and the right to convene and direct the meetings of the senate. The third clause upheld the legality of all decrees passed at extraordinary meetings of the senate which had been convened at his request, and the fourth confirmed that his chosen candidates for public office should be elected unopposed. Then the fifth and sixth allowed him to extend the *pomerium*, the sacred boundary of Rome, whenever he so wished, and granted him the right and power (*ius* and *potestas*) to do whatever he saw fit for the benefit of the state. The last two declared his exemption from certain (unspecified) laws, and provided retrospective legality to any acts he had ordered before being constitutionally invested as *princeps*. In short, they invested the *princeps* with the puissance of an absolute monarch even if they expected him to act as nothing other than the first citizen.

The *lex imperii* left the senate bereft of any real power, and made its constitutional position a legal absurdity. While it ordered business whenever there was a crisis in the succession, and retained the mechanism for selecting and approving the *princeps*, it was powerless to control or supervise his actions thereafter. This was most obviously so in the matter of the empire. The army was the principal instrument for enforcing affairs abroad, and as the supreme commander to whom all soldiers swore their allegiance, and who was responsible – in principle at least – for each and every commissioned appointment, it was the *princeps* who dictated foreign policy, not the senate. None the less, technically, the consuls remained the heads of state,[3] and while the *lex imperii* gave the ruler the absolute authority to rule by fiat, Trajan and most of his predecessors were careful to maintain propriety and the delicate balance of power whereby the *princeps* should at least present the appearance of consultation and discussion with the *Curia*.

This was principally achieved through the *consilium*, an *ad hoc* council formed from among the emperor's personal friends, the past and present consuls (or the other one, when the emperor himself shared the curule chair) and the more distinguished senators and equestrians.[4] It was not a cabinet in the modern sense, but a cabal, which on the one hand served to advise the emperor in criminal cases brought before him, and on the other allowed him to canvass public opinion.[5] Among its members in the early years of Trajan's reign were the generals and experienced provincial administrators L. Licinius Sura, Julius Frontinus, Claudius Livianus, C. Pompeius Planta; the distinguished jurists L. Javolenus Priscus, L. Neratius Priscus and Titius Aristo; and the noted orators Dio Chrysostom, Junius Mauricus and C. Plinius Secundus. The remaining participants spanned all classes of society, and while principally Roman in origin, may also have included a number of Jews from the Greek-speaking part of the empire. That at least is the import of a papyrus which purports to be the verbatim record of a hearing held before Trajan and his *consilium*. In it, the lawyer acting for a group of Alexandrian Greeks, charged with riotous behaviour, arouses Trajan to anger by insinuating that his clients would not get a fair hearing as the emperor was governed in his decision by his *consilium*, many of whom were 'impious' Jews.[6] In fact, while equestrian Jews are known from the reign of Nero onwards, of the over forty members of Trajan's *consilium* who can be identified, not all of them permanent, only one seems to have been of Jewish origin: Ti. Julius Alexander Julianus, ex-procurator of Crete, if he is indeed the son of the renegade Jew Ti. Julius Alexander, Nero's prefect of Egypt.

While the system of government had worked (after a fashion) for all his predecessors, it would appear that Trajan determined to resolve the legal paradox resulting from his position as an honorary *ex officio* magistrate in what was technically the supreme legislative body of the Roman state. His intentions were made clear when he accepted his third consulship in 100. Even as he made a public display of humility and accountability in accepting the honour, it did not escape notice that he qualified the consular oath by observing that 'those things unlawful for others are unlawful for Caesar *while he is consul*' (*my italic*).[7] In other words, once he relinquished the consulship he again resumed the legal right and power as *princeps* to direct affairs of state. Then in 103 he took steps to formalize the precise relationship between *princeps* and senate. That can be inferred from the appearance late that year – probably in the autumn – of low-denomination coins bearing his name in the dedicatory dative, *TRAIANO*, instead of the usual nominative, *TRAIAN(us)*, together with the legend *SPQR OPTIMO PRINC(ipi)* (for the legend, cf. Pl. 1B).[8] It is a remarkable, indeed unique, formulary which merits careful attention and scrutiny for its precise meaning, especially as the emperor himself was probably personally responsible for the legends which appeared on his coinage, and regularly used specie to disseminate official policy.

To begin with, the appellation *Optimus* was normally restricted to the premier god of Rome, Jupiter, *Optimus Maximus* – 'best and greatest' – and therefore subsumes god-like qualities. In its transferred sense of 'perfect', it had occasionally been incorporated as a personal cognomen, for example by Lucius Scipio, and it had been unofficially employed in this way to describe certain of Trajan's predecessors.[9] Pliny attached the epithet to Trajan as early as February 98, and used it in his *actio gratiarum* as the fairest expression of the emperor's worth to Rome.[10] It attributed an exceptional moral influence to him, and by assimilating the emperor with Jupiter, transformed him from a mere mortal into a leader destined by providence.[11] Once it was given wider currency – for Pliny was assuredly reflecting popular usage – it was natural that the title should quickly appear on unofficial inscriptions, becoming fairly common in this medium from 101 onwards.[12] But its appearance on the coinage testifies to something more – particularly so given the use of the rubric *SPQR*, the customary abbreviation for identifying acts undertaken by and on behalf of the Roman Senate and People – *S(enatus) P(opulus) q(ue) R(omanus)* – the ultimate authority from whom all legitimate power derived. The combination of formula and dedicatory dative suggests the passage of a resolution expressing a spirit of homage and devotion from the paramount jurisdiction of Rome to their *princeps*, whose virtues made him rank only just after the supreme deity. For that reason, then, the choice of legend would seem to advertise a concordat whereby the senate publicly and perpetually entrusted all affairs of state to the guidance of the emperor. Trajan, for his part, accepted the legal fiction that the senate remained the source of all legitimate power, as is evidenced by his use of *Optimus* as an *agnomen*, and careful avoidance of the practice of Domitian and others of usurping honorifics and taking them into their official nomenclature.[13] Stripped of obfuscation, what it meant was that so long as he was allowed a free hand to implement his personal policies without question, he was prepared to recognise the senate's rights in the governance of Rome. Thus, even if we do not know the precise details and circumstances of the agreement, it seems that it marked a significant change in the constitutional relationship of *princeps* and senate.

In truth, Trajan already controlled the *Curia* through the nomination of trusted senators to the consulship. He likewise administered the *urbs* through his placemen, the *praefectus urbi* and *cura aquarum*, both senior ex-consuls, and the three senior equestrian commands in the city, the *praefectus praetorio*, the *praefectus annonae* and the *praefectus vigilum*. Whatever the terms of the concordat agreed in 103, therefore, it was no great revolution: just the simple recognition that the relentless march and unbroken continuity of imperial power had irrevocably replaced the republic, and that the senate had effectively become clients of the *princeps*.[14] As Tacitus wryly observed, a new kind of absolutism had appeared, combining military powers with internal compromise. The principate symbolized by Nerva (not to mention the dominate of Domitian) had become under Trajan the even more powerful imperiate, supervised by an *imperator* who possessed greater public powers than any of his predecessors.[15] The appearance and adoption of the new title was nothing less than a carefully calculated political act, designed to signal to Trajan's contemporaries that the new reign was the apogee of the existing system, marking a disjunction between what came before and what was to follow.[16]

Whatever the terms of the new polity, Trajan publicly maintained a studious respect for the dignity of the senate, choosing to exercise his influence through measured prerogative rather than authoritarian dictum. Since he was possessed of the real power, simple courtesy towards the *Curia* cost him nothing, and his extraordinary civility to Rome's governing body became a byword in later times; by the mid-third century it was customary to welcome each new emperor with the approbation that he be 'More felicitous than Augustus, and much greater than Trajan'.[17] One way in which he showed *civilitas* (deference) towards the senate was in his attitude towards the consulship. Domitian, like many of his predecessors, had made a point of repeatedly holding the *fasces*, and had alienated senatorial opinion in doing so.[18] Trajan was careful to placate their feelings. Having held the ordinary consulship twice before becoming *princeps*, he displayed due moderation by only taking the curule chair on four more occasions in his nineteen-year reign: in 100, by popular demand to establish consular precedence; in 101, in preparation for the First Dacian War; in 103, in celebration of that conflict, and finally in 112, to celebrate his quindecennium. In terms of practical power it was not necessary for him to repeat the gesture: it tells us much about his sense of constitutional propriety that two of the last three occasions on which he took it were connected with his foreign policy.

His *civilitas* was further expressed by his energetic participation in the proceedings of the *Curia* and the promotion of its authority. He asked that it take an active part and share in the care of Rome's empire,[19] and supported the reintroduction of secret balloting in the selection of the annual magistrates (even though some abused the process by scribbling obscenities on the voting tablets): both measures were influenced by a genuine concern that the senate should be seen to act as an independent body.[20] He evidently sought to govern with a high degree of openness, most strikingly demonstrated by his decision in 100 that the daily acts of the senate should be compiled and published on bronze plates as a permanent record for all to see.[21] Then, in 105, his scrupulous concern for senatorial propriety was recognized by the request that he intervene and remedy the situation after serious allegations were made concerning cases coming before the Centumviral Court.[22] The following year, he took steps against electoral bribery and stipulated that senators should invest a third of their capital in real estate within Italy,

> [T]hinking it unseemly, as indeed it was, that candidates for magisterial office should be seen to treat Rome and Italy not as their *patria*, but as a simple inn or lodging-house for them when on their visits.[23]

Despite his real authority, Trajan was well aware of the need to maintain the acquiescence of the senate and its senior officials. Consequently, like his predecessors, he exercised a strong influence on the election of both ordinary and suffect consuls and made a special point of using the consulship to reward his intimates and confidants. As we have seen, Sex. Attius Suburanus Aemilianus was honoured in this way in 101 shortly after he had been adlected into the senate – if he was not directly adlected *inter consularis* – and another friend and supporter, the Pergamene C. Julius Quadratus Bassus, took the ordinary consulship in 105. Nor was Trajan loath to award the accolade of an iterated consulship to those suitably distinguished: L. Julius Ursus Servianus and L. Licinius Sura in 102,[24] M'. Laberius Maximus in 103, Sex. Attius Suburanus Aemilianus in 104, Ti. Julius Candidus Marius Celsus and C. Antius A. Julius Quadratus in 105, Q. Sosius Senecio in 107, A. Cornelius Palma Frontonianus in 109 and L. Publilius Celsus in 113. The supreme honour of a third consulship was granted no fewer than three times during his rule to Sex. Julius Frontinus and L. Julius Ursus in 100 and to L. Licinius Sura in 107.

On the other hand, there is no clear evidence that Trajan did anything to influence the composition of the *Curia*, as is frequently alleged of certain of his predecessors. While the absolute number of new men continued to grow at the expense of the old republican nobility during his reign, this is only to be expected as second- or even third-generation provincials achieved prominence through their own ability. Thus, the admission of *novi homines*, such as T. Mustius Hostilius Fanricius Medulla Augurinus, C. Julius Antiochus Philopappus and Pliny's candidate Bruttius Praesens, continued as before, and the patriciate continued to be maintained through the adlection of men like C. Eggius Ambibulus (*cos. ord.* 126). That said, Trajan certainly showed a partiality towards men from the Greek East for several senior positions, men like C. Julius Quadratus Bassus and his kinsman A. Julius Quadratus rising high in the emperor's service, and his reign saw the senate develop an increasingly cosmopolitan nature.[25]

The clearest demonstration of Trajan's respect for the *Curia* and his desire that it should be free to deliberate at will can be found in his refusal to try any senators for *maiestas*. It had become customary for each *princeps* to make an accession oath not to put any senators to death. Trajan followed suit, and further swore not to exile and disenfranchize any senator, although he did add the important proviso that these oaths were personal to him alone, allowing the senate to bring forward such charges and penalties if they saw fit.[26] His sincerity may be gauged by his repeated affirmation of the oath, and is confirmed by the circumstance that no senators are known to have forfeited their life for *maiestas* during his reign, despite the discovery of at least one plot. This was led by that inveterate conspirator C. Calpurnius Crassus Frugi, a descendant of the republican Crassi, and previously implicated in a conspiracy against Nerva.[27] It probably included M'. Laberius Maximus, Trajan's general in the First Dacian War and consular colleague in 103, for he is found in exile at the beginning of Hadrian's reign.[28] In accordance with the emperor's personal wishes, however, the charge against the conspirators was brought by the senate without his knowledge, and despite the magnitude of their crimes, and especially the personal treachery involved on Laberius' part, those involved were sentenced to exile instead of being summarily condemned by the *imperator*.[29]

Trajan's amazing civility to the senate was in many ways surpassed by his efforts to enhance the dignity of the equestrian order. It was during his reign that the equestrian career, the *tres militiae*, was effectively formalized, as the knights were given an escalating importance in the administration of Rome and the empire. From the first, the monarchical characteristic of the principate had encouraged the development of an 'imperial secretariat'. Originally, it was predominantly staffed with imperial freedmen, men whose political loyalty remained exclusively with their master, despite the circumstance that they often held posts nominally within the senatorial jurisdiction, for example as mint officials or as provincial procurators. While an greater number of equestrians had been appointed to such positions from Claudius' reign onwards, and Domitian positively encouraged their advancement in an increasingly compartmentalized administration, it appears that they greatly extended and consolidated their place under Trajan and he was the first to appoint them to the principal offices of state on a consistent basis. There were two principal reasons why this may have been so. Firstly, there was the increasing complexity and recognized importance of the posts involved, which warranted their replacement by a more organized bureaucracy. Secondly, by replacing imperial freedmen with equestrians and making many of these new posts a regular part of the *tres militiae*, Trajan changed them from semi-private to public appointments, emphasizing his *civilitas* with regard to his constitutional position within the new polity.[30]

Whether Trajan should be given all the credit for formally organizing the *tres militiae* cannot be proved. The exact dating of administrative institutions and reforms in the Roman world is notoriously troublesome, for it rests principally on the evidence of epigraphy. The complication is quite simply that the earliest record we might have for a particular post need not date to its inception. However, it is generally agreed that in those cases where the earliest surviving document for an office is followed by a reasonably regular series of other inscriptions recording it, then the chances are that it was only recently introduced. Hence, while it is well known that Domitian, for one, had encouraged the practice of sharing imperial appointments between freedmen and equestrians, the increasing number of documents recording new equestrian duties during Trajan's reign is likely to reflect a real regularization and enhancement of the equestrian career at his instigation. The deed would certainly be especially consistent with his particular mode of government, always personal and beneficial, and favouring a general improvement in administrative competence. Consequently, it should come as no surprise that while the grades of sexagenarian, centenarian and ducenarian procurators are registered in earlier reigns, the practice of describing the rank in such particular terms became more usual from Trajan's reign onwards. Thus, even while any argument *e silentio* from epigraphic material alone is hazardous and rightly notorious, the overwhelming body of relevant evidence strongly supports the contention that Trajan significantly reorganized the *tres militiae*.

With these provisos in mind, it would appear that the most senior of Trajan's new equestrian posts was that of *a rationibus*, whose duties were analogous to a modern chief financial secretary. Before Trajan's reign it is last certainly recorded as being held by the palace freedman Atticus, but at some early date in the period 103–14 it was given to an equestrian, either Cn. Pompeius Homullus or L. Vibius Lentulus.[31] Then, Trajan might well have been responsible for subdividing the secretarial post *ab epistulis* into two discrete offices, as it is during his reign that we first hear of the position *ab epistulis Graecis*, with one Dionysius Alexandrinus in the duty, which could imply that he was working in tandem with an equivalent equestrian *ab epistulis Latinis*, even if firm evidence is lacking.[32] At the same time another new junior post was created within the palace, that of *a studiis*, in charge of the palace library. It was granted to a man later to achieve a certain degree of notoriety as a biographer, the African C. Suetonius Tranquillus, later made *a bibliothecis*, in charge of the imperial libraries.[33]

Several of the junior administrative grades were also reorganized by Trajan. In some cases, he did little more than formally establish existing posts as regular appointments within the equestrian hierarchy. For example, the *procurator ludi magni*, in charge of the imperial *ludi*, and the *procurator vehiculorum*, responsible for the official postal service, both hitherto *ad hoc* positions, appear as regular posts from his reign onwards.[34] Other positions once held exclusively by imperial freedmen were now completely passed over to equestrians. Principal among these was that of *procurator monetae*, a centenarian duty, charged with overseeing the imperial mint, whose first equestrian holder was that same L. Vibius Lentulus later elevated to *a rationibus*, and who was replaced in the post *c.* 106 by P. Besius Betuinianus C. Marius Memmius Sabinus.[35]

Then there were a number of sexagenarian offices which were instituted during Trajan's rule. Many of these were concerned with relatively minor administrative procedures, for example the *procurator hereditatum*, responsible for death duties, and the *subpraefectus vigilum*, assigned to the *vigiles*, the urban fire brigade. Others confirm his reputation for a concern with responsible government and the care of his people. Thus, to improve the distribution of grain from his new port at Ostia, he appointed an equestrian as *procurator annonae Ostiae*, and to ensure a better apportionment at Rome he appears to have inaugurated the position of *procurator minuciae*, charged with distributing the corn-dole at the eponymous basilica.[36]

Similarly, Trajan might be credited with introducing the equestrian duty of *procurator aquarum*, who controlled the imperial workforce employed on repairs to the city's water supply.[37] The increase in the amount of good water coming into the *urbs* was of equal importance to the provision of adequate grain, and both *princeps* and senate had taken a commensurate share in the administration of the water supply from the beginning of the principate. Previously, all water brought into the city went to the public fountains for communal use, although the senate had the prerogative of allocating water rights for private use. Augustus appointed Agrippa to establish an effective administration, and when he died in 12 BC, his staff was reorganized as a commission charged with maintaining all Rome's aqueducts under a consular *cura aquarum*. Sex. Julius Frontinus held that position in 97, and with his passion for detail and public duty produced a work entitled *On the Aqueducts of Rome*. While containing no specific recommendations as such, it did describe his comprehensive review of Rome's water supply and its administrative procedure, and it would be entirely characteristic of Trajan to have used the work as the basis for a comprehensive reorganization of the water commission.

Whatever the precise extent of Trajan's reforms to the equestrian career, just as with his senators, those equestrians who performed their duties well were destined to go far, regardless of their origin. The case of Suburanus has already been adduced. Another who stands out is the Dalmatian Q. Marcius Turbo.[38] In 103 he was perhaps still a legionary centurion at Aquincum, and probably came to Trajan's attention during the Second Dacian War, by when he was *primus pilus*. At any event, he was rapidly made *procurator vehiculum*, before returning to military service as tribune of first the *cohors VII Vigilum*, then the *equites singulares Augusti* and finally the Praetorian Guard, after which he was commissioned one more time as *primus pilus* in an unknown legion. Service as Trajan's *procurator ludi magni* subsequently followed, before he was appointed to command the imperial fleet at Misenum (Miseno, Italy) sometime before 114. Afterwards, he held a series of high military commands in the east, before another series of extraordinary commands under Hadrian, ending his career as that emperor's Praetorian Prefect. Then there was that same Suetonius, whose successive appointments as *a studiis* and *a bibliothecis* have already been mentioned. Pliny had secured for him a military tribunate which he transferred to a relative in favour of a literary career, yet by 111, without having gone through the necessary equestrian military posts, he was on Pliny's staff in Bithynia. While there, Pliny won for him from Trajan the rights of *ius trium liberorum*, the privileges attached to a man with three children.[39] Pliny's encomium ('[he is] a very fine scholar, and a man of the highest integrity') probably won him adlection *inter selectos* to serve as a juror in Rome, after which he became *a studiis*, then *a bibliothecis*, before being made *ab epistulis* when Hadrian became emperor in 117, a position he subsequently lost owing to overfamiliarity with Hadrian's wife, Sabina.[40]

Trajan's administrative responsibilities and reforms were not restricted to his countrymen in Rome and Italy. A recognized part of the first citizen's duty was a due care and watchfulness for the welfare of his subjects in the provinces, for in the last resort the stability and prosperity of Rome and her citizens depended to a great extent on the good management of her peregrine territories.[41] After all, Rome was essentially a parasitic city, containing a sixth of the population of Italy,[42] and was essentially maintained by the proceeds of tribute exacted from abroad, which supplied the wherewithal for the extensive grain distributions and the provision of public works and entertainment for the *plebs urbana*. Trajan was doubtless aware of this reality. Moreover, while he was not the most peripatetic of Rome's emperors, his experience as soldier and administrator in the provinces was rivalled only by that of Vespasian, and had provided him with first-hand experience of the day-to-day problems of managing a vast overseas hegemony, a particular requirement given that the enterprise was achieved with a remarkably small number of men, none of whom were specifically trained for the post.

This came about through historical reasons. The provinces derived their name from the circumstance that each was the *provincia*, the sphere of command or responsibility, of a duly appointed magistrate. Since the settlement of 27 BC, they had been divided into two groups, the 'public' provinces, which theoretically remained within the fief of the senate, and the 'imperial', those entrusted to the *princeps*. In practice, while there was a certain amount of exchange between the two groups for a variety of reasons (usually strategic) at different times, the difference between the two was in how their administrators were appointed and the length of their tenure.[43] Thus, the public provinces were essentially those domains which had their governors elected by lot according to the republican system, even though the emperor could influence who was actually appointed by exercising (discreetly or not) his superior *imperium maius*. Holding office for a single year, these men derived their title of *proconsul* from the fact that they governed the territory in place of the consuls at Rome. The junior proconsulships – Achaia, Baetica, Creta-Cyrenaica, Cyprus, Macedonia, Gallia Narbonensis, Sardinia (for a short period), Sicilia and Pontus-Bithynia (until *c.* 110) – were open to propraetors of at least five years' seniority; the senior, Asia and Africa (the last being the single senatorial province which retained a legion), were restricted to ex-consuls, and nomination to either of these was considered the 'crown of the public career'.[44]

The imperial provinces, on the other hand, came directly under the authority of the *princeps* by virtue of his proconsular *imperium maius*, and he alone designated their governors. Most were territories that had contained a legionary garrison at the time of the Augustan settlement, even if it was now without, along with those areas which had since come under Roman rule by one means or another. Their governors were known by the title of *legatus*, for they were 'delegated' to that particular mission or duty (*legatio*) as deputies of the *princeps*. As with the public provinces, there was a hierarchy of sorts, some provinces being regulated by men of praetorian rank, other by consulars. During Trajan's rule, the praetorian provinces were: Arabia (added in 106), Aquitania, Belgica, Cilicia, Galatia (divided from Cappadocia in 113), Judaea, Lycia-Pamphylia, Lugdunensis, Lusitania, Pannonia Inferior (divided from Pannonia in 106) and Thrace (from *c.* 105). The consular provinces, generally those with a garrison of two legions or more, comprised: Britannia, Cappadocia (with Galatia until 113), Dacia (after 106), Germania Inferior and Superior, Moesia Inferior and Superior, Pannonia (Superior after 106) and Syria. A further three provinces, although lacking legionary garrisons, were given consular governors for historical or other special reasons: Bithynia (from *c.* 110), Dalmatia and Hispania Tarraconensis. Whether praetorian or consular, the *legati* remained subordinate to the *princeps*, who alone had proconsular power over the area they administered. Hence they all took the title *legatus Augusti pro prateore*, 'imperial legate of propraetorian rank'.

Then there were those territories which came under imperial jurisdiction, but which were managed by equestrian members of the emperor's household. All except one were either relatively small or represented military districts of minor importance which did not have a regular legionary garrison. As such they were administered by a *procurator* (literally, 'one for cares for something on another's behalf', in this case, the emperor). There were eight of these minor equestrian jurisdictions: the three small Alpine provinces of Cottia, Graiae et Poeninae and Maritima; Thrace (until *c.* 105); the important Danubian frontier provinces of Noricum and Raetia; the African provinces of Mauretania Tingitana and Mauretania Caesariensis. The senior equestrian command, the single exception to the general rule that an equestrian imperial province should be neither large nor contain a legionary garrison, was Egypt, administered by a *praefectus*, who was also uniquely in command of the legion stationed there, all the other legions being commanded by senators. The reason for this situation was again historical. On the suicide of Cleopatra, Augustus had replaced the Ptolemies as the divine heir of the pharaohs, and in so doing inherited a centuries-old monarchical system of government with a highly developed and organized taxation and agricultural infrastructure. Already recognized as the bread basket of Rome, the land was also the sole source for papyrus, the 'paper' of the time, a prerequisite for efficient bureaucracy, and was the main starting point for the lucrative trade with the Orient, making it a territory of enormous strategic and economic importance. Because of this, Augustus and his successors treated it as their own personal domain, and lest they foment revolt, no senator was allowed to visit the province without the emperor's express permission. Hence, it was felt best to keep it firmly under direct imperial control by appointment from among the senior equestrians, all of whom owed their prominence to the *princeps* alone, and until Severan times it remained the only province with a legion regularly commanded by an equestrian.

There is no surviving evidence for a unitary constitutional or judicial code which direct-ed the administration of the provinces. Instead, there was a body of regulations of various kinds which established the parameters of a governor's responsibilities. In the first instance there were the provincial and municipal charters, the canons which established the organization of the territory concerned and the cities within it.[45] Then there were the *senatus consulta*, the resolutions of the senate, which applied throughout the empire unless specifically restricted, and which remained valid without time limit.[46] Third were the *constitutiones principum*, decisions of the successive emperors in various matters which effectively formed a *corpus* of binding precedent, as 'that which has been decided by the emperor has the force of law', on the grounds that 'he is given his (superior) *imperium* by statute'.[47] They took three principal forms, the *decreta*, texts of judicial resolutions made by the emperor after due process; the *edicta*, proclamations made on his behalf by his officials on what he wanted done, both in legal and other matters, and which often stemmed from oral pronouncements made by the emperor in person to municipal depu-tations;[48] the *rescripta*, written documents addressed to individuals or corporations (cities or provinces) in response to a petition, either as *epistulae* (personal letters) or *subscripta* (literally, decisions written at the foot of the original invocation). Finally, there were the imperial *mandata*, issued by the emperor to his governors when they departed for their assignment, and frequently cited by jurists as a source of law.[49] The last seem to have been the nearest thing there was to an official code of instructions available to guide a governor in the administration of his province, although he could refer to the *edictum perpetuum*, a list of legal principles passed by each governor to his successor, and which incorporated all previous judgements concerning the province.[50]

All the provincial governors were peripatetic, fulfilling their varied duties in the principal cities of their jurisdiction.[51] They were assisted by a remarkably limited staff.[52] In the junior public provinces, each proconsul could appoint a single juridical or adminis-trative deputy, the *legatus proconsulis*, usually a man of praetorian rank, although the proconsuls of the prestigious African and Asian provinces could command the services of respectively three and two such subordinates.[53] Then there were the individual military commanders in those few public provinces which retained an armed garrison, all of them auxiliary, except in the case of Africa; and a financial secretary, who would be one of the eleven provincial quaestors appointed annually by the senate to each proconsular administration. In addition there was the imperial procurator. Always of a lesser social rank than the governor, for he was usually an equestrian, but sometimes a freedman, this man was responsible for any imperial properties within the province, and reported to the *princeps* alone.[54]

The *legati* of the imperial provinces, on the other hand, were themselves already 'deputies' to a proconsul – the emperor – and had no juridical or administrative subordi-nates as such. Being senior in rank to any army commanders within their command, however, they could assign junior officers to these specific tasks within their overall administration. Financial matters, by contrast, were the responsibility of an imperial procurator, answerable only to the emperor. He was charged with collecting the taxes due to the imperial government, from which he financed the standing garrison and any public works ordered or authorized by the emperor. He was also served by a limited clerical staff formed out of soldiers on secondment from their own units, some of whom could even be called upon in their own right as *iudices dati* to adjudge fairly straightforward matters of fact, for example, boundary disputes and the like.[55]

What enabled the system to work with such a small administrative staff was precisely the Roman procedure of self-governing urban communities directly accountable to the provincial governor, who in turn was personally answerable to the emperor. There was no system of permanent functionaries to be circumvented at any intervening level, so it was a straightforward matter of 'government without bureaucracy', as P. Garnsey and R. Saller have aptly termed it.[56] Thus it was essential that the provinces were governed in an honest and conscientious fashion. Trajan, unfortunately, inherited some particularly bad administrators from Nerva. At the beginning of his reign, for example, Pliny the Younger was asked to act in the trial of an unknown senatorial official assigned to Baetica.[57] The next two years, 99 and 100, witnessed the trials for malversation of, first, the African proconsul Marius Priscus and his deputy Hostilius Firmus, and then Caecilius Classicus, proconsul of Baetica.[58] Then, in 103, Julius Bassus, proconsul of Bithynia, was tried before the senate for alleged extortion and theft; by his own admission guilty of corruption, he was acquitted of the principal charges on what some saw as a legal technicality, but convicted for the lesser and his *acta* in the province rescinded.[59] Three years later Bassus' own prosecutor, Rufus Varenus, now himself proconsul of Bithynia, was accused of similar iniquitous behaviour. In this case, however, the Bithynians decided to drop the proceedings, ostensibly because they felt it would cost them more to prosecute than they would recover from the accused were he convicted. Trajan, after hearing both sides of the argument, concurred, suggesting there was little evidence to support the charge.[60]

As P. Brunt and B. Levick have observed, Bithynia, along with Asia Minor, was a province notorious throughout the empire for cases of corruption, in part because of its wealth and articulate ruling class, and the contentiousness of local politics.[61] On the other hand, we are particularly well-informed about events in the territory, thanks to the reports of Dio Chrysostom and Pliny the Younger, and it could well be that it was no more and no less prone to corruption than other wealthy provinces. The remark of Suetonius, that Domitian may have been a bad emperor, but he was well-served by his delegates, comes to mind, suggesting that Trajan's reign may have been characterized by an unusual number of cases of malversation throughout the empire.[62] Perhaps this was especially true of the public provinces, as in republican times, for it later became routine for the emperors to appoint their administrators directly rather than by relying on the lottery. Some men selected by this method had proved to govern 'badly', a euphemism which disguises corruption rather than simple incompetence.[63] One might suspect that the heads of these quasi-autonomous dominions, governing their fief without any external regulation, had by Trajan's time won a well-deserved reputation for embracing the politics of greed and envy. Certainly, the lack of adequate independent supervision seems to have prompted Trajan to demonstrate a greater and more paternalistic interest in the affairs of imperial properties throughout the empire. And particularly so in the east, where the number of equestrian and freedmen imperial procurators in the various administrations was increased from the forty-five of Domitian to not less than sixty-two.[64] It seems that these men now also shared in the collection of provincial tariffs as a whole, just as their counterparts did in the imperial provinces, putative evidence for mistrust of the existing procedures.[65] Likewise, it might not have been coincidental that a *promagister* was now appointed to take charge of the tithe-corn from Sicily, a responsibility managed since republican times by a senatorial procurator.[66]

Trajan might also have been responsible for an increasing reliance upon two hitherto irregular provincial appointments within his prerogative, the *curatores rei publicae* and the *iuridici*.[67] Both offices are attested before his time, yet from his reign onwards occur with increasing frequency, suggesting the recognized need for their periodic placement.[68] Moreover, from epigraphic evidence the *curatores*, at least, are known to have been operating in Italy, pointing to an extension of the emperor's powers into territory that the senate traditionally considered its own.[69] Again, as with so much concerning Trajan's reign, caution is necessary when using inscriptions alone to determine the introduction or importance of a particular post. However, both positions, while irregular, were of high standing in the senatorial *cursus*, and their reiteration in the epigraphic register from Trajan's reign onwards strongly suggests an appropriate concern over the state of municipal and provincial affairs – specifically that 'what was Caesar's remained Caesar's' and was not misappropriated on the way: in effect, a recognition of the maxim *Quis custodiet ipsos custodes?*

That said, we know little in detail of the doings of these men. The *curatores rei publicae*, drawn equally from the ranks of the ex-quaestors and the equestrian order in Trajan's time,[70] were charged with supervising the financial affairs of designated cities, even if *civitates liberae*.[71] Current doctrine would hold that their powers did not transcend those of the locally elected authorities; rather they were appointed as surrogates to assist in the correct and speedy passage of justice in disputed matters.[72] This might well be the case with those appointed to certain of the Italian cities. Legal responsibility for the peninsula outside the one-hundredth milestone from Rome devolved entirely upon the Praetorian Prefect, and it would be expected he might need some professional assistance given the extent of his duties.[73] Yet such a limit to their responsibilities, whether in Italy or outside the peninsula, is not borne out by their commissions, which specifically covered the *supervision* of city funds,[74] the letting of public lands, the correct use of public buildings and property, the prevention of peculation and malversation, and the payment of debts owed or financial pledges made but not yet collected.[75]

The *iuridici*, meanwhile, generally jurists of senatorial status at this time, were assigned as independent legal assessors to certain of the imperial provinces. Now, there are well-documented delays in the juridical administration within such territories, owing to the enormous burden placed upon the governor, who alone was 'delegated' with the responsibility for dispensing justice in non-capital cases.[76] Thus, it would be simple to see the necessity for *iuridici* as a means of lightening the duties of the provincial *legati*, the interpretation favoured by most modern scholars. However, the *iuridici* remained subordinate to the emperor rather than to the provincial governor, in which case, it would not be unreasonable to suppose that they were also charged with rooting out malversation. No certainty is possible. But what can be said is that Trajan's increasing use of both *curatores* and *iuridici*, to alleviate and perhaps reciprocally check on the duties of the designated governor, heralded an eventual loss of provincial autonomy and the consequent imposition of uniform government by the central authority.[77]

No clearer is the development towards central government seen than in Trajan's response to an appeal by certain citizens of Bithynia to examine and correct the province's 'confused' financial affairs. He promptly initiated a *senatus consultum* abrogating the territory's status as a public dominion to allow the appointment of his own nominee, Pliny the Younger, to conduct the necessary audit.[78] Unfortunately, although we learn from the *Letters* that Pliny arrived in his province on 17 September, there is no indication of which year. Various internal references, however, allow it to be deduced as either 109, 110 or 111, and the *Letters* end abruptly with Pliny's death before two full years had elapsed.[79] As A. N. Sherwin-White has observed, the year 109 seems most likely for his appointment as in Letter 100, the second and last New Year's address to the emperor, Pliny does not register the consulship Trajan took up on 1 January 112.[80] In support of the claim, we might also adduce Pliny's failure to register Trajan's designation as consul in the elections of late 111, and also the lack of any reference to the death of Plotina on 29 August 112.

The precise circumstances which occasioned Pliny's commission are not known. His posthumously published official correspondence reveals he was primarily concerned with extravagance and corruption in the administrations of certain cities within the province, together with the disorder fomented between various political claques, a sorry situation independently confirmed by several of Dio Chrysostom's *Orations*.[81] It was a unique appointment, and Pliny was meticulous in recording the dignity of his station, as *legatus Augusti pro praetore consulari potestati*, that is, 'emperor's deputy, with propraetorian rank and consular powers'.[82] As such, he presumably brought to what was otherwise a legate's office the superior outward dignity of his proconsular predecessors, namely their right to a deputy and, perhaps, their entitlement to six *lictores* instead of the five that regular *legati* were assigned.

On the one hand, the correspondence itself would appear to provide a unique insight into provincial administration. It is effectively the complete official file of letters addressed by a governor, Pliny, to his superior, Trajan, together with the emperor's replies. On the other, it needs to be continually remembered that the content is likely to be atypical to some extent. The particular circumstances that prompted Pliny's assignment and his constant need to appear the model of integrity (for he doubtless intended eventual publication of the letters) meant that he naturally sought guidance on each and every matter where there was any potential for accusations of malversation or subjectivity. Consequently, aside from the fifteen or so letters taken up with personal requests and congratulatory messages on important state occasions, the overwhelming majority concern Pliny's need for direction in establishing legal precedent.[83] A substantial number are in a similar vein, for example detailing his anxiety about maintaining his personal integrity with regard to imperial privileges;[84] reporting on and obtaining permission for proposed public works;[85] and his apprehension over the correct use of auxiliary troops for detached duties.[86] The remainder, the minority, deal more obviously with his stated assignment, namely his studious examination of the financial accounts of the cities and suggestions for reducing extravagance and recovering debts;[87] his apprehension about the lack of skilled surveyors to alleviate waste and reduce the cost of public building works;[88] his desire to improve the infrastructure of the province;[89] and his disquiet about potentially subversive bodies.[90]

As for Trajan's replies, these are generally limited to confirming Pliny's suggestions and making decisions on matters of legal precedent. Nowhere is there the slightest hint that the emperor was in the habit of sending instructions to Pliny on how to administer his province: these had been detailed in the *mandata* Pliny received upon appointment. Only occasionally do we see evidence of what Trajan's 'policy' towards Bithynia was, namely that 'you must above all examine the accounts of the communities: for it is an established fact that they have been in confusion'.[91]

If Pliny's correspondence with Trajan was typical of what passed between an emperor and his deputies, then it would appear that the emperor kept the firmest personal control over the actions and decisions of each one of his subordinates, even down to the most mundane of matters. The pressure of work on the emperor must have been enormous: Trajan sent at least forty-eight *rescripta* to sixty-one *libelli* dispatched by Pliny – as many as thirty in a single year – and he seems to have been remarkably prompt in replying. Yet Bithynia was but one of the forty-two territories outside of Italy which Trajan controlled at the time, and was by no means the largest. Hence, some have doubted that Trajan himself could have personally composed answers to all his imperial correspondence, or that he was even more than superficially aware of its content. However, the familiarity of Trajan's replies to Pliny, to the extent of using an oath in exasperation at Pliny's procrastination, signifies that the majority of the replies were at least dictated by him, if not actually autographed.[92] This should not come as a surprise: Pliny was a special case. A friend of the emperor, a member of his *consilium*, he had been appointed to a specific commission as the emperor's special representative, and thus can be expected to have been a more regular correspondent than his peers. Allied to which was his understandable and transparent concern for probity in a province seemingly ridden with financial and administrative malpractice and a source of recurrent tribulation to the *princeps*. Indeed, the polite rebukes, the thinly veiled sarcasm and even the elements of irritation that punctuate and illuminate Trajan's replies to Pliny surely reveal that in normal circumstances a governor was expected to act with a significant degree of independence and on his own responsibility rather than be continually referring decisions back to the emperor.[93] In other words, Pliny stands revealed as an unmitigated temporizer. Whether or not this resulted from the circumstances of his commission, the quantity and nature of the matters on which he sought guidance and a decision from the emperor should not be considered characteristic of a normal governor.[94] Hence, the general tenor of the correspondence cannot be unreservedly used as evidence for Trajan's attitude towards the role of the provinces in the Roman hegemony – his provincial policy, as it were.

X

LAW, FINANCE AND
LITERATURE

Later sources credit Trajan with an active and diligent part in the formulation and administration of justice. He was particularly praised for his introduction of new laws, while
scrupulously reinforcing those which already existed and renewing many which had been
suppressed by Domitian and other unprincipled tyrants.[1] His legal rulings were issued
through imperial *edicta*, pronouncements that had the same authority as a modern papal
encyclical, giving orders in the guise of 'considered advice'. Their judicial supremacy was
unquestionable for, as remains the case with the Roman Catholic Pope, the *imperator*, as
Pater Patriae, was the *paterfamilias* of the citizen community, and literally a father to his
children. Thus,

> What the emperor decides has the same authority as the law of the people, because
> the people have made him their sovereign.[2]

It would be reasonable to assume that the learned jurists in Trajan's *consilium* played a
major part in his legal reforms, as the *Digest* testifies.[3] Yet none was rewarded with the
consulship, which suggests that their views were peripheral to his own will. This being so,
it is strikingly obvious that most of Trajan's judicial measures – like his introduction of
the alimentary system – were dictated more by humanitarian considerations
than political expediency, so often the leitmotif of contemporary *fin de siècle* regimes.
To begin with, he removed the insecurity that resulted from Domitian's reliance on
delatores, the anonymous paid informers whose usually unsigned and unsupported
allegations had resulted in the prosecution for treason of any who opposed him. The
delatores, whose name derived from their function, 'to give the name' – *delatio nominis* –
of a suspect to the relevant *quaestio perpetua*, frequently came from the highest ranks of
society, and were thus able to accumulate the evidence by which many of their peers
were brought before the magistrates on charges of treason. Most *principes* found them
useful for one reason or another; to the general citizenry, on the other hand, they seemed
intent on destroying the state, and were never adequately controlled by law or even
severe penalties.[4] Titus enacted certain measures, revised by Nerva, that improved
the security of the people, but it was Trajan who added force to the law, first by publicly
condemning several of the minor *delatores* at the Flavian Amphitheatre on his return to
Rome in 99, and then by introducing the corps of *frumentarii*, officially appointed
investigators drawn from the military.[5] Then he enabled provisions which banned
anonymous allegations of the sort favoured by the *delatores*, and proscribed the use
of bribery and torture on an individual's slaves in cases of treason, although slaves might
still be tortured if murder or suspicious death occurred.[6] By these measures, Trajan

effectively enacted that cornerstone of modern justice whereby defendants should have a fair trial and not be convicted in their absence, often as a result of charges brought by *delatores*. It was better that the crime of a guilty person should go unpunished than that an innocent person be convicted in his place.[7] As Pliny wryly noted, the subsequent reduction in the number of convictions for *maiestas*, and the consequent diminution in the amount and value of property seized on conviction, had an adverse effect on the state treasury.[8]

But the area in which Trajan made his greatest contribution to Roman jurisprudence was in the legislation he effected to protect the rights of minors and abandoned infants.[9] The modern concerns for child welfare simply did not exist in the classical world, and until the reign of Trajan there were few legal checks on the powers of the *paterfamilias*. A major change initiated by him was in the laws relating to the exposure of new-born children. The practice of infant exposure was a routine and perfectly legal method in the Roman world, used to dispose of deformed children; those whose paternity might be suspect; or simply as a means of limiting the size of the family.[10] It arose from the privileges of *patris potestas*, which gave the *paterfamilias* the *ius vitae necisque*, the absolute right of life and death over his children. On occasion, however, a foundling would be brought up as an *alumnus* (sometimes free, sometimes as a slave) by a childless couple in order to provide for their own old age. Trajan returned the rights of these children so that they could claim their due inheritance from their real parents, and were no longer obliged to compensate their foster-parents for the maintenance they had received in the meantime.[11]

Other changes, no less important, have become enshrined in modern law. Heads of families now lost their right of *patris potestas* over any sons they maltreated, and were obliged to emancipate them with a due share of the family's inheritance.[12] The laws relating to guardianship were tightened and as a means of protecting the inheritance, statutes were brought in to prevent municipal magistrates giving such responsibilities to insolvent fidejussores.[13] With regard to wills, greater security was given to actual and potential heirs through an injunction which prevented a single testator from inheriting all without due probate.[14]

Similar concerns with the welfare of children resulted in reforms relating to the rights of soldiers to make wills. During their term of service, usually twenty years for a legionary but twenty-five or more in the case of the *auxilia*, soldiers below the rank of centurion could not contract a legal marriage and any existing marriage was broken off on enlistment.[15] Nature would have its way, and unions were formed and children produced, a circumstance which Claudius recognized by granting the privileges of married men to the legionaries, all of whom were citizens.[16] Yet as any children were illegitimate in the eyes of Roman legislation, they were barred from inheriting their father's estate, chiefly their accumulated *deposita* or savings, unless they were made testamentary heirs, in which case they became liable to the *vicesima hereditatum*. To alleviate the hardship this caused, Trajan decreed that soldiers who made anomalous wills should have their intentions fulfilled, thus allowing them to make peregrines, such as their wives and children, their heirs or legatees.[17] However, as a corollary, it was also decided that a soldier could no longer simply assign his belongings by naming an heir, but instead had to swear this before witnesses.[18]

But while many of Trajan's legal reforms exemplify his concern with the spirit as well as the letter of the law, a rather unsavoury development in the application of justice should perhaps be laid at his door. A direct consequence of his reforms to the equestrian *tres militiae* was an increasing formalization in the hierarchy of Roman society. By the time of Hadrian the distinction between the *honestiores*, literally, the 'distinguished ones', and the *humiliores*, the 'humble', had been legally recognized, and it had become common to apply one class of penalties to the one group and more extreme sanctions against the other. Nowhere is the exact definition of who belonged to which clique precisely defined, except that the decurions (and presumably all those above them) were classed among the *honestiores*, and that the *humiliores*, no matter how wealthy, were regarded as an inferior social class. The distinction between the two groups is best brought out by the penalties that could be applied to them: *honestiores* were usually exempt from capital punishment, but *humiliores* could be executed by crucifixion, burning or even being thrown to the beasts; *honestiores* might be exiled for up to five years, but *humiliores* could be sent to work in the imperial mines, for life.[19]

In addition to formulating law, Trajan also played an active part in its practice. A significant change made by him to modify legal procedure was his decision to alter the date on which he renewed the tribunician power. In the republic, the people's tribunes were elected or had their powers renewed on 10 December each year,[20] and the successive grants had served the purpose of providing an absolute chronology for any legal enactments during their term of office – much as Queen Elizabeth II's regnal years are used for dating pronouncements in the United Kingdom's Parliament, or the years of the republic are used for the same reason in the United States of America. Augustus, however, had assumed the perpetual tribunician power on a different date, namely 1 July 23 BC, yet he sought to establish continuity in chronology by annual renewal in republican fashion. All subsequent *principes* had followed his practice, usually by renewing the grant on the anniversary of its original award, normally their accession date.

It occasionally happened that the grant of tribunician power did not coincide with a *princeps'* accession. In Trajan's case, for example, he first acquired *tribunicia potestas* some three months before his accession. Thus, anyone drawing up any form of legal or public document which they wished dated by his tribunician years could only do so by knowing the exact date of the award; and anyone dealing with the same document several years in the future would need what F. Lepper has called a 'suitable almanack in hand' to provide the correct reckoning.[21] Now, it has long been known that the number of times Trajan acquired the tribunician power does not directly tally with his regnal years. He was first elected to the power in the autumn of 97 and was *trib. pot. ii* at the end of 98. An annual renewal each autumn thereafter would make him *trib. pot. vi* by the end of 102, but coins issued after September 102 show him as *trib. pot vii*, indicating an incremental advance in the count during the intervening period. The most likely explanation is a change in the date of renewal, for by the reign of Antoninus Pius, and probably earlier, it had again become usual to extend the tribunician power on the traditional date of 10 December. Given the frequent use of *trib. pot.* figures to provide an absolute chronology and the evidence for a shift in Trajan's numbering before September 102, it seems reasonable to conclude with M. Hammond and others that Trajan personally instituted the change, and that it was done for administrative convenience as a further example of his 'republican' *civilitas.*[22]

Trajan was not averse to imposing his personal will in other respects through the medium of imperial *edicta*. For example, there was his decision to suppress the *ludi scaenici*, the stage plays in the theatres, which often formed part of the celebrations paid for by incoming praetors. A form of opera cum ballet, and introduced to Rome from Greece in 22 BC, they had rapidly acquired a reputation for softness and obscenity – they were, in fact, the forerunners of modern burlesque and public pornography. Tiberius, in a fit of excessive righteousness, had them banned, but they were reinstated by Gaius. Domitian, the militant moralist, had seen fit to ban them again, from the public stage at least, for he allowed the actors to perform in private, but Nerva, bowing to popular demand, revoked the edict to demonstrate publicly the new liberality that characterized his political theory of pluralism. Now, Trajan suppressed them one more time, and refused their performance at his accession gala:

> You removed all these ludicrous shows from the honours paid to you. Instead of a moment's disgraceful publicity, serious poetry and praise for the everlasting glory of our historic past was offered to you, and theatre audiences rose to show their respect.[23]

But it should not be thought that Trajan's revocation of Nerva's decree was in any way an act of censorship or expression of illiberality worthy of Domitian's tyranny. On the contrary, Pliny assures us, in a superb display of dialectical aerobatics, for both measures were equally just. Nerva, in restoring the shows in the first place, had demonstrated that the unjust deeds of a bad ruler could be reversed; Trajan, in suppressing them again, showed that the *princeps* was the defender of public morality:

> And so the same public, which had once applauded [...] now turned away from the pantomimes and damned these effeminate performances as unworthy of the new age.

That he was later to reverse his own edict was at that time inconsequential.[24]

Aside from such administrative measures to facilitate the new spirit of justice and morality, Trajan often personally conducted trials in and outside of Rome.[25] Pliny describes three *cognitiones* (trials) in which he was invited to attend the emperor as an assessor, supplying a first-hand account of 'our ruler's justice and wisdom', while confirming the impression that the *princeps'* decision as to legal procedure was absolute. One case concerned municipal law, namely whether or not a local magistrate had the power to suppress and then abolish the gymnastic games set up under the terms of a will at Vienna, Gallia Narbonensis (Vienne-sur-le-Rhône, France); the eloquence of the magistrate concerned, Trebonius Rufinus, won the case in his favour, not least because they had become 'a corrupting influence in the town'.[26]

A more important matter involved two senators holding proconsular office in the same unnamed senatorial province. The one, Lustricius Bruttianus, had detected the involvement of his junior associate and confidant, Montanius Atticinus, in certain criminal offences, probably extortion, deception and forgery. Atticinus then sought to discredit his accuser by corrupting a witness (a slave of Bruttianus), by intercepting papers relating to the case, and by falsifying documents, which he then used to bring forward counter-charges. Pliny records:

The trial came on and I acted as an assessor. Each side conducted their case dealing with the allegations serially, the quickest way to establish veracity ... [Bruttianus] cited a number of shocking charges, all clearly proved, and being unable to refute them, Atticinus responded with counter-allegations, but merely showed himself a rogue in his defence and a scoundrel by his accusations ... [in] ... directing a indictment intended for himself against his friend. Caesar dealt with him admirably, and asked for an immediate verdict on Atticinus but none on Brut-tianus: found guilty, he was banished to an island.[27]

In all likelihood these two cases took place at Rome and the specific charges were dealt with in a single day. But Trajan also travelled with his court outside the *urbs* as if he were some circuit judge, holding sittings lasting for lengthier periods and dealing with a variety of cases. The third *cognitio* described by Pliny was held at Centum Cellae (Civitavecchia, Tuscany), where Trajan was overseeing the construction of a new harbour.[28] The first day was devoted to the case of a leading Ephesian, Ti. Claudius Aristion, who had elected for the citizen's right of trial before the emperor after envious compatriots had suborned an informer against him. He was cleared of the charge and acquitted. On the second day, Trajan dealt with a case of adultery involving one Gallitta, the wife of a military tribune of senatorial rank about to petition for public office, and a centurion in the same provincial command. The affair had been reported to the provincial governor, who passed it to the *Curia* for a decision because of the differences in social class of those implicated. On account of the public disgrace involved, the senate avoided their responsibility for dealing with the case in the standing courts (*quaestiones perpetuae*) and referred the matter to Tra-jan, who, finding the centurion guilty on the evidence already heard, had him cashiered and banished.[29] The husband, meanwhile, had forgiven his wife and dropped his civil case against her, thus ignoring the statutory requirement that she be divorced and prosecuted within sixty days of the affair's discovery.[30] He was censured for condoning her conduct, and compelled to complete the proceedings. Gallitta was duly found culpable and sen-tenced under the *lex Julia de adulteriis* to banishment on an island and the forfeiture of half her dowry and a third of her property.[31]

The third day's proceedings involved a contemporary *cause célèbre*, the validity of the will of one Julius Tiro.[32] Certain codicils were agreed to be genuine, but others were allegedly forged by two members of the imperial secretariat, Sempronius Senecio, an equestrian, and Eurythmus, an imperial freedmen and procurator. Because of the status of the accused, Tiro's heirs had asked Trajan to deal with the case, but some of them now wished the matter to be dropped, and only two appeared at the court, asking that either all should be present or they should be allowed to end the proceedings. The counsel for Senecio and Eurythmus, however, argued that by abandoning the case his clients were neither exonerated or convicted, and would be left under suspicion. Trajan for his part, conscious of the positions of the accused as members of the imperial household, expressed concern that he too could come under suspicion if the matter were ended then and there. So it was agreed to adjourn the proceedings one more time until all the heirs could be summoned either to complete the case or individually to give adequate reasons for drop-ping the matter; otherwise, all would be declared guilty of instituting false charges. In the event either the case was dropped or Senecio, at least, found not guilty, as his career, which included service as procurator for the *census* in Thrace and then Aquitaine, and a term as Trajan's *procurator monetae*, ended with his appointment as procurator of Judaea during the reign of Hadrian.[33]

As the personification of supreme justice, Trajan on occasion would direct and return cases to the senate. Pliny once acted for the defence in an action which involved unspecified procedures never before tested in the courts. It came about when a woman charged her deceased son's freedmen, who were co-heirs with her, with his murder and with forging the will. She brought the allegation direct to the emperor, and asked for and won the services of L. Julius Ursus Servianus as examining magistrate to judge on the correct process. In the event, when the case was brought to trial the freedmen were acquitted, although she later won an appeal based on new evidence she had discovered.[34]

The emperor also determined legal precedent. Two cases Pliny was involved in when legate of Bithynia afford a glimpse as to the *princeps*' role in this field, and reveal his own inflexible if fundamentally humane attitude towards the letter and application of existing law. The first case concerned two men who had enlisted in the army. After they had taken the military oath, but before their names were entered on the nominal rolls, they were found to be slaves and thus ineligible for military service. As Pliny saw it, the moot point was whether they were to be tried as slaves, with the capital offence of seeking citizenship by illegal means, or, having taken the military oath, whether they were exempt from the charge. He referred the matter to the emperor partly because he was doubtful of their status, and partly because only those who held the *imperium* could pass a death sentence on the military, but 'especially because this [case] will establish a precedent'. Trajan's reply was quite specific. That the men were not yet formally enrolled was held to be immaterial, for their status should have been verified the day they enlisted. On the other hand, whether or not they deserved to be put to death depended on how they had entered the army. If they had been directly conscripted, then the examining officer was at fault for not establishing their legal status; if they had been substituted for other conscripted men, then the persons who put them forward were to blame; but if they had volunteered in full knowledge of their slave-status, then they were to executed forthwith.[35]

The case exemplifies Trajan's personal attitude to legal matters, that the letter of the law was supreme, but the spirit of humane justice should prevail. Hence, when Pliny sought the emperor's advice concerning the prosecution of members of the Christian community within his *provincia*, it was again blunt and uncompromising concerning the matter of the law, but emphasized magnanimity where possible. The particular litigation, which coincidentally provides the earliest non-Semitic evidence for the Christian Church, arose from the trial of a group of believers in one of the Pontic towns, perhaps Amisus. We are not told the particular circumstances involved, but they can be guessed at. The emperor, as supreme pontiff, embodied *sancrosanctitas*, which in some regions of the empire, especially the east, gave him a near-divine status. Recognition of this, therefore, became a test of political loyalty and personal integrity, not least because all legal documents were sworn by the emperor's fortune. The Christians, however, refused to swear by his name, believing it to be tantamount to worship. To any rational Roman official, such as Pliny, this was seen as perverse behaviour at the very least; to eastern fundamentalists who believed in the emperor as a living god, it was blasphemy of the worst kind. Hence Pliny's forthright dealing with those Christians now brought before him: those who admitted their beliefs were summarily executed according to the existing law, and those who denied ever having been believers were pardoned.[36]

What remained to be resolved, though, was what Pliny should do about those who had previously admitted their Christianity but who had now recanted; what should he do about unsigned letters identifying other Christians within the community, given the short shrift Trajan had given to the methods of the *delatores*; and, if such anonymous charges were to be pursued, should any be exempt from trial on the grounds of age, sex or apostasy? In the first instance, Pliny considered that those who had apostatized should also be pardoned, an adjudication the emperor agreed with. As to the second and third, Trajan was quite specific about the matter. Anonymous charges were not to be entertained, nor should Christians be specifically sought out: but if publicly charged, and if they recanted after accusation, they should be pardoned; obstinacy in the face of the law, however, was to be severely punished.[37]

Finance

Several of Trajan's laws and administrative reforms continued the strict spirit of public accountability in public finance expounded by Nerva, and had proved to be a simple way of winning popularity. Some of these have already been discussed: for example, Trajan's retention and encouragement of the office of *praetor fiscalis*, and the measures taken to resolve certain iniquities in the application of the inheritance tax. New measures seem to have been connected with clarifying the distinction between his own financial resources, the *fiscus* or *patrimonium*, and those of the state, the *aerarium*. This was a notoriously obscure area of imperial administration as many of his predecessors freely used funds from both without rendering any formal account, at least not after the reign of Gaius. As Seneca observed, even if the *fiscus* alone was the personal wealth and property of the *princeps*, his constitutional position meant that state expenditure as with all manner of things came under his direct control.[38] Thus Dio, when speaking of Augustus' road-building schemes, was unable to establish if the monies involved came from the *fiscus* or the *aerarium*, for 'the people and the *autokrator* use each other's funds freely'; and Tacitus, commenting on the frequent transfers of cash from one account to the other, wryly questions whether there was any real difference between the two.[39] Nero for one, however, always tried to maintain a clear distinction, as did Galba, during whose brief reign the equestrian office of *procurator patrimonio* is first attested.[40] Likewise, Frontinus noted that of the two gangs working on the aqueducts of Rome, one was paid *ex aerario*, 'from the treasury', the other *ex fisco*, 'from the [emperor's] purse', and describes how Domitian had diverted the water rates from the *aerarium* to the *fiscus*, an allotment subsequently reversed by Nerva, indicating that a clear distinction was asserted between the two.[41] The distinction was evidently maintained into Trajan's reign. Pliny informs us that the *a rationibus*, the emperor's financial secretary, was responsible for the *fiscus* alone, and that Trajan was careful to distinguish between funds drawn from the 'private' *fiscus* and those taken from the 'public' aerarium.[42]

Yet, as is clear from Frontinus, both funds were resourced for similar projects. Consequently, many problems remain in differentiating between their relative constituencies and in defining their parameters, while no clear answer is available to the question of their precise constitutional standing.[43] The *aerarium*, however, represented the imperial version of the republican treasury. Originally administered by senatorial quaestors, it was now overseen by praetors, men effectively selected by the emperor: thus, while all expenditure was traditionally authorized by the senate, it was personally controlled by the *princeps*.[44] After the abolition of direct taxation in Italy in AD 38, the *aerarium* derived its principal revenue from three main sources: customs dues; the *tributa*, taxes – cash and in kind – paid by the 'public' provinces, such as Spain, Africa, Syria, Cilicia, Judaea, Egypt, Sicily, Sardinia, Asia and Phrygia; and the *indictiones*, levies exacted at irregular intervals to finance special needs.[45] It was responsible for all state expenditure, and included a special department, the *aerarium militare*, established by Augustus expressly to finance the army. This, however, was funded from the *centesima rerum venalium*, the 1 per cent sales tax, and the *vicesima heriditatum*, the 5 per cent inheritance tax, although it also received payment in kind, for example the grain sent from Baetica direct to the garrisons of the Mauretanias.[46]

The *fiscus*, on the other hand, was the personal wealth of the emperor, to be distributed as and when he saw fit (hence its name, from *fisci*, travelling bags containing cash and valuables). It was a combination of two distinct funds, the *ratio privata* and the *patrimonium*.[47] The first was the personal fortune of whoever became *princeps*, and was traditionally increased by the war booty (*manubiae*) that devolved to the emperor as commander in chief. It was supplemented to a great extent by gifts, for example the gold crowns voted to the *princeps* on his accession and at other times by the various cities and provinces, and also by personal legacies, for it was customary for successful administrators to leave the emperor a gift in acknowledgement of his patronage.[48] The *patrimonium*, however, consisted of the private wealth and property that had originally belonged to Augustus, and which had passed legally through all his heirs until its seizure by Vespasian: hence it was always referred to as being of the *Caesares*, that is, all the legitimate heirs to the *imperium*.[49] As Suetonius reveals, it was boosted by *tributa* from the 'imperial' provinces, and further enlarged, from the reign of Tiberius onwards, by the legal acquisition, through *bona vacanta* and *bona caduca*, of estates forfeited for intestacy or lack of a valid will; or *bona damnatorum*, confiscated for treason.[50] Vespasian in his turn left the *patrimonium* to his son and successor Titus, and it eventually passed through Domitian and Nerva to Trajan, as Vespasian's heirs.[51] It remained a private fortune passed on by personal legacy so that Augustus' successors should not lack the wherewithal to perform their public duty of *liberalitas*, namely the distribution of gifts in cash or kind as an expression of their personal patronage.[52] Even so, no emperor after Claudius seems to have made a will, and the existing *ad hoc* method of personal imperial inheritance was not legally formalized until the principate of Antoninus Pius.

Yet, despite the determined efforts of Trajan's predecessors to distinguish between *fiscus* and *aerarium*, we might agree with Tacitus that it was impossible to define the boundary between them. While taxes and tribute from the empire went into the *aerarium*, the *princeps* was entitled to an annual allowance from it on account of the ventures he undertook in his capacity as proconsul with *imperium maius*. Thus, as expenditure from both funds evidently sometimes went towards the same projects, it may not always have been clear whether the *princeps* had paid for the measure as an officer of the state or as a private individual.

Nor do we know what kinds of sums might have been involved. In 62 BC, the annual income of the *aerarium* was said to have been increased from *HS* 200,000,000 to 340,000,000, thanks to the acquisition by Pompey of the eastern territories; in 14, Augustus was able to deed *HS* 240,000,000 from the *fiscus*; in 33, Tiberius loaned out HS 100,000,000 from his own reserves to alleviate a cash crisis; in 37, Gaius had no problems in squandering the *HS* 2,700,000,000 accumulated by Tiberius, the total reserves, it would seem, of both *aerarium* and *fiscus*; while in 70, Vespasian calculated that not less than *HS* 40,000,000,000 was needed to restore the treasury after the ravages of the Civil War.[53] The validity of these figures cannot be proved: on the other hand, the persuasive analysis of K. Hopkins suggests that in the early principate, taxation in any one year produced about *HS* 824,000,000.[54]

Whatever the sums available, tradition demanded that the liberality which ensured the popularity and immortal reputation or otherwise of successive rulers should come from their own resources, the *fiscus*, for which reason several *principes* retained officials (*dispensatores*) who maintained a record of the emperor's personal largesse.[55] It was perhaps with this in mind that Trajan determined upon a policy of financial accountability, symbolized at the very beginning of his reign by his decision to publish his own travelling expenses. One later source credits him with appointing an official specifically to supervise and budget for the imperial post and official journeys outside the capital.[56] It was this desire for public accountability that no doubt prompted him to change the position of *a rationibus* from an office held by an imperial freedman to a senior grade in the equestrian *tres militiae*. To all intents and purposes, therefore, it would seem that Trajan at the very least laid the groundwork for the financial reforms which Antoninus Pius was later to formalize by imperial edict.

Trajan's consistent public attitude of deference and accountability to the senate likewise provides the occasion for his reorganization of the imperial mint. Originally housed in the Temple of Juno Moneta on the Capitoline, by Trajan's reign it had been transferred to the Coelian Hill, where the church of S. Clemente now stands.[57] The move could well have been authorized by Domitian in the aftermath of the fire of 80, but Pliny seems to imply that the temple ceased to be the repository for imperial cash only during Trajan's rule.[58] At any rate, it may not be coincidental that the first epigraphic evidence for its new location belongs to his reign, as does the first record of the equestrian *procurator monetae* and his subordinate, the *optio et exactor auri argenti et aeris*, an imperial freedman responsible for the minting of specie in all three metals.[59]

It can be assumed that Trajan had probably inherited a reasonably secure treasury. The economies and seizures of Domitian and the parsimony of Nerva certainly left sufficient funds in the *fiscus* to provide the wherewithal to pay for an accession *donativium* and *congiarium* only sixteen months after funding like bequests on Nerva's accession. Confirmation of the basic soundness of the financial situation is found in the measures taken by Trajan to lighten the tax burden on the public at large. He was able to restrict the scope of the inheritance tax, cancel outstanding debts owed to the *aerarium* (the scene is shown of the *Anaglypha Traiani*: Pl. 4), and refuse personal gifts of money for the *fiscus* as well as remitting for the whole empire the *aurum coronarium*, the golden crown traditionally given to each *princeps* by the individual provincial communities on his accession.[60] Pliny praised the general good order of the imperial finances under Trajan (and since he was an ex-treasury official, his testimony can be accepted as reasonable and accurate), but expressed qualified concern that the revenues were suffering as result of his generosity:

> You will bear with my anxieties, Caesar, and my concern as consul, for I have thought on your refusal to accept gifts of money, your distribution of the *donativium* and *congiaria* […] and your reduction of taxes, and I must ask if you have computed the effect on the imperial revenues? Are there sufficient reserves to compensate your frugality in receiving income and your paying out of such large sums?[61]

Numismatic analysis suggests that in the longer term Pliny's fears may have been well-founded. Trajan's reign saw two substantial currency reforms in which the weight and purity of the Roman imperial coinage was significantly diminished, a devaluation, in so far as modern economic terminology can be applied to ancient monetary systems. The first involved the gold *aureus*. Under Augustus, forty had been minted from a *libra* of gold at an average weight of 8.03g each.[62] Successive emperors had allowed a gradual reduction in heaviness by an average of 0.2g per reign, ostensibly, it is held, to retain parity by mass with older coinage still in circulation, now reduced in weight by the wear resulting from frequent use.[63] Then, in 64, the serious financial difficulties consequent upon the Great Fire of that year prompted Nero to lower the weight sharply from the existing 7.54g to allow forty-five *aurei* to be minted per *libra* at an average weight of 7.26g, allowing existing bullion stocks to be used to greater effect, as more was now achieved using the same resources.[64] After his death, the *aureus* continued to be progressively reduced in weight, and stood at around 7.19g by the reign of Titus. Then, in 84/85, Domitian restored it to its pre-64 standard, a level meticulously maintained for the rest of his reign, and retained by Nerva and in Trajan's first gold issue of 98. At some time before the end of 99, however, its weight was sharply reduced by 5 per cent to around 7.20g, returning to the early Flavian standard.[65]

From Pliny the Elder we learn that it was not uncommon for the state to reduce the weight or purity of the bullion coinage in times of fiscal stress in order to meet its pecuniary obligations. From other sources we learn that there was also a general awareness that a shortage of coinage resulted in higher interest rates and prices.[66] However, Pliny the Younger has nothing to say about the change in the gold coinage in his *actio gratiarum*, which is superficially surprising, as the reform happened the year before his consulship. Evidently it was deemed best to keep silent on the circumstances. In fact, the date of the reform suggests a probable reason: the *donativium* paid out to the army on Trajan's return to Rome at the end of 99. As G. R. Watson has noted, in every donative where the amount is known the sum is specified in *denarii*, but the figure given is always a multiple of twenty-five, the number of *denarii* equal to an *aureus*.[67] Given the volume of currency involved, this fact raises the probability that *donativia* were paid entirely in gold *aurei*, a single coin much lighter in weight, at about 7.20g, than the twenty-five *denarii* it represented, equivalent to around 80g, and therefore correspondingly easier to transport in the bulk required. Now, the most obvious motive for any debasement is a desperate shortage of ready cash and bullion. It may have been, therefore, that Trajan quite simply did not have sufficient gold coin or bullion to meet the demands of the donative, a possibility strengthened in the knowledge that the army only received half the expected amount –

and the duly enrolled plebs had to wait a little while longer for their *congiarium*. This should not be too surprising. There were, after all, periodic shortages of coin in the Roman world, resulting partly from the prevalence of hoarding in a system where there were no banks, and partly from the continued drain of currency outside the empire for trade, well evidenced in the many hoards of Roman coins found beyond the frontiers.[68] Rome signally failed to control the dispersal of its bullion reserves, and in a bullion currency, money could not be simply minted without the necessary metallic resources. In which case, it can be assumed that Trajan was forced to reduce the weight of the *aureus* to achieve more with the limited stockpile of bullion available, in effect devaluing the coin, hence Pliny's reticence on the subject.

Some confirmation that this was indeed the case is suggested by the inflationary process that resulted, for the *denarius* was retained at the existing standard. Now, the Roman monetary system was based on a tri-metallic coinage in which each unit was tied to the others by the relative value of the metal involved, even if all classes of coinage had long been somewhat overvalued in practice – gold and silver by perhaps as much as 20–5 per cent. Thus, while reducing the *actual* value of the *aureus*, Trajan had retained its *relative* value with regard to the other specie: twenty-five *denarii* at the existing standard still equalled one *aureus* of the new reduced gauge.

Five years later, however, in 104, Trajan did rectify the proportional weight of the silver currency, but only as a temporary measure. Like the *aureus*, the *denarius* had gradually lost weight from the time of Augustus, when eighty-four were struck per *libra* of silver, at around 3.73g each, to the early reign of Nero, when they weighed an average of 3.37g. When Nero brought down the weight of the *aureus* in 64, he was careful to maintain nominal parity between it and the *denarius*, so that it too was reduced in weight to around 3.18g. He also coined it with a significantly reduced silver content, from about 98 per cent to 93 per cent, allowing ninety-six to be minted per *libra* and enabling him to recover the surplus for his own means.[69]

It was further reduced in gradual steps in subsequent reigns, although Domitian restored the coin to its pre-Neronian standard, minting *denarii* weighing about 3.33g at 98 per cent purity. Events forced him to return to the Neronian reformed weight, but the metallic fineness of his second reform issue was maintained by Nerva and Trajan, whose first *denarii* weigh on average 3.22g with a silver content of about 92.60 per cent. In 104, however, while the weight of the coin was not significantly reduced, more alloy was added and the silver content reduced to an average of 89.89 per cent, although in 105 it was restored to its earlier fineness.[70] It will be noted that these dates correspond with the Second Dacian War, a conflict forced on Trajan rather than one he had prepared for. Now, it was usual to reduce the size of the army in peacetime: thus, in order to remobilize it, a substantial increase in the amount of money was needed to pay for the materials, equipment and provisions required.[71] In the event of a forced mobilization, the demands on the treasury must have been considerably greater. It seems likely, therefore, that the temporary debasement of the *denarius* in 104 was a direct consequence of the unplanned resumption of hostilities with Dacia, and Trajan's need to raise a large sum of cash at short notice, from limited stocks, to effect a rapid recall to arms.

A much more serious change in the silver coinage came about in late 107. While the weight of the *denarius* was maintained at about 3.20g, the bullion content was now reduced to around 89.23 per cent, the balance being made up with copper, effectively returning the coin to the purity standard favoured by the early Flavians. Further, it seems probable that the base metal coinage was sharply debased at the same time, even though Titus, Domitian and Nerva had already affected thorough recoinages of the *aes* denominations. The once pure copper *asses* of Augustus, for example, which had shown a progressive but gradual decline in fineness down to Trajan's reign, were reduced in weight and now appear alloyed with up to 15 per cent tin and lead. Likewise with the *sestertius* and *dupondius*: originally golden-coloured owing to the high proportion of zinc they contained, not less than 23 per cent, they too had shown a slight but gradual decline in standard since the reign of Augustus. Now, however, they were minted with less than 11 per cent zinc, becoming almost indistinguishable in colour from each other and from the *asses*, and it became regular to show the emperor with a radiate crown on the *dupondius* and a laurel wreath on the *as* and *sestertius* to prevent any confusion between the three.

The 107 currency reform was no temporary expedient. Indeed, it set the standard for the denominations involved for the next forty years. Moreover, the comparatively large output of the new coinage, coupled with a relative shortage of pre-Neronian reform silver coinage in post-Trajanic hoards, suggests that the earlier issues were comprehensively recalled at this time. In which case, the measure can be associated with Dio's remark that Trajan called in obsolete specie for recoinage, with the intention of removing from circulation those coins worn beyond recognition.[72] It was not a wholesale demonetization, however, for even republican silver is found in later hoards. But some idea of its short-term impact is provided by a document of about this time from Pergamum, a recognized financial centre of the period, where the moneychangers now sold one *denarius* for eighteen *asses* and bought in at seventeen: given that the official rate was sixteen to the *denarius*, it suggests a serious shortage of *denarii*, the principal coin used to pay taxes.[73]

Superficially, the effective devaluation resulting from the 107 reform is surprising. Trajan had only recently returned from Dacia bringing with him, it is safe to assume, Decebalus' Royal Treasure, a quantity of gold and silver commensurate to more than 4 billion *denarii*. Further, he had only recently begun to exploit the gold and silver mines in Dalmatia and Dacia. As it is, there is some documentary evidence to show that the amount of gold now available had resulted in a drop in its bullion value, and the Romans were well aware that a sudden increase in available bullion had a dramatic effect on price.[74] Thus the effective devaluation of the silver and *aes* coinage may well have been initiated to restore parity between them and the *aureus*. Yet other factors were doubtless involved. Despite the amount of booty brought back by Trajan, it might well have proved inadequate to match the demands placed upon it. Considerable expenses had been incurred in raising the two new legions and paying for the celebratory games and buildings, let alone the third *congiarium*. And while the massive increase in public expenditure may well have boosted the economy, it surely had a detrimental effect on the absolute value of the currency involved. None the less, the reform itself was evidently well thought out. The early Flavian standard to which Trajan reverted for both the *aureus* and the *denarius* lasted for another forty years until the reforms of the Severan dynasty, and his effective demonetization removed virtually all the existing earlier coinage from circulation. Hence the Palestinian Talmud of *c.* 250/270 drew a clear distinction between two types of *denarii* acceptable for settling dowries, those of the reformed weight introduced by Trajan and maintained by his successors, and those of the later reduced weight characteristic of the later Severan period.[75]

None the less, Trajan saw the need to assure the public about his remonetization, as is demonstrated by his issue of a 'restored coinage' the same year. In general, such 'restored' coins bear motifs redolent of the glorious past, and most numismatists would agree that recoinages of this type were intended to advertise, explain and commend current policies by linking them to great events and people of yore. Vespasian, for example, had used the method to assert his legal succession by issuing coins which stressed the Augustan qualities of his reign, and he was followed in the practice by Titus, Domitian and Nerva, all of whom used *aes* coinage to disseminate the chosen messages as widely as possible. Yet while these restorations were fairly specific in their choice of type and were limited to *aes*, the everyday small change, Trajan's 'restored coinage' was restricted to silver *denarii* and gold *aurei*, the very coins withdrawn in his recoinage, and was far more extensive in the choice of types issued. Thus, while the liberal selection of images Trajan authorized makes his 'restored coinage' one of the more interesting and attractive coinages of the early Roman empire, it is also one of the most difficult to interpret, partly because of our ignorance of what may have influenced the original choice of the types now being reproduced.[76]

To begin with, the coinage is characterized by the reverse legend *IMP CAES TRAIAN AUG GER DAC PP REST(ituit)*: that is, that Trajan had 'restored' the coin-type in question to circulation. A clear political message was intended from the outset by his deliberate choice of the *denarius*, as the favoured coin of the republic, to reproduce favoured legends and types of that period, while the *aureus*, a coin firmly associated with the principate, was chosen to disseminate the policies of the 'good' emperors. Hence, it is no coincidence that the only overlap between the two series are the *denarii* and *aurei* that commemorate Julius Caesar, the dictator who marked the transitional point from republic to principate.

The *denarii*, therefore, reproduce representations characteristic of the better-known republican coins. Some types are of mythical interest – Aeneas and Anchises, Ulysses, the dog Argos, the foundation of Rome and some of the early kings. Others commemorate the great generals, for example Caecilius Metellus (victor in the First Punic War in 251 BC), Marcellus (who defeated Viridiomarus in 221 BC), Aemilius Paullus (conqueror of Macedonia in 167 BC), M. Metellus (who smashed Andriscus in 148) and Marius (whose Jugurthine War of 105 BC was the first time Rome fielded a systematically organized, trained and equipped professional army). A third series records great families of the past – the moneyers M. Tullius and C. Marius, the consul Galba, father of the later emperor, and even Caesar's political opponents Pompey and Brutus. Then there are representations of the chief divinities of Rome, and types commemorative of Rome's principal republican buildings – the temple of Vesta, founded in the fourth century BC, the Basilica Aemilia-Fulvia of 179 BC and the Aqua Marcia of 144 BC. In sum, therefore, the republican 'restorations' appear to provide a pageant of Rome's consummate antiquity and the benevolence of the divinities. By issuing these specific types, it would seem Trajan probably wished to broadcast that his own reign was endowed with the same virtues.

The imperial 'restorations', on the other hand, seem more specific. The obverse in each case is restricted to those of Trajan's predecessors who embodied particular moral attributes for the benefit of the state, such as *liberalitas*, the virtue of generosity, and complementary merits like *parsimonia*, the virtue of frugality as opposed to *luxuria*, extravagant living and meanness, and *avaritia*, greed. Those chosen to appear are Caesar, Augustus, Tiberius, Claudius, Galba, Vespasian, Titus and Nerva. In some cases the corresponding reverses are distinctive of the person commemorated, but frequently they are types neither struck by nor categorically exclusive to him. This suggests a deliberate decision to associate current policies and themes with the worthies of the past in order to lend them greater respectability in the public consciousness. A few examples will suffice to illustrate the practice. Caesar, ambiguously named as *imperator*, is shown with *Venus Victrix*, honouring the tradition that he was descended from her through Aeneas, and also with *Pax Augusta*, even though the spirit of Augustan peace was introduced by his successor. Augustus himself appears with legionary standards to symbolize the primary allegiance of the imperial army to the *princeps* alone (although the type actually owes much to the coinage of his enemy Antony), and also with a crocodile, to represent his addition of Egypt to the *imperium*. Tiberius is now paired with *Justitia Augusta*, the spirit of imperial justice, and Claudius with *Concordia*, the civil concord brought about by his accession after the trials and tribulations of Gaius' short reign. Nero is passed over for obvious reasons, as are Otho and Vitellius, but prominence is given to Galba, shown with *Libertas* to celebrate his part in ending the tyranny of Nero, just as Nerva and Trajan had restored *liberalitas* after the reign of Domitian. Vespasian is associated with Jupiter and Mercury, representative of wise government and the extension of trade, while Titus is commemorated with Mars and Minerva, to celebrate his part in the destruction of Jerusalem and the crushing of the Jewish revolt. Finally, Nerva is remembered with the clasped hands which signify concord. As H. Sutherland observed, Trajan had thus skilfully used the withdrawal of obsolete coinage and the issue of the 'restored coinage' of 107 to provide an interpretation of Roman history which he wished propagated, that the

> legendary glories of the republic descend through the line of great republican generals and statesmen and after them through the 'good' emperors to the 'optimus princeps' who guarantees the 'optimus status rerum', which had been the dream of the Roman patriots for ages.[77]

Literature

In reality, even before he had resolved the issues of constitutional propriety, the *optimus princeps*' disposition towards order and duty had prompted a sense of peace and security that was expressed in a renaissance in Roman literature. Several of his predecessors had made it almost a divine mission to punish any who made derogatory allusions to the *princeps* and the system he represented, no matter how real or how supposed, and Roman writers had evolved a style that was concerned not so much with content as with pure and simple rhetoric. Nerva had been famed in his time for his literary pursuits, and while Trajan himself was not, apparently, a student of the liberal arts,[78] he and his wife Plotina were at least favourably disposed towards them, especially the allied subjects of rhetoric and writing, and later established two new libraries, the bibliothecae Ulpiae.

Many writers welcomed the air of liberty that characterized the new regime. Prime amongst them was the historian P(?). Cornelius Tacitus, even if he lugubriously acknowledged that autocratic rule was here to stay, and throughout his writings displayed a concern about how a senator might fulfil his traditional duty in what was nominally a republic without showing sycophancy or giving offence to the ruler.[79] He was born *c*. 56 in Gallia Narbonensis, the son of an equestrian procurator, and ended his public career under Trajan as proconsul of Asia *c*. 113. To his contemporaries he was better known as an orator, but despite his curmudgeonly nature, he is by common consent now recognized as the greatest and most original of the Roman historians. His five surviving works were published over a period of about twenty years. The first, released at the beginning of 98, is the eponymously titled short biography of his father-in-law, Domitian's general Gn. Julius Agricola. Superficially it is a eulogistic work of piety to a much-loved relative, comparable to a funeral oration, but towards the end it incorporates material deliberately chosen to blacken Domitian's character, reinforcing a persistent subtext defending the subservience that Tacitus and others had shown during the dominate. The *Agricola* was quickly followed by the *Germania*. It is precisely what its title states, an ethnography of the German people, yet Tacitus manages to make it also serve as a moral and political essay, contrasting the virtues of the Germans, which recall the morality of the republic, with the tendency towards degeneracy (as he saw it) that had come to symbolize contemporary Rome. But as in the *Agricola*, there is a second strand to the work, that of political comment intended to bring home to his readers the threat the Germans could become were they to discipline their undoubted valour and if Rome ever rested on its laurels. Some have argued this was Tacitus' principal reason for writing the text; unlikely, for Trajan was with the army in Germany at the time taking steps to resolve any threat, and Tacitus' narrative merely reflects what was already imperial policy. The third of his works was the *Dialogus*, a work which follows the accepted tradition of placing an author's own compositions in the mouths of historic personages. It was composed between 102 and 109, but the work's dramatic date is 74/75, and it purports to recount a series of dialogues concerning the decline in oratory between Curiatius Maternus on the one hand and Marcus Aper, Julius Secundus and Vipstanus Messalla on the other. This was a subject of some concern to Tacitus, for as the proceedings in the senate became less and less important, the art of rhetoric began to take their place – indeed, there even developed a fashion for reading plays aloud rather than performing them. Instead of impassioned debate, the *Curia* now resounded to verbal antitheses, and, especially, *sententiae* – those apothegms or epigrammatic sayings, suitably honed to give the least offence. As far as Tacitus was concerned, the root of the matter was whether the decline in political oratory resulted from a lowering of moral standards, or if it came about because there was no place for contentious oratory, even under the stable rule of an enlightened ruler (*sc.*, Trajan). Yet again, the essay serves as a political testament of sorts, in this case in concluding that whatever the reason for the decline, forensic and political oratory still had a necessary part to play in the senate despite the absolutism of the principate.

Tacitus' chief claim to fame as a historian rests upon his most revered works, the *Histories*, published *c*. 106, and the '*Annals*', probably written after 114.[80] Of the first, effectively an account of the Flavian regime, only the first four books and part of the fifth survive from at least twelve originally written, and these are invaluable for the events of 69/70; would that more had survived. In his Introduction, Tacitus was careful to stress that although he had secured political advancement under all three Flavians, including the worst – Domitian – he chose to eschew partisanship for integrity, making a clear claim to fame as an unbiased historian.[81] Using the staccato sentences that characterize his prose, his masterly control of language brilliantly interweaves both subjective and objective elements to give a subtle and lucid narrative which cannot fail to excite the reader – even in translation – with its immediacy. The *Annals*, on the other hand (there is no ancient authority for the medieval ascription), provocatively begin with the death of Augustus and end with the death of Nero. Of the eighteen books, only eight survive complete with fragments of another three. Hexadic in structure – although not rigidly so – each surviving book is more polished in its writing than the *Histories*, but they none the less oversimplify the reigns of those concerned. For some a dichotomic approach is adopted, dividing the reign into a 'good' and a 'bad' half: for Tiberius the division occurred in 23 and the instigator was the Praetorian Prefect Sejanus. For others Tacitus unashamedly followed a tradition of senatorial hostility towards the principate: the regimes of Claudius and Nero are condemned from the very beginning. Consequently, it comes as no surprise that while both works contain several allusions to the critical balance between senatorial freedom and executive privilege and authority, some have seen in the *Annals* a projection of Tacitus' personal disenchantment with the barely concealed absolutism of Trajan's rule, as confirmed by the protocol of 103.

While about his works, Tacitus frequently received letters from his virtual contemporary (he was six or so years his junior) Pliny the Younger. Indeed, it is an allusion in one of these that provides the crucial evidence for ascribing the *Dialogus* to Tacitus.[82] As we have seen, Pliny was an inveterate correspondent. He wrote to over a hundred named individuals, and his ten volumes of *Letters* provide an invaluable insight into Roman society at the turn of the second century, no matter how circumscribed his personal circle.[83] The order of the ten volumes is broadly chronological, although that of the missives within them is not, and the first nine were published in his lifetime after careful revision and selection. They are invaluable, providing essential evidence which exists nowhere else for the organization of Roman civil and state bureaucracy, legal procedure and the rural economy; and valuable insights into the structure and workings of Roman society. As already discussed, the tenth book, published posthumously and unrevised, contains his correspondence with Trajan after Pliny was given a special appointment as proconsular legate of the province of Bithynia. No matter the specific circumstances of his duty, they too are unrivalled as a source, in this case for the administration of the empire.

The first nine books of the *Letters* expose Pliny as a rather Pickwickian character. He is fond of himself and his doings, dutifully affectionate towards his wife, a loyal friend, tolerant of everyday foibles, a caring landowner and diligent master, and a considerate and conscientious public servant.[84] Well aware that his talents are not of the first order (the few verses that survive of his poetry are execrable), yet of undoubted integrity, he comes across as a *bon viveur* equally at home in Club and Pub. The majority of his epistles follow a single theme, whether it be political or legal, an appreciation or a criticism of literary or other events, or simply descriptions of natural phenomena or summaries of local news. Like Tacitus', his publications are often studious: he can be a stylist, reproducing what seem to be trifles in a pedantic fashion, occasionally allowing himself a somewhat more poetic expression. One cannot avoid the suspicion that no matter how revised, the letters were written with future publication in mind; consequently, as with Trajan himself, the modern reader can be forgiven for feeling that 'it is evident, my dearest Secundus, that you have spared neither forethought nor effort in the matter [before you]', gently raising the question why the letter was written in the first place.[85] None the less, when it is considered alongside the *Panegyricus*, the modern historian, otherwise denied a comprehensive contemporary account of the reigns of both Nerva and Trajan, cannot fail to be grateful for Pliny's invaluable contribution.

It is not known if either Tacitus or Pliny was acquainted with Mestrius Plutarchus, the other great historian of antiquity, although it seems likely as the Greek philosopher lectured at Rome during the Flavian period, quite possibly during the dominate. Born in Chaeronea (Heronia, Greece) about the year 48, he published at least 250 works, of which only the 48 '*Lives*' and over 70 short essays, the '*Ethika*' (better known as the '*Moralia*'), survive.[86] Little is known about his personal life, but his greatest literary activity was during the reigns of Nerva and Trajan, by when he was resident at Delphi, where he died early in Hadrian's reign. He was an unashamed Platonist who became enormously popular in the Byzantine period, his works being frequently cited as an exemplar by contemporary moralists. Indeed, many considered the '*Moralia*', a series of polemical treatises against Stoicism, the formative ethical work of the western world, even if its mixture of moral austerity and somewhat cloying sentiment often conceals Plutarch's fundamental humanism and desire to improve society. But the '*Lives*', contrasting the virtues and vices of the great statesmen and soldiers of antiquity, were held in equal esteem. Freely used as a primary historical source after his death, not least by Shakespeare, they were in fact intended to complement the '*Moralia*' by examining the *ethos*, the moral code that characterized his subjects as revealed by their 'way of life'. As he noted about Alexander the Great, '[A] battle with ten thousand dead might tell us less about a man's character than a single brief anecdote.' Even so, the dramatic and evocative narrative he employs to describe the personalities examined is in vivid contrast to the more austere '*Moralia*', which helps explain why the '*Lives*' are usually viewed more as history than moral primer.

Another literary man of Greek origin who came to the fore at this time was Dio Chrysostom, whose career and *Peri Basileias* have already been discussed. Nothing survives of his histories, but the seventy-three other discourses that can be assigned to him fall into three classes. Those of a sophistic nature belong to his early years, and are typical of their kind. Among them are *The Trojan Discourse*,[87] and his famed *Eulogy on Hair*, both exploiting the principle of rhetoric to prove in the first that the Greeks never took Troy, and in the second that all bald men should be banned from appearing in public. To judge from their titles, the *Eulogy of a Parrot* and the *In Praise of a Gnat* probably belong to this branch of polemics, but are sadly no longer extant. A second group, the political essays, provided the bulk of the surviving *corpus* and can all be assigned to the reign of Trajan. Several deal with the affairs of his home town in particular and those of Bithynia and Asia Minor in general, and illuminate the often turbulent state of affairs that existed between their respective citizens. Their titles are self-explanatory: *On Concord between the Nicome-dians and the Niceaeans; On Concord in Nicaea after Civil Strife; On Concord between Prusa and the Apameians.*[88]

Chrysostom frequently uses this medium to rebut allegations against himself, for example his *Speech in the Public Assembly at Prusa.*[89] To avoid lagging behind other cities in Asia Minor which were then being embellished with fine public buildings,[90] he had instituted a series of urban developments which brought about charges of impiety as a result of his planned destruction of landmarks that some considered sacred. Further, it was scandalously alleged that he was motivated more by personal pride and ambition than by civic duty! The accusations were probably based on jealousy, and in a notably sarcastic and bitter speech, Chrysostom skillfuly used irony to destroy the case of his main opponent.[91]

The final class of Chrysostom's work is the moral discourses, products of his last years. Of these, *The First Tarsic Discourse*[92] stands supreme for its skilful use of humour to inveigh against wantonness and moral decay. It was delivered, by invitation, at Tarsus, the home city of the Apostle Paul. Half of it is taken up with the subject of what he calls '*regeiu*' – '*regeiu*', an onomatopocia which might be translated as 'snorting'. He uses the theme to expound upon the subject of bad or low moral standards, for not only is the noise made by men of the most debased sort, but it can also be taken to imply the presence of a brothel, and was thus not the type of sound that should be heard in decent cities.[93]

Tacitus frequently bemoaned the lack of genius and learning that resulted from the years of enforced artifice under Domitian. It was evidently the complaint of an intellectual curmudgeon, for Pliny averred that the literary arts were flourishing as never before, each year bringing forth new poets. None the less, in one sense, Tacitus' complaint was perfect-ly valid; Pliny had occasion to rebuke his protégé C. Suetonius Tranquillus for 'a culpable reluctance to publish'.[94] The original 'scholar and gentleman' by nature, Suetonius was the son of an equestrian tribune from Hippo Regius, Numidia (Annaba, Algeria), where he was born *c.* 70. He became a friend of Pliny the Younger, who sometime before 97 helped him buy a small Italian estate where he could reflect and work in peace among the vines and fruit trees.[95] By 105 he had completed one major work which Pliny encouraged him to publish: '[It] is already finished and perfect: further revision will not improve it but only dull its freshness.'[96] It is unlikely, as is often claimed, that his misfortune in writing in the shadow of Tacitus was responsible for his reluctance to publish, as analysis reveals his style and audience to be quite different. More probably, as the tone of Pliny's letter sug-gests, this unnamed piece, possibly the three-volume *On Games*, was his first major publication.[97] Yet by 111/12, he was evidently a well-known author, as he likely won then the rights of *ius trium liberorum* for his literary merits, and probably owed his posi-tion as Trajan's *a studiis* to his literary and forensic skills.[98]

The work for which Suetonius is best known today, *de vita Caesarum*, the lives of the twelve Caesars from Julius to Domitian, was published in the early years of Hadrian's reign. Frequently derided for their exploitation of trivia, when set against Tacitus the indi-vidual sections certainly come across as little more than a catalogue of colourful items, a 'tabloid' history, as it were. Viewed as their author intended them to be – a series of biographies in the Hellenistic fashion intended to inform – they actually provide many interesting and fascinating insights, not least about their subjects. By using traditionally 'unhistorical' details, often derided as trivia, they illuminate important aspects of contemporary life. Hence we learn about the Shavian system of spelling employed by Augustus; the methods and materials used in imperial correspondence; the liberality or otherwise of the various *principes*; even the pay scales of the imperial lyre players. While aiming to inform his readers, however, Suetonius assumes they possessed a high standard of knowledge, for he often fails to provide or explain the precise context of any single subject, whether it be details concerning a conspiracy, the organization of the imperial finances, or even why Augustus twice considered restoring the republic.

The *vita Caesarum* was a product of Suetonius' mature years and presumably reflects his developed style. Yet the Byzantine *Suda* includes it as almost a minor work in an extensive catalogue of works credited to him, and A. Wallace-Hadrill has shown that it draws upon several of these earlier publications, most of which must have been prepared during the reign of Trajan. Few have survived, but the fragments and known titles allow them to be divided into three categories: lexicographical, antiquarian and biographical.[99] Among the first, *On Words of Insult* was an erudite tract, classifying insulting names into types, then analysing the word in question, providing its meaning, derivation and literary citations for its usage. The antiquarian works are chiefly concerned with the organization of institutions, and the surviving parts of *On Greek Games* indicates a similar approach was employed to each subject. Likewise with his biographical works, of which the essay *On Grammarians and Rhetors* serves to explain the rise in prestige attached to these men in his own day, rather than to provide a comprehensive appraisal of each man's individual contribution.

Throughout one has to admire the scholarship of Suetonius and his contemporaries. When preparing their works they depended chiefly upon a prodigious memory, even if they did have access to well-organized libraries and archives. The principle of the index was not yet established, while the scrolls recording earlier events anyway lacked numbered pages to provide convenient reference points. Moreover, the practice of punctuation, the separation of words in a text with clear distinguishing marks to denote syntax and structure, was completely wanting. Added to all this, the disadvantages and sheer inconvenience of unrolling and then rolling a papyrus scroll on average some 40ft (12.20m) long in order to check a text or citation meant that the verbatim learning of many texts was a prerequisite, especially when initiating any new field of research; we should therefore be grateful for the relatively few inaccuracies in detail which can be identified in the few works which have survived to this day.

The liberation from oppression brought about by Trajan, the new political concordant of 103 and the sense of order he encouraged in the two senior ranks of Roman society lie at the root of this renaissance in literature. Aside from the major literary figures just discussed, many other men were inspired to produce works which were highly regarded by their contemporaries, even if only fragments now survive. They include Titinius Capito, *ab epistulis* to Domitian, Nerva and Trajan, acclaimed as a leading light in literary circles by Pliny and praised for his encouragement of studies, who is known to have written verses as well as a prose work on *Deaths of Famous Men*;[100] and T. Statilius Crito, Trajan's physician during the Dacian Wars, who wrote at least two scholarly works, the *Getica* and *Cosmetica*. The mood of freedom within regulated order fostered rational study of flights of rhetoric. Hence, Trajan's reign encouraged the continuance of the Second Sophistic

Movement, which was to reach its apogee under Hadrian, and the love of analysis and forensic detail his regime encouraged were the foundation for the climate that sanctioned the great works of synthesis that characterized the last half of the second century. Thus, the rebirth of literature mirrored the desire for systemization in the prevailing judicial and fiscal dogma which Trajan sought, and complemented his other continual efforts to improve the wherewithal of his hegemony.

XI

PATER PATRIAE

One of the principal ways in which Augustus manifested his authority as *princeps* was through the construction and provision of public amenities at Rome and throughout Italy. A practical demonstration of *liberalitas* (generosity) and *beneficium* (benefaction), it helped win for him popularity and the title of *Pater Patriae* – father of his country. Hardly surprising, therefore, that his successors chose to emulate the method, and public patronage, as a means of reinforcing the position of the *princeps* as the principal benefactor of the Roman people, became an established principle. *Noblesse oblige* was henceforth the leitmotiv of the principate.

Outside of the *urbs*, the ruling emperor's *beneficium* was most obviously expressed in the upkeep of the roads that criss-crossed the Italian peninsula. Originally provided for military purposes, they were not of major economic consequence, for most long-distance commercial traffic was sustained by water-borne transport. Their greater significance was social and administrative, in facilitating the unification of the disparate regions and providing a speedy means of communication both for the imperial *cursus publicus* and for the general traveller. Augustus himself had shown a keen interest in their upkeep as early as 20 BC, when he organized a board of propraetors as road-commissioners, making the maintenance and repair of public highways a state service. A due concern with this particular function of the state henceforth became expected of each emperor – indeed, Dio Chrysostom considered it one of the more important aspects of good government.[1]

Trajan was no exception to the rule. Throughout his reign he showed a keen interest in the upkeep of existing roads and bridges throughout the peninsula as well as the development of new arterial systems to facilitate both local and long-distance communications. The early years were given over to the completion of a programme begun by his immediate predecessors, namely a renewal of the via Appia, the principal route south to Brundisium (Brindisi), a project initiated by Domitian and continued by Nerva.[2] Even so, Trajan consciously favoured the application of new solutions to old problems, and it was his surveyors who were responsible for the major feats of engineering involved in remaking the road: first, forging a successful crossing of the malaria-infested Pontine marshes, and then devising and fabricating an easier route to circumvent the steep slope into Tarracina.[3] Elsewhere, he continued the tradition of judicious piecemeal renovations. In 100/101 at least one bridge along the via Aemilia was restored, and in 102 Nerva's improvements to Domitian's via Puteoli were completed.[4] The via Sublacensis, a branch of the via Valeria, was revamped in 103–5, and the via Labicana in 105.[5] The via Salaria south of Rieti was resurfaced in 111, and the bridge on the via Flaminia near modern Fossombrone restored the same year.[6]

These enterprises were sporadic and continued the firm tradition set by his predecessors in improving existing routes. The bounty recovered from Dacia allowed more substantial measures. One may well have been administrative, for it was probably now that Trajan implemented the provision of a systematic series of staging posts for the imperial post, further evidence of his concern in maintaining effective communications, and the likely reason for his establishment of the office of *praefectus vehiculorum* as a regular duty.[7] Other measures were practical. In 107/8, he initiated work on a series of minor routes in Etruria, creating a completely new road, the via Traiana Nova, linking Volsinii (Bolsena) and Clusium (Chiusi), as the principal contribution to what became the viae Tres Traianae. The work in this remote rural region was quite possibly carried out by using Dacian prisoners of war as a source of cheap labour, and the emperor established an equestrian procuratorship to oversee future upkeep.[8] At the same time he ordered the upgrading of the ancient minor western road from Beneventum (Benevento) to Brundisium along the Puglian plain by way of Barium (Bari), an enterprise in which he took particular pride.[9] Work on the 205-mile highway, which was renamed the via Traiana, was well in hand in 109, in which year milestones were erected at regular intervals beside the route. They carry a standard formula, which includes the statement *VIAM ET PONTES A BENEVENTO BRUNDISIUM PECUN(ia) SUA FECIT*, proclaiming in no uncertain terms that both the road and the bridges involved along the way were ordered and paid for out of the emperor's private funds:[10] coins issued in 112/113, showing a reclining woman holding a wheel, with the rubric *VIA TRAIANA*, might seem to commemorate its formal dedication, when it was placed under the direct charge of a praetorian *curator*. At the same time, to mark the emperor's *beneficium* in providing the new route, work began 'by command of the Senate and People of Rome' on a triumphal arch at Beneventum, an enterprise completed between 29 August and 9 December 114.[11]

Trajan's concern with the upkeep and development of the road system in Italy was not, however, simply a matter of *noblesse oblige* in the manner of his predecessors. Instead, it reflected a personal policy designed to improve communications as a means of promoting trade. Pliny firmly connects Trajan's road improvements with his programme for establishing new harbours, 'to link far distant peoples by commerce so that the natural products of any place now seem to belong to all'.[12] The most concrete expression of the strategy was the new commercial haven Trajan caused to be built north of the ancient colony at Ostia.[13] Lying at the mouth of the Tiber, twelve miles (19km) distant from Rome as the crow flies, but nearly twice as far by river, Ostia had long been the principal port of Rome, but already by the reign of Claudius it could no longer handle the large vessels that were now being constructed as a result of rapid advances in ship-building technology. Some of these freighters were leviathans. Claudius' regulations concerning the building of corn-transports, for example, envisages the smallest having a capacity of 70 tons (71 tonnes), and Lucian records the Alexandrian corn-freighter *Isis* as having a length of 180ft (54.9m), a beam of 45ft (13.7m) and a hold 44ft (13.4m) deep, figures implying a capacity of 1,200–1,300 tons (1,220–1,320 tonnes). Yet even these are dwarfed by the ship Gaius ordered built to convey the obelisk from Heliopolis to Ostia and thence Rome: measuring 340ft (104m) stem to stern, 65ft (20.3m) abeam, with a displacement of about 7,400 tons (7,520 tonnes),[14] it was somewhat larger than many of today's smaller luxury passenger ships.

Ostia was unable to take these large vessels, because the harbour frontage was limited and because the river mouth was prone to silting, and the larger ships began to make increasing use of the more extensive and deep-water facilities at Puteoli (Pozzuoli), on the north side of the Bay of Naples. To restore commercial viability to Rome's own port, Claudius revived a project of Julius Caesar's and commissioned a new harbour. Appropriately named Portus, it comprised a 160 acre (65ha) basin enclosed by twin travertine moles, the entrance being protected from the fierce westerlies by a breakwater surmounted by a lighthouse.[15] It was directly linked to the Tiber by at least one canal, allowing transhipment of goods to Rome using lighters. The canal also served a secondary but no less important purpose as a throughflow channel, preventing the heavily silted river mouth from backwatering and thus inundating the *urbs* during the flood season, and at the same time reducing build-up of silt within the harbour entrance.[16]

Claudius may well have hoped that his enterprise would provide a safe anchorage and prevent further flooding at Rome. It significantly failed to do either. A severe storm in 62 wrecked over two hundred ships moored within the harbour, and seven years later the Tiber backwatered to create one of the worst floods ever recorded.[17] Little surprise, therefore, that literary sources reveal Puteoli maintaining its dominance over Ostia as the principal destination of the corn fleet, so much so that Domitian built the via Domitiana to allow speedy consignment of goods from the port to the capital. Or that Trajan should concern himself with improving the existing facilities to provide a safe harbour for the grain ships currently unloading at Puteoli, thereby simultaneously eliminating the need for transhipment and securing Rome's food supply. The Portus Traiani Felicis, 'Trajan's auspicious harbour', as it became known, was positioned south-east of the Claudian installations, a locale dictated by the upstanding structures surrounding Claudius' waterfront and the decision to utilize the existing canal as an entrance to the new haven (Fig. 3). The centrepiece was a land-locked hexagonal mooring, now the placid lake of the Villa Torlonia, clearly visible from the air as one flies into Rome's Leonardo da Vinci (Fiumcino) airport. It was in excess of 76 acres (30ha) in area; its excavation required the removal of not less than 600,000 tons of earth.[18] The hexagonal shape, with sides 1,174ft (358m) long, allowed the most equitable distribution of mooring facilities, the twenty-four travertine stanchions embedded in each of the five principal quays providing mooring points for over a hundred ships at any one time. Numbered pillars around the basin identified the individual berths, and access to the 20ft (6m) wide quay, built of tufa revetted with concrete, was controlled by a high brick wall with five entrances on each land side.

Beyond the quay were substantial *horrea* on at least three and probably a fourth side. Entered by means of a colonnaded peristyle, each conformed to a standard plan of long narrow rooms set back to back, with at least one upper storey entered by means of a ramp. The raised ground floor of one allows it to be confidently identified as a granary, but the port was also used for the import of other materials, unworked blocks of marble, for example, from the African and other provinces. Transhipment of goods to the capital was achieved either by waggon, using the existing via Campana and via Portuensis; or by lighter, via a channel which linked the basin to a 150ft (44m) wide concrete-lined canal, and thence the Tiber.

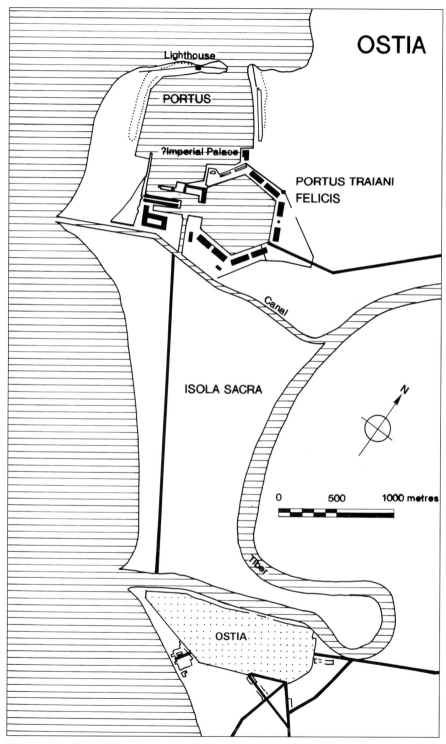

Fig. 3 Ostia (after Meiggs and Sear)

Aside from substantial monolithic columns marking each of the angles, and a colossal statue of the emperor in military dress opposite the harbour entrance, the practical appearance of the installations as originally built was only relieved on the north-west side. Here, overlooking the entrance, and commanding views of both the new and the old havens, was a complex of richly decorated buildings, which included a bath-house, a small theatre, a temple and a large atrium flanked by grand rooms. The fine reticulate masonry and brick-stamps date it to the final years of Trajan's reign, and the various structures are conceivably the component parts of an imperial residence: the lack of any contemporary private buildings at Portus Traiani Felicis rules out its identification as a public structure.

There is no agreement as to when the building of Portus Traiani began. Despite Pliny's apparently explicit reference to the harbour in the published version of his *gratiarum actio*, the prevalent assumption is that work started after the conquest of Dacia, when Trajan had the funds to finance what was evidently a major project. Nor is the date of its dedication certain. Coins issued in 112, with a representation of the harbour and the legend *PORTUM TRAIANI*, are generally held to provide a *terminus ante quem*.[19] But they could well belong to a general commemorative series emanating that year, which opened his quindecennalia, and which celebrated a number of earlier auspicious events in his reign, for example the annexation of Arabia in 106. Even so, the immediate effect on Ostia was to make it a boom town, and there are ample traces of building projects of Trajanic date, especially at its western end, where the road and ferry from the new port entered the settlement, signalling its accelerated prosperity through the increase in commerce.[20] Among them were an impressive temple-like building, identified as the *Curia*, and a new Basilica, both incorporating grey and white marble columns and white marble facings and furnished with polychromatic marble floors. A nymphaeum was constructed to fill the awkward junction of the Decumanus and the via del Tempio Rotondo, the brick-faced concrete used for its walls being concealed behind white marble panels, while Trajanic work on the *Area Sacra* involved the reconstruction of the temple to Hercules and another public building. Then at least four public bathing establishments were begun if not all finished during his reign. Also a series of store-houses, some with upper storeys and typically with a large central court suitable for the heavy waggons utilized in the transport of grain; a number of what might best be called porticoed shopping arcades; and several apartment blocks, which routinely incorporated *tabernae*, the cubicles used as shops or offices, on the ground floor.

Portus Traiani did not exist in isolation. Pliny tells us that it was but one of several such works initiated as a single comprehensive plan. Chief among them was the brand-new harbour which Trajan ordered built at Centum Cellae (Civitavecchia), 30 miles to the north. The locale had previously been noted solely for the therapeutic value of its thermal springs, which accounts for the existence of an imperial villa overlooking the site. Trajan now set about the establishment of a harbour and new town, complete with an aqueduct to ensure an adequate supply of fresh water, and providing direct access to the Etrurian heartland, an area which hitherto had apparently been serviced by road from the capital:[21] as fate would have it, it is now the principal seaport for Rome. The harbour seems to have copied the Portus design on a smaller scale, with an inner basin (now used as a coastguard and fishing harbour: Pl. 9A), entered from a larger outer haven whose entrance was protected by a breakwater, reflecting Pliny's reference in the *Panegyricus* to Trajan enclosing

PLATE 1A Trajan idealized; *denarius* of 98

PLATE 1B *Dacia Capta*;
denarius of 107

PLATE 1C Trajan realized;
denarius of 116

PLATE 1D *Fortuna Redux*;
denarius of 116

PLATE 2A Idealized provincial bust of Trajan, from Ephesus

PLATE 2B Idealized provincial bust of Trajan, from Aphrodisias

PLATE 2C Trajan as *Triumphator*, statue from Perge

PLATE 2D Trajan shortly before his death,
bronze bust from Ankara

PLATE 3 Dedication to Ti. Claudius Classicus, Ephesus

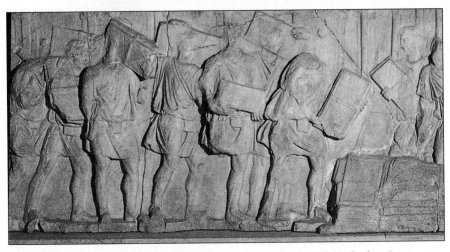

PLATE 4 The 'Burning of the Account Books', Rome (photograph by J. C. N. Coulston)

PLATE 5 Trajan's Column, Rome (photograph by J. C. N. Coulston)

PLATE 6A Trajan's Column: the Battle
of 'Tapae' (photograph by J. C. N. Coulston)

PLATE 6B Trajan's Column:
Apollodorus' bridge at
Drobeta (photograph by
J. C. N. Coulston)

PLATE 7 The reconstructed Tropaeum Traiani, Adamklissi

PLATE 8A The Tropaeum Traiani: Trajan with auxiliary soldiers

PLATE 8B The Tropaeum Traiani: a Dacian armed with a *falx* (photograph by C. M. Daniels)

PLATE 9A Trajan's harbour at Civitavecchia

PLATE 9B Trajan's Arch at Ancona

PLATE 10A Caryatid head of Dacian *pileatus* from Trajan's Forum
(Hermitage Museum, St Petersburg)

PLATE 10B Caryatid head of Dacian *comatus* from Trajan's Forum
(Hermitage Museum, St Petersburg)

PLATE 11A Trajan in battle, the 'Great Trajanic Frieze', Rome (photograph by J. C. N. Coulston)

PLATE 11B Trajan's Markets, Rome (photograph by C. M. Daniels)

PLATE 12A Milestone from
the via Nova Traiana, now in
Aqaba Museum

PLATE 12B The Colonnaded Street, Petra

PLATE 13A Trajan in Parthia, ivory frieze from Ephesus

PLATE 13B Trajan in Parthia, ivory frieze from Ephesus

PLATE 14A The Arch at Beneventum

PLATE 14B The Dacian triumph on the Beneventum Arch

PLATE 15A Trajan on the northern frontier, the Beneventum Arch

PLATE 15B Trajan and northern barbarians, the Beneventum Arch

PLATE 16A Trajan and the new provinces, the Beneventum Arch

PLATE 16B Trajan and the army, the Beneventum Arch

'the sea within the shore'.[22] Pliny, in fact, witnessed its construction while staying at Trajan's villa, and has left a valuable description of the works:

> [A] natural bay is being converted at the moment into a great harbour. The left arm has already been secured with a mole of solid masonry, and the right is now being built. At the entrance to the harbour an artificial island is being raised, so that when the wind blows inland it will break the force of the waves and give safe passage to ships entering from either side. Its construction is well worth seeing: immense rocks are brought out by barges and heaved out opposite the harbour; their weight keeps them in place and the dump rises like a rampart. Already there is a mound against which the waves are dashed and tossed into the air with a resounding crash, surrounding it with a sea of white foam. Later, piles will fix the stone foundation, and give it the appearance of an island. Here indeed is a port, that will be named after its maker, and is already so-called by his name; it will save countless lives by providing a haven on this long stretch of harbourless coastline.[23]

Ostia and Centum Cellae were completely new installations. Elsewhere, Trajan restricted his activities to the improvement of existing port facilities. The Porta Romana at Tarracina, for example, condemned as inadequate in Vespasian's reign, was reorganized about now, as is evidenced by typically Trajanic brick-reticulate work in one of the moles and an adjacent porticoed building, together with the re-routing of the via Appia to give better access to the harbour.[24] Similarly, Trajan inaugurated extensive alterations to the anchorage at Ancona, even if little is known of the magnitude of the work or what structures were involved;[25] excepting, of course, the commemorative arch marking the end of one mole, which still adorns the structure, even though now hidden among the piers and cranes of the modern commercial port (Pl. 9B). It was an elegant and graceful composition, and its impressive height was influenced by the need to provide a landmark for ships entering from the Adriatic. The four angle columns have their own pedestals, as do those flanking the single opening, and between them are inverted V-shaped insets, which once held bronze representations of *rostra*, skeuomorphs of the rams of captured enemy ships used to dedicate the eponymous tribunal at Rome. Their Corinthian capitals support an attic that once carried a *quadriga* with flanking statues, perhaps of Marciana and Plotina, given that their names are inscribed on the arch, and the landward side of the entablature bears a dedication panel, stating that it was voted and consecrated by the senate in 114/115 to mark the emperor's *providentia* in

> building the port at his own expense, to give better access to Italy and to protect the ships returning from overseas.[26]

Rome: Trajan's Buildings before 106

Inevitably it is in Rome that the full extent of Trajan's public patronage is best seen. There had long been a convention for victorious generals to embellish the city with grandiose public structures paid for *ex manubiis*, from the booty won in foreign wars: it was an effortless way of keeping their names before the public and of winning public support in times of political crisis. Sulla, for example, had reorganized the west end of the Forum Romanum, and Pompey added a new theatre and enclosed garden in the Campus Martius. Caesar, the most ambitious of the republican benefactors, implemented work on a reconstruction of the Saepta Julia, the voting-place for the *tribus*; relocated the *Curia*; and began the imposing Forum Julium, with its Temple of Venus Genetrix and the Basilica Julia. Augustus, having inherited the tradition and Caesar's vision, proceeded to monopolize the planning of Rome and transformed the face of the city, leaving no major public space without some evidence of his liberality.[27] More secure in his position than any of the victorious generals of yore, with no need to temporize and use public work programmes solely as a means of winning short-term political popularity, he capitalized on Caesar's agenda by building grandiloquent monuments dignified by their unity and placement within a comprehensive urban plan. Central to his blueprint was the innovative Forum Augustum. Based upon the traditional rectangular piazza with a temple (to Mars Ultor) at one end, it was embellished with statues of celebrated *triumphatores* on one side and members of the *gens Iulii* on the other, and the surrounding colonnades were crowned with caryatids flanking *imagines clipeatae* of various dignitaries, and broken by great hemicyclical exedrae.[28] Noteworthy was the use of white marble-cladding for this and the more important public buildings, a deliberate and resourceful programme to exalt and advertise Rome's position as world capital of a wealthy and continually expanding hegemony: it is with good reason that Augustus boasted 'I found the *urbs* built of brick, and left it made of marble.'[29]

Augustus' example in ornamenting the capital with grandiose public buildings was followed by his successors. Their major construction projects similarly confirmed their responsibility for the general improvement of Rome by virtue of the extraordinary patron–client relationship which existed between *princeps* and the urban plebs. It was Trajan more than any other, however, who exemplified the maxim, and monumental architecture within the city virtually ceased after the completion of the series of magnificent architectural schemes he initiated. Indeed, he effectively established the appearance of Rome for the next two centuries, and brought to its fulfilment 'the great building programme in the capital initiated over a century before by Augustus'. This was recognized by contemporary and later writers, who praise the splendour of his constructions, even if Juvenal spewed forth a diatribe about how the incessant night traffic involved in bringing materials to the various projects condemned him to insomnia.[30]

Yet while it cannot be denied that Trajan's contributions to the urban topography of Rome were splendid additions to the city, justifying his extensive use of the imperial coinage to publicize the grandeur and scale of the programme, they mani-fested much more than his personal *beneficium* or even bombastic self-aggrandizement. The devastation caused by the fire of 64 had hardly begun to be remedied when the great conflagration of 80 added to the task, and while Domitian had made exceptional efforts to repair the situation, considerable work remained to be done. Thus, many of the building schemes that marked Trajan's reign were really the completion of enterprises launched by his predecessors, most notably Domitian, or represented restorations of earlier works. Little wonder it was later alleged of him that he carved his name on so many buildings erected by others, as if he were 'a creeper growing over the monuments of the past'.[31]

In fact, the epigraphic evidence for the buildings erected during Trajan's reign is very thin. Lacking a comprehensive catalogue of his principal renovations and new erections, historians have been forced to rely on the evidence of the contemporary specie, in which field the pioneering work of P. V. Hill in clarifying the chronology of Trajan's coinage and identifying several of the buildings represented thereon has proved both exemplary and of great importance.[32] That said, some of these edifices, and many others, have been independently recognized as Trajanic by virtue of their particular construction technique, and especially through the somewhat unsatisfactory evidence of brick-stamps.[33] However, while many brickmakers – private and imperial – customarily stamped their products, they rarely included the consular date until the reign of Hadrian. Consequently, while over a hundred and fifty individual brick-stamps are known for Trajan's reign, the majority can only be broadly dated by their use in buildings reliably dated by other means, such as a dedicatory inscription. Even then, there is no guarantee that the bricks used were freshly made for the purpose they were actually used for, as they could have come from a stockpile.[34]

If such limitations are accepted, brick-stamps and literary evidence combine to suggest that Trajan's first major building project at Rome was a purely functional measure, the rectification of severe flood damage. Indeed, our principal ancient source claims that it was partly on account of this work that he 'was worthy of being called *Pater Patriae*'.[35] Rome was notoriously prone to flooding, for without the stone embankments that now contain it, the Tiber was then over 330ft (100m) wide with infamous and treacherously strong currents.[36] It could (and still does) rise on occasion with remarkable rapidity, especially in spring-time with the snow-melt, and in other seasons after heavy rain. It flowed principally between marshy banks, with few embankments to channel the current; severe and destructive floods had occurred several times in the city's history, prompting various remedial works. Claudius for one had paid conscientious regard to engineering works designed both to keep the river channel open to traffic and to control inundations. His measures alleviated the matter, but did not prevent it: the Tiber overflowed its banks during Nerva's short reign and again shortly after Trajan became *princeps*, necessitating substantial financial and material assistance to the people affected.[37]

As befits the solid and eminently practical person he was, Trajan resolved on prevention rather than cure through a series of administrative and practical reforms. Paramount was the decision before 101 to create the office of *curator alvei et riparum Tiberis et cloacarum urbis*, combining the existing duty of overseeing the banks of the Tiber with the responsibility for the city's drains, which took both sewage and storm water to the river. The first holder was Ti. Julius Ferox, and his initial duty was to set in place a comprehensive resurveying of the boundary between public and private property along the river banks.[38] Then, according to a poorly preserved inscription, Trajan ordered the building of a relief channel, the *fossa Traiana*, to reduce the danger of further inundations at Rome. The project probably began after the floods which opened his reign, and was certainly completed before 107, when Pliny observed in a letter to Caecilius Macrinus that:

> The Tiber has again overflowed its bed and has flooded the lower areas to some depth, so that even while it is being drained by the canal that the emperor dug with his usual foresight, it is flooding the valleys and inundating the fields: wherever there is level ground there is nothing to see but water.[39]

Once the river frontage had been resurveyed, Trajan activated a programme of improving the urban harbour facilities at the Emporium to further constrain the Tiber and ameliorate the possibility of flooding.[40] This at least might be assumed from the construction of a series of wharves in typically Trajanic concrete and brick-reticulate masonry on the left bank of the river, downstream of the so-called 'Porticus Aemilia', and a little south of the present Ponte Sublicio. Paved with travertine and provided with travertine mooring rings, they incorporated symmetrical pairs of loading ramps, and were backed by a uniform series of barrel-vaulted chambers, presumably used for storage.[41] More certainly Trajanic in date is a substantial *horreum* on the opposite bank of the Tiber in the grounds of the Villa Farnesina, dated by an inscription to 102. This, the *Cellae Vinariae Novae*, was purpose-built for the wholesale storing and distribution of wine, and excavations have disclosed that it comprised a series of vaulted chambers with large storage jars, over which were rooms arranged in rows around colonnaded courts adorned with stuccoed travertine columns.[42]

The public water supply was another early concern of Trajan's. The *curator aquarum* at the time of his accession was no less a person than Sex. Julius Frontinus, appointed to the office by Nerva. He had used his period in office to write a treatise on the city's water supply, the *de Aquae ductu*, and it could well have been his suggestion that Trajan initiated works to improve the clarity and standard of the existing resources. The water carried by the Aqua Anio Novus, for example, was often found to be cloudy. Frontinus gives Trajan the credit for ordering the intake to be moved back to the Subiaco lakes, effectively adapting these decorative features of Nero's Villa Sublacensis as vast settling tanks, consequent upon which the water supplied by the Anio Novus rivalled that of the Aqua Marcia in clarity and freshness. The supply to the Aventine from the Aqua Marcia was also improved: it had been obstructed by Nero's changes to the Aqua Marcia, but a new reservoir of five vaulted chambers was built about now to ensure an adequate and continuous supply.[43]

Having inaugurated those projects necessary to improve the city's infrastructure, Trajan turned his attention to its embellishment. A priority was the completion of those building projects begun by Domitian but left unfinished for one reason or another, and in particular the restoration of the public buildings damaged in the two great conflagrations of 64 and 80. At several sites, repair work was well in hand, as at the temple of Augustus, whose library was replaced by Trajan before he rededicated the building in *c.* 101, and the Flavian amphitheatre, probably finished at the same time.[44] More substantial work was required on the Circus Maximus, almost completely destroyed in the inferno of 64, which began in a shop on its north-eastern side. Occupying the Vallis Murcia between the Palatine and Aventine, and traditionally founded by the Tarquinian dynasty in the sixth century BC, it was the oldest and largest venue for the *spectacula*, being used principally for the seventeen annual *ludi circenses*, by far the most exciting and popular events of the period. It thus held an important place in the urban psyche, and so both Nero and Domitian had made makeshift repairs to bring it back into use. Trajan, however, completely rebuilt it between 98 and 103, using masonry which was retrieved from Domitian's *naumachia*, now demolished for this purpose. By extending the length of the Circus on the Palatine side, and carrying the tiers of seats up the slope of the hill over the street that ran there, he was able to provide another 5,000 places. In order to commemorate his generosity, the twenty-five tribes of Rome erected a statue in his honour.[45]

At other monuments, restoration work had perhaps hardly progressed beyond the early stages. This was probably the case with the Temple of Jupiter Victor, thought to lie on the north slope of the Palatine where S. Sebastiano now stands, whose renovation was not completed until 105/106; also with the Temple of Venus Genetrix, eventually reconsecrated on 12 May 113.[46] Elsewhere, more substantial work was needed, as with the Ludus Magnus, the largest of the four gladiatorial training schools founded by Domitian, which Trajan effectively rebuilt before 112.[47] Likewise with the Odeum: probably situated beneath today's Palazzo Massimo alle Colonne, it was apparently a very impressive covered building, able to hold between five and seven thousand spectators for musical and theatrical shows.[48]

Then there were the projects Trajan initiated on his own behalf. Among the first was at least one temple erected in honour of the deified Nerva, which Pliny indicates was under way before *c.* 100.[49] It has not been located, but it could well be the otherwise unidentified octostyle temple whose completion was commemorated on coins of 105–107.[50] Set on a podium of two or three steps, the coins reveal it contained a standing male cult figure apparently holding a sceptre and *cornucopia*, the latter a particular attribute of Nerva, while the pediment, surmounted by five statues, contained a seated figure between two reclining ones, surrounded by shields and more *cornucopiae*. Of a similar date is a second unlocated temple also depicted on coins of the period 105–107.[51] Again octostyle, with Corinthian columns, flanked with covered porticoes, it was set on a high podium of three steps, and housed a statue of a seated (?) female deity. An altar stood in front of the podium and statues in the pronaos, and the pediment contained one seated and two reclining figures, with a standing male figure positioned on the gable apex and *acroteria* in the form of (?)Victories at the corners. It was evidently a building of some substance, but its location remains an enigma; the seated female cult statue within it suggests it may well be the Temple of Fortuna which Lydus attributes to Trajan.[52]

Two ceremonial arches can also be attributed to this period. The first, shown on coins of 100, was probably voted by the senate to celebrate the emperor's return to Rome in 99. Known to have been situated in *Regio I*, it had three openings, each flanked by simple columns, and the whole was surmounted by a plain attic which supported a ten-horse chariot framed by twin trophies. Despite the fact it survived into the fourth century, its precise location is unknown – unless it is indeed to be identified with the 'Arco di Druso', the name given in the sixteenth century to a travertine arch, originally panelled with marble, just inside the Porta S. Sebastiano.[53] The second, which appears on coins dating to 105–107, can probably be attributed to Trajan's own initiative. By contrast with the first it had a single opening flanked by heavily decorated columns and metopes, and the pediment contained a standing figure between giants. The attic carried the abbreviated dedication *IOM* (*Jupiter Optimus Maximus*), and supported a six-horse chariot, flanked by trophies, captives and eagles. The dedication suggests it stood on the Capitoline, marking the formal entrance to the temple of Jupiter, and it might reasonably be assumed that Trajan ordered its construction, at his own expense, both on account of the importance of the place in the events leading up to his public adoption, and to celebrate his Dacian triumph.[54]

Aside from the riverine projects and these 'lost' structures known only from coins, very few other public works can be attributed to the early years of Trajan's reign. One was an extension to the Atrium Vestae, the House of the Vestal Virgins in the Forum Romanum, which brick-stamps suggest was begun *c.* 101/2.[55] The existing *tabernae* on the east side were replaced with three contiguous rooms, the middle one, with a transverse barrel vault open to the sky at the centre, having flanking *cubicula* on either side with windows opening on to lateral courts containing fountains. Another construction would have been the fort and barracks Trajan built for the *equites Singulares*, the élite cavalry unit he re-formed as the imperial bodyguard; dedicated before 27 October 113, and later known as the Castra Priora, it lay on the Caelian Hill.[56] A third might well have been the Arch of Titus. It was completely re-assembled and much restored after being disengaged from the Fortalezza Frangipani in 1822/3; the surviving dedication in the east side of the attic informs us it was voted by the Senate and People of Rome as a memorial to the deified Titus, thus providing a *terminus post quem* for the structure of 13 September 81, the day he died. Yet the overall form of the monument, an elegantly proportioned single *fornix*, flanked by massive piers with engaged fluted columns and composite capitals, is strikingly similar to the Arch of Trajan at Beneventum, while the comparatively pure and elegant lines of the façade are remarkably close to the functional simplicity of the Arch at Trajan at Ancona. Consequently, several scholars have entertained the suspicion that the Arch of Titus might in fact be Trajanic in date, a suspicion heightened by the existence of a fragmentary Trajanic inscription of 102–14 of comparable dimensions to the dedication which remains *in situ*, and therefore possibly its missing pendant.[57] If it was indeed built so late after Titus' death, it would signify that although the structure had been voted in his memory, Domitian had conspicuously failed to build it out of envy and spite at his elder brother denying him – or so he thought – any due share in the imperial power. Thus it may have been left to Trajan to see the senate's intentions brought to fruition.[58]

Rome: Trajan's Buildings after 106

It was the gold and silver brought from Dacia, however, which allowed Trajan to unleash any suppressed pretensions he may have had as Augustus' successor as connoisseur and patron of fine architecture. His intentions were unmistakably revealed shortly after his return to Rome in 106 when, on the strength of his annexation of Dacia, he enacted a redefinition of the *pomerium*, the sacred boundary of the city.[59] The act was tantamount to a symbolic refoundation of the *urbs*, and by performing it Trajan unequivocally demonstrated his position as master of the city and his aim of literally rebuilding Rome as a visible token of his achievements. During the next seven years, his longest stay in the capital as emperor, he proceeded to adorn it with a succession of buildings worthy of the apogee of the known world. Yet, while they were intended to provide a tangible reminder of his own greatness and dominance, Trajan was consistently careful to avoid allegations of megalomania or selfishness. He studiously did not add to the Domus Tiberiana and refused to build palaces on any scale, never mind anything comparable to the excesses perpetuated by Nero and Domitian. Instead, he deliberately reinforced his reputation and increased his popularity as *Pater Patriae* by erecting structures distinguished by their usefulness to the plebs as public amenities.

Among the first was the Naumachia Traiani, an artificial basin built for simulated naval battles, dedicated on 11 November 109.[60] It was provided as a replacement for the similar structure of Domitian's (torn down at his behest to provide material for the Circus Maximus); its precise location is uncertain, although topography and the lack of space within the *urbs* for such a structure suggest it is likely to have been situated in the Ager Vaticanus. In which case, it can probably be identified with the massive rectangular complex, lined with waterproof *opus signinum*, known as the Naumachia Vaticana, just north-east of the later Mausoleum Hadriani (Castel Sant' Angelo). This structure is faced with brickwork in a style usually identified as Trajanic; its principal feature is a large basin, with rounded internal and external corners, measuring 330ft wide by at least 1,000ft long (100×>300m), with submerged conduits, also lined with *opus signinum*, leading into and out of it. It was surrounded and retained at ground level on the three known sides with a series of vaulted corridors and chambers, originally service rooms and *tabernae*, which in turn supported at least four rows of tiered seating for the spectators.[61]

Of about the same date as the Naumachia Traiana was the Balneum Surae, which Trajan caused to be built on the demise of L. Licinius Sura. The emperor's intimate friend and trusted confidant, Sura had lived on the Aventine, near to the Temple of Diana, in a house which overlooked the Circus Maximus.[62] After his death, *c.* 108, he was granted the rare honour of a public funeral and statue in the Forum. According to Aurelius Victor, Trajan founded a bath-house in his memory, an act which encapsulated the principle of euregetism in the Roman world, demonstrating as it did the emperor's due concern, as *Pater Patriae*, with the welfare of the commonality, whether rich or poor.[63] Communal bathing was an especial characteristic of Roman life, the nudity of the bathers allowing all to meet as social equals for a minimal admission fee. The tradition had been adopted from the Greeks sometime in the second century BC, and provided a pleasant way for citizens to spend the early afternoon. The bather, perhaps having previously exercised with weights or in ball games, undressed in the *apodyterium* (changing room), and made his way to the *tepidarium* (warm-room) and then the *caldarium* (hot-room), each being provided with plunge baths at the corresponding temperature, heated through a complicated system of hypocausts and wall-ducts. A period in a steam-bath, the *laconicum*, sometimes followed before the massage and the scraping-off of dead skin with a strigil, after which the bather reversed the sequence, ending with a swim in a large open pool (*natatio*) or a covered cold bath (*frigidarium*) to seal the skin pores. Afterwards the male bather could choose from a wide variety of pastimes – gossip, swimming, sex, lectures and poetry readings, to give some documented examples. Seneca, once forced to spend a night next to a provincial bath-house, provides a vivid glimpse of the goings-on. There were

> all sorts of uproar, fit to make you hate your ears! Toughs are put through their paces, throwing their hands about laden with dumb-bells, and I hear their grunts and gasps each time they expel their precious breath [. . .] The picture is not complete without some quarrelsome fellow, or a thief caught in the act, or the man who loves the sound of his own voice in the bath - not to mention those who jump in with a tremendous splash. Besides them [there is] the high strident cry of the depilator, continually advertising his presence, never quiet except when he plucks someone's armpits and makes his customer shriek out for him: or the shouts of the pastry cook, the sausage seller, the confectioner and all those hawkers of refreshments selling their wares.[64]

Agrippa had been the first to commission a public bathing complex on any grand scale as an easy way of demonstrating concern for the well-being of the *plebs urbana*. Nero had capitalized on the principle, as had Titus, and thus Trajan, in establishing the Balneum Surae, was consciously emulating the *beneficium* of his predecessors. As to the structure itself, four fragments of the *Forma Urbis Severiana*, the Severan marble plan of the city, show it to have been of conventional Pompeian type, with a rectangular colonnaded palaestra and a single row of bathing rooms to one side, separated from the street by an arcaded row of shops.[65] If, as seems likely, Trajan had inherited the Domus Surae and used the site for the baths he founded in memory of his friend, then the Balneum Surae can probably be identified with a bath-house found on the Aventine just north of Santa Prisca, near to the Domus Traiani. Not only does the location afford a fine view over the Circus Maximus, but the complex itself is built of typical Trajanic brick-and-concrete, and is supplied by a branch of Trajan's Aqua Marcia.[66]

A number of other minor public buildings which probably belong to the period 106–12 are known solely from documentary or numismatic evidence. One was a theatre, perhaps located in the Campus Martius, and referred to in the mid-fourth century *Historia Augusta*, where it is claimed that Hadrian had it razed in 117/18 out of spite for his predecessor. It is much more likely that work had not advanced very far on the structure, and that it was demolished on Trajan's own instructions, as Hadrian indeed claimed, to release the site and materials for another purpose. Assuming this to be the case, the several unused yet decorated Luna marble blocks and alabaster columns discovered in the Antonine *ustrina* at Montecitorio, all seemingly originally designed for a building of mixtilinear form, may have been intended for the superstructure.[67] A second theatre of Trajan, however, does seem to have been completed, as it is described by Pausanias, the mid-second-century Greek historian, who considered it one of Trajan's more important buildings. On the other hand, Pausanias quite specifically describes it as circular, and not as semi-circular, which suggests it was in fact an elliptical amphitheatre. In which case it may just possibly be identified with the Amphitheatrum Castrense, south of the Sessorium, a work now generally attributed to Elagabalus but whose brickwork allows for it being conceivably a Trajanic foundation.[68] Finally there was the Ara Pudicitia, an altar erected to the goddess by Plotina, depicted on coins of *c.* 112 as a comparatively plain structure of traditional form, and a Gymnasium, known only from an incidental reference in the *Roman History*.[69]

These structures were all doubtless impressive in design and scale, but the culmination of Trajan's ambitions to glorify the *urbs* was the new baths he initiated on the Oppian hill, and the Forum complex he commissioned in the valley between the Quirinal and the Capitoline. The largest series of constructions Rome had ever known, these monuments excited and aroused the admiration of visitors to Rome for at least the next four centuries, and their magnificent if dilapidated remains still impress the modern tourist. Yet while Trajan is to be credited with their creation, since antiquity their design has been linked with the name of one man, Apollodorus of Damascus, the architect responsible for Trajan's bridge across the Danube at Drobeta, and for building the aforementioned Odeum and Gymnasium.[70]

The first to be completed was the Thermae Traiani, dedicated on 22 June 109 and laid out on the southern brow of the Esquiline.[71] Apollodorus adroitly used the surviving lower storey of Nero's Domus Aurea, destroyed by fire in 104, to provide a terraced extension to the available site, filling the remaining rooms with rubble and consolidating the shell with substantial parallel walls to provide a firm foundation for his own construction (Fig. 4).[72] This structure, often claimed to be the first of the great imperial baths, as the Thermae Antoninianae, Diocletiani and Constantinii owe much to its design, actually brings to a logical conclusion the resourceful double-circulation layout employed in the earlier and adjacent Thermae Titi, itself an analytical development of the Thermae Neronis.[73] What was new, however, justifying its claim to originality, was the sheer scale of the complex, for the Thermae Traiani occupied an area three times greater than the Thermae Titi, previously the largest bath-complex in the empire. Sadly, little enough of the structure has survived above ground, a particularly galling verity given that it preserves almost intact much of Nero's Domus Aurea below its own paltry remains.[74] Even so, the plan and the construction techniques involved are both tolerably well-known from the extant remains, archaeological excavations and the antiquarian surveys of Alessandro Palladio and others, especially Piranesi.[75]

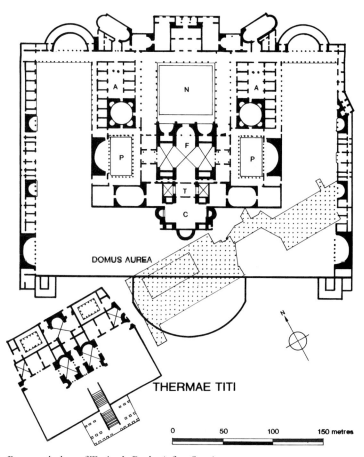

Fig. 4 Restored plan of Trajan's Baths (after Sear)

The complex, which covered a maximum area of $1,033 \times 1,082$ft (315×330m), was built principally from concrete and brick. Tiles were used for the internal roofing of the minor vaulted areas, square or hexagonal coffering for the principal barrel- and cross-vaults, and stucco or marble for the exterior facings, with clay tiles for the roof. Orientated to the south-west to take maximum advantage of the afternoon sun, especially in the wintertime, the principal rooms, which occupy an area 623×696ft (190×212m), were accordingly set in the centre of the north-eastern side, and project into the main court. Intending bathers, both male and female in the time of Trajan, even if public bathing was primarily a male practice, entered the compound by a substantial barrel-vaulted vestibule. They were immediately confronted by an ample open-air almost square *natatio* surrounded on all four sides by porticoes which opened on to *apodyteria* and two symmetrically disposed quatrefoil rooms.[76] Beyond lay a vast cruciform *frigidarium*, the focus of the entire complex, occupying the twin axes of the building. It contained oblong cold plunge baths in each of the four corners, and the main cross-axial hall itself was divided into three bays by eight enormous semi-engaged columns, perhaps up to 50ft high. They supported cross-vaults spanning 66ft (20m) wide voids, probably the first use of the technique on such a large scale. At the opposed ends were open peristyle *palaestrae*, for gymnastic exercises, with vaulted hemicycles along the long side, possibly intended for boxing matches. Ahead lay the *tepidarium*, which gave on to flanking sweating rooms. Then came the oblong *caldarium*, with not less than seven hot baths, the principal three of which were semi-circular vaulted tubs. Outside was an open area, flanked by a peribolus, and containing running tracks and gardens. The two opposing sides were divided into small rooms and cubicles, and broken by two half-domed twin-storeyed hemicycles with niches, probably libraries. The third side may well have contained similar rooms, but it was dominated by a great semi-circular exedra with tiered seating, which probably served as a theatre for gymnastic and other displays; a timber balcony supported on travertine corbels on the external chord may well have been provided for the use of fire-fighters, should the need arise.

The Thermae Traiani vastly increased the amount of water required for a city which already suffered from periodic shortages, despite the existence of nine aqueducts which together brought in over 2,182,600 gallons (992,200 cubic metres) of water per day.[77] While the baths probably appropriated much of their initial supply from the nearby Aqua Anio Vetus, Trajan initiated an entirely new aqueduct to augment the city's reserves by a tenth, the Aqua Traiana delivering an additional 250,593 gallons (113,920 cubic metres) of water from Lake Bracciano to the Trastevere region of Rome.[78] It was inaugurated on 24 June 109, two days after the Thermae Traiani, and celebrated by coins bearing the legend *AQUA TRAIANA* and a representation of the river god reclining in a grotto, perhaps an attempt to portray the terminal basin at the Janiculum, in the vicinity of the modern Villa Spada.[79] From here it is believed that subsidiary channels powered the grain mills lower down the hill,[80] and supplied the large feeder reservoir on the via Aurelia, while a pipe was laid towards the east to maintain a reserve for the Thermae Traiani at the so-called Sette Sale (Le Capocce), a series of seven barrel-vaulted settling chambers. Other feeder channels are suspected, but those known confirm the claim in the *Fasti Ostienses*, that the Aqua Traiana was provided to supply water 'to every part of the city', as indeed is proclaimed on another inscription of the same period.[81]

Trajan's supreme achievement in the urban planning of Rome was the forum and basilica he inaugurated on 1 January 112.[82] The last and greatest of the imperial *fora*, it covers an area of 606 × 984ft (185 × 300m), almost as great as all the others put together (Fig. 5). Straddling the valley between the Quirinal and the Capitoline, thus uniting the area between the Atrium Libertatis on the north-west and the Forum Augustum and Forum Julium on the south-east and south-west, it brings to a completion the series of monumental squares, porticoes and temples that Caesar and Augustus had planned for this

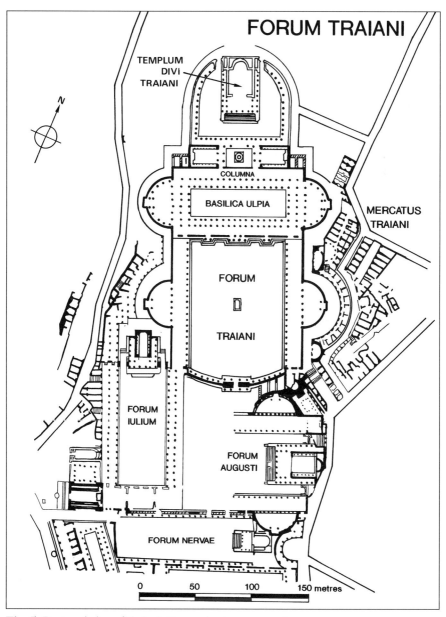

Fig. 5 Restored plan of Trajan's Forum (various sources)

region. Sadly, much of it is fragmented or even concealed by gardens and Mussolini's grand via dei Fori Imperiali, while little has yet been achieved on publishing the excavations of the 1930s, creating considerable problems in its interpretation.[83] Even so, it is clear that the credit for opening the space actually belongs to Domitian, for it was during his reign that the area was cleared and the slope north-west of the Forum Augustum cut back, indicating he planned some monumental construction on the land. But, whatever Domitian's intentions, Trajan's development, as designed and completed by Apollodorus, is a complex whole, perfectly integrated axially and spatially with its immediate neighbours, the Cluvius Argentarius on the south side providing a covered link with the Forum Julium.

On one level, the Forum Traiani is a clever adaptation of, and return to, the more creative architectural features of the Forum Augustum, for example, certain structural details, such as the *exedrae* and the use of caryatid-like figures to support the upper storey of the flanking porticoes, or the ornamental motifs, specifically the use of *imagines clipeatae*, and decoration with a distinctive dentil and *cyma reversa* mouldings. In other ways it was a radical development in public architecture, for it abandoned the traditional oblong *templum-in-foro* plan used for its immediate neighbours (and throughout Italy and most of the empire), in favour of an almost square layout. It brought together in one construction for the first time in the capital the Greek-inspired agora, a piazza where commercial and financial business was transacted in the open air, and the Roman-preferred aisled basilica, where legal and other business took place under cover. Now, in traditional Roman architecture, the basilica had almost always stood alone: but in the Forum Traiani, Apollodorus, perhaps inspired by the plan of a military *principia*, or headquarters building, took the revolutionary step of combining it in a unified construction with the open square. In effect, he made the basilica a roofed extension of the forum, providing a single complex where politicians, lawyers and businessmen could conduct their intrigues, in the open during the balmy spring and autumnal months, and under cover in the insufferable heat of the Italian summer and the intolerable damp of the Roman winter. It proved a most eminent and practical layout, and was quickly adopted in many of the northern provinces.[84]

Approaching from the Forum Augustum, the visitor first came to a convex marble wall broken only by a single albeit monumental entrance of five aediculated bays, the central one with the single opening. Coins indicate it was heavily decorated, each niche containing a statue framed by columns with composite capitals and surmounted with an *imago clipeus*.[85] The deep attic carried a long inscription, and was surmounted by a four- or six-horse chariot, flanked with trophies, soldiers and Victories. Passing through the archway, the visitor then entered the Forum Traiani proper, a vast oblong courtyard, paved with white marble flags and measuring some 291 × 387ft (89 × 118m). It was here that Constantius II, visiting Rome for the first time in 357, stopped in amazement, letting his eyes wander over the vast series of buildings, such as to beggar description and never again to be embarked upon by mortal men.[86] His astonishment was understandable. Dominated by a colossal gilded equestrian statue of the emperor, the piazza, intended as a place for public business and ceremony, was given over to numerous statues of generals and other distinguished men. Behind the front wall was a single narrow colonnade, perhaps the *porticus Purpuretica* (?porphyry) known from a later source.[87] The two long sides took the form of galleried porticoes, 40ft (12m) wide, entered by a flight of three steps of yellow giallo antico and floored with polychrome marbles. Fluted columns of pavonazetto, with alternating Ionic and Corinthian capitals, supported entablatures based upon those used in the Forum Augustum. Above them the deep attics were broken by caryatid figures of Dacian captives, the intervening spaces alternating with windows and *imagines clipeatae*, perhaps representing prominent heroes of the Dacian Wars. According to Gellius, the attics were crowned with gilded statues of horses and military standards individually identified as *EX MANUBIIS*, '[paid for] from the spoils [of the Dacian war]', a description confirmed by fragmentary inscriptions which also reveal that the bases bore the names of army units known to have been involved in the Dacian Wars.[88] Each portico was broken at the centre by an immense half-vaulted *exedra*, geometrically paved with giallo, africano and pavonazzetto, panelled with Luna marble, and with central aedicular niches framed by grey granite columns. Clearly inspired by the similar apses in the Forum Augustum, as were the *imagines* and the caryatid figures of Dacian captives used in the entablature, these exedra were perhaps where the consuls held court.[89]

The north-west side of the Forum was filled by the transverse Basilica Ulpia, standing on a podium approached by a broad flight of steps of giallo antico. There were three porticoed entrances; the principal one, on the same axis as the main gateway and equestrian statue, was tetrastyle, the four monolithic grey Egyptian granite columns *in antis* supporting an inscribed and heavily decorated attic crowned by a *quadriga* flanked by Victories. Equidistant on either side were secondary distyle porches, each with a *biga* and trophies on the attic, and travertine bases set on the podium probably bore bronze statues of the emperor, for they are inscribed with his titles and the formula *OPTIME DE REPUBLICA MERITO DOMI FORISQUE*: 'to the best [of emperors] for his meritorious service to the republic at home and abroad'. Then, continuing the theme of homage to Trajan's victory over Dacia, the principal attic of the Basilica was broken by further caryatid figures of Dacian prisoners – at 10ft (3m) high, somewhat larger than those decorating the Forum colonnades, and of pavonazetto, giallo and porphyry, with heads and hands of Luna marble (Pls 10A,10B). The three entrances opened into an aisled building, twice as long as it was broad, at 180×360ft (55×110m). The largest hall hitherto built in Rome, it provided an enclosed space comparable to the Romanesque nave and choir of the Cathedral of the Virgin Mary at Durham, England, though wider; or the basilican church of S. Paolo fuori le Mura at Rome, except longer. The central nave, 80ft (25m) wide, was panelled and floored with Luna marble, and was divided from the paired side aisles by columns of granito del foro, brought from Mons Claudianus in the Egyptian eastern desert. The lesser diameter of the alternating cipollino, giallo antico and pavonazetto shafts used for the lateral aisles and their second-storey galleries indicates a clerestory roof, perhaps 80ft (25m) high, covered on the outside with tiles of gilded bronze.[90] Corinthian capitals of white Luna marble were used for the principal columns, and they were crowned with a Pentelic marble entablature of two orders, framed with bead-and-reel, the lower adorned with a continuous floral scroll, the upper embellished with a figured frieze in Augustan style, of lion-headed griffins, alternating with Victories shown sacrificing bulls and adorning candelabra with floral garlands.[91] At each end of the nave were apses of an equal size to the hemicycles flanking the Forum, but apparently only of a single storey. They were no less lavishly decorated than the main structure, however, the walls being covered with Luna marble, the floors with polychrome marbles set in an elaborate geometric pattern, and the central aedicular niche which formed the focus in each flanked by a colonnade creating a series of shallow bays. These may have been used to contain scrolls, for the Severan marble plan reveals that the two hemicycles replaced the Atrium Libertatis, originally the headquarters of the republican censors and the repository of their records, and more recently used as a national library. More certainly they were used for the manumission of slaves, and perhaps replaced the Forum Romanum as the location where boys were advanced to manhood on the festival of the Libertatis.[92]

Beyond the Basilica Ulpia were two rectangular rooms flanking an open court, the three conforming to the *tabularii* and *aedes* of a military *principia*. The two rooms, each of two storeys, constituted the Bibliotheca Ulpia, where Trajan's imperial archives were kept,[93] and were thus built of brick and concrete for protection against fire and damp: brick-stamps indicate they were begun *c.* 110. Their façades, with four columns *in antis*, were of plain if finely finished brickwork, but their galleried interiors were superlatively decorated with white and polychrome marbles, ornamented with a double order of Corinthian-style pilasters, of mixed pavonazetto and giallo antico, framing the numbered niches containing the scrolls. In the usual fashion, one of the rooms was given over to works in Greek, the other to Latin, and according to one later writer, the interiors of both were embellished with statues of famous authors.[94]

The court between the two libraries measured 52 × 75ft (16 × 23m), and contained the eponymous Column (Pl. 5). Dedicated on 12 May 113, it could well have been added as an afterthought, as its foundation cuts into the existing atrium paving, known from excavations to be contemporary with the construction of the libraries.[95] The shaft, of seventeen drums of Luna marble, each averaging 12ft 3in (3.74m) in diameter, and giving a total height of 100 Roman feet (97ft 9in; 29.78m), was raised on a 17ft 6in (5.37m) high rectangular podium, decorated with military trophies carved in low relief. A small doorway on one side of the base gives on to a vestibule within the podium, later used as the resting place for the golden urn containing Trajan's remains. From here a spiral staircase of 185 steps, lit by 43 slit windows, allows access to the summit, some 115ft 3in (35.15m) above the level of the pavement.[96] Yet, while the Column now soars conspicuously above the surrounding buildings, this was not always so, for originally it was totally concealed from the Forum by the clerestory roof of the Basilica Ulpia, and only the monumental statue of Trajan on top of the Column, now replaced by one of St Paul, might have been universally visible from all vantage points. Indeed, as the inscription on the Column's base confirms, it was intended not so much to dominate the surrounding terrain as to be used as a vantage point to view the 'great works' that had been necessary to clear the area used for the entire complex and to build the Forum Traiani.[97] Thus, in order to examine the figured scroll itself, it was necessary to leave the court and ascend the stairwells behind each of the flanking libraries, which gave access both to their upper galleries and to the external ambulatory, from where a relatively unimpeded view of the frieze was possible.

The fourth side of the library court was occupied by a transverse colonnade, perhaps of two storeys, forming a corridor at ground level and a gallery above. The outer entablature of this structure was quite possibly the original location for the 'Great Trajanic Frieze'. A work originally not less than 100ft long (30m) and 10ft high (3m), and hence the third largest relief frieze from antiquity, it is generally recognized as being one of the formative sculptures of the High Imperial period.[98] Several pieces from the Frieze, including two substantial panels, were later incorporated into the Arch of Constantine, a *fornix* erected to celebrate the victory of the Mulvian Bridge using a number of reliefs expropriated from several earlier structures whose precise locations are now lost. The overall size of the Frieze, however, and the fact that one section is known to have come from Trajan's Forum, suggest that it formerly belonged to the Forum complex, although precisely where is uncertain. Unless it was originally much longer, at about 754ft (230m), it is unlikely to belong to the colonnade surrounding the Forum, while it cannot easily be fitted into the known arrangements of the attic in the Basilica or of the Temple to the Deified Trajan and Plotina further to the north. Hence, in the absence of any evidence for another substantial monument which it may have embellished within the complex, a location on the outer face of the library court's colonnade seems as likely as any other situation.

As for the piece itself, it is truly stunning, a masterpiece of sculpture. Like the Column, it uses the traditional device of packing equal-sized figures behind one another on progressively higher levels to give the illusion of depth, completely ignoring all the rules of conventional perspective, yet somehow making a comfortably harmonious whole. In contrast to the diachronous frieze on the Column, it is synchronous, with no separation between the various scenes it carries. Instead, it presents an episodic synthesis. In mid-picture, the emperor is shown on horseback, bare-headed and with his cloak spread out behind him, in the thick of the action, lifting his right hand to throw a spear, as if Jupiter about to dispatch a thunderbolt against Rome's enemies (Pl. 11A). To the right Roman soldiers are shown with Dacian captives and offering severed heads to the emperor, while on the left is an *Adventus* scene, in which the emperor, followed by lictors, is shown being crowned by Victoria as Roma leads him into the capital for the triumph.

In default of excavation, there is simply no agreement as to what Apollodorus intended in the colonnaded piazza beyond the library. An inscription reveals that Hadrian dedicated a temple to the deified Trajan and Plotina in this space between the years 121/122 and 127/8, the only building at Rome, apparently, on which he allowed his own name to appear. There is some evidence to suggest it was octostyle peripteral, set in a courtyard flanked by colonnades, which perhaps could be independently entered from the Campus Martius by a monumental gateway, conceivably the archway decreed to Trajan by the senate 'in his Forum' in 116.[99] Whether or not the temple was part of Apollodorus' original plan is unclear. Certainly, it would be unheard of for a living emperor to arrange the construction of a temple to himself, which superficially rules out the possibility that Trajan had intended such a structure.

At least, not one erected in his own name. It needs to be remembered that Hadrian is specifically said to have dedicated the structure to Trajan and Plotina, not to have built it. Therefore, taking into account that the Temple harmoniously completes the Forum complex as known, it is of interest to note that before 29 August 104, Trajan had ordered the construction of a monumental building which required monolithic 50 Roman foot (48ft; 19m)-high column-shafts of rose Aswan granite (Syene), pieces of such magnitude they could only be intended for an octostyle Imperial Temple.[100] It just so happens that whoever built the Forum temple evidently used columns of a similar mass. This is demonstrated by the existence at the site of two fragments of column-shafts in grey Mons Claudianus granite, together with part of a Corinthian capital in white marble, all of the appropriate diameter for columns the same magnitude as that brought from Aswan. They are amongst the largest of their kind (they are, for example, larger than those used by Hadrian in his rebuilding of the Pantheon); it is possible that they were intended for use in an octostyle façade of up to twenty-six alternating grey and rose granite columns, as was later employed for the portico of the Pantheon, but in this case the Forum temple.[101] It may be, of course, that they belonged to one of those octostyle temples commemorated on Trajan's early coinage. On the other hand, their enormous scale suggests they were intended for a monument somehow connected with the emperor himself. In which case the date of the Aswan monolith would suggest it was originally cut for some building intended to commemorate the First Dacian War, but then the Second Dacian War supervened, and after the conquest of Decebalus, it was decided to incorporate the monument into the Forum complex instead, and thus provide the religious focus that tradition demanded. If so, it is conceivable that the Forum temple, presumably originally vowed to Victoria, thus continuing the theme of the Dacian victory which runs throughout the Forum complex, was not completed until the reign of Hadrian, who took the opportunity to rededicate it to the memory of his adoptive parents.[102]

North-east of the Forum, a succession of terraces had been cut into the slopes of the Quirinal to accommodate the *exedra* on this side, and were now exploited for the erection of a great complex of buildings, known today as the Mercati di Traiano, or Markets of Trajan (Fig. 6 and Pl. 11B).[103] Built from brick-faced concrete with travertine details, and contemporary with the Thermae Traiani, on the evidence of the brick-stamps, it is an elaborately planned yet utilitarian construction. It has more than 170 barrel-vaulted rooms in at least 6 storeys, accessible by streets on two principal levels, and with interconnecting stairways and corridors. Occupying an area of about 360×490ft (110×150m), it is a remarkably unified building, tailored to conform to an irregular plot of land with a sharp slope to the north-east, and successfully integrating curving, trapezoidal and radial blocks into a composite whole that contains the thrust imposed by the unstable clay subsoil of the Quirinal. At ground level the centrepiece is a hemicyclical façade of two orders. Originally this would have been seen from the side approaches only, as it conforms to the outer curve of the Forum's northern *exedra*, although as it was laid out on a different chord the two are not concentric. Bordered by semi-domed halls, perhaps used as schools or *auditorii*, a series of ten wide-doored rooms open off the lowermost street. A pair of stairwells at either end lead to the second storey, composed of a barrel-vaulted corridor divided into ten rooms, lit by twenty-five windows set within Tuscan pilasters, and crowned with an entablature incorporating alternating triangular, lunette and segmental pediments.

The third storey, largely destroyed, is recessed from the principal façade by a gallery, which backed on to individual rooms that faced the opposite direction, opening on to the upper street, paved with basalt and bordered with travertine pavements. Known in medieval times as the via Biberatica, a name perhaps derived from the presence of drinking establishments here at that time, it follows a gentle downhill course best likened to a shallow W-shape, resulting in a less symmetrical arrangement for the upper levels. The buildings on the opposite side of the street mark an abrupt change in perspective, the graceful curve of the hemicycle giving over to a multi-faceted and angular façade. At the north or lower end, the street is fronted by a trapezoidal basilican hall, now known as the Aula Traiana. The ground level, which at this point corresponds to the gallery level of the hemicycle, is taken up with a single row of six rooms which face comparable chambers on the opposite side of the via Biberatica. A stairway at the south end gives access to an upper storey, with opposing rows of six rooms, perhaps offices, on either side of a cross-vaulted hall, 92×32ft (28×9.80m). The galleries above them repeat the plan, with the addition of longitudinal access corridors, and the groins for the six-bayed cross-vaulted roof spring from their pavement level, a space being left over the hallways to allow for lighting the

TRAJAN'S MARKETS

FORUM TRAIANI

Fig. 6 Trajan's Markets (after Boethius)

concourse and the shops below. A series of seven arched buttresses were installed over each corridor to stabilize the cross-vaulting, and vaulted staircases were provided to give access to a further two storeys set back and above it.

The north-eastern block, of at least three storeys, is less uniform in plan and more obviously conditioned by the local topography. Incorporating a semi-circular chamber and a row of irregular and interconnecting rooms with wall niches, perhaps offices, the rooms are all joggled into position to adapt to the space available and, being at the same level as the uppermost storey of the hemicycle, could thus be entered directly from the level of the pavement in the Aula Traiana. The upper storey conforms substantially to the lower in layout, and can be entered by means of a staircase at the south end or via the galleries of the market hall. Completing this range was a shallow arcade facing the eastern leg of the via Biberatica, again with a few chambers of standard type.

The entire complex has no known parallel, nor is its original function clear. Opinion remains divided as to its original purpose, but most authorities now favour its use as an administrative building, even though the rooms are so much like the known *tabernae*, or shops, at Ostia.[104] But whatever its purpose, it articulates the victory of concrete and brick in the development of Roman building techniques, and marks a distinct change in architectural principles. Hitherto, Roman architecture was dominated by the use of columns, whether engaged or free-standing, to support vaults whenever these were needed – even the cross-vault used for the *frigidarium* in the Thermae Traiani springs from semi-engaged pillars, while vaulting was completely avoided for the principal roof of Trajan's Basilica. The use of brick-faced concrete vaults, first seen on any scale at the Domus Aurea and in Domitian's palace, was the most important advance made by Rome on existing (Greek) architectural principles, and the practice comes to fruition in the Markets, which totally reject columnar support in favour of centred vaulting throughout. Then, it had been traditional to cover the substance of all public buildings with marble panels or stuccoed facings, when they were not built of marble throughout. But the crisp mouldings and carvings of the brickwork and travertine details in the Markets, while in low-relief, reveal that they were never intended to be concealed. Instead, they were meant to present a purely functional appearance, the warm colour and texture of the brickwork with its travertine embellishments making a vivid chromatic contrast, and divorcing the complex completely from the marble-encased walls of the adjacent Forum. More significantly, the planning of the complex marked a radical change in the prevailing concepts of utilitarian architecture. The strictly symmetrical and axial thinking that governed the Forum and the Baths was rejected in favour of a whole series of new ideas in layout and composition. Repudiating the rigid application of a formalized plan to the landscape, the Markets instead adapt the area available to create a series of closely interrelated yet spatially and visually distinct modules, with remarkably few straight axes of any length. Unity in composition is none the less stressed by repeated details, the standardized size and plan of the separate rooms and their travertine details. As J. Ward-Perkins observed, while

> The Forum and Markets of Trajan were contemporary and complementary monuments, the two halves of a single plan [...] yet it would be hard to imagine two groups of buildings that were more different in every respect. [...] The contrast is, of course, symptomatic of an age in transition.[105]

XII

'REDACTA IN FORMAM PROVINCIAE ...'[1]

The occasion of a severe drought and consequent famine in Egypt, *c.* 99, gave Trajan an early chance to demonstrate his concern for provincial matters, which he did by dispensing a *beneficium* in the form of a grain subsidy to those affected. Pliny applauded the act. To him it proved that the provinces had not become the indispensable servants of Rome; rather, Rome had become indispensable to the provinces, thanks to the existence of a well-managed polity whose chief executive, the *princeps*, was able to divert supplies from one place to another as occasion and necessity demanded.[2] If the truth be known, the converse was probably correct. Aside from the matter of external security, the generally accepted motive for conquering new territories was economic, to provide for the demands of Rome, although personal prestige did play its own part on occasion.[3]

The successful economic exploitation of any territory was achieved through the imposition of the correct administrative machinery, the means which enabled the proper collection of the appropriate provincial *tributum*, 'contributions', or taxes. Chief among these was the *tributum capitis*, a poll tax based upon the provincial census of the indigenous population. Provincial census had perhaps been carried out on a regular basis from the reign of Augustus onwards, and was probably immediately extended to all those areas subsequently brought into the Roman hegemony – and even, on occasion, to client-kingdoms. What limited evidence we have demonstrates that in some areas it could be paid in cash, and in others in kind, but almost nothing is known concerning how it was actually collected and delivered to the emperor's representative in any province.[4] That said, it is abundantly clear, from a variety of sources, that a significant part of the responsibility lay with the elected authorities in the individual communities of the territory concerned.[5] Hence the fundamental basis for the maintenance of the Roman empire was the system of provincial cities it encouraged, rather than the provincial territories themselves. It follows, therefore, that the extent to which any one province was 'Romanized' can be gauged in the first instance from the existence of recognized communities, together with the attention paid to its internal and external security, and secondly from the degree to which its indigenous population was assimilated within the overall framework of Roman administration.

To begin with, the provinces were sub-divided into autonomous communities, the *civitates*, each usually with its own principal city. They were self-governing, with a recognized constitution executed by annually elected magistrates answerable to a council of their peers. Their duty, within the framework of the Roman administration, was to supervise and provide a recognized juridical and fiscal centre for the *civitas*, which concomitantly included the proper collection of imperial taxes along with meeting any other demands the emperor placed on them. Yet while Rome doubtless aimed for a similarity in the constitutions and institutions of the provincial communities, there was a great contrast between the territorial and urban organization of the eastern and the western parts of the empire. In the east there were many urban communities, usually Greek foundations, self-governing enclaves (*poleis*) with an existing legal constitution and territorial rights, and generally with three tiers of government: the *ekklesia*, the open assembly of all male citizens, who elected the *boule*, or council, which was supervised by the *archons*, the annual magistrates. The *polis*-system of administration was easily adapted to the needs of Roman government, and after assimilation within the Roman empire, the *poleis* were soon charged with acting as the agents of Rome in fiscal and other matters. In return, they were awarded certain privileges, such as that of *civitates liberae* (in rare cases), which placed them outside the provincial governor's jurisdiction where urban matters were concerned, or of *civitates immunes*, which gave them freedom from taxation. A few were even elevated to the status of *metropolis*, which may well have involved the imposition or grant of certain Latin rights as a *de facto municipium*, with all the rights and privileges that entailed. Others had a Roman *colonia* founded next to them, with the full rights of the *ius Italicum*, making it and its territory a part of Rome, which among other things gave the inhabitants certain exemptions from provincial taxation, but left them exposed to the other taxes levied on Roman citizens alone. In all other ways they were left to their own devices, except where outside intervention was necessary to maintain order or fiscal probity. It is for this reason that Greek, being the long-established *lingua franca* in these parts, remained the principal language of everyday intercourse and of administrative procedure.

In the west, on the other hand, at least outside those areas on the Mediterranean littoral settled by Greek or Phoenicians in pre-Roman times, there was a much more limited tradition of urban life, and no 'democratic' system of self-government. In these regions, therefore, Rome was forced to foster the development of communities, a process well described by Tacitus, who also candidly describes its purpose in a well-known phrase: 'the unsuspecting Britons welcomed the novelties of "civilization", when in fact they were only a feature of their enslavement'.[6] Where there were existing urban centres which could be assimilated within the Roman model, they were often granted rights as *civitates foederatae*, federated communities, usually as a preliminary to being awarded the status of *municipium*. As *civitates foederatae*, they kept their own laws but adopted an administrative system modelled on that of Rome. Once they were advanced to municipal status, however, a version of the Latin law was applied, with due exceptions on occasion to assimilate local customs, and Latin or Roman citizenship could be granted to the more prominent and wealthy among the municipal élite. Otherwise, the practice was to establish *coloniae*, settlements of retired legionaries, often founded in redundant legionary fortresses and governed by a Roman constitution, although with time the title was increasingly awarded to existing communities, especially the *municipia*, not least because it conveyed a certain social cachet.[7] Whether *colonia* or *municipium*, these chartered foundations played a fundamental part in introducing a vigorous urban life and juridical and fiscal control into the west. Moreover, along with acquainting the indigenous population with the institutions and amenities of Rome, the administrative system they represented brought a homogeneity of thought and language to the outer regions. Hence

Latin, while not replacing all traces of the local languages, was adopted in place of native speech, establishing itself as the *lingua franca* of the western empire.[8]

It follows, therefore, that the relative success of Romanization in any newly occupied territory might be assessed in the first instance by the strength or otherwise of urbanization. And we are fortunate in that Trajan's reign provides two examples from opposite parts of the empire – Dacia and Arabia – where the process of Romanization in this limited sense, and its relative success, or otherwise, can be examined through a combination of archaeological and semi-documentary evidence.[9] It is not for one moment held that any coherent or tangible picture will emerge. For one thing, the available material is usually either too explicit or too ambiguous for any rational generalized or deterministic interpretation. For another, there is the matter of geography and history: Arabia was a client-kingdom in the 'civilized' east, long accustomed to bureaucratic procedure, and apparently peacefully incorporated into the empire; Dacia was a client-kingdom in the 'barbarian' west, with a feudal system, and forcibly assimilated by Rome. Yet the exercise remains of interest, not least because both territories were added to the Roman hegemony within two years of each other, but also precisely because it highlights the effect of geographical and cultural diversity on the procedure, and how these factors were adapted, where necessary, to allow for the imposition of a recognizably Roman administration.

Dacia

The first of the two territories to be 'received and formed into a province' was Dacia (Fig. 7), assimilated into the empire after two extremely bloody wars. As we have seen, the Second Dacian War was intended from the outset to be a campaign of conquest, and thus the apparatus for transforming the kingdom into a fully functioning Roman province was already to hand before hostilities were completed. By 11 August 106, within weeks of the *Basileion*, or royal capital, at Sarmizegethusa Regia being reduced, and a month or more previous to the elimination of Decebalus and his last band of resisters, one D. Terentius Scaurianus had already been inducted as propraetorian governor of Dacia.[10]

It was an immense sphere of responsibility, forming a marked extension north of the Lower Danube marches, all of which had to be organized in an acceptable Roman fashion. Scaurianus' first task, therefore, was to secure the territory from external aggression. The potential threat came from two nomadic Sarmatian tribes of Scythian origin, the Iazyges to the west of the province, and the Roxolani to the east. Their mode of life, reconstructed from archaeology and documents, indicates they were semi-nomads, living in ox-drawn waggons and on horseback, and camping out in felt yurts or leather tents.[11] With few material possessions beyond their weapons and livestock, and disparaged by the Greeks as uncouth *hippemolgi* and *galactophagi* – horsemilkers and milk-eaters – they moved with the seasons. In the winter they camped beside the Pontus or in river valleys; in summer they roamed the pasture lands of the transdanubian steppes. It was a harsh and precarious existence, even if the menfolk could perhaps take pleasure in a common Scythian method of relaxation, namely communal drug-use: Herodotus describes what was evidently a 'pot-party' involving the roasting of *cannabis sativa* in a sealed felt tent![12] Drawing on such hardship, however, they proved a fierce

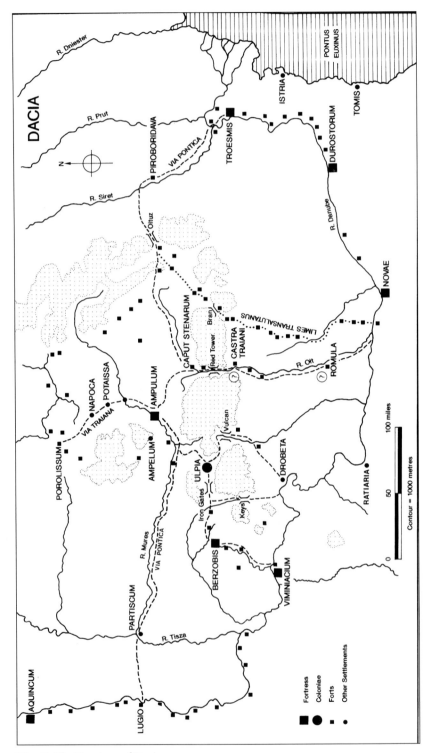

Fig. 7 The Province of Dacia

enemy. Mares were used in warfare, for the ease with which they could urinate while galloping,[13] and by the Roman period they were using as their principal weapons the long cavalry lance and, for close combat, the two-handed sword. Having by then also adopted the iron scale armour of their Central Asian relatives, they presumably used identical shock tactics in battle, the close formations of *clibanarii* proving irresistible on open ground.

Of the two tribes, the Iazyges, centred on the Hungarian Alfold, were the less predictable. Responsible for the loss of the *legio XXI Rapax* during the reign of Domitian, more recently they had allied themselves with Rome on account of Decebalus' occupation of the prime grasslands of the western Banat. They now proved fractious again, partly because of Trajan's refusal to restore to them those territories as he had previously agreed; and partly because of the Roman occupation of Oltenia, which threatened their access to the seasonal migration routes into and across Wallachia and thence to the Black Sea.[14] Simmering discontent erupted into open rebellion as early as 107, in which year Hadrian, as governor of Pannonia Inferior, undertook a punitive campaign against them and other groups to the north, after which it would seem that a judicious treaty restored their lands and consequently peace to the area.[15]

The Roxolani, of Wallachia and Moldavia, on the other hand, had proved consistently hostile to Rome. They had supported Decebalus in the insurrection of 105, and now found as much as half of their traditional southern grazing grounds incorporated into the Roman province of Dacia. In their case a similar confrontation over land rights was averted by diplomacy. While the Romans had needed to occupy the vast and featureless Wallachian and Moldavian steppes in order to attack Dacia from the east, the territory was not necessary for the subsequent development or protection of the province. True, the steppes were useful in their own right, as prime grazing land, but it was also realized that they could not sustain settled occupation, and would be almost impossible to hold and control permanently without the deployment of several cavalry units, backed by a network of established forts and linear obstacles.[16] Consequently, as archaeological excavations have shown, most of the forts in Wallachia and Moldavia may well have been quickly abandoned after the province was formed, a few being retained as outposts, indicating that these territories, the transdanubian extension of Moesia Inferior, were restored to the Roxolani. Oltenia, however, was retained, to secure the right flank of the province, in return for which Trajan granted a subsidy to the tribe.[17] By *c.* 108, therefore, the province of Dacia had probably already taken on the outline familiar from modern text books, an amorphous bubble-shaped northern protuberance based upon the Lower Danube, and ringed by the Carpathians.[18]

Once the limits of the province had been determined, it was possible to complete work on the building of the road network. Provincial road systems were essential for two reasons: in the first instance for security, to allow the adequate movement of the garrison when the necessity arose, and only secondly to allow for commerce. Some of these networks, the arterial systems, followed existing natural routes of communication, often the principal lines of initial advance during the conquest of the territory. The others, the peripherals, while using natural trails wherever possible, were generally driven through the countryside specifically to link military outposts, and usually mark the outer boundary of a fully consolidated area. As such, the peripheral roads were sometimes known by the term of *limes*, a word originally used to denote the cross-paths between fields in an agricultural estate, and which might still be correctly used to denote this particular form of boundary track.

It is safe to assume that the existing natural routes of communication into Dacia were quickly paved in Roman fashion, and that work soon set about establishing a more comprehensive network in the rest of the province. So far as documentary evidence is concerned, however, only two routes can unequivocally be assigned to Trajan's directive. The one was the arterial road between Potaissa (Turda) and Napoca (Cluj), marked by a milestone indicating work in 107/108, and probably part of a longer length later recorded as the via Traiana Pataesina.[19] The second was a more substantial arterial road which, according to Aurelius Victor, Trajan built using the 'wild peoples' of the region (presumably prisoners of war) to allow a direct overland link between the Black Sea and 'Galliam', by which Gaul is to be understood.[20] The eastern course of this 'via Pontica' through the territory of the Roxolani has not been ascertained, but it probably ran from Troesmis along the Siret to Piroboridava and thence west over the Oituz Pass. It then probably followed the headwaters of the Olt to Caput Stenarum, before crossing over the intervening saddle to Apulum (Alba Julia). West of Apulum the road's course is clear, even if untested by the spade: it followed the Mureş downstream to Partiscum (Szeged), at the confluence with the Tisza, where an inscription attests to a road station under the charge of a *vicilis* who, in turn, was responsible to the region's *praefectus vehiculorum*.[21] From this place the road presumably ran directly across the intervening territory of the Iazyges to Lugio (Dunaszekcsö), in Pannonia Inferior.

The initial work on the road system was a natural responsibility for the garrison of Dacia, now considerably reduced in size from the force needed for the conquest. We are fortunate in that three military diplomas – 'discharge certificates' – survive for the early years of the occupation, providing a nominal muster for 14 October 109, and 17 February and 2 July 110.[22] They list 6 quingenary *alae*, one composed of Ituraean archers from the Anti-Lebanon; 5 *cohortes milliaria equitatae*, one of Ituraean archers; 2 *cohortes milliaria*; 9 *cohortes quingenaria equitatae*, one of Commagene archers; 6 *cohortes quingenariae*, one of Ituraean and one of Cretan archers; and a single *numerus*, formed from various detached elements which originally made up part of the personal guard of the governor of Britain. To this auxiliary force of about 15,000 can be added 2 legions, the *IIII Flavia* and the *XIII Gemina*, making a total garrison of about 27,000 troops.

The disposition of the legionary forces in Dacia indicates where the main concern for the security of the province was vested. The *IIII Flavia* was at Berzobis (Berzovia-Resita), from where it could easily strike against the Iazyges, and the *XIII Gemina* at Apulum, in the centre of the former Dacian kingdom, allowing it to move against any threat from north, west or east. The retention of the standing legionary garrisons at Aquincum in Pannonia Inferior and (?)Singidunum and Viminiacium in Moesia Superior on the one hand, and at Novae, Durostorum and Troesmis in Moesia Inferior on the other, meant that the twin threats posed by the Iazyges and Roxolani were thus effectively nullified, although as events in 117 were to show, they were not completely eliminated.

The distribution of the auxiliary garrisons would seem to reflect more obviously a concern with attack from the two neighbouring Sarmatian tribes, although the serious lack of firm evidence for the chronology and even the very existence of certain claimed sites hinders an adequate review. To begin with, the ring of forts along the boundary of the territory, concentrated as they are in the mountain passes and river valleys, and linked by the peripheral road systems, would appear to have been garrisoned by cavalry and equitate units. This suggests the primary interest was in the control of migrating mounted nomads, whether or not they came with hostile intent. Advance warning of such movements may well have been provided (in one sector, at least) by an outer screen of watch-towers, and the peripheral roads themselves, while not constituting a frontier or military installation as such, allowed for the control of any groups moving across the boundary they formed. With this in mind, it is not inconceivable that Trajan adopted the *clausurae* system he had used with such success during the conquest of Dacia to impede further uncontrolled migrations in the east of the province. A series of disconnected lengths of earthen barrier in the east of the province, of uncertain but early Roman date, dignified with the name *limes Transalutanus*, directed movement towards nearby permanent forts as if to allow for supervision of cross-border traffic.[23]

By way of contrast, however, as far as it can be established, those units stationed within the province were principally peditate and universally stationed along the arterial highways. Such a spatial distribution of infantry troops, if real, would demonstrate that the interior forts and their garrisons were primarily concerned with close observation and general policing duties. Together, the placement of the individual types of unit, therefore, might point to a stated aim at promoting security within the province, denying unauthorized entry and controlling internal movement.

While the measures taken for the security of Dacia were the most significant responsibility of the new governor, it is to be expected that its urbanization was more obviously the interest of the emperor. He, after all, gave the authority and provided from the *fiscus* the necessary monies for the creation of new towns and cities and the means for their successful administration. As it is, while the evidence for the urbanization of Dacia is even more circumstantial than for its military organization, it does suggest that a minimal approach was adopted. For example, while many of the sophisticated hill-top *oppida* within the kingdom were now abandoned, there is little evidence for the foundation of a commensurate number of new towns at lowland sites to accommodate their populations. In fact, only one is known for certain, Colonia (Ulpia Traiana Augusta) Dacica, a settlement founded solely for veteran legionaries. Even so, it quickly attracted the epithet Sarmizegethusa, doubtless to symbolize its status as the metropolis or chief city of the province.[24]

Located on the eastern side of the Iron Gates Pass, 18 miles (30km) west of Decebalus' now abandoned and levelled *Basileion*, the site chosen for Colonia Dacica had first been used for the fortress of the *Legio IIII Flavia Felix* during the First Dacian War. An inscription reveals that Scaurianus was responsible for founding the colony, and Ulpian tells us that it was awarded the *ius Italicum*.[25] As we have already seen, Scaurianus is known have been in office by 11 August 106, and another document manifests that he still held the duty on 2 July 110, which would signify that he was not replaced until the spring of 111 at the earliest.[26] A later date is possible, as the next known governor of Dacia is C. Avidius Nigrinus, appointed in the year 113 at the earliest.[27] In fact, a later date is probable. While Trajan did not generally allow any of his governors to exceed the usual term of three or at the most four years, the one exception he is known to have made was in the case of Arabia, where C. Claudius Severus, who had supervised the military occupation of the territory in 106/107, remained in office as governor until 115/116, presumably in order to supervise the installation of the Roman administrative machinery. Perhaps Scaurianus' commission was similarly extended for the same reason, which would therefore allow for the Colonia Dacica being founded any time between the years 106 and 111/113.[28]

Conversion of the site from a fortress into a civil settlement followed the standard practice of adapting or replacing the existing military buildings. Three sides of the upstanding earthen military defences were retained while the fourth was demolished to allow an extension on that side, a stone wall then being constructed around the entire 80-acre (32.5ha) area (Fig. 8).[29] Early inscriptions attest to the usual magistrates and civic priests, confirming the rapid establishment of an organized municipal élite and the social and political system it represented.[30] It was also provided from the start with suitable public buildings, for example a temple to the Imperial Cult, later known as the *aedes Augustalium*, while outside the city was an amphitheatre capable of holding 5,000 spectators.[31] This last structure formed the focus for a number of extramural shrines, the largest being for the worship of Aesculapius and Hygieia, the Greek deities of medicine and health. It was evidently a popular cult centre, for it contained a workshop where supplicants could purchase votaries, statues, lamps and religious dedications, and it even attracted a medical practitioner of Greek origin from Pergamum in Asia Minor, who went on to become a priest at the shrine.[32] Yet while the temple to Aesculapius and Hygieia was

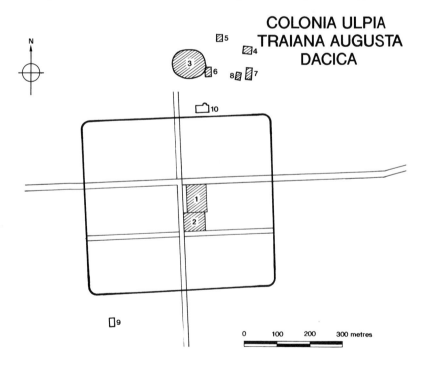

Fig. 8 Sarmizegethusa Ulpia

undoubtedly popular, it has produced far fewer sculptural representations than one of its neighbours, which was rather enigmatically dedicated to Liber Pater, an ancient Roman god associated with the vine, and assimilated with Dionysus-Bacchus, the Roman god of wine.[33] Now, the Carpathians are at the very limit of modern vine cultivation, the area around Suceava in the extreme north of modern Romania, for example, producing a somewhat sharp but wholesome white wine, and it may be that the temple reflects the Roman introduction of vine-growing to the area. Certainly, viticulture was practised in the general region in the later Roman period, as is demonstrated by a dedication to Liber Pater found in Pannonia Secunda, recording the planting of some 200 *iugera* (100 acres; 40.4ha) of grapes, and listing the names of at least four distinct varieties of wine produced on the estate.[34] That the quality of these northern wines might well have been disparaged by those at Rome, or even today's oenophile, is, in this context, irrelevant; what is important is the proof that Roman social fashions were quickly assimilated and even provided for locally by astute entrepreneurs.[35]

The odds are against Colonia Dacica being the only settlement of its type founded by Trajan in the new province. His practice elsewhere was to raise the number of *coloniae* to the equal number of legions the territory contained,[36] and as Dacia had two legions until the reign of Hadrian, a second Trajanic colony should be sought. Epigraphic evidence supplies the names of at least seven other Dacian *coloniae*, of which six – Drobeta, Napoca, Potaissa, Romula and the two successive foundations at Apulum – are demonstrably Hadrianic or later. The seventh, Malva, is undated, and thus putatively Trajanic, although it is nowhere recorded as a colony until the year 230. The city was certainly founded before that date, however, for before 168/169, when Dacia was sub-divided into three provinces, it gave its name to the third, Dacia Malvensis, the other two being named Dacia Porolissensis, after Porolissum, and Dacia Apulensis, after Apulum.

Nothing more is known about the origins or status of Malva for the quite simple reason that it has not yet been positively identified. As Dacia Porolissensis and Dacia Apulensis take up the whole of Transylvania, however, it can reasonably be assumed that Dacia Malvensis, and hence Malva, was south of the Carpathians, namely in Oltenia. As for Malva itself, it may be, as M. P. Speidel has argued, that the colony is to be equated with that town otherwise known as Romula, where a *Numerus Syrorum Malvensium* was later stationed, the suggestion being that the unit took its eponymous epithet from the town.[37] But there are cogent reasons for doubting the inference, in which case an alternative location might still be sought. Now, a clue for the settlement's whereabouts might be found in its name. Assuming it to be toponymic, it could derive from the pre-Celtic **mala*, for mountain, which would rule out a location in the centre of a plateau, but little else.[38] On the other hand, the cryptically named Castra Traiani, just south of the Red Tower Pass on the upper Olt, might have some connection, for the toponymic use of imperial *nomen* is usually associated with civil establishments rather than military sites. Might it be that Castra Traiani took its name from an adjacent chartered settlement which incorporated the emperor's *cognomen* in its title – perhaps Colonia Malva Traiana?[39] The site is, after all, overlooked by the nearby Capatinei mountain range. It is freely admitted that there is nothing whatsoever to support this tentative proposal – except that it is one explanation for the origin of the fort's appellation. And its location, on a major arterial route from Moesia Inferior, fits the requirement for such a major civil settlement to be located on a principal highway, matching that of Colonia Dacica, built on the main road from Moesia Superior.[40]

No other urban foundations in Dacia can certainly be assigned to the period of Trajan, although Hadrian granted the title and rank of *municipium* to the settlements at Drobeta and Napoca, which suggests they should represent *civitates peregrinae* first established during Trajan's reign. By the reign of Severus, both had been advanced to colonial status, as were the post-Hadrianic municipal foundations of Apulum, Potaissa and Romula, while Ampelum, Dierna, Porolissum and Tibiscum had been made *municipia* in their turn. In each case, however, the gradual change in the legal status of these communities indicates a slow if certain climb in prosperity, rather than a strong centralized influence on urban development and the immediate and profitable exploitation of the territory. More significantly, none of these settlements, with the possible exception of Porolissum, seem to have developed from existing native communities, although the dearth of evidence concerning their origins does not rule it out. Instead all but one of them apparently owe their origin to the tendency for retired auxiliaries and legionaries – already Roman citizens all – to inhabit the *vici* and *canabae* which sprang up adjacent to their former stations; the single exception is Ampelum, the gold-mining community in the west of the province, administered by imperial procurators. True, many of these towns have names derived from the Geto-Dacian language, but this is probably of little relevance in this context. Local names for topographical features, even if freely adopted by alien colonists, indicate nothing more than the presence of a few aborigines able to pass them on to any who asked. As with so many names of Indian origin on the eastern seaboard of the United States of America (Manhattan, Chappaquiddick), they hardly even attest to the existence, never mind the survival, of permanent indigenous settlements left in place after conquest and consolidation.[41]

Superficially, therefore, it would seem that in Dacia, Rome was slow in establishing the formal civic institutions which constituted a functioning province. This cannot have resulted from the territory being of marginal economic significance, for Dacia was a thriving kingdom before the conquest, and there is every reason to believe that Rome quickly exploited the gold and silver mines in the west of the province. Nor can it be explained by the lack of an existing social structure which could be adapted to Roman needs, as Dacia had a defined hierarchy living in settled communities until the conquest of 106. From this it might be concluded that the relative lack of an urban structure in Dacia results from a combination of two things: an underdeveloped economy which never advanced beyond a subsistence level for most of the population, and the absence of an indigenous élite ready and capable of adapting to the machinery of Roman administration and the realities of a stratified social system. Such a conclusion is seemingly reinforced by a statement of Eutropius, who notes that a decade after the conquest, when Hadrian allegedly considered abandoning Dacia, he was dissuaded from doing so on the grounds that

> so many Roman citizens resident there would be left at the mercy of the barbarians; for Trajan, after his victory, had transferred thereto an enormous number of people from all over the Roman world in order to [re-] establish agrarian and urban life on a firm footing, as Dacia, through the two wars against Decebalus, had totally exhausted its manpower.[42]

Many have considered Eutropius' observation to be an exaggeration. This is to deny the documented dispatch to Rome of as many as 50,000 Dacian prisoners, several thousand, perhaps 10,000, to fight and be slaughtered as gladiators, never mind the losses incurred in combat during the two wars.[43] Added to which, a significant number of the able-bodied survivors were enrolled into auxiliary units before the decade was out. Documents attest to the existence of at least one Dacian *ala* and a mounted *numerus*, and at least six Dacian *cohortes*, one of which (if not more) was raised to milliary status by Hadrian, and sent to garrison the north of Britain.[44] These were probably raised by conscription from among the surviving population. While it was traditional for the *auxiliaries* to be constituted from volunteers within the provinces, or from non-provincials provided by treaty obligations, there is substantive evidence that the levy and forced conscription were often resorted to during this period, when few heeded the call to arms.[45]

Yet, assorted Dacian-type artefacts continued to be made and used to a significant extent in the aboriginal and Roman settlements of Dacia in the post-conquest period, which suggests some degree of survival among the native population.[46] Indeed, the mid-second century *Geography* of Ptolemy lists no fewer than twelve tribes with Geto-Dacian names.[47] But what does seem to be missing in this period is a native aristocracy. For example, of the named élite at Napoca whose origins can be verified, a quarter are evidently immigrant citizens who received the franchise before Trajan's rule, while other immigrants within the province include Galatians (at Napoca), Syrians (at Colonia Dacica and Apulum) and Illyrians (at the gold mines of Alburnus Minor and Ampelum). Of greater significance is the marked tendency for Dacian provincials – none of recognizably Geto-Dacian origin – to hold municipal office in more than one city. It would confirm that there was a fairly small governing élite which easily accumulated civic honours. The failure of native Dacians to appear among this group cannot be simply attributed to their backwardness: as we have seen, there was a highly stratified social structure in pre-Roman times. It is surely symbolic of an absence of a native aristocracy in the newly formed province.[48]

The evidence for rural settlement might seem to confirm this rather grim picture. For a start, there are comparatively few Roman-style villas in the countryside, and those that exist are remarkably modest and poorly appointed when compared with equivalent structures in other Danubian provinces.[49] It may be that they were principally used by bailiffs for non-residential owners, responsible for managing comparatively small estates. These might well have been exploited as vineyards (hence the obsession with Liber Pater at Colonia Dacica), which gave the surest and quickest cash return on any investment and required minimal labour most of the year, although a large work-force was required during the harvest. But, however they were worked, the comparative rarity of any subsidiary rural settlements, whether or not of native character, points to both a lack of habitation and an underdeveloped economy, in which case, whatever rural population there was lived at subsistence level.

Then there is other testimony which points to large parts of the province being expropriated as imperial estates. Inscriptions reveal that the gold-mines, for example, were imperial property, as is to be expected, as were the iron-workings. In addition, the emperor owned extensive areas of rich pasture lands and salt-pans, sublet for grazing and exploitation to others. Now, most of the inscriptions relating to these properties belong to a later period. But both Trajan and Hadrian, and most of their successors, generally favoured the use of the Mancian Law to dismember imperial estates in aid of the indigenous population, rather than consolidating large tracts of agricultural land for their own purpose. Consequently, it is reasonable to assume that the imperial lands in Dacia were established upon a *tabula rasa* early in the province's history, and remained imperial owing to the lack of a viable population to work them in their own name.

More significant in this respect is the question of language survival. The late President Nicolae Ceausescu made a virtue of advertising how the people of Romania formed a tenacious Latin-speaking island in an ocean of Slavonic peoples. In fact, a modern tourist with a good knowledge of spoken Italian and Spanish can communicate on a basic level with remarkable ease in even the most isolated of Transylvanian villages. While it is true that nineteenth-century and later nationalists were responsible for reintroducing many Latin loan-words into 'modern' Romania, in order to assert their independent ethnicity from their Slav and Magyar neighbours and former rulers, the high proportion of existing Latin cognates in the language is proof of a remarkable degree of linguistic stability. Amazingly so, given that Dacia was only within the Roman hegemony for two hundred years. In that short time, the local language of the original population had entirely disappeared to be replaced by Latin, the language of social rank and officialdom. As such, despite the existence of many Slavic cognates in Romanian, it stands comparison with the Romance-speaking areas of western continental Europe, all subject to direct Roman rule for more than twice as long. By contrast there is Britain, occupied by Rome for some three hundred and fifty years, and where the Latin element in modern English – and much of Gaelic, Welsh and Cornish, for that matter – is almost entirely medieval in origin, and derived from Norman French at that. Now the population of Britannia never seems to have been converted *en masse* to the use of Latin, and the language as used in the province was particularly archaic, with few exchanges between the introduced and the native language, which, *pace* J. C. Mann, could indicate a lack of everyday use.[50] For the lower classes of Britannia, the British language remained the common means of communication. Surviving the Roman occupation, it has been maintained to a greater or lesser degree in outlying highland areas, despite the imposition and assimilation of other official languages – 'Anglo-Saxon' and Norman French – on the lowland part of the island. It even survived emigration to France, where Breton remains the language of choice in the north-west. The apparent dominance and subsequent vigorous development of Latin in Dacia, on the other hand, would indicate a radical conversion to its everyday use, and a near-complete replacement of the local Geto-Dacian. This in turn is prima facie evidence for the complete loss or suppression of the local culture and a lack of political or social will for its maintenance. It might also attest just as surely to the effective displacement of large numbers of the indigenous population by Latin-speaking immigrants, corroborating the documentary evidence already adduced that the process of conquest had considerably reduced the size of the aboriginal community.

Arabia

Arabia, by contrast with Dacia, came to Rome as part of a logical expansion of her hegemony rather than through forced acquisition for reasons of security. It was formed out of Nabataea, a realm centred on what is today the Hashemite Kingdom of Jordan, but which also encompassed the Sinai and Negev in the north-west, and the al-Hijaz mountains and the Hisma and an-Nafud deserts of the north-western Arabian peninsula in the south-east (Fig. 9).[51] The Nabataeans were originally pastoral nomads of Semitic origin. They first enter the historical record in 312 BC, in which year the Levantine Greeks attempted to take control of their principal centre, Petra – 'The Rock' – already an important emporium for the traffic in frankincense and myrrh. Thwarted by its natural defences, and the cunning of the menfolk in dispersing themselves and their livestock into the remote bulwarks and canyons of the sandstone plateau where it is located, the frustrated hoplites instead vented their wrath on the Nabataean women and children, but never again seriously sought their submission.[52]

By the end of the first century AD, a part of the people had become sedentary, with a recognized king and an established legal system and constitution, and lived in conditions of luxury, especially at Petra (Wadi Musa, Jordan).[53] What brought about the change was an accident of geography: Nabataea occupied the crossroads between Africa and Mesopotamia, and Arabia and the Mediterranean. To begin with, the Nabataean territory straddled the Eastern Rift Valley, the only conduit for trans-Levantine contact, and until comparatively recently the richest and most important trade route in the region.[54] The late Roman (and modern) terminus was Aila, now 'Aqaba (Jordan), at the head of the eponymous Gulf, but in earlier times the trail extended along the south side of the Gulf by way of Haql' and el-Bad' to Leuke Kome, 'the White Village', an unlocated haven on the eastern shores of the Red Sea, thought to be located in the vicinity of Aynunah (Saudi Arabia).[55] At this time, Leuke Kome was an important entrepôt for the aromatic perfumes and incense brought from the Sabaeans of Arabia Felix (modern Saudi Arabia and the Yemen) as well as all manner of goods from India, and contained a customs station where the Nabataeans exacted a 25 per cent *portarium*.[56] From Leuke Kome, cargoes were transported to Aila by water or land, and then carried north on the trans-Levantine trail along the eastern rim of Wadi 'Araba, the edge of the Jordanian pre-desert, to the emporium at Petra, the marshy conditions of the Wadi 'Araba hampering use of the valley itself. The trail then continued to Bostra, and thence east of the Lebanon across the forbidding el-Leja' lava plateau and the stony treeless plains to the oasis of Efca and finally Palmyra (Tadmor, Syria), the 'City of Palms'. Already legendary for its wealth, Palmyra was the goal for traders on the Silk Road from China, and was the single most important trading centre of the northern Levant.[57]

Petra and Bostra grew rich from being situated at important road junctions where west–east itineraries met the trans-Levantine trail. One of these, the western trans-Arabian route was the overland trail from Arabia Felix. It ran across the sandstone plateau of the Hejaz and the Hisma on its west, then along the valleys leading to the Nabataean centre of Hegra (Mada'in Salih) and Wadi al-Saba', and then through Wadi Rumm and Ma'an on the Shara' to meet the King's Highway just east of Petra. Then there was the trans-Negev route, which brought Egyptian traders to Petra from the Mediterranean ports of Rhinocolura (el-'Arish, Egypt) and Gaza, by way of Elusa (Bar Mashash) and the icy waters of the en-Avdat oasis and the adjacent hill-top city of Oboda ('Avdat). From here, the road continued across the Makhtesh Raman of the central Negev, an area of bare rocky sandstone peaks and plateau, to the lower Nahal Paran, where it was possible to cross Wadi 'Araba to Petra. This last was evidently a popular route: the correspondence of Julius

Apollinaris reveals that in early 107 it was in regular use by Egyptian traders from Pelusium, at the north-eastern head of the Nile delta.[58] Bostra (Busra ash-Shaam, Syria) was equally fortunate in its location. Situated half-way between Petra and Palmyra, it commanded one of the exits from Wadi as-Sirhan, the final section of the eastern trans-Arabia trade route used by traders carrying spices from India via the Persian Gulf or incense from Oman. From Bostra they could then enter the Decapolis; or move north or south along the trans-Levantine trail; or continue to the west, along Wadi Yarmuk to Tiberias and thence to the Mediterranean port of Ptolemais (Akko, Israel).

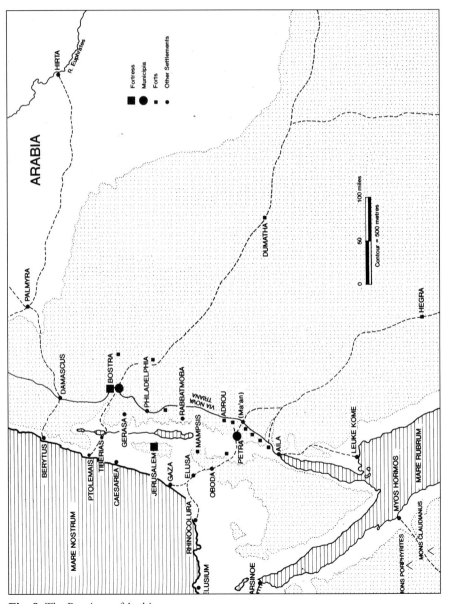

Fig. 9 The Province of Arabia

Rome first came into direct contact with the Nabataean kingdom in 64 BC, when Pompey annexed Syria after the collapse of the Seleucid dynasty. Two years later, his deputy Aemilius Scaurus led an expeditionary force against Nabataea, but it could not contend with the arid and desolate landscape, and he eventually sought peace terms. Despite their 'victory', the episode probably resulted in the Nabataeans entering into a client relationship with Rome, as 300 talents of silver were paid to Scaurus as part of the accord and Pompey was to claim Arabia among his conquests.[59] Later, during the triumvirate, Antony felt empowered to cede a part of Nabataea to Cleopatra, presumably the Gulf of 'Aqaba and the adjacent territory.[60] In c. 26 BC, Augustus, through the agency of Aelius Gallus, tried to monopolize the overland trade from Arabia Felix, an enterprise which ended in ignominious failure in the wasteland of the Hisma, leaving the Nabataeans in unchallenged command of the region and its hazardous trade routes.[61] In 9 BC, however, Rome directly intervened in the affairs of the domain by ratifying Aretas IV Philopatris – 'lover of his people' – as king, and five years later, briefly incorporated the territory during the troubled period that followed the death of Herod of Judaea. Taken together, these two episodes confirm that the kingdom was by now an established Roman client-state, and only the combination of Tiberius' reluctance to expand the empire and then his inopportune death prevented its formal annexation.[62]

It was during the benevolent rule of Aretas IV that Nabataea blossomed and reached a level of unprecedented prosperity and growth.[63] At this time it was taking a large share in the trade between the Orient and Rome, and a significant amount of the taxes paid by traders on this route must have got into the Nabataean coffers.[64] The principal urban centres of Petra and Bostra assumed their final Nabataean appearance now, as the architectural tastes of the Hellenistic and Roman world were adopted and glorified in such monuments as, at Petra, the Qasr el-Bint temple, the theatre, and the el-Deir and el-Khazneh tomb façades; and at Bostra, the twin commemorative arches and, probably, the theatre.[65] Comparable grandeur no doubt existed at other Nabataean centres, for example Oboda, Mampsis (Kurnub) and Hegra. Prosperity continued under Aretas' successor, Rabbel II, during whose reign the royal residence may well have been transferred to Bostra.[66]

Coincidentally, Rome became a more obvious and ominous neighbour. In 92/93, Domitian extended the boundaries of Syria into the Trachonitis, that roughly triangular area bounded by the Anti-Lebanon and the Jordan valley to the north-west, deserts and the Jabel ad-Duruz mountains to the east, and the black basalt plain of the Hauran to the south.[67] As a result, the Nabataean kingdom now manifested a topographical and administrative anomaly, forming the sole gap in Rome's direct command of the Mediterranean littoral and the pre-desert hinterland. Even so, the kingdom was allowed to retain its quasi-autonomy for another twelve years. Client-kingdoms were, after all, considered to be unincorporated extensions of the empire, their kings ruling by dispensation.[68] While the favour could be withdrawn at any time, the status quo usually lasted until there was a perceived weakness in native control, as when dynastic succession was in dispute; or where a more direct regulation was considered necessary, usually for military and administrative reasons.

According to Dio, Trajan decided to appropriate the kingdom at about the time the Second Dacian War was coming to an end, which allows for either 106 or early 107:

although 105, or early 106 at the latest, seems the more likely.[69] His reasons are nowhere stated and are probably unknowable.[70] On the face of it, the annexation does not seem to have been brought about by any obvious problems in the succession, as King Rabbel II may have had a son, by the name of Obodas. Yet while the event was commemorated with coins bearing the legend *ARAB(ia) ADQ(uisita)* – 'Arabia gained [for the empire]' – as if to convey the impression that the process was essentially peaceful, there are allusions to a 'Nabataean war' which might suggest an element of forcible persuasion. Dio, for example, in the single direct documentary reference to the event, claims that land was 'subjugated'. The suspicion of some conflict is somewhat reinforced by the knowledge that A. Cornelius Palma, governor of Syria, earned triumphal insignia and a statue in the Forum Augusti for his part in the operation, and also from the apparent secrecy which surrounded the episode, the commemorative coins not being issued until some four years *post eventum*.[71] Yet whatever military action was required, it could not have been serious, as Trajan did not adopt the *agnomen* 'Arabicus'.

In the absence of any direct evidence, further speculation as to Trajan's motive for annexation, and the failure to mark it at the time, is pointless. But whatever the circumstances, Arabia was formally recognized as a province in the course of 107, a fact supplied by provincial inscriptions and documents, even if it was not proclaimed publicly on the Roman coinage for at least another four years.[72] The first governor was the praetorian C. Claudius Severus, simultaneously *legatus* of the province and its sole legion, the *legio III Cyrenaica*, now detached from its base in Egypt.[73] From the correspondence of Julius Apollinaris, *librarius* – 'secretary' – in the *III Cyrenaica*, we learn of his involvement in military building projects at the very beginning of the Roman occupation. These can hardly be anything other than the construction of a network of forts to control the new province, notwithstanding that the garrison might at first have usurped existing Nabataean strongholds for the purpose. At any rate, the correspondence demonstrates that some time before 26 March 107, legionaries were cutting stone in the southern part of the province, somewhere in the vicinity of Petra, and perhaps for the nearby military installation of Adrou (Udhruh), a site claimed as Trajanic in origin.[74] By the time Apollinaris wrote the letter, however, he had transferred to Bostra, where a legionary fortress, presumably the base for the *III Cyrenaica*, has been identified on the north side of the known ancient settlement.[75]

It has been cogently argued that in addition to the *III Cyrenaica* there were perhaps as many as twelve auxiliary units in the original garrison, among them an *ala dromedariorum* (a unit of camel-scouts) and the *ala Veterana Gaetulorum*; at least two equitate units (*cohortes I Augusta Thracum* and *I Augusta Canathenorum*); and one milliary and three quingenary regiments (*I Thracum milliaria, I Hispanorum, VI Hispanorum* and *I Thebaeorum*).[76] This list provides for an auxiliary garrison of some four and a half thousand, marginally below the paper strength of the legion, hence the belief that other units remain to be identified. It is possible that existing Nabataean militia units were now absorbed into the Roman army, making up the apparent shortfall. How they might have been distributed, however, is unknown. Apart from the putative Trajanic sites at Adrou and Bostra, nothing is known concerning Trajan's arrangements for the security of the province, as military remains of the period have proved extremely difficult to identify on the ground. Then the documentary evidence for the activities of the known units themselves is ambiguous. The two *alae*, for example, are both known to have operated in the vicinity of Hegra (Mada'in Salih) in the Hijaz, the most southerly Roman frontier post so far recorded, but the *ala Veterana* is also known to have spent some time at Gerasa (Jerash), perhaps its principal base.[77] On the basis of one document in the Babatha archive, another if not the same *ala* can be postulated at Rabbathmoba, the capital of Moab, the district east of the Dead Sea, although this reference is fixed to 127 and need not be relevant to the matter in question.[78] Likewise, a (probably) early-second-century gravestone recording a soldier of the *cohors I Augusta Thracum* at Mampsis in the Negev need not prove the unit was stationed at the site. Consequently, when set against the almost complete absence of military structures assignable to this period, there has understandably been an over-readiness to dismiss the slim body of evidence which can be assembled for the early military arrangements in the province.[79] This is to ignore the fact that bases should exist for at least the two auxiliary units certainly attested here in Trajanic times, and that the fleet which Trajan established in the western 'Red Sea', presumably based at Aila or Leuke Kome, could not have functioned in isolation.[80] In fact, it remains true that there has still been far too little fieldwork and even less excavation in the Jordanian pre-desert, which allows for the postulate that, as at Adrou, early fort-sites might yet lie concealed beneath the better-known but little investigated debris of later *castra*.

In the absence of firm evidence for the distribution of the early garrison, the most conspicuous feature relating to the province's early history has to be the via Nova Traiana, which links Aila and the Red Sea to the Trachonitis. It was begun in the year 111 under the direction of Claudius Severus, and milestones along it record how the route was opened and surfaced 'from the border of Syria to the Red Sea' after Arabia had been 'received and formed into a province' (Pl. 12A).[81] It seems unlikely that a north–south road needed to be cut and paved on the edge of the pre-desert solely for everyday communications and trade. In the first place, a paved road was anathema for that principal beast of burden, the camel, whose feet would slip on the exposed stone. Roman horses too were generally unshod. Then, if the main purpose of the road was simply communications, the Roman skill at engineering would have allowed it to be built along the comparatively level bottom of the marshy Wadi 'Araba, the course followed by the modern road between 'Aqaba and Safi. Instead, the via Nova adapted the existing trans-Levantine caravan-trail, the King's Highway, as it became known, providing a fixed line which could be easily patrolled on foot and which facilitated the use of (Roman) wheeled traffic between the individual communities along its route, many of which would have some form of official and military presence. Climbing a series of ridges and crossing bare plateau to form what is still the main north–south thoroughfare in the Middle East, it is the single most conspicuous monument in the region to the manifest destiny of Rome.[82]

As we have already seen, while roads in themselves do not constitute a frontier or military installation, they do allow for the control of any groups moving along or across it. This is why in other regions of the Roman empire they often formed the backbone of a flexible military system specifically designed to control the movement of nomadic societies. The Stanegate in Britain is a good example, as is the road along the western bank of the Olt in Dacia.[83] This may have been the reason for Trajan's via Nova ignoring the lower Wadi 'Araba in favour of the edge of the pre-desert. The line chosen corresponds with the eastern limit of sedentary occupation, and – in the north, at least – with the 100–250mm isohyet line of precipitation, the zone where there was just sufficient water to guarantee the continuance of existing sedentary farming.[84] The coincidence is unlikely to have been accidental, and it may be that the alignment was deliberately decided upon to assist in controlling the east–west passage of seasonal pastoralists, as they migrated from desert to sown. Certainly, the modern replacement of the via Nova is used much in this way today, the Royal Jordanian Police maintaining isolated stations to the east on the natural west–east seasonal trails, such as Wadi Rumm, to supervise the movement of Bedouin semi-nomads. The posts are designed and situated not so much as to resist or control the threat of raiding as to prevent smuggling between Jordan and Saudi Arabia, and to ensure that the appropriate levies are paid on goods coming in and out of the country, and that the Bedouin fulfil their taxation obligations to central government. Human nature rarely changes, even if rulers do, and it is known that from at least the mid-second century, the Romans – following the earlier practice of the Nabataeans – maintained a similar apparatus in the pre-desert, presumably for the same reason, rather than simply for defence, as often assumed.[85] Some of these later bases were situated a considerable way in advance of the main arterial route: both Hegra, in the Hijaz, and Dumatha (al-Jawf/Dumat), in Wadi Sirhan, are not less than 300 miles (482km) southeast of the via Nova. The known sites seem to be Antonine, but they may well have Trajanic predecessors. In which case, it would seem possible that the via Nova may have provided the effective *limes* (in the sense of a formal 'boundary') to the province, and it is at least plausible that from the first it was intended to provide the baseline for an outer shield of military installations, mainly concerned with police activities.[86]

By contrast with the lack of material proof for the initial military organization of the Arabia, physical evidence for its urban development is comparatively plentiful, even if individual chronologies are not always as secure as might be wished.[87] To begin with, it should be remembered that the Nabataean kingdom was already significantly urbanized before the Roman annexation.[88] Despite that, the change in the kingdom's status seems to have resulted in certain immediate major changes to the urban infrastructure at a number of sites. At Petra, for example, the Colonnaded Street, in its present form, is probably a Trajanic innovation (Pl. 12B). That, at least, might be deduced from the triumphal arch erected in the year 114 at the entrance to the so-called Upper Market; as this would appear to be contiguous with the adjacent buildings, it implies that the entire complex of structures on the south side of the Colonnaded Street is of like date.[89] Of greater significance, however, is the Greek inscription carried on the arch, for it records that Trajan elevated Petra to the status of *metropolis Arabia* – 'mother city of Arabia' – and the change in name is likely to reflect a change in the city's administration.[90] At any rate, by the year 124, Petra had a recognizable Greek city-constitution, with a council which issued public acts, and the grant may have included certain Latin rights equivalent to a *municipium*, given Petra's later elevation to the rank of *colonia*.[91]

Yet despite Petra's new dignity, other evidence would counsel that the city had already lost its privileged position as principal Nabataean centre to Bostra. This is implicit in the Madaba tomb inscription of 110, which records (in Nabataean) that it was erected in the 'third year of the province [of] Bostra'.[92] Now, F. Millar would urge caution on using this item as proof that the administrative centre for the territory had been relocated: yet as he notes, it does 'reflect a consciousness that [Bostra] was where the main Roman base was'.[93] Bostra was, after all, where the single legion in Arabia was stationed, and it follows, therefore, that it was also the *de facto* headquarters for the province's governor and his gubernatorial offices. One might expect this to be reflected in the subsequent development of the town, especially as coins and inscriptions reveal it to have been renamed Nova Traiana Bostra, putative testimony for direct imperial stimulation in the establishment of nothing less than a new town.[94] The very limited evidence of urban topography does, in fact, suggest that a new city – presumably the self-same Nova Traiana Bostra – was initiated by Trajan to the west of the existing Nabataean settlement, itself now buried beneath the modern Arab town.[95] It was formed around a semi-regular street-grid, the precise alignments being conditioned to a certain extent by the existing roads leading from the Nabataean town, and the principal axial streets, lined with shops and warehouses built in a plain and functional style, were both colonnaded, an architectural design newly introduced into the province (Fig. 10). A large open-plan building, which appears to have served a marketing and administrative function, stood to one side of their intersection, and south of it was a large bath-house. Two other public buildings might just belong to the same period, the so-called *naumachia* and the hippodrome. If so, they would suggest direct imperial intervention, but they are likely to belong to a later date, as comparable structures in the region seem generally to belong to the late Antonine revival.[96] None the less, the structural evidence for a planned Trajanic city at Bostra, together with the documented evidence for its name, suggests that Nova Bostra was given a Roman constitution, presumably as a *municipium*, as might be reflected in its award of colonial status towards the end of the second century.[97]

Other possible changes in the urban infrastructure of the new province are less clear, although there is proof of some radical reorganization of the new territory. For example, it seems that at least two cities of the former Decapolis were now ceded from Syria to Arabia, Philadelphia (Amman) and Gerasa (Jerash).[98] Little is known of Philadelphia, buried as it is beneath the modern city of Amman.[99] It may well have already been highly Hellenized by the time of Trajan, for it issued its own coinage until its formal annexation by Rome. During that period and later, the place is frequently named in Greek inscriptions as 'Philadelphia of Coele Syria', which suggests it retained its own constitution as a *civitas libera*, although the right to its own coinage does not seem to have been restored until the time of Hadrian. That the city attained some degree of prosperity, however, is certified by the substantial theatre and other public buildings erected in the course of the second and third centuries AD, which at the very least attests to a thriving community in the immediately preceding period. Gerasa, by comparison with Philadelphia, is well explored.[100] The visible city plan seems to be a product of the early first century AD, thus before Roman domination, and excavation and inscriptions show a steady improvement in urban facilities culminating in the later second century, when the more substantial public buildings were constructed. Like Philadelphia, it had its own coinage before and after the Trajanic period, which suggests that a Greek constitution was retained at this date, and that it too was considered a 'free community'.

The urban centres of Arabia, therefore, reflect a mixture of Roman imposition and Hellenistic continuity. The vigour with which Petra and Bostra were redeveloped and the steadily growing prosperity of Gerasa and, perhaps, Philadelphia might be contrasted with the apparent decline in rural settlements east of the via Nova.[101] This could have resulted from a variety of factors, the most extreme of which would either be climatic change (specifically drought conditions), forcing movement of groups living in marginal catchment areas; or official intervention, the resettlement of the population within an artificially created administrative network for purposes of control, taxation, and so on.[102] Alternatively, it could symbolize the successful Romanization of a province as defined by Strabo, in that the development of the urban centres encouraged the movement of isolated rural populations into the territories surrounding them. Further work needs to be done before any judgement can be made.

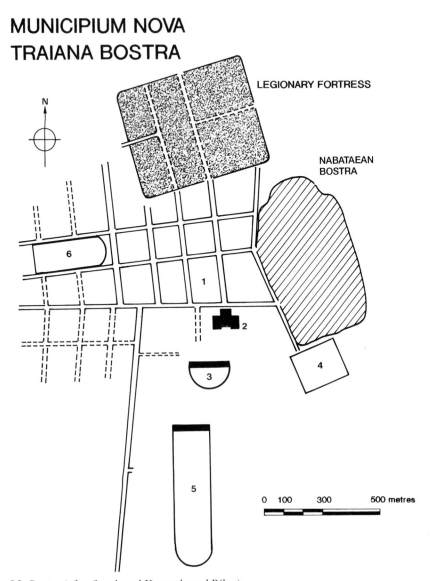

Fig. 10 Bostra (after Segal, and Kennedy and Riley)

That said, more substantive evidence for the effect of annexation on the population, both rural and urban, is supplied by a military diploma of the year 139. It records the discharge of veterans from a number of units, including the *cohortes IV* and *VI Ulpia Petraeorum*, after the usual twenty-five years' service.[103] The implication is that at least six new auxiliary units were raised in the province sometime before 114. They may have been formed for a specific purpose, namely Trajan's forthcoming invasion of Parthia, although an earlier mobilization cannot be discounted. Even so, while each regiment was probably formed around a nucleus of experienced troops seconded from other *cohortes*, a substantial number of recruits must have been required to bring them to full strength.

As it is, the most vivid demonstration of the changes brought about by the incorporation of Nabataea into the Roman hegemony is contained in the Babatha archive. This series of documents, hidden in a cave in the Negev around the year 132 and not recovered by their eponymous owner, contains a wealth of information pertaining to the legal and administrative framework of the newly constituted province. For example, they reveal that by 127, the inhabitants of Nabataea were liable to the Roman census and direct taxation, and it has been inferred that this was the third taken on a ten-year cycle since the province was incorporated in 107.[104] Some idea of the potential revenue it may have brought to Rome might be extrapolated from the case of Commagene, a not especially rich province, if of comparable size, which over a twenty-year period paid some *HS* 5,000,000 in taxes and tributes to Rome, an average of *HS* 250,000 each year.[105]

Of greater significance, however, is that the Babatha archive would seem to confirm a statement of Ammianus Marcellinus, that Trajan ordered the people of Arabia to follow the Roman legal system from the date of their annexation, even if certain adaptations were made to accommodate local practices, as, indeed, was usual.[106] For example, the first four documents, which pre-date the Roman annexation, are in Nabataean, and reveal the existence of an already sophisticated legal system within the kingdom. The next series of documents belong to the period 110–24, and use a combination of dating systems, consular, imperial and provincial, mute recognition of the new political reality. Broadly speaking, they can be divided into two distinct groups according to their content and language: those concerning private transactions are generally written in Aramaic; while those relating to public settlements tend to be in Greek – and at that are apparently direct transcriptions of documents originally written in either Nabataean or Aramaic. The choice of language for the different class of documents, private or public, can only reflect a clear acceptance of the new status of the territory and the formal acceptance of Roman institutions and legal forms in public matters. So does the use of the relevant Aramaic or Greek equivalent of Roman provincial titles where this is required. From the year 124 onwards, however, whether public or private, the entire archive is in Greek, several of the documents evidently being official translations from Aramaic originals, and in one case from Latin, thus registering that Greek had replaced any of the local Semitic dialects as the established means of legal communication in the province. Coincidentally, although graffiti in Nabataean script are found in later contexts throughout the region, the use of the name 'Nabataean' as a means of identifying the ethnic origin of the people in Arabia almost disappears from the epigraphic record. At the very least, this suggests that there was a total assimilation of the new reality by the literate classes throughout *Provincia Arabia*.[107]

Trajan's 'provincial policy', therefore, as expressed in Dacia and Arabia, would seem to conform to what is known about the nature of early Roman imperialism. Essentially less centralized than is often supposed, it relied upon the adaptation of existing autonomous societies to administer their own territories under the overall control of Roman officials. Direct intervention was limited to what was necessary to establish the underlying basis of 'Romanization', the *civitas* or *polis*. Thus, where an existing urban élite could be conditioned to conform with the interests of Rome, this was done; where not, immigration was encouraged, as was veteran settlement. All that the central authority then needed to do was to provide the indispensable infrastructure, through founding planned towns; and a sufficient military presence to ensure compliance and political security, by controlling the borders and the interior. What it did not do, as the studies of K. Hopkins and M. Millet in particular have shown, was to encourage any systematic economic exploitation of the provinces, and their productive power remained in the main unchanged.

XIII

PARTHICUS [1]

On 1 January 112, Trajan took his sixth and final consulship. He shared the curule chair with T. Sextius Africanus, an otherwise undistinguished patrician, probably the son of the equally obscure T. Sextius Magius Lateranus, ordinary consul in the year 94, and grandson of the otherwise unknown homonymous who was an Arval Brother in the reign of Nero. Why this seemingly colourless individual was chosen at this time is not at all clear, except that he is likely to have been a favourite of Trajan's, for the year opened with a series of celebrations to mark the quindecennalia of the emperor's accession.

The festivities began the same day that Trajan and Africanus took office, with the formal dedication by the emperor of the Forum and Basilica built in his name.[2] Then, on 28 January, the anniversary of his succession, Trajan inaugurated fifteen days of extraordinary *ludi* in the '*theatris tribus*', and on 1 March, the senate and Equestrian Orders jointly commissioned thirty races at the Circus in his honour.[3] Before 29 August, Plotina and Marciana, wife and sister of the *imperator*, had coins issued in their own right. Both are now officially signalled with the epithet *Augusta* that Pliny had so earnestly asked for in his *actio gratiarum*, directly associating them with the *auctoritas* and *dignitas* of the *imperator*, and subtly stressing the emergence of a dynastic principle.[4] The dynastic theme is advertised on the coins themselves. Plotina is shown with Genius and Vesta, symbolic of the imperial hearth and household, and the altar of Pudicitia, which she apparently restored, the embodiment of modesty and virtue; Marciana is shown with her daughter, Salonia Matidia, also entitled *Augusta*, and her two granddaughters, Vibia Sabina, wife to Hadrian, and her spinster sister, Mindia Matidia.[5] The coins were released into circulation towards the end of 111 as part of a new series in which the name of Nerva is dropped from Trajan's titulature, allowing his triumphal *agnomina* of *Germanicus* and *Dacicus* to be given greater prominence. Many of the reverses used in the new coinage repeat the general theme of earlier issues, but a few new varieties appear, notably those commemorating the dedication of the Forum and Basilica, and two distinct types which commemorate earlier events in Trajan's reign not previously dignified in this way, namely the acquisition of Arabia in 106 and the completion of the via Traiana in 108/109.[6]

These new coin-types convey the general sense of festivities and celebration appropriate for Trajan's quindecennalia. Allied to them, and in the same mintage, are others which commemorated Trajan's deification of his father, Ulpius Traianus, *triumphator* over the Parthians when governor of Syria, one showing his bare-headed bust facing that of the laurel-wreathed Nerva, the two signalled as *DIVI NERVA ET TRAIANVS PAT(er)*.[7] A fourth type, belonging to the identical issue, is more enigmatic: it is that of *FORT(una) RED(ux)* – 'May Fortuna return you [safely]' – presumably heralding an impending imperial journey overseas.[8] It is natural to associate it with more ominous reverse-types of the same period, all usually held to be harbingers of war: Mars, with his spear and trophy; eagles and legionary standards; Victory, and a representation of the great equestrian statue in the recently dedicated Forum, showing the emperor trampling upon his vanquished enemies. They in their turn are doubtless to be associated with the documented departure about now of the emperor's cousin Hadrian – then in his mid-thirties – to the eastern provinces, perhaps as governor of Syria, on what might have been a commission connected with making logistical preparations for a potential campaign.

Hadrian's appointment to such an assignment is substantiated by a single documentary source, which expressly notes that he was assigned to Syria with the responsibility of 'preparing for the Parthian War', presumably reconnaissance and logistical matters.[9] It does not indicate precisely when or why Hadrian was nominated to the task, although as direct hostilities with Parthia commenced in the spring of 114, preparations must have begun the previous year at the very latest. His departure from Italy in the autumn of 111, however, can be deduced from his election as eponymous archon of Athens that winter.[10] Only five or so Roman citizens had been thus distinguished in the two hundred years Athens had been under Rome's dominion, and all except one were almost certainly of Greek origin and domicile, the exception being the emperor Domitian, who took the title *in absentia* through imperial prerogative. Consequently, it is legitimate to infer that the decision to honour Hadrian testifies to his presence in the city and to the high status that accrued to him, perhaps to his being in the province as the emperor's representative, that is, on imperial duty. In which case, it might not be simple coincidence that the via Egnatia, the principal overland route from Italy to the eastern provinces via the Greco-Balkan peninsula, was ordered to be restored during the course of 112.[11]

But whether or nor Trajan had indeed sent Hadrian east as early as the year 111 to pre-pare for war with Parthia, it certainly seems reasonable to infer from his coinage that he had intended on such a campaign by 112. It was finally occasioned, we are told, by the intervention of the Parthian 'king of kings' into the Armenian succession, the very matter which had first brought the two powers into conflict during the Triumvirate.[12] Under terms negotiated by Augustus and reaffirmed by Nero, it had been accepted that the ruler of Armenia was to be nominated by Parthia, but Rome alone had the power to approve the choice and effect the installation. However, in 113, Osroes, who had recently suc-ceeded his brother Pacorus II as the Parthian king of kings, deposed the Armenian ruler Exedares, the younger son of Pacorus, in favour of Exedares' own older brother Parthamasiris. That Parthia should now unilaterally elect to abrogate the agreement, especially during the emperor's quindecennalia, could be seen by many as nothing other than an unparalleled affront to the dignity of the empire.

No matter what prompted Trajan to intervene directly in the Armenian situation, con-flict between Rome and Parthia was probably inevitable. After all, for three centuries, the Parthians had been the single hegemony – outside of China – comparable to the burgeoning Roman empire, and Armenia and the Mesopotamian kingdoms constituted the border marches between the two. At this time primarily pastoralists, the Parthians were originally nomads of Asian origin, a branch of the Scythian peoples who had settled in southern Turkestan about 220 BC after displacing the Parthava, an Achaemenid satrapy.[13] They have left virtually no written records, and their political history is deduced principally from their coinage. Other details about them and their history are derived from an astonishingly wide selection of works produced in the Greek- and Latin-speaking world together with some documents from China. As might be expected, these are unanimously hostile, depicting the Parthians as treacherous, barbarous and arrogant, consistently and exceedingly bellicose by nature. Acknowledged as excellent horsemen (they were alleged to go continually mounted, whether to war or to banquets, whether travelling or resting), they dressed in the usual Asian nomadic fashion of a kaftan and loosely fitting trousers when riding, simple tunics when not. They were especially noted for their apparent vanity and considered somewhat meretricious. The nobility frequently used cosmetics and painted their faces, and all ranks wore long beards and often had their tonsure dressed in curls or otherwise elaborately styled.[14]

Not enough is known about Parthian social organization to pronounce on its structure with any certainty, a topic that would well reward further investigation. It seems to have been feudal, and based on the extended family with a single absolute ruler over seven principal clans. The ruler had to be a member of the Arsacid family, and was elected by two councils, one drawn from the nobility (effectively the Arsacids and their cadet branches), the other from the Magi, or 'Wise Men'. He was chosen for his worthiness to lead in battle and by example. The system did not ensure undisputed succession, and resulted in habitual internecine feuding, as the king could only count on the unprincipled loyalty of his own clan. At any time he might be usurped by the joint council in favour of another candidate – yet be re-elected at a later date. Then, as in several Iranian societies, the principle of fratrigeniture, in which brother followed brother, was often espoused at the expense of primogeniture, frequently arousing simmering discontent as the dispossessed elder son later challenged his uncle's succession. In either case, problems over the matter of succession seem often to have degenerated in internal bickering with no clear conclusion, one effect of which was to obscure further the historical record. For example, to judge from the coinage, it was not unknown for a king to be made, unmade, and then made again in quick succession, or even for a ruler to continue issuing coinage regardless of the fact that he had actually been legally usurped and replaced by another.

The semi-autonomous nobility occupied the top tier of society in a like manner to the clan chiefs of Highland Scotland. Below them were their 'dependants', a group which corresponds to the tacksmen of the Highlands, the petty nobility and their retainers; and then an underclass, who were known to the ancient writers as 'slaves'. In fact, true slavery was not a feature of Parthian society, and the social position of these men and their families conforms best to that of the sub-tenants of the Highland clan system – slaves in all but name. Some groups remained firmly transient. Others established prosperous communities of mud-brick houses at those places where local environmental conditions proved favourable for pastoralism, especially in the Azerbaijan plains around Lake Urnia, and the southern watershed of the Elburz, where Iran's present-day capital of Tehran is situated. Rainfall in the area was slight, but the early inhabitants developed an ingenious system of irrigation schemes which allowed substantial areas of marginal land to be turned over to agriculture, by now the principal source of Parthian wealth. By the beginning of the Christian era, however, the Parthians were able to capitalize on western demands for eastern luxuries – silk, perfumes, ointments, trinkets, etc. – traded along the Silk Route through their territory. As middlemen, individual communities grew wealthy through the imposition of taxes and the provision of supplies for those passing through their domains.[15]

The bulk of the Parthian army was formed of lightly armed infantry levied from among the lower orders. They were of indifferent worth and very much subordinate to the élite cavalry, the principal means for Parthia's success in the field of war. Two tactical mounted units can be recognized, both riding exceedingly strong and powerful Asian ponies. The principal arm was the heavy cavalry, or *clibanarii*, formed from among the nobility and their tacksmen. The horses wore chamfrons and trappers of interlocking bronze or iron scales, wired on to a fabric backing. Their riders were dressed in a full panoply of iron helmet and aventail, with iron corselets, vambraces, cuisses and chausses, usually of either laminate or mail, sometimes in combination. Their principal weapon was the long lance, with long swords and maces for close combat. The subsidiary division, the more numerous, were the horse-archers, drawn from among the retainers and followers of the nobility, and on occasion from the true nomads of the Iranian steppes. Neither horses nor riders had anything but the absolute minimum of defensive armour, and the only weapon these light cavalrymen carried was a powerful long-range reflex bow, made from a combination of wood and bone or antler, and which could penetrate most types of armour from within 100 yards (92m).

The fighting tactics of the Parthians were those of the nomadic east – simple but brutally and bloodily effective. The basic principle was to break an enemy's dense formations into smaller units by using hit-and-run tactics. With kettle-drums controlling each manoeuvre, the horse-archers would be the first to attack, discharging a shower of arrows as they galloped forward. Their reflex bows allowed them to shoot with deadly effect from outside the range of their opponents' throwing weapons, before swerving off to return to the flanks, firing over their horse's rump as they did so, the proverbial 'Parthian shot'. Persistence was the secret: by repeated attacks it was hoped to demoralize their opponents and break their formation or, by retreating, lure them into a counter-attack.[16] Then the *clibanarii* would charge in an attempt to crush their normally lightly armed adversaries. By these tactics, on their own ground, a force of Parthians could prove the undoing of armies three or even four times their own size.

The Parthian rulers had managed to extend their influence across Persia by taking advantage of internal divisions amongst the Seleucids. By 140 BC, under Mithridates I, they had annexed Media and much of Babylonia, and then Seleucia itself. Mithridates chose to retain the existing Seleucid system of semi-independent satrapies and eparchies (principalities). He installed his younger Arsacid relatives as rulers of the minor kingdoms and illustrious Parthian nobles as governors of the several cities, taking as his own title 'great king'. He consolidated his rule, as did the later Ottomans in the Balkans and the Mongols in Russia, by the simple but effective procedure of preserving local customs and existing constitutions where there was no resistance: and exacting bloody revenge where there was.

Mithridates' death brought about a series of reverses and advances, eventually resolved by Mithridates II, who proceeded to overrun Mesopotamia and Armenia. For these exploits he took the epithet 'king of kings', signalling his suzerainty over the region and its satraps, reinforced by his placement of a nominee, Tigranes, on the throne of Armenia in 94 BC. Soon, the adjacent territories of Adiabene, Gordyene and Osrhoëne, among others, had been formally annexed. Shortly thereafter, negotiations with embassies from the Han dynasty laid the basis for the Silk Route, permitting overland trade from the Orient to the Occident. In return for their horses, the Parthians received gold and silk, which was then exchanged with merchants from the Mediterranean world, greatly enriching the Parthian empire in the process.

Coincidentally, Rome was beginning to show a greater interest in eastern matters. The Parthian involvement in Armenia and Mesopotamia occasioned a treaty between L. Cornelius Sulla and Mithradates II in 92 BC, which recognized the Euphrates, the most convenient landmark, as the boundary between the two empires. Then, in 64 BC, Sulla's protégé, Pompey, after bringing Pontus and Syria into the *imperium*, established a series of protectorates along the river to strengthen Rome's influence in the region. Having assured the Parthian king, Phraates III, that Rome had no designs on the buffer states between the two hegemonies, Sulla came to a separate arrangement with Armenia, and unilaterally transferred the domain of Gordyene to the kingdom, in the process expelling the Parthian governor. Shortly after, Pompey's former legate Gabinus, now pro-consul of Syria, took an army across the Euphrates to occupy Mesopotamia, probably to establish the Tigris as the boundary between Parthia and Rome. Then, in 54 BC, the elderly and megalomaniac consul M. Crassus, seeking to emulate Alexander the Great, moved an army into Mesopotamia, and the next year, with the connivance and promised military support of the Armenian king, advanced towards Seleucia and Ctesiphon, only to be confronted by a Parthian cavalry brigade in the plains near Carrhae (Harran, Turkey). The resulting battle was an unmitigated disaster for Rome. Repeatedly attacked by 10,000 Parthian cavalry – mainly horse-archers – over a three-day period, Crassus' army of 35,000 was annihilated. The episode precipitated the collapse of the triumvirate, and forced Rome to withdraw to the Euphrates.

Caesar's untimely, yet some would say deserved, death ended Roman plans for exon-erating the disaster at Carrhae, and the Parthians decided to take advantage of the confusion at Rome to avenge the earlier duplicity. Before 40 BC, they had attacked Roman territory in force for the first and only time, a large cavalry division ranging almost unhindered over Anatolia until brought to book by Ventidius Bassus at Gindarus in 38 BC, on the very anniversary of Carrhae. Mark Antony used the episode as a pretext to invade Parthia itself, but his expedition ended in dismal failure in 35 BC, when the Parthians, under Phraates IV, cut down his supply train, forcing him to retreat ignomin-iously over the mountainous terrain of Azerbaijan. The men were plagued by lack of food and water; his version of the 1812 retreat from Moscow cost him a third of his army, more than was lost with Crassus at Carrhae, without even the excuse of a single battle. He rallied sufficiently from this humiliation and other preoccupations (Cleopatra, the war with Octavian) to occupy Armenia briefly in 34 BC, but for the next few years both Rome and Parthia found themselves having to contend with internal problems which took precedence over external affairs. Events culminated in 20 BC, when Augustus took advantage of a further bout of dynastic feuding among the Parthians to propose a diplo-matic solution satisfactory to all. The principal bone of contention being Rome's continued interference in Armenian affairs, Augustus accepted the territory's inalienable status as a minor kingdom within the Parthian hegemony, subject to Rome's approval of the chosen Parthian nominee for the throne.

It seemed a fair and equable solution. Despite it, Augustus' successors continued to find reasons to interfere in Armenian affairs, usually taking advantage of the frequent internal divisions endemic to the Parthian system of decentralized authority and administration, based as it was upon semi-autonomous satrapies and eparchies: Tiberius, for example, in securing the election of the approved pro-Roman candidate to the throne in 17; Gaius, in deposing the mutually agreed ruler Mithridates in 37; Claudius, in restoring him in 41 with Roman military support,[17] then seeing him replaced by the Arsacid Radamistus in 51, after Claudius' own intervention into the Parthian succession. Each time the matter was eventually resolved diplomatically, to the mutual benefit of the two hegemonies, even though Parthia was usually the injured party. Until, that is, the year 58, when Corbulo entered Armenia, expelled Tiridates from the capital Artaxata, laid it waste, and made the kingdom a protectorate with a Roman garrison and Roman nominee, Tigranes, on the throne.[18] To add further insult to the injury, Rome provided support for Tigranes when he unwisely attempted a *coup d'état* against Vologaeses, the Parthian ruler. Furious at yet another example of Roman chicanery, Vologaeses forced the outnumbered Roman garrison of Armenia into another ignominious retreat. Despite the deceit, he deigned to renegotiate the Augustan settlement. It was agreed that henceforth the Parthians would select a king for Armenia from among the Arsacid dynasty, usually a younger son of the ruling Parthian king of kings, and that Rome's sole involvement in the process would be to confer the royal diadem on the person nominated.

The new arrangement seems to have been broadly satisfactory to both parties. Even so, Rome continued to test Parthian sensibilities. Another crux in the relationship came during Vespasian's rule, when he decided to station two legions at the eastern limit of Cappadocia; then to annex the neighbouring kingdom of Commagene, bordered on the east by the Upper Euphrates and the Parthian sub-kingdom of Osrhoëne; then to expropriate – probably under M. Ulpius Traianus – Palmyra as an integral part of Syria; finally, in 75, to detach legionaries to construct the fortifications of Harmozica (Mtzhete, Georgia), in Iberia. These events may well have occasioned the unrest among the Parthians which resulted in the award of *ornamenta triumphalia* to Traianus in 73/76, yet the Parthians seem otherwise to have maintained by and large an uneasy peace with their bellicose neighbour. After all, an optimistic (Parthian) interpretation of these acts could view them as reasonable organic stages in the Roman consolidation of the natural frontier of the Euphrates as the agreed boundary between the two hegemonies. In one way, it could be said, they actually served to reassure the Parthians of Rome's good intentions, in that they reflected an attempt to unify territories already incorporated, as opposed to the massing of troops on the marches, which hitherto had presaged further expansion by Rome. Hence, the Neronian arrangements resulted in a generally unbroken – if uneasy – peace between Rome and Parthia. Until, that is, they were shamelessly violated by Trajan.

If we are to believe Dio Cassius, as abbreviated by Xiphilinus, Trajan had no valid excuse for waging war against Parthia. Instead, he used the πρόφασις (pretext) that the Parthian king of kings had pre-empted Rome in presenting the new Armenian king with the royal diadem symbolizing his sovereignty. By way of explication, it is added that Trajan's real motivation for opening hostilities against Parthia was quite simply his desire 'to win renown'. After all, it was common knowledge that Trajan was a man who 'delighted in warfare'.[19] On the other hand, Arrian is quite specific that Trajan, while mindful of Rome's dignity, did all he could to avoid conflict with Parthia, and only went to war when the Parthians refused to revert to the *status ante quo*.[20]

Dio's explanation seems the more tenable. The stated justification seems unquestionably specious and superficial, not least because it would appear that Rome and Parthia had already agreed on the choice for the Armenian throne. It was simply the matter of the actual coronation which seems to have offended Trajan's *amour propre*, and as we have seen in quite recent times, such a factor has often resulted in violent and quite unnecessary armed conflict in place of reasoned diplomacy. Certainly, no strategic need can be discerned for a war with Parthia at this time. The treaty between the two powers had worked thus far to the advantage of both sides, and none of the admittedly few sources even hints that Parthia was making threatening moves against Rome. Indeed, as B. Isaac has shown, there is surprisingly little evidence for believing that Parthia ever sought open conflict with Rome.[21] On the contrary, the consecutive Parthian kings of kings, often distracted by internal squabbles over their own succession, appear to have been universally desirous of peaceful co-existence with Rome. More often than not they initiated the various treaties between the two empires, in the knowledge that the Parthian people lacked both the cohesion and determination for expansion beyond the territories already ruled. Instead, it was the megalomania of successive Roman *viri militares*, prompting expeditions across the Euphrates, abrogating existing agreements in the process, which usually brought about confrontation between Parthia and her imperious neighbour.

To accuse Trajan of megalomania, of being a pathological warmonger as it were, would contradict the assessment of his contemporaries, namely that he endeavoured to avoid hostilities whenever he could.[22] But that judgement belongs to the earlier years of his reign. While it is undeniable that Trajan's studied aversion to the trifles of illustrious titles suggests a modest and thoughtful maturity rather than the infantile omnipotence of a Domitian – or even a Crassus or a Mark Antony – it so happens that a frequent (and natural?) characteristic of the combination of mature age and absolute authority is the desire to emulate, if not surpass, the vigour and exploits of past youth.[23] Trajan, like his contemporaries and many since, was all too aware that Alexander had triumphed over the eastern peoples when in his thirties, and that several Roman *viri militares* older than the Macedonian general had since tried and singularly failed to imitate his success. Trajan was also doubtless aware that Alexander traced his lineal descent from Zeus/Jupiter and Heracles/Hercules, the two gods who, more than any, Trajan had identified with himself. In which case it could well have been, as Dio implies, that Trajan, as a descendant of the Baetican Hercules, sought to climax the celebrations for the conquest of Dacia, now coming to their conclusion with the dedication of the Forum and the Column, with the promise of further victory, succeeding where other Roman generals had failed in reducing Parthia to tributary status. After all, the potential for victory could not have seemed better: Parthia was riven yet again by internecine strife.[24]

The thesis finds support in three significant occurrences. First, there was Hadrian's apparent appointment as *generalissimo* in the eastern provinces from April 112, a commission seemingly connected with the logistical preparations for war with Parthia. Second, there were the military themes which characterized the mintage of 111/112–13, announcing the emperor's imminent departure on campaign. Third, there was the deification of Trajan's own father, one of the few Roman generals who received triumphal decorations for an eastern campaign, a brazen attempt at manipulating the national will towards recognizing and approving Trajan's familial duty to subordinate Rome's last remaining enemy. When this is considered together, the additional knowledge that active hostilities did not commence until the spring of 114, after Parthia had twice offered a diplomatic solution, only serves to confirm the thesis that the war was premeditated as early as 111, and merely awaited a suitable and felicitous *casus belli*.

That vindication was provided by the Parthian intervention into the Armenian succession, an event which can be assigned to the latter part of the year 113, two years after Hadrian's departure for Syria. In between times, it seems that Trajan had remained at Rome, having relinquished his duty as consul in favour of (M.?) Lincinius Ruso. On 29 August that same year, however, he was struck by personal tragedy, the death of his sister Marciana, then in her mid-sixties. It evidently affected him deeply, for breaking all precedent, she was immediately deified, and the *Fasti Ostienses* record that on the same day her granddaughter Matidia was given the *cognomen Augusta* in her stead.[25] Her funeral took place on 3 September, coins showing her body taken to the crematory in a *carpentum*, a two-wheeled carriage drawn by a pair of mules. Her effigy followed on a chariot pulled by two elephants, and her formal apotheosis was celebrated by coins showing an eagle about to rise to the heavens.[26]

The following year, 113, opened with L. Publilius Celsus as consul for the second time and C. Clodius Crispinus for the first. The *Fasti Ostienses* are complete for the early part of the year, and record the conclusion of the third set of the Dacian *lusiones*, involving 1,202 pairs of gladiators, in early May, and that on 12 May, the emperor formally dedicated the eponymous Column and the newly restored Temple of Venus.[27] For the chronology of subsequent events, we must turn to the information supplied by a variety of documentary sources, chief among which is again Xiphilinus' epitome of Dio Cassius' *Roman History*, considerably augmented in this instance, however, by the *Excerpta* of the same work assembled in the mid-tenth century for the Byzantine emperor Constantine VII Porphyrogenitus. Together they enable a broad chronology to be determined, although there remain many uncertainties about where certain individual episodes belong. Only slightly less important are the surviving fragments of the *Parthica* published by Arrian, Hadrian's governor of Cappadocia. A Bithynian, born in Nicomedia, he may have been personally involved in Trajan's eastern campaigns and, to judge from his *Periplus Maris Euxini*, was a conscientious and discriminating scholar.[28] Then there are the secondary sources, of which the most useful are the mutilated remains of M. Cornelius Fronto's *Parthica*; the summaries in the *Breviarii* of Eutropius and his contemporary, Rufius Festus; and the *Chronographia* assembled in the sixth century by John Malalas of Antioch. Unfortunately, these authors were habitually inconsistent and circumstantial, and even inaccurate on occasion, particularly Malalas, a careless scribbler who evidently failed to check his primary sources. Despite that, they provide important incidental and ancillary information, such as calendar dates and inconsequential 'facts' which flesh out an otherwise bald narrative. Together, whatever their inadequacies and contradictions, and despite several difficulties over chronology, they allow a broadly coherent account to be reconstructed for Trajan's Parthian War, even if there are problems in placing certain of the minor events within the overall sequence.

From Arrian we learn that Trajan set out from Rome for Parthia amid scenes of jubila-tion in the autumn of 113, quite probably choosing the anniversary of his adoption for the *profectio*.[29] Dio, for his part, informs us that the emperor's journey east to Antioch (Antakya, Turkey), the principal base and imperial residence for the campaign, was by way of Athens. Assuming Trajan travelled with a small entourage, the probable route was along the via Appia and via Traiana to Brundisium, then by ship for Corinthus (Corinth, Greece) and thence overland to the Greek *metropolis*. He was met on arrival by an embassy from Osroes, who proposed that as Exedares 'was satisfactory to neither the Romans nor the Parthians' (we are not told why), Parthamasiris should be allowed to retain the Armenian throne. To resolve the issue, it was suggested that Trajan should now offer him the royal diadem in accordance with the Neronian compact. Trajan was studiously deaf to the proposition, refusing to discuss the matter, or to accept any of the gifts sent by Osroes; the embassy was sent packing with the remark that friendship and diplomacy were deter-mined not by words but by deeds, and that Trajan would review the matter after he arrived at his forward base in Syria – further confirmation, were it needed, that Trajan had decid-ed upon war with Parthia at any cost.[30]

The next stage of the emperor's journey probably took him across the Aegean to Eph-esus, the grandest marine emporium west of the Taurus Mountains.[31] From Ephesus the rational route east was overland via Aphrodisias to one of the ports of Lycia-Pamphylia, perhaps Attaleia (Antalya) or Side (Selimiye), thereby avoiding the treacherous seas off south-west Anatolia, with their many reefs and rocks on which many a ship had come to grief in antiquity, especially in winter.[32] Dio implies that Trajan then continued by ship, by way of the coastal towns of Asia Minor, to Seleucia in Pieria (Samandag), the seaport for Antioch. Hadrian was present to meet him when he arrived late that December. Together they went at once to nearby Mount Kasios, where the emperor dedicated spoils from the Dacian War to Zeus, with a prayer for divine intervention on his side in the forthcoming campaign.[33] Sacrifices made and oracles read, the two proceeded to Antioch, which the emperor entered on 7 January 114.[34]

It can be inferred that Hadrian had by now assembled a substantial army at Antioch for the coming campaign. The city is the obvious concentration point for those legions drawn from the south-eastern provinces which are known to have participated in the war, the *legio X Fretensis* from Jerusalem in Judaea, the *III Cyrenaica* from Bostra in Arabia, and the *III Gallica* from (?)Raphanaea in southern Syria. Trajan probably remained at the city until the beginning of April, as the passes north to Armenia through the rough terrain of the Taurus mountains, at altitudes approaching 6,000ft (1,800m), are usually blocked with snow and rockfalls until that month.[35] During that interval, Antioch served as the imperial capital, in the same way that Viminacium did during the Dacian Wars. Conse-quently, while the emperor's time was doubtless fully occupied with the continued administration of the empire, and supervising preparations for the forthcoming crusade against Parthia, he also entered into diplomatic negotiations with the kingdoms of the border marches. Early on he received an embassy from Abgarus, king of Osrhoëne, who balked at coming in person in hopes of remaining neutral, but who sent gifts and a message of friendship.[36] Other embassies came from Mannus, king of the Scenite Arabs, and Sporaces, ruler of the adjacent kingdom of Anthemusia.[37] A fourth was sent by Osroes to receive Trajan's decision on the terms proposed in Athens, but it found that the emperor's resolve had, if anything, hardened. While protesting, for the record, that he personally had no wish for war, he now announced that Osroes' terms were unsatisfactory and were accordingly rejected.[38] Soon afterwards he left with his divisions for Satala (Kelkit), his chosen campaign base for the year, leaving Hadrian behind to administer the strategically and logistically important province of Syria.[39]

It is deduced that Trajan's journey from Antioch to Satala was made in two stages, Melitene (Malatya, Turkey) marking the mid-way point (Fig. 11). The first leg took Trajan by way of Beroea (Aleppo, Syria) to the fortress of Zeugma (Bireçik), headquarters of the *legio IV Scythica*.[40] From Zeugma, the constraints of local topography suggest a crossing of the Euphrates and the route over the Kanliavşar watershed to Samosata (Samsat), the base of the *legio VI Ferrata*. After he crossed to the left bank of the Euphrates, a march over the Malatya Dağlari followed, bringing Trajan to the fortress at Melitene, at this time garrisoned by the *legio XII Fulminata*. Founded by Vespasian to control the Euphrates crossing on the principal trade route between Armenia and Cilicia, it was set in a relatively fertile and prosperous area which encouraged the growth of a substantial *canabae legionis*, now honoured by Trajan with the rank of *municipium*.[41]

About now Trajan received a letter from Parthamasiris, suggesting that the *fait accompli* of his own enthronement be accepted and that Parthamasiris should come to Trajan to be formally presented with the Armenian royal diadem. Trajan, for his part, considered the letter peremptory in tone, not least because of Parthamasiris' perceived audacity in signing himself 'king [of Armenia]', and did not even deign to reply.[42] A second, more conciliatory epistle was remitted for the emperor's consideration, this time leaving out the royal title, and asking that the governor of Cappadocia, M. Junius Homullus, be empowered to open negotiations in Trajan's place. The emperor would not agree to this, but instead dispatched Junius' son to verify the terms being offered by Parthamasiris. He then continued on the second leg of his advance to Satala, crossing the Euphrates again and then the Elazig Pass to the southern Armenian city of Arsamosata (Palu), which was now occupied without resistance.[43] Making his way north through the Pülümür Pass, he crossed the Euphrates once more at, probably, Eriza (Erzincan), after which a day's march brought him to Satala, the headquarters of the *legio XVI Flavia Firma*, where he very probably arrived late in the month of May 114.[44]

Satala that spring must have witnessed the greatest concentration of Roman legions ever known, even though the partial evidence available precludes the preparation of a complete muster. It is generally agreed, however, that seven legions from the eastern armies were present in full or slightly reduced strength: the *III Gallica*, *IIII Scythica* and *VI Ferrata* from Syria; the *XII Fulminata* and *XVI Flavia Firma* from Cappadocia; the *X Fretensis* from Judaea; and the *III Cyrenaica* from Arabia. They were supported by a substantial contingent drawn from the Danubian armies, some of whom travelled overland from the Balkans by way of Ancyra (Ankara), in the winter of 113/114: most, or at least the bulk, of the logistical supplies probably travelled by ship from Tomis (Constanta), along the coast of the Black Sea, to Trapezus (Trabzon), and then overland via the Zigana Pass and thence Satala.[45] Some of these legions were almost certainly present in full strength, for example the *I Adiutrix* and *XV Apollinaris*; others were probably represented by vexillations: *VII Claudia*, *XI Claudia*, *XIII Gemina*, *II Traiana fortis*, *XII Primigenia*, *XXX Ulpia victrix*, *I Italica* and *V Macedonica*. Yet even if only half of each of the seventeen legions enumerated was present at Satala, the army Trajan amassed there represented the equivalent of eight full legions, to which should be added at least an equal number of auxiliaries: in all, therefore, perhaps 80,000 men.

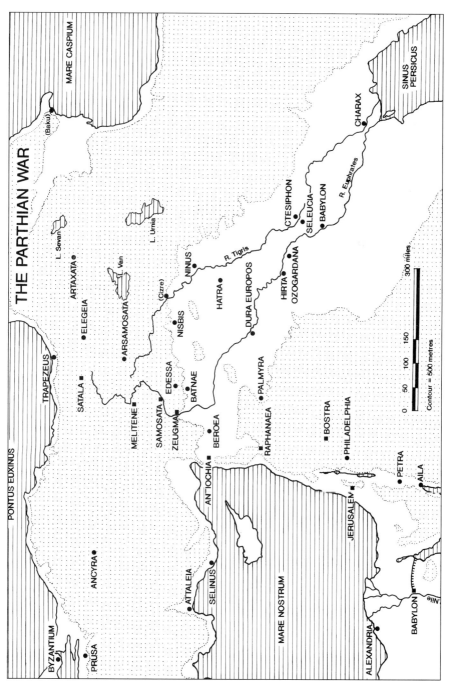

Fig. 11 The Parthian War

After assembling his army, and receiving the homage of Anchialus, ruler of the Heniochi, and Machelones, of the Coruh Nehri, Trajan advanced into Armenia.[46] His destination was the Armenian city of Elegeia, 110 miles (180km) east of Satala, and 180 miles (300km) west of the Parthamasiris' capital at Artaxata (Artasat, Armenia). It had been agreed that Parthamasiris and the leading Armenian nobility should rendezvous with Trajan at the city, but in an astounding display of *lèse-majesté*, the Arsacid ruler and his entourage arrived late for the convention, a delay he blamed on the need to avoid attacks from marauding bands of Exedares' supporters.[47] Coming before Trajan, who was seated upon a tribunal in the camp, he saluted, removed the royal diadem and laid it at the emperor's feet in confident expectation of its return.[48] Trajan pointedly left it on the ground, at which the assembled soldiers, having witnessed an Arsacid deposed without the need for battle, hailed Trajan *imperator* 'just as if he had won a military victory'.[49] Despite Parthamasiris' private and public entreaties, that he was the lawful Parthian *nomineé* to the Armenian throne, who had come voluntarily to Trajan to be crowned, not as a captive or as one vanquished in battle, Trajan proclaimed the annexation of Armenia as a Roman province. Declaring that he would surrender the territory to no one, he then appointed the distinguished ex-consul L. Catilius Severus as its first governor.[50]

Trajan ordered those members of the Armenian nobility who had accompanied Parthamasiris to remain at Elegeia, as 'they were already his subjects'. The Arsacid prince, however, was sent on his way with an escort of Roman cavalry for protection from Exedares' supporters, only to lose his life outside Elegeia in uncertain circumstances. Rumour had it that Trajan was responsible for the assassination, although in a letter to Osroes the emperor maintained that Parthamasiris had brought about his own death by trying to escape his escort.[51] Whatever his alleged involvement in the matter, Trajan had meanwhile mandated his generals to complete the process of reforming Armenia as a province. A variety of sources reveal that Roman armies ranged far and wide across the land during the rest of the year. One division, commanded by Lusius Quietus, is heard of fighting the Mardi, who occupied the highlands south of Lake Van and the access to the vital Bitlis Pass. A second, led by C. Bruttius Praesens, legate of the *VI Ferrata*, is known to have been operating in the Armenian highlands, where the men adopted the native snowshoes as they campaigned late in the year in wintry conditions and deep snow. A third advanced far to the east, eventually reaching the Caspian Gates: it might well have been the *IIII Scythica*, known from an inscription to have remained in Armenia until at least the spring of 116, when it was building a stone fortress at Artaxata. A fourth, perhaps involving the young Arrian, seems to have advanced beyond Armenia as far as the Dariel Pass.[52] By the end of 114, then, it seems that all of Armenia had been consolidated, the key valleys and river crossings occupied, and any remaining resistance isolated in the highlands around Lake Van by the divisions led by Quietus and Praesens.

While his commanders set about the subjugation of Armenia, Trajan remained that summer at Elegeia, receiving the homage of local satraps and minor kings (Pl. 13B). One brought as a gift a horse taught to do obeisance by kneeling on its forelegs.[53] From Arrian's *Periplus*, a work commissioned towards the end of Hadrian's reign, we learn that it was about now that Trajan appointed a certain Julianus as king of the Apsilae, and nominated a king to the Albani.[54] Arrian goes on to report that in his own time, the kings of three other tribes along the eastern Pontic coast – the Lazi, Abasci and Sanigae – all received their authority from Rome, from which it might be inferred that all five had initially acknowledged Roman supremacy at the same time, namely in 114. This, at any rate, seems to be implicit in an observation of Dio/Xiphilinus, that once Trajan had annexed Armenia, he went on to receive the submission of many of the local satraps. It is also consistent with Eutropius' comment that during his reign, Trajan received the submission of the kings of the Pontic Iberians, the Crimean Bosphorans and the Colchi.[55] Moreover, it seems that the Iberians may have provided Trajan with a detachment of soldiers, as one Amazaspos, nephew of the king, died the following year while on campaign with the emperor.[56] Viewed together, these disparate sources suggest a concentrated effort was now being made to exercise Roman supremacy over the tribes that occupied the eastern Euxine littoral.[57] True, some had been clients of Rome since the time of Pompey (indeed, Tiberius – and probably Vespasian as well – had induced the Alani to attack Parthia when it suited them), and Rome had even on occasion dispatched troops to the Caucasian kingdoms for engineering works and other duties.[58] Perhaps Trajan now attempted to formalize the existing *ad hoc* arrangements, and might even have been instrumental in developing the network of permanent garrisons in the Caucasian hinterland.[59] It was surely on account of all these diplomatic successes – the annexation of Armenia included – that in the high summer of 114, the senate once more voted Trajan *Optimus*, an epithet he henceforth formally adopted into his nomenclature and in which he took 'greater pride than all the rest [of his titles], insofar as it referred to his personal abilities rather than his military prowess'.[60]

There are many problems in the Dio/Xiphilinus account for the sequence of events after Elegeia. For one thing, it is implied that Trajan went on that same year, 114, to capture the Mesopotamian cities of Nisbis and Batnae, for which he was voted the title *Parthicus*, and then continued to the Osrhoënian capital of Edessa; for another, hardly any military activity is recorded in the following year, 115. Now, it so happens that the *Fasti Ostienses* firmly date the events leading to the award of the title *Parthicus* to 115, as indeed is implied elsewhere in the Dio/Xiphilinus account, while Trajan is known to have received no fewer than four imperial salutations during that year, his eighth through to his eleventh.[61] The simplest solution to the conundrum, adopted here, is to assume that Xiphilinus has obscured the passing of the winter 114/115, which Trajan probably spent at either Elegeia or Artaxata, and therefore to attribute the Mesopotamian campaign, his second, to 115.[62] That being so, it can be said that the late spring of 115 saw Trajan marching south with his army over the central Taurus mountains to consolidate the territory between the Euphrates and the upper Tigris, permanent garrisons being left at opportune points along the way to secure the region. It would seem he journeyed on foot with his men, fording rivers with them and using the opportunity of an unopposed progress to practise manoeuvres and marching dispositions. The anecdote does not read like a *topos* – unless it is misplaced in Xiphilinus' reduction of Dio's narrative – and thus might well be true.[63] By the summer, it might be expected that he had reached upper Mesopotamia, and was ready to set about its annexation.

This was achieved by a pincer movement on a grand scale. Lusius Quietus, after vanquishing the Mardi, continued south into Adiabene, where he fought and defeated King Mebarsapes, and then advanced into eastern Mesopotamia.[64] Trajan, meanwhile, having skirted Osrhoëne, set about the reduction of the western part of the territory.

Batnae (Incidere), the capital of Anthemusia, was quickly taken, in order to punish King Sporaces for his earlier failure to offer fealty to Rome, and the occupation of Nisibis (Nusaybin) soon followed. Osrhoëne itself, however, was left as an autonomous enclave, as the king, Abgarus VII, prompted by his son Arbandes, now offered homage as a means of making amends for his failure to do so the previous year. If we are to believe Dio, Trajan had met Arbandes on an earlier occasion (presumably as a member of the Osrhoënian embassy dispatched to Antioch in 114), and had become deeply enamoured of him. What is certain is that after meeting Abgarus outside his capital at Edessa (Sanliurfa), Trajan pardoned the king, granted his realm the status of a protectorate, and then went on to be entertained at a banquet where the royal youth performed 'some barbaric dance'.[65]

Faced with such clear evidence of Trajan's evident determination to achieve total conquest, Mannus, king of the Scenite Arabs, one of the rulers who had singularly failed to appear at Antioch on Trajan's arrival, now dispatched peace envoys to the emperor. His overtures were viewed with some suspicion, however, as he was known to have sent auxiliaries to support Mebarsapes against Lusius Quietus.[66] Another envoy came to Trajan from Manisarus, a ruler usually accepted as king of Gordyene. Evidently a member of the Arsacid dynasty, he had made an armed challenge for the Parthian throne. Now he was being counter-attacked by Osroes, and he proposed to Trajan that they should unite against their common enemy, in return for which he would cede to Rome the parts of Armenia and Mesopotamia already taken from Osroes' supporters. Trajan, however, refused to negotiate with either Mannus or Manisarus until they came to him in person, which both had frequently promised but had signally failed to do. He then left to join Lusius Quietus in Adiabene, having arranged that the two should meet him there. The outcome seems to have favourable, for Lusius was peacefully allowed to possess the Scenite Arab town of Singara (Gebel Sinjar, Iraq) and certain other cities, probably including Dura Europos, thus completing the occupation of Mesopotamia.[67] This, at any rate, might be inferred from Trajan's dispatch of a 'laurelled letter' to the senate before the end of the year, which they received on 21 February 116. It probably announced the annexation of Parthian territory to form the two new provinces of Armenia and Mesopotamia, as coins were subsequently issued proclaiming these territories as 'subjected to the power of the people of Rome'. Trajan was now voted the title *Parthicus*, prayers were offered for his safety, and he was further honoured with thirty *ludi* at the Circus on 25, 26 and 28 February.[68]

Trajan, meanwhile, had returned to Antioch for the winter 115/116, where he nearly lost his life in a great earthquake which devastated the region. Dio provided a detailed account of the episode, evidently copied from an eyewitness account, which Xiphilinus seems to have reproduced in full.[69] It begins:

> While the *autokrator* was resting that winter in Antioch, a dreadful earthquake occurred: many cities suffered injury from it, but Antioch was the most unfortunate of all. As Trajan was spending the winter there, myriad soldiers were present, and many civilians had flocked there from all corners of the empire to prosecute law suits, embassies, business and just from curiosity; thus not a single nation or class [of society] was left untouched by the catastrophe, and the whole Roman world suffered disaster. There had been several thunderstorms and portentous

winds, but none had expected so many evils to result from them. First there was a sudden and great bellowing roar; it was followed by a tremendous quaking of the land. The ground was heaved up, and buildings thrust into the air; some were carried aloft only to collapse on themselves and be broken in pieces; others were tossed every which way as if by the swell of the sea, and then overturned; and the wreckage was spread out to a great extent, even into the open countryside. The frightful grinding and splintering of timbers, tiles and stones and the inconceivable quantity of dust which arose made it impossible to see anything or to speak or hear a word. As for the people, many were hurt, even those outside the houses being snatched up and tossed violently and then dashed to the ground as if from a cliff. Some were maimed, others killed. Even trees, roots and all, were thrown into the air. The number of those who were trapped and perished in their houses was impossible to establish; multitudes were killed by the force of the falling debris, others suffocated in the ruins. The worse off were those trapped by stones or timbers, who suffered a lingering death.

Nevertheless, many of the trapped were saved, as was to be expected with such a throng, but not all were unscathed. Several lost legs or arms, some had their heads broken, others vomited blood from internal wounds; Pedo, the consul,[70] was one of the latter and he quickly expired. In a word, there was no kind of violent experience that these people did not go through at the time. And as the after-shocks continued for several days and nights, the trapped were in dire straits and helpless, some of them eventually crushed and perishing under the weight of the ruined buildings; others, while preserved from injury by being in clear spaces, formed of fallen timbers or even upstanding colonnades, most miserably died of hunger. When at last the evil had subsided, one who ventured to climb the rubble caught sight of a woman trapped yet still alive. She was not alone, but had by her an infant, and had kept themselves alive by feeding herself and her child with her milk. She was dug out with her child, and her rescuers quickly sought other rubble heaps for others in like circumstances; yet found none still living, save one child suckling at the breast of her dead mother. And as they dug out the dead, even those who lived could find little pleasure at their own escape.

Trajan miraculously escaped through a window in the room in which he was staying. Some entity, of greater than mere human stature, came to him and led him forth, so that he only suffered slight injuries. And on account of the after-shocks which continued for several days, he lived out of doors in the hippodrome. So great were the calamities that racked Antioch at the time. Even Mount Kasios was so shaken that its peaks seemed to lean over and break off and be falling on the city. Other hills were lowered, and many new streams appeared as old ones dried up.

Early 116 saw Trajan march forth from Antioch for the Tigris, and his third and final campaign against the Parthian hegemony.[71] It seemed a rash move. To vanquish Parthia required a long and arduous march, much of the way through hostile terrain, leaving the Roman forces dangerously over-extended. Trajan could well have stopped and been satisfied with the two new provinces to his credit, both of which anyway required consolidation. None the less, perhaps encouraged by the total lack of Parthian resistance to date, the emperor was to have his way, and made his first objective the subjugation of Adiabene.

Now, Lusius Quietus had already entered the kingdom the previous year, but was forced to halt his advance when it proved impossible to obtain the materials needed for a bridge across the river and take the war to the Adiabene capital. To overcome the problem, Trajan brought with him a waggon train carrying prefabricated pontoons built the previous winter at Nisibis, where plentiful wood was available from the forests of Mount Massius (Tur 'Abdin) north of the city. The river was eventually crossed, but with some difficulty, as the engineers had to contend with both the strength of the stream and fierce opposition from the Adiabenes, ranged along the opposite bank. However, with the pontoons used in a series of feints, some moored mid-stream, with legionaries and archers to provide covering fire, the crossing was eventually effected, probably in the vicinity of modern Cizre.[72]

Our sources are particularly confused for the following events, not the least because not all the places named have been securely identified. It seems that one division swept south through the kingdom, using the road taken by Alexander, capturing Ninus (Nineveh, the capital), Arbela and Guagamela, where Alexander had defeated Darius III in 331 BC. It also managed to seize Adenystrae, which fell without a fight, owing to the circumstance that a Roman centurion held prisoner there managed to escape with some others, killed the garrison commander and opened the gates to the Roman forces arrayed outside.[73] Adiabene was now formally occupied, probably the occasion for Trajan's twelfth imperial salutation; and, according to Eutropius and Festus, Trajan then proceeded to form the territory into the province of Assyria.[74] A second division, meanwhile, seems to have continued along the western bank of the Tigris as far as Babylon, meeting no opposition on the way, as the Arsacid dynasty was again distracted and riven by internal dissent.[75]

Trajan, however, accompanied neither group. Once the Tigris crossing was achieved, he made his way overland to Dura Europos, where a commemorative arch was erected in his honour to the north of the town early in 116.[76] This at least might be inferred from Arrian's *Parthica*, for it lists towns along the Euphrates, on the route of the Ten Thousand, perhaps parallel stages in Trajan's own journey south. A similar itinerary can be deduced from the Dio/Xiphilinus account, for it records Trajan's visit to asphalt wells, probably those at Hit, while Ammianus Marcellinus records how, in the fourth century, visitors were still being shown Trajan's tribunal at Ozogardana, even further down the Euphrates.[77] More conclusive, perhaps, is that Dio/Xiphilinus specifically notes how Trajan was accompanied by a river fleet on the Euphrates during his advance to Ctesiphon. Then, Arrian provides the important information that the fleet was made up of fifty ships, divided among three squadrons, the van containing four vessels carrying the imperial *vexilla*. He goes on to tell us that the largest craft was the emperor's flagship, about the length of a trireme, with a beam and draught comparable to that of the largest Egyptian or Nicomedian merchantman: it was provided with 'adequate' living quarters, the stem and stern posts were decorated with gold, and the sail carried the emperor's name and titles in gold letters.[78]

Trajan's intention was to use this fleet to cross the Tigris and attack Ctesiphon, for which purpose he proposed to cut a canal between the Euphrates and the Tigris at (?)Sippar, where the two rivers flow within 20 miles (33km) of each other. In the event, inspection on the ground suggested that at this particular point the Euphrates flowed at a higher elevation than the Tigris. Fearing that the proposed canal might drain the one and flood the other, and choosing not to use the existing Naharmalcha, or 'Royal River', the artificial watercourse which already linked the two rivers somewhat further south of Ctesiphon, the emperor instead elected to have his fleet dragged overland by means of 'engines', presumably a combination of capstan devices and rollers.[79] That mission satisfactorily accomplished, Trajan took Seleucia on the west bank, and then crossed the Tigris unopposed and entered the city of Ctesiphon without a fight. Osroes and his entourage had fled, leaving behind his daughter and golden throne to be captured by the emperor.[80] It was a moment of personal triumph for the emperor, and one recognized as such by his army, who saluted him *imperator* as he 'established his right to be acclaimed *Parthicus*'.[81]

The capture of Ctesiphon marked the official culmination of Trajan's third campaign and of the war. Even though he had not once encountered any resistance from the king of kings or his cavalry, for Osroes had followed the traditional tactic of his ancestors, withdrawing over the Zagros Mountains in the face of a superior enemy, the emperor ordered the issue of coins with the legend *PARTHIA CAPTA*. He then set about reviewing and consolidating the occupied territory, perhaps intending to form a province of Babylonia.[82] Using ships from his Euphrates 'fleet', Trajan next sailed down the Tigris to the Erythraean Sea, or Persian Gulf, pausing on the way to take homage from Athambelus and the inhabitants of Mesene and Spasinus. After nearly losing his life in a tidal bore, the emperor eventually arrived at Charax (Basra), a town located at the river's mouth, arriving there just in time to see a merchant ship sailing for India, whereupon he publicly lamented that he was no longer young enough to follow in Alexander the Great's footsteps. This episode evidently signalled his personal consummation of the Parthian War, for he now dispatched another 'laurelled letter' to the senate, announcing his accomplishments, and erected a statue marking the limit of his advance.[83] For his achievements, the senate in their turn voted him a triumph over as many nations as he wished and many other honours, which probably included his thirteenth imperial salutation, and issued coins with the legend *FORT(una) RED(ux)*, wishing the emperor a safe return to Italy (Pl. 1D).[84]

Trajan, however, had not finished with matters in the east. He now made his way up the Euphrates to Babylon. He had conceived the desire to visit the site and view the tomb of Semiramis and make a sacrifice in the house where Alexander had died in 323 BC. He left his ships behind with the apparent intention of a future campaign eastwards.[85] But when he arrived at Babylon, he found that in his absence the shock caused by the capture of Ctesiphon had caused the Parthians to resolve their internal differences. They were now inciting widespread revolt, probably at the instigation of one Sanatrukes, another nephew of Osroes, who had apparently been nominated by the Parthians as king-in-exile of the Armenians in place of Parthamasiris. Sanatrukes could not have chosen a better time. Trajan had yet again advanced too far and too quickly without making sure he had sufficient resources to consolidate his gains, and then had absented himself on the lower Euphrates before securing his perimeters. Added to which, if the evidence of Malalas and Dio is to be accepted, Sanatrukes was a superb organizer, for rebellion broke out simultaneously at a number of widely spread locations, Roman garrisons being expelled or slain throughout Mesopotamia and Armenia.[86]

The emperor immediately ordered at least three divisions against the rebels. One was led by a consular officer who may have been T. Julius Maximus, perhaps the governor of Mesopotamia, but he perished in battle shortly thereafter.[87] The second came under Trajan's most single-minded general, Lusius Quietus, who quickly recovered Nisbis and a number of cities, including Edessa, which he sacked and burnt, either on account of Abgarus' treachery or because he had been replaced by a pro-Parthian substitute; for these exploits he was promised a consulship in the following year.[88] The third division, meanwhile, under the joint command of two legates, Erucius Clarus and Julius Alexander, captured and burnt Seleucia, in Babylonia. They were then joined by Trajan himself, if we are to believe Malalas, who claims to have got the information from Arrian's *Parthica*, and the three then went on to defeat a Parthian host somewhere in the vicinity of Ctesiphon, after which Sanatrukes was killed in somewhat suspicious circumstances.

Despite these successes, however, Armenia was now threatened by a Parthian army under the command of Vologaesus, the son of Sanatrukes. The situation there must have been extremely critical, for when an armistice was offered in return for a part of the territory, Trajan quickly agreed. Then, in an effort to avoid further insurrection in Babylon, and perhaps to assert some authority over Vologaesus, Trajan went to Ctesiphon and appointed one Parthamaspates, a son of Osroes', as client-king of Parthia. He personally crowned him with the royal diadem, after which Parthamaspates did obeisance to Trajan in the traditional manner in full view of the assembled population, confirming his subordinate status. Even so, some may well have thought this episode marked the abandonment of all the territory so recently won for Rome, but in a letter to the senate, Trajan explained and justified his action:

> So vast and infinite is this domain, and so immeasurable the distance that separates
> it from Rome, that we do not have the compass to administer it. Let us then
> [instead] present the people with a king who is subject to Rome.[89]

With both Parthia and the major part of Armenia restored to client-kings, Trajan hurried north to recover what he could of Mesopotamia. A priority was the reduction of Hatra, whose population had also revolted, for this citadel, occupying the site of a perennial spring, controlled the steppes west of the Tigris and the vital road between Mesopotamia and Babylon. Its possession was indispensable for the restoration of Roman rule beyond the Tigris, and Trajan accordingly set about investing the site, which Dio describes, inaccurately, as neither large nor prosperous.[90] He is correct in saying, however, that the surrounding desert provides insufficient water, and that of poor quality, and neither timber nor fodder for a besieging army. Added to which the Roman force was further troubled by the flies which swarmed over their food and drink, bringing discomfort and illness to many. Despite such deterrents, Trajan persisted with the siege. He even managed to breach the defences at one point with a cavalry charge using his own *equites singulares*, during which the emperor's unmistakable 'majestic grey head' attracted the attention of Hatrian archers, who managed to kill a trooper in his escort.

But by now, winter was evidently approaching, and the besiegers had to contend with sudden cloudbursts, hailstorms and thunderstorms in addition to all their other troubles, causing Trajan to lift the siege and retire west, probably to Antioch, where he began to fail in health.

Coinciding with the Parthian revanche – whether by design or accident is not clear – certain of the Jewish communities in the Greek-speaking diaspora began their own revolt. Their rigid monotheistic belief had always occasioned some localized anti-Semitism, but throughout antiquity the Greeks in particular had been notorious for their manifestations of hostility, which on more than one occasion deteriorated into pogroms. The principal source of tension had originally been the privileged positions held by Jews in many of the eastern communities, for they were often favoured by the nobility both as merchants and for their military skills. Then, with Roman domination, it seems that some Jewish communities were granted a separate legal status, which allowed them to enjoy the benefits of city life without having to subscribe to the regular constitution, an attempt, it would seem, at trying to eliminate religious tension between differing neighbourhoods in the same city. Instead, it served to isolate the Jews even more, as did the lack of religious tolerance endemic among certain Jewish groups, making them the focus for attacks by Greek chauvinists. Serious but isolated disturbances had previously occurred at individual cities in the eastern empire, especially at Alexandria, where particularly bloody riots had taken place in 29 BC and AD 41. Now, it would seem, religious tensions between the two communities flared into open riot at a number of places.[91] Our main source for these, however, is the Greek pantheist Dio Cassius, as abbreviated by the Greek Christian Xiphilinus, and it is hardly surprising that they place the blame firmly on the Jewish population. At Cyrene, for example, it was claimed that they had killed up to 220,000 Greeks and Romans, and were eating their flesh and making belts from their entrails. Similar outrages were told of the Jewish community in Alexandria and in Cyprus, and it was said that a further 240,000 had perished at their hands in Cyprus alone. While the alleged atrocities are likely to be grossly exaggerated, as is usual in such cases, some measure of the seriousness that Trajan attached to the matter was his dispatch of Marcius Turbo to (probably) Alexandria to help subdue the disturbances.

Despite these problems, Trajan none the less intended to march into Mesopotamia again in 117, but was dissuaded by his ill-health.[92] A remarkably well-preserved bust of the emperor from about this time, once hanging in the forum at Ankyra, shows him to have become already somewhat gaunt of feature (Pl. 2D).[93] The full cheeks of his middle age have sagged and become jowly; his hair has receded, and his cheek-bones and nose project from a thin covering of skin. Now, it appears, he was dropsical, by which peripheral oedema is meant, perhaps worsened by arteriosclerosis, as it was said that he suffered from haemostasis in his nether regions. He had also suffered a stroke, which left him partially paralysed, all these symptoms hinting at congestive heart failure, perhaps brought on by hypertension.[94] Given the nature of his lifestyle, the stresses and strains of active campaigning – in which he insisted on sharing all the hardships of his men, marching through the Anatolian mountains, and camping in the Arabian desert with them, when only noxious water was available – had evidently proved too much for his 60-year-old frame. His recovery was hardly helped by the almost daily arrival of news concerning fresh disturbances across the *imperium*: insurrection in Mauretania; a threat of war from the

Roxolani and Iazyges; raids by British brigands in the north of that province; and signs of rebellion in Judaea. Then to cap it all, Parthamaspates was faced with civil war. With Jewish revolts throughout the east, Armenia already lost and the fate of Mesopotamia hanging in the balance, and in some pain on account of his ailment, the emperor decided to return to Rome to celebrate his Parthian triumph, appointing Hadrian to the overall command of the armies in the east.[95]

It must have been a very dejected emperor who boarded the royal yacht at Seleucia in Pieria that summer, when climatic conditions were most favourable to sea travel. With all that he achieved in the east apparently lost, and the great climacteric of his sixty-third year fast approaching, it is no wonder that symptoms of paranoia began to appear, and he began to suspect that his malady was induced by poison. Sometime about the beginning of August, however, as they coasted along the shores of Rough Cilicia, his condition suddenly worsened. The ship pulled into the nearest harbour, Selinus (Gazipasha), in Rough Cilicia, where the emperor took to his bed and subsequently died.[96] Without certain proof of poisoning, a diseased heart was probably the principal factor in his demise, but the immediate cause of death could well have been a debilitating infection contracted in the east. This, at least, is implied by Eutropius, who suggests that Trajan's extinction was attended by internal haemorrhaging and bloody diarrhoea.[97] The possibility is given greater credence by the sudden death at about the same time (on 12 August, to be precise) of one M. Ulpius Phaedimus, who was at Selinus with the emperor's entourage. A close personal servant of Trajan – he had been successively the emperor's chief table- and wine-servant, and then personal assistant and secretary – he had presumably travelled with the emperor throughout the east, before dying at the comparatively early age of 28, which suggests that he too may have contracted some internal ailment.[98]

Trajan had left no clear instructions concerning the succession; the thought of his imminent death had evidently never occurred to him. On 9 August, however, Hadrian, while at Antioch, was able to produce documents which announced his adoption by the emperor, and then two days later, when he learnt of Trajan's actual demise, he announced his own accession. The proclamation was not challenged: after all, Hadrian had a considerable army at his command, as many were aware. None the less, the circumstances surrounding the adoption and accession seemed to many to be precipitate and deliberately obscure, and it was popularly believed that the succession was foisted on the empire. The belief was based on the conviction that Trajan had favoured the jurist Neratius Priscus as regent, should he suddenly die, in order to give the senate an opportunity to select a successor from a list of the great and good he proposed sending to them. Like Alexander, he eschewed directly naming his own choice. The story might be true, and if so would confirm Trajan's avowed respect of constitutional principle; he himself, it should be remembered, had been selected and approved as Nerva's successor, ostensibly without any knowledge of the matter. Even so, suspicions were increased by the circumstance that the imperial correspondence at this time was being signed by Plotina in Trajan's name. Apparently, it was said, he had never previously resorted to the practice, although an objective observer might note that Trajan's paralysing stroke would probably have occasioned the matter. None the less, rumour begot rumour: perhaps Plotina, who was popularly believed to be enamoured of Hadrian, had actually concealed Trajan's death and smuggled in someone to impersonate the emperor with a suitably feeble voice, so that she could consort with the Praetorian Prefect, Attianus, Hadrian's former co-guardian, and ensure that Hadrian's adoption could be announced before news of the death was made public.

These accusations, however, originate principally in the prevailing senatorial historical tradition, which is consistently hostile to Hadrian. When the facts are examined, it can be seen that Trajan had shown an unwavering tendency to favour his cousin and only male heir as his successor. When Hadrian was but a military tribune, for example, he had been included in the imperial entourage, and then given the emperor's own great-niece as his wife. He succeeded to the right public offices at the earliest opportunity, went with the emperor as his imperial quaestor in the First Dacian War, and was then charged with announcing to the senate the progress of the first season's campaigning.[99] Then, in the Second Dacian War, he was entrusted with the command of the *legio I Minervia*, and the emperor presented him with a diamond which he, Trajan, had been given by Nerva, an act which in both cases was taken as indicating that the recipient was the designated successor.[100] Command of the new province of Pannonia Inferior followed, with the real chance of acting on his own initiative; and he was then made consul at the earliest opportunity, possibly as a replacement for one who died in office.[101] Sura, Trajan's closest confidant, chose that opportunity to tell him that the emperor intended to adopt him, and he accordingly developed his friendship with Plotina, and also with Attianus, his former guardian and Trajan's friend of over twenty years, now Praetorian Prefect and an influential member of the imperial *consilium*. Finally, Trajan's evident trust in and reliance upon Hadrian is demonstrated by Hadrian's appointment to command the expeditionary force in Syria on the emperor's departure for Rome in 117, and by the eastern armies' immediate acclamation of Hadrian in his place when news of Trajan's decease was broadcast.[102]

What occasioned senatorial hostility towards Hadrian was quite simply his pragmatism. On receiving the news of Trajan's death, the new *princeps* at once reverted to the late Augustan policy, the *consilium coercendi intra terminos imperii*, which stipulated that the empire should be kept within its natural boundaries. He justified his actions by quoting the dictum of Cato, that those who could not be held subject should be made free.[103] There was no place in the new order for some of Trajan's more aggressive marshals, and in a short time many were replaced – and some died in mysterious circumstances, notably A. Cornelius Palma, former commander of Asia, Hispania Citerior and Syria; L. Publilius Celsus; C. Avidius Nigrinus, governor of Dacia; and Lusius Quietus, governor of Judaea. Then, all the territory east of the Euphrates was immediately relinquished, as was the Syrian pre-desert, Dura Europos, for example, being abandoned before 30 September 117.[104] Parthamaspates, meanwhile, having been comprehensively rejected by the Babylonian Parthians, was reassigned to another unnamed client-kingdom, probably Osrhoëne, in place of Abgarus; Vologaesus, the son of Sanatrukes, was allowed to retain Armenia, and Mesopotamia was released from provincial status and had the tribute lifted.[105] The new emperor even considered giving up Dacia, presumably on account of internal disturbances, perhaps in connection with the Iazyges and/or Roxolani, which had led to the death in combat of Q. Julius Quadratus Bassus, only recently dispatched there to replace Nigrinus. He was dissuaded from doing so by the number of colonists who had settled in the province.[106] Not only could all these acts be construed as an outright denial of Rome's manifest destiny and a renunciation of Trajan's achievements, but they also directly affected the senators in reducing the number of high-ranking administrative posts they could aspire to; reason enough to damn him proleptically.

In the meantime, Plotina, Matidia and Attianus brought Trajan's corpse to Seleucia in Pieria. Hadrian viewed the body, and then had it cremated and the ashes conveyed to Rome in a golden urn, which was placed in the vestibule of the Column. Subsequently offered the triumph and games that the senate had previously voted Trajan in commemoration of his Parthian victories, Hadrian asked that the *Optimus Imperator* – the 'best of emperors' – should not be denied in death what was his due honour when alive, and arranged that Trajan's effigy should be carried in the triumphal chariot at the ceremony.[107] Before the year was out, the late emperor had been deified, and coins were issued depicting the transference of power from Trajan to his adopted son.[108] Hadrian then set about resolving the several disturbances that troubled the disparate regions of the empire, and, with all military opposition removed, the new frontier policy of passive defence could be instituted. 'Thus it was', as Dio/Xiphilinus noted, in a possibly unconscious imitation of Tacitus, 'that the Romans, in conquering Armenia, most of Mesopotamia, and the Parthians, had undergone severe hardships and dangers for naught.'[109]

XIV

A PERFECT PRINCE?

As we have seen in an earlier chapter, Pliny's *Panegyricus* and Dio Chrysostom's *Peri Basileias* present those aspects of Trajan's personal doctrine and policies that he desired publicly disseminated at the beginning of his rule. An equally clear impression of how he aspired to be remembered in his later years is presented on one of the finest surviving works of antiquity, the Arch at Beneventum, which stands to the south of the eponymous town on the very crest of the hill where the via Traiana leaves for Brindisi.[1] At the time of writing it is sadly shrouded in plastic and scaffolding, to protect it from the insidious and invisible menace of atmospheric pollution and the continual and all-pervading vibration of motor traffic (Pl. 14A). Otherwise, it is extremely well preserved, having survived virtually without damage the conflicts of the Italian Middle Ages, when it was incorporated into the town's defences, and even the heavy bombardment inflicted on the city in 1944.

From a distance the most prominent features of either side of the Arch are the inscribed panels in its attic. Each carries an identical text, originally emphasized with bronze letters, probably gilded, recording that the monument was erected by the Senate and People of Rome on behalf of their *FORTISSIMO PRINCIPI,* their 'bravest *princeps*'. It incorporates the appropriate imperial titulature for the period 29 August to 9 December 114, but construction must have been begun sometime earlier, perhaps in 112, when the via Traiana was officially commemorated on coinage. The Arch might well have been conceived even before then. Certain scenes on it would appear to relate directly to Trajan's second Dacian triumph of 107 and the colonization of that province, as if it were designed with the building of the road in mind and as a thank-offering for the victory which allowed its construction from the emperor's own share of the booty – 'pecunia sua fecit'.

In its general details, the Beneventum Arch is broadly analogous to the Arch of Titus at Rome and the Harbour Arch at Ancona. The single archway (*fornix*) is supported by a pair of pylons, the two principal faces of which were embellished with four engaged fluted columns, with composite capitals, standing on plain dado plinths. These framed the lower carved panels and carried a continuous frieze and cornice, above which rested the attic, only the two short ends and the dados of the pylons being devoid of elaborate sculpture. As was divined by K. Fittschen in 1972, the principal metopes are given over to what is effectively a paraphrase of Trajan's ideology – a lavish decoration and detailed catalogue of his *auctoritas* and *beneficium*, and his *pietas* and *virtus*. Nothing less, in fact, than an illustrated manifesto of the regime.[2] Fittschen was able to show that the Arch is not a canonical and historical account of the reign, as was previously thought, but rather an allegorical treatise, the panels being *topoi*, symbolic of Trajan's political tenets – a panegyric in stone, as it were. Hence, many of the qualities of the 'good ruler', as enumerated by Pliny and Dio Chrysostom, are reaffirmed on the monument, and especially the emperor's duty and responsibility to care for his people as benefactor, not their master; to serve as their protector, and not oppressor; and to work constantly for their betterment, rather than taking pleasures in the prerogatives of temporal power.

The largest panels are set within the *fornix* passageway, and directly express the *pietas* and *humanitas* of Trajan. On the one side he is seen presiding over a sacrifice, emblematic of his *pietas* towards the gods. On the other he is shown giving out bags of coins (*fisci*) to children who are accompanied by their parents. Trees show it to be a country scene. It can be nothing less than a record of the *alimenta*, paid for from the emperor's own *fiscus*, symbolic therefore of his *humanitas* and *beneficium* towards the common people of Italy.

The soffit of the coffered barrel-vault over the two panels contains a single relief slab, portraying Victory crowning Trajan with a laurel wreath and giving him the palm of victory. He 'faces' towards Beneventum, indicating that the town side of the Arch is the principal façade, and wears a moulded cuirass, the only time he appears on the Arch in full military garb, here signifying *virtus*. The representation seems to be directly linked with the relief frieze on the architrave, which shows a triumphal procession (Pl. 14B). The van has just reached the Capitoline, leading a cavalcade formed of chariots carrying chained prisoners, soldiers carrying boxes of valuables, and *victimarii* leading bulls to the slaughter, while Trajan brings up the rear of the parade in a triumphal chariot. It is the only detailed illustration of such a scene; there are valid reasons, as we will see, for believing it to record the triumph celebrated for the conquest of Dacia in 107, not least because the prisoners are shown as bearded northern barbarians.

Other emblems on the theme of victory are interspersed between the main series of reliefs on the pylons. Such are the intermediate panels which occur on both faces, paired upper metopes of *victimarii* and acolytes at sacrifices, and lower sets showing Victories slaughtering bulls in front of *candelabra*. Other winged Victories with *vexilla* occupy the spandrels on the town side of the Arch, with river gods symbolic of the travels involved in campaign in the corresponding position on the country side. Then there are personifications of the four seasons, allegorically confirming that Trajan's victories have brought about a *felicitas temporum*.

The principal reliefs, both those on the pylons and those in the attic, follow differing themes according to which side they are on. Those on the town side depict the administration of Italy; those on the country side relate to the government of the provinces. The lowest two metopes on the town side, for example, both illustrate an *adventus*. On the right Trajan is shown, with the imperial lictors, approaching a city gate.[3] It is probably Rome, for the corresponding panel on the left-hand side shows Trajan in front of the (?)Curia Julia being welcomed by men in togas. With them are three *genii*: that of the People of Rome, the *Genius Populi Romani*, shown as a youth holding a cornucopia; that of the Equestrian *Ordo*, the *Genius Equester*, mural-crowned, and with a wreathed 'swagger-stick'; and that of the senate, the *Genius Senatus*, offering the emperor a globe, symbol of the senate's trust in their *princeps* to exercise temporal power for the good of the people.[4] The two plaques together, therefore, represent Trajan's return from the Danubian provinces late in the year 99, and the *providentia* which gave the Senate and People of Rome the ideal successor to Nerva.

Thus legitimized with absolute power, the emperor was able to set about his reforms to existing institutions in Italy, and it is this which forms the subject of the medial panels on the town side. To the right Trajan is depicted with Portunus, the god of harbours, and Hercules and Apollo, deities both commonly associated with business affairs. The subject, then, is Trajan's reforms to commerce through his maritime policy, as expressed at Ostia, Ancona, Civitavecchia and elsewhere. Across the archway, Trajan takes on the role of benefactor of the army in a relief which shows him with his lictors taking leave of legionary veterans, their status revealed by the representation of a legionary *vexillum*, crowned with five eagles. The presence of Diana, goddess of the hunt, Silvanus, god of the forest, and (?)Abundantia, goddess of prosperity, all three tutelar gods of the provinces, indicate that the legionary colonies in the overseas territories are being represented. Here, then, we have an allegorical illustration of Trajan's policy in founding overseas colonies for his veterans, both for their personal benefit and for the further extension and future well-being of *Romanitas*, the Roman hegemony.

The top tier of metopes, on either side of the inscription, is somewhat more ethereal in content, but continues the theme of *providentia* and Trajan's divinely inspired rule. On the right Trajan is shown being welcomed to the Capitoline Temple, identified by its frieze bearing weaponry and a thunderbolt in the pediment. Having just entered the precinct through the arch he caused to be erected there, he is welcomed by the two consuls, shown on a much reduced scale, with Roma, the goddess of Rome, Romulus, the city's founder, and the Penates, the two deities which watch over the urban community, all in attendance. They are about to lead the emperor inside the Temple itself, the subject of the left panel, where Jupiter, as *Optimus Maximus*, awaits with his lightning bolt, ready to give it to Trajan as a token of the emperor's divine power, as one directly chosen by the greatest of the gods to rule the Roman people, and consequently his earthly counterpart.[5] As witnesses, Jupiter has in attendance the other members of the Capitoline triad, Juno and Minerva, while standing around are Hercules, Bacchus, Ceres and Mercury, symbolic of the way the welfare of the state has been entrusted to Trajan.

The country side of the Arch likewise bears paired images. The lowest on the right (Pl. 15A) shows Trajan, wearing a short tunic and *paludamentum*, the military cloak, with his lictors in attendance, surrounded by soldiers, identifiable as such by the animal skin one of them wears, denoting that he is a legionary standard bearer. The remainder are in undress uniform, yet the oak trees in the background indicate far-away territories, specifically the northern frontier provinces. The parable, therefore, is of the emperor ensuring the *securitas* of the *imperium* through his personal exercise of *disciplina*, discipline.[6] Hence the subject of the opposite metope (Pl. 15B), which represents Trajan, still in military undress uniform, talking to a group of tunic-clad bearded barbarians with Jupiter as an intermediary. Trees again symbolize the frontier territories, and Jupiter is present as the god of oaths, indicating that we are witnessing the agreement of treaties with client states on the periphery of the empire. Consequently, *securitas* through *concord*, not through *bellum*, force of arms.

The middle reliefs continue the provincial theme. To the right is a highly metaphorical metope which seems to refer to the fecundity of the provinces, for it shows Mother Earth ploughing a furrow from which spring forth a boy and a girl (Pl. 16A). Trajan is again shown with the *paludamentum*, confirming the frontier domains are at point, and he welcomes the children as Mars, Abundantia and Felicitas watch on. Their presence suggests that the relief is emblematic of the role of the provinces in providing an expanding population at the service of Rome. And the interpretation may well be confirmed by the matching panel to the left, which illustrates Trajan welcoming new recruits to the army (Pl. 16B). The trees in the background are symbolic of the provinces, and the status of the initiates is manifested by the presence of Honos, the personification of military honour, watching over the scene as one man is measured against a rod to ensure he conforms to the minimum height requirement.[7]

The uppermost panels on the country side are, if anything, even more allegorical concerning the emperor's virtues. On the right Trajan, still in military undress, is shown receiving the homage of a kneeling female figure, evidently the embodiment of a province. She is flanked by two beardless river gods, while in the background men march over a bridge. Oak trees symbolize the northern regions, and it is logical and reasonable to assume that the personification is that of Dacia, no longer dejected, but now imploring the emperor for his benefaction. In which case, the men marching over the bridge are the new colonists sent forth (or bribed) to settle the *tabula rasa* of the new province, itself symbolized by the two river gods, apparently the Olt and the Tisza, which demarcated the western and eastern limits of the newly acquired territory. As such, the scene would conform with the badly damaged relief on the other side of the *fornix*. This shows Trajan (or did: the figure is now missing), with the imperial lictors, in the presence of Diana, Silvanus, Ceres and Bacchus, the tutelar deities of the new and old provinces. It is nothing less than the embodiment of Trajan's desire to see the empire he ruled as a commonwealth, in which 'the natural products in any place now seem to belong to all'.[8]

This, then, is the ostensible message of the Arch of Beneventum. Trajan is the perfect prince of almost superhuman excellence, who embodies the equilibrium brought to constitutional, economic and military matters by the emergence of the principate. In successfully welding the ostensibly republican system of government, as symbolized by the senate, with the Augustan concept of the first citizen, simultaneously at the service of the state and guiding its destiny, Trajan had fulfilled the deepest wishes of the people by providing the sound rule of an autocrat, advised by a council of the wise, and continually working for the benefit of the people. Hence Dio Chrysostom's proclamations concerning how well Trajan fitted the ideal theoretical form of government as agreed by the sophists. Hence too the joyous rhetoric pronounced by Pliny in his *actio gratiarum* before the senate, relishing the new 'liberty' brought about by the emperor's liberality.

In fact, when all is said and done, the Roman people had been the victim of a well-managed confidence trick. And while Pliny and Dio Chrysostom were doubtless happy in their service to the emperor, and the several ideologies and policies they find so invigorating were undoubtedly real and genuinely welcomed by the majority, not all were fooled by or welcomed the new reality.[9] For in truth, Trajan's rule was no less and perhaps more autocratic than that espoused by the detested Domitian, and some of the procedures and programmes Trajan assiduously pursued, and brought to fruition, were not noticeably different from those initiated by his predecessors, both the 'good' and the 'bad'. He most certainly did not cultivate or even encourage a climate of compliance. It was all a matter of presentation, and Trajan deserves credit for successfully managing and advertising his own ideology in such a way that instead of being accused of creating an absolute monarchy, he was seen to be restoring the Augustan ideal of a guided autocracy.[10]

To begin with, there was the subtle projection of the emperor's status as anything but adoxiac. Domitian had been called both *dominus* and *deus* in his lifetime, and was rightly condemned for it, as it publicly announced the absolutism of his regime. Trajan managed to avoid the charge, even as he made it clear that he was some superhuman, divinely chosen, who could therefore be entrusted with sole and supreme rule as the representative of the gods. For example, early in his reign he 'allowed' his coinage to carry the title *Optimus* voted to him by the senate, with its overtones of affiliation with Jupiter Optimus Maximus, the supreme deity, even if he was careful not to incorporate it into his formal titulature.[11] Then he deified both his natural and adoptive father, along with his sister Marciana, becoming uniquely the son of two deities and the brother of a third. Further substance to the belief in his divinity is provided by the personification of the Baetican Hercules on his coinage, and is emphasized by his formal adoption of the title *Optimus* in 114, after the senate had once again implored him to accept their award. The purpose of all these allusions to the emperor's near-divine status, as Pliny, Dio Chrysostom and the designer of the Beneventum Arch were only too aware, was to promulgate and consummate the supreme and semi-divine nature of Trajan's rule. Chosen by providence, he is Jupiter's earthly equal, entrusted with the rule of the temporal world through fiat, his autocracy reinforced by the acknowledgement of the senate of his position as *primus inter pares*. It is for this reason that in the eastern provinces, and especially at Pergamum, the citizens of the various free cities celebrated him along with Zeus, as literally being a god on earth.[12]

On a more mundane level, the emperor developed to a fine art the existing procedures of imperial benefactions to the Roman people as a means of presenting himself as the perfect ruler. Whether these be his glorious buildings at Rome, in themselves a conscious imitation of the *beneficium* of Augustus, or the *alimenta*, he was careful to let it be known on inscriptions and on his coinage that these were personal gifts of a benign and all-providing *princeps*. It is in this context that we should see his reforms to the civil administration, promoting the view that it was now more public, as the imperial freedmen were gradually replaced in the important offices of the *imperium* by ostensibly independent equestrians. Hence, as the perfect ruler, he could promise a programme of radical change and institutional reform for the benefit of the people.

Now, while his public benefactions encouraged the love of the people, in reality, his change to the administration served to consolidate the absolute nature of the regime by giving senior duties to men who were answerable to the emperor alone. This is nowhere more clearly expressed than in his decision to regulate the twin posts of the *iuridici* and the *curatores*. Their duties were now extended even into the supervision of matters within Italy in addition to the provinces, where they were increasingly used to intervene in the actual administration of the nominally 'free cities'. It is also seen in the incremental change of equestrian offices as fundamental pillars of imperial administration. These assignments began increasingly to outnumber the senatorial posts available, and they acquired a greater importance, not least because they were held without formal time limit, but at the dispensation of the *princeps*. The change portended, in fact, the appearance of a professional civil service, answerable to the emperor alone.

The same determination to secure direct control is seen in Trajan's relationship with the senate. Competition for the various offices declined, as the emperor increasingly used his prerogative, formalized by the concordat of 103, to intervene directly in the selection of the junior and senior senatorial posts and the public administrators and his more surreptitious direction in the matter of selecting the consuls.[13] Moreover, just as in Domitian's time, so in Trajan's the *novi homines* seem consciously favoured over the *nobilitas*. Several held a longer and more extensive series of imperial offices, substantiating a thesis of the increasing centralization of the emperor's powers, as exercised through his *auctoritas*. It may well have been intended to improve bureaucratic procedures: Trajan was, after all, badly served by certain of his proconsular administrators. Even so, as W. Eck has convincingly demonstrated, Trajan's reign was notorious for the facility with which the *princeps* changed the constitutional basis of several provinces, individual public territories becoming imperial almost overnight with no apparent dissent by the senate.[14] The lines of prerogative and responsibility had become increasingly blurred, which suggests that the legislative body had effectively, if not legally, accepted the overriding nature of imperial authority, the pernicious advance of *auctoritas* which had caused Domitian's memory to be damned in perpetuity. In Trajan, therefore, as the astute Tacitus recognized, the process of transforming the *principatus* into the *dominatio*, albeit now masquerading as the due exercise of *imperium*, was made complete.

Yet Trajan was careful throughout to maintain constitutional proprietary and tactfulness in his dealings with the *Curia*, for there is no trace of a crisis in the relations between first citizen and governing body. To begin with, he believed in allowing it to deliberate as it saw fit, promoted secret voting, and ostensibly only intervened in procedures at their request, instead of directly and obviously imposing his own demands on the body: as Pliny noted, Trajan 'bid us be free, and we were free'.[15] This is why the emperor was careful to remain approachable to the individual senators, and why he showed a studious observance to, and personal affirmation of, the consular oath. He did not act in a confrontational manner; what happened was much more subtle. He allowed his wishes to be propagated through his consuls and *consilium*: for what the emperor wished was law on account of his semi-divine status, as the *Digest* was to later affirm. This accounts for his 'failure' to adopt Hadrian formally as his heir; he let it be known that the matter would be left in the hands of the senators to choose from a nominal roll of those he thought best to inherit his own powers. Denied a son and heir himself, he instead promoted the standing of Hadrian, seemingly his closest male kinsman, by authorizing his marriage to his own closest eligible female relative, and deliberately elevating him to duties which assured his place in the *consilium* right from the very beginning of his reign.[16]

But in spite of these absolutist measures, Trajan brought a particularly even-handed approach and sense of humanist duty to his polity, which transcended the mere usurpation of the remaining shreds of senatorial power. As Fronto observed, 'none have excelled and few equalled Trajan in his popularity with the people'.[17] Some of his specific domestic proposals, as we have seen, were improvements in what we would now recognize as fundamental human rights: those concerning the treatment and rights of foundlings and children, for example, or his measures dealing with the torture of slaves. Then there was the *alimenta*, a social welfare policy intended primarily to benefit the poor of Italy while encouraging a degree of self-sufficiency among the populace at large.

Coupled with it was a determination to improve the supply of the most basic of food stuffs, grain. Even if the corn-dole distributed among the 'deserving' proletariat at Rome, the *plebs frumentaria*, was primarily a political act, the procedure served to reinforce his obvious concern for the interest of the people at large. It is in this context that we should see his decision to extend certain rights of citizenship to promote an increase in the number of bakers at Rome, and it seems highly likely that the series of corn mills on the Janiculum at Rome, powered by a branch of the Aqua Traiani, were another direct result of his *beneficium*.[18]

Allied to all this was Trajan's policy to ameliorate internal and external communications. It is best seen through the new road systems and the wholesale programme of harbour improvements he inaugurated in Italy. But it was also extended to the provinces, as witnessed by the recutting of the Ptolemaic canal linking the Nile to the Bitter Lakes, greatly facilitating sea trade with the east.[19] For, while his efforts to reduce reliance on the overseas provinces for basic foodstuffs were genuine, he was well aware of the need to promote and secure trade in all commodities at all points of his polity. At the same time, the measures implanted in the public consciousness that (as Pliny observed, even if he could not quite bring himself to admit it) Rome was becoming but one city, if the principal, amongst a commonality of peoples and communities.[20] It was the first faltering step along the road which eventually brought about the *constitutio Antoniniana*, granting citizenship to all men of free-born status.

Then, Trajan consistently affirmed his concern for the security of his people, at Rome and abroad, through his intimate relationship with the army and his specific regard to *securitas*. Not for nothing did he exploit his facility at remembering names to greet his men personally; or that he wore his hair in that strict military fashion preferred by Vespasian, as opposed to the curls and waves of Domitian. As Sir Ronald Syme ascertained, Trajan conceived and expressed his affinity with his soldiers in a most paternal and personal fashion, as was demonstrated by his reforms to the procedures relating to soldiers' wills and his rescript allowing monotesticular men to join the legions.[21] Furthermore, he made certain reforms to military procedure, most now sadly lost to us, although remarked upon by Vegetius. Among them, probably, was the decision to raise the *numeri*, companies drawn from external allies, principally as regular army units to garrison many of the minor fortifications on the frontiers, but also to play a vital part in campaigning and in the matter of maintaining logistical matters. A second was presumably his well-attested reforms to the imperial horse guard, while a third was the practical pains he took at restoring military discipline.[22]

As it was, no *princeps* before him played such an innovative part in the formulation of what became a specific policy for the frontier provinces of the Roman empire. His commission in 98 to restore the frontier in Germania Superior undoubtedly sprang from his experiences in the aftermath of the Saturninian revolt in 89. His preoccupation with security against external attack is exemplified by his review of the Danubian provinces immediately after he became *princeps*, when many thought that by rights he should have turned his steps to Rome. The decision to replace many of the existing timber forts and fortresses throughout the provinces with permanent bases of masonry construction, where the appropriate materials were to hand, reveals his comprehension that the empire had, indeed, already reached manageable limits in most of the provinces.[23] Nowhere is this better seen than in Trajan's decision to formalize the Stanegate line in Britain as the northern limit of Roman expansion, as a network of forts and fortlets, together with a simplified system of advance observation posts, gradually developed out of the existing Domitianic dispositions.[24] Likewise in Africa, where Trajan initiated an advance south of the Aures to create an in-depth military zone, rather than a formal limit, to cope with the nomadic tribes crossing the area.[25] Indeed, when his reforms of the Rhine and Danube frontier works are taken into account, along with the measures he adopted in Arabia and in Africa south of the Aures, there is good reason for believing that the policy of preclusive 'defence' – in reality, the direct control of cross-frontier movement – commonly attributed to Hadrian should rightly be assigned to Trajan. Hadrian's return to Augustan values concerning the empire's security was nothing less than the wholesale application of an already developing policy.

In which case, why, then, did Trajan throw so much away, in terms of material and manpower, in the inconclusive First Dacian War and his later campaign against Parthia? To the first, it can be said in his favour that he wished to repair the indignity done to Rome by the policy of appeasement forced on Domitian in 91. Bruised *amour propre* has had more than a slight part in hostilities between even mature states, as comparatively recent events in the southern hemisphere have revealed. Yet Trajan had quite clearly seriously miscalculated the strength and determination of his opponents when he began the First Dacian War, as conclusive victory after the second battle of Tapae in 101 was denied him through the losses his overstretched forces had sustained, requiring him to extend the campaign into 102. It was an uneasy peace which prevailed thereafter, which explains Decebalus' provocation in the following years and Trajan's need to restore his personal prestige through direct conquest. Thus, while Trajan's Dacian triumphs may well have been honourably accomplished, they were no more deserved than the ones Domitian had claimed for his own. Their only solid achievement was the acquisition of Dacia, a territory lost to barbarian inroads within two centuries because of its very indefensibility, and the glorious Tropaeum Traiani the emperor caused to be erected south of the eponymous *municipium* in Moesia Inferior (Pl. 7).

But while the initial campaign against Dacia could at least be justified by the real need to restore Roman prestige, and it could be said that the eventual conquest was forced upon Trajan by the recalcitrant nature of Decebalus, there is no verifiable political or military justification for Trajan's war with Parthia. It seems to have been brought about by the need for personal glory alone, a contemporary Falklands Factor, and conforms to a worrying and well-recognized tendency among established political leaders of any period, if especially so of the present, to seek internal prestige by diverting attention away from matters at home and interfering in the affairs of foreign states. Even so, Trajan had once more seriously miscalculated the strength of the opposition. While the Parthians were quarrelling amongst themselves, he rapidly advanced through their hegemony: when they provided a concerted resistance, his own strategy was quickly proved useless. It would have been a very hollow triumph, less deserved than any of Domitian's, in fact, if Trajan had indeed survived to return to Rome in 117.

The subject of any biographical prospection cannot emerge unscathed from cold, forensic analysis. While the eminence of Trajan rightly remains secure and supreme amongst the virtuous emperors, for his glorification of Rome yet survives to impress us, and his legal and administrative measures to improve the lot of the *plebs urbana* had far-reaching and long-lasting effects, in the end, as K. Waters noted, he emerges as an unmitigated autocrat from the same mould as Domitian.[26] His absolute success was owed in the main to his maturity, which defined his subtle methodology. He brought to his task a well-versed policy concerning the administration of the empire, which he owed to his own unparalleled field experience in the protection of the state. Thus most of his reforms were in the main creditable, in their attempts at formalizing an ever-growing and increasingly complex polity, hitherto run by the most *ad hoc* of systems. Likewise he deserves praise for the way he effectively brought about, if not intentionally, a dynasty of adoptive emperors, and Gibbon's period of great prosperity. Then, Trajan alone developed the principle of the *imperium*, a conscious policy of internal trade within a commonwealth of nations, firmly protected through a well-trained and positioned army. His successor, Hadrian, merely inherited this tradition wholesale and brought it to its logical conclusion. Which is why Hadrian's detractors sought to disparage his military courage with faint praise, and denigrate his accomplishments at recovering the adverse situation caused by Trajan's over-expansion through surrendering the eastern territories. Hence the need for Hadrian to take such swift, if disguised, action against certain highly discontented members of the senate. But on any objective analysis, most would agree that Hadrian's peripatetic regime was made both necessary and possible by Trajan, who correctly foresaw that the betterment of Rome was best achieved through the autocratic government of the *urbs* and the security and development of the provinces – even while carefully disguising the policies behind a façade of republican and Augustan standards. To Trajan, then, belongs the praise for bringing the developing principate to its zenith, and the embryonic *imperium* to its nascence. As such, he was assuredly Trajan, *Optimus Princeps*.

DIO'S ACCOUNT OF THE DACIAN WARS

The broad details of the two Dacian Wars can be reconstructed from the relevant passages of Dio's History as these survive in two quite different sources: the *Excerpta* prepared by unknown abstractors for the Byzantine emperor Constantine VII Porphyrogenitus (912–59); and the *Epitome* produced by Xiphilinus of Trabzon for the emperor Michael VII Parapinaces (1071–8).[1] The *Excerpta* were originally chosen for their instructive or moral value, and are usually quite comprehensive abstracts from the original. Xiphilinus, on the other hand, was only concerned in his *Epitome* with giving a brief outline of Roman history, and was totally unconcerned with the minutiae of campaigns etc. None the less, where these disparate sets of information can be compared with the surviving unabridged text of Dio's History, it would seem that they preserve the original wording fairly closely, save at the beginnings and ends of passages. On the other hand, it is not certain that the citations presented in the *Excerpta* and the *Epitome* faithfully reflect their original order, for a close comparison with the unabridged text does reveal errors in chronology.[2] That said, there is sufficient overlap between the two sets of abstracts to allow some reconstitution of the original text with a reasonable degree of confidence, and the following text merges the constituent elements of the two principal sources to make a single narrative, using intrinsic clues wherever possible (bold type is used to identify the passages from the *Excerpta*).

The First Dacian War

(Dio 6.1) Trajan, after spending some time in Rome, made an expedition against the Dacians: he had taken stock of their previous record, he resented the sums of money that they received annually, and he saw that their powers and their pride were on the increase.

(Dio 6.2) When Decebalus learnt of his approach, he was afraid, for he realized that, whereas before he had been victorious not over Rome but only over Domitian, he now had Rome and Trajan as emperor to make war against.

(Exc Val 286) **For Trajan was distinguished for his justice, his valour and the simplicity of his manners. He was physically robust – he was in his forty-second year when he began to reign – and on equal terms with all in enduring hard labour, and was mentally in his prime, without either the impetuosity of youth or the torpor of old age.**

(Dio 7.5.2) And that all-too-familiar feature of [previous] regimes, the arrogance and licence of the soldiery, never took shape in his time: under such firm discipline did he keep them.

(Dio 8.1) For these reasons Decebalus had good cause to be afraid of him. And when Trajan was on the march against the Dacians and drawing near to Tapae, where the barbarians were encamped, a large mushroom was brought to him on which a message was written in Roman lettering saying that the Buri and the rest of the [Dacian] allies advised Trajan to go home and keep the peace.

(Dio 8.2) But Trajan joined battle with them, and while he saw many wounded on his own side, yet slew many of the enemy; and at this time too, when the field dressings gave out, he is said not to have spared even his own clothing, but cut it into strips for bandages; and he set up an altar in honour of the soldiers who had fallen in the battle and ordered yearly sacrifices to be made on it.

(Exc. UG 47.1–3) **Even before this defeat Decebalus had sent an embassy, not as previously, of the *comati* class, but of the *pileati*.[3] They threw down their arms and cast themselves upon the ground and besought Trajan, if possible, to let Decebalus come into his presence and to speak with him in person, undertaking he would do everything that he was ordered to do; otherwise, to send someone to arrange terms of peace with him. Sura and Claudius Livianus, the Prefect, were duly sent. However, nothing came of this, for Decebalus did not venture to meet them either, but once again sent intermediaries. Trajan meanwhile stormed some mountain strongholds and in them found the captured arms and engines and the standard that had been lost in the time of Fuscus.**

(Dio 8.3.1)[4] And he set about scaling the very peaks of the mountains, capturing, not without danger, crest after crest, and drew near the Royal City of the Dacians; and Lusius, attacking from another direction, killed many of them and took still more prisoners.

(Exc. UG 47.4) **For these reasons, and especially because at the same time Maximus captured his sister and a certain stronghold.**

(Dio 8.3.2) Decebalus then sent an[other] embassy of the top-class *pileati* and through them appealed to the emperor, and was ready to accept any terms imposed on him without exception.

(Exc UG 47.4–7) **Not that he intended to abide by them, but needed them to give him a respite from his present reverses. So he reluctantly agreed to surrender the arms and the engines and the engineers, to return the deserters, to dismantle the forts, to relinquish the [Dacian] territory already captured [by Rome], and for the future to have the same friends and foes as the Romans, and neither give refuge to any deserter nor enlist any soldier from the Roman's dominions: for he had acquired the bulk and the pick of his troops by attracting men from Roman territory into his service. And he came into**

Trajan's presence and prostrated himself and did obeisance to him and cast aside his arms. He also sent envoys to the senate about these matters so that the peace might be ratified by that body also. Having thus made peace, Trajan returned to Italy, leaving behind the main body of his army at Zermizegethusa and distributing smaller garrisons over the rest of the country.

(Dio 10.1) And the envoys from Decebalus were brought before the senate: laying down their arms they placed their hands together like manacled prisoners and uttered words of supplication; and thus they concluded the peace and received back their arms.

(Dio 10.2) But Trajan celebrated a triumph, and took the name 'Dacicus'. In the theatre he matched pairs of gladiators in single combat, a sport he took much pleasure in.

The Second Dacian War

(Dio 10.3) But Decebalus was reported to him to be doing many things in breach of the peace – and indeed, he was procuring arms, receiving deserters, restoring the forts, sending embassies to neighbouring peoples, maltreating his political opponents without provocation, and he had even deprived the Iazyges of a piece of their territory, land which later Trajan did not give back when they asked for it.

(Dio 10.4) In these circumstances, the senate again voted Decebalus an enemy and Trajan once again took command in person, instead of leaving it to others, and took the field in person against him.

(Exc.UG 48) **And great numbers of the Dacians came over to Trajan's side; for this and other reasons Decebalus again sued for peace. But he would not agree to surrender his weapons and his own person. Instead he began to openly assemble his forces and to call upon his neighbours for their help. He pointed out to them that if they left him in the lurch, they would be imperilled, but by joining forces with him now, while his kingdom was intact, they would preserve their own freedom more surely and easily than by looking on idly while the Dacians were eliminated, only to be subjugated later in their turn without any allies left to help them.**

(Dio 11.3) Now, as far as the fighting went, Decebalus did badly. But by guile and treachery he came near to taking Trajan's life: he sent some deserters to Moesia to see if they could assassinate him, seeing he was always easily approachable and at that time, even with all the requirements of waging war, he used to grant interviews to anyone who asked for one. However, this plan did not come off, for one of the men was arrested on suspicion and under torture revealed the whole plot.

(Dio 12.1) So Decebalus then sent an invitation to a certain Longinus, the commander of the Roman force, and an officer who had served with particular distinction in the wars against him, and persuaded him to come to a conference with him, professing himself ready to meet whatever terms of accommodation he might propose. He then seized him, and interrogated him publicly about Trajan's plans, and when Longinus refused to reveal anything placed him under open arrest.

(Exc UG 49.2–5) **He sent a message to Trajan demanding that he should get the territory as far as the Danube and the expenses so far incurred by him on the war in exchange for Longinus. Trajan gave him an ambiguous answer, from which Decebalus could not infer either that Longinus was of great or little importance to him, so that he would neither be put to death nor have to be ransomed at a high price. At this Decebalus hesitated, considering what he should do next. But meanwhile Longinus contrived to obtain some poison from his [sc., Decebalus'] freedman; he then promised Decebalus that he would persuade Trajan to come to terms, so that Decebalus would not have the slightest suspicion of what was going to happen, in case he put him under closer confinement, and he gave the freedman, to ensure the man's safety, a letter to take to Trajan, which contained his petition. Then when the man had departed, he drank the poison during the night and died. Thereupon Decebalus demanded the freedman back from Trajan, promising to give him in exchange the body of Longinus and ten prisoners of war, and sent him at once the centurion who had been captured with Longinus, so as to arrange these exchanges. From him, Trajan learnt the whole story of Longinus' fate. But he did not send the centurion back, nor did he give back the freedman, accounting the saving of his life more important for the good name of the empire than the burial of Longinus' corpse.**

(Dio 13.1) But Trajan had built a bridge of stone over the Ister and it is beyond my powers to express adequately my admiration for him for this. For while his other works are magnificent enough, this puts even them in the shade. It has piers, of squared stone, twenty in number, one hundred and fifty feet in height above the foundations and sixty feet in breadth.

(Dio 13.2) These piers were set one hundred and seventy feet apart from each other and they were connected by arches. How could anyone fail to marvel at the amount of money spent on them? Or at the technical skill by which each of them was placed in a great river and in turbulent waters and upon a muddy bottom? For there was no possibility there of diverting the stream into another channel.

(Dio 13.3) As to the distance across the river, what I said must not be taken to indicate its normal width – for in places it is twice that width, and it can flood over three times that figure – but I meant only that this was the distance at this particular point in its course, which was the narrowest and best adapted to be bridged in the whole of that region.

(Dio 13.4) But the more straightly the river is contracted at this point in its downward course from a great flood of water into a narrow gorge, to expand further downstream into a greater flood again, the more violent and deep do its waters become, as you may well suppose: so that this factor too added to the difficulty of building this bridge.

(Dio 13.5) And this is additional proof of the grand scale of Trajan's enterprise. But the bridge does not provide any sort of service for us today; instead its piers stand idle with no roadway spanning them, as though they were created for no other purpose than to show there was nothing that human ingenuity could not accomplish.

(Dio 13.6) But Trajan had been concerned that at some time when the Danube was frozen over an attack might be made on the Romans on the further bank, and he had built the bridge so that reinforcements could easily be got across to them over it.[5] But Hadrian on the contrary was afraid that the barbarians might overpower the men on guard at the bridge and thus have an easy crossing over into Moesia, so he removed its superstructure.

(Dio 14.1) Trajan then crossed the Danube by this bridge, and conducting his campaign with caution rather than dash, in due time and not without difficulty, vanquished the Dacians. He himself performed many instances of good generalship and bravery while his soldiers likewise faced many dangers and displayed much valour under his command.

(Dio 14.2) An instance of this indeed was given by a certain cavalryman: badly wounded, he had been carried off the field as a case not beyond treatment; but when he realized that his wound was mortal, he leapt out of the tent, for the onset of death was not yet upon him, took his place in the line and met a hero's death in battle.

(Dio 14.3) Decebalus, when his Royal City and the whole of his country had been overrun and he himself was in danger of being taken prisoner, committed suicide, and his head was brought to Rome. And thus Dacia became subject to the Romans and Trajan settled some cities there.

(Dio 14.4) Decebalus' treasure was also found, though it had been hidden beneath the waters of the river Sargetias that flowed past his Royal City. For he had diverted the course of this river, using some captives as labour, and dug a hole in its bed, and there he had deposited much silver and gold and other most precious valuables such as could survive wetting, and then heaped stones over them and piled up earth on top and finally brought the river back into its old channel.

(Dio 14.5) And he got the same labourers to deposit his robes and suchlike articles in the caves there. And all these things having been done, he slew the men, to prevent them from talking too much. But one of his companions, a man called Bikilis, knew what had been done: he was captured and revealed the whole story.

(Dio 14.6) About this same time, Palma, the governor of Syria, subdued the part of Arabia around Petra, and made it subject to the Romans.

(Dio 15.1) Upon Trajan's return to Rome, ever so many embassies came to him from various barbarians, including the Indi. And he gave spectacles on one hundred and twenty-three days, in the course of which some eleven thousand animals, both wild and tame, were slaughtered, and ten thousand gladiators fought.

ABBREVIATIONS

ADAJ	*Annual of the Department of Antiquities of Jordan*
AE	*L'Année épigraphique*
AJA	*American Journal of Archaeology*
AJP	*American Journal of Philology*
AK	*Antike Kunst*
Anc.Hist.Bull.	*Ancient History Bulletin*
ANRW	*Aufstieg und Niedergang der römischen Welt*
ArchN	*Archaeological News*
BARIS	*British Archaeological Reports Supplementary (International) Series*
Birley, Fasti	Birley, A. R., 1981, *The* Fasti *of Roman Britain* (Oxford 1981)
BJ	*Bonner Jahrbuch*
Blake, *Roman Construction*	Blake, M. E. and Bishop, D. T., 1973, *Roman Construction in Italy from Nerva through the Antonines* (Philadelphia 1973)
BMC	*A Catalogue of the Coins of the Roman Empire in the British Museum* (vol. 3, *Trajan* (1966), unless otherwise stated)
Bowersock, *Arabia*	Bowersock, G. W., 1983, *Roman Arabia* (Cambridge, Mass. and London 1983)
BRGK	*Bericht der römisch-germanischen Kommission*
Brit	*Britannia*
Campbell, *Emperor*	Campbell, J. B., 1984, *The Emperor and the Roman Army* (Oxford 1984)
Cataniciu, *Evolution*	Cataniciu, I. B., 1981, *Evolution of the System of Defence Works in Roman Dacia* (= *BARIS* 116, Oxford 1981)
Cichorius	Cichorius, C., *Die Reliefs der Trajanssäule*, II (Berlin 1896)
CIL	*Corpus Inscriptionum Latinarum*
CJ	*Classical Journal*
CQ	*Classical Quarterly*
Devijver, *Prosopographia*	Devijver, H., 1976–80, *Prosopographia militiarum equestrium quae fuerunt ab Augusto ad Gallienum* I–III (Leuven 1976–80)

Duncan-Jones, *Economy*	Duncan-Jones, R., 1974, *The Economy of the Roman Empire: Quantitative Studies* (Cambridge 1974, 2nd ed., 1982)
Eck, *Senatoren*	Eck, W., 1970, *Senatoren von Vespasian bis Hadrian: Prosopographische Untersuchungen mit Einschluss der Jahres- und Provinzialfasten der Statthalter* (= *Vestiga* 13, Munich 1970)
Eck, *Statthalter*	Eck, W., 1985, *Die Statthalter der germanischen Provinzen vom 1–3. Jahrhunderts* (= *ES* 14, Cologne 1985)
Eck, *Stattliche Organisation*	Eck, W., 1979, *Die stattliche Organisation Italiens in der Organisation hohen kaiserzeit* (= *Vestiga* 28, München 1979)
EE	*Ephemeris Epigraphica*
ES	*Epigraphische Studien*
Garnsey and Saller, *Roman Empire*	Garnsey, P. and Saller, R., 1987, *The Roman Empire: Economy, Society and Culture* (Trowbridge 1987)
G&R	*Greece and Rome*
HA	*Scriptores Historiae Augustae*
HAC	*Historia-Augusta-Colloquium* (with year and publication date)
Halfmann, *Itinera*	Halfmann, H., 1986, *Itinera Principum: Geschichte und Typologie der Kaiserreisen in römischen Reich* (Stuttgart 1986)
Hammond, *Monarchy*	Hammond, M., 1959, *The Antonine Monarchy* (= *Papers and Monographs of the American Academy in Rome* 19, Rome 1959)
Hill, *Monuments*	Hill, P. V., 1989, *The Monuments of Ancient Rome as Coin Types* (London 1989)
ILS	*Inscriptiones Latinae Selectae*
Isaac, *Limits*	Isaac, B., 1992, *The Limits of Empire: the Roman Army in the East* (2nd ed., Oxford 1992)
JDAI	*Jarhbuch des Deutschen Archäologischen Institutes*
JÖAI	*Jahreshefte des Österreichischen Archäologischen Institutes*
Jolowicz and Nicholas, *Roman Law*	Jolowicz, H. F. and Nicholas, B., 1972, *Historical Introduction to the Study of Roman Law* (3rd ed., Cambridge 1972)
Jones, *Domitian*	Jones, B. W., 1992, *The Emperor Domitian* (London 1992)
Jones, *Senatorial Order*	Jones, B. W., 1979, *Domitian and the Senatorial Order: A Prosopographical Study of Domitian's Relationship with the Senate, AD 81–96* (= *Memoirs of the American Philosophical Society* 132, Philadelphia 1979)
Jones, *Titus*	Jones, B. W., 1984, *The Emperor Titus* (London and New York 1984)
JRA	*Journal of Roman Archaeology*

JRMES	*Journal of Roman Military Equipment Studies*
JRS	*Journal of Roman Studies*
Lepper, *Parthian War*	Lepper, F. A., 1948, *Trajan's Parthian War* (Oxford 1948, reprinted Westpoint, Conn. 1979)
Lepper and Frere, *Column*	Lepper, F. A. and Frere, S. S., 1988, *Trajan's Column: A New edition of the Cichorius Plates* (Gloucester 1988)
Les Empereurs Romains	*Les Empereurs Romains d'Espagne* (= *Colloques du Centre National de la Recherche Scientifique*, Paris 1965)
LF	*Listy Filologické*
MAAR	*Memoirs of the American Academy at Rome*
McCrum and Woodhead, *Documents*	McCrum, M. W. and Woodhead, A. G., 1961, *Selected Documents of the Principates of the Flavian Emperors including the Year of Revolution, AD 68–96* (Cambridge 1961)
MacDonald, *Architecture*	MacDonald, W. L., *The Architecture of the Roman Empire 1: An Introductory Study* (2nd ed., New Haven, Conn. and London 1982)
Maxfield, *Decorations*	Maxfield, V. A., 1981, *The Military Decorations of the Roman Army* (London 1981)
MEFR	*Mélanges de l'Ecole Française de Rome, Antiquité*
Meiggs, *Ostia*	Meiggs, R., 1973, *Roman Ostia* (2nd ed., Oxford 1973)
Millar, *Emperor*	Millar, F. G. B., 1992, *The Emperor in the Roman World, 31 BC – AD 337* (2nd ed., London 1992)
Millar, *Near East*	Millar, F. G. B., 1993, *The Roman Near East, 31 BC– AD 337* (Cambridge, Mass. and London 1993)
Mócsy, *Pannonia*	Mócsy, A., 1974, *Pannonia and Upper Moesia: A History of the Middle Danubian Provinces of the Roman Empire* (London 1974)
Mon.As.Min.Ant.	*Monumenta Asiae Minoris Antiqua*
NC	*Numismatic Chronicle*
PBA	*Proceedings of the British Academy*
PBSR	*Papers of the British School at Rome*
Pflaum, *Carrières*	Pflaum, H.-G., 1960–1, *Les carrières des procuratoriennes équestres sous le haut-empire romain* I–III (Paris 1960–1)
Pflaum, *Procurateurs*	Pflaum, H.-G., 1950, *Les procurateurs équestres sous le haut-empire romain* (Paris 1950)
PIR	*Prosopographia Imperii Romani Saec I–III*
PP	*La Parola de Passato*
Raepsaet–Charlier, *Prosopographie*	Raepsaet-Charlier, M.-T., 1987, *Prosopographie des femmes de l'ordre sénatorial (Ier–II siècles)* (Louvain 1987)

RE	Pauly–Wissowa–Kroll: *Real-Encyclopädie der classischen Altertumswissenschaft*
Rev. Et. Anc.	*Revue des Études Anciennes*
Richardson, *Ancient Rome*	Richardson, L., 1992, *A New Topographical Dictionary of Ancient Rome* (Baltimore and London 1992)
RP 1–7	Syme, R., *Roman Papers* 1–7 (Oxford 1979–91)
Segal, *Town Planning*	Segal, A., 1988, *Town Planning and Architecture in Provincia Arabia: The Cities along the Via Traiana Nova in the 1st–3rd Centuries C.E.* (= *BARIS* 49, Oxford 1988)
Sherwin-White, *Letters*	Sherwin-White, A. N., 1966, *The Letters of Pliny: A Historical and Social Commentary* (Oxford 1966)
Smallwood, *Documents*	Smallwood, E. M., 1966, *Documents Illustrating the Principates of Nerva, Trajan and Hadrian* (Cambridge 1966)
Strack, *Untersuchungen*	Strack, P. L., 1931, *Untersuchungen zur römische Reichsprägung des zweiten Jahrhunderts I: Die Reichsprägung zur zeit des Traian* (Stuttgart 1931)
Strobel, *Dakerkriegen*	Strobel, K., 1984, *Untersuchungen zu den Dakerkriegen Trajans: Studien zur Geschichte des mittleren und unteren Donauraumes in der Hohen Kaiserzeit* (= Antiquitas 1.33, Bonn 1984)
Syme, *Tacitus*	Syme, R., 1958, *Tacitus* (Oxford 1958)
Talbert, *Senate*	Talbert, R. J. A., 1984, *The Senate of Imperial Rome* (Princeton 1984)
TAPA	*Transactions of the American Philological Association*
VdH	van den Hout, M. P. J. (ed.), *M. Cornelius Fronto: epistulae* (Teubner, Leipzig 1988)
Veyne, *Bread and Circuses*	Veyne, P., 1990, *Bread and Circuses* (St Ives 1990)
Williams, *Correspondence*	Williams, W., 1990, *Pliny: Correspondence with Trajan from Bithynia (Epistles X)* (Warminster 1990)
ZPE	*Zeitschrift für Papyrologie und Epigraphik*

NOTES
AND REFERENCES

Preface and Prolegomenon (pp. xii–xvii)

[1] *Optimus Princeps*: Pliny *Pan.* 88.4; Eutr. 8.5 and 13.4. E. Gibbon, *The History of the Decline and Fall of the Roman Empire* (1776), ch. 3. Septimius Severus: *ILS* 420.

[2] R. Syme, *Cambridge Ancient History* 11 (1936), 200.

[3] The works of Pliny and Dio Chrysostom are discussed in Chapter 6.

[4] Pliny and Dio Chrysostom: see Chapter 6. Cassius Dio: F. G. B. Millar, 1964, *A Study of Cassius Dio* (Oxford 1964).

[5] The 'kaisergeschicte': A. Enmann, *Philologus* Suppl. 4 (1884), 337–501, and T. D. Barnes, 1978, *The Sources of the Historia Augusta* (Brussels 1978), *passim*. Eutropius: cf. H. W. Bird, *Eutropius: Breviarium* (1993), vii–lvii; Barnes, *op. cit.*, and C. P. Jones, *JRS* 60 (1970), 99. Aurelius Victor: id. *Sextus Aurelius Victor: A Historiographical Study* (1984).

[6] Dedication of *Essay concerning Human Understanding*.

[7] Trajan's popularity: Fronto *Princ. Hist.* 19 (= VdH 213). His integrity and fortitude: *Epit.* 13.4. The accession oath: Eutr. 8.5. The Forum: Amm. Marc. 16.10; Cass. *Var.* 7.6.

[8] S. Gallen *Vita* 29; Joh. Diac. *Vita* 2.44. The modern literature is not extensive: see G. Paris, *Mélanges publiés par l'Ecole des Hautes Etudes Sciences, philologiques et historiques* 35 (1878), 261–94; and F. H. Dudden, *Gregory the Great*, I (1905), 48–9, with further references; and for a modern commentary, G. Whatley, *Viator* 15 (1984), 25–63.

[9] Dante, *Purgatorio* 10.70–96; *Paradiso* 20.43–8 and 106–17.

[10] *Piers Plowman*: B 11.140–71 and 12.280–92; Wycliff, *De Eccl.*, *passim*, among other works.

[11] A. von Mandach, *Der Trajan- und Herkinbald Teppich* (1987). For an embossed leather bridal trunk of similar date, quite possibly influenced by a painting of Mantegna's, cf. R. Milesi, *Mantegna und die Reliefs der Brauttruhen Paola Gonzangas* (1975).

[12] I am grateful to Justice Sandra Day O'Connor for her comments on the reliefs in the Supreme Court. For the 'Justice of Hadrian', see Dio 69.6.

1 The Making of a New Aristocracy (pp. 1–10)

[1] Dio 68.4.1: 'Italiot' was the somewhat pejorative term applied to Italians of Greek descent, but strictly speaking, Trajan was a *Hispaniensis*, that is, an Italian domiciled or born in Spain, as opposed to a *Hispanus*, a citizen of Spanish stock. Tuder: *Epit.* 13.1; Syme, *Tacitus*, 786. The most recent discussion on the origins of the Ulpii of Italica is A. Caballos Rufino, *Los senadores hispanorromanos y la romanizacion de Hispana (siglos I–II)* (1990), 309–11.

2   For the derivation of Ulpius, G. Bonfante, *Latomus* 3, 1939, 81–3, and Syme, *Tacitus*, 786; and for Traianus, I. Kajanto, *The Latin Cognomina* (1965), 32–6 and 157, and H. Krahe, *Lexicon altillyrischer Personennamen* (1929), 245. Cf. *Epit.* 13.1 for the claim that the *cognomen* Traianus was introduced through marriage.
    The possible ties with the Ameria region are considered by Syme, *Tacitus*, 786, and A. Caballos Rufino, op. cit., 310–11.

3   Eutr. 8.2.1–2. For an Augustan M. Trahius at Italica, possibly a collateral ancestor, see A. Caballos Rufino, op. cit., 309–10.

4   B. Caven, *The Punic Wars* (1980) is the standard work on the events leading up to the battle of Ilipa, while S. J. Keay, *Roman Spain* (1988), 27–9, and L. A. Curchin, *Roman Spain: Conquest and Assimilation* (1991) 24–8, add more recent data on Spain's pivotal role in the Carthaginian Wars. For the foundation of Italica: Appian *Iber.* 38, Vict. *Caes.* 13.1, and Eutr. 8.2; and for the origins of the first settlers, P.A. Brunt, *Italian Manpower, 225 BC–AD 14* (1971), 420. Pliny *NH* 37.78 (203) remarked upon Iberia's riches, and with due justice, Gibbon termed the peninsula the Peru and Mexico of the Roman world.

5   Strabo 3.2.6 (144) and Pliny *NH* 15.3.8. For the Baetican oil trade, see Keay, op. cit., 98–104; and D. J. Mattingly, *JRA* 1 (1988), 38–44.

6   D. J. Mattingly, op. cit., 55, would caution against using the Monte Testaccio evidence for making firm pronouncements about the volume of the oil trade to Rome from the main supply areas, yet the inference from the deduced proportion of Baetican amphorae in the dump does give some idea of the magnitude of that particular trade.

7   Gell. *NA* 16.13.4.

8   The origins of the Italian settlers in Iberia and elsewhere are discussed by A. J. N. Wilson, *Emigration from Italy in the Republican Age* (1966), 22–7, 29–42, and Brunt, op. cit., 204–64. For Trajan's kinsmen, the Aelii, as descendants of a Scipionian veteran, *HA Had.* 1.1. Vell. 1.15.4 (157), claims that the first overseas colony for veteran soldiers was not founded until 123 BC.

9   Brunt, op. cit., 602.

10 For a workman's pay, Cato 22.3 provides the figure of *HS* 2, and Cic. *Ros.* 28 gives *HS* 3. For the legionary's salary at this time, G. R. Watson, *The Roman Soldier* (1969), 91.

11 Note the case of Pliny. He claimed to be of modest means (*Ep.* 2.4), but could raise *HS* 3,000,000, even when short of ready cash (*Ep.* 3.19), and found no difficulties in obtaining sums of between 100 and 300,000 to assist friends (*Ep.*1.19). Cicero considered *HS* 50,000 a sum too small to be concerned with (*Ros.* 22).

12 L. A. Curchin, *The Local Magistracies of Roman Spain* (1990) has discussed the process by which local families achieved senatorial rank. *CIL* 1.6257, n. 199, from Ilici, attests to the manufactory of Traius.

13 The *lacunae* in our early sources mean that the best evidence for the development of the system relates to the Flavian period, by when the complex whole was fully developed. Even though the separate stages – as detailed here – existed when Tiberius succeeded Augustus, it should not be presumed that they already formed a strictly regulated and authoritative norm.

14 For a discussion of the 'restoration', see E. A. Judge, *Polis and Imperium* (1974), 279–312.

[15] Cf. Dio 53.12–15.

[16] R. Syme, *Roman Revolution*, 407, would hold that already under Augustus the senate was no longer a sovereign body, but merely the organ of government. That view is perhaps a little extreme. While the senate had doubtless been cowed by Augustus, it still retained various legislative powers superior to those of the *princeps*. Compare, for example, the senate's decision to condemn Nero when that emperor's political situation had become untenable: Suet. *Nero* 48.2. The modern analogy is, of course, the Supreme Soviet of the late USSR, which always had the power to overrule or even depose the Chairman, even though it never attempted to exercise it until the rule of Gorbachev.

[17] J. Morris, *LF* 88 (1965), 23.

[18] Cic. *Bal.* 51.

[19] Pliny *Ep.* 1.19.

[20] The fundamental study of the equestrian order remains A. Stein, *Der römische Ritterstand* (1927), but see also G. Alföldy, *The Social History of Rome* (1985), 122–6; Hammond, *Monarchy*, 129–30; Millar, *Emperor*, 279–82. For more detail, the seminal works are Pflaum, *Carrières*, and Devijver, *Prosopographia*. The equestrian *militiae* are discussed by E. B. Birley, *Roman Britain and the Roman Army* (1953), 133–53, especially 138–9 and 148–50.

[21] G. L. Cheeseman, *The Auxilia of the Roman Imperial Army* (1914, reprinted 1975) remains the definitive work, if now outdated and defective in places. See also D. B. Saddington, *The Development of the Roman Auxiliary Forces from Caesar to Vespasian, 49 BC–AD 79* (1982); and P. A. Holder, *Studies in the Auxilia of the Roman Army from Augustus to Trajan* (1980) and id., *The Roman Army in Britain* (1982).

[22] Pflaum, *Procurateurs*, 54, with additions.

[23] It has been objected that the 'top-heavy distribution' identified here is more apparent than real, in that the higher posts are more likely to be reported on inscriptions than those lower-ranking, the supposition being, presumably, that those of lower rank were less likely to leave comprehensive epigraphic records of their career. The objection is valid: yet it would be remarkable if all those who achieved the thirty or so higher offices epigraphically attested went through precisely the same twenty or so lower-ranking grades beforehand.

[24] This was the pattern from the Flavian period onwards, but previously the Egyptian and Praetorian prefectures were apparently taken in reverse order.

[25] D. McAlindon, *JRS* 47 (1957), 192, discusses irregular entry into the senate, and J. Devreker, *Latomus* 39 (1980), 70–87, is of particular importance in a consideration of the Flavian period.

[26] Tac. *Ann.* 3.29. Birley, *Fasti*, 4–35, provides a lucid account of the senatorial career during the principate and detailed references; see also the relevant parts of Talbert, *Senate*, and Hammond, *Monarchy*. The decemvirate and the *candidati Caesaris* are fully discussed by S. Brassloff, *JOAI* 8 (1905), 65–70. The seminal study of the viginitivirate, and its relevance to a man's later career, is E.B. Birley, *PBA* 39 (1953), 197–214: cf. Birley, *Fasti*, 4–8, for further details and references.

[27] *Dig.* 50.4.8; 36.1.76. Cf. G.V. Sumner, *Latomus* 26 (1967), 422–3.

[28] Birley, *Fasti*, 9.

[29] Pliny *Ep.* 2.9.1.

[30] Birley, Fasti, 16–17, provides a list of propraetorian offices. See the discussion by Sherwin-White, *Letters*, 74, on the workings of the *ius trium liberorum*: Galba, for one, was notoriously stingy in granting the right (Suet. *Galba* 14.3).

[31] J. Morris, *LF* 87 (1964), 335.

[32] For the consular career, see Birley, Fasti, 26–9. Cf. Cic. *Mur.* 9.22, on the glories of the military career, and Suet. *Vesp.* 4, on the prestige attached to the African and Asian proconsulship.

[33] For Seneca the Elder's origins and career, M. Griffin, *JRS* 62 (1972), 1–19, and *Seneca: A Philosopher in Politics* (1976), 29–34. Mela: Tac. *Ann.* 16.17, perhaps malicious gossip (cf. Sen. *Cont.* 2, Pref. 3). Novatus: *Acts* 18.12. Seneca the Younger: M. Griffin, op. cit. (1976), 34–128.

[34] Dio 59.9.5. Recruitment at this time was perhaps necessary because of omissions by Tiberius during his long absences from Rome: Suet. *Tib.* 4.1. It can be conjectured that a certain Marullinus, *atavus*, or great-great-great-grandfather, of the future emperor Hadrian, and the first member of the Aelius family to enter the senate, was elected now: *HA Hadr.* 1.1.

[35] M. Griffin, op. cit. (1976), 254–5, has examined the charge, but found no secure evidence to prove or disprove it. None the less, the suspicion remains, and is justified.

[36] Strabo 3.5.3 (169), reporting the situation early in Augustus' reign, notes some 500 *equites* in Gades alone. Keay, op. cit., 83, provides an useful discussion of when and how these were appointed, with detailed references to individual cases.

II The Rise of the Ulpii (pp. 11–26)

[1] The unsatisfactory accounts of R. Hanslik, *RE* Suppl. 10 (1965), 1032–5, and G. Alföldy, *Fasti Hispanienses* (1969), 157–9, have been replaced by B. Thomasson, *Op.Rom.* 15 (1985), 136–8; cf. P.M.M. Leunissen, *ZPE* 89 (1991), 235, n. 58. See also T. Franke, *Die Legionslegaten der römischen Armee* (1991), 191–6, and A. Caballos Rufino, *Los senadores hispanorromanos* (1990), 305–13.

[2] J. Morris, *LF* 87 (1964), 334, and id., *LF* 88 (1965), 28: cf. Syme, *Tacitus*, 65–6.

[3] Perhaps as *decemvir stlitibus iudicandis*, given his later position as *quindecimvir sacris faciundis*: cf. L. Schumacher, *ANRW* 2.16.1 (1978), Taf. 1 and 2.

[4] R. Syme, *Historia* 36 (1987), 318 (= *RP* 5, 232).

[5] She is alluded to on inscriptions: McCrum and Woodhead, *Documents* (1961), no. 264. For her probable age at marriage, cf. S. Treggiari, *Roman Marriage* (1991), 39–43.

[6] The cogent arguments of E. Champlin, *Athenaeum* 61 (1983), 257–64, are followed.

[7] Servilia: Tac. *Ann.* 16.30.4. Furnilla: Jones, *Titus* (1984), 19–20.

[8] As Champlin, op. cit., 264, implies. Cf. M.-T. Raepsaet-Charlier, *Prosopographie* (1987), no. 52, pp. 439–41.

[9] Tac. *Ann.* 16.30.4.

[10] *CIL* 1:1, pp. 255 and 329; cf. Pliny *Pan.* 92.4. For a detailed discussion of this document, see M. R. Salzman, *On Roman Time* (1990). Curiously, Eutropius (8.3) implies that Trajan's birthday was on 7 November, perhaps a confusion with the date of Trajan's adoption?

[11] The sources: Mal. 11.12; *Chron. Pasch.* 253.4; *Epit.* 13.4; Eutr. 8.5; Dio 68.6.3. For Dio's use of the cardinal and ordinal systems of enumeration, cf. 61.3; 66.18.4; 77.17.4, etc. Xiphilinus seems to have faithfully reproduced those incidents

which interested him (cf. Lepper and Frere, *Column*, 226), but Dio was not infallible: he claims that Pedanius Fuscus was eighteen when he died (69.17.1–3), yet documents indicate he was probably twenty-five: cf. E. Champlin, *ZPE* 21 (1971), 79–89.

[12] T. D. Barnes, *The Sources of the Historia Augusta* (1978). Cf. C. P. Jones, *JRS* 60 (1970), 99.

[13] That neither is indicated on his *cursus honorum* need not be significant, as few senators seem to have recorded the fact.

[14] *ILS* 8970; cf. B. Thomasson, *Op.Rom.* 15 (1985), 137 and P. M. M. Leunissen, *ZPE* 89 (1991), *passim*, especially 235 and n. 58.

[15] G. Alföldy, op. cit., 270; but see P. M. M. Leunissen, op. cit., 234.

[16] Tac. *Ann.* 16.30.4.

[17] Jones, *Titus*, 19–20.

[18] The contemporary account by Flavius Josephus, *The Jewish War*, has hardly been bettered, confused though it is in places. Jones, *Titus*, 34–55, provides a useful study of the campaign and further references.

[19] Cf. Tac. *Hist.* 2.37.

[20] Cf. Jones, *Domitian*, 11. They may have been advanced by Nero's greatest general, Cn. Domitius Corbulo, whose preferential treatment of *novi homines* is touched on by Jones, *Titus*, 94, and whose daughter was married to Marcia Servilia's own brother-in-law, Annius Vinicianus. Corbulo, like his son-in-law Vinicianus, was another implicated by the Pisonian conspiracy, and forced to commit suicide as a result.

[21] K. Wellesley, *The Long Year* (1975), provides a readable account of the events of AD 68/69.

[22] Suet. *Galba* 17; cf. *HA Avid.* 8.5.

[23] Tac. *Hist.* 1.4.2.

[24] For the events of July 69, cf. Suet. *Vesp.* 6.3. Tac. *Hist* 2.79 gives Vespasian's *dies imperii* as 1 July, and his assumption of the principate as 21 December. For Traianus in Judaea in this period, cf. B. Isaac and I. Roll, *JRS* 66 (1976), 15–19 = *AE* 1977, 829. For the rank of *comes*, see H. Halfmann, *Itinera* (1986), 92–103.

[25] *CIL* 6.930 = McCrum and Woodhead, *Documents*, 1.

[26] Syme, *Tacitus*, 593.

[27] For the year of Traianus' consulship, previously assigned to 72, see W. Eck, *ZPE* 45 (1982), 146–8, and A. Caballos Rufino, op. cit., 306–7. P. A. Gallivan, *CQ* 31 (1981), 187–99 and 213, considers the length of the consulates under Vespasian, and suggests the months September and October for Traianus. For the *quindecimviri sacris faciundis*, cf. W. Eck, *Senatoren*, 33, n. 14; a useful introduction is M.W. Hoffman Lewis, *The Official Priests of Rome under the Julio-Claudians* (1955), and L. Schumacher, *ANRW* 2.16.1 (1978), 655–819, gives further references and lists.

[28] Suet. *Vesp.* 8.4, although there is still no agreement over the date at which Cappadocia was made a consular province. Syme, *Tacitus*, 31, n. 1, originated the idea that Traianus was its first governor and was convinced of Traianus' significant role in Vespasian's eastern policy, as was G.W. Bowersock, *JRS* 63 (1973), 140, but T. B. Mitford, *JRS* 64 (1974), 173, n. 90, and W. Eck, *Chiron* 12 (1982), 287, among others, have expressed qualified doubts. See also A. Caballos Rufino, op. cit., 307, and Isaac, *Limits*, 36–7.

29 Pliny *Pan.* 9.2; A. Caballos Rufino, op. cit., 307. See Jones, *Titus*, 82–4, for the date of Vespasian and Titus's joint censorship, and Suet. *Vesp.* 9.2, for the need to replenish the corps. For adlection as a method of rewarding partisans, cf. Tac. *Hist.* 2.88: the circumstances are discussed further by Eck, *Senatoren* (1970), 103–5, and 108–9. See also J. Devreker, *Latomus* 39 (1980), 70–87, and G.W. Houston, *AJP* 98 (1977), 35–63.

30 W. Eck, *Chiron* 12 (1982), 293–9, collates the evidence for Traianus' term of office and F. Grosso, *RIL* 91 (1957), 318–42, has discussed individual aspects of his administration. R. Syme, *ZPE* 41 (1981), 134, suggested he replaced A. Marius Celsus on the latter's premature death. As for Traianus' triumphal insignia, see *ILS* 8970, Pliny *Pan.* 14, and Maxfield, *Decorations* (1981), 102; and for *triumphalia ornamenta* awarded in irregular circumstances, cf. Tac. *Ann.* 11.20. For the inscriptions in eastern Armenia cf. McCrum and Woodhead, *Documents*, 237, of 75 (Mtzhete, Georgia); *AE* 1951.263, of 84 (Baku, Azerbaijan): they are discussed by R. K. Sherk, *ANRW* 2.7.2 (1980), 996–7; E. Dabrowa, *Klio* 62 (1980), 379–88, 387 and n. 60; J. G. Crow, in *The Defence of the Roman and Byzantine East* (1986), 77–91, *passim*; and Jones, *Titus*, 156–7. Regarding Vespasian's eastern policy, cf. Dio 65.15.3; Suet. *Dom.* 2.3; Syme, *Tacitus*, 30.

31 W. Eck, *ZPE* 45 (1982), 147: according to Hammond, *Monarchy*, 298, senatorial proconsuls had to leave Rome by 13 April of the year they were appointed to their exceedingly well-paid position (it had a salary of *HS* 1,000,000 – Dio 78 22.5). For 'Marcia' in the East, see McCrum and Woodhead, *Documents* (1961), no. 264. For Traianus' administration, cf. Laodicea, *IGRR* 4. 845; Miletus, *ILS* 8970; Smyrna, *IGRR* 4. 1411, 1412; Ephesus, *ILS* 8797.

32 Jones, *Titus*, 138–9, discusses the cases of several men passed over by Vespasian and advanced by Titus: given the lack of an iterated consulship for Traianus, he is surely wrong in asserting that Traianus was one of Titus' *amici*. The Flavian cult is discussed by K. Scott, *The Imperial Cult under the Flavians* (1975), 80–1.

33 *BMC* 498–508 (cf. Strack, *Untersuchungen*, 199–202) and *ILS* 307, from Djemila-Cuicil. Cf. Smallwood, *Documents*, 22, lines 40–1, and M. Durry, *Pline le Jeune* (1938), 233.

34 Pliny *Pan.* 89.2. Again, the credit goes to Durry, op. cit., 234, for realizing the implications.

35 Plut. *Cato Maj.* 20. Mart. 8.68; Pliny *Ep.* 3.3.3. General overviews of Roman education are provided by A. Gwynn, *Roman Education from Cicero to Quintilian* (1964), and S. F. Bonner, *Education in Ancient Rome* (1977).

36 I. J. Murphy, *Quintilian* (1987), xi–xvi, provides a useful introduction.

37 Suet. *Vesp.* 18.

38 Quint. *Inst.Or.* 1.1.15.

39 *Inst.Or.* 1.1.12-14.

40 *Inst.Or.* 1.9.1, and 1.10–11; cf. Cic. *Or.* 1.42.

41 *Inst.Or.* 2.1.7.

42 Dio 52.26.1–2; Ver. *Aen.* 7.162–5.

43 Pliny *Ep.* 6.31.12.

44 Dio 68.7.4; *Epit.* 13. Both Licinius Sura and Hadrian are attested amongst his speech-writers: Jul. *Caes.* 327b, and *HA Hadr.* 3.8. Phil. *Vit.Soph.* 1.7.2.

45 Most believe in Trajan's authorship: e.g., L. Vidman, *Etude sur la correspondence de Pline le Jeune avec Trajan* (1960); Sherwin-White, *Letters*, 536–46; F. Millar, *JRS* 57 (1967); Williams, *Correspondence*, 16–17 (1990): for a contrary view, K. H. Waters, *ANRW* 2.2 (1975), 411–12. Firm evidence is lacking: Trajan certainly sent autograph *libelli* on occasion (Dio 68.5.2 and 68.12), even if it was later claimed that he 'never answered letters' (*HA Macr.* 13.1). See also A. Henneman, *Der Aussere und innere Stil in Trajans Briefen* (1935), and H. Bardon, *Les Empereurs et les Lettres Latines D'Auguste à Hadrien* (1940), 345–57.

46 Cf. Lepper and Frere, *Column* (1988), 226–8; E. Cizek, *L'Epoque de Trajan* (1983), 30, n. 5. Prisc. *Inst. Gramm.* 6.13 preserves the single surviving sentence in a discussion of nominative singulars that end in -*i*: its relevance to reconstructing Trajan's first Dacian campaign is considered in Chapter 8.

47 R. Paribeni, *Optimus Princeps* I (1926), 50.

48 *Epit.* 13.

49 The military tribunate, while not compulsory, might well have enhanced an individual's further senatorial career: cf. Dio 67.11.4, where he speaks of the tribunate being used as 'a stepping stone to the senate'.

50 H. M. Cotton, *Chiron* 11 (1981), 237–8; Birley, *Fasti*, 11.

51 Tac. *Agr.* 5.2. For the contrasting opinions on the length of the tribunate, cf. E.B. Birley, op. cit., 200, with W. Eck, *ANRW* 2.1 (1974), 175, and B. Campbell, *JRS* 65 (1975), 18.

52 Pliny's service is attested by *ILS* 2927, and in *Ep.* 3.11.5 and 7.31.2.

53 Pliny *Ep.* 4.4.2.

54 *Ep.* 1.10; 3.11; 7.31.2. Cf. Birley, *Fasti*, 9, n. 19.

55 R. Syme, *Danubian Papers* (1971), 204–5.

56 Birley, *Fasti*, 9.

57 *Pan.* 14.1.

58 *Pan.* 15.1–3.

59 The case of Trajan and Traianus should therefore be added to the list supplied by Birley, *Fasti*, 11.

60 Birley, *Fasti*, 9.

61 Pliny *Ep.* 8.23. Cf. Birley, *Fasti*, 8–9, with n. 18.

62 For the last, cf. the case of Titus, who, perhaps, took reinforcements from Germany to Britain in 60–1: Birley, *Fasti*, 269.

63 The Black Forest: H. Schönberger, *BRGK* 66 (1985), 363–5. The Bructeri: Stat. *Silv.* 1.4.88–9.

64 Syme, *Tacitus*, 31. Cf. Poly. 6.19.2 and Plut. *Grac.* 2 for the *stipendia decem* as a requirement for entering the senate. Perhaps Pliny was also using the reference as a literary conceit to signal Trajan's ostensible republican *mores*, contrasted with the blatant monarchical aspirations of Domitian.

65 Syme, *Tacitus*, 603; M.-T. Raepsaet-Charlier, *Prosopographie* (1987), no. 631, pp. 511–12. For the Nîmes basilica, *HA Hadr.* 12.2.

66 She is recorded on two wax tablets, with two other Ulpii, at Herculaneum: G. P. Carratelli, *PP* 1 (1946), pp. 383–4, no. 8; *AE* 1955.198. Syme, *Tacitus*, 603, suggested this lady might be an older sister of Traianus' or even a daughter from a previous marriage: the latter can be discounted, in view of Traianus' deduced age.

[67] Augustus established the minimum age for the quaestorship as the twenty-fifth year, effectively permitting election after a candidate's twenty-third birthday, as Roman law allowed that 'a year once begun counts as a year completed': *Dig.* 50.4.8; 36.1.76. Judicious use of accepted legal procedures, therefore, meant that the relevant statutes could be interpreted to discount almost two full years: cf. G.V. Sumner, *Latomus* 26 (1967), 422–3. For the quaestors' duties: Talbert, *Senate*, 17; and for the date of their election: op. cit., 204–7.

[68] For the *quaestores Caesaris*, see S. Brassloff, *JOAI* 8 (1905), 65–70.

[69] *HA Hadr.* 1.4. For the preferential use of the ordinal in the *Historia Augusta*, see R. Syme, *JRS* 54 (1964), 142.

[70] Talbert, *Senate*, 59–63, provides a useful summary.

[71] Tac. *Agr.* 6.

[72] *HA Sev.* 3.5.

[73] Sen. *Benef.* 2.21.5.

[74] Birley, Fasti, 15–16, with detailed references.

[75] *HA Hadr.* 10.1.

[76] The early history of the legion is provided by A. Garcia y Bellido, *Legio VII Gemina* (1970), 305–29.

[77] *Pan.* 14.5.

[78] K. H. Waters, *ANRW* 2:2 (1975), 381–431.

III Imperial Expansion and Crisis (pp. 27–41)

[1] Domitian's reputation was much restored in a series of papers by K. H. Waters: *Phoenix* 18 (1964), 49–77; *AJPh* 90 (1969), 385–404; *ANRW* 2:2 (1975), 381–431. Cf. Jones, *Senatorial Order*, and id., *Domitian*. See also T. A. Dorey, *G&R* 7 (1960), 66–71, and R. Urban, *Historische Untersuchungen zum Domitianbild des Tacitus* (1971), for the distortions evident in Tacitus' view of the reign. The need to justify the principicide explains the hostility of so many contemporary commentators.

[2] Suet. *Dom.* 7.2; cf. Pflaum, *Procurateurs*, 167–9, for Domitian's fundamental role in formalizing a graduated equestrian career. The senate: Jones, *Senatorial Order*, 51–2. Domitian's appointees: Suet. Dom. 8.2. K. H. Waters, *AJP* 90 (1969), 385–404; H.W. Pleket, *Mnemosyne* 14 (1961), 296–315. Flavius Sabinus: Suet. *Dom.* 10.4; citing later sources, Jones, *Domitian*, 47, argues that Sabinus died between 1 October 82 and 28 September 83. For the *lex Julia de Maiestatis*, which at this time provided for death in the case of seditious slander, cf. J. E. Allison and J. D. Cloud, *Latomus* 21 (1962), 711–31.

[3] Suet. *Dom.* 10.1. Cf. Eutr. 7.23.1; R. Urban, op. cit., Jones, *Senatorial Order*, 83–7; R. Syme, *Chiron* 13 (1983), *passim*.

[4] Suet. *Dom.* 9.2–3. Cf. McCrum and Woodhead, *Documents*, 466.

[5] Suet. *Dom.* 8.3; Dio 67.13.1.

[6] Tac. *Germ.* 30–1. The most recent survey of the campaign is that by K. Strobel, *Germania* 65:2 (1987), 423–52.

[7] Tac. *Agr.* 6.1; Dio 67.4.1; Strobel, op. cit., 427–8. Cf. Tac. *Germ.* 30.3: 'You might see other Germans going to battle, but the Chatti going to war.'

[8] Dio 67.6.1 and 5.

9 Suet. *Dom.* 12.1–2; Dio 67.4.5; Oros. *Adv Pag.* 7.10.2. For a discussion of Domitian's currency reforms, see I. Carradice, *Coinage and Finances in the Reign of Domitian, AD 81–96* (1983), Ch. 5 (152–66).

10 Dio 67.3.5 and 4.1–2. Cf. Tac. *Agr.* 39.1

11 Suet. *Dom.* 6.1; Jord. *Get.* 13.77; Oros. *Adv. Pag.* 7.10.4: cf. Juv. 4.111–12. The 'army' (*exercitus* is the term used) was presumably a brigaded force of praetorians and legionaries, and Orosius confirms the magnitude of the disaster.

12 Tac. *Hist.* 1.2.

13 The Septemberists: *CIL* 6.2065, line 62. The removal and execution of the proconsul of Asia, Sex. Vettulenus Civica Cerealis, along with the alleged exile of many senators in 88/89, might be connected with the conspiracy: cf. Jones, *Domitian*, 182–3. For Tapae and Julianus: Dio 67.10; it was Julianus, according to Dio, who ordered the legionaries to inscribe their names and those of their centurions on their shields so that they could be recognized in battle. A failure to complete the rout of the Dacians after Tapae because of the season seems more likely than the explanation offered by Dio 67.10.3, that the Romans were tricked into believing the Dacians had uncommitted reserve forces. The Dacian *Basileion*, or 'Royal City', can be identified as the modern Gradistea Muncelului – amongst other locations! Cf. Lepper and Frere, *Column* (1988), 304–6.

14 For the date of the revolt, see E. Ritterling, *Westdeutsche Zeitschrift* 12 (1893), 218–19. For Saturninus, see Ael. fr. 112; *Epit.* 11.9; Dio 67.11.4. Cf. Eck, *Senatoren*, 103; R. Syme, *JRS* 68 (1978), 12–21 (= *RP* 3, 1070–84); Suet. *Dom.* 6.2.

15 Domitian's departure: McCrum and Woodhead, *Documents*, p. 27, no. 15. Trajan's role: Pliny *Pan.* 14.5.

16 Suet. Dom. 6.2. The Arval Brethren celebrated the victory on 29 January: cf. G. Walser, *Chiron* 19 (1989), 455.

17 Suet. *Dom.* 10.5.

18 Dio 67.11.1; W. Eck, *Chiron* 12 (1982), 316.

19 For the putative conspiracy, cf. Suet. *Dom.* 10.5; Dio 67.11.2; G. Walser, in *Provincialia: Festschrift Laur Belart* (1968), 497–510. Lappius: Jones, *Senatorial Order*, 33, with further references. Julius Calvaster, a tribune, and a centurion were the most senior of the conspirators recorded: Suet. *Dom.* 10.5 and Dio 67.11.4.

20 Dio 67.7.1.

21 They included the Lygians, who were also involved in some conflict with the Suebi and the Semnones: Dio 67.5.2–3. The treaty was probably agreed that October, a month renamed Domitianus in honour, we are told, of his Dacian 'victory': Vict. *Caes.* 11.4.

22 Tac. *Hist.* 1.2; Dio 67.5.2.

23 Suet. *Dom.* 6; Eutr. 7.23.4; Tac. *Agr.* 41. It is possible that the cenotaph erected at Adamklissi during Domitian's reign relates to this episode.

24 For Domitian on the Danube: Mart. 7.8; cf. 7.2 and 9.31. For the march across Dacia: *ILS* 9200. For the *ovatio*: Suet. *Dom.* 6.1; Mart. 8.8; Eutr. 7.23.4.

25 Dio 67.7.4.

26 This is the import of *ILS* 2720, dated to 98, which implies that the *bello Suebicorum* had only recently been concluded.

27 Tac. *Agr.* 44–5; Epic. *Disc.* 4.15.5.

28 Dio 65.12.1.

29 Epic. *Disc.* 1.19–21; Tac. *Hist.* 4.5–8.43; Dio 65.13.1.

30 Suet. *Dom.* 10.3–4; Pliny *Ep.* 3.11.3; Dio 67.13.2–3; Philo. *Vit. Apol.* 7.11.

31 Suet. *Dom.* 14.1 and 4.15.1; Dio 67.4 and 14.1–2.

32 Cf. J. C. Mann, *Legionary Recruitment and Veteran Settlement During the Principate* (1983), 54–5. Even in times of peace, a legion with a nominal strength of 5,000 could expect to lose an average of 200 men per year through the expiration of their period of service, while as much as 66 per cent of any army unit could be unavailable for duty at any one time because of illness, detached duties, and the like: J. Bennett, 'The Setting, Development and Function of the Hadrianic Frontier in Britain' (1990), 91 and 486–7.

33 Suet. *Dom.* 14.4; Pliny *Pan.* 53.4; Dio 67.14.4.

34 Dio 67.15.3.

35 Dio 67.14.1–2; Oros. *Adv. Pag.* 7.10.1–6; Mal. *Chron.* 10.48 (262); Jord. *Rom.* 265.

36 Eutr. 7.15.2; Vict. 11.2; Oros. *Adv. Pag.* 7.10.2 and 5; Jord. *Rom.* 265.

37 Suet. *Dom.* 8.3–4; Pliny *Ep.* 4.11.

38 Dio 67.12.1, and 14.3; Juv. 4.99–101; Fronto *ad M.Caes.* 5.37. Syme, *Tacitus*, 33, surprisingly dismisses Glabrio as an undistinguished 'relic of the republican nobilitas'.

39 Dio 67.14.2–3. Cf. P. Keresztes, *V.Chr.* 27 (1973), 7–15.

40 Cf. Sulp. *Sev. Chron.* 2.31; Suet. *Claud.* 25.4 and *Dom.* 12.2; and Euseb. *Hist. Eccl.* 3.18, where Domitilla is incorrectly described as the niece of Clemens. P. Pergola, *MEFR* 90 (1978), 407–23, discusses the matter. While perhaps not decisive, it might not be entirely coincidental that an early Christian cemetery at Rome was named after Domitilla.

41 Suet. *Dom.* 15.1; Dio 67.14.1–2.

42 The continued support for Domitian is admitted by Pliny, *Pan.* 62.3–5. Petronius Secundus: Dio 67.14.4 and 68.3.3. Clemens: Suet. *Dom.* 15.1.

43 Pliny *Ep.* 3.5.5; *Pan.* 57.2.

44 Dio 67.15.4. Suet. *Dom.* 17.2 and Dio 67.15.1 for the principals. Suetonius adds Maximus, an imperial freedman, Clodianus, a *cornicularius* and an unnamed gladiator, while Dio refers to Entellus, another freedman. Philo. *Vit. Apol.* 8.25 claims that Stephanus' desire was to avenge Clemens and prevent the planned execution of Domitilla.

45 *CIL* 15.548a–549d. Cf. Jones, *Senatorial Order*, 33–8.

46 The Praetorian Prefects: Dio 67.15.2 (cf. Eutr. 8.1.1); *Epit.* 12.2.8.

47 Dio 67.15.5. Cf. Eutr. 8.1.1, and Epict. *Diss.* 4.13.5, for the claim that Petronius was instrumental in offering the throne to Nerva.

48 Cf. D. Kienast, *Historia* 17 (1968), 61. It might legitimately be speculated if Larginius Proculus, who was arrested and brought before Domitian at Rome for predicting (correctly, as it turned out) the date of his assassination, had some foreknowledge of the plot: cf. Dio 67.16.2.

49 Suet. *Dom.* 17; Dio 67.17.1.

50 Suet. *Dom.* 23. Their continued affection for Domitian surfaces on *ILS* 2034, of 99/100.

51 Pliny *Pan.* 52.4–5; Smallwood, *Documents*, 27a. But note H. Hammond, *MAAR* 19 (1949), 46, where it is cogently argued that Nerva's *dies imperii* was 19 September.

52 *Epit.* 12.3.

[53] Pace Eutr. 8.1.1.

[54] Tac. *Ann.* 15.72; Smallwood, *Documents*, 90.

[55] Vict. *Caes.* 13.10; Mart. 8.70 and 9.26.

[56] Nomenclature suggests that Salvius Cocceianus, one of Domitian's victims, may have been the son of Nerva's sister and a brother or cousin of Otho: Syme, *Tacitus*, 628.

[57] Suet. *Dom.* 1.1.

[58] Smallwood, *Documents*, 90.

[59] Philo. *Vita Apoll.* 7.8 and 11. Cf. Vict. 12.2.

[60] Dio 67.5–6.

[61] Suetonius says nothing, as does Martial, whose eulogy to Nerva (12.6) and other references (8.70 and 9.26) show him unharmed between the years 93 and 95. Syme, *Tacitus*, 3, bluntly regards Nerva's alleged exile as 'plain fiction'.

[62] Mart. 5.28.4 and 8.70.1; Pliny *Ep.* 10.58.7.

[63] Pliny *Ep.* 4.22.4–7.

[64] Dio 68.1.3–4; Aus. *Caes.* (Tetra.) 13.

[65] Pliny *NH* 6.24 (89).

[66] The concept of dyarchal rule is no longer as fashionable as it once was. Yet it seems abundantly clear that the senate thought that by approving Nerva as *princeps*, they were installing a place-man who would be amenable to their various demands.

[67] Eutr. 8.1.1.

[68] Dio 68.3.1.

[69] Tac. *Agr.* 3.1.

[70] D. C. Shotter, *G&R* 25 (1978), 156–67.

[71] *BMC, Nerva*, 4–9.

[72] Dio 68.3.3. Cf. the similar action taken by Hadrian after the death of the four consulars: *HA Hadr.* 9.4.

[73] *BMC, Nerva*, p.14.

[74] *BMC, Nerva*, 87. The *congius* was a liquid measure, the *congiarium* originally referring to a gift in kind, although this was now usually given in the form of coin: cf. Strack, *Untersuchungen*, 84–5.

[75] *Epit.* 1.4; Pliny *Pan.* 37–9. Cf. *BMC, Nerva* 88: *FISCI IUDAICI CALUMNIA SUBLATA*, 'An end to the abuses of the Jewish tax'; and *BMC, Nerva*, 119, *VEHICULATIONE ITALIAE REMISSA*, 'Remission of Italy from the charges for the imperial post', a particularly charming reverse which shows the imperial mules freely grazing while the post-cart is tilted on its shafts behind them.

[76] Smallwood, *Documents*, 477; *BMC, Nerva*, 118, with the legend *TUTELA ITALIAE*, 'For the care of Italy'; Dio 68.1.1 and 2.2; Front. *Aq.* 64; *BMC, Nerva*, 115, *PLEBEI URBANAE FRUMENTO CONSTITUTO*, 'Fixing (or securing) the corn supply for the plebs of the city (of Rome)'; *BMC, Nerva*, 127, *AEQUITAS AUGUST(i)*, and a design including corn ears, signifying 'The emperor's reform of equity (in the corn-distribution)'; *ILS* 1627.

[77] Pliny *Pan.* 46.2; and *Pan.* 47.4 (the new name is confirmed by *ILS* 9538). *CIL* 6.32254; *BMC, Nerva*, 132, *NEPTUNO CIRCENS(es) CONSTITUT(i)*; *Epit.* 13.12; and 12.4; Pliny *Pan.* 37.6.

[78] Pliny *Ep.* 2.1.9; *Pan.* 62.2; Dio 68.1.1 and 2.3: cf. Smallwood, *Documents*, 434.

[79] Dio 68.1.1–2 and 2.1; cf. Pliny *Ep.* 9.13.21.

[80] Pliny *Ep.* 9.13.

[81] Cf. A. R. Birley, *CR* 12 (1962), 197–9.
[82] Suet. *Dom.* 23; Dio 68.1.2; Eus. *Hist. Eccl.* 3.20.8; Oros. *Adv. Pag.* 7.11.12; Pliny *Ep.* 1.5.10, 15–16, 4.9.2, 4.11.14 and 7.19.10.
[83] Pliny *Ep.* 4.23.3–7.
[84] Front. *Aq.* 1.1.
[85] For Spurinna, see R. Syme, *RP* 7 (1991), 541–50.
[86] Pliny *Ep.* 9.13.1 and 22; cf. *Pan.* 5.7 and 6.2.
[87] Smallwood, *Documents*, 218, with *AE* 1908.237. For the governor's identification, cf. W. Eck, *Chiron* 12 (1982), 324. Note also Pliny's reference to rioting and mutiny amongst the army: *Pan.* 5.7 and 6.2.
[88] Dio 68.3.2; *Epit.* 12.6. Crassus was an incorrigible conspirator, and eventually put to death by Hadrian for attempted usurpation: *HA Hadr.* 5.6.
[89] Pliny *Pan.* 6.1; Dio 68.3.3; *Epit.* 12.6–8. Cf. K.-H. Schwartz, *BJ* 79 (1979), 139–75.
[90] Smallwood, *Documents*, 248; for a laurelled wreath to signify victory, cf. Pliny *NH* 15.133–4.
[91] Pliny *Pan.* 6.3, 8.1–3 and 5, 10.1 and 6, and 47.5; Dio 68.2.3 and 3.3–4; Eutr. 8.1.1–2; Vict. *Caes.* 13.1; Oros. *Adv. Pag.* 7.11.1. According to *Epit.* 12.9, the adoption was three months before Nerva's death, thus 27/28 October, but 18/19 September, Nerva's *dies imperii* (cf. H. Hammond, *MAAR* 15 (1938), p. 40, n. 186), or even 8 November, when Nerva entered his sixty-third year, are also possible (for the last, cf. Eutr. 8.3., where he gives Trajan's birthday as 7 November: perhaps the date of Trajan's formal adoption is meant).

IV Domitian's General, Nerva's Heir (pp. 42–52)

[1] Dio 67.12 (cf. *Epit.* 13) and 68.5; Pliny *Pan.* 1.5 and 5.3–4.
[2] Pliny *Pan.* 6.3 and 8.5.
[3] Pliny *Pan.* 14. 2–3. Why Pliny refers to Trajan marching *cum legionibus*, that is with two or more legions, is unclear, as it is thought that the garrison of Spain was reduced to a single legion at the beginning of Vespasian's reign. On the other hand, it is just possible that the *legio I Adiutrix* had returned to the peninsula after its involvement in the Chattan War, for it is not securely attested in Pannonia until late Flavian times at the earliest.
[4] G. Walser, *Chiron* 19 (1989), 455.
[5] Pliny *Pan.* 14.5.
[6] Chariomerus: Dio 67.5.1 (10.4), but note that it is said there that the king received no military support from Rome, only money; cf. H. Schönberger, *JRS* 59 (1969), 159. The Taunus 'frontier': V. A. Maxfield, in *The Roman World* (1987), 149–54. It is just possible, if unlikely, that Eutr. 8.2.7, a fourth-century reference to Trajan restoring forts across the Rhine, should correctly refer to this stage in his career rather than the period 98/99, as generally assumed.
[7] *ILS* 1006. The honour is best seen in connection with a series of armed interventions rather than simply as a veiled reference to the suppression of the mutiny alone: cf. Jones, *Domitian*, 150. But note Tac. *Ann.* 15.72, where the suppression of a conspiracy was celebrated as a military victory.
[8] Birley, Fasti, 28.
[9] Pliny *Pan.* 95.3.

10 Lepper, *Parthian War*, 106, n. 1, among others, has adduced from Pliny's silence on the matter that Trajan might well have been lacking in experience of active warfare and military command: the argument is negated by Pliny's failure to mention certain otherwise well-documented stages in Trajan's early career, in particular his consulship, already referred to.

11 Pliny *Pan.* 44.1. Tacitus, for all his faults, at least has the honesty to admit his advancement under Domitian: *Hist.* 1.1.

12 Pliny *Pan.* 14.5.

13 *HA Alex.* 65.5.

14 Millar, *Emperor*, 117–22; Campbell, *Emperor*, 355–7; Halfmann, *Itinera* (1986), 92–103.

15 Pliny *Pan.* 9.2, the relevant part of which might be translated as 'Will future generations believe that a man [. . .] who commanded a formidable, great and adoring army became *imperator* without using it? and who, when he governed Germany, was granted the *cognomen Germanicus* from here [*sc.*, Rome]? that he did not stir up some activity to become emperor, but only earned his pay and obeyed orders?': note that the references to the 'formidable army' and Trajan's command in Germany are in separate clauses.

16 *HA Hadr.* 2.5. For the traditional view of Trajan's German command, cf. Eck, *Statthalter*, 45–6.

17 Pliny *Pan.* 13. For the Pannonian *fasti*: W. Eck, *Chiron* 12 (1982), 322–7. For Trajan's absence from Rome: Pliny *Pan.* 6.4 and 8.2; Dio 68.3.4. The laurelled letter presumably marked the end of the *bellum Germanicum et Sarmaticum*, commemorated on *CIL* 11.5992.

18 Cedr. *Comp. Hist.* 433.20–434; Georg. *Mon. Chron. Breve* 3.338. Cf. Pliny *Pan.* 8.2: 'so that the symbol [of the Pannonian] victory could decorate the rise of the undefeated commander'; and 16.1: 'Your own father had been granted triumphal honours, and the day of your adoption was marked by the dedication of a laurel wreath at the Capitoline, yet you never sought opportunity for triumphs [as emperor].'

19 Others have independently come to the same view (cf. *AE* 1985 722): it is hoped to present the full argument in a more appropriate place.

20 There are many problems in reconciling the principal literary sources concerning Trajan's adoption with one another: they are often contradictory. Pliny's *Panegyricus* is here favoured over the various epitomes of Dio's *Roman History*, although that is used where relevant. On the choice of Trajan: Pliny *Pan.* 8.6, 7.6–7 and 8.1; Dio 68.3.4 and 68.4; *Epit.* 12.9. For epigraphic evidence of Trajan being styled Caesar during Nerva's lifetime, cf. the Pergamum inscription honouring Ti. Claudius Classicus: P. C. Weaver, *Antichthon* 14 (1980), 143–56; also Smallwood, *Documents*, 185. For the possibility of a usurpation, cf. *Epit.* 13.7; and Pliny *Pan.* 9.2, noting that the relevant part discussed here is in a separate clause from that detailing Trajan's command of Germany; C. P. Jones, *JRS* 60 (1970), 99; and for Trajan's reluctance: Pliny *Pan.* 5.7.

21 Pliny *Pan.* 8.5. The stylistic affinities between Pliny's account of Trajan's adoption (*Pan.* 7–8) and Tacitus' Piso's adoption by Galba (*Hist.* 1.15–16) might have been a deliberately veiled reminder of the comparable pressures behind the final choice. Given that it is generally accepted that the *Histories* were written at a later date, then

unless Pliny and Tacitus were drawing upon a common source, it might be (surprisingly) assumed that Pliny's account was the model for Tacitus'.

22 Cf. Pliny *Pan.* 60.5: 'In times of war this honour [*sc.*, the third consulship] was granted to allies, in times of danger companions, and then only in rare cases, but you granted it upon outstanding individuals [*sc.*, Frontinus and Ursus] who served you well and bravely but as civilians.'

23 *HA Hadr.* 3.7; Dio 68.3.4. Cf. Hom. *Il.* 1.43.

24 Suet. *Tib.* 16.1 and Dio 55.13.2. Tac. *Ann.* 1.3.3 and 10.7; Suet. *Tib.* 21 and 68.3.

25 *ILS* 244; P. A. Brunt, *JRS* 67 (1977), 95–116.

26 Pliny *Pan.* 9.3. Cf. the Pergamum inscription honouring Ti. Claudius Classicus, where Trajan is entitled *CAESAR GERMANICUS* in the period before Nerva's death: P. C. Weaver, *Antichthon* 14 (1980), 143–56; and Smallwood, *Documents*, 185, listing Trajan as *CAESAR* before Nerva's death. On the other hand, Pliny (*Pan* 9.2) specifically associates the title *Germanicus* with Trajan's German command.

27 Pliny, *Pan.* 6.4 and 8.6; cf. 9.3. Note the case of Antoninus Pius, who was formally adopted a full four weeks after the initial announcement.

28 Pliny *Pan.* 8.4, 8.6, 9.1 and 10.3–4. There can be no scintilla of doubt that the adoption of Trajan effectively raised him to a co-regency. See B. Parsi, *Désignation et investiture de l'empereur romain* (1963), 46 and 174–82.

29 Cf. Pliny *Pan.* 5.4 and 10; *HA Hadr.* 2.5; Pliny *Pan.* 5.7.

30 Pliny *Pan.* 9.2; cf. R. Paribeni, *Optimus Princeps* I (1926), 85–91.

31 Tac. *Germ.* 33.1.

32 Eutr. 8.2.7; Oros. *Adv. Pag.* 7.12.2. Cf. E. Schallmayer, *Der Odenwald Limes vom Main bis an der Neckar* (1984), 19.

33 For Trajan in Colonia: Eutr. 8.2; *Epit.* 13.2. Nerva's health, lifestyle and death: Dio 68.1.3 and Vict. 13.10; *Epit.* 12.10–11. The date of 28 January for Trajan's *dies imperii* is provided by the Fer. Dur. col. 1.15 (*Yale Classical Studies* 7 (1940), 41), making that or the previous day the occasion of Nerva's death, pace Eutr. 8.1 (15 January) and Dio 68.4.2 (16 January).

34 Smallwood, *Documents*, 109; *HA Hadr.* 2.5. Servianus: Pliny *Ep.* 8.23. *HA Hadr.* 2.12, 6–10: Hadrian's notorious love of hunting and similar activities when younger had already caused Trajan some concern, even if Trajan was fond of the chase himself (Cf. Pliny *Pan.* 81.1–3). But, that agreed, the passage may well be a malicious insertion to explain Hadrian's hostility towards Servianus at the end of his reign. *HA Hadr.* 2.7: the matter of Trajan's sexual preferences is discussed further in Chapter 5.

35 Dio 68.5. Cf. A. R. Birley, *CR* 12 (1962), 197–9.

36 *Epit.* 12.12; cf. Suet. *Aug.* 100–1. Pliny *Pan.* 10.5 and 11.1–3; Eutr. 8.1: nothing is known of the temples, although an octostyle building depicted on coins of 112 might be one: see Chapter 11.

37 Herod. *Hist.* 4.2.

38 Pliny *Pan.* 21 and 84.6.

39 Dio 68.5.

40 *Pater Patriae*: *BMC* 25, and Pliny *Pan.* 57.5, not, apparently, a prolepsis in this otherwise much-revised speech. *Augusta*: Pliny *Pan.* 84, 6–8; the first epigraphic instance is Smallwood, *Documents*, 106, of 104/105.

[41] Mart. 10.7; Pliny *Pan.* 22.
[42] Aelianus: Philo. *Vit. Apol.* 7.18; Dio 68.5.4. Pliny *Pan.* 67.8; Dio 68.16.1; Vict. *Caes.* 13.9.
[43] Cf. Smallwood, *Documents*, 434.
[44] Pliny *Pan.* 18.1 and 10.1–2; cf. *Ep.* 8.14.7 and 10.29.1. It is not clear exactly which 'legates' were visited, those in charge of the provinces (*legates augusti pro praetore*) or the legionary commanders (*legates legiones*): perhaps both.
[45] Cf. Tac. *Ann.* 1.49 and Dio 47.6.1.
[46] Dio Chrys. *Or.* 12.16–20.
[47] Pliny *Pan.* 12 and 16.2. While ostensibly dealing with the winter of 98/99, the events described are proleptically linked with the First Dacian War and must be used with caution. For an earlier use of the specific tactic to overawe an enemy, cf. *RG* 30.2.
[48] Smallwood, *Documents*, 413; *AE* 1973, 475; J. Sasel, *JRS* 63 (1973), 80–1. Cf. Pliny *Ep.* 10.41–2.
[49] Pliny *Pan.* 20.1 and 22; Mart. 10.6.7.

▼ The New Ruler (pp. 53–62)

[1] Pliny, *Pan.* 20.
[2] Pliny *Ep.* 10.8 and 10.10 indicates his return was not before September 99: Sherwin-White, *Letters*, 571–5, *passim*; a rescript issued from Antium (Anzio) before the Ides of November that year demonstrates he was probably in Rome before then: cf. *Fouilles de Delphes* 3, 4.288, and A. Henneman, *Der Äussere und innere Stil in Traians Briefen* (1940), 14, fr. 34. Halfmann, *Itinera*, 185, favours October.
[3] Aside from the many coin portraits and sculptures, both Pliny (*Pan.* 22.2) and Malalas (*Chron.* 11.1) provide descriptions.
[4] This was the usual approach to the city from the north-eastern provinces, and Mart. *Ep.* 10.6, seems decisive.
[5] Pliny *Pan.* 22.
[6] Pliny *Pan.* 23 and *Ep.* 3.7.6–7; Tac. *Hist.* 1.38, *Ann.* 16.27.
[7] Suet. *Aug.* 72.1–2. Cf. Millar, *Emperor*, 18–24.
[8] Cf. Ovid *Met.* 1.175–6; Suet. *Tib.* 54.2; *Gaius* 41.1; *Vit.* 15.2.
[9] The Domus Tiberiana is tolerably well known, despite lying beneath the Farnese Gardens. For a review of the evidence, see Richardson, *Ancient Rome*, 136–7.
[10] For the women in Trajan's household, see H. Temporini, *Die Frauen am Hofe Trajans* (1978).
[11] Tac. *Ann.* 3.33–4; for Marcia's presence in Asia, cf. McCrum and Woodhead, *Documents*, 264.
[12] Pliny *Pan.* 83.5–8, and *Ep.* 9.28.1; Dio 68.5.5. Cf. Raepsaet-Charlier, *Prosopographie*, 631.
[13] Pliny *Pan.* 84. For Ulpia Marciana, cf. Raepsaet-Charlier, *Prosopographie*, 824.
[14] For a discussion of the matter, see A. Birley, *Marcus Aurelius: A Biography* (revised edition: 1987), 241. Mindius: his *gens* is deduced from the nomenclature of (Mindia) Matidia's *libertus*, L. Mindius Damaleius, charged with overseeing her private property: H. Solin, *Epigraphische Untersuchungen* (1975), 66–9, no. 112: some form of relationship with L. Mindius Balbus and L. Mindius Pollio of Claudian times seems probable. For Salonia Matidia, cf. Raepsaet-Charlier, *Prosopographie*, 681, and for

(Minidia) Matidia, op. cit., 533: she herself lived to a considerable age by contemporary standards, for she died sometime between 161 and 169, the subsequent litigation over her will causing considerable difficulties to the joint emperors Marcus Aurelius and Verus: cf. Fronto *Ad Ant Imp*. 2.1 and 4.1.1 (= VdH, p.95).

15 Cf. Raepsaet-Charlier, op. cit., 802.
16 *HA Hadr*. 12.1; Dio 69.10.3; Smallwood, *Documents*, 114.
17 Cf. *Dig*. 9.3.5.1. and 33.9.3.6.
18 Martial (10.10) complains that the sum distributed by one patron – 21 asses, or *HS* 6.25 – was not enough to buy a dinner.
19 For the inheritance of imperial slaves, cf. P. R. C. Weaver, *CQ* 15 (1965), 45; and id., *Familia Caesaris* (1972), *passim*.
20 Smallwood, *Documents*, 270.
21 Cf. P. C. Weaver, *Antichthon* 14 (1980), 143–56.
22 Aeglus: Smallwood, *Documents*, 185; Eutychius: 183; Hermius: 184; Thaumastus: 182; Vernius: 181.
23 Pliny *Pan*. 55; *CIL* 6.8686. Cf. Pliny *Ep*. 10.9.
24 Gell. *NA* 4.1.1. The Roman day was divided into twelve equal hours, beginning with sunrise and ending at sunset, with true noon marking the division between morning and afternoon. Thus the length of the hour varied from about 45 minutes in the winter to 75 in the summer. The passage of time was commonly measured by sun-dials (cf. S. L. Gibbs, *Greek and Roman Sundials* (1971), *passim*), but by Trajan's time the use of an adjustable water clock had become relatively widespread and was a symbol of status and wealth: cf. Pet. 26.
25 Vespasian continued to greet his clients at the *salutatio* after becoming emperor (Pliny *Ep*. 3.5.9), and there is every reason to believe that Trajan continued the practice. Cf. Pliny *Pan*. 24.2, 47.5–6 and 48.1.
26 Pliny *Pan*. 24.2–3.
27 Pliny *Pan*. 49.5 and 7, and *Ep*. 6.31.13.
28 Dio 68.7.4.
29 Fronto *Fer.Als*. 5 (= VdH, p.230); *HA Hadr*. 3.2; *HA Alex.Sev*. 39.1; Dio 68. 7.4; Jul. *Caes*. 327c.
30 Pliny *NH* 14.62 and 71; 17.213. For a modern study, cf. A. Tchernia, *Le Vin de L'Italie romaine* (1986).
31 Dio 62.6.4; Anacreon 3.43.
32 Vict. *Caes*. 13.10.
33 It has been usual to dismiss the reports of Trajan's homosexuality as circumstantial denigratory gossip, yet the evidence is prolific: cf. Dio 68.10.2; *HA Hadr*. 2.7 and 4.5; Jul. *Caes*. 311.
34 Dio 68.10; *HA Hadr*. 2.7–8 and 4.5–7; Smallwood, *Documents*, 173, with Fronto, *De Fer. Als*. (= VdH, p. 229.5). Cf. Mart. 12.15; Arr. *Diss. Epict*. 3.17.4. One of Trajan's own appointees, Vibius Maximus, prefect of Egypt in AD 103–7, was remarkably indiscreet with a certain Theon, a 17-year-old Alexandrian: *P. Oxy*. 471 = H. A.Musurillo, *The Acts of the Pagan Martyrs* (1954), 152–6.
35 Cat. 10 and 28; cf. Mart. 1.58, 92 and 96; 2.62, 71, 73; and 4.48.
36 Dio 62.64.
37 Xen. *Banquet*, 468–71; similar sentiments are expressed in Plut. *Erotikos* 750.

38 Cf. Suet. *Dom.* 10.5.

39 B. Levick, *Claudius* (1990), 130–1.

40 Cf. *HA Avid.* 8.5.

41 Pliny *Pan.* 25.3. What it amounted to cannot be resolved: Mucianus, acting on Vespasian's behalf, had given 'no more than the others did in time of peace', a paltry 25 *denarii*, an amount equivalent to the annual tip made to the Praetorians by Claudius, but he at least was able openly to claim insolvency: cf. Tac. *Hist.* 2.82 and Dio 64.22.2. Nero, on the other hand, distributed the same amount as Claudius: Tac. *Ann.* 12.69 and Dio 61.3.1.

42 Cf. Suet. *Caes.* 38; Dio 43.21.

43 G. R. Watson, *The Roman Soldier* (1969), 89–102. Cf. M. Speidel, *JRS* 63 (1973), 141–7, and R. Alston, *JRS* 84 (1994), 113–23.

44 Pliny *Pan.* 25.2 and 26.1–4. Trajan is still signalled as *COS II* on the coins celebrating the event, which reveals that it took place before the end of that year, and possibly before October/December: cf. Strack, *Untersuchungen*, 79 and 88–9.

45 Pliny *Pan.* 25.2.

46 *BMC* 712: cf. Veyne, *Bread and Circuses* 388–9, for the political significance of the act.

47 Pliny *Pan.* 25.

48 R. Hanslik, *RE Suppl.* 10, 1083. In all, Trajan disbursed a total of *HS* 2,600 in the three *congiaria* of his principate.

49 Cf. Strack, *Untersuchungen*, 85.

50 Pliny *Pan.* 25.3; Fronto *Princ. Hist.* 20 (= VdH, p.213).

51 Dio 38.13: perhaps as many as 320,000 benefited.

52 Cf. Suet. *Aug.* 41.

53 Dio 68.10.2.

54 Cf. Cic. *Domo Sua* 43.110, *Mun.* 18, *passim*, and 26.53, *Off.* 2.16–17 and *Verr.* 1.12.36; also Livy 6.42.12.

55 Fronto *Princ. Hist.* 20 (= VdH, p.213).

56 Pliny *Pan.* 33. The Venerable Bede gave the Colosseum its popular name from the giant statue of Nero, converted to represent the sun god Sol, moved nearby during the reign of Hadrian from its original location in the centre of the vestibule of Nero's 'Golden House'.

57 Pliny *Pan.* 34.3–4. For the *venationes*, see especially G. Jennison, *Animals for Show and Pleasure in Ancient Rome* (1937).

58 Hence the infamy attached to Drusus and to Claudius for the obvious pleasure they derived from such shows.

59 Cic. *Tusc.* 2.41; Pliny *Pan.* 33.1, and 34.4.

60 Pliny *Pan.* 34.

61 Pliny *Pan.* 34.2; cf. 35.2.

VI A Public Ideology (pp. 63–73)

1 The views of K. H. Waters, in *Polis and Imperium* (1974), 233–52, seem a little too emphatic in rejecting the validity of Pliny's and Dio Chrysostom's treatises as an important contribution to understanding the character of Trajan's reign. The fact remains that they and the class they represent were evidently more than content with Trajan's rule.

2 The title is certainly not his, but comes from the work's inclusion in a collection known as the *XII Panegyrici*, the other eleven of which – all true panegyrics – were written in the fourth century.

3 For his career, Smallwood, *Documents*, 230.

4 Originally, these men were chosen by lot, but by the early third century they were directly selected by the ruler: cf. Dio 55.25.2–3. While it is not known exactly when the change took place, Pliny's account of his own election indicates that the emperor was directly responsible for their selection from at least the reign of Nerva.

5 Pliny *Pan.* 90.6.

6 For example, *Pan.* 17, which seems to be a reference to Trajan's triumph at the end of 103. On the other hand, even Martial, in his first greetings, welcomed the new ruler with allusions to forthcoming triumphs: 12.8.

7 *Ep.* 3.18.2; cf. *Pan.* 4.1, and 63.1.

8 *Pan.* 1.5; 5.3–4; 8.3; 23.4; 94.3–4. Cf. 88.7–8, possibly an anachronistic coupling of Jupiter as *Optimus Maximus* with Trajan's first nomination as *Optimus* by the senate, an event dated to 103.

9 *Pan.* 1.3–5; 52.6.

10 *Pan.* 4.4–6.

11 *Pan.* 44.2.

12 *Pan.* 21.

13 *Pan.* 13.1.

14 *Pan.* 81.1 and 3.

15 *Pan.* 81.4–82.3.

16 *Pan.* 49.5 and 82.9.

17 *Pan.* 82.6–7.

18 *Pan.* 14.5.

19 *Ep.* 10.1.2.

20 *Pan.* 66.2.

21 *Pan.* 6.2–5; cf. *Ep.* 8.14.8.

22 *Pan.* 62.2 and 5; 71.4.

23 *Pan.* 13.4.

24 *Pan.* 15.5; 19.3.

25 *Pan.* 12.1.

26 *Pan.* 18; cf. 6.2 and 13.5, and *Ep.* 8.14.7.

27 *Pan.* 2.3; 16.1; 63.2.

28 *Pan.* 85.6. Cf. Tac. *Hist.* 4.7.

29 *Pan.* 45.2–3. This is another example of how Pliny contrives to exculpate those who advanced their careers under Domitian, implying that they only served in office because they were forced to do so.

30 *Pan.* 86. The name of this man escapes identification, but he may have been selected as Suburanus' replacement: Claudius Livianus was presumably appointed in his place.

31 *Pan.* 53.3 and 76.1–3.

32 *Pan.* 47.1-2.

33 The standard account is Jones, *Dio Chrysostom* (1978). See also Jones, *Domitian*, 66, and A. Gowing, *CPh* 85 (1990), 49–54.

34 Pliny *Ep.* 10.58

35 *Or.* 13.1. In view of Dio Chrysostom's intimacy with both Vespasian and Titus, the victim is generally identified as T. Flavius Sabinus: cf. Jones, *Dio Chrysostom*, 46 and n. 2. The exile may have been voluntary: cf. Philo Vit Soph. 1.7.

36 A long-standing friendship is deduced from *Or.* 18, a letter suggesting which authors to read, and usually considered to have been addressed to Nerva before he became emperor.

37 Jones, *Dio Chrysostom*, 52.

38 *Ep.* 10.81 and 82.

39 It is usual (and proper) to translate the Greek *Basileus* as 'king', and to render the title of these four Discourses as *De regno*, 'On Kingship'. But, as the stated idea of a monarchy was anathema to the Roman senate and public, 'On Sovereignty' is to be preferred. That said, while most of the orations usually refer to the ideal ruler as *autokrator*, the Greek equivalent of *princeps* (for example, *Or.* 3.2), the title *Basileus* is also used on occasion (cf. *Or.* 1.5).

40 *Or.* 1.5.

41 For the order and date, see Jones, *Dio Chrysostom*, 114–23 *passim*, and 136, although he would date the *First Discourse* to 100 and the *Fourth* possibly as late as 115. Cf. Lepper, *Parthian War*, 203, where it is argued that the *Fourth* in its present form could well date to after Hadrian's accession.

42 *Or.* 1.15; 3.12–24 and 50.

43 Jones, *Dio Chrysostom*, 116–21, provides a detailed analysis of the four discourses in their numerical order. Here, they are examined thematically.

44 *Or.* 1.11–12; cf. Hom. *Il.* 2.205–6.

45 *Or.* 1.38–9; cf. Hom. *Il.* 2.169 and 407.

46 *Or.* 2.75–7.

47 *Or.* 1.49–84.

48 *Or.* 1.84.

49 *Or.* 3.43–4.

50 *Or.* 3.45.

51 *Or.* 3.46–7.

52 *Or.* 3.50.

53 *Or.* 1.17 and 22; *Or.* 3.41.

54 *Or.* 1.13 and 23; 3.83 and 127.

55 *Or.* 1.21; 3.57, 83 and 124–6.

56 *Or.* 1.5; 2.47; 3.10, 28, 54 and 62.

57 *Or.* 1.26 and 40–1.

58 *Or.* 1.15–16 and 3.51–2; cf. 2.64.

59 *Or.* 1.13–14.

60 *Or.* 2.55–6; 3.53.

61 *Or.* 1.20, 25 and 35.

62 *Or.* 3.119–22 and 130–2.

63 *Or.* 1.30–1.

64 *Or.* 3.87–9.

65 *Or.* 1.32 and 3.92–107.

66 *Or.* 1.27.

67 *Or.* 1.22 and 28; 2.49; 3.127. Cf. Pliny *Pan.* 15.5 and 19.3.

68 *Or.* 1.25 and 27–9; 2.52.

69 Cf. *Or.* 2.55–64.

70 *Or.* 2.34–6 and 64.

71 Always bearing in mind that the military were usually paid with precious metal coinage, whereas the populace had a greater demand for base metal token specie for everyday transactions, which is why the contestants in the Civil Wars of 68/69 concentrated on producing *aurei* and *denarii* rather than the smaller denominations.

72 Strack, *Untersuchungen*, 4–5. Dio (47.25.3) shows the custom was established in the republican period, and Eusebius (4.73) shows its use under Constantine. The practice was not restricted to the ancient world. Compare the United Kingdom, where there are six separate versions of the one-pound piece, four with 'nationalistic' emblems (the oak of England, the leek of Wales, the flax-plant of (Northern) Ireland and the thistle of Scotland, together with their appropriate mottoes), one bearing the Royal Crest and the last with the Royal Arms, as a symbol of the unified provinces.

73 Pliny *Pan.* 21.1; Dio Chrys. *Or.* 1.22.

74 Cf. Strack, *Untersuchungen*, 43–4.

75 Cf. G. G. Belloni, *ANRW* 2.1 (1974), 1076–1138.

76 *BMC* 53, with Trajan's titulature as *TR P COS II P P*.

77 *BMC*, p. 38.

78 Strack, *Untersuchungen*, 62–5.

79 *BMC* 742a.

80 *BMC* 6; cf. lxvi for the correct identification of this figure, more usually recognized as either Abundantia, Fortuna or Annona Secura. Pliny alludes to the glory of the new age at its very beginning: cf. *Ep.* 10.1.2.

81 *BMC* 56. The coincidence in the date of these issues and the delivery of the *Panegyricus* and the *Second Discourse*, both of which emphasize the connection between Trajan and Hercules/Heracles, is to be noted.

82 Cf. Strack, *Untersuchungen*, 95–105, for the identification.

83 *BMC* 94 (*Mars Ultor*), 1 (*Roma Victrix*), 8 (*Germania*) and 731 (*Pax Augusti*).

84 *BMC* 19 (*Victrix*), and p. 149 (*Decursio*).

VII The Inauguration of a New Era (pp. 74–84)

1 Cf. *RG* 34, which is usually rendered as 'I had no more power than my fellow consuls, but I excelled all in *auctoritas*', although the Latin terminology is somewhat ambiguous. See Pliny *Pan.* 57.1–2 on the practices of the emperors before Trajan. Augustus held the consulship five times in succession at the beginning, and then twice more in a 41-year reign; Tiberius three times in 23; Gaius three times in 4; Claudius twice in succession then twice again in 13; Nero four times in 14; Vespasian eight times in 10; Titus once in 2; Domitian seven in succession then three more in 15; Nerva twice in his two years.

2 Pliny *Pan.* 57.1. For the third consulship as the *summum fastigium*, the pinnacle of the senatorial career, cf. Pliny *Ep.* 2.1.2.

3 R. Syme, *JRS* 20 (1930), 61. Cf. Jones, *Senatorial Order*, 104, and id., *Domitian*, 53–4.

4 Pliny *Pan.* 58.1–2; 59.1–2; 60.1–3.

5 *Pan.* 63.1 and 64. This is not quite true, since Claudius, for one, is known to have sworn an oath to the acts of Augustus.

6 *Pan.* 64.3–4.

7   *Pan.* 65.1.

8   Cf. *Pan.* 57.5.

9   Pliny *Ep.* 4.8.3

10 Front. *Strat.* 4.3.1–4. For further details of his career, see Birley, Fasti, 69–72.

11 This is inferred from the contents of the *Strategemata* and his subsequent elevation to command Asia 85/86.

12 Pliny *Pan.* 62.2.

13 Syme, *Tacitus*, 635–6; F. Zevi, in *Akten des VI internationalen Kongresses für griechische und lateinische Epigraphik* (1972), 438.

14 Jones, *Titus*, 137–8.

15 Cf. Dio 67.3.1 and 4.2.

16 Pliny *Pan.* 60.6.

17 Cf. *Pan.* 70–1.

18 Cf. *Pan.* 70.8.

19 Suet. *Dom.* 8.2; cf. Dio 68.1.3.

20 Pliny *Ep.* 2.11 and 3.9.4. The trial is dated by the involvement of Cn. Pompeius (Iulius) Ferox Licinianus, *cos. suff.* September–October 98, and at the time *cos. des.*: cf. *ILS* 3355.

21 Cf. Juv. *Sat.* 1.49, and Pliny *Ep.* 2.11.21.

22 Pliny *Ep.* 3.4 and 9. Priscus was a Baetican and Classicus an African, which gave rise to a saying amongst the Baetici that 'We gave as good as we got': *Ep.* 3.9.3.

23 *Epit.* 42.21; Suet. *Dom.* 8.3. and 12.1; Pliny *Pan.* 42.1.

24 *Dig.* 1.2.2.32.

25 Pliny *Pan.* 36. 3–5 and 41.3.

26 *Pan.* 37.3–4.

27 Dio 55.25.5.

28 Pliny *Pan.* 37.3–4.

29 Gai. *Inst.* 1.93 and 2.135a. Cf. Pliny *Ep.* 10.11.2.

30 A reluctance to fill the local magistracies is seen as early as Vespasian's reign: cf. *ILS* 6089.51 and J. Gonzalez, *JRS* 76 (1986), 214.

31 Pliny *Pan.* 37.6. As preserved, the latter part of the text reads: 'At the same time immunity from the tax was granted between father and a free-born son, provided he was in *patris potestatem*.' This makes no sense as it stands, for if already in *patris potestatem*, the son was already exempt: an error in transmission is to be assumed, and confirmed by the rest of the passage, on redressing the injustice of destroying the natural relationship between son and father.

32 *Pan.* 38.2 and 6–7.

33 *Pan.* 39.1–2.

34 *Pan.* 39.5, and 40.1–3 and 5 (cf. 37.5). The event is commemorated by a scene on the *Anaglypha Traiana*.

35 *Pan.* 41.

36 *Pan.* 39.5.

37 *Pan.* 50.5 and 50.2–5. Cf. Suet. *Cal.* 38–9, Dio 68.20, and Sen. *Ben.* 7.6.2, for the careful distinction between properties belonging to the *patrimonium* and the *imperium*.

38 Cf. Dio 60.11. The thesis was formulated by M. Rostovtzeff, *The Social and Economic History of the Roman Empire* (2nd ed., 1957), 19–22, 30–6, 54–75, 91–105,

165–75, 192–204. See also A. Sirago, *L'Italia agraria sotto Traiano* (1958), 250–74, and R. Martin, *Recherches sur les agronomes latins et leurs conceptions économiques et sociales* (1971), 257–310 and 370–5.

39 Cf. Pliny *NH* 18.35; for the potential returns, see Duncan-Jones, *Economy*, 51 and 59. Settefinestre: T. W. Potter, *Roman Italy* (1987), 106–9.

40 Suet. *Dom.* 7.2 and 14.2.

41 Stat. *Silv.* 4.3.11–12; Philo. *Vit. Soph.* 520.

42 A. Tscheria, *Le vin de l'Italie romaine* (1986), Ch. 5.

43 A. Tchernia, in *Roman Seaborne Commerce, MAAR* 36 (1980), 305–12; J. R. Paterson, *PBSR* 55 (1987), 116–17 (but cf. Duncan-Jones, *Economy*, 35, n. 4).

44 Dio 68.2.1; Pliny *Ep.* 7.31.4; *ILS* 1019; *Dig.* 47.21.3.1; Mart. 12.6.9–11.

45 Pliny *Ep.* 10.8; Duncan-Jones, *Economy*, 20.

46 *Ep.* 2.4.3.

47 *Ep.* 2.15.2.

48 *Ep.* 4.6.1.

49 *Ep.* 7.30.3.

50 *Ep.* 8.1–4.

51 *Ep.* 9.16.1.

52 *Ep.* 9.20.2.

53 *Ep.* 9.27.2.

54 *Ep.* 9.37.1–2, dated to 107.

55 *Ep.* 10.8.5, dated to 98/99.

56 Dio 60. 11; Pliny *NH* 18.35.

57 Cf. *CIL* 10.5055, a private scheme of Augustan date.

58 Vict. *Caes.* 12.4 is the only evidence, although it has been argued that the undated Veleian scheme could be Nervan: cf. Duncan-Jones, *Economy*, 292–3.

59 Pliny *Ep.* 1.8.10 (presumably of *c.* 97), and 7.18.2; cf. Smallwood, *Documents*, 230.

60 *CIL* 9.1455 and 11.1147. The bibliography is extensive: P. Veyne, in *Les Empereurs romaines* (1965), 163–79; P. Garnsey, *Historia* 17 (1968), 367–381; M. Pfeffer, *Einrichtungen der sozialen Sicherung in der griechischen und römischen Antike* (1969), 122–7 and 175; R. Duncan-Jones, *PBSR* 32 (1964), 123–46; id., *Economy*, 288–319 and 333–42; Eck, *Staatliche Organisation* (1979), 146–89.

61 The figures come from the Veleia tablet, but are assumed to be standard throughout the scheme. The amount was sufficient for a subsistence diet only.

62 One of the first was the consular T. Pomponius Bassus, appointed to Ferentinum (Ferentino) in 100/101 (Smallwood, *Documents*, 437), and also responsible for administering the primary (?Nervan) scheme at Veleia (*CIL* 11.1149: cf. 1151).

63 Duncan-Jones, *Economy*, 307–10.

64 *CIL* 9.1455 = Smallwood, *Documents*, 435 (part text); the number of beneficiaries is calculated from the interest involved. The *Ligures Baebiani* themselves were the descendants of Ligurians transplanted from northern Italy to Samnium in 181/180 BC by the consul M. Baebius Tamphilus: cf. E. T. Salmon, *Samnium and the Samnites* (1967), 310–11.

65 R. Duncan-Jones, *PBSR* 32 (1964), 145.

66 CIL 11.1147 = Smallwood, *Documents*, 436 (part text).

67 Duncan-Jones, *PBSR* 32 (1964), 145.

68 Cf. Pliny's comments with regard to his perpetual scheme at Comum, where he takes care to allow and provide for the reduction in the market value of the land he donated in order to provide a permanent subsidy: *Ep.* 7.18.

69 Cf. *Dig.* 34.1.14.1, although this is of Hadrianic date and refers to a private scheme.

70 Pliny *Pan.* 26.3 and 28.5.

71 Cf. *CIL* 6.1492; 9.1455; and 11.1147.

72 Pliny *Pan.* 26.1–4.

73 Pliny *Pan.* 26.5–6; the incentives for the rich that he refers to are the provisions enshrined in the *lex Iulia de maritandis ordinibus*, the *lex Papia Poppaea* and the *ius trium liberorum*.

74 Cf. Smallwood, *Documents*, 437.

75 For example, Pliny *Pan.* 27.1: 'in spem alimentorum, in spem congiariorum'. A. Garzetti, *From Tiberius to the Antonines* (1974), 313, on the other hand, suggests confusion between the two, arising because Pliny was attempting to avoid anachronisms in the published version of his *actio gratiarum*. This seems unlikely, for the alimentary scheme was in operation in the Macchia district by 101 (cf. *CIL* 9.1455), which indicates that it was organized during the course of 100, the year the speech was delivered.

76 Cf. R. Duncan-Jones, *PBSR* 32 (1964), 146. Smallwood, *Documents*, 386, shows that the Thermae Neptuni at Ostia cost *HS* 2,000,000, and K. Hopkins, *JRS* 70 (1980), 125, has put forward the convincing figure of about *HS* 445,000,000 for the annual cost of the army, and estimated that the imperial revenue (at the time of Claudius) was in the order of *HS* 824,000,000.

77 Pliny *Pan.* 28.4; the possible minimum juvenile population of Rome is calculated by adopting the then current demographic rule of thumb that the active male population was one-quarter of the whole (cf. Caes. *BG* 1.29), and assuming that one-half of the remainder were children.

78 Duncan-Jones, *Economy*, 301–2.

79 Duncan-Jones, *Economy*, 310, and P. Veyne, *Bread and Circuses* (1990), 373–5, both argue for a natalist purpose. It remains possible that Trajan was deliberately favouring the rural population, and was attempting to avoid an agricultural crisis caused by depopulation of the rural centres of Italy.

80 Veyne, *Bread and Circuses*, 369, adopts a more neutral position.

81 Jones, *Senatorial Order*, 98.

82 This might be deduced from Pliny *Pan.* 85.1–8. Suburanus may have been adlected *inter consulares*, but the earliest instance known is Tarrutenus Patternus, likewise a Praetorian Prefect, adlected by Commodus: Dio 72.5.1.

VIII Dacicus (pp. 85–103)

1 The most recent and authoritative accounts of the Dacian wars are Strobel, *Dakerkriegen*, and Lepper and Frere, *Column*.

2 Móscy, *Pannonia* (1974), 27.

3 Jord. *Get.* 12.74; Flor. *Epit.* 28.18.

4 I. H. Crisan, *Burebista and his Times* (1978).

5 Dio Chrys. *Or.* 12.19. Fronto *Princ. Hist.* 10 (= VdH, p. 207) speaks of the terrible wounds inflicted by this weapon, regarded as more dangerous than the reflex bows used with deadly effect by the Parthians.

[6] Strabo 7.3.5 and 11; Suet. *Caes.* 44, and *Aug.* 8 and 63; App. *BC* 2.110 and 3.25; Liv. *Per.* 117; Front. *Strat.* 1.40.4; Plut. *Ant.* 63; Pliny *NH* 3.147; Dio 51.22.7–8; Vell. Pat. 2.59.4; Ptol. 3.7.1 and 8.1.

[7] Strabo 7.3.13. Following Caes. *BG* 1.29 and Vell. Pat. 2.110.3, which provide the broad equation of one warrior for every three civilians within the prehistoric communities of central Europe, Strabo's figures suggest that the total Dacian population was not less than 800,000 and 160,000 respectively in these years.

[8] *RG* 30; Dio 54.36.2; *ILS* 8965; Strabo 7.3.10; Flor. *Epit.* 2.28–9; Tac. *Ann.* 4.1.

[9] Strabo 7.3.10 and 13; Tac. *Hist.* 2.83, 3.46 and 4.4; Dio 55.30.4, 67.7.3–4 (cf. 67.6.5, where it is indicated that the subsidy may have been as much as two obols for each Roman citizen).

[10] Cf. Lepper and Frere, *Column*, 277–82.

[11] Cic. *Man.* 16.

[12] Dio 68.6.1. Note also Jul. *Caes.* 22, where it is claimed that there had been Getic (*sc.,* Dacian) incursions.

[13] It may have been now that the unique post of *legatus Augusti pro praetore regionis Transpadanae* was created and C. Julius Proculus installed as its (apparently) sole holder (*EE* 7, 397, n. 7). It is not heard of after the First Dacian War, which suggests the perceived need for direct control of the area at that time alone, presumably in connection with the marshalling of supplies for the forthcoming campaign. As Proculus was *cos. suff.* in 109 (Smallwood, *Documents*, 212), then despite some doubt, a likely historical context for Transpadane office would be in connection with the First Dacian War.

[14] Smallwood, *Documents*, 1: identical prayers were consecutively offered to Juno, Minerva and other deities.

[15] C. P. Jones, *JRS* 60 (1970), 98–104, has cogently argued that the *cursus honorum* on the acephalous inscription *CIL* 6.1444, generally ascribed to Sura, is in fact that of Q. Sosius Senecio; either man might still be possible. For further discussion see id., *Gnomon* 45 (1973), 690; W. Eck, *Chiron*, 329, n. 190; and Strobel, *Dakerkriegen*, 62–4 and 228–30.

[16] For a discussion of the duty of *legatus pro praetore* without a specific provincial command, see Strobel, *Dakerkriegen*, 67, n. 40.

[17] Four in Pannonia: *XIII Gemina*, *XV Apollinaris*, *I* and *II Adiutrix*; three in Moesia Superior: *XIV Gemina Martia Victrix*, *IV Flavia felix* and *VII Claudia pia fidelis*; two in Moesia Inferior: *V Macedonica* at Oescus and *I Italica*. As for the size of Trajan's army, it might be noted that Caesar used a mere ten legions for the whole of Gaul, Augustus six for Germany, and Claudius four only for Britain. For an overview of the legions, see the relevant parts of Y. le Bohec, *The Imperial Roman Army* (1994).

[18] There can be no hard and fast rule on what body armour was usually worn by the legionaries. While *lorica segmentata* is shown throughout on Trajan's Column, the Tropaeum Traiani shows them wearing both *hamata* and *squamata*, and laminated vambraces. On this subject in general, and the weaponry of the legions, see M. C. Bishop and J. C. N. Coulston, *Roman Military Equipment* (1993).

[19] Veg. 2.25.

[20] There is no standard modern account on the auxiliary infantry, but see the relevant sections in Y. le Bohec, op. cit., and M. C. Bishop and J. C. N. Coulston, op. cit.

21 The standard work on the Roman cavalry is K. Dixon and P. Southern, *The Roman Cavalry* (1992). A. Hyland, *Equus* (1990), may also be consulted with profit.

22 The figures for the *auxilia*, which have to be used with caution, are derived and adapted from Strobel, *Dakerkriegen*, 81–153, and Lepper and Frere, *Column*, 289–95.

23 For contrasting views on the date of *de Metatione Castrorum*, see S. S. Frere, *Brit* 11 (1980), 51–60 and E. B. Birley, *Brit* 12 (1981), 287. The fact that the document refers to camel troops at one point need not date it to the Trajan's Parthian War or later as is sometimes assumed: camels were early on recognized as excellent beasts of burden, although as anyone familiar with them will know, they are creatures adapted by nature for soft terrain, and cannot traverse rocky ground with any ease.

24 See Appendix.

25 For a general introduction, see Lepper and Frere, *Column*, 1–43. See also A. Claridge, *JRA* 6 (1993), 5–22, for the entirely reasonable argument that the decoration might have been commissioned by Hadrian. The frieze on the Tropaeum Traiani has been restored to illustrate the ebb and flow of the two Dacian Wars on the basis of the Column, but, as will be shown elsewhere, the several metopes are more likely to have formed a continuous narrative representing a *profectio*, a war and a triumphal *adventus*.

26 Cichorius, Casts 12–16. Twin bridges were needed on account of the size of Trajan's army. When Grant's Army of the Potomac crossed the much wider James River by a single pontoon bridge in June 1864, for example, it took some four days for the 70,000 strong force to complete the crossing of the 2,100ft-wide river.

27 Jord. *Get.* 12.74. Prisc. *Inst. gram.* 6.13 records the citation *Inde Berzobim deinde Aizi processimus* as coming from *I Dacicorum*: while a campaign in the First War is evidently referred to, it need not necessarily be that of spring 101.

28 Cichorius, Cast 23.

29 On army transport, cf. Jos. *BJ* 2.546, 3.90 and 165; *HA Sev. Alex.* 47.1. *De Met. Cast.* 1 allows a space of 9 by 12ft in front of each tent for a baggage animal, manifesting that each *contubernium* was assigned a pack-animal, presumably to carry the leather tent itself – which must have weighed some 40–5lbs (18–20 kg: cf. C.van Driel-Murray, *JRMES* 1 (1990), 118) – as well as the common hand-mill and sundry cooking equipment.

30 Both Josephus, *BJ* 3.115–27 and 5.47–50, and Arrian, *Ectaxis*, 1 11, provide useful accounts of the Roman army on the march.

31 Veg. 1.9 and Jos. *BJ* 3.72.

32 Comparable figures have been independently arrived at by D. J. Breeze, *Talanta* 18/19 (1986/87), 11–13 and 23: I am indebted to Charles Daniels for drawing my attention to this obscure but important reference.

33 *De Mun. Cast.*, *passim*.

34 Cichorius, Casts 54–63.

35 Tac. *Agr.* 35.

36 The taking of heads was common amongst the tribes of barbarian Europe, from whom many of the auxiliaries were drawn: cf. J. Filip, *Celtic Civilization and its Heritage* (1962), 157; Diod. 14.115; Livy 10.26; Strabo 4.4.

37 Cichorius, Cast 70, perhaps the first of three dispatched by Decebalus during the First Dacian War: cf. Dio 68.9.1.

38 Cichorius, Casts 73–6: a parallel scene is shown on the *Anaglyphia Traiana*. Many have seen this scene as evidence for a major counter-attack by the Dacians and their Sarmatian allies into Roman territory: cf. Lepper and Frere, *Column*, 79–80. For a spirited rebuttal of the belief, cf. A. Poulter, in *Studien zu den Militärgrenzen Roms* III (1986), 519–28.

39 *De Met. Cast.* reports the progress of a mixed army group along the banks of the Danube, perhaps the same occasion, the Column only showing the emperor's water-borne advance with the vanguard.

40 The time is indicated by the appearance of the goddess of night within the scene.

41 Dio 8.2; Cichorius, Cast 99; Dio 68.9.2.

42 Cichorius, Casts 101–10.

43 Cichorius, Casts 102–3; Dio 8.1–2.

44 His first proclamation in late 97 was synonymous with his adoption of the *praenomen imperator*. *ILS* 285, which dates to after 10 December 101, provides the terminus post quem for the second.

45 The annual celebrations that marked the traditional end of the campaigning season began at Rome on 1 October, the date in the republican period when the citizens who formed the army became civilians again, and ended on the nineteenth, when the Salii performed a dance that commemorated the ritual cleansing of sacred weapons dedicated to Mars.

46 Smallwood, *Documents*, 109.

47 Smallwood, *Documents*, 214.

48 Cichorius, Casts 123–5. For the 'parallel defences' here, cf. F. Blume et al., *Die Schriften der römischen Feldmesser* I (1848, repr. 1967), 92–3, lines 7–10.

49 Dio 68.8.3.1. Cf. Pliny *Ep.* 8.4.

50 Cichorius, Casts 165–72. The occasions for which Trajan won his third imperial salutation? *ILS* 285 shows only two before the end of 101, and Smallwood, *Documents*, 352 reveals the fourth was awarded before 19 November 102.

51 Jord. *Get.* 12.74 gives the Red Tower Pass as one of the two access routes into Dacia, the other being that via the Iron Gates Pass. Callidromus: Pliny *Ep.* 10.74: a less charitable but more realistic explanation for Callidromus' presence in Asia Minor is that he was a runaway, who concocted the story of his capture and transfer to escape punishment.

52 Cichorius, Casts 191–2, for the spring; Dio 8.3.2.

53 Dio 68.9.4–7. This was presumably the event which occasioned Trajan's fourth imperial salutation, received before 19 November 102: Smallwood, *Documents*, 352.

54 *BMC* 191, 236 and 242.

55 Lepper and Frere, *Column*, 295.

56 Dio 13.1 and 6; Proc. *De Aed.* 4.6.13. It occasioned great admiration at the time: cf. Pliny *Ep.* 8.4.

57 For example, the actions of Aelius Catus, during the reign of Augustus: Strabo 7.303; and Ti. Plautius Silvanus between 57 and 67: *ILS* 986.

58 *AE* 1972.572.

59 *P. Lon.* 2851 (Hunt's Pridianum): the most recent discussion of the document is Lepper and Frere, *Column*, 244–59.

60 Dio 68.10.1.

61 Dacicus: Strack, *Untersuchungen*, 344–9. Cf. Halfmann, *Itinera*, 184; *AE* 1978.61.

62 Coins with the legend *CONGIAR(ium) SECUN(dum)*, with a reverse showing
    Trajan distributing the largesse, bear the consular date for 103; cf. *BMC* 767.
    For the shows, see Dio 68.10.2.

63 Cf. *BMC* 853–6 and 827–8, all of 103; Smallwood, *Documents*, 374a, of 103, noting
    how Trajan had 'liberally and commodiously enlarged' the Circus; and Dio 7.1, 'he
    put up an inscription in the Circus saying merely that he had made it adequate for the
    Roman people, when in fact it had got into a ruinous state in places [after the fire of
    80] and he had both enlarged and embellished it'.

64 Dio 68.10.3; Pliny *Ep.* 10.74.

65 Smallwood, *Documents*, 3, lines 40–1, and 19, line 5.

66 Cichorius, Casts 258–62.

67 Lepper and Frere, *Column*, 254–9. Not all these casualties need have occurred across
    the Danube.

68 Cichorius, Casts 249–57. *Clausurae* are generally considered to be a later
    phenomenon: their use by Caesar in controlling the movements of the Helvetii
    demonstrates their antiquity: Caes. *BG* 1.8. See D. J. Mattingly, *Tripolitania* (1995),
    106–7, and 113–14, for their name and purpose.

69 Cichorius, Cast 257. The general cannot be Trajan, as often assumed, for the figure is
    shown at the same scale as his companions, whereas the emperor – like Decebalus – is
    always shown at a slightly larger size throughout the Column.

70 Dio 68.11.3.

71 Dio 68.12.1; cf. Fronto *B. Parth.* 2 (= VdH p.220).

72 Dio 68.12.1.

73 J.C. Mann, *Hermes* 91 (1963), 483–9.

74 J.C. Mann, *Legionary Recruitment and Veteran Settlement during the Principate*
    (1983), 55, suggests that these legions were raised in Italy. However, Trajan is known
    to have excused the Spanish provinces from the military levy as so many men had
    already been conscripted from there (*HA Marc.* 11.7): a likely reason for his edict was
    that a significant proportion of the men raised for the two new legions came from the
    peninsula.

75 The connection was first made by T. Mommsen, *Hermes* 19 (1884), 219–34.
    P. Southern, *Brit* 20 (1989), 81–140, is the definitive study of the *numeri*, although
    it retains a careful neutrality on their origins; I am grateful to Ms Southern for her
    comments on the matter.

76 P. Southern, op. cit., 104.

77 Dio 68.11.2.

78 Cichorius, Casts 262–3.

79 The camp at Schela Cladovei, a little upstream from the bridge at Drobeta, encloses
    92.5 acres (37.44ha), large enough to contain the equivalent of four legions:
    cf. D. Tudor, *Oltenia Romana* (1978), 300. *CIL* 16.52 for the fifth salutation.

80 Cichorius, Cast 291, perhaps in this case a *topos*.

81 Cichorius, Casts 325–8.

82 Cf. Strobel, *Dakerkriegen*, 45–6: tiles suggest *legio IIII Flavia Felix* was the garrison.
    News of some imperial success, most probably this victory, given the apparent
    chronology, reached Cyrene before 30 July 106, prompting the organization that
    day of a commemorative meal: cf. J. Reynolds, *Report for the Society of Libyan Studies*
    1975/6 (1976), 11.

83 J. Carcopino, *Les Etapes de l'imperialisme romain* (1961), 106–17. Trajan did not recover everything: later discoveries at Sarmizegethusa Regia have included 1,543lb (700kg) in *aurei* alone between 1540 and 1759, more being discovered in the nineteenth century: Strobel, *Dakerkriegen*, 221, n. 23.

84 Cf. Lepper and Frere, *Column*, 242. The scene is shown on the Column: Cichorius, Cast 385; cf. Dio 68.14.3, and Pliny *Ep.* 8.4.2.

85 M. Speidel, *JRS* 60 (1970), 142–53.

86 Smallwood, *Documents*, 20, lines 1–2.

87 Again, the figure has probably been exaggerated by a factor of 10, and a total of 50,000 prisoners is to be preferred: cf. J. Carcopino, op. cit., 106–17.

88 Eutr. 8.6.2, referring to Dacia as Scythia.

89 *HA Hadr.* 3.8, for which he received a subsidy of *HS* 2,000,000.

90 *HA Hadr.* 3.9.

91 F. B. Florescu, *Das Siegesdenkmal von Adamklissi: Tropaeum Traiani* (1965), is the standard text.

92 For the altar, see E.Dorutiu-Boilu, Dacia 5 (1961), 345–63. But cf. A. Poulter, in Unz, C. (ed.), *Studien zu den Militärgrenzen Roms III* (1986), 519–28.

93 *BMC* 381.

94 *BMC* 381 and 439.

95 T. Schafer, *JDAI* 104 (1989), 283–317; and M. Labrousse, *Apulum* 19 (1981), 57–63.

96 Cf. Strack, *Untersuchungen*, 130–1, with the legend *ADVENTUS AUG(usti)*; 131–2, depicting *Fortuna Redux*, encapsulating the desire for the emperor's safe journey home; and 132–3 for the Circus Maximus. For the date of his return, cf. Pliny *Ep.* 6.5.5 and 13.2; Halfmann, *Itinera*, 184 and 187.

97 Dio 15.1; Pliny *Ep.* 8.4.2.

98 For the *congiarium*: *BMC* 769, with the legend *CONGIARIUM TERTIUM*, and Smallwood, *Documents*, 21, lines 2–3. For the *ludi*, loc.cit., lines 4–6. When one gladiator was killed another took his place: hence the final number who fought did not always equal an even number of pairs.

99 Smallwood, *Documents*, 22 and 23, lines 13–14. Dio 68.15.1 says that they lasted 123 days, and besides supplying the number of animals, claims that 10,000 gladiators were involved, without specifying whether pairs or singles.

100 Smallwood, *Documents*, 22, lines 15–16.

101 Fronto *Princ. Hist.* 20; consciously or not, Fronto was reflecting a common theme about how to satisfy the plebeians: cf. Juvenal's *panem et circenses* (Sat. 10.81) and Dio Chrysostom's 'plenty of bread and a seat at the chariot-races' (*Or.* 31.31).

IX *Optimus Princeps* (pp. 104–17)

1 Talbert, *Senate*, 432–3; Suet. *Tib.* 30; Tac. *Ann.* 13.49: under the Constitution adopted by the USSR (as with that of the United States), each one of the federal regions had the power to break away from the Union, but none dared to do so until the advent of *glasnost*. For entrance to the senate as a prerequisite for further office: Tac. *Ann.* 2.33; Dio 48.53; cf. Cic. *Verr.* 2.2.

2 *ILS* 244. Among the many modern discussions, P. A. Brunt, *JRS* 67 (1977), 95–116, provides a comprehensive account and further references.

3 Cf. Suet. *Gai.* 26.3.

4   *Dig.* 27.1.30 pr. indicates the *ad hoc* nature of its membership. The standard work remains J. Crook, *Consilium Principis* (1955), but see also Millar, *Emperor*, *passim*. For Trajan's *consilium*, Crook, op. cit., 53–5; and G. Galleazzo Tissoni, *Stud.Doc. Hist.Iuris* 31 (1965), 222–45, and id., *Stud.Doc.Hist.Iuris* 32 (1966), 129–52.

5   Crook, op. cit., 29 and 115: indeed, it should not be forgotten that Trajan owed his own advancement to the advice given by members of Nerva's *consilium*. Helvidius Priscus, hardly a supporter of the principate as a system of government, none the less considered the *consilium* 'the most valuable instrument of good government': Tac. *Hist.* 4.7.

6   *P.Oxy.* 1242 (H. A. Musurillo, *Acts of the Pagan Martyrs*, 161–78): 'impious', that is, with respect to the Greek worshippers of Serapis who were making the complaint.

7   Pliny *Pan.* 65.1. Cf. Mart. 10.72.8–9, for the observation that as a senator, Trajan was a servant of the senate, the corollary being that as *princeps* he was not.

8   It does not appear on bullion specie until 104: *BMC* 156 etc. For the date of issue, cf. P. V. Hill, *NC* 130 (1970), 59.

9   Lucius Scipio: *CIL* 1(2).2.9; Augustus: *CIL* 2.472; Tiberius: *CIL* 11.3872 = *ILS* 159; Caligula: Suet. *Cal.* 22.1 and Quint. *Inst.* 1.7.21; Claudius: Pliny *Ep.* 8.6.13 and (with 'princeps') *CIL* 10.1401; Nero: Sen. *Clem.* 1.19.9 and *CIL* 10.7852; Domitian: *ILS* 3546; Nerva: Pliny *Ep.* 9.13.23.

10 Pliny *Ep.* 10.1.2; *Pan.* 2.7 and 88.4.

11 Thus Paribeni, *Optimus Princeps*, II, 156–7. It is used in this way on the alimentary table of 101 for the *Ligures Baebiani*, that from Veleia of 101, and an inscription from Rome of the same year: Smallwood, *Documents* 374a, and 436.

12 For example Mopsuestia, Cilicia, in 99: *IGRR* 3.914, and the above-mentioned *Tabula Ligures Baebiani* of 101. For other early irregular inscriptions, cf. Smallwood, *Documents*, 435, of 101, and 436, of 102. For a discussion, see V. A. Georgescu, *Studii Clasice* 10 (1968), 187.

13 Trajan did not formally adopt it into his personal nomenclature until 114 (see above, p. 118), although Pliny uses it unofficially as a *cognomen* in the *actio gratiarum* (*Pan.* 2.7).

14 Cf. Pliny *Ep.* 3.20.12: 'Everything today, it is true, depends on the will of that one man (*sc.*, Trajan) who has taken upon himself for the general good all our cares and responsibilities': cf. *Pan.* 72.1 and Tac. *Dial.* 41.4 for a similar sentiment.

15 Tac. *Hist.* 1.1.6. Cf. E. Cizek, *L'Epoque de Trajan* (1983), 211–12.

16 Cf. Cizek, op. cit., 213–14.

17 Eutr. 8.2 and 5.

18 Pliny *Pan.* 58.4.

19 *Pan.* 4.2; 66.2 and 5; 69.2–5; 71.1–3; 76.2. Cf. Dio 68.5–6. Note also his decision to send Dacian envoys to the senate to ratify the peace treaty after the First Dacian War, a gesture symbolic of the republican tradition whereby only the *Curia* could confirm treaties agreed by generals in the field.

20 Pliny *Ep.* 3.20 and 4.25.

21 *Pan.* 75.1–3.

22 *Ep.* 5.13.6–8: cf. 5.9.3.

23 *Ep.* 5.13.7 and 6.19. According to Pliny, the result of the last edict was a tremendous increase in the price of land in Italy.

24 For a discussion of these two men, see R. Syme, *HAC* 1986/1989 (1991), 189–200.

25 R. Syme, *The Classical Outlook* 62 (1986/87), 41, and *RP* 4, 13–14; also the relevant sections in H. Halfmann, *Die Senatoren aus dem östlichen Teil des Imperium Romanum* (1979). It may have been that Trajan developed his friendship with many of these men during his military service in Syria: cf. R. Syme, *Athenaeum* 59 (1981), 273.

26 Dio 68.5.2; cf. A. R. Birley, *CR* 12 (1962), 197–9, who holds that the oath was usually a formality: as we can demonstrate, in Trajan's case it was emphatically not.

27 Dio 68.3.2 and 16.2; for an oblique reference to this plot in a letter of the emperor Severus, cf. *HA Alb.* 12.10.

28 *HA Hadr.* 5.5.

29 Eutr. 8.4 (which only mentions one senator in the plot), *HA Hadr.* 5.5, and *HA Avid.* 8.6: Crassus was put to death shortly after Hadrian's accession, allegedly for planning yet another revolt.

30 It is tempting to see Suetonius' lost *de Institutione Officiorum* ('On the Institution of Offices') as a study prompted by Trajan's reforms to the equestrian service.

31 For Atticus: Jones, *Domitian*, 63. For Pompeius Hommulus, cf. Pflaum, *Carrières*, no. 89; and for Vibius Lentulus (who may have been a tribune of Trajan's in the *legio VII Gemina*), op. cit., no. 66 = Devijer, *Prosopographia*, V.97: it is not certain which of these men held the post of a *rationibus* first, although it is likely to have been Hommulus as Lentulus was *procurator monetae, c.* 99–106.

32 Alexandrinus: Pflaum, *Carrières*, no. 46. Most would not agree that the division in the post occurred this early.

33 Cf. Pflaum, *Carrières*, no. 96 = Devijer, *Prosopographia*, S.84.

34 For the *procurator vehiculorum*, cf. Vic. Caes. 13.5.

35 *PIR* 2, B.112 = Pflaum, *Carrières*, 73 = Devijer, *Prosopographia* B.21. Cf. M. Peachin, *NC* 146 (1986), 94–106; D. W. McDowall, in *Scripta Nummaria Romana* (1978), 32–47, and id., *Num. Notes and Monog.* 161 (1979), 111–29. See P. V. Hill, *The Dating and Arrangement of the Undated Coins of Rome, AD 98–148* (1970), 2–5, for the organization of the mint.

36 The position of *procurator annonae Ostis* was established by Claudius (Suet. Claud. 24.2 and Dio 60.24.3), but the first known equestrian holder is the African M. Vettius Latro, in post between 112 and 117: Pflaum, *Carrières*, 104 = Devijer, *Prosopographia*, V.76. The first attested *procurator Minuciae* is C. Camrius Clemens, in post *c.* 110 after service in Britain, where he had commanded the *ala Petriana*, the largest cavalry regiment in the province: Pflaum, *Carrières*, 87 = Devijer, *Prosopographia*, C.72.

37 Pflaum, *Procurateurs*, 55, n.11.

38 For his career, E. Frézouls, *Syria* 30 (1953), 247–78; *AE* 1955.225; Pflaum, *Carrières*, 94 = Devijer, *Prosopographia*, F 54; R. Syme, *JRS* 52 (1962), 87–96.

39 Pliny *Ep.* 3.8 and 10.94 and 95; *AE* 1953.73.

40 Cf. Pflaum, *Carrières*, no. 96 = Devijer, *Prosopographia*, S.84.

41 This was recognized by Aelius Aristides: *Or.* 26.63–5.

42 K. Hopkins, *Conquerors and Slaves* (1978), 68–9.

43 F. Millar, *Ancient World* 20 (1983), 93–7.

44 Suet. *Vesp.* 4.

45 None of the several *leges provinciarum* have survived to the present day, although there are several references to them in other sources: cf. F. F. Abbott and A. C. Johnson, *Municipal Administration in the Roman Empire* (1926), 49, and A. Lintot, *Imperium Romanorum* (1993), 28–32.

46 Jolowicz and Nicholas, *Roman Law*, 363–5; Talbert, *Senate*, 394; Millar, *Emperor*, 342–9.

47 *Dig.* 1.4.1.*pr*; Gai. *Inst.* 1.5. For the *constitutiones*, cf. Jolowicz and Nicholas, *Roman Law*, 365–73; J. H. Oliver, *Greek Constitutions of Early Roman Emperors* (1989); and Millar, *Emperor*, 228–57 and 317–41.

48 Cf. W. Williams, *ZPE* 22 (1976), 240–5, and Millar, *Emperor*, 228–40. For two contrasting examples of the range of Trajan's *edicta*, cf. that of 104/112 concerning the penalties for neglecting specified religious observations: W. Cureton, *Ancient Syriac Documents* (1864), 41; and the Aphrodisias text releasing T. Julianus Attalus from a civic liturgy at Smyrna: J. Reynolds, *Aphrodisias and Rome* (1982), 113–15.

49 *Dig.* 29.1.1.*pr*; cf. Sherwin-White, *Letters*, 589–91, and G. P. Burton, *ZPE* 21 (1976), 63; Talbert, *Senate*, 402–7; Jolowicz and Nicholas, *Roman Law*, 370–1; Millar, *Emperor*, 313–17.

50 Cf. Jolowicz and Nicholas, *Roman Law*, 97–101 and 358–9.

51 Cf. the case of Pliny, recorded as being involved in official work at Prusa, Nicomedia and Nicaea, among other locations: *Ep.* 17A, 33 and 37, and 81; also the Babatha archive, referring to meetings before the governor of Arabia at Petra and Rabbathmoab: N. Lewis, in *The Documents from the Bar-Kokhba Period in the Cave of Letters* (1989), 23 and 25.

52 It has been suggested that there was one senatorial or equestrian administrative official for every 300,000 people in the Roman empire, compared with one for every 15,000 in twelfth-century China, an empire of comparable size and technology: K. Hopkins, *Death and Renewal* II (1983), 186.

53 H.-G. Pflaum, in *Hommages à Albert Grenier* (1962), 1232–42. Also, B. E. Thomasson, *Legatus* (1991), 73–84.

54 For a reassessment of his role, cf. G. P. Burton, *Chiron* 23 (1993), 13–28.

55 A. H. M. Jones, *Studies in Roman Government and Law* (1960), 161–4; for examples of *iudices dati*, cf. CIL 3.2882, 2883, 8472, 9833, 9973 and 12794.

56 Garnsey and Saller, *Roman Empire*, 20; cf. G. P. Burton, *Chiron* 23 (1993), 25, 'Rome's control over her provinces [was] characterised by a substantial deficit of administrative resources.'

57 Pliny *Ep.* 1.7.2.

58 See above, p. 77.

59 Pliny *Ep.* 4.9, 5.20.1, 6.29.10 and 10.56 and 57.

60 *Ep.* 5.20; 6.5, 13 and 29.11; 7.6, and 10.

61 Brunt, *Historia* 10 (1961), 224–7; B. Levick, *Claudius* (1990), 164.

62 Suet. *Dom.* 8.2. There was certainly a marked increase in the number of recorded trials for maladministration during the period (P. A. Brunt, *Historia* 10 (1961), 227): as a Tacitus or Suetonius would not have hesitated to use such evidence of corruption to damn certain of Trajan's predecessors, the increase now is likely to be real rather than merely apparent.

63 Dio 53.14.1.

64 Pflaum, *Procurateurs*, 54–7.

65 G.P. Burton, *Chiron* 23 (1993), 19 and *passim*.

66 Cic. *Verr.* 2.3.172 and *ILS* 7193–5.

67 For the *curatores rei publicae*, cf. W. Liebnamm, *Philologus* 56 (1897), 290–325; Eck, *Staatliche Organisation*, 190–246; G. P. Burton, *Chiron* 9 (1979), 465–88; R. Duthoy, *Ancient Society* 10 (1979), 171–239; F. Millar, *Phoenix* 40 (1986), 3160; G. Camodeca, *ANRW* 2:13 (1980), 453–534; F. Jacques, *Les curateurs de cités dans l'Occident romain de Trajan à Gallien* (1983) and id., *Le privilège de liberté* (1984), 3–4; M. Sartori, *Athenaeum* 67 (1989), 5–20. For the *iuridici*, Eck, *Staatliche Organisation*, 247–66, and id., *Senatoren*, 3; Alföldy, *Fasti Hispanienses*, 236–42; Birley, Fasti, 405.

68 For *curatores* under Nero and Domitian: R. Syme, *JRS* 67 (1977), 38–49; for *iuridici* during the Augustan and Flavian periods: Strabo 3.4.20 (167), Pliny *NH* 19.35, and *ILS* 1011 (cf. *ILS* 1015).

69 Smallwood, *Documents*, 475. For the senate's control over the peninsula, cf. Dio 52.22.1.

70 The analysis provided by R. Duthoy, *Ancient Society* 10 (1979), 171–238, *passim*, reveals that Trajan's *curatores* were equally split between equestrians and propraetorian senators.

71 Cf. Pliny *Ep.* 8.24.2, to a Maximus, on his appointment as (presumably) *curator rei publicae* to set in order the constitutions of certain free cities in Achaia.

72 For example, F. Millar, *Phoenix* 40 (1986), 316.

73 Within this distance, it was the responsibility of the Urban Prefect: *Dig.* 1.12.

74 Smallwood, *Documents*, 475; cf. R. K. Sherk, *The Municipal Decrees of the Roman West* (Buffalo, 1970), 51 and 65–6.

75 *Dig.* 22.1.33; 50.8.11.2; 50.8.12.1–2; and 50.10.5.1.

76 G. P. Burton, *JRS* 65 (1975), 99–102.

77 J. Colini, *Les villes libres de l'orient gréco-romain* (1965), 67, has argued that Trajan did not favour the free cities, and by inference thus sought to reduce their privileges, but an inscription from Aphrodisias recording an edict of Trajan's controverts this, as it upholds the rights of free cities: J. Reynolds, *Aphrodisias and Rome* (1982), 113–15.

78 Pliny *Ep.* 10.18.2–3.

79 Williams, *Correspondence*, 13, for a discussion.

80 Sherwin-White, *Letters*, 81.

81 For example, *Or.* 38.33–7; 39.4; 48.7. The most recent commentary on Pliny's letters from Bithynia is Williams, *Correspondence*.

82 Smallwood, *Documents*, 230; Pliny *Ep.* 10.25.

83 *Ep.* 10.29; 31; 49; 56; 58; 65; 68; 72; 79; 81; 92; 110; 112; 114; 116; 118.

84 *Ep.* 10.45; 63; 120.

85 *Ep.* 10.23; 75; 98.

86 *Ep.* 10.19; 21; 27.

87 *Ep.* 10.17A; 43; 47; 54; 108; 110.

88 *Ep.* 10.17B; 37; 39.

89 *Ep.* 10.41; 61; 90.

90 *Ep.* 10.33; 92; 96.

91 *Ep.* 10.18.3.

92 *Ep.* 10.38.1. For the contrasting views on their authorship, cf. K. H. Waters, *ANRW* 2:2 (1975), 411, A. N. Sherwin-White, *JRS* 52 (1962), 114–25, and id., *Letters*,

536–46 (against); and F. Millar, *JRS* 57 (1967), W. Williams, *Latomus* 38 (1979), 67–89, and id., *Correspondence*, 16–17 (for).

93 *Ep.* 10.40.1: 'You could have been in no uncertainty, my dearest Secundus, about ...';
Ep. 10.82: 'As the man on the spot, you are the best person to decide ...'
Cf. *Ep.* 10.18.3; 32.1; 34.1; 38.1; 40.3; 60.2; 62; and 117.

94 Cf. *Ep.* 10. 18.2: 'For you [*sc.*, Pliny] will see to it that they [sc., the Bithynians] know you have been picked out to be sent to them to act in my place.'

x Law, Finance and Literature (pp. 118–37)

1 *Epit.* 13.
2 *Dig.* 1.4.1. *pr.*
3 *Dig.* 37.12.5, recording the involvement of Aristo and Neratius in formulating an edict of Trajan's.
4 Tac. *Ann.* 4.30.
5 Suet. *Tit.* 8.5; Pliny *Pan.* 35.1–5. For the *frumentarii*, who were sadly to acquire their own sinister reputation at a later date, see *HA Hadr.* 11.4
6 Pliny *Ep.* 10.97 and *Pan.* 42.1–4: cf. Tac. *Hist.* 1.2.6. *Dig.* 29.50 and 48.18.1.11–12 and 19.
7 *Dig.* 48.19.5.
8 Pliny *Pan.* 42.1.
9 Pliny *Ep.* 10. 66–7; *Dig.* 48.19.5.
10 Sen. *de Ira* 1.15; Cic. *de Leg* 3.19; Livy 27.37; Soranus *Gyn.* 2.9–10; Tac. *Germ.* 19; *Dig.* 40.4.29; Juv. 6.603; Aul. Gell. *NA* 12.1.23. Cf. Tac. *Hist.* 5.5. and *Germ.* 19.5; Strabo 17.824. For the subject in general, J. Boswell, *The Kindness of Strangers* (1989), and W. V. Harris, *JRS* 84 (1994), 1–22.
11 Pliny *Ep.* 65 and 66.
12 *Dig.* 37.12.5.
13 *Dig.* 26.7.12.1; 27.1.17; and 41.4.2.8.
14 Pliny *Pan.* 43.1.
15 Dio 60.24; *Dig.* 24.1.60–2.
16 Dio 60.24.3.
17 *Dig.* 29.1.1.*pr*; Gai. *Inst.* 2.110.
18 Just. *Inst.* 2.11.
19 *Dig.* 48.19.15 and 22.5.3; cf. P. Garnsey, *Social Status and Legal Privilege in the Roman Empire*, 87–8 and 152–78.
20 Livy 39.52.4.
21 Lepper and Frere, *Column*, 232.
22 The arguments are fully rehearsed by H. Hammond, *MAAR* 15 (1938), 23–61, and id., 19 (1949), 36–76. See also the discussion in Lepper and Frere, *Column*, 232–6.
23 Pliny *Pan.* 46.4 and 54. 2. Cf. *Ep.* 7.24; Luc. 35; App. *Met.* 10.29–34; Suet. *Gai.* 57.4, and *Dom.* 7.1; Mart. *Spect.* 7.
24 Pliny *Pan.* 46.3–4; cf. A. Garzetti, From *Tiberius to the Antonines* (1974), 313. Cf. Dio 68.10.2; Fronto *Princ. Hist.* 20.
25 Dio 68.10.2.
26 Pliny *Ep.* 4.22.
27 *Ep.* 6.22.

[28] *Ep.* 6.31. Sherwin-White, *Letters*, 391–6.

[29] The decision was later codified as *Dig.* 3.2.2.3, which provided for the immediate dismissal of any soldiers detected in adultery.

[30] *Dig.* 48.5.4. pr. and 16(15).2 allowed a third party to proceed with a case involving adultery after the sixty days had elapsed.

[31] The penalty is specified in the *Sent. Pauli* 2.26.14.

[32] Usually identified as C. Julius Tiro Gaetulicus: *PIR* (2), I.603

[33] *AE* 1975.849; cf. H.-G. Pflaum, *Carrières* (Supplement: 1980), 103a and 114.

[34] Pliny *Ep.* 7.6.7–13. Sherwin-White, *Letters*, 409–10, provides a valuable discussion.

[35] *Ep.* 10.29 and 30. The usual *summum supplicum* for a slave was to be burnt alive (*crematio*) or crucifixion (*crux*).

[36] *Ep.* 10.96 and 97; P. Keresztes, *Imperial Rome and the Christians* I (1989), 107–10.

[37] *Ep.* 10.96 and 97. Cf. Sherwin-White, *Letters*, 691–712; G. E. M. de Ste. Croix in M. Finlay, *Studies in Ancient Society* (1974), 210–49 and 256–62; A. N. Sherwin-White, op. cit., 250–5; T. D. Barnes, *JRS* 58 (1968), 32–84. Beyond this particular case, objective evidence for Trajan's personal attitude towards Christianity is lacking. While later chroniclers spoke of his reign marking the 'third great persecution' (after those of Nero and Domitian), during which St. Ignatius of Antioch and Simeon, second bishop of Jerusalem, were martyred, any oppression seems to have been sporadic and popular rather than official in origin: cf. P. Keresztes, op. cit., 103–5. That said, despite the reservations of F. Lepper (*Parthian War*, 93–5), the evidence of the so-called *Acts of Sharbil and Barsamya*, which purport to recount how these two men suffered martyrdom at the hands of one Lysanias (?Lusius Quietus) in Edessa *c.* 116/117, for failing to observe an edict of Trajan's concerning the observance of official religious ceremonies, might be of some relevance to the matter in question: W. Cureton, *Ancient Syriac Documents* (1864), 41.

[38] Sen. *Ben.* 7.17.3; cf. 7.6.3. See also G. Boulvert, *Labeo* 18 (1972), 201–6.

[39] Dio 53.22; Tac. *Ann.* 6.2.1.

[40] Tac. *Ann.* 15.18; *ILS* 1447.

[41] Front. *Aq* 2.116–18.

[42] *Ep.* 8.6.7; *Pan.* 36.3.

[43] The literature is, predictably, extensive. See in particular F. Millar, *JRS* 53 (1963), 29–42, *JRS* 54 (1964), 33–40, and *Emperor*, 133–201 and 623–5; P. A. Brunt, *JRS* 56 (1966), 75–91; and Veyne, *Bread and Circuses*, 321–77 and 380–418.

[44] Dio 55.25.2–3.

[45] Tributa: Spain and Africa: Cic. *Verr.* 2.3.12; Syria, Cilicia: App. *Syr.* 50; Judaea: Jos. *AJ* 14.202–6 and 18.3, and Tac. *Ann.* 2.42; Egypt and Sicily: Cic. *Verr.* 2.3.172; Sardinia: *B.Afr.* 98; Asia: App. *BC* 5.4.17 and *pro lege Man.* 45; Phrygia: Tac. *Ann.* 4.13. *Indictiones*: HA Marc. 17.4.

[46] Strabo 3.4.13; *B.Hisp.* 42; Dio 60.24.5.

[47] The term *ratio privata* is not officially registered until the reign of Hadrian or Antoninus Pius (*CIL* 8.8810), and is used here for descriptive purposes only.

[48] Hence the existence of an imperial freedman responsible for claiming and receiving legacies: *ILS* 1520 and 1523–7. Cf. Pliny *Pan.* 43.5, on the obligation to restore to the *princeps* that proportion of a man's estate which derived specifically from the effect of imperial patronage.

[49] *RG* 15.1, 17.2 and 18; Vell. Pat. 2.130.2; *ILS* 1447; *CIL* 11.3885 and 5028. Cf. H. Nesselhauf, *HAC* 1963 (1964), 73; A. Masi, *Richerches Sulla 'Res Privata' del 'Princeps'* (1971), 31–53.

[50] *Tributa*: Suet. *Aug.* 40.3; cf. Dio 53. 15.3 and 54.21.2–8; Pliny *Pan.* 29.4–5; *Dig.* 2.14.42, 8.1.27.3, 39.4.1.1, 49.14.46.5, 50.4.18.26 and 15.5.pr. Property seizures: Tac. *Ann.* 2.48, 4.20, 6.2 and 6.19; Dio 58.22.2; and Pliny *Pan.* 42.1.

[51] Veyne, *Bread and Circuses*, 331.

[52] Tac. *Ann.* 1.8; J. Beranger, in *Mélanges offerts à Georges Bonnard* (1966), 151–60. Cf. Pliny *Pan.* 27.3 and 41–2; *Dig.* 43.8.2.2. Note, for example, how the *Tabula alimentaria Ligurum Baebianorum* differentiates between land which was *adfinis populo*, that is, which belonged to the 'people', and the imperial estates, *adfinis Caesari nostro*. Also the differences before the law in public cases, private cases, and those involving the *fiscus*: *Cod.Just.* 7.49.1.

[53] Plut. *Pomp.* 45.3–4; *RG*; Tac. *Ann.* 13.31.2 and Dio 58.21; Suet. *Gaius* 37.3 and Dio 59.2.6; Suet. *Vesp.* 16.3.

[54] K. Hopkins, *JRS* 70 (1980), 119.

[55] Suet. *Galba* 12.3 and *Vesp.* 22.

[56] Vict. *Caes.* 13.5, perhaps recording the formalization of the post rather than its establishment, for it is recorded as early as the reign of Claudius.

[57] The epithet *moneta*, from which we derive the word money, seems to derive from *monere*, 'to remind'.

[58] *Pan.* 36.1.

[59] Pflaum, *Carrières*, nos. 66 and 73 = Devijer, *Prosopographia*, B.21 and V.97; cf. M. Peachin, *NC* 146 (1986), 94–106. For a discussion, D. W. McDowall, in *Scripta Nummaria Romana* (1978), 32–47, and *Num.Notes and Monog.* 161 (1979), 111–29; and P. V. Hill, *The Dating and Arrangement of the Undated Coins of Rome, AD 98–148* (1970), 5.

[60] B. H. Grenfell, et al., *Fayum Towns and their Papyri* (1900), no. 20, Col. 2.3: the document is assigned to the reign of Severus Alexander, 222–35, on internal evidence, and to the period 270–350 on palaeographical grounds, but is accepted as a copy of an earlier document.

[61] *Pan.* 41.1.

[62] The Roman pound (*libra*) consisted of 12 *unciae*, each *uncia* of 24 *scripula*, and equalled 11.5 imperial ounces or 321g.

[63] S. Bolin, *State and Currency in the Roman Empire to 300 AD* (1958), Tables 15 and 16.

[64] M. T. Griffin, *Nero: The End of a Dynasty* (1984), 198.

[65] Its purity, however, was not affected. For the change in weight, cf. S. Bolin, op. cit., Table 16.

[66] Pliny *NH* 33.3.47; *Dig.* 13.4.3. Cf. the credit crisis of 33, when a shortage of coin resulted in high interest rates, resolved by Tiberius loaning without interest *HS* 100,000,000 from his own reserves: Tac. *Ann.* 13.31.2 and Dio 58.21.

[67] G. R. Watson, *The Roman Soldier* (1969), 114.

[68] R. Duncan-Jones, in *Rhythmes de la production monétaire de l'antique à nos jours* (1989), 235–54; cf. Pliny *NH* 12.84 and 6.101. It is the fate of any hard currency: note the comparable modern situation where it is estimated that half of the US dollar bills ever printed are – as a favoured hard currency – stored outside the United States.

69 Pliny *NH* 33.132. These and the following figures are derived from the tables provided in D. R. Walker, *The Metrology of the Roman Silver Coinage Part I: From Augustus to Domitian* and *Part II: From Nerva to Commodus* (*BARIS* 22 1977).

70 Walker, op. cit., I, 56.

71 P. A. Brunt, *Scripta Classica Israelica* 1 (1974), 90–115.

72 Cf. P. V. Hill, *The Dating and Arrangement of the Undated Coins of Rome, AD 98–148* (1970), and Dio 68.15.3.

73 D. Sperber, *NC* ser 7, 10 (1970), 111–15. For the Pergamum inscription, cf. *Or.Graeci Ins.Sel.* 484

74 *P.Bad.* 37, of 107–11: for an alternative explanation see L. C. West and A. C. Johnson, *Currency in Roman and Byzantine Egypt* (1944), 92–4. Suet. *Jul.* 54.2 and Jos. *BJ* 6.6.1 (317).

75 D. Sperber, *NC* ser 7, 17 (1977), 153–5.

76 The fundamental study of Trajan's 'restored coinage' remains H. Mattingley, *NC* ser. 5, 61 (1926), 232–78.

77 *BMC*, p. xciii.

78 Pliny *Pan.* 47.1–3 and 49.8; *Ep.* 9.28.1. Cf. A. Henneman, *Der Aussere und innere Stil in Trajans Briefen* (1940), *passim*, and H. Bardon, *Les Empereurs et les lettres latines* (1940), 357–89, for Trajan's own literary attainments, best described as adequate.

79 Tac. *Agr.* 3.1; the principal studies are Syme, *Tacitus*, and Martin, *Tacitus*.

80 The probable date of the *Annals* was deduced by R. Syme, in *Historiographia Antiqua* (1977), 262–3.

81 *Hist.* 1.1.

82 Martin, *Tacitus*, 58–9.

83 Cf. Syme, *Tacitus*, 86–99.

84 He epitomizes a Romanian saying: 'My friends are those who forgive me my faults.'

85 *Ep.* 10.62.

86 The principal biographies and studies are C. P. Jones, *Plutarch and Rome* (1971), and D. A. Russell, *Plutarch* (1972). Again, there is no ancient authority for the popular titles given to these works.

87 *Or.* 11.

88 *Or.* 38-40.

89 *Or.* 47.

90 *Or.* 40.11.

91 The eventual outcome of the case is not clear. For other problems raised by Chrysostom's building programme, cf. *Or.* 40 and 45, and Pliny *Ep.* 10. 81 and 82.

92 *Or.* 33.

93 *Or.* 33. 60 and 36.

94 *Ep.* 1.10.1; 3.5–11; and 1.13.1. *Ep.* 5.10; the phrase is Syme's. Suetonius' life and work are best assessed by A. Wallace-Hadrill, *Suetonius* (1983). For his dealings with Trajan, cf. G. Bowersock, in J. Bibauw (ed.), *Hommages à Marcel Renard* 1 (1969), 119–25.

95 *Ep.* 1.24: as *Ep.* 2.1 can be dated to 97 by the death of Verginius, it is generally accepted that the contents of *Ep.* 1 precede that year. For Suetonius' career, see above, pp. 135–6.

96 *Ep.* 5.10.3.

[97] A. Wallace-Hadrill, *Suetonius* (1983), 47. An ancient 'volume' (from *volvere*, to roll), equalled a single scroll, and Homer's *Iliad* and *Odyssey* are said to have filled at least thirty-six such rolls.

[98] Martial was granted the like distinction of the *ius trium liberorum* for his services to poetry.

[99] A. Wallace-Hadrill, op. cit., 46–9; 43 and n. 22.

[100] *Ep.* 1.17 and 8.12.

xi *Pater Patriae* (pp. 138–60)

[1] Dio Chrys. *Or.* 3.127.

[2] Smallwood, *Documents*, 406. But see now G. di Vita-Eurard, *La Via Appia* (1990), 73–93.

[3] Dio 68.15.3. For the Terracina cutting (Pesco Montana), cf. *CIL* 10.6839 and 6849, and Blake, *Roman Construction*, 280–1.

[4] Via Aemilia: *CIL* 11:2.6813; Via Puteoli: *CIL* 10:1.6926–8 and 6931.

[5] Via Sublacensis: *CIL* 9.5971; Via Labicana: *CIL* 10:1.6890 and 6887–9;

[6] Via Salaria: *CIL* 9.5947; Via Flaminia: *ILS* 299.

[7] Cf. Dio 68.15.3, where it is claimed that Trajan 'provided the roads with many buildings'. For the *praefectus vehiculorum*, cf. Pflaum, *Carrières* 1029.

[8] Smallwood, *Documents*, 407: cf. *ILS* 1059 and 1093; *AE* 1926.77.

[9] Cf. Hor. *Sat.* 1.5, for the hazards of this route in earlier times.

[10] For example, Smallwood, *Documents*, 408a; over thirty-two similar milestones are known from the route.

[11] *BMC* 484; Smallwood, *Documents*, 408b; F. J. Hassel, *Der Traiansbogen in Benevent* (1966), 9; F. A. Lepper, *JRS* 59 (1969), 250–61: the symbolism of the Beneventum reliefs is considered in Chapter 14.

[12] Pliny *Pan.* 29.2. Cf. Dio 68.7.2 on Trajan's repairs to roads and harbours.

[13] The standard work is Meiggs, *Ostia* (1960).

[14] Gai. *Inst.* 1.32c; Luc. *Navig.* 5, cf. L. Casson, *TAPA* 81 (1950), 43–56. I am grateful to Dr Cheryl Haldane for her helpful discussions on ancient shipping.

[15] Suet. *Claud.* 20.3; Dio 60.11.4. Cf. Meiggs, *Ostia*, 153–61.

[16] Pace Meiggs, *Ostia*, 161, topography dictated that canals and overflow cuts should be below the capital rather than above it, as the principal cause of floods at Rome was the silted-up channel of the Tiber at Ostia, which caused it to backwater when in spate.

[17] Tac. *Ann.* 15.18.3, and *Hist.* 1.86.

[18] Meiggs, *Ostia*, 161–6. The location conforms with Pliny's comment that Trajan effectively 'opened the shore to the sea': cf. Suet. *Nero.* 31.3.

[19] *BMC* 770a; cf. Strack, *Untersuchungen*, 212. As Meiggs, *Ostia*, 489, observes, there is no reference to the work in the *Fasti* for 112, which suggests that it was dedicated either before or after that year.

[20] Blake, *Roman Construction*, 144–58, and Meiggs, *Ostia*, 133–5.

[21] For Centum Cellae, see S. Bastianelli, *Centumcellae, Castrum Novum* (1954), and Blake, *Roman Construction*, 275 and 292, with further references.

[22] *Pan.* 29.2, evidently anachronistic: see below, n. 26.

[23] *Ep.* 6.31.15–17, whose literary date is *c.*107; S. Bastianelli, op. cit., and Blake, *Roman Construction*, 292–2, detail the physical remains. There is no evidence to support Pliny's assertion that the port took Trajan's name.

24 Tac. *Hist.* 3.76–7; cf. *ILS* 282 of 101, from the town, recording Trajan's *PROVIDENTIA*. Blake, *Roman Construction*, 292–3, provides a summary of the structural evidence.

25 Blake, *Roman Construction*, 293–4, discusses the physical remains of the harbour.

26 Smallwood, *Documents*, 387. The similarity of phrasing between the inscription and Pliny's encomium is to be noted. Ancona and Centum Cellae are the only two places where Trajan could be said to have 'enclosed the sea within the shore' (Pliny *Pan.* 29.2): given that the second was in process of construction in 107, and work at Ancona was not completed until *c.* 114, it would seem possible that Pliny was making an anachronistic reference to Centum Cellae in the published version of his *actio gratiarum*.

27 Cf. *RG* 19–21.

28 Suet. *Aug.* 31.5; cf. P. Zanker, *Forum Augustum* (1968); Richardson, *Ancient Rome*, 16–162.

29 Suet. *Aug.* 28.3.

30 J. B. Ward-Perkins, *Roman Imperial Architecture* (2nd ed., 1981), 84; MacDonald, *Architecture* (1982), 41–6; Juv. *Sat.* 3.254–61; cf. Mart. 5.22.

31 *Epit.* 41.13–14; cf. Amm. Marc. 27.3.7.

32 P. V. Hill, *NC* 144 (1984), 34–89, *NC* 145 (1985), 82–92, and *Monuments*, *passim*.

33 The fundamental work on the brick-stamps is H. Bloch, *I bolli laterizi e la storia edilizia romana* (1947), supplemented by M. Steinby, *Bullettino della Commissione archeologia comune di Roma* 84 (1974/5), 7–132, and *AE* 1978.10; also T. Helen, *Organization of Roman Brick Production in the First and Second Centuries AD* (1975).

34 For example, bricks with the consular date of 123 were used in Hadrian's new Temple of Venus and Rome, still under construction in 134.

35 *Epit.* 13.

36 Dio. Hal. *Rom. Antiq.* 9.68.2; Hor. *Car.* 1.2.13–6. J. Le Gall, *Le Tibre, fleuve de Rome dans l'antiquité* (1953), 29–53, lists the known floods.

37 *CIL* 6.31545 and 14.85; *Epit.* 13.12–13.

38 Smallwood, *Documents*, 381a; cf. Pliny *Ep.* 2.11.5.

39 Meiggs, *Ostia*, 172; Pliny *Ep.* 8.17.1–2. This flood could well have destroyed the Pons Sublicius, the oldest bridge at Rome, frequently washed away in severe inundations yet always replaced; a coin of 105–7 showing a single-span bridge might well indicate a reconstruction carried out by Trajan: cf. P. V. Hill, *NC* 145 (1985), 86–7, citing *BMC*, 847–52.

40 Smallwood, *Documents*, 381a; cf, Pliny *Ep.* 2.11.5.

41 Richardson, *Ancient Rome*, 144.

42 *ILS* 7672. Blake, *Roman Construction*, 39; Richardson, *Ancient Rome*, 80.

43 Front. *Aq.* 2.87 and 2.93; cf. E.B. van Deman, *The Building of the Roman Aqueducts* (1934), 271–330.

44 Templum Augustum: Mart. 12.3.8; Amphitheatrum Flavium: *CIL* 6.32255.

45 Pliny *Pan.* 51; Dio 68.7.2; Paus. 5.12.6; Smallwood, *Documents*, 374a; P. V. Hill, *NC* 145 (1985), 83, and id., *Monuments*, 47–8, citing *BMC* 853–6 and 827–8; Suet. *Dom.* 5; Richardson, *Ancient Rome*, 85. For a full discussion, see J. H. Humphrey, *Roman Circuses* (1986), 102–6.

46 Jupiter Victor: P. V. Hill, *NC* 144 (1984), 49, citing *BMC* 863–5, and Richardson, *Ancient Rome*, 227. Venus Genetrix: Smallwood, *Documents*, 23 line 55; cf. MacDonald, *Roman Construction*, 102–3; Richardson, *Ancient Rome*, 166.

47 Blake, *Roman Construction*, 110, and Richardson, *Ancient Rome*, 237.

48 Suet. *Dom.* 5; Dio 69.4.1; Amm.Marc. 16.10.14; cf. Richardson, *Ancient Rome*, 276.

49 Pliny *Pan.* 11.

50 *BMC* 354, 857–62, 915–18 and 955–7; P. V. Hill, *NC* 144 (1984), 34–5, and id., *Monuments*, 8–9, considers this to represent the Aedes Honos et Virtus, but the iconography does not agree. It is a moot question whether or not Roman 'architectural' coins, such as this, could ever anticipate the completion of a construction, as some have claimed, but to this writer, and others, it seems unproven.

51 *BMC* 193, 863–6 and 958.

52 Lydus *de.Mens.* 4.7; P. V. Hill, *NC* ser. 7, 5 (1965), 158–60, and id., *Monuments*, 33–6, however, has identified this as a Temple of Jupiter Ultor.

53 Richardson, *Ancient Rome*, 30–1; P. V. Hill, *NC* 144 (1984), 35–6; Strack, *Untersuchungen*, 152.

54 P. V. Hill, *NC* 144 (1984), 42–3, citing *BMC* 842–6.

55 Richardson, *Ancient Rome*, 43.

56 *ILS* 2205 and 3196. For the unit in general, M. Speidel, *Die Equites Singulares Augusti* (1965) and id., *Riding for Caesar* (1994); for the remains of the fort, op. cit. (1994), 127–8. Many of Trajan's first *equites* were raised from among the Baetasii, a German tribe who may have been partially displaced by the establishment of Colonia Ulpia Traiana (Xanten) in 98/106.

57 *CIL* 6.946.

58 Cf. F. Magi, *Mitt. Deutsche Arch. Inst. Ab. Rom.* 82 (1975), 100; and A. Bonanno, *Portraits and Other Heads on Roman Historical Reliefs up to the Time of Septimius Severus* (1976), 62. For a rebuttal, cf. M. Pfanner, *Der Titusbogen* (1983), 16 and 91–2.

59 *CIL* 6.1231 and Tac. *Ann.* 12.23–4; *BMC* 829 and *HA Aur.* 21. Cf. Var. *Ling. Lat.* 5.143.

60 Smallwood, *Documents*, 22, lines 15–16.

61 Richardson, *Ancient Rome*, 266.

62 Mart. 6.64.12–13.

63 Dio 68.15.3: the gymnasium attributed to Sura was probably that elsewhere credited to Trajan, cf. Dio 69.4.1. For the date of Sura's death, cf. F. Zevi, *PP* 34 (1979), 193–4, n. 30; and Syme, *Tacitus*, 232; and id., *HAC 1986/1989* (1991), 199–200. See also Vict. *Caes.* 13.5, and *Epit.* 13.6.

64 Sen. *Ep.Mor.* 61.1–2.

65 For the Severan marble plan, see A. M. Colini et al., *La pianta marmorea di Roma antica* (Rome 1960); and for the Balneum Surae, ibid., fr. 21.

66 Blake, *Roman Construction*, 33; Richardson, *Ancient Rome*, 395–6.

67 *HA* Hadr. 9.1–2; Blake, *Roman Construction*, 34 and 36; Richardson, *Ancient Rome*, 385.

68 Paus. 5.12.6; Richardson, *Ancient Rome*, 7.

69 Ara Pudicitia: P. V. Hill, *NC* 145 (1985), 88, and id., *Monuments*, 64, citing *BMC* 529; Gymnasium: Dio 69.4.1.

70 Dio 68.16.3 and 69.4.1; Paus. 5.12.6. For a discussion of this man and his works, see MacDonald, *Architecture*, 129–37; C. Leon, *Apollodorus von Damaskus und die trajanische Architektur* (1961); and Lepper and Frere, *Column*, 187–93. Many of the premier architects of the time were from the Greek-speaking half of the empire, a fact Trajan was well aware of: cf. Pliny *Ep.* 10.40.

71 Smallwood, *Documents*, 22, lines 10–11.

72 Hier. *Abr.* 2120.

73 For these constructions, see Richardson, *Ancient Rome*, 387–97, *passim*. How much of the known plan of the Thermae Neronianae is the result of rebuilding by Severus Alexander after a later fire is unclear, but it seems unlikely he fundamentally altered the overall arrangements and plan.

74 Yet one must be grateful that this allowed the artists of the Renaissance to explore the subterranean rooms of the Domus Aurea, and exploit the styles they found there in a glorious rebirth of art and architecture after the sombre temperance of the late Gothic. Indeed, the distorted anthropo- and zoomorphic grotesques, which Raphael and others adapted from the frescoes in the Domus Aurea, took their very name from the 'grottoes' in which they were studied.

75 See K. de Fine Licht, *Untersuchungen an den Trajans- thermen zu Rom* (1974); Richardson, *Ancient Rome*, 397–8. I am grateful to Charles and Miriam Daniels for showing me their private collection of Piranesi engravings.

76 Cf. *Schol. ad Iuv.* 6.154, which indicates that clay figurines (*sigillaria*) were sold in the porticoes of the Thermae Traiani during Saturnalia; and *Chron.* 146, which tells us of mixed bathing at the same place.

77 The figures are computed from various sources, with help from Capitano di Macchina Antonio Pepe.

78 E. B. van Deman, *The Building of the Roman Aqueducts* (1934), 331–40; Richardson, *Ancient Rome*, 18–19.

79 Smallwood, *Documents*, 22, line 11; *BMC* 873-6 and 975–6; Strack, *Untersuchungen*, 192–4.

80 F. Gregorovius, *Geschichte der Stadt Rom in Mittelalter* II (1859), 424; the idea has been rejected in a more recent study by O. Wikander, *Opuscula Romana* 12 (1979), 24–7.

81 Smallwood, *Documents*, 22 and 382. Cf. A. M. Colini, *Bull. Comm.* 66 (1938), 244–5; L. Cozza, *Atti d. pontif. Acad. di Archaeologia ser* 3, Rend. 47 (1974/75), 79.

82 Smallwood, *Documents*, 22, lines 34–5. See Hill, *Monuments*, 42–4, for the coin evidence.

83 For summaries, cf. Blake, *Roman Construction*, 12–18; C. Leon, *Die Bauornamentik des Trajansforums*; P. Pensabene, *Foro Traiano* (1989); J. Packer, *AJA* 96 (1992), 151–62; Richardson, *Ancient Rome*, 175–6. For the Forum Traiani's status as the most impressive group of buildings in ancient Rome, cf. Cass. 7.6 and Vict. *Caes.* 13.5.

84 G. Rodenwaldt, *Gnomon* 2 (1926), 338–9; cf. C. F. Leon, op. cit., 33–4. There is, however, evidence to suggest the plan may already have been in use in north Italy and the provinces during the republican and early imperial periods.

85 *BMC* 509, with the legend *FORUM TRAIAN(i)*.

86 Amm. Marc. 16.10.15.

[87] For the (?)porphyry corridor, *HA Prob.* 2.

[88] Gell. *NA* 13.25. Eight of the caryatid statues were subsequently incorporated into the Arch of Constantine.

[89] Gell. *NA* 13.25.2; *HA Comm.* 2.1. To raise money for his Parthian campaign, Marcus Aurelius later used the forum to auction off various imperial properties: *HA Marc.* 17.4.

[90] Paus. 5.12.6 and 10.5.11, although it is possible that these formed an internal ceiling.

[91] For the decoration, see C. F. Leon, *Die Bauornamentik des Trajansforums* (1971).

[92] Richardson, *Ancient Rome*, 41: as the library of the Atrium Libertatis retained its name into the sixth century, it is unlikely to have been renamed the Bibliotheca Ulpia, pace Richardson, op. cit., 176. Manumission: Sid. *Apoll.* 2.544–5.

[93] *HA Aur.* 1.

[94] Cf. Vop. *Tac.* 8.1. The contents may well have come from Pollio's library, formerly housed in the now demolished Atrium Libertatis. For the statues: Sid. *Apoll. Ep.* 9.16.25–8.

[95] Smallwood, *Documents*, 22, lines 55–6. An important review of the matters involved in the Column's construction has been presented by M. Wilson Jones, *JRA* 6 (1993), 23–38. See also A. Claridge, op. cit., 5–22, for a discussion of its original form and the possible Hadrianic date of the carvings which now decorate it. For the Column on contemporary coinage, see Hill, *Monuments*, 57–8. It remains a moot point whether the column shown surmounted by an eagle on some Trajanic coins was an earlier version of this or another structure altogether: cf. Hill, *Monuments*, 60–1.

[96] Dio 69.2.3; Eutr. 8.5.2; Vict. *Caes.* 13.11. Burial within the *pomerium* was only allowed for those who had celebrated a triumph, but whether Trajan had always intended the vestibule to be his tomb is debatable: cf. Lepper and Frere, *Column*, 21–2.

[97] Smallwood, *Documents*, 378a. See Lepper and Frere, *Column*, 203–7, for a discussion.

[98] A.-M. Leander Touati, *The Great Trajanic Frieze* (1987); G. Koeppel, *BJ* 185 (1985), 173–95. The first and second longest friezes are respectively that from the Parthenon, now in the British Museum, London, and that from the Altar of Zeus at Pergamum, now in the eponymous museum in Berlin.

[99] Smallwood, *Documents*, 141. Cf. *HA Hadr.* 19.9. For the controversy over the dating of the temple: cf. Lepper and Frere, *Column*, 197–203; Richardson, *Ancient Rome*, 177. For the arch of 116: Dio 68.29.2.

[100] The evidence is in the form of a Greek inscription on the base of the monolith eventually used for the Column of Antoninus Pius: J. B. Ward-Perkins, in *Mélanges d'histoire ancienne et d'archéologie offerts à Paul Collart* (1976), 345–52. The unprovable assumption is that this piece, one of a pair, was but one of several 'spares' in case of damage: hence its availability for another use some fifty-six years later. It is just possible that it and its fellow(s) might have been originally intended for Trajan's Baths, which could have required columns of this size to support the roof over the *frigidarium*, although these, being semi-engaged, were more likely to have been composite rather than monolithic.

[101] Lepper and Frere, *Column*, 199.

[102] See J. T. Pena, *JRA* 2 (1989), 126–32, for a discussion of *P. Giss* 69, which details the extraction and transport of 50-foot monolith columns from Egypt, and the suggestion that it might relate to the building of this temple.

[103] The most accessible description of the complex, whose ancient name is not known, is that of MacDonald, *Architecture*, 76–93. Study of the brick-stamps suggest it was completed before the Forum: Blake, *Roman Construction*, 28; MacDonald, *Architecture*, 76.

[104] Cf. Richardson, *Ancient Rome*, 252.

[105] J. B. Ward-Perkins, *Roman Imperial Architecture* (1981), 94.

XII 'Redacta in formam Provinciae...' (pp. 161–81)

[1] Smallwood, *Documents*, 420. Compare an alleged oath of Trajan's, 'Sic in provinciarum speciem redactam ...': Amm. 24.3.9.

[2] Pliny *Pan.* 30–2.

[3] App. *BC pr.* 5; Strabo 2.5.8. (115–16); Tac. *Agr.* 21.

[4] Duncan-Jones, *Structure*, 187–94; cf. W. Goffart, *Caput and Colonate* (1974), 7–21.

[5] A. H. M. Jones, *The Cities of the Eastern Roman Empire* (2nd ed., 1971), 314–42.

[6] Tac. *Agr.* 21.

[7] Cf. Gell. *NA* 16.13.4–5.

[8] Cf. Strabo 3.2.15 (151); Tac. *Agr.* 21.

[9] M. Millett, *The Romanisation of Britain* (1990), for a masterly analysis of the procedure in general in a peripheral Celtic province; and J. Bennett, in *Settlement and Society in the Roman North* (1984), 34–8, and id., *The Setting, Development and Function of the Hadrianic Frontier in Britain* (1990), 543–63, for a regional analysis of the process in northern England. It is not proposed to examine here the longer-term aspects of the workings and success of Romanization, best dignified by the name of acculturation.

[10] Smallwood, *Documents*, 344; cf. *AE* 1969/70.583. He replaced Julius Sabinus, the military commander who followed Longinus: J. G. Garbsch, in V. A. Maxfield and M. J. Dobson (eds), *Roman Frontier Studies 1989* (1991), 283. For the dates of the reduction of Sarmizegethusa and the death of Decebalus, see pp. 99–101.

[11] Strabo 7.3.17 (306–7); Tac. *Germ.* 46; Amm. Marc. 17.12.

[12] Herod. 4.73–5.

[13] Pliny *NH* 8.165.

[14] Cf. Dio 71.18–19.

[15] Dio 68.10.3; *HA Hadr.* 3.9; Eutr. 8.3.1; Cf. Mócsy, *Pannonia*, 95, for the archaeological evidence.

[16] The fact was also well appreciated by the post-war Romanian government, as is clear when flying across the region: the many wide, deep and concrete-lined fresh-water canals that cross the area stand revealed as linear obstacles to invasion from the north-east.

[17] But note that Cataniciu, *Evolution*, 21, would date the final abandonment of Wallachia and Moldavia to the reign of Hadrian. For the subsidy: *HA Hadr.* 6.6.

[18] To ancient commentators, overwhelmed by the magnificence of the Carpathians, it always seemed a much larger piece of territory than was really the case: cf. Eutr. 8.2,

'this province is contained by a perimeter of thousands of miles', whereas the actual distance was probably little more than 620 miles (1,000 km).

19 Smallwood, *Documents,* 414; *CIL* 9.2600 = *ILS* 6523.

20 Vict. *Caes.* 13.3.

21 Móscy, *Pannonia*, 100–1.

22 J. G. Garbsch, in V. A. Maxfield and M. J. Dobson (eds), *Roman Frontier Studies 1989* (1991), 281–4; *CIL* 16. 57 and 163. Cf. *CIL* 16.160, of 11 August 106 (110).

23 Even if forts were retained in Wallachia at this time, as I. B. Cataniciu and others believe, the *limes Transalutanus* could still be Trajanic. Compare the contemporary situation south of the Aures in Numidia, where forts and organized tribal lands of Trajanic date are well south of the *clausurae* and 'border roads' Trajan (probably) initiated, creating a defence-in-depth: cf. P. Trousset, *Ant.Afr.* 12 (1978), 125–77, and P. Salama, in *Limes: Akten des XI Internationaler Limeskongresses 1976* (1977), 577–95, especially 586. Also D. J. Mattingly, *Tripolitania* (1995), 106–15.

24 Smallwood, *Documents,* 479, and Lepper and Frere, *Column*, 304–9, especially 308–9.

25 *CIL* 3.1443; *Dig.* 50.25.1.9.

26 *CIL* 16. 160 and 163.

27 W. Eck, *Chiron* 12 (1982), 355.

28 A closer date might just be argued from the evidence of the military diplomas, which reveal a mass discharge of auxiliaries in February and July of 110. While coloniae in the strict sense were founded exclusively for the benefit of time-expired legionaries, it may have been that Colonia Dacica was established in part to accommodate some of the many auxiliaries released at this time, now all Roman citizens whatever their individual ethnic origin.

29 Lepper and Frere, *Column*, 119–20 and 303. The process is discussed in the several papers contained in G. Webster, *Fortress into City* (1988), although certain of these need to be used with some caution.

30 For example, *ILS* 3437 and 7141.

31 C. and H. Daicoviciu, *Ulpia Traiana* (1966).

32 D. Aliciu and E. Nemesh, *Roman Lamps from Sarmizegethusa* (1977), 7; D. Aliciu, et. al., *Figured Monuments from Sarmizegethusa* (1979), 11–12 and 67–71. Cf. *ILS* 3854.

33 D. Aliciu et. al., op. cit., 15–16 and 80–6.

34 *CIL* 3.10275; Móscy, *Pannonia*, 298–9. Note *BMC* 960–4, *DACIA AUGUSTA*, with grapes and wheat.

35 Dio 49.36.2.

36 Móscy, *Pannonia*, 118. Compare Germania Inferior, where Colonia Ulpia Traiana (Xanten) was founded *c.* 98/102–5/106 for veterans of the *legio X Gemina*, then stationed at the adjacent fortress of Vetera: H. G. Horn (ed.), *Die Römer in Nordrhein und Westfalen* (1987), 631. Also Africa, where Colonia Marciana Traiana Thamugadi (Timgad) was founded in 100 in the newly annexed territory some 15 miles (25km) east of the legionary fortress at Lambaesis. At both places, study of the available early inscriptions reveals, as is to be expected, a preponderance of good Roman names.

37 M. P. Speidel, in *Akten des VI internationalen Kongresses für griechische und lateinische Epigraphik* (1972), 545–7.

38 Cf. A. L. F. Rivet and C. Smith, *The Place-names of Roman Britain* (1979), 409 and 417.

39 The use of the genitive case, 'the fort of Trajan', would allow for another, that Trajan personally directed its construction.

40 It seems unlikely, no matter how attractive, that the nearby modern settlement of Malaia, in the Lotru valley, between the Lotrului and Capatinei mountain ranges, derives its name from the lost Malva, although it could come from the same root.

41 By way of marked contrast is Argentina, where the modern place-names are predominately Spanish in origin, with few indigenous names (Pampas, Ushuaia), despite the existence of a settled and substantial native population until comparatively recently.

42 Eutr. 8.6.2.

43 See above.

44 *RIB* 1872, etc.

45 Tac. *Hist* 4.14 and *Germ.* 29; *HA Hadr.* 12.4. Cf. P. A.Brunt, *Scripta Classica Israelica* 1 (1974), 90–115. Trajan issued an edict to the effect that Spain, having supplied so many men for the legions, was specifically exempt from the military levy: *HA Marc.* 11.7. Note how Pliny, while governor of Bithynia, adjudged a case involving conscripts (*Ep.* 10.29 and 30), and because of the shortage of willing recruits, Trajan himself brought in a law that punished fathers who deliberately mutilated their own sons so that they would escape conscription, and even provided for the recruitment of monotesticular men, hitherto denied the right to serve in the military (*Dig.* 49.16.4.12 and 49.16.4 *pr*).

46 D. Protase, *ANRW* 2.6 (1977), 1002.

47 Ptol. *Geog.* 3.8.3; Lepper and Frere, *Column*, 318. See also D. Protase, *Autohtonii in Dacia* (Bucharest 1980), and id., op. cit., 990–1015.

48 Lepper and Frere, *Column*, 317–18 and 320–1 discuss the matter and provide further references.

49 For a review, I. Glodariu, *ANRW* 2:6 (1977), 950–89.

50 J. C. Mann, *Brit.* 2 (1971), 219. But note the surprising number of archaisms that survive in that most vigorous of dialects, American English: this, however, results primarily from greater literacy, publications preserving earlier forms while neologisms are introduced.

51 As is well known, different approaches to transliteration from Arabic result in different spellings of the same place name from one authority to another: those adopted here are in general use.

52 Diod. 19.94–8. Bowersock, *Arabia*, is the principal modern work, along with A. Negev, *ANRW* 2.8 (1977), 520–686. On the matter of the origins of the Nabataeans, cf. J. F. Healey, *Aram* 1 (1989), 38–44, who concludes they were Arabs, and D. F. Graf, *Aram* 2 (1990), 54–75, more specifically narrowing them down to north-east Arabia.

53 Strabo 16.4.21 (779).

54 For an overview of the Middle Eastern trade routes, cf. D. L. Kennedy, *Archaeological Explorations on the Roman Frontier in North-east Jordan* (1982), 137–97, especially 140–2.

55 D. Kirkbride, *Aram* 2 (1990), 256–7 and 261, has made the attractive suggestion that Leuke Kome was in fact 'Aqaba, and Myos Hormos might be Safaga.

56 *Per.Mar.Eryth.* 19.
57 Palmyra was also the ultimate objective of the Chinese envoy Pan Ying, dispatched to Syria in the year 97 by General Pan Chao, although in the event, the Parthians prevented him from crossing into Roman-held territory and accomplishing his mission: D. L. Kennedy, op. cit. (1982), 137–8.
58 *P.Mich.* 465.
59 Plut. *Pomp.* 45.2; Pliny *NH* 7.97; Bowersock, *Arabia*, 28–40.
60 Jos. *AJ* 15.96; Plut. *Ant.* 36.2; Dio 49.32.5; Bowersock, *Arabia*, 40–1.
61 Strabo 16.4.22–4 (780–2).
62 Jos. *AJ* 16.355; Bowersock, *Arabia*, 53–7.
63 Bowersock, *Arabia*, 58–75; P. J. Parr, *Aram* 2 (1990), 14.
64 According to Pliny *NH* 6.101, goods from the east increased in value a hundred fold before they reached Rome on account of the various taxes levied upon them on the way.
65 For the probable date of the Petra theatre, cf. P. Hammond, in *Bull.Am.Schools Or.Res.* 174 (1964), 66; and for the Gasr el-Bint, G. R. H. Wright, *Pal.Exp.Quarterly* 93 (1961), 8–37. Comparison with the substantial series of dated rock-cut façades at Mada'in Salih suggests the date for the developed monuments in Petra: cf. J. Mackenzie, *The Architecture of Petra* (1990), 51–2, and P. C. Hammond, *Anc.Hist.Bull.* 5 (1991), 36–46. For the Bostra theatre, cf. H. Finsen, *Le levé du théâtre romain à Bostra, Syrie* (1972).
66 Bowersock, *Arabia*, 73, with further references.
67 Millar, *Near East*, 91–2.
68 Strabo 6.4.2 (288); P. A. Brunt, in *Imperialism in the Ancient World* (1978), 168–70.
69 *Chron.Pasch.* 472; A. Negev, *ANRW* 2.8 (1977), 520–686.
70 J. W. Eadie, in *The Craft of the Ancient Historian* (1985), 407–23, suggested it was in reaction to an expansionary policy of the Nabataean king Rabbel II. A common belief, that the province was annexed as a strategic preliminary for Trajan's later campaign against Parthia, is to ignore the fact that the annexation of Arabia added to the burdens of an already over-extended army.
71 *BMC* 474–7 etc.; Dio 68.14.5; cf. G. W. Bowersock, *Arabia* (1983), 79–82. For Palma's honours, Smallwood, *Documents,* 202.
72 For the date of the *ARAB(ia) ADQ(uisita)* coinage: W. Metcalf, *Amer.Num.Soc. Mus.Notes* 20 (1975), 99–109. For the provincial dating system, cf. J. T. Milik, *Syria* 35 (1958), 243, no. 6; A. Negev, *IEJ* 13 (1963), 117, no. 11; and the Babatha archive, *P.Yad.* 5. For caution on the use of 'provincial era' dating, cf. P. Freeman, in *Studies in the History of the Roman Province of Arabia* (1986), 38–46.
73 M. Speidel, *ANRW* 2:8 (1977), 691–7.
74 *P.Mich.* 466 and 465; the Apollinaris correspondence is usually considered to refer to the construction of the via Nova, but the date of the milestones along the road mitigate against the inference. For an *eques* of the *III Cyrenaica* buried at Petra about this time, cf. C.-M. Bennett and D. Kennedy, *Levant* 10 (1978), 163–5. For Udhruh, cf. A. Killick, *Levant* 15 (1983), 110–31, where the site is claimed as a Trajanic legionary fortress in origin, which might imply that two legions were involved in the annexation of Arabia: further information is urgently needed to resolve the matter.
75 D. Kennedy and D. Riley, *Rome's Desert Frontier from the Air* (1990), 124–5: the *III Cyrenaica* is not actually attested there until the late Hadrianic period.

76 M. Speidel, *ANRW* 2:8 (1977), 700. To be quite precise, these units are those later found as part of the provincial garrison, but it would be pedantic to the point of absurdity not to accept that they had probably been in the province from the time of its annexation. Even so, it should also be noted that the *cohors I milliaria Thracum* is attested in Judaea by 124: *P.Yad.* 11. See also F. Zayadine and Z. T. Fiema, *ADAJ* 30 (1986), 199–202.

77 J. Bowsher, in *The Defence of the Roman and Byzantine East* (1986), 23.

78 *P.Yad.* 16.

79 For a discussion of the matter, see S. T. Parker, *Romans and Saracens* (1986), 125–8, and id., *The Roman Frontier in Central Jordan* (1987), 798–801.

80 Eutr. 8.3.2; Festus 20. The name 'Red Sea' was used indiscriminately to mean the Persian Gulf and the present Red Sea and Gulf of 'Aqaba: the last is to be preferred in the general context.

81 Smallwood, *Documents*, 420. Cf. P. Thomsen, *Zeitschrift des Deutschen Palästina-Vereins* 40 (1917), 1–103.

82 Cf. D. Kennedy and D. Riley, op. cit., 85–8.

83 J. Bennett, 'The Setting, Development and Function of the Hadrianic Frontier in Britain' (1990), 69–73.

84 A. Poidebard, *La trace de Rome dans le désert de Syrie* (1934), 22. See now, C. R. Whittaker, *Frontiers of the Roman Empire* (1994), 96.

85 Isaac, *Limits*, 68–77, has conclusively shown that claims of an external threat in this region before the fourth century are very much exaggerated.

86 For the use of auxiliaries (and legionaries) in this and similar ways, cf. R. W. Davies, *Service in the Roman Army* (1989), 54–63. Even when the Romans relied on fixed artificial boundaries, it was usual to have a forward screen of 'police posts'. For the use of such a 'defence-in-depth' in a somewhat similar locale, compare the situation south of the Aures in Numidia at this time, where Trajan initiated the construction of *clausurae* and 'border roads' to mark the official 'limit' of the province, with a series of forts and organized tribal territories beyond them to allow control of those nomadic tribes who wandered 'far and wide' (Oros. *Adv. Pag.* 6.21.18). Cf. P. Trousset, *Ant.Afr.* 12 (1978), 125–77, and P. Salama, in *Limes: Akten des XI Internationaler Limeskongresses 1976* (1977), 577–95, especially 586. But note that D. J. Mattingly, *Tripolitania* (1995), 106–15, believes the African *clausurae* to be no earlier than Hadrian.

87 For an overview, see Segal, *Town Planning* (1988).

88 Bowersock, *Arabia*, 60–1.

89 The arguments of D. Kirkbride, *ADAJ* 4/5 (1960), 119–20, remain persuasive, as noted by P. J. Parr, *Aram* 2 (1990), 14–16, but cf. J. McKenzie, *The Architecture of Petra* (1990), 35–6.

90 G. W. Bowersock, *JRS* 72 (1982); Millar, *Near East*, 95; I. Browning, *Petra* (1989), 145.

91 *P.Yad.* 12; S.Ben Dor, *Berytus* 9 (1948/49), 41–3.

92 J. T. Milik, *Syria* 35 (1958), 243, no. 6.

93 Millar, *Near East*, 94: but note P. Freeman, in *Studies in the History of the Roman Province of Arabia* (1986), 38–46, for the limited and localized use of such methods of dating.

94 *IGLS* 13.1.19; A. Kindler, *The Coinage of Bostra* (1983), 105–6, 2 and 4.

95 Segal, *Town Planning*, 51–63 and 104.

96 J.H. Humphrey, *Roman Circuses* (1986), 492–5, has suggested that the Bostra hippodrome, the third largest in the Eastern provinces (it is 400ft (120m) wide and 1470ft (440m) long), might have been constructed as late as the reign of Philip Arabicus (244–9).

97 S. Ben Dor, *Berytus* 9 (1948/49), 41–3.

98 M. Sartre, *Trois études sur l'Arabie romaine* (1982), 45–7.

99 Segal, *Town Planning*, 5–18.

100 Segal, *Town Planning*, 21–48.

101 Isaac, *Limits*, 122–3.

102 Cf. A. Negev, *ANRW* 2.8 (1977), 646. For evidence of the process in Moesia Inferior, cf. A. G. Poulter, in *Roman Frontier Studies* 1979 (1980), 736 and 738.

103 *CIL* 16.87; the full title is given on *CIL* 16.106, of 156.

104 Cf. Millar, *Near East*, 97; N. Lewis, in *The Documents from the Bar-Kokhba Period in the Cave of Letters* (1989), 16, and id., *Scripta Classica Israelica* 8/9 (1985/1988), 132–7.

105 Tac. *Hist.* 2.81.1; Suet. *Cal.* 16.3; Dio 59.8.2.

106 Amm.Marc. 14.8.3; H. Cotton, *JRS* 83 (1993), 94–108.

107 Millar, *Near East*, 414.

XIII *Parthicus* (pp. 183–204)

1 The standard work is Lepper, *Parthian War*, now supplemented by the valuable study of C. S. Lightfoot, *JRS* 80 (1990), 115–26. Cf. also K.-H. Ziegler, *Die Beziehungen zwischen Rom und dem Partherreich* (1964); and J. Wagner, *Die Römer an Euphrat und Tigris* (1985).

2 Smallwood, *Documents*, 22, line 34.

3 Smallwood, *Documents*, 23, lines 35–7.

4 Pliny *Pan.* 84.6; for earlier unofficial instances of the title, cf. *ILS* 288, with *trib. pot.* dates of 104/105.

5 *BMC* 525–30 and 531. Marciana is named on her coin without the epithet *Diva*, which Trajan granted her on her death on 29 August, hence it at least should have been issued before then; cf. *BMC* 647–57, with *DIVA AUGUSTA MARCIANA*.

6 *FORUM TRAIANA*: *BMC* 509; *BASILICA ULPIA*: *BMC* 492; *ARAB(ia) ADQ(uisita)*: *BMC* 474; *VIA TRAIANA*: *BMC* 484.

7 *BMC* 498; Strack, *Untersuchungen*, 199–202.

8 Strack, *Untersuchungen*, 215–16.

9 Dio 69.1.1. There is a lacuna in the Syrian *fasti* between L. Fabius Justus, whose term of office ended 111/112, and C. Julius Quadratus Bassus, appointed 114/115 (cf. W. Eck, *Chiron* 12 (1982), 353–7), and the possibility that Hadrian was appointed as the interim governor is reasonable. It has been suggested that Julius Quadratus Bassus, appointed to command Cappadocia about now, was charged with organizing the northern armies in readiness for the campaign: cf. R. K. Sherk, *ANRW* 2.7 (1980), 1066.

10 Smallwood, *Documents*, 109: the date of Hadrian's archonate is provided by Phlegon of Tralles, *Fr.Gr.H* 2B, 257, 36.25.

11 Smallwood, *Documents*, 415. It was a substantial undertaking. One milestone records that work was necessary on the entire 250-mile-long route, from Dyrrachium in the

west to Acontisma in the east, and was brought about by the circumstance that the road 'had long been neglected'.

12 Dio 68.17; cf. Jul. *Caes.* 333a.

13 There is no single comprehensive modern account of the Parthians, but much useful detail is supplied by N. C. Debevoise, *A Political History of Parthia* (1938); E. Yarshater (ed.), *The Seleucid, Parthian and Sassanian Periods* (1983); and M .A. R. Colledge, *The Parthians* (1967).

14 It seems that the Romans were as shocked by the effeminate appearance of the Parthian Suren, the victor over the Romans at Carrhae, as they were by the magnitude of their own losses: cf. Plut. *Crass.* 24.1–2.

15 As we have already seen, Pliny *NH* 6.101 records that oriental merchandise increased in value a hundred fold on its way to Rome because of the taxes levied en route.

16 Cf. Arr. *Parth.* 53.

17 Tac. *Ann.* 12.43 records a Roman garrison under a tribune in Gornea, central Armenia, in 51.

18 *ILS* 232, of before 64, from Harput, western Armenia, records the building of what might have been an intended permanent fortress for the *legio III Gallica*.

19 Dio 68.7.5 and 17.1; Jul. *Caes.* 333a; Fronto *Princ. Hist.* 17 (= VdH, p.212).

20 Arr. *Parth.* 33.

21 Cf. Isaac, *Limits,* 22–33.

22 Pliny *Pan.* 16.1; Dio Chrys. *Or.* 1.27.

23 As Isaac, *Limits,* 376, astutely observed.

24 Cf. Dio 68.26.4.

25 Smallwood, *Documents,* 22, lines 39–41. Strictly speaking, the *Fasti* only report that a Matidia was given the *cognomen* that day. However, as we have previously seen, coins issued before Marciana's death already record the elder Matidia as Augusta, and the logical way to reconcile the *Fasti* and the coins is to assume that the *cognomen* passed to her unmarried homonymous granddaughter.

26 *BMC* 647 and 653 (with the legend *DIVA AUGUSTA MARCIANA/ CONSECRATIO*), and 1088. For the date: Smallwood, *Documents,* 22.

27 Smallwood, *Documents,* 22, lines 54–6.

28 A. G. Roos, *Studia Arrianea* (1912), 4–64: cf. P. A. Stadter, *Arrian of Nicomedia* (1980), 142–4. Some ten books of the *Parthica*, more than half, were devoted to Trajan's Wars.

29 Arr. *Parth.* Cf. *BMC* 511, *PROFECTIO AUG(usti)*, and Strack, *Untersuchungen,* 218.

30 Dio 68.17.2–3.

31 Dio 68.17.3 confirms the general route; cf. Pliny *Ep.* 10.15. It could not have been a comfortable journey, even for Trajan, allegedly an enthusiastic sailor: cf. Pliny *Pan.* 81.3–4. As Pliny himself discovered (*Ep.* 10.17A), it was a far from easy or comfortable sail in the late summer, and in winter was especially stormy and effectively closed for shipping from November to March or April: cf. Duncan-Jones, *Structure,* 8–29, for times and seasons involved in ancient sea-travel in general, and 25–9 for passage across the eastern Mediterranean in particular.

32 I am grateful to Dr Cheryl Haldane and Captain Giuseppe Casini-Lemmi for their personal observations on this matter.

33 A letter of Hadrian's, in Greek elegiac couplets, records the occasion: *Anth. Pal.* 6.332; cf. D. L. Page, *Further Greek Epigrams* (1981), 562.

34 Mal. *Chron* 2.272.

35 Lightfoot, op. cit., 16–17.

36 Dio 68.18.1.

37 Dio 68.21.1, which logically refers to events at this time.

38 Arr. *Parth.* 33; Jul. *Caes.* 328.B.

39 Seleucia emerges as a major naval base during the second century: cf. D. van Berchem, *BJ* 185 (1985), 77, and Millar, *Near East*, 103–4. Perhaps Q. Marcius Turbo, prefect of the Misenum fleet before serving in Trajan's Parthian War, was originally transferred to develop the naval facilities here.

40 For the military distributions in the area, cf. J. Crow, in *The Defence of the Roman and Byzantine East* (1986), 79–81 and 84.

41 Proc. *Aed.* 3.4.17; cf. Lightfoot, op. cit., 17. To be quite precise, Procopius actually states that Trajan removed the garrison and made Melitene a *colonia*, but this is unlikely given that a legion is attested here in the fourth century.

42 Dio 68.19–20.

43 Thus Lightfoot, op. cit., 17.

44 loc. cit., n.11.

45 Ancyra: Smallwood, *Documents,* 215, whose context can only really be 113/114 (cf. R. D. Sullivan, in *Studien zur Religion und Kultus Kleinasiens* II (1978), 931–6). Trabzon: Tac. *Ann.* 13.39.1. Cf. T. B. Mitford, *ANRW* 2.7 (1980), 1196–8, for a partial listing of the legions epigraphically or otherwise attested in the Parthian War.

46 Dio 68.19.2.

47 Arr. *Parth.* 38–40.

48 Dio 68.19.2–20 describes the main events at Elegeia. For the symbolic crowing of a client king, cf. the ritual adopted when Diegis acted as Decebalus' proxy to receive the Dacian crown from Domitian in 89: Dio 67.7.3.

49 Dio 68.19.3; evidently Trajan's seventh imperial salutation, dated to before 1 September 114, by *CIL* 16.61. The humiliation of Parthamasiris was commemorated on a coin with the legend *REX PARTHICUS*, showing him making obeisance to Trajan: Strack, *Untersuchungen*, 218–20.

50 *ILS* 1041. Severus was simultaneously governor of Cappadocia, now divided from Galatia: cf. R. K. Scherk, *ANRW* 2.7 (1980), 1026.

51 For these events, see Arr. *Parth.* 40; Fronto *Princ. Hist.* 18 (= VdH, p. 212).

52 Arr. *Parth.* 5, 85 and 87 (cf. Them. *Or.* 16.250); cf. L. Dilleman, *Haute Mésopotamie orientale et pays adjacents* (1962), 278. For the Artaxata inscription, see J. G. Crow, in *The Defence of the Roman and Byzantine East* (1986), 80. See also P. A. Stadter, *Arrian of Nicomedia* (1980), 143, for Arrian's possible involvement in events at this time.

53 This seems the most logical place for the events recorded as Dio 68.18.2 and 3.

54 Arr. *Per.* 2.2–3.

55 Dio 18.2 should really belong to this stage of the campaign. Cf. Eutr. 8.3; Festus *Brev.* 20. From Pliny *Ep.* 10.63, 64 and 67, it is clear that the Crimean Bosphorans were already in some form of allied status with Rome.

56 *IG* 14.1374; A. I. Boltunova, *Klio* 53 (1971).

57 Isaac, *Limits*, 42–50. If so, then it may have been that Trajan did not complete the task, hence Arrian's gentle reminder to Hadrian about the importance of the region: A. B. Bosworth, *Har. Stud. Class. Phil.* 81 (1971), 240.

58 Tac. *Ann.* 6.31–6. For Roman troops in the Caucasus, see *SEG* 20. 112, of AD 75 from Harmozica, near Tbilisi, Georgia; and *AE* 1951.263, of Domitianic date, from near Baku.

59 Arr. *Per.* 6.1–5. Cf. M. P. Speidel, in *Studien zu den Militärgrenzen Roms III* (1986), 657–60; also, J. Bennett, *JRMES* 2 (1991), 63, n. 43. Arrian might even have been dispatched to Iberia in command of a garrison supervising the Dariel Pass: cf. P. A. Stadter, op. cit., 142.

60 Dio. 68.23.1; the arguments concerning the date are summarized by Lepper, *Parthian War*, 34–9, esp. Table 1 and p. 38.

61 Cf. *ILS* 299, in which Trajan's titulature included *IMP.IX* and *TRIB.POT. XIX*, indicating the ninth imperial salutation was awarded before December 115. For a discussion of the problems relating to Trajan's later imperial salutations, cf. Lepper, *Parthian War*, 44–5.

62 As was divined by A. G. Roos, *Studia Arrianea* (1912), 42.

63 Dio 68.23.1–2: if it is a *topos*, it would rightly belong with the character assessment provided at 68.6.1–8.

64 His movements are inferred from his known activities around Lake Van and the events described in Dio 68.22.2; his success was rewarded by adlection into the senate as praetor: Dio 68.32.5.

65 Arr. *Parth.* 42–8, where it is noted that Arbandes wore gold ear-rings; Dio 68.21. If the evidence of the so-called 'Acts of Sharbil and Barsamya' is to be believed, it would confirm that Edessa was in a tributary relationship with Rome before this date: cf. W. Cureton, *Ancient Syriac Documents* (1864), 41, and Lepper, *Parthian War*, 93–4.

66 Dio 68.21.1 and 22.1–2.

67 A milestone found north of Singara, with the appropriate imperial titulature for spring 116, at the earliest, shows that the territory was being consolidated before then: *AE* 1927.161.

68 *BMC* 1033–40; Smallwood, *Documents*, 23, lines 9–12. At this time of the year, it could take as long as ten weeks or even more for official letters between Rome and the eastern Mediterranean to arrive at their destination: cf. *Fontes Iuris Romani Anteiustiniani* 1 (2nd ed., 1940), 80.

69 Dio 68.24–5; Lepper, *Parthian War*, 65–83, provides a masterly analysis of the problems involved in the chronology.

70 M. Pedo Vergilianus, *cos. ord.* for 115, probably at Antioch to assist the emperor in the many legal cases requiring decisions.

71 Dio 68.26 for this and the following events.

72 Arr. *Parth.* fr. 7; Dio 68.26.2 notes that the crossing was dominated by the 'Gordyaean Mountains'.

73 The location of Adenystrae is particularly uncertain: cf. Lightfoot, op. cit., 118, n. 20, for two possibilities.

74 Trajan's twelfth salutation can be dated to 20 February – 9 December 116: *CIL* 2.5543. For the province of Assyria, see Eutr. 8.3.2 and 8.6.2; Fest. 14 and 20. Not all are convinced of its existence: for opposing views, cf. A. Maricq, *Syria* 36 (1959),

254; and Lightfoot, op. cit., 121–4. Both Eutropius and Festus also talk of Trajan forming Arabia into a province about this time: the claim is usually dismissed as a substantially *post eventum* reference to the earlier assimilation of Nabataean Arabia, but it could just refer to the formal – if short-lived – integration of the Scenite Arabs and Arabia Deserta within (presumably) Provincia Assyria.

75 Dio 68.26.42.

76 S. Gould, in *The Excavations at Dura Europos: Fourth Season* (1933), 56–65. The arch lacks the title *Parthicus*, so should date to before late April at the latest, if one allows for the news taking six weeks to reach here from Rome.

77 Arr. *Parth.* 8, 10 and 64; Dio 68.27: for the debate on whether these or the similar wells at Kirkuk are meant, see the discussion and references supplied by Lightfoot, op. cit., 120. Ozogardana: Amm. Marc. 24.2.3.

78 Arr. *Parth.* 67.

79 Dio 68.28.1–2. On the Naharmalcha, see Ptol. 5.18; Pliny *NH* 5.90; Amm. Marc. 24.7; and Lepper, *Parthian War*, 133.

80 Hadrian restored the daughter *c.* 128, and at the same time promised to return the throne, but in the event he failed to do so, and Antoninus Pius later refused a direct request for it: *HA Hadr.* 13.8 and *HA Ant.* 9.7.

81 Dio 68.28.2–3: this should be the twelfth salutation, but see Lepper, *Parthian War*, 44–5, for the problems.

82 *BMC* 606. For the sequence of events after Ctesiphon, see Dio 68.29. It seems plausible that the later references which talk of Trajan establishing a frontier along the banks of the Tigris (cf. Fest. *Brev.* 14) were inspired by a belief that he intended to form a province out of the fertile territory of the lower Euphrates and Tigris. For Trajan's personal activities in forming the province, cf. Fronto's comment, not necessarily a *topos* in this context, that the emperor spent some time 'making more stringent the ferry dues for camels and horses on the Euphrates and Tigris': *Princ. Hist.* 19 (= VdH, p. 212).

83 Jord. *Rom.* 268. The statue was apparently yet upstanding in 569, when recorded by John of Ephesus in his *Ecclesiastical History.*

84 Smallwood, *Documents*, 105, shows that Trajan was awarded no more than thirteen imperial salutations.

85 Arr. *Parth.* 74; Jord. *Rom.* 268.

86 The principal sources are Dio 68.30–2 with 75.9, and Mal. 11.273–20.274.

87 Fronto *Princ Hist* (= VdH, pp. 206 and 212); Syme, *Tacitus*, 239, n. 9.

88 Dio 68.32.5. The end of Abgarus' reign, and presumably the fall of Edessa, can be closely dated to between 6 June 116 and 1 July 117 (see Lepper, *Parthian War*, 92–5), but this is of little help in determining when the Parthian revanche began.

89 The status of Parthamaspates was advertised on coins issued late that year bearing the legend *REX PARTH[ic]US DATUS*, 'A King is given to the Parthians': *BMC* 1054.

90 Dio 68.31, for the events at Hatra. The city's walls actually enclose an area of about 400ha (1000 acres), and it was a rich caravan city: cf. D. Kennedy and D. Riley, Rome's *Desert Frontier from the Air* (1990), 106–7 and Pls 53 and 54; Isaac, *Limits*, 152–6.

91 A. Fuks, *JRS* 51 (1961), 98–104; where attention is drawn to the apparent widespread destruction of pagan shrines by the Jews.

92 For the events of this period, see Dio 68.33; and *HA Had.* 4–7 and 11.2.

93 L. Budde, *Antike Plastik* 4 (1965), 103–17. Not all would agree this is of Trajan: cf. R. Winckes, *Clipeata Imago: Studien zu einer römische Bildnisform* (1969), 73–80. However, the likeness bears comparison with other depictions of the general period, while the claim that it is of Trajan's father can be rejected on account of the laurel wreath the individual wears, a symbol appropriate to an emperor alone: cf. the representations of Traianus on the *Divus Pater* coinage, for example *BMC* 498 etc.

94 I am grateful to Dr Michael Margolies for his comments on what seems the likely cause of Trajan's ill-health.

95 Arr. *Princ. Hist.* 6 (= VdH, p. 206); Dio 68.33.1.

96 The date of his death is not certain, but as we will see, it was before 11 August 117.

97 Eutr. 8.5.

98 Smallwood, *Documents*, 1176. For an attractive if unprovable theory concerning the events surrounding the deaths of Trajan and Phaedimus and the matter of Hadrian's succession, namely that Trajan was assassinated, and Phaedimus murdered to ensure silence, see Paribeni, *Optimus*, 2, 310, n. 16, and Syme, *Tacitus*, 240, n. 7.

99 J. Bennett, forthcoming, surveys Hadrian's career as *privatus*.

100 Cf. Dio 53.30.

101 Syme, *Tacitus*, 233.

102 There remains the problem of the enigmatic coin of Trajan with his titulature for mid-114–early 116, which depicts Hadrian on the reverse with the legend *HADRIANO TRAIANO CAESARI* (*BMC*, p.124): if genuine, it directly contradicts the documentary evidence in signalling Hadrian's adoption during that period.

103 Tac. *Ann.* 1.11; *HA Hadr.* 5.1–5.

104 Smallwood, *Documents*, 53.

105 *HA Hadr.* 5.4 and 20.10–12; cf. Dio 68.33.2.

106 For Bassus, see Smallwood, *Documents*, 214; H. Halfmann, *Die Senatoren aus dem östlichen Teil des Imperium Romanum* (1979), 26; and Strobel, *Dakerkriegen*, 64–6. For Hadrian's thoughts on Dacia, Eutr. 8.6.2.

107 *HA Hadr.* 5.9 and 6.3; Dio 69.2.3; Eutr. 8.5; *Epit.* 14.11. The triumph was celebrated with coins showing the bust of Trajan on the obverse and a *quadriga* with his effigy and a palm-branch on the reverse, the legend reading *DIVO TRAIANO PARTH(ico) AUG(usto) PATRI/TRIUMPHUS PARTHICUS*: *BMC, Hadrian,* 47. One of those who took part in the funeral games was M. Antonius Exochus, a Thracian: *ILS* 5084.

108 *BMC* 5 and 49. For the events surrounding Trajan's deification and Hadrian's accession, see W. den Boer, *Ancient Society* 6 (1975), 203–12.

109 Dio 68.33.1; cf. Tac. *Hist.* 1.2.

xiv A Perfect Prince? (pp. 205–13)

1 For a detailed analysis and commentary, see J. F. Hassel, *Der Traiansbogen in Benevent* (1966), with F. A. Lepper, *JRS* 59 (1969), 250–61; and M. Rotili, *L'Arco di Traiano a Benevento* (1972).

2 K. Fittschen, *AA* 87 (1972), 742–8; cf. W. Gauer, *JDAI* 89 (1974), and T. Lorenz, *Leben und Regierung Trajan auf dem Bogen von Benevent* (1973), *passim*.

3 Cf. G. Koeppel, *BJ* 169 (1969), 158–70 and 181–2.

4 The scene is paralleled by early coin types, for example *BMC* 38. For the identification of the *Genius Equester*, see G. Koeppel, *BJ* 169 (1969), 162–3; and H. Kunckel, *Der römische Genius* (1974), 41. For an alternative view, see H. Gabelmann, *JDAI* 92 (1977), 445, and id., *JDAI* 96 (1981), 363. J. Béranger, BJ 165 (1965), 85, n. 54, would dispute that there was such a *Genius*.

5 Cf. Pliny *Pan.* 1.5; 5.3–4; 8.3; 23.4; 94.3–4. Also Dio Chrys. *Or.* 1.11–12.

6 Cf. Pliny *Pan.* 12.1; Dio Chrys. *Or.* 1.25 and 27–9, and 2.52.

7 Cf. Veg. 1.5; and *P.Dura* 89.i.15, recording how the stature of two recruits had been measured and recorded.

8 Pliny *Pan.* 29.2.

9 Cf. Mart. 10.6, 7, 34, 72, and 12.8.

10 Cf. Dio 53.17.1–18.3 and 21.3.7.

11 Whatever the official policy, the fact remains that Trajan was most commonly associated with Zeus/Jupiter in dedicatory inscriptions in the eastern world: J. Beaujeu, *La religion romaine à l'apogée de l'empire* I (Paris 1955), 72–3. It will be noted that Hercules, the son of the supreme deity, was chosen as the symbol of one of Trajan's new creations, the *legio II Traiana*.

12 For a discussion of the imperial cult in the east, see especially S. R. F. Price, *Rituals and Power* (1984).

13 J. Morris, *LF* 87 (1964), 316–37, and id., *LF* 88 (1965), 22–31, *passim*; cf. K. H. Waters, *ANRW* 2:2 (1975), 396 and 402; and B. M. Levick, *Historia* 16 (1967), 207–21.

14 Eck, *Senatoren*, Ch. 1.

15 Pliny *Pan.* 66.4.

16 We can discount the claim that the marriage was arranged against Trajan's will by a determined Plotina, a fiction brought about by the need to denigrate the method of succession: *HA Hadr.* 4.10.

17 *Princ. Hist.* 19 (= VdH, p. 213).

18 Gai. *Inst.* 1.34.

19 Ptol. 4.5; J. Lesquier, *L'Armée romaine d'Egypt d'Auguste à Diocletien* (1918), 396; and S. E. Sidebotham, in D. H. French and C. S. Lightfoot (eds), *The Eastern Frontier of the Roman Empire* (1989), 487–9. The surviving Roman lighthouse at La Coruña, popularly believed to be Trajanic, is not in fact dated: T. Hauschild, *Madrider Mitteilungen* 17 (1976), 253–6.

20 Pliny *Pan.* 32.

21 Syme, *Tacitus*, 38; cf. Pliny *Pan.* 15.5 and 19.3. For the reforms concerning military wills, see *Inst.* 2.12; for that concerning monotesticular men, see *Dig.* 49.16.4. *pr.*

22 Veg. 1.8: the work itself is sub-titled 'Institutorum rei militaris ex commentariis Catonis, Celsi, Traiani, Hadriani et Frontonis'; for the *equites singulares*, see M. P. Speidel, *Die equites singulares Augusti* (1965), and id., *Riding for Caesar* (1994), *passim*; Pliny *Pan.* 18.

23 Cf. J. Lander, *Roman Stone Fortifications* (1984), 30–9.

24 See J. Bennett, *The Setting, Development and Function of the Hadrianic Frontier in Britain* (1990), 55–73.

25 Cf. P. Salama, in *Limes: Akten des XI Internationaler Limeskongresses 1976* (1977), 577–95, and P. Trousset, *Ant.Afr.* 12 (1978), 125–77.

26 K. H. Waters, *AJP* 90 (1969), 385–404.

Appendix (pp. 214–18)

1 The standard text for what follows is that of U. P. Boissevain, *Cassii Dionis Cocceiani Historiarum Romanorum quae supersunt III* (2nd ed., Berlin 1955). Cf. Lepper and Frere, *Column*, 211–17 for the constituent elements and further discussion.

2 Cf. Lepper and Frere, *Column*, 211.

3 Cf. *Petr.Patr. exc. de leg.* 4: 'Decebalus then sent *pileati* as envoys to Trajan; for these are the most honourable men among them. Previously he had been sending the *comati*, who are held of less repute among them. When these latest envoys came to Trajan, they threw down their arms, and binding their hands behind their backs after the manner of captives, they begged Trajan to hold a conference with Decebalus.'

4 Cf. Tzetz. *Chil.* 2.62, for what might be a missing sentence that belongs here: 'And Trajan immediately ferried the Romans across the Ister in merchantmen against the Dacians.'

5 This passage is somewhat confusing. In this context it most certainly does not imply that the river could be crossed by an army when frozen over, even though that was possible – apparently – at other locations. On the contrary, the import is that the river could not be crossed in the depths of winter, and that the bridge was built to replace the usual method of crossing, namely by boat, impossible in the depths of winter when the Danube was frozen, and hazardous in the early spring, when the river was full of floating ice.

BIBLIOGRAPHY

Abbott, F. F. and Johnson, A. C., 1926, *Municipal Administration in the Roman Empire* (Princeton)

Alföldy, G., 1967, *Die Legionslegaten der römischen Rhienarmeen* (= *ES* 3, Köln)

Alföldy, G., 1969, *Fasti Hispanienses: Senatorische Reiches–beamte und Offiziere in den spanischen Provinzen des römischen Reiches von Augustus bis Diokletian* (Wiesbaden)

Alföldy, G., 1985, *The Social History of Rome* (3rd ed., London)

Alföldy, G. and Halfmann, H., 1973, 'M. Cornelius Nigrinus Curiatius Maternus, General Domitians und Rivale Trajans', *Chiron* 3, 331–73

Aliciu, D., Constantin, P. and Wolfmann, V., 1979, *Figured Monuments from Sarmizegethusa* (= *BARIS* 55, Oxford)

Aliciu, D. and Nemesh, E., 1977, *Roman Lamps from Sarmizegethusa* (= *BARIS* 18, Oxford)

Allison, J. E. and Cloud, J. D., 1962, 'The Lex Julia Maiestatis', *Latomus* 21, 711–31

Alston, R., 1994, 'Roman Military Pay from Caesar to Diocletian', *JRS* 84, 113–23

Amici, C. M., 1982, *Foro di Traiano: basilica Ulpia e biblioteche* (Rome)

Anderson, J. C., 1981, 'Domitian's Building Programme: Forum Iulium and Markets of Trajan', *ArchN* 10, 41–8

Anderson, J. C., 1985, 'The Date of the Thermae Traiani and the Topography of the Oppius Mons', *AJA* 89, 499–509

Arnold, T., 1882, *History of the later Roman Commonwealth, from the end of the second Punic War to the death of Julius Caesar; and of the reign of Augustus; with a life of Trajan* (2nd ed., London)

Ashby, T., 1935, *The Aqueducts of Ancient Rome* (Oxford)

Bachrach, S., 1973, *A History of the Alans in the West* (Minnesota)

Balil, A., 1960, 'Sobre los miembros hispánicos del senado romano durante el Imperio de Nerva', *Zephyrus* 10, 215–24

Bardon, H., 1940, *Les Empereurs et les Lettres Latines d'Auguste à Hadrien* (Paris)

Barnes, T. D., 1968, 'Legislation Against the Christians', *JRS* 58, 32–84

Barnes, T. D., 1978, *The Sources of the Historia Augusta* (= *Collections Latomus* 155, Brussels)

Bastianelli, S., 1954, *Centumcellae, Castrum Novum* (= *Italia romana; municipi e colonie ser.* 1.14) (Rome)

Beaujeu, J., 1955, *La religion romaine à l'apogée de l'empire I* (Paris)

Bebelon, I., 1962, 'Note sur un buste de Trajan père conservé au Cabinet des Médailles', *Rev.Et.Anc.* 64, 49–53

Belloni, G. G., 1973, *Medagliere milaneses: le monete di Traiano* (Milano)

Belloni, G. G., 1974, 'Significati storico–politici delle figurazioni e delle scritte delle monete da Augusto a Traiano (Zecche di Roma e'imperatorie)', *ANRW* 2.1, 997–1144

Ben Dor, S., 1948/49, 'Petra Colonia', *Berytus* 9, 41–3

Bennett, C.–M. and Kennedy, D., 1978, 'A New Roman Military Inscription from Petra', *Levant* 10, 163–5

Bennett, J., 1984, 'The North-east in the Second Century', in P. Wilson et al. (eds), *Settlement and Society in the Roman North* (Bradford), 34–8

Bennett, J., 1990, 'The Setting, Development and Function of the Hadrianic Frontier in Britain' (unpublished Ph.D. thesis, the University of Newcastle upon Tyne)

Bennett, J. 1991, '*Plumbatae* from Pitsunda (Pityus), Georgia, and some Observations on their Probable Use', *JRMES* 2, 59–63

Béranger, J., 1965, 'Der "Genius populi Romani" in der Kaiser Politik', *BJ* 165, 72–87

Béranger, J., 1966, 'Fortune privée impériale et État', in *Mélanges offerts à Georges Bonnard* (Geneva), 151–60

Berchem, D. van, 1939, *Les distributions de blé et d'argent à la plèbe romaine* (Geneva)

Berchem, D. van, 1952, *L'armée de Dioclétien et la réforme constantinienne* (Paris)

Berchem, D. van, 1983, 'Une inscription flavienne du Musée d'Antioche', *Museum Helveticum* 40, 185–96

Berchem, D. van, 1985, 'Le port de Séleucie de Piérie et l'infrastructure logistique des guerres partiques', *BJ* 185, 47–87

Berge, C. de la, 1877, *Essai sur le règne de Trajan* (Paris)

Birley, A. R., 1962, 'The Oath not to put Senators to Death', *CR* 12, 197–9

Birley, A. R., 1981, *The Fasti of Roman Britain* (Oxford)

Birley, A. R., 1987, *Marcus Aurelius: A Biography* (revised ed., London)

Birley, E. B., 1953, 'Senators in the Emperor's Service', *PBA* 39, 197–214

Birley, E. B., 1953, *Roman Britain and the Roman Army* (Kendal)

Birley, E. B., 1966, '*Alae* and *cohortes milliariae*', in *Corolla Memoriae Erich Swoboda Dedicata* (= *Römische Forschungen in Niederösterreich* 5, Graz), 54–67

Birley, E. B., 1981, 'Hyginus and the First Cohort', *Brit* 12, 287

Bishop, M. C. and Coulston, J. C. N., 1993, *Roman Military Equipment: From the Punic Wars to the Fall of Rome* (London)

Blake, M.E., 1959, *Roman Construction in Italy from Tiberius through the Flavians* (Washington, DC)

Blake, M. E. and Bishop, D. T., 1973, *Roman Construction in Italy from Nerva through the Antonines* (Philadelphia)

Blazquez Martínez, J. M., 1980, *Produccion y Comercio del Aceite en la Antigüedad, Primer Congreso Internacional* (Madrid)

Blazquez Martínez, J. M. and Remesal Rodríguez, J., 1983, *Produccion y Comercio del Aceite en la Antigüedad, Segundo Congreso Internacional* (Madrid)

Bloch, H., 1947, *I bolli laterizi e la storia edilizia romana: contributi all'archeologia e alla storia romana* (Rome)

Blume, F., Lachmann, K. and Rudorff, A., 1848, Gromataci Veteres: *Die Schriften der römischen Feldmesser* I (Berlin, reprinted Hildesheim)

Boer, W. den, 1975, 'Trajan's Deification and Hadrian's Succession', *Anc.Soc.* 6, 203–12

Bogaers, J. E., 1979, 'King Cogidubnus: Another Reading of RIB 91', *Brit* 10, 243–54

Bohec, Y. le, 1994, *The Imperial Roman Army* (London)

Boissevain, U. P., 1955, *Cassii Dionis Cocceiani Historiarum Romanorum quae supersunt III* (2nd ed., Berlin)

Bolin, S., 1958, *State and Currency in the Roman Empire to 300 AD* (Uppsala)

Boltounova, A. I., 1971, 'Quelques notes sur l'inscription de Vespasien trouvée à Mtskhetha', *Klio* 53, 213–22

Bonanno, A., 1976, *Portaits and Other Heads on Roman Historical Reliefs up to the Age of Septimius Severus* (= *BARIS* 6, Oxford)

Bonfante, G., 1939, 'Le Latin Ulpius et le nom osco-ombrian du loup', *Latomus* 3, 79–83

Bonner, S. F., 1977, *Education in Ancient Rome, from the Elder Cato to the Younger Pliny* (London)

Boswell, J., 1989, *The Kindness of Strangers* (London)

Bosworth, A. B., 1971, 'Arrian and the Alani', *Harv. Stud. Class. Phil.* 81, 217–55

Boulvert, G., 1972, 'Le *fiscus* chez Sénéque *de beneficiis*', *Labeo* 18, 201–6

Boulvert, G., 1981, 'La carrière de Tiberius Claudius Augusti libertus Classicus', *ZPE* 43, 31–41

Bowersock, G. W., 1969, 'Suetonius and Trajan', in Bibauw, J. (ed.), *Hommages à Marcel Rennard* I (= *Collections Latomus* 101, I, Brussels), 119–25

Bowersock, G. W., 1973, 'Syria under Vespasian', *JRS* 63, 133–40

Bowersock, G. W., 1982, 'Review of A.Spijkerman, *The Coins of the Decapolis and Provincia Arabia*', *JRS* 72, 197–8

Bowersock, G. W., 1983, *Roman Arabia* (Cambridge, Mass. and London)

Bowsher, J., 1986, 'The Frontier Post of Medain Saleh', in P. Freeman and D. J. Kennedy (eds), *The Defence of the Roman and Byzantine East* (= *BARIS* 297, Oxford), 23–9

Brassloff, S., 1905, 'Die Grundsätze bei der Commendation der Plebjer', *JÖAI*, 65–70

Breeze, D. J., 1986/87, 'The Logistics of Agricola's Final Campaign', *Talanta* 18/19, 7–28

Bringmann, K., 1971, '*Imperium proconsulare* und mitregentschaft im frühen Prinzipat', *Chiron* 7, 219–38

Browning, I., 1989, *Petra* (3rd ed., London)

Brunt, P.A., 1966, 'Charges of Provincial Maladministration under the Early Principate', *Historia* 10, 189–227 (= Brunt, 1990, 53–95)

Brunt, P. A., 1966, 'The "Fiscus" and its Development', *JRS* 56 (1966), 75–91 (= Brunt, 1990, 134–62)

Brunt, P. A., 1971, *Italian Manpower, 225 BC–AD 14* (London)

Brunt, P. A., 1974, 'Conscription and Volunteering in the Roman Army', *Scripta Classica Israelica* 1, 90–115 (= Brunt, 1990, 188–214)

Brunt, P. A., 1975, 'Stoicism and the Principate', *PBSR* 43, 7–35

Brunt, P. A., 1977, 'The lex de imperio Vespasiani', *JRS* 67, 95–116

Brunt, P. A., 1978, 'Laus Imperii', in P. D. A. Garnsey and C. R. Whittaker (eds), *Imperialism in the Ancient World* (Cambridge), 159–91

Brunt, P. A., 1980, 'Free Labour and Public Works at Rome', *JRS* 70, 81–100

Brunt, P. A., 1981, 'The Revenues of Rome: review of L. Neesen, *Untersuchungen zu den Direkton Staatsabgaben der römischen Kasierzeit*, *JRS* 41, 161–72 (= Brunt, 1990, 324–46)

Brunt, P. A., 1990, *Roman Imperial Themes* (Oxford)

Budde, L., 1965, 'Imago Clipeata des Kaisers Traian in Ankara', *Antike Plastik* 4, 103–17

Burton, G. P., 1975, 'Proconsuls, Assizes, and the Administration of Justice under the empire', *JRS* 65, 92–106

Burton, G. P., 1976, 'The Issuing of Mandata to Proconsuls and a New Inscription from Cos', *ZPE* 21, 63–8

Burton, G. P., 1979, 'The curator rei publicae: towards a reappraisal', *Chiron* 9, 465–87

Burton, G. P., 1993, 'Provincial Procurators and the Public Provinces', *Chiron* 23, 13–28

Caballos Rufino, A., 1990, *Los senadores hispanorromanos y la romanizacion de Hispana (siglos I–III)* (Seville)

Cagnat, R., 1923, 'La Colonie romaine de Djemila (Algérie)', *Musèe Belge: revue de philologie classique* 27, 113–29

Calder, W. M., 1956, *Monuments from Eastern Phrygia* (= *Mon.As.Min.Ant.* 7, Manchester)

Camodeca, G., 1980, 'Richerche sui curatores rei publicae', *ANRW* 2:13, 453–534

Campbell, J. B., 1975, 'Who were the Viri Militares?', *JRS* 65, 11–31

Campbell, J. B., 1984, *The Emperor and the Roman Army* (Oxford)

Carcopino, A. J., 1961, *Les étapes de l'impérialisme romain* (2nd ed., Paris)

Carcopino, A. J., 1963, *Recontres de l'histoire et de la littérature romaine* (Paris)

Carradice, I., 1983, *Coinage and Finances in the Reign of Domitian, AD81–96* (= *BARIS* 178, Oxford)

Carratelli, G. P., 1946, 'Tabulae Herculanenses', *PP* 1, 379–85

Casson, L., 1950, 'The Isis and her Voyage', *TAPA* 81, 43–56

Casson, L., 1978, 'Unemployment, the Building Trade, and Suetonius, Vesp. 18', *Bulletin of the American Society of Papyrologists* 15, 43–51

Cataniciu, I. B., 1981, *Evolution of the System of Defence Works in Roman Dacia* (= *BARIS* 116, Oxford)

Caven, B., 1980, *The Punic Wars* (London)

Champlin, E., 1971, 'Hadrian's Heir', *ZPE* 21, 78–89

Champlin, E., 1981, 'Owners and Neighbours at Ligures Baebiani', *Chiron* 11, 239–64

Champlin, E., 1983, 'Figlinae Marcianae', *Athenaeum* 61, 257–64

Chastagnol, A., 1992, *Le senat Romain à l'Epoque Impériale* (Paris)

Cheeseman, G. L., 1914, *The Auxilia of the Roman Imperial Army* (Oxford, reprinted Chicago, 1975)

Christol, M., and Demougiu, S., 1988, 'Note de Prosopographie Equestre V–VI: V, Les Ornements de Ser. Sulpicius Severus', *ZPE* 74 (1–14)

Cichorius, C., 1896, *Die Reliefs der Trajanssäule, II* (Berlin)

Cizek, E., 1983, *L'époque de Trajan: circonstances politiques et problèmes idéologiques* (Paris)

Claridge, A., 1993, 'Hadrian's Column of Trajan', *JRA* 6, 5–22.

Coarelli, F., 1968, 'L'identificazione del'Area Sacra dell'Argentina', *Palatino* 12, 365–78

Colini, A. M., Cozza, L. and Gatti, G., 1960, *La pianta marmorea di Roma antica (Forma Urbis Romae)* (Rome)

Colini, J., 1965, *Les villes libres de l'orient gréco-romain* (= *Coll. Latomus* 82, Brussels)

Colledge, M. A. R., 1967, *The Parthians* (London)

Corzo, R., 1982, 'Organizacion del territorio y la evolución urbana en Italica', in *Italica: Actus de las primeras jornadoa sobre excavaciones arqueológicas en Italica* (= *Excavaciones Arqueológicas en España* 121)

Cotton, H. M., 1981, 'Military Tribunates and the Exercise of Patronage', *Chiron* 11, 229–38

Cotton, H., 1993, 'The Guardianship of Jesus, son of Babatha: Roman and Local Law in the Province of Arabia', *JRS* 83, 94–108

Cozza, L., 1974/75, 'I recenti scavi della sette sale', *Atti della pontifici Accademia Romana di archaologia* 46/47, 1974/5, 79–102

Crişan, I.H., 1978, *Burebista and his Times* (Bucharest)

Crook, J. A., 1955, *Consilium Principis: Imperial Councils and Counsellors from Augustus to Diocletian* (Cambridge)

Crook, J. A., 1967, '*Patria potestas*', *CQ* 17, 113–22

Crow, J. G., 1986, 'A Review of the Physical Remains of the Frontier of Cappadocia', in Freeman, P. and Kennedy, D. (eds), *The Defence of the Roman and Byzantine East: Proceedings of a Colloquium held at the University of Sheffield in April 1986* (= *BAR IS* 297, Oxford), 77–91

Curchin, L. A., 1990, *The Local Magistracies of Roman Spain* (Toronto)

Curchin, L. A., 1991, *Roman Spain: Conquest and Assimilation* (London)

Cureton, W., 1864, *Ancient Syriac Documents* (London and Edinburgh)

Dabrowa, E., 1980, 'Le limes anatolien et la frontière caucasienne au temps des Flaviens', *Klio* 62, 379–88

Daicoviciu, C. and H., 1968, *Columna lui Traian* (2nd ed., Bucharest)

Daicoviciu, C. and H., 1966, *Ulpia Traiana* (Bucharest)

Davies, R.W., 1989, *Service in the Roman Army* (ed. D. J. Breeze and V. A. Maxfield: Oxford)

Debevoise, N. C., 1938, *A Political History of Parthia* (Chicago)

de Fine Licht, K., 1974, *Untersuchungen an den Trajansthermen zu Rom* (= *Analecta Romana Instituti Danici* suppl. 7, Rome)

Degrassi, A., 1947, *Fasti consulares et triumphales* (Rome)

de la Berge, C., 1877, *Essai sur le règne de Trajan* (Paris)

Deman, E. B. van, 1934, *The Building of the Roman Aqueducts* (Washington, DC)

den Boer, W., 1975, 'Trajan's Deification and Hadrian's Succession', *Anc. Soc.* 6

De Robertis, F. M., 1972, *Storia delle corporazioni e del regime associativo nel mondo romano* (Bari)

de Ste Croix, G. E. M., 1974a, 'Why were the Early Christians Persecuted?', in M. Finlay (ed.), *Studies in Ancient Society* (London and Boston, Mass.), 210–49

de Ste Croix, G. E. M., 1974b, 'Why were the Early Christians Persecuted?: A Rejoinder', in M. Finlay (ed.), *Studies in Ancient Society* (London and Boston, Mass.), 256–62

Devijver, H., 1976–80, *Prosopographia militiarum equestrium quae fuerunt ab Augusto ad Gallienum* I–III (Leuven)

Devreker, J., 1980, 'La Composition du sénat romain sous les Flaviens', in W. Eck, H. Galsterer and H. Wolff (eds), *Studien zur antiken Sozialgeschicht: Festchrift Friedrich Vittinghoff* (= *Kölner Hist. Abh.* 28, Köln), 257–68

Devreker, J., 1980, 'L'*adlectio in senatum* de Vespasien', *Latomus* 39, 70–87

de Waele, F. J. M., 1976, *Marcus Ulpius Traianus: veldheer, bouwheer, rijksheer* (Antwerp)

Dillemann, L., 1962, *Haute Mésopotamie Orientale et pays adjacent* (Paris)

Dittenberger, G., 1960, *Sylloge Inscriptionum Graecarum* (Hildesheim)

di Vita-Eurard, G., 1990, 'La Via Appia', *Quad. centro di Studi per l'archeol. Etrusco-Ital.* 18, 73–93

Dixon, K. and Southern, P., 1992, *The Roman Cavalry: From the First to the Third Century AD* (London)

Dorey, T. A., 1960, 'Agricola and Domitian', *G&R* 7, 66–71

Dorutiu-Boila, E., 1961, 'Some Observations on the Military Funeral Altar of Adamclissi', *Dacia* 5, 345–63

Driel-Murray, C. van, 1990, 'New Light on Old Tents', *JRMES* 1, 109–37

Dudden, F. H., 1905, *Gregory the Great: His Place in History and Thought, I* (London, New York and Bombay)

Duncan-Jones, R., 1964, 'The Purpose and Organisation of the Alimenta', *PBSR* 32, 123–46

Duncan-Jones, R., 1974, *The Economy of the Roman Empire: Quantitative Studies* (Cambridge, 2nd ed., 1982)

Duncan-Jones, R., 1989, 'Weight-loss as an Index of Coin-wear in the Currency of the Roman Empire', in G. Depeyrot and T. Hackens (eds), *Rhythmes de la production monétaire de l'antiquité à nos jours* (Louvain), 235–54

Duncan-Jones, R., 1990, *Structure and Scale in the Roman Economy* (Cambridge)

Durry, M., 1938, *Pline le jeune: Panégyrique de Trajan* (Paris)

Durry, M., 1965, 'Sur Trajan père', *Les Empereurs Romains* (Paris), 45–54

Dušanić, S. and Vasić, M. R., 1977, 'An Upper Moesian Diploma of AD 96', *Chiron* 7, 291–304

Duthoy, R., 1979, 'Curatores rei publicae en Occident durant le principat', *Ancient Society* 10, 171–238

Eadie, J., 1985, 'Artifacts of Annexation: Trajan's Grand Strategy and Arabia', in J. Eadie and J. Ober (eds), *The Craft of the Ancient Historian: Essays in Honour of Chester G. Starr* (Lanham, Maryland), 407–23

Eck, W., 1970, *Senatoren von Vespasian bis Hadrian: Prosopographische Untersuchungen mit Einschluss der Jahres- und Provinzialfasten der Statthalter* (= *Vestiga* 13, München)

Eck, W., 1974, 'Beförderungskriterien innerhalb der senatorischen Laufbahn, dargestellt an der Zeit von 69 bis 138 n.Chr.', *ANRW* 2:1, 158–228

Eck, W., 1979, *Die stattliche Organisation Italiens in der hohen Kaiserzeit* (= *Vestiga* 28, München)

Eck, W., 1982, 'Prokonsuln von Asia in der Flavisch–Traianischen Zeit', *ZPE* 45, 139–53

Eck, W., 1982, 'Jahres- und Provinzialfasten der senatorischen Statthalter von 69/70 bis 138/139: I', *Chiron* 12, 281–362

Eck, W., 1985, *Die Statthalter der germanischen Provinzen vom 1–3. Jahrhunderts* (= *ES* 14, Cologne)

Etienne, R., 1965, 'Les sénateurs espagnols sous Trajan et Hadrien', in *Les Empereurs romains* (Paris), 55–86

Eurard, G. di Vita, 1990, 'La via Appia', *Quad. centro di Studi per l'archeol. Etrusco-Ital.* 18, 73–93

Fell, M., 1992, *Optimus Princeps?: Anspruch und Wirklichkeit der imperialen Programmatik Kaiser Traians* (München)

Filip, J., 1962, *Celtic Civilization and its Heritage* (Prague)

Fine Licht, K. de, 1974, *Untersuchungen an den Trajansthermen zu Rom* (= *Analecta Romana Instituti Danici*, suppl. 7, Rome)

Finsen, H., 1972, *Le levé du théâtre romain à Bostra, Syrie* (= *Analecta Romana Instituti Danici*, suppl. 6, Copenhagen)

Fittschen, K. 1972, 'Das Bildprogramm des Trajansbogen zu Benevent', *AA* 87, 742–88

Florescu, F. B., 1965, *Das Siegesdenkmal von Adamklissi: Tropaeum Traiani* (Bonn)

Ford, G. B., 1965, 'The Letters of Pliny the Younger as Evidence of Agrarian Conditions in the Principate of Trajan', *Helikon* 5, 381–9

Forni, G., 1985, *Le tribu romane* (Paris)

Franke, T., 1991, *Die Legionslegaten der römischen Armee in der Zeit von Augustus bis Traian* (= *Bochumer historische Studien, Alte Geschichte*, 9, Bochum)

Frankfort, T., 1962, 'La retour de Trajan aux apparences républicaines', *Latomus* 21, 134–44

Freeman, P., 1986, 'The Era of the Province of Arabia: Problems and Solution?', in H. I. MacAdam (ed.), *Studies in the History of the Roman Province of Arabia: The Northern Sector* (= *BAR IS* 295, Oxford), 38–46

Frere, S. S., 1980, 'Hyginus and the First Cohort', *Brit* 11, 51–60

Fuks, A., 1961, 'Aspects of the Jewish Revolt in AD 115–17', *JRS* 51, 98–108

Gabelmann, H., 1977, 'Die ritterliche Trabea', *JDAI* 92, 322–72

Gabelmann, H., 1981, 'Römische ritterliche Offiziere in Triumphzug', *JDAI* 96, 436–65

Galleazzo Tissoni, G., 1965, 'Sul *consilium principis* in età traianea', I, *Stud. Doc. Hist. Iuris* 31, 222–45

Galleazzo Tissoni, G., 1966, 'Sul *consilium principis* in età traianea', II, *Stud. Doc. Hist. Iuris* 32, 129–52

Gall, J. Le, 1953, *Le Tibre, fleuve de Rome dans l'antiquité* (Paris)

Gallivan, P. A., 1981, 'The Fasti for AD 70–96', *CQ* 31, 186–220

Garbsch, J. G., 1991, 'The Oldest Military Diploma for the Province of Dacia', in V. A. Maxfield and M. J. Dobson (eds), *Roman Frontier Studies 1989* (Exeter), 281–4

Garcia y Bellido, A., 1965, 'La Italica de Hadriano', *Les Empereurs romains* (Paris), 7–26

Garcia y Bellido, A., 1970, 'Nacimiento de la légion VII Gemina', in *Legio VII Gemina* (Leon), 305–29

Garnsey, P., 1968, 'Trajan's Alimenta: Some Problems', *Historia* 17, 367–81

Garnsey, P., 1970, *Social Status and Legal Privilege in the Roman Empire* (Oxford)

Garnsey, P. and Saller, R., 1987, *The Roman Empire: Economy, Society and Culture* (Trowbridge)

Garzetti, A., 1974, *From Tiberius to the Antonines: A History of the Roman Empire, AD 14–192* (trs. by J. R. Foster; London)

Gaudemet, J., 1962, *Indulgentia Principis* (Trieste)

Gauer, W., 1974, 'Zum Bildprogramm des Trajansbogen', *JDAI* 89, 308–35

Georgescu, V. A., 1968, 'Optimus si Optimus Maximus in technia juridica romana: optima lex, optima jus, fecundus optimus maximus', *Studii Classice* 10, 155–206

Gephardt, R. F. C., 1922, C. Suetonii Tranquilli Vita Domitiani: *Suetonius' Life of Domitian, with Notes and Parallel Passages* (Philadelphia)

Gibbon, E., 1776, *The History of the Decline and Fall of the Roman Empire* (London)

Gibbs, S. L., 1971, *Greek and Roman Sundials* (New Haven, Conn. and London)

Glodariu, I., 1976, *Dacian Trade with the Hellenistic and Roman World* (= *BAR IS* 8, Oxford)

Glodariu, I., 1977, 'Die Landwirtschaft im römischen Dakien', *ANRW* 2:6, 950–89

Goffart, W., 1974, Caput *and Colonate* (Toronto), 7–21

Gonzalez, J., 1986, 'The Lex Irnitana: A New Copy of the Flavian Municipal Law', *JRS* 76, 147–243

Gordon, A. E., 1983, *Illustrated Introduction to Latin Epigraphy* (New York)

Gould, S., 1933, 'The Triumphal Arch', in P. V. C. Bauer, M. I. Rostovtzeff and A. R. Bellinger (eds), *The Excavations at Dura Europos: Preliminary Report of the Fourth Season of Work, October 1930–March 1931* (New Haven and London), 56–65

Gowing, A., 1990, 'Dio's Name', *CPh* 85, 49–54

Graf, D. F., 1990, 'The Origin of the Nabataeans', *Aram* 2, 45–75

Gregorovius, F., 1859, *Geschichte der Stadt Rom in Mittelalter: vom 15. Jahrhundert bis zum 16. Jahrhundert* II (Stuttgart)

Grelle, F., 1972, *L'autonomia cittadina fra Traiano e Adriano: teoria e prassi dell' organizazione municipale* (Naples)

Grenfell, B. H., Hunt, A. S. and Hogarth, D. G., 1900, *Fayum Towns and their Papyri* (London)

Griffin, M., 1972, 'The Elder Seneca and Spain', *JRS* 62, 1–19

Griffin, M., 1976, *Seneca: A Philosopher in Politics* (Oxford)

Griffin, M.T., 1984, *Nero: The End of a Dynasty* (London)

Grosso, F., 1957, 'M. Ulpio Traiano, Governatore di Siria', *RIL: Classe di lettere, scienze morali e storiche* 91

Gwynn, A., 1964, *Roman Education from Cicero to Quintillian* (New York)

Halfmann, H., 1979, *Die Senatoren aus dem östlichen Teil des Imperium Romanum bis zum Ende des 2.Jahrhunderts n.Chr.* (= *Hypomnemata* 58, Göttingen)

Halfmann, H., 1986, *Itinera Principum: Geschichte und Typologie der Kaiserreisen in römischen Reich* (Stuttgart)

Hammond, M., 1938, 'The Tribunician Day during the Early Empire', *MAAR* 15, 23–61

Hammond, M., 1949, 'The Tribunician Day from Domitian through Antoninus: a Re-examination', *MAAR* 19, 35–76

Hammond, M., 1956, 'The Transmission of the Powers of the Roman Emperor from the Death of Nero to that of Alexander Severus in AD 235', *MAAR* 24, 61–131

Hammond, M., 1959, *The Antonine Monarchy* (= *Papers and Monographs of the American Academy in Rome* 19, Rome)

Hammond, P. C., 1965, 'The Excavation of the Main Theater at Petra', *Bulletin of the American Schools of Oriental Research* 174, 59–66

Hammond, P. C., 1991, 'Nabataean Settlement Patterns inside Petra', *Anc.Hist.Bull.* 5, 36–46

Hanslik, R., 1965, 'Ulpius Traianus', *RE* Suppl. 10 (Stuttgart), 1032–5

Harris, W. V., 1994, 'Child Exposure in the Roman Empire', *JRS* 84, 1–22

Hassel, F.J., 1966, *Der Traiansbogen in Benevent: ein Bauwerk des römischen Senates. Archäologisch–historische Untersuchungen zu seiner Chronologie und kunstgeschichtlichen Stellung* (Mainz)

Hauschild, T., 1976, 'Der römische Leuchtturm von La Coruña(Torre de Hercules): Probleme seiner Rekonstruktion', *Madrider Mitteilungen* 17, 238–56

Healey, J. F., 1989, 'Were the Nabataeans Arabs?', *Aram* 1.1, 38–44

Helen, T., 1975, *Organization of Roman Brick Production in the First and Second Centuries AD* (Helsinki)

Henneman, A., 1935, *Der Äussere und innere Stil in Trajans Briefen* (Giessen)

Hill, P. V., 1965, 'Some Architectural Types of Trajan', *NC* Ser. 7, 5, 155–60

Hill, P. V., 1970, *The Dating and Arrangement of the Undated Coins of Rome, AD 98–148* (London)

Hill, P. V., 1970, 'The Bronze Coinage of 103–111', *NC* 130, 57–70

Hill, P. V., 1984, 'Buildings and Monuments of Rome on the Coins of the Second Century, AD 96–192: part 1', *NC* 144, 33–51

Hill, P. V., 1985, 'Buildings and Monuments of Rome on the Coins of the Second Century, AD 96–192: part 2', *NC* 145, 82–101

Hill, P. V., 1989, *The Monuments of Ancient Rome as Coin Types* (London)

Hoffman Lewis, M. W., 1955, *The Official Priests of Rome under the Julio–Claudians: A Study of the Nobility from 44 BC 68 AD* (= *American Academy at Rome Papers and Monographs* 16, Rome)

Holder, P. A., 1980, *Studies in the Auxilia of the Roman Army from Augustus to Trajan* (= *BAR IS* 70, Oxford)

Holder, P. A., 1982, *The Roman Army in Britain* (London)

Hopkins, K., 1965, 'Age of Roman Girls at Marriage', *Population Studies* 18, 309–27

Hopkins, K., 1978, *Conquerors and Slaves* (Cambridge)

Hopkins, K., 1980, 'Taxes and Trade in the Roman Empire (200 BC–AD 400)', *JRS* 70, 100–25

Hopkins, K., 1983, *Death and Renewal: Sociological Studies in Roman History* II (Cambridge)

Horn H. G. (ed.), 1987, *Die Römer in Nordrhein und Westfalen* (Stuttgart)

Houston, G. W., 1977, 'Vespasian's Adlection of Men *in senatum*', *AJP* 98, 35–63

Humphrey, J. H., 1986, *Roman Circuses: Arenas for Chariot Racing* (London)

Hyland, A., 1990, *Equus: The Horse in the Roman World* (London)

Isaac, B., 1992, *The Limits of Empire: The Roman Army in the East* (2nd ed., Oxford)

Isaac, B. and Roll, I., 1976, 'A Milestone of AD 69 from Judaea: The Elder Trajan and Vespasian', *JRS* 66, 15–19

Jacques, F., 1983, *Les curateurs des cités dans l'Occident romain de Trajan à Gallien: études prosopographiques* (Paris)

Jacques, F., 1984, *Le privilège de liberté: Politique impériale et autonomie municipale dans le cités de l'Occident romain (161–244)* (Rome and Paris)

Jennison, G., 1937, *Animals for Show and Pleasure in Ancient Rome* (Manchester)

Jolowicz, H. F. and Nicholas, B., 1972, *Historical Introduction to the Study of Roman Law* (3rd ed., Cambridge)

Jones, A. H. M., 1950, 'The Aerarium and the Fiscus', *JRS* 40, 22–9

Jones, A. H. M., 1960, *Studies in Roman Government and Law* (Oxford)

Jones, A. H. M., 1971, *The Cities of the Eastern Roman Empire* (2nd ed., Oxford)

Jones, B. W., 1979, *Domitian and the Senatorial Order: A Prosopographical Study of Domitian's Relationship with the Senate, AD 81–96* (= *Memoirs of the American Philosophical Society* 132, Philadelphia)

Jones, B. W., 1984, *The Emperor Titus* (London and New York)

Jones, B. W., 1990, 'Domitian and the Exile of Dio of Prusa', *PP* 254, 348–57

Jones, B. W., 1992, *The Emperor Domitian* (London)

Jones, C. P., 1970, 'Sura and Senecio', *JRS* 60, 98–104

Jones, C. P., 1971, *Plutarch and Rome* (Oxford)

Jones, C. P., 1978, *The Roman World of Dio Chrysostom* (Cambridge, Mass. and London)

Jones, M. W., 1993, 'One Hundred Feet and a Spiral Staircase: The Problems of Designing Trajan's Column', *JRA* 6, 23–38

Judge, E. A., 1974, '"Res Publica Restituta": A Modern Illusion?', in J. A. S. Evans (ed.), *Polis and Imperium: Studies in Honour of Edward Togo Salmon* (Toronto), 279–312

Kajanto, I., 1965, *The Latin Cognomina* (Helsinki)

Keay, S. J., 1988, *Roman Spain* (London)

Kennedy, D. L., 1982, *Archaeological Explorations on the Roman Frontier in North–east Jordan: The Roman and Byzantine Military Installations and Road Network on the Ground and from the Air* (= *BARIS* 134, Oxford)

Kennedy, D. and Riley, D. 1990, *Rome's Desert Frontier from the Air* (London)

Keresztes, P., 1973, 'The Jews, the Christians and the Emperor Domitian,' *V.Chr.* 27, 1–28

Keresztes, P., 1989, *Imperial Rome and the Christians* I (Lanham, Md. and London)

Kienast, D., 1968, 'Nerva und das kaisertum Trajans', *Historia* 17, 51–71

Killick, A., 1983, 'Udruh – the Frontier of an Empire: 1980 and 1981 Season, a Preliminary Report', *Levant* 15, 110–31

Kindler, A., 1983, *The Coinage of Bostra* (Warminster)

Kirkbride, D., 1960, 'A Short Account of the Excavations at Petra in 1955–56', *ADAJ* 4/5, 119–21

Kirkbride, D., 1990, 'The Nabataeans, Trajan and the Periplus', *Aram* 2, 252–65

Kloft, H., 1970, *Liberalitas Principis* (Boehlau)

Kneissl, P. 1969, *Die Siegestitulatur der römischen Kaiser* (= *Hypomnemata* 23, Göttingen)

Koeppel, G., 1969, 'Profectio und Adventus', *BJ* 169, 130–95

Koeppel, G., 1985, 'Die Historische Relief der römischen Kaiserzeit', *BJ* 185, 143–213

Krahe, H., 1929, *Lexikon altillyrischer Personennamen* (= *Indo-Germanische Bibliothek: Untersuchungen* 9, Heidelberg)

Kränzlein, A., 1965, 'Patrimonium', *RE* supp. 10, 493–500

Kunckel, H., 1974, *Der römische Genius* (Heidelberg)

Labrousse, M., 1981, 'Les potiers de la Graufessenque et la gloire de Trajan', *Apulum* 19, 57–63

Lambrechts, P., 1936, 'Trajan et le recrutement du sénat', *L'Antiquité Classique* 5, 105–14

Lander, J., 1984, *Roman Stone Fortifications: Variation and Change from the First Century AD to the Fourth* (= *BARIS* 206, Oxford)

Last, H., 1944, 'The Fiscus: A Note', *JRS* 34, 51–9

Leander Touati, A.-M., 1987, *The Great Trajanic Frieze* (= *Acta Instituti Romani Regni Sueciae*, ser. 4, 45, Stockholm)

Le Bohec, Y., 1994, *The Imperial Roman Army* (London)

Le Gall, J., 1953, *Le Tibre, fleuve de Rome dans l'antiquité* (Paris)

Leon, C., 1961, *Apollodorus von Damaskus und die trajanische Architektur* (Innsbruck)

Leon, C., 1971, *Die Bauornamentik des Trajansforums und ihre Stellung in der früh– und mittelkaiserzeitlichen Architekturdekoration Roms* (= *Publikationen des österreichischen Kulturinstituts in Rom* 1.4, Vienna, Köln and Graz)

Lepper, F. A., 1948, *Trajan's Parthian War* (Oxford, reprinted Westpoint, Conn., 1979)

Lepper, F. A., 1969, Review of F. J. Hassel, *Der Traiansbogen in Benevent: ein Bauwerk des römischen Senates*, *JRS* 59, 250–61

Lepper, F. A. and Frere, S. S., 1988, *Trajan's Column: A New Edition of the Cichorius Plates* (Gloucester)

Lesquier, J., 1918, *L'Armée romaine d'Egypt d'Auguste à Diocletien* (= *Inst.franc.d'arch.orient.Mem* 41)

Leunisson, P. M. M., 1991, 'Direct Promotions from Proconsul to Consul under the Principate', *ZPE* 89, 217–60

Levick, B. M., 1967, 'Imperial Control of the Elections under the Early Principate: *commendatio, suffragatio* and *nominato*', *Historia* 16, 207–21

Levick, B. M., 1990, *Claudius* (London)

Lewis, M. W. Hoffman, 1955, *The Official Priests of Rome under the Julio–Claudians: A Study of the Nobility from 44 BC– 68 AD* (= *American Academy at Rome Papers and Monographs* 16, Rome)

Lewis, N., 1985/1988, 'A Jewish Landowner in Provincia Arabia', *Scripta Classica Israelica* 8/9, 132–7

Lewis, N., 1989, 'Greek Papyrii', in *The Documents from the Bar-Kokhba Period in the Cave of Letters* (= *Judean Desert Studies* 2, Jerusalem), xi–133

Liebnamm, W., 1897, 'Curator Rei Publicae', *Philologus* 56, 290–325

Lightfoot, C. S., 1990, 'Trajan's Parthian War and the Fourth Century Perspective', *JRS* 80, 115–26

Lintott, A., 1993, Imperium Romanorum: *Politics and Administration* (London)

Lorenz, T., 1973, *Leben und Regierung Trajans auf dem Bogen von Benevent* (Amsterdam)

Luttwak, E. N., 1976, *The Grand Strategy of the Roman Empire, from the First Century AD to the Third* (Baltimore and London)

McAlindon, D., 1957, 'Entry to the Senate in the Early empire', *JRS* 47, 191–5

McCrum, M. W. and Woodhead, A. G., 1961, *Selected Documents of the Principates of the Flavian Emperors including the Year of Revolution, AD 68–96* (Cambridge)

McDermott, W. C., 1969, 'SHA Vita Hadriani II, 1–6', *Mnemosyne*, Ser. 4, 22, 186–90

MacDonald, W. L., 1982, *The Architecture of the Roman Empire 1: An Introductory Study* (2nd ed., New Haven, Conn. and London)

McDowall, D. W., 1978, 'The Organisation of the Julio-Claudian Mint at Rome', in R. A. G. Carson and C. M. Kraay, (eds), *Scripta Nummaria Romana: Essays presented to Humphrey Sutherland* (London), 32–47

McDowall, D. W., 1979, 'The Western Coinages of Nero', *Numismatic Notes and Monographs* 161, 111–29

MacKenzie, J., 1990, *The Architecture of Petra* (Oxford)

MacMullen, R., 1963, 'A Note on Roman Strikes', *CJ* 58, 269–71

Magi, F., 1975, 'L'inscrizione perduta dell'arco di Tito. Una ipotesti', *Mitt. Deutsche Arch. Inst. Ab. Rom.* 82, 99–116

Mandach, A. von, 1987, *Der Trajan- und Herkinbald Teppich: die Entdeckung einer Internationalen Portraitsgalerie des 15. Jahrhunderts* (Bern)

Mann, J. C., 1963, 'The Raising of New Legions during the Principate', *Hermes* 91, 483–9

Mann, J. C., 1971, 'Spoken Latin as Evidenced in the Inscriptions', *Brit.* 2, 218–24

Mann, J. C., 1974, 'The Frontiers of the Principate', *ANRW* 2:1, 508–33

Mann, J. C., 1983, *Legionary Recruitment and Veteran Settlement during the Principate* (ed. M. M. Roxan = *University of London, Institute of Archaeology Occasional Publications* 8, London)

Maricq, A., 1959, 'Classice et Orientalia 6: La province d'Assyrie créée par Trajan', *Syria* 36, 254–63

Martin, R., 1971, *Recherches sur les agronomes latins et leurs conceptions économiques et sociales* (Paris)

Martin, R., 1989, *Tacitus* (London)

Masi, A., 1971, *Richerches Sulla 'Res Privata' del 'Princeps'* (= *Università di Cagliari, Pubblicazioni della facoltà di Giurisprudenza* 11, Milan)

Mattingly, D. J., 1988, 'Oil for Export? A Comparison of Libyan, Spanish and Tunisian Olive Oil production in the Roman Empire', *JRA* 1, 33–56

Mattingly, D. J., 1988, 'The Olive Boom: Oil Surpluses, Wealth and Power in Roman Tripolitania', *Libyan Studies* 19, 21–42

Mattingly, H., 1926, 'The Restored Coins of Trajan', *NC* Ser. 5, 61, 232–78

Maxfield, V. A., 1981, *The Military Decorations of the Roman Army* (London)

Maxfield, V. A., 1987, 'Mainland Europe', in J. Wacher (ed.), *The Roman World* 1 (London), 139–97

Meiggs, R., 1973, *Roman Ostia* (2nd ed., Oxford)

Merlin, A., 1944, *Inscriptions latines de la Tunisie* (Paris)

Metcalf, W., 1975, 'The Tell Kalak Hoard and Trajan's Arabian Mint', *American Numismatic Society Museum Notes* 20, 39–109

Milesi, R., 1975, *Mantegna und die Reliefs der Brauttruhen Paola Gonzangas* (Munich)

Milik, J. T., 1958, 'Nouvelles inscriptions nabatéenes', *Syria* 35, 227–51

Millar, F. G. B., 1963, 'The Fiscus in the First Two Centuries', *JRS* 53, 29–42

Millar, F. G. B., 1964, *A Study of Cassius Dio* (Oxford)

Millar, F. G. B., 1964, 'The Aerarium and its Officials under the Empire', *JRS* 54, 33–40

Millar, F. G. B., 1967, 'Emperors at Work', *JRS* 57, 9–19

Millar, F. G. B., 1969, 'Havennius Dixippus: The Greek World and the Third-century Invasions', *JRS* 59, 12–29

Millar, F. G. B., 1986, 'Italy and the Roman Empire: Augustus to Constantine', *Phoenix* 40, 295–318

Millar, F.G.B., 1989, ' "Senatorial" Provinces: An Institutional ghost', *Ancient World* 20, 93–7

Millar, F.G.B., 1992, *The Emperor in the Roman World 31 BC–AD 337* (2nd ed., London)

Millar, F.G.B., 1993, *The Roman Near East, 31 BC–AD 337* (Cambridge, Mass. and London)

Millett, M., 1990, *The Romanisation of Britain: An Essay in Archaeological interpretation* (Cambridge)

Mitford, B. H., 1974, 'Some Inscriptions from the Cappadocian Limes', *JRS* 64, 160–75

Mitford, T. B., 1980, 'Cappadocia and Armenia Minor: The Historical Setting of the Limes', in *ANRW* 2.7, 1169–1228

Mócsy, A., 1974, *Pannonia and Upper Moesia: A History of the Middle Danubian Provinces of the Roman Empire* (London)

Mommsen, T., 1884, 'Die Konskriptionsordnung der römischen Kaiserzeit', *Hermes* 19, 219–34

Moore, F. G., 1950, 'Three Canal Projects, Roman and Byzantine', *AJA* 64, 97–111

Morris, J., 1964, 'Leges Annales under the Principate: Legal and Constitutional', *LF* 87, 316–37

Morris, J., 1965, 'Leges Annales under the Principate: Political Effects', *LF* 88, 22–31

Mrozek, S., 1977, 'Die Goldbergwerke im römischen Dazien', *ANRW* 2:6, 95–109

Murphy, I. J., 1987, *Quintillian: On the Teaching of Speaking and Writing* (Carbondale and Edwardside)

Musurillo, H. A., 1972, *The Acts of the Pagan Martyrs* (Oxford)

Negev, A., 1963, 'Nabataean Inscriptions from 'Avdat (Oboda)', *Israel Exploration Journal* 13, 113–24

Negev, A., 1977, 'The Nabateans and the Provincia Arabia', *ANRW* 2.8, 520–686

Nesselhauf, H., 1964, 'Patrimonium und res privata des römischen Kaisers', *Historia-Augusta-Colloquium 1963* (Bonn), 73–94

Nielsen, I., 1990, Thermae et Balnea: *The Architecture and Cultural History of Roman Public Baths* (Aarhus)

Oliver, J.H., 1989, *Greek Constitutions of Early Roman Emperors* (= *Memoirs of the American Philosophical Society* 178, Philadelphia)

Orgeval, B. d', 1950, *L'empereur Hadrian: oeuvre législative et administrative* (Paris)

Packer, J., 1992, 'Trajan's Forum in 1989', *AJA* 96, 151–62

Page, D. L., 1981, *Further Greek Epigrams* (Cambridge)

Paladini, M. L., 1962, 'Divinizzazione di Traiano padre', in *Hommages à Albert Grenier* (= *Collections Latomus* 58, Brussels), 1194–1206

Panciera, S., 1972, 'L. Pomponius L. F. Horatia Bassus Cascus Scribonianus', *APARA*, R.45, 105–31

Paribeni, R., 1926/1927, *Optimus Princeps: Saggio sulla storia e sui tempi dell' imperatore Traiano*, I–II (Messine)

Paris, G., 1878, 'La Légende de Trajan', *Mélanges publiés par l'Ecole des Hautes Etudes Sciences, philologiques et historiques* 35, 261–94

Parker, S. T., 1986, *Romans and Saracens: A History of the Arabian Frontier* (Winnalake)

Parker, S.T. (ed.), 1987, *The Roman Frontier in Central Jordan: Interim Report on the Limes Arabicus Project, 1980–1985* (= *BARIS* 340, Oxford)

Parr, P. J., 1990, 'Sixty Years of Excavation at Petra', *Aram* 2, 7–23

Parsi, B., 1963, *Désignation et investiture de l'empereur romain (Ier & IIe Siècles après J. -C.)* (= *Publ.Inst.de Droit romain de l'Univ.de Paris* 31, Paris)

Patterson, J. R., 1987, 'Crisis: What crisis? Rural Change and Urban Development in Imperial Appenine Italy', *PBSR* 55, 115–46

Peachin, M., 1986, 'Procurator Monetae', *NC* 146, 94–106

Peña, J. T., 1989, '*P.Giss 69*: Evidence for the Supplying of stone Transport Operations in Roman Egypt and the Production of Fifty-foot Monolithic Shafts', *JRA* 2, 126–32

Pensabene, P., 1989 (ed.), 'Foro Traiano: contributi per una riconsruzione storica e architettonica', *Arch. Cl.* 41, 27–291

Pergola, P., 1978, 'La Condamnation des Flaviens "Chrétiens" sous Domitien: Persécution religieuse ou répression à caractère politique?', *MEFR* 90, 407–23

Perret, L., 1935, *Essai sur la carrière d'Hadrien jusqu'à son avènement à l'Empire 76–117* (= *Mémoires de la Société Nationale des Antiquaiers de France*, ser. 8, 9, Paris)

Pfanner, M., 1983, *Der Titusbogen* (Mainz)

Pfeffer, M., 1969, *Einrichtungen der sozialen Sicherung in der griechischen und römischen Antike* (Cologne)

Pflaum, H.-G., 1950, *Les procurateurs équestres sous le haut-empire romain* (Paris)

Pflaum, H.-G., 1960–61, *Les carrières des procuratoriennes équestres sous le haut-empire romain*, I–III (Paris)

Pflaum, H.-G., 1962, 'Légats impériaux à l'intérieur de provinces sénatoriales', in M. Renard (ed.), *Hommages à Albert Grenier* (= *Collections Latomus* 58, Brussels), 1232–42

Pflaum, H.-G., 1963, 'De nouveau sur les *agri decumantes* à la lumière d'un fragment de Capoue, CIL X.3872', *BJ* 163, 234–7

Pflaum, H.-G., 1982, *Les carrières procurationnes équestres sous le haupt-empire romain: supplément* (Paris)

Plecket, H. W., 1961, 'Domitian, the Senate and the Provinces', *Mnemosyne* 14, 296–315

Poidebard, A., 1934, *La trace de Rome dans le désert de Syrie* (Paris)

Ponsich, M., 1974, *Implantation rurale antique sur le Bas-quadalcuivir* I–II (Paris, 2nd ed., 1979)

Potter, T. W., 1987, *Roman Italy* (London)

Poulter, A. G., 1980, 'Roman Communities (Vici and Komai) and their Role in the Organisation of the Limes of Moesia Inferior', in W. S. Hanson and L. J. F. Keppie (eds), *Roman Frontier Studies XII* (= *BARIS* 79, Oxford), 729–44

Poulter, A. G., 1986, 'The Lower Moesian Limes and the Dacian Wars of Trajan', in C. Unz (ed.), *Studien zu den Militärgrenzen Roms III* (Stuttgart), 519–28

Preisigke, F. and Bilabel, F., 1926, *Sammelbuch griechisches Urkunden aus Aegypten*, III:1

Price, S. R. F., 1984, *Rituals and Power: The Roman Imperial Cult in Asia Minor* (Cambridge)

Protase, D., 1977, 'Der Forschungstand zur kontinuität der bodenständigen Bevölkerung im römischen Dazien (2–3 Jh.)', *ANRW* 2.6

Protase, D., 1980, *Autohtonii in Dacia* (Bucharest)

Radice, B., 1968, 'Pliny and the *Panegyricus*', *G&R* 15, 166–72

Raepsaet-Charlier, M.-T., 1987, *Prosopographie des femmes de l'ordre sénatorial (Ier–II siècles)* Louvain

Reynolds, J., 1976, 'Lunch at Cyrene in AD 106 and the Closing Incidents of Trajan's Second Dacian War', *The Society for Libyan Studies: Seventh Annual Report, 1975–6*, 11–18

Reynolds, J., 1982, *Aphrodisias and Rome: Documents from the Excavation of the theatre at Aphrodisias conducted by Professor Kenan T. Erim together with some related texts* (= *JRS* Monograph 1, Hereford)

Richard, J. C., 1966, 'Incinération et inhumation aux funérailles impériales: histoire du rituel de l'apothéose pendant le Haut-empire', *Latomus* 25, 784–804

Richard, J. C., 1966, 'Les funérailles de Trajan et le triomphe sur les Parthes', *Revue Etudes Latines* 44, 351–62

Richardson, L., 1992, *A New Topographical Dictionary of Ancient Rome* (Baltimore and London)

Richmond, I. A., 1935, 'Trajan's Army on Trajan's Column', *PBSR* 13, 1–40

Richmond, I. A., 1969, 'The Arch of *Beneventum*', in P. Salway (ed.), *Roman Archaeology and Art: Essays and Studies by Sir Ian Richmond* (London), 229–38

Rickman, G. E., 1971, *Roman Granaries and Store Buildings* (Cambridge)

Rickman, G. E., 1980, *The Corn Supply of Ancient Rome* (Oxford)

Ritterling, E., 1893, 'Zur römischen Legionsgeschichte am Rhein: der Aufstand des Antoninus Saturninus', *Westdeutsche Zeitshrift für Geschichte und Kunst* 12

Rivet, A. L. F. and Smith, C., 1979, *The Place-names of Roman Britain* (London)

Robathan, D. M., 1942, 'Domitian's Midas Touch', *TAPA* 73, 130–44

Robinson, D. M., 1924, 'A New Latin Economic Edict from Pisidian Antioch', *TAPA* 55, 5–20

Rockwell, P., 1983, *A Preliminary Study of the Carving Techniques on the Column of Trajan* (Rome)

Rodenwaldt, G., 1926, Review of H. Lehner, *Das Römerlager Vetera*, *Gnomon* 2, 337–43

Rodenwaldt, G., 1942, 'Römische Staatsarchitektur', in E. Berve (ed.), *Das neue Bild der Antike*, II (Leipzig), 356–73

Rogers, P. M., 1984, 'Domitian and the Finances of State', *Historia* 33, 60–78

Roos, A. G., 1912, *Studia Arrianea* (Leipzig)

Roos, A. G. (ed.), 1928, *Scriptora Minora et Fragmenta* (Leipzig)

Rossi, R. F., 1966/67, 'Sulla "abdicazione" di Nerva', *Fac.Lett. e.Fil.Trieste* 3, 43–68

Rostovtzeff, M., 1957, *The Social and Economic History of the Roman Empire* (2nd ed., Oxford)

Rotili, M., 1972, *L'arco di Traiano a Benevento* (Rome)

Rufino, A. Caballos, 1990, *Los senadores hispanorromanos y la romanizacion de Hispana (siglos I–III)* (Seville)

Russell, D. A., 1973, *Plutarch* (London)

Saddington, D. B., 1982, *The Development of the Roman Auxiliary Forces from Caesar to Vespasian, 49 BC–AD 79* (Harare)

Salama, P., 1977, 'Les déplacements sucessifs du Limes au Maurétanie Césarienne', in *Limes: Akten des XI Internationaler Limeskongresses 1976*, 577–95

Saller, R. P., 1980, 'Patronage and Promotion in Equestrian Careers', *JRS* 70, 44–63

Saller, R. P., 1987, 'Men's Age at Marriage and its Consequences in the Roman Family', *CP* 82, 21–34

Salmon, E. T., 1967, *Samnium and the Samnites* (Cambridge)

Salzman, M. R., 1990, *On Roman Time: The Codex-calendar of 354 and the Rhythms of Urban Life in Late Antiquity* (Berkeley)

Sander, E., 1958, 'Das Recht des römischen Soldaten', *Rheinsiches Museem* 101, 187–234

Sartori, M., 1989, 'Osservazioni sul ruolo del curator rei publicae', *Athenaeum* 67, 5–20

Sartre, M., 1982, *Trois études sur l'Arabie romaine et byzantine* (= *Collections Latomus* 178, Brussels)

Sasel, J., 1973, 'Trajan's Canal at the Iron Gate', *JRS* 63, 80–5

Sauciuc-Saveanu, T., 1946, 'L'empereur Trajan et la mer Noire', *Revista Istorica Romána* 16, 119–28

Saxer, R., 1967, *Die Vexillationen der römischen Kaiserheeres von Augustus bis Diokletian* (= *ES* 1, Wien)

Schafer, T., 1989, 'Die Dakerkriege Trajans auf einer Bronzekanne (ein Auftragsarbeit für den Praetorianerpraefekt Ti. Claudius Livianus)', *JDAI* 104, 283–317

Schallmayer, E., 1984, *Der Oldenwald Limes vom Main bis an der Neckar* (Stuttgart)

Schönberger, H., 1969, 'The Roman Frontier in Germany: An Archaeological Survey', *JRS* 59, 144–64

Schönberger, H., 1985, 'Die römischen Truppenlagen der frühen und mittleren Kaiserzeit zwischen Nordsee und Inn', *BRGK* 66, 321–498

Schulze, W., 1904, *Zur Geschichte lateinische Eigennamen* (= *Abhandlungnen der königlichen Gesellschaft der Wissenschaften zu Göttingen, Philogisch–Historische Klasse*, Neue Folge, 5.5: Göttingen)

Schumacher, L., 1978, 'Die vier hohen römischen Priesterkollegien unter den Flavien, den Antoninien und den Severen (69–235 n. chr.)', *ANRW* 2.16.1, 655–819

Schwartz, K.–H., 1979, 'Trajans Regierungsbeginnund', *BJ* 79, 139–75

Scott, K., 1975, *The Imperial Cult under the Flavians* (2nd ed., New York)

Segal, A., 1988, *Town Planning and Architecture in Provincia Arabia: The Cities along the Via Traiana Nova in the 1st–3rd centuries CE* (= *BARIS* 49, Oxford)

Sherk, R. K., 1970, *The Municipal Decrees of the Roman West* (Buffalo)

Sherk, R. K., 1980, 'Roman Galatia: The Governors from 25 BC–AD 114', *ANRW* 2.7.2, 954–1052

Sherwin-White, A. N., 1962, 'Trajan's Replies to Pliny: Authorship and Necessity', *JRS* 52, 114–25

Sherwin-White, A. N., 1966, *The Letters of Pliny: A historical and Social Commentary* (Oxford)

Sherwin-White, A. N., 1973, *The Roman Citizenship* (2nd. ed., Oxford)

Sherwin-White, A. N., 1974, 'Why were the Early Christians Persecuted?: an Amendment', in M. Finlay (ed.), *Studies in Ancient Society* (London and Boston), 250–5

Shotter, D. C., 1978, 'Roman Historians and the Roman Coinage', *G&R* 25, 156–67

Sidebotham, S. E., 1989, 'Ports of the Red Sea and the Arabia–India Trade', in D. H. French and C.S. Lightfoot (eds), *The Eastern Frontier of the Roman Empire*, 485–513

Sijpesteijn, P. J., 1983, 'Traianus Dacicus and the Papyri', *Mnemosyne*, ser 4, 36, 359–66

Sijpesteijn, P. J., 1987, *Customs Duties in Graeco-Roman Egypt* (Zuthphen)

Sirago, A., 1958, *L'Italia agraria sotto Traiano* (Louvain)

Skydsgaard, J. E., 1983, 'Public Building and Society in Ancient Rome', in *Città e architettura nella Roma imperiale* (= *Analecta Romana Instituti Danici* suppl. 10, Copenhagen), 223–7

Smallwood, E. M., 1966, *Documents illustrating the Principates of Nerva, Trajan and Hadrian* (Cambridge)

Solin, H. 1975, *Epigraphische Untersuchungen im Rom und Umgebung* (= *Annales Academiae Scientiarium Fennicae*: Helsinki)

Southern, P., 1989, 'The Numeri of the Roman Imperial Army', *Brit* 20, 81–140

Speidel, M. P., 1965, *Die equites singulares Augusti: Begleittruppe der römischen Kaiser des zweiten und dritten Jahrhunderts* (= *Antiquitas* 1:11, Bonn)

Speidel, M. P., 1970, 'The Captor of Decebalus: A New Inscription from Philippi', *JRS* 60, 142–53 (= M. P. Speidel, *Roman Army Studies* (Amsterdam), 173–88)

Speidel, M. P., 1972, 'Malva and Dacia Malvensis Located through the Discovery of a Numerus Syrorum Malvensium in Mauretania', in *Akten des VI internationalen Kongresses für griechische und lateinische Epigraphik* (= *Vestiga* 17, Munich), 545–7

Speidel, M. P., 1973, 'The Pay of the Auxilia', *JRS* 63, 141–7 (= Speidel, 1984, 83–90)

Speidel, M. P., 1977, 'The Roman Army in Arabia', *ANRW* 2:8 (1977), 687–730 (= Speidel, 1984, 229–72)

Speidel, M. P., 1978, *Guards of the Roman Armies: An Essay on the* Singulares *of the Provinces* (= *Antiquitas* 1:28, Bonn)

Speidel, M. P., 1984, *Roman Army Studies* (Amsterdam)

Speidel, M. P., 1986, 'The Caucasus Frontier: Second Century Garrisons at Apsarus, Patra and Phasis', in C. Unz (ed.), *Studien zu den Militärgrenzen Roms III* (Stuttgart), 657–60

Speidel, M. P., 1994, *Riding for Caesar: The Roman Emperor's Horse Guard* (London)

Sperber, D., 1970, 'New Light on the Problem of Demonetization in the Roman Empire', *NC* Ser. 7, 10 (= 130:), 111–15

Sperber, D., 1977, 'Mehaginot = Trajanic Tetradrachms', *NC* Ser. 7, 17 (= 137), 153–5

Stadter, P. A., 1980, *Arrian of Nicomedia* (Chapel Hill)

Stambaugh, J. E., 1988, *The Ancient Roman City* (Baltimore and London)

Stein, A., 1918, 'Ser. Sulpicius Similis', *Hermes* 53, 422–33

Stein, A., 1927, *Der römische Ritterstand: Ein Beitrag zur Sozial und Personengeschichte des römischen Reiches* (München)

Steinby, M., 1974/5, 'La cronologia dalle "*figlinae*" doliari urbane dalla fine del l'età repubblicana fino all'inizio del III secolo', *Bullettino della Commissione Archeologia del comune di Roma* 84, 7–132

Strack, P. L., 1931, *Untersuchungen zur römische Reichsprägung des zweiten Jahrhunderts I: Die Reichsprägung zur Zeit des Traian* (Stuttgart)

Strobel, K., 1984, *Untersuchungen zu den Dakerkriegen Trajans: Studien zur Geschichte des mittleren und unteren Donauraumes in der Hohen Kaiserzeit* (= *Antiquitas* 1.33, Bonn)

Strobel, K., 1987, 'Der Chattenkrieg Domitians: historische und politische Aspekte', *Germania* 65:2, 423–52

Strobel, K., 1988, 'Zu Fragen der frühen Geschichte der römischen Provinz Arabia und zu einigen Problemen des Imperium Romanum zu Beginn der 2 Jh. n. Chr.', *ZPE* 71, 251–80

Strobel, K., 1989, *Die Donaukriege Domitians* (= *Antiquitas* 1.38, Bonn)

Stucchi, S., 1956, 'Il ritratto di Traianus pater', *Studi in onore di A.Calderini e R. Paribeni* III (Milan), 527–40

Sullivan, R. D., 1978, 'Priesthoods of the Eastern Dynastic Aristocracy', in *Studien zur Religion und Kultus Kleinasiens 2: Festschrift für Friedrich Karl Dörner* (Leiden), 914–39

Sumner, G. V., 1967, 'Germanicus and Drusus Caesar', *Latomus* 26, 413–35

Sutherland, C. H.V., 1945, '*Aerarium* and *Fiscus* during the Early Empire', *AJP* 66, 151–70

Swoboda, E., 1965, 'Trajan und der pannonische Limes', in A. Piganiol and H. Terrase (eds), *Les empereurs romains*, 195–208

Syme, R., 1930, 'The Imperial Finances under Domitian, Nerva and Trajan', *JRS* 20, 55–70 (= *RP* 1, 1–17)

Syme, R., 1936, 'Nerva and Trajan', *Cambridge Ancient History* 11 (Cambridge), 189–222

Syme, R., 1938, 'The First Garrison of Trajan's Dacia', in *Laureae Aquincenses: Memoriae Valentini Kuzsinsky Dicatae*, 1 (*Diss. Pann.* Ser. 2 10) (Budapest), 275–86

Syme, R., 1949, 'Personal Names in Annals I–IV', *JRS* 39, 6–18

Syme, R., 1954, 'The Consuls of AD 97: Addendum', *JRS* 44

Syme, R., 1958, *Tacitus* (Oxford)

Syme, R., 1962, 'The Wrong Marcius Turbo', *JRS* 52, 87–96 (= *RP* 2, 541–56)

Syme, R., 1964, 'Hadrian and Italica', *JRS* 54, 142–9 (= *RP* 2, 617–28)

Syme, R., 1971, *Danubian Papers* (Bucharest)

Syme, R., 1977, 'The Enigmatic Sospes', *JRS* 6, 38–49 (= *RP* 3, 1043–62)

Syme, R., 1977, 'How Tacitus Wrote Annals I–III', in *Historiographia Antiqua: Commentationes Lovanienses in honorem W. Peremans septuagenarii editae*, 262–3 (= *RP* 3, 1014–42)

Syme, R., 1978, 'Antoninus Saturninus', *JRS* 68, 12–21 (= *RP* 3, 1070–84)

Syme, R., 1980, 'Guard Prefects of Trajan and Hadrian', *JRS* 70, 64–80 (= *RP* 3, 1276–1302)

Syme, R., 1981, 'Governors Dying in Syria', *ZPE* 41, 125–44 (= *RP* 3, 1376–92)

Syme, R., 1981, 'Hadrian and the Vassal Princes', *Athenaeum* 59, 273–83 (= RP 3, 1436–46)

Syme, R., 1983, 'Domitian: The Last Years', *Chiron* 13, 121–46 (= *RP* 4, 252–77)

Syme, R., 1985, 'The Dating of Pliny's Last Letters', *CQ* 35, 176–85 (= *RP* 5, 478–89)

Syme, R., 1986/87, 'Human Rights and Social Status at Rome', *The Classical Outlook* 62, 37–41 (= *RP* 6, 182–92)

Syme, R., 1987, 'Marriage Ages for Roman Senators', *Historia* 36, 318–32 (= *RP* 6, 232–46)

Syme, R., 1988, 'Greeks Invading the Roman Government', *RP* 4, 1–20

Syme, R., 1991, 'Hadrian's Autobiography: Servianus and Sura', *Historia-Augusta-Colloqium 1986/1989* (Bonn), 189–200 (= *RP* 6, 398–408)

Syme, R., 1991, 'Vestricius Spurinna', *RP* 7, 541–50

Talbert, R. J. A., 1984, *The Senate of Imperial Rome* (Princeton)

Taylor, L. R., 1960, *The Voting Districts of the Roman Republic* (= *Papers and Monographs of the American Academy in Rome* 20, Rome)

Taylor, L. R., 1961, 'Freedmen and Freeborn in the Epitaphs of Imperial Rome', *AJP* 82, 113–32

Tchernia, A., 1980, 'Quelques remarques sur la commerce du vin et les amphores', in J. H. D'Arms and E. C. Kopff (eds), *Roman Seaborne Commerce* (= *MAAR* 36, 305–12)

Tchernia, A., 1986, *Le vin dans l'Italie romaine: Essai d'histoire économique d'après les amphores* (Rome)

Temporini, H., 1978, *Die Frauen am Hofe Trajans: Ein Beitrag zur Stellung der Augustae im Principat* (Berlin)

Thomasson, B. E., 1985, 'Zur Laufbahn einiger Statthalter des Prinzipats', *Op.Rom.* 15, 109–42

Thomasson, B. E., 1991, *Legatus: Beiträge zur römischen Verwaltungsgeschichte* (Stockholm)

Thomsen, P., 1917, 'Die römischen Meilensteine der Provinzen Syria, Arabia und Palaestina', *Zeitschrift des Deutschen Palästina-Vereins* 40, 1–103

Tissoni, G. Galleazzo, 1965, 'Sul *consilium principis* in età traianea,' I, *Stud. Doc. Hist. Iuris* 31, 222–45

Tissoni, G. Galleazzo, 1966, 'Sul *consilium principis* in età traianea,' II, *Stud. Doc. Hist. Iuris* 32, 129–52

Torelli, M., 1982, *Typology and Structure of Roman Historical Reliefs* (Ann Arbor)

Touati, A. -M. Leander, 1987, *The Great Trajanic Frieze* (= *Acta Instituti Romani Regni Sueciae*, Ser. 4, 45, Stockholm)

Townend, G. B., 1961, 'The Hippo Inscription and the Career of Suetonius', *Historia* 10, 99–109

Toynbee, J. M. C. and Ward-Perkins, J. B., 1957, *The Shrine of St Peter and the Vatican Excavations* (New York)

Treggiari, S., 1991, *Roman Marriage*: Iusti Coniuges *from the Time of Cicero to the Time of Ulpia* (Oxford)

Trousset, P., 1978, 'Les bornes du Bled Segui: nouveau aperçus sur la centuriation romaine du Sud Tunisien', *Ant.Afr.* 12, 125–77

Tschernia, A., 1986, *Le vin de l'Italie romaine: Essai d'histoire économique d'après les amphores* (Paris)

Tudor, D., 1978, *Oltenia Romana* (4th ed., Bucharest)

Urban, R., 1971, *Historische Untersuchungen zum Domitianbild des Tacitus* (München)

van Berchem, D., 1939, *Les distributions de blé et d'argent à la plèbe romaine* (Geneva)

van Berchem, D., 1952, *L'armée de Dioclétien et la réforme constantinienne* (Paris)

van Berchem, D., 1983, 'Une inscription flavienne du Musée d'Antioche', *Museum Helveticum* 40, 185–96

van Berchem, D. 1985, 'Le port de Séleucie de Piérie et l'infrastructure logistique des guerres partiques', *BJ* 185, 47–87

van Deman, E. B., 1934, *The Building of the Roman Aqueducts* (Washington, DC)

van Driel-Murray, C., 1990, 'New Light on Old Tents', *JRMES* 1, 109–37

Vermeule, C. C., 1979, 'An Imperial Commemorative Monument Never Finished: A Possible Memorial of Trajan's Eastern "Conquests" at Salamis on Cyprus', in *Studies presented in Memory of Porphyrios Dikaios* (Nicosia), 189–93

Veyne, P., 1957, 'La Table des Ligures Baebiani et l'Institution Alimentaire de Trajan: I', *MEFR* 69, 81–135

Veyne, P., 1958, 'La Table des Ligures Baebiani et l'Institution Alimentaire de Trajan: II', *MEFR* 70, 177–241

Veyne, P., 1965, 'Les Alimenta', in *Les Empereurs romaines*, 163–79

Veyne, P., 1990, *Bread and Circuses* (St Ives)

Vidman, L., 1960, *Etudes sur la correspondence de Pline le Jeune avec Trajan* (Prague 1960, reprinted Rome)

Vita-Eurard, G. di, 1990, 'La via Appia', *Quad. centro di Studi per l'archeol. Etrusco-ital.* 18, 73–93

von Mandach, A., 1987, *Der Trajan- und Herkinbald Teppich: die Entdeckung einer Iternationalen Portraitsgalerie des 15 Jahrhunderts* (Bern)

Vulpe, R., 1988, *Columna lui Traian: Monument al etnogenezei Romanilor* (Bucharest)

Waele, F. J. M. de, 1976, *Marcus Ulpius Traianus: veldheer, bouwheer, rijksheer* (Antwerpen)

Wagner, J., 1985, *Die Römer an Euphrat und Tigris* (= *Antike Welt* Sondernummer 16)

Waldstein, W., 1964, *Untersuchungen zum römischen Begnadigungsrecht:* abolitio, indulgentia, venia (Innsbruck)

Walker, D. R., 1977, *The Metrology of the Roman Silver Coinage I: From Augustus to Domitian* and *II: From Nerva to Commodus* (= *BARIS* 22, Oxford)

Wallace-Hadrill, A., 1983, *Suetonius: The Scholar and his Caesars* (London)

Walser, G., 1968, 'Der Putsch Saturninus gegen Domitian', in *Festschrift für Laur Belart* (= *Provincialia* 40, Basel), 497–510

Walser, G., 1989, 'Kaiser Domitian in Mainz', *Chiron* 19, 449–56

Ward-Perkins, J. B., 1976, 'Columna Divi Antonini', in *Mélanges d'histoire ancienne et d'archéologie offerts à Paul Collart* (Lausanne), 345–52 (= H. Dodge and B. Ward-Perkins, *Marble in Antiquity: Collected Papers of J. B. Ward-Perkins* (= *Archaeological Monographs of the British School of Archaeology at Rome* 6, London, 107–14)

Ward-Perkins, J. B., 1981, *Roman Imperial Architecture* (2nd ed.)

Waters, K. H., 1964, 'The Character of Domitian', *Phoenix* 18, 49–77

Waters, K. H., 1969, 'Traianus, Domitiani Continuator', *AJP* 90, 385–404

Waters, K. H., 1970, 'Juvenal and the Reign of Trajan', *Antichthon* 4, 62–77

Waters, K. H., 1975, 'The Reign of Trajan and its Place in Contemporary Scholarship', *ANRW* 2.2, 381–430

Watson, G. R., 1969, *The Roman Soldier* (Bath)

Weaver, P. R. C., 1965, 'The Father of Claudius Etruscus: Statius, *Silvae* 3.38', *CQ* 15, 145–54

Weaver, P. R. C., 1972, Familia Caesaris: *A Social Study of the Emperor's Freedmen and Slaves* (Cambridge)

Weaver, P. R. C., 1980, 'Two Freedmen Careers', *Antichthon* 14, 143–56

Webster, G., 1988, *From Fortress into City: The Consolidation of Roman Britain in the First Century* (London)

Wellesley, K., 1975, *The Long Year* (London)

West, L. C. and Johnson, A. C., 1944, *Currency in Roman and Byzantine Egypt* (Princeton and London)

Whatley, G., 1984, 'The Uses of Hagiography: The Legend of Pope Gregory and the Emperor Trajan in the Middle Ages', *Viator* 15, 25–63

Whittaker, C. R., 1994, *Frontiers of the Roman Empire* (Baltimore)

Wiedemann, T., 1992, *Emperors and Gladiators* (London and New York)

Wikander, O., 1979, 'Water-mills in Ancient Rome', *Opuscula Romana* 12, 13–36

Williams, W., 1976, 'Two Imperial Pronouncements Reclassified', *ZPE* 22, 240–5

Williams, W., 1979, 'Caracalla and the Authorship of Imperial Edicts and Epistles', *Latomus* 38, 67–89

Williams, W., 1990, *Pliny: Correspondence with Trajan from Bithynia (Epistles X)* (Warminster)

Wilson, A. J. N., 1966, *Emigration from Italy in the Republican Age* (Manchester)

Wilson Jones, M., 1993, 'One Hundred Feet and a Spiral Staircase: The Problems of Designing Trajan's Column', *JRA* 6, 23–38

Winkes, R., 1969, *Clipeata Imago: Studien zu einer römischen Bildnisform* (= *Klassiche Archäeologie* 1, Bonn)

Wiseman, T. P., 1970, 'The Definition of "Eques Romanus" in the Late Republic and Early Empire', *Historia* 19, 67–83

Wiseman, T. P., 1971, *New Men in the Roman Senate, 139 BC–AD 14* (Oxford)

Wistrand, E., 1979, 'The Stoic Opposition to the Principate', *Studii Classice* 18, 92–101

Wright, G. R. H., 1961, 'The Structure of Qasr Bint Far'un', *Palestine Exploration Quarterly* 93, 8–37

Yarshater, E. (ed.), 1983, *The Seleucid, Parthian and Sassanian Periods* (= *The Cambridge History of Iran 3:1 and 2*, Cambridge)

Yegül, F., 1992, *Baths and Bathing in Classical Antiquity* (Cambridge, Mass.)

Zanker, P., 1968, *Forum Augustum: Das Bildprogramm* (Tübingen)

Zanker, P., 1969, 'Das Trajansforum in Rom als Monument kaiserlicher Selbstdarstellung', *AK* 12, 120–1

Zanker, P., 1970, 'Das Trajansforum', *AA* 85, 499–544

Zayadine, F. and Fiema, Z. T., 1986, 'Roman Inscriptions from the Siq at Petra', *Ann. Dept. Antiq. Jordan* 30, 199–206

Zevi, F., 1972, 'Nuovi Frammenti dei Fasti Ostienses', in *Akten des VI internationalen Kongresses für griechische und lateinische Epigraphik* (= *Vestiga* 17, Munich), 437–9

Zevi, F., 1973, 'I consuli del 97 d.Chr in due frammenti già editi dei Fasti Ostienses', *LF* 96, 125–37

Zevi, F., 1979, 'Un frammento dei *Fasti Ostienses* e i consolati dei primi anni di Traiano', *PP* 34, 179–210

Ziegler, K.-H., 1964, *Die Beziehungen zwischen Rom und dem Partherreich: Ein Beitrag zur Geschichte des Völkerrechts* (Wiesbaden)

INDEX OF
PERSONAL NAMES

Emperors, classical authors and non-Roman citizens are listed under their common name; all others are listed under their *nomen*.

GENERAL INDEX

iron, 171
roads, 165–6
rural settlement, 171
silver mines, 129, 170
urbanization, 167–70
viticulture, 169, 171
Dacia Apulensis, 169
Dacia Malvensis, 169
Dacia Porolissensis, 169
Dacian War, First, 67, 87–95
reason, 87
Dacian War, Second, 97–101
reason, 97, 128, 163
Dacians, 24, 28, 29
army, 85–6
origins, 85
prisoners of war, 97, 102, 139, 155, 166, 171, 206
royal treasury, 100–1, 129, 191, 218
Dalmatia, 112, 129
Danaans, 47
Danube, 26, 29, 30, 31, 45, 51, 52, 86, 87, 90, 95, 97, 99, 101, 212, 217
fleet, 52, 95
Danuvius, 90
Dariel Pass, 194
Decapolis, 175, 179
decreta, 113
decurion, 3, 120
delatores, 118, 119, 124
Delphi, 134
denarius, 127, 128, 129
deposita, 119
Diana, 207, 208
Dierna (Osrova), 93, 170
Digest, 210
dignitas, 183
diplomas, 166, 181
disciplina, 207
dispensatores, 126
divus, 3
Djerdap, 52, 87
domestici, 56
donativium, 59, 126, 127
Drobeta (Turnu-Severin), 95, 97, 98, 99, 169, 170

Dumatha (al-Jawf/Dumat), 178
duovir, 5
dupondius, 129
Dura Europos, 196, 198, 203
Durostorum (Silistra), 95, 166
Dyrrachium (Dures), 97

Edessa (Sanliurfa), 195, 196, 200
edicta, 104, 113, 118, 120
edictum perpetuum, 113
education, 19–20
Efca, 173
Egypt, 6, 17, 51, 75, 76, 112, 125, 131, 155, 161, 176, 210
ekklesia, 162
el-Leja', 173
Elbe, 28
Elegeia, 194, 195
Elusa (Bar Mashash), 173
en-Avdat, 173
eparchies, 186, 188
Ephesus, 18, 191
Epitome de Caesaribus, xiii, 13
equestrian order, 17, 49, 108–11, 206
career, 5–6, 10
equites singulares Augusti, 110, 148, 200
erastes, 35, 58
Eriza (Erzincan), 192
eromenos, 35, 58
Euphrates, 18, 22, 187, 188, 189, 192, 195, 199, 203
fleet, 198–9
expeditio, 43

felicitas temporum, 206
Felicitas, 208
fiscus, 38, 79, 124, 125, 126, 167
fleets
Alexandrian, 6
Danube, 52, 95
Euphrates, 198–9
Ravenna, 6
Red Sea, 177
fossa Traiana, 145
Fossombrone, 138
frumentarii, 118, 210

Jabel ad-Duruz, 175
Japha, 15
Jericho, 15
Jerusalem, 131, 191
Jewish Revolt (AD 116–17), 201
Jewish War (AD 66–70), 12, 14–15, 17, 18
Jotapta, 15
Judaea, 5, 14–15, 17, 51, 76, 112, 123, 125, 175, 191, 192, 202, 203
Judaism, 32, 105, 200
Juno, 207
Jupiter, 46, 64, 67, 68, 70, 71, 106, 207, 209
    Tonans, 92

'kaisergeschicte', xiii
Karatash–Gradac canal, 87
Keys Pass, 93

Lake Van, 194
Laodicea, 18
latifundia, 79, 81
Latin, 19, 20
latus clavius, 5
Lazi, 194
Lebanon, 173
Lederata (Palanka), 90, 94
legatus, 112, 113
    Augusti pro praetore, 8, 9, 17, 112, 116
    legionis, 7, 8, 43
    proconsulis, 113
    pro praetore, 8
Legio (Léon), 26
legions, 3, 5, 16–17, 51, 88, 112
    I Adiutrix, 192
    I Flavia Minervia pia Fidelis, 88, 93, 203
    I Italica, 192
    II Adiutrix, 22, 29, 88
    II Traiana fortis, 72, 99, 192
    III Cyrenaica, 176, 191, 192
    III Gallica, 21, 23, 191, 192
    IIII Ferrata, 23, 192, 194
    IIII Flavia Firma, 95, 166, 167
    IIII Scythica, 23, 40, 94, 192, 194

    V Macedonia, 14, 22, 45, 49, 88, 95, 192
    VII Claudia, 25, 101, 192
    VII Galbiana, 25
    VII Gemina, 25–6, 30, 43
    VIII Augusta, 30
    X Fretensis, 13, 14, 191, 192
    XI Claudia pia fidelis, 30, 88, 94, 95, 192
    XII Fulminata, 18, 94, 192
    XII Primigenia Pia Fidelis, 22, 45, 49, 192
    XIII Gemina, 88, 95, 166, 192
    XIV Gemina Martia Victrix, 29
    XV Apollinaris, 14, 192
    XVI Flavia Firma, 23, 192
    XXI Rapax, 29, 31, 101, 165
    XXX Ulpia victrix, 99, 192
Leja': *see* el-Leja'
Leuke Kome (?Aynunah), 173, 177
lex agraria, 38
lex de imperio Vespasiani, 17, 47, 104
lex Julia de adulteriis, 122
liberalitas, 83, 125, 131, 138
libertas, 37, 65, 73
lictors, 53, 54, 116, 207, 208
Ligures Baebiani, 82, 83
limes, 49, 166, 178
    limes Transalutanus, 167
ludi, 60, 61, 110, 183, 196
    circensis, 146
    honorarii, 60
    Magni or *Romani*, 25
    scaenici, 120
Lugdunensis: *see* Gallia Lugdunensis
Lugio (Dunaszekcsö), 166
lusiones, 101, 102, 190
Lusitania, 15, 112
luxuria, 131
Lycia-Pamphylia, 112, 191

Ma'an, 173
Macedonia, 111
Machelones, 194
Madaba, 178
Magi, 185
maiestas, 31, 39, 108, 119

Main, 49
Makhtesh Raman, 173
Malva, 169–70
Mampsis (Kurnub), 175, 177
mandata, 113, 116
Mannus, 191, 196
manubiae, 125, 143, 156
Marcomanni, 30, 87, 99
Mardi, 194, 195
Maritima (Alpes), 112
Mars, 208
Mauretania Caesariensis, 6, 112, 125,
  202
Mauretania Tingitana, 112, 125, 202
Media, 186
Melitene (Malatya), 192
Mercury, 207
Mesene, 199
Mesopotamia, 184, 186, 187, 196, 200,
  201, 204
    abandonment, 203
    conquest, 195, 196
    Roman province, 196
metropolis, 162, 167, 178
Miletus, 14, 18
military wills, 119
Minerva, 207
minuendis publicis sumptibus, 38
Misenum (Miseno), 111
Moesia, 26, 28, 88, 99, 216
    Inferior, 44, 86, 87, 96, 97, 101,
      112, 165, 166, 169
    Superior, 30, 76, 86, 87, 95, 97, 98,
      112, 166
    partition, 29
Moguntiacum (Mainz), 29, 30, 31, 43,
  45, 49
Moldavia, 86, 96, 165
Mongols, 186
Mons Claudianus, 155, 158
Mother Earth, 207
Mount Kasios, 191, 197
Mount Massius (Tur 'Abdin), 198
municipia/municipium, 4, 162, 170,
  178, 179, 192
Municipium Tropaeum Traiani
  (Adamklissi), 102

munificienta, 61
munus/munera, 61, 102
    gladiatoria, 61
Mures, 166, 169
murus Dacicus, 85

Nabataea, 172–6
Nafud: *see* an-Nafud
Nahal Paran, 173
Naharmalcha, 199
Napoca (Cluj), 166, 169, 170, 171
Narbonensis: *see* Gallia Narbonensis
Narnia, 34
nationes (*see also symmachiarii*), 89, 92,
  93, 94, 99
    Balearic slingers, 89, 94, 100
    British, 89
    Cantabri, 89
    Daci, 89
    Getae, 89
    Moors, 88, 89, 94
    Palmyrene archers, 89, 94, 100
Neckar, 49
Negev, 173, 177, 181
Neumausus (Nîmes), 24
Nicaea (Iznik), 18, 135
Nicomedia (Izmit), 135, 190
Nile, 174
Nineveh, 198
Ninus: *see* Nineveh
Nisbis (Nusabayin), 195, 196, 198,
  200
Noricum, 31, 112
Nova Traiana Bostra: *see* Bostra
Novae, 166
novi homines, 4, 6, 7, 8, 9, 11, 14, 25, 27,
  49, 65, 75, 108, 210
Noviodunum (Issacea), 95
numerus/numeri, 99, 166, 171
    Syrorum Malvensium, 169
Numidia, 28–9, 75, 135

Oboda ('Avdat), 173, 175
Odenwald, 49
Oescus, 95
Oituz Pass, 166
olive oil, 2, 3, 79, 224